GREENS
SOLICITORS
PROFESSIONAL HANDBOOK
1999/2000

This book belongs to

GILLIAN SHAW

AUSTRALIA
LBC Information Services
Sydney

CANADA and USA
Carswell
Toronto

NEW ZEALAND
Brooker's
Auckland

SINGAPORE and MALAYSIA
Sweet & Maxwell Asia
Singapore and Kuala Lumpur

Reprinted from the *Parliament House Book*, published in looseleaf form
and updated quarterly by W. Green, the Scottish Law Publisher
The following paperback titles are also available in the series:
Mercantile Statutes 1999/2000
Conveyancing Statutes 1999/2000
Family Law Statutes 1999/2000
Scottish Licensing Handbook 1999/2000
Sheriff Court Rules 1999/2000
Greens Annotated Rules of the Court of Session 1999/2000

also

Criminal Law Statutes 1999/2000
reprinted from *Renton & Brown's Criminal Procedure Legislation*

Parliament House Book consists of the following Divisions:
A Fees and Stamps
B Courts, Upper
C Rules of the Court of Session (annotated)
D Courts, Lower
E Licensing
F Solicitors
G Legal Aid
H Bankruptcy and other Mercantile Statutes
I Companies
J Conveyancing, Land Tenure and Registration
K Family Law
L Landlord and Tenant
M Succession, Trusts, Liferents and Judicial Factors
N Tribunals, Inquiries etc
O Valuation for Rating

GREENS
SOLICITORS
PROFESSIONAL HANDBOOK
1999/2000

Reprinted from
Division F (Solicitors)
of the *Parliament House Book*

W. GREEN/Sweet & Maxwell Ltd
EDINBURGH
1999

Published in 1999 by W. Green & Son Ltd
21 Alva Street
Edinburgh EH2 4PS

Typeset by Mendip Communications Ltd, Frome, Somerset.
Printed and bound in Great Britain by Redwood Books Ltd,
Kennet Way, Trowbridge, Wiltshire.

No natural forests were destroyed to make this product;
only farmed timber was used and replanted

A CIP catalogue record for this book is available from the British Library

ISBN 0 414 01322 0

© W. Green & Son Ltd 1999

DIVISION F

Solicitors

Alphabetical and chronological indexes of all statutes and regulations in *Parliament House Book* can be found at the beginning of this binder.

Statutes

Statutory Instruments

Rules and Subordinate Legislation

Codes etc.

Practice Guidelines

Delegated Powers Law Society Contacts and Index

Rules, Codes, Practice Guideliness and Index reproduced with kind permission of the Law Society of Scotland.

Statutes

Solicitors (Scotland) Act 1980

(1980 c. 46)

An Act to consolidate certain enactments relating to solicitors and notaries public in Scotland.   [1st August 1980]

PART I

ORGANISATION

The Law Society of Scotland

Establishment and objects of Law Society of Scotland

1.—(1) The Law Society of Scotland (referred to in this Act as "the Society") shall continue to exist and shall exercise the functions conferred upon it by this Act.

(2) The object of the Society shall include the promotion of—

    (*a*) the interests of the solicitors' profession in Scotland; and

    (*b*) the interests of the public in relation to that profession.

(3) The Society may do anything that is incidental or conducive to the exercise of these functions or the attainment of those objects.

(4) Schedule 1 shall have effect in relation to the Society.

Membership of Society

2.—(1) Every solicitor having in force a practising certificate shall be a member of the Society.

(2) Notwithstanding any other provisions of this Act, the Council may admit as a member of the Society any solicitor not having in force a practising certificate on such terms and conditions (including the payment by him of a reduced annual subscription) as they may determine.

(3) Subject to subsection (2), a solicitor shall—

    (*a*) be treated as if he were not a member of the Society while suspended from practice as a solicitor under any enactment;

    (*b*) cease to be a member of the Society when his practising certificate ceases to have effect.

The Council of the Law Society

Establishment and functions of Council of Law Society

3.—(1) The business of the Society shall continue to be conducted by the Council of the Society (referred to in this Act as "the Council") the members of which shall be elected in accordance with the provisions of the scheme made under paragraph 2 of Schedule 1.

[THE NEXT PAGE IS F 5]

(2) The Council shall have the functions conferred upon them by this Act.

PART II

RIGHT TO PRACTISE AS A SOLICITOR

Qualifications and Training

Qualifications for practising as solicitor

4. No person shall be qualified to practise as a solicitor unless—
  (*a*) he has been admitted as a solicitor; and
  (*b*) his name is on the roll; and
  (*c*) subject to section 24, he has in force a certificate issued by the Council in accordance with the provisions of this Part authorising him to practise as a solicitor (referred to in this Act as a "practising certificate").

Training regulations

5.—(1) The Council may, with the concurrence of the Lord President, make regulations for—
  (*a*) practical training;
  (*b*) attendance at a course of legal education;
  (*c*) the passing of examinations.
  (2) Regulations under this section—
      (*a*) may make such incidental, consequential and supplemental provisions as the Council consider necessary or proper in relation to the matters specified in subsection (1);
      (*b*) may include provision for the charging by the Council of fees and the application thereof; and
      (*c*) may make different provisions for different circumstances.

Admission

Admission as solicitor

6.—(1) Subject to the provisions of this section, no person shall be admitted as a solicitor in Scotland unless—
  (*a*) he is aged 21 years or over; and
  [1] (*b*) he has satisfied the Council—
          (i) that he has complied with the provisions of any regulations made under section 5 that apply to him, and
          (ii) that he is a fit and proper person to be a solicitor, and has obtained from the Council a certificate to that effect; and
  (*c*) he has paid such sum in respect of his admission as has been fixed by the Council with the approval of the Lord President.
  [1a] (2) Where
  (*a*) a person has complied with the requirements of subsection (1); but
  (*b*) the Council have not lodged a petition for his admission as a solicitor within one month of his having so complied,
he may apply by petition to the court for admission as a solicitor; and if he produces the certificate mentioned in paragraph (*b*) of subsection (1) the court shall make an order admitting him as a solicitor.
  (3) If any person has not obtained from the Council a certificate to the effect mentioned in paragraph (*b*) of subsection (1) but has otherwise satisfied the requirements of that subsection the court, on such an application being made by him and on being satisfied after such inquiry as it thinks fit, that—
  (*a*) he is a fit and proper person to be admitted as a solicitor, and
  (*b*) he is competent to be a solicitor,
may make an order admitting him as a solicitor.

[2] **(3A)** The Council may petition the court for the admission as a solicitor of an applicant who has complied with the requirements of subsection (1) above; and, where it does so it shall lodge the petition not later than one month after the applicant has first so complied.

[2] **(3B)** The Court shall, on a petition being made to it under subsection (3A) above, make an order admitting the applicant as a solicitor.

(4) Any order admitting a person as a solicitor under this section shall include a direction to the Council to enter the name of that person in the roll.

(5) Nothing in this section affects the operation of the Colonial Solicitors Act 1900 or any Order in Council made under that Act (admission as solicitors in Scotland of solicitors of certain overseas territories).

(6) Every person who has been enrolled as a law agent shall be deemed to be admitted as a solicitor.

NOTES

[1] As amended by the Law Reform (Miscellaneous Provisions) (Scotland) Act 1985, Sched. 1, Pt. II, para. 2(*a*) and Sched. 4.

[1a] As substituted by the Law Reform (Miscellaneous Provisions) (Scotland) Act 1990, s.37(1) (effective 20th July 1992: S.I. 1992 No. 1599).

[2] Inserted by the Law Reform (Miscellaneous Provisions) (Scotland) Act 1985, Sched. 1, Pt. II, para. 2(*b*).

The Roll

Keeping the roll

7.—(1) The Council shall continue to be the registrar of solicitors and shall keep at the office of their secretary a roll of solicitors (in this Act referred to as "the roll").

(2) The roll shall consist of the names in alphabetical order of all solicitors entered on it in accordance with section 8.

(3) Any person may inspect the roll during office hours without payment.

[1] (4) Schedule 2 (powers of Council in relation to roll of solicitors) shall have effect.

NOTE

[1] Added by the Solicitors (Scotland) Act 1988, Sched. 1, para. 2.

Entry in the roll

8.—(1) On production to the Council of an order under section 6 admitting a person as a solicitor and directing that his name be entered on the roll the Council shall enter the name of that person on the roll.

(2) Any solicitor whose name is entered on the roll (in this Act referred to as "an enrolled solicitor") shall, on such enrolment, inform the Council in writing of the address of his place of business, and shall on any change of that address, inform them in writing of his new address.

(3) The Council shall issue a certificate of enrolment to any enrolled solicitor who applies for it.

Removal of name from roll on request

[1] **9.** An enrolled solicitor who wishes his name, or any annotation made against his name under section 25A(3), to be removed from the roll of solicitors may make an application to the Council in that behalf, and the Council shall on the solicitor satisfying the Council that he has made adequate arrangements with respect to the business he has then in hand, remove the name of that solicitor or, as the case may be, the annotation against his name, from the roll.

NOTE

[1] As amended by the Solicitors (Scotland) Act 1988, Sched. 1, para. 3, and the Law Reform (Miscellaneous Provisions) (Scotland) Act 1990, Sched. 8, para. 29(2).

Restoration of name to roll on request

[1] **10.**—(1) A solicitor whose name has been struck off the roll other than by order of the court, shall only be entitled to have his name restored to the

roll, if on an application in that behalf made by him to the Tribunal and after such inquiry as the Tribunal thinks proper, the Tribunal so orders.

(1A) On an application to the Council from a solicitor whose name, or any annotation against whose name, has been removed from the roll under section 9 the Council may, after such inquiry as they think proper, restore the name of that solicitor or, as the case may be, the annotation, to the roll.

(2) Rules made by the Tribunal under section 52 may—

    (*a*) regulate the making, hearing and determining of applications under subsection (1);

    (*b*) provide for payment by the applicant to the Council of such fee in respect of restoration to the roll as the rules may specify.

NOTE
[1] As amended by the Solicitors (Scotland) Act 1988, Sched. 1, para. 4, and the Law Reform (Miscellaneous Provisions) (Scotland) Act 1990, Sched. 8, para. 29(3).

Directions by Lord President

11.—(1) The Lord President may give directions to the Council in relation to the carrying out of their duties in connection with the keeping of the roll and they shall give effect to any such directions.

(2) [Repealed by the Solicitors (Scotland) Act 1988, Sched. 2.]

Power of court to prescribe fees

12. [Repealed by the Solicitors (Scotland) Act 1988, Sched. 2.]

Practising Certificates

Applications for practising certificates

13.—(1) Subject to this section and sections 14 to 24, the Council may make rules with respect to—

    (*a*) applications for practising certificates;

    (*b*) the issue of practising certificates;

    (*c*) the keeping of a register of applications for and the issue of practising certificates.

(2) Any person may inspect the register during office hours without payment.

(3) The making of a false statement by a solicitor in an application for a practising certificate may be treated as professional misconduct by him for the purposes of Part IV, unless he proves the statement was made without intention to deceive.

Issue of practising certificate

14.—(1) The Council shall issue to an enrolled solicitor on application being duly made by him, a practising certificate in accordance with rules made by them under section 13.

(2) The Council shall not issue a practising certificate to a solicitor while he is suspended from practice.

Discretion of Council in special cases

15.—(1) In any case where this section has effect, the applicant shall, unless the Council otherwise order, give to the Council, not less than 6 weeks before he applies for a practising certificate, notice of his intention to do so; and the Council may in their discretion—

    (*a*) grant or refuse the application, or

    (*b*) decide to issue a certificate to the applicant subject to such conditions as the Council may think fit.

(2) Subject to subsections (3) and (4), this section shall have effect in any case where a solicitor applies for a practising certificate—

    (*a*) [Repealed by the Law Reform (Miscellaneous Provisions) (Scotland) Act 1985, Sched. 1, Pt. II, para. 3 and Sched. 4.]

(*b*) not having held a practising certificate in force within the period of 12 months following the date of his admission; or

(*c*) when a period of 12 months or more has elapsed since he held a practising certificate in force; or

(*d*) without having paid in full any fine imposed on him under Part IV; or

(*e*) without having paid in full any expenses for which he has been found liable under section 38 or Part IV; or

(*f*) when, having been suspended from practice, the period of suspension has expired; or

(*g*) when, having had his name struck off the roll, his name has been restored to the roll; or

(*h*) after his estate has been sequestrated or he has granted a trust deed for behoof of creditors, whether he has obtained his discharge or not; or

(*i*) when, after a complaint has been made—

  (i) relating to his conduct of the business of a client his attention has been drawn by the Council to the matter, and he has not replied or has not furnished a reply which would enable the Council to dispose of the matter; or

  (ii) of delay in the disposal of the business of a client he has not completed that business within such period as the Council may fix as being a reasonable period within which to do so,

  and in either case has been notified in writing by the Council accordingly; or

[1] (*j*) while any thing required to be done by him by a direction of the Council under section 42A or of the Tribunal under section 53A (including any such direction as confirmed or varied on appeal) remains undone.

(3) Where a practising certificate free of conditions is issued by the Council under subsection (1) to a solicitor in relation to whom this section has effect by reason of any such circumstances as are mentioned in paragraphs (*b*), (*c*), (*f*), (*g*) or (*h*) of subsection (2), this section shall not thereafter have effect in relation to that solicitor by reason of those circumstances.

(4) Where the Council decide to issue a practising certificate subject to conditions, they may, if they think fit, postpone the issue of the certificate pending the hearing and determination of an appeal under section 16.

NOTE
[1] Inserted by the Solicitors (Scotland) Act 1988, Sched. 1, para. 5.

Appeals from decisions of Council
  16.—[1] (1) Where

  (*a*) an application for a practising certificate is duly made to the Council otherwise than in a case where section 15 has effect and the Council refuse or neglect to issue a practising certificate, the applicant;

  (*b*) the Council refuse to recognise a body corporate as being suitable in terms of section 34(1A)(*b*), the body corporate

may apply to the court, who may make such order in the matter as it thinks fit.

(2) Where the Council in exercise of the power conferred on them by section 15, refuse to issue a practising certificate, or issue a practising certificate subject to conditions, the applicant may appeal to the court against that decision within 14 days of being notified of it.

(3) On an appeal to the court under subsection (2) the court may—

  (*a*) affirm the decision of the Council; or

  (*b*) direct the Council to issue a practising certificate to the applicant subject to such conditions if any as the court may think fit; or

  (*c*) make such other order as it thinks fit.

NOTE
[1] As amended by the Law Reform (Miscellaneous Provisions) (Scotland) Act 1985, Sched. 1, Pt. I, para. 1.

Date and expiry of practising certificates

17.—(1) Every practising certificate issued in November of any year shall bear the date of 1st November in that year, and every other practising certificate shall bear the date of the day on which it was issued.

(2) Every practising certificate shall have effect from the date it bears under subsection (1).

(3) Subject to subsection (4), every practising certificate shall expire on 31st October next after it is issued.

(4) On the name of any solicitor being struck off the roll or on a solicitor being suspended from practice as a solicitor, any practising certificate for the time being in force of that solicitor shall cease to have effect, but in the case of suspension, if he ceases to be so suspended during the period for which the practising certificate would otherwise have continued in force, the certificate shall thereupon again have effect.

Suspension of practising certificates

18.—[1] (1) If—
    (*a*) in pursuance of the Mental Health (Scotland) Act 1984 a solicitor is, by reason of mental disorder, admitted to a hospital and becomes liable to be detained there or becomes subject to guardianship;
    (*b*) a *curator bonis* is appointed on the estate of a solicitor;
    (*c*) the estate of the solicitor is sequestrated;
    (*d*) a solicitor grants a trust deed for behoof of creditors;
    (*e*) a judicial factor is appointed on the estate of the solicitor under section 41;
any practising certificate for the time being in force of that solicitor shall cease to have effect, and he shall be suspended from practice as a solicitor.

[2] (1A) If—
    (*a*) an administration or winding up order, or an appointment of a provisional liquidator, liquidator, receiver or judicial factor has been made in relation to the incorporated practice; or
    (*b*) a resolution has been passed for the voluntary winding-up of an incorporated practice (other than a resolution passed solely for the purposes of reconstruction or amalgamation of the incorporated practice with another incorporated practice),
the recognition under section 34(1A) of the incorporated practice shall be thereby revoked.

[3] (2) On the occurrence of any of the circumstances mentioned in subsection (1), the solicitor in question shall intimate those circumstances to the Council in writing immediately.

(3) On the occurrence of the circumstances mentioned in paragraphs (*d*) or (*e*) of subsection (1) the trustee or as the case may be the judicial factor shall intimate his appointment to the Council in writing immediately.

[2] (3A) On the occurrence of the circumstances mentioned in—
    (*a*) paragraph (*a*) of subsection (1A), the administrator, provisional liquidator, liquidator, receiver or, as the case may be, judicial factor appointed in relation to the incorporated practice;
    (*b*) paragraph (*b*) of subsection (1A), the incorporated practice
shall immediately intimate that fact to the Council.

NOTES
  [1] As amended by the Mental Health (Scotland) Act 1984, Sched. 3, para. 46.
  [2] Inserted by the Law Reform (Miscellaneous Provisions) (Scotland) Act 1985, Sched. 1, Pt. I, para. 2.
  [3] As amended by the Solicitors (Scotland) Act 1988, Sched. 2.

Further provisions relating to suspension of practising certificates

19.—(1) The provisions of this section have effect in relation to a practising certificate which has ceased to have effect by virtue of section 18 during the period when that certificate would, but for that section, have continued in force.

(2), (3) [Repealed by the Solicitors (Scotland) Act 1988, Sched. 2.]

(4) A practising certificate which has ceased to have effect by virtue of paragraphs (*c*) or (*d*) of section 18(1) shall again have effect on the solicitor being granted his discharge.

(5) A practising certificate which has ceased to have effect by virtue of paragraph (*e*) of section 18(1) shall again have effect on the judicial factor being granted his discharge.

[1] (5A) Where a solicitor is suspended from practice as a solicitor by virtue of paragraph (*a*) or (*b*) of section 18(1), the period of suspension shall, for the purposes of section 15(2)(*f*), expire on the solicitor ceasing to be liable to be detained or subject to guardianship or, as the case may be, on the *curator bonis* being discharged.

(6) Where a solicitor is suspended from practice as a solicitor by virtue of paragraphs (*c*), (*d*) or (*e*) of section 18(1), he may at any time apply to the Council to terminate the suspension.

(7) On an application under subsection (6), the Council may either—

    (*a*) grant the application with or without conditions; or

    (*b*) refuse the application.

(8) If on an application by a solicitor under subsection (6), the Council refuse the application or grant it subject to conditions, the solicitor may appeal against the decision to the court, who may—

    (*a*) affirm the decision; or

    (*b*) vary any conditions imposed by the Council; or

    (*c*) terminate the suspension either with or without conditions.

NOTE
[1] Inserted by the Solicitors (Scotland) Act 1988, Sched. 1, para. 6.

Council's duty to supply lists of solicitors holding practising certificates

[1] **20.**—(1) The Council shall send a list of all solicitors holding practising certificates for the practice year then current—

    (*a*) to the Keeper of the Registers of Scotland;

    (*ab*) to the Principal Clerk of Session;

    (*b*) to each sheriff clerk;

as soon as practicable after 1st December in each year.

(2) The Council shall send a list of all solicitors who have rights of audience in—

    (*a*) the Court of Session, to—

        (i) the Principal Clerk of Session;

        (ii) the Principal Clerk of the Judicial Office of the House of Lords; and

        (iii) the Registrar to the Judicial Committee of the Privy Council; and

    (*b*) the High Court of Justiciary, to the Principal Clerk of Justiciary,

as soon as practicable after 1st December in each year; and where, by virtue of an order under section 53(2)(*ba*), 53A(2)(*ba*) or 55(1)(*ba*), a solicitor's right of audience in any of those courts is suspended or revoked, the Council shall forthwith inform the persons mentioned in this subsection of that fact.

(3) The Council shall notify those persons to whom they have sent lists under this section of any changes in those lists.

NOTE
[1] As amended by the Law Reform (Miscellaneous Provisions) (Scotland) Act 1990, Sched. 8, para. 29(4) and Sched. 9.

Consultants to hold practising certificates
21.—(1) A consultant shall be treated for the purposes of this Act as a practising solicitor and the provisions relating to practising certificates and, subject to subsection (2), the Guarantee Fund shall apply to him.

(2) The Council may if they think fit exempt a consultant from any of the provisions of section 43 or Schedule 3 (the Guarantee Fund).

[1] (3) In this section "consultant" means any solicitor who
   (a) not being in partnership with a solicitor or other solicitors causes or permits his name to be associated with the name of that solicitor or those solicitors or their firm's name,
   (b) not being a director of an incorporated practice, causes or permits his name to be associated with that incorporated practice,
whether he is described as a consultant or adviser or in any other way.

NOTE
[1] As amended by the Law Reform (Miscellaneous Provisions) (Scotland) Act 1985 (c. 73), Sched. 1, Pt. I, para. 3.

Evidence as to holding of practising certificates
22.—(1) Any list purporting to be issued by the Council and to contain the names of solicitors in Scotland who have before 1st December in any year obtained practising certificates for the period of 12 months from 1st November in that year shall, until the contrary is proved, be evidence that the persons named in that list are solicitors holding such certificates.

(2) The absence from any such list of the name of any person shall, until the contrary is proved, be evidence that the person is not qualified to practise as a solicitor under a certificate for the current year, but in the case of any such person an extract from the roll certified as correct by the Council shall be evidence of the facts appearing in the extract.

Offence to practise without practising certificate
23.—(1) Any person who practises as a solicitor or in any way holds himself out as entitled by law to practise as a solicitor without having in force a practising certificate shall be guilty of an offence under this Act unless he proves that he acted without receiving or without expectation of any fee, gain or reward, directly or indirectly.

(2) Without prejudice to any proceedings under subsection (1), failure on the part of a solicitor in practice to have in force a practising certificate may be treated as professional misconduct for the purposes of Part IV.

Saving of public officials
24. Nothing in this Act shall require a practising certificate to be taken out by a person who is by law authorised to act as a solicitor to a public department without admission, or by any assistant or officer appointed to act under the direction of any such solicitor.

Rights of Solicitors

Rights of practising
25. Every person qualified to practise as a solicitor in accordance with section 4 may practise as a solicitor in any court in Scotland.

Rights of audience in the Court of Session, the House of Lords, the Judicial Committee of the Privy Council and the High Court of Justiciary
[1] **25A.**—[2] (1) Without prejudice to section 103(8) of the Criminal Procedure (Scotland) Act 1995 (right of solicitor to appear before single judge) and section 48(2)(b) (extension of rights of audience by act of sederunt) of the Court of Session Act 1988, a solicitor who—
   (a) seeks a right of audience in, on the one hand, the Court of Session, the House of Lords and the Judicial Committee of the Privy Council or, on the other hand, the High Court of Justiciary; and

(*b*) has satisfied the Council as to the requirements provided for in this section,

shall have a right of audience in those courts or, as the case may be, that court.

(2) The requirements mentioned in subsection (1), in relation to the courts or, as the case may be, the court in which a solicitor seeks a right of audience, are that—

(*a*) he has completed, to the satisfaction of the Council, a course of training in evidence and pleading in relation to proceedings in those courts or that court;

(*b*) he has such knowledge as appears to the Council to be appropriate of—

(i) the practice and procedure of; and

(ii) professional conduct in regard to,

those courts or that court; and

(*c*) he has satisfied the Council that he is, having regard among other things to his experience in appropriate proceedings in the sheriff court, otherwise a fit and proper person to have a right of audience in those courts or that court.

(3) Where a solicitor has satisfied the Council as to the requirements of subsection (2) in relation to the courts or, as the case may be, the court in which he seeks a right of audience the Council shall make an appropriate annotation on the roll against his name.

(4) The Council shall make rules under this section as to—

(*a*) the matters to be included in, the methods of instruction to be employed in, and the qualifications of the person who will conduct, any course of training such as is mentioned in subsection (2)(*a*); and

(*b*) the manner in which a solicitor's knowledge of the practice and procedure and professional conduct mentioned in subsection (2)(*b*) is to be demonstrated,

and separate rules shall be so made in relation to, on the one hand, the Court of Session, the House of Lords and the Judicial Committee of the Privy Council and, on the other hand, the High Court of Justiciary.

(5) The Council shall make rules of conduct in relation to the exercising of any right of audience held by virtue of this section.

(6) Where a solicitor having a right of audience in any of the courts mentioned in subsection (1) is instructed to appear in that court, those instructions shall take precedence before any of his other professional obligations, and the Council shall make rules—

(*a*) stating the order of precedence of those courts for the purposes of this subsection;

(*b*) stating general criteria to which solicitors should have regard in determining whether to accept instructions in particular circumstances; and

(*c*) securing, through such of their officers as they think appropriate, that, where reasonably practicable, any person wishing to be represented before any of those courts by a solicitor holding an appropriate right of audience is so represented,

and for the purposes of rules made under this subsection the Inner and Outer Houses of the Court of Session, and the High Court of Justiciary exercising its appellate jurisdiction, may be treated as separate courts.

(7) Subsection (6) does not apply to an employed solicitor whose contract of employment prevents him from acting for persons other than his employer.

(8) Subject to subsections (9) and (10), the provisions of section 34(2) and (3) apply to rules made under this section as they apply to rules made under that section and, in considering any rules made by the Council under subsection (5), the Lord President shall have regard to the desirability of there being common principles applying in relation to the exercising of rights of audience by all practitioners appearing before the Court of Session and the High Court of Justiciary.

(9) The Council shall, after any rules made under subsection (4) have been approved by the Lord President, submit such rules to the Secretary of State, and no such rules shall have effect unless the Secretary of State, after consulting the Director in accordance with section 64A, has approved them.

(10) The Council shall, after any rules made under subsection (5) have been approved by the Lord President, submit such rules to the Secretary of State.

(11) Where the Secretary of State considers that any rule submitted to him under section (10) would directly or indirectly inhibit the freedom of a solicitor to appear in court or undertake all the work preparatory thereto he shall consult the Director in accordance with section 64A.

(12) The Council may bring into force the rules submitted by them to the Secretary of State under subsection (10) with the exception of any such rule which he has, in accordance with section 64B, refused to approve.

(13) Nothing in this section affects the powers of any court in relation to any proceedings—

(*a*) to hear a person who would not otherwise have a right of audience before the court in relation to those proceedings; or

(*b*) to refuse to hear a person (for reasons which apply to him as an individual) who would otherwise have a right of audience before the court in relation to those proceedings, and where a court so refuses it shall give its reasons for that decision.

(14) Where a complaint has been made that a solicitor has been guilty of professional misconduct in the exercise of any right of audience held by him by virtue of this section, the Council may, or if so requested by the Lord President shall, suspend him from exercising that right pending determination of that complaint under Part IV.

(15) Where a function is conferred on any person or body by this section he or, as the case may be, they shall exercise that function as soon as is reasonably practicable.

NOTES

[1] Inserted by the Law Reform (Miscellaneous Provisions) (Scotland) Act 1990 (c. 40), s. 24.

[2] As amended by the Criminal Procedure (Consequential Provisions) (Scotland) Act 1995 (c. 40), Sched. 4, para. 31 (effective 1st April 1996: s. 7(2)).

Restriction on rights of practising

Offence for solicitors to act as agents for unqualified persons

26.—[1] (1) Any solicitor to whom this subsection applies who or incorporated practice which upon the account or for the profit of any unqualified person—

(*a*) acts as agent in any action or proceedings in any court, or

(*b*) permits or suffers his or, as the case may be, its name to be made use of in any way in any such action or proceedings; or

(*c*) draws or prepares any writ to which section 32 applies; or

(*d*) permits or suffers his or, as the case may be, its name to be made use of in the drawing or preparing of any such writ; or

(*e*) does any other act to enable that person to appear, act or practise in any respect as a solicitor or notary public,

knowing that person not to be a qualified solicitor or notary public, as the case may be, shall be guilty of an offence.

(2) Subsection (1) applies to any solicitor, not being a solicitor who is employed full-time on a fixed salary by a body corporate or employed by a law centre.

[1] (3) In this section "person" includes a body corporate but "unqualified person" does not include an incorporated practice.

NOTE
[1] As amended by the Law Reform (Miscellaneous Provisions) (Scotland) Act 1985 (c. 73), Sched. 1, Pt. I, para. 4, and the Law Reform (Miscellaneous Provisions) (Scotland) Act 1990 (c. 40), Sched. 8, para. 29(5)(c) (effective 17th March 1993: S.I. 1993 No. 641). Prospective amendments in para. 29(5)(a), (b) and (d), which states:
"(5) In section 26 of the 1980 Act (offence for solicitors to act as agents for unqualified persons)—
(a) in subsection (1)(c), at the beginning there shall be inserted 'subject to subsection (4),';
(b) in subsection (1)(d), at the beginning there shall be inserted 'subject to subsection (4),';
...
(d) after subsection (3) there shall be inserted—
'(4) Subsection (1)(c) and (d) shall not apply in relation to—
(a) writs relating to heritable or moveable property drawn or prepared upon the account of or for the profit of independent qualified conveyancers providing conveyancing services within the meaning of section 23 (interpretation of sections 16 to 22) of the Law Reform (Miscellaneous Provisions) (Scotland) Act 1990; or
(b) papers to found or oppose an application for a grant of confirmation in favour of executors drawn or prepared upon the account of or for the profit of an executry practitioner or recognised financial institution providing executry services within the meaning of the said section 23.' "

Offence for solicitors to share fees with unqualified persons
27. [Repealed by the Law Reform (Miscellaneous Provisions) (Scotland) Act 1990 (c. 40), Sched. 9 (effective 17th March 1993: S.I. 1993 No. 641.]

Offence for solicitors who are disqualified to seek employment without informing employer
[1] **28.** Any person who—
(a) has been struck off the roll; or
(b) suspended from practice as a solicitor,
and while so disqualified from practice seeks or accepts employment by a solicitor in connection with that solicitor's practice or by an incorporated practice without previously informing him or, as the case may be, it that he is so disqualified shall be guilty of an offence.

NOTE
[1] As amended by the Law Reform (Miscellaneous Provisions) (Scotland) Act 1985 (c. 73), Sched. 1, Pt. I, para. 6.

29. [Repealed by the Law Reform (Miscellaneous Provisions) (Scotland) Act 1990 (c. 40), s. 39 and Sched. 9.]

Liability for fees of other solicitor
[1] **30.** Where a solicitor, or an incorporated practice authorised by and acting for a client employs another solicitor or incorporated practice he or, as the case may be, it shall (whether or not he or, as the case may be, it discloses the client) be liable to the other solicitor or incorporated practice for that other solicitor's or incorporated practice's fees and outlays, unless at the time of the employment he or, as the case may be, it expressly disclaims any such liability.

NOTE
[1] As amended by the Law Reform (Miscellaneous Provisions) (Scotland) Act 1985 (c. 73), Sched. 1, Pt. I, para. 7.

Unqualified persons acting as solicitors

Offence for unqualified persons to pretend to be solicitor or notary public
[1] **31.**—(1) Any unqualified person (including a body corporate) who either by himself or together with others, wilfully and falsely—
(*a*) pretends to be a solicitor or notary public; or
(*b*) takes or uses any name, title, addition or description implying that he is duly qualified to act as a solicitor or a notary public or recognised by law as so qualified;
shall be guilty of an offence.

In this section, "unqualified person" does not include an incorporated practice.

(2) Any person (including a body corporate) who either by himself or together with others, wilfully and falsely—
(*a*) pretends to be an incorporated practice;
(*b*) takes or uses any name, title, addition or description implying that he is an incorporated practice,
shall be guilty of an offence.

(3) [Repealed by the Law Reform (Miscellaneous Provisions) (Scotland) Act 1990 (c. 40), Sched. 9.]

NOTE
[1] As amended by the Law Reform (Miscellaneous Provisions) (Scotland) Act 1985 (c. 73), Sched. 1, Pt. I, para. 8. Modified by the Copyright, Designs and Patents Act 1988 (c. 48), s. 278 (patent attorneys).

Offence for unqualified persons to prepare certain documents
[0] **32.**—(1) Subject to the provisions of this section, any unqualified person (including a body corporate) who draws or prepares—
(*a*) any writ relating to heritable or moveable estate; or
[1] (*b*) any writ relating to any action or proceedings in any court; or
(*c*) any papers on which to found or oppose an application for a grant of confirmation in favour of executors,
shall be guilty of an offence.

(2) Subsection (1) shall not apply—
(*a*) to an unqualified person if he proves that he drew or prepared the writ or papers in question without receiving, or without expecting to receive, either directly or indirectly, any fee, gain or reward (other than by remuneration paid under a contract of employment); or
(*b*) to an advocate; or
(*c*) to any public officer drawing or preparing writs in the course of his duty; or
(*d*) to any person employed merely to engross any writ; or
[2] (*e*) an incorporated practice.

(2A) Subsection (1)(*a*) shall not apply to a qualified conveyancer providing conveyancing services within the meaning of section 23 of the Law Reform (Miscellaneous Provisions) (Scotland) Act 1990.

(2B) Subsection (1)(*b*) shall not apply to a person who is, by virtue of an act of sederunt made under section 32 (power of Court of Session to regulate procedure) of the Sheriff Courts (Scotland) Act 1971, permitted to represent a party to a summary cause.

(2C) Subsection (1)(*c*) shall not apply to an executry practitioner or a recognised financial institution providing executry services within the meaning of section 23 of the Law Reform (Miscellaneous Provisions) (Scotland) Act 1990.

(3) In this section "writ" does not include—
(*a*) a will or other testamentary writing;
(*b*) a document *in re mercatoria,* missive or mandate;

    (*c*) a letter or power of attorney;
    (*d*) a transfer of stock containing no trust or limitation thereof.

NOTES
  [0] As amended by the Law Reform (Miscellaneous Provisions) (Scotland) Act 1990 (c. 40), Sched. 8, para. 29(6).
  [1] As amended by the Solicitors (Scotland) Act 1988 (c. 42), Sched. 1, para. 7.
  [2] Added by the Law Reform (Miscellaneous Provisions) (Scotland) Act 1985 (c. 73), Sched. 1, Pt. I, para. 9.

Unqualified persons not entitled to fees, etc.
  [1] **33.** No fee, reward, outlay or expenses on account of or in relation to any act or proceeding done or taken by any person who—
    (*a*) acts as a solicitor or as a notary public without being duly qualified so to act; or
    (*b*) not being so qualified, frames or draws any writs to which section 32 applies,
shall be recoverable by any person in any action or matter.
  This section does not apply to an incorporated practice or in relation to writs framed or drawn by a person who is, by virtue of an act of sederunt made under section 32 of the Sheriff Courts (Scotland) Act 1971, permitted to represent a party to a summary cause.

NOTE
  [1] As amended by the Law Reform (Miscellaneous Provisions) (Scotland) Act 1985 (c. 73), Sched. 1, Pt. 1, para. 10, the Solicitors (Scotland) Act 1988 (c. 42), Sched. 1, para. 8 and Sched. 2, and the Law Reform (Miscellaneous Provisions) (Scotland) Act 1990 (c. 40), Sched. 8, para. 29(7).

Privilege of incorporated practices from disclosure etc.
  [1] **33A.**—(1) Any communication made to or by an incorporated practice in the course of its acting as such for a client shall in any legal proceedings be privileged from disclosure in like manner as if the body had at all material times been a solicitor acting for the client.
  (2) Any enactment or instrument making special provision in relation to a solicitor or other legal representative as to the disclosure of information, or as to the production, seizure or removal of documents, with respect to which a claim to professional privilege could be maintained, shall, with any necessary modifications, have effect in relation to an incorporated practice as it has effect in relation to a solicitor.

NOTE
  [1] Inserted by the Law Reform (Miscellaneous Provisions) (Scotland) Act 1985 (c. 73), Sched. 1, Pt. I, para. 11.

PART III

PROFESSIONAL PRACTICE, CONDUCT AND DISCIPLINE OF SOLICITORS

Practice rules

Rules as to professional practice, conduct and discipline
  [1,3] **34.**—(1) Subject to subsections (2) and (3), the Council may, if they think fit, make rules for regulating in respect of any matter the professional practice, conduct and discipline of solicitors and incorporated practices.
  [2] (1A) Rules made under this section may—
    (*a*) provide as to the management and control by—
      (i) solicitors holding practising certificates or their executors;
      (ii) other incorporated practices

of bodies corporate carrying on businesses consisting of the provision of professional services such as are provided by individuals and firms practising as solicitors being bodies the membership of which is restricted to such solicitors, executors and other incorporated practices;

(*b*) prescribe the circumstances in which such bodies may be recognised

[THE NEXT PAGE IS F 15]

by the Council as being suitable to undertake the provision of any
such services;
  (c) prescribe the conditions which (subject to any exceptions provided by
      the rules) must at all times be satisfied by bodies corporate so
      recognised if they are to remain so recognised (which bodies, when
      and for so long as so recognised, are in this Act referred to as
      "incorporated practices");
  (d) regulate the conduct of the affairs of incorporated practices; and
  (e) provide—
      (i) for the manner and form in which applications for recognition
          under this section are to be made, and for the payment of fees in
          connection with such applications;
      (ii) for regulating the names that may be used by incorporated
           practices;
      (iii) as to the period for which any recognition granted under this
            section shall (subject to the provisions of this Act) remain in
            force;
      (iv) for the revocation of any such recognition on the grounds that it
           was granted as a result of any error or fraud;
      (v) for the keeping by the Society of a list containing the names and
          places of business of all incorporated practices and for the
          information contained in any such list to be available for
          inspection;
      (vi) for the rules made under any provision of this Act to have effect
           in relation to incorporated practices with such additions, omis-
           sions or other modifications as appear to the Council to be
           necessary or expedient;
      (vii) for empowering the Council to take such steps as they consider
            necessary or expedient to ascertain whether or not any rules
            applicable to incorporated practices by virtue of this section are
            being complied with; and
  (f) make such additional or different provision as the Council think fit in
      relation to solicitors who, or incorporated practices which, are
      partners in or directors of multi-disciplinary practices.
(2) The Council shall, before making any rules under this section or
section 35—
  (a) send to each member of the Society a draft of the rules; and
  (b) thereafter submit the draft rules to a meeting of the Society; and
  (c) take into consideration any resolution passed at that meeting relating
      to amendments to the draft rules.
(3) Rules made under this section or section 35 shall not have effect unless
the Lord President after considering any objections he thinks relevant has
approved the rules so made.
(3A) Without prejudice to subsection (3), any rule made, whether before
or after the coming into force of this subsection, by the Council under this
section or section 35 which has the effect of prohibiting the formation of
multi-disciplinary practices shall not have effect unless the Secretary of
State, after consulting the Director in accordance with section 64A, has
approved it.
(4) If any solicitor fails to comply with any rule made under this section
that failure may be treated as professional misconduct for the purposes of
Part IV.
  [2] (4A) A certificate purporting to be signed by an officer of the Society and
stating that any body corporate is or is not an incorporated practice shall,
unless the contrary is proved, be sufficient evidence of that fact.
  [2] (4B) Subject to the provisions of this Act, the Secretary of State may, by
order made by statutory instrument subject to annulment in pursuance of a
resolution of either House of Parliament, provide for any enactment or
instrument passed or made before the commencement of [sub]section (1A)

above and having effect in relation to solicitors to have effect in relation to incorporated practices with such additions, omissions, or other modifications as appear to him to be necessary or expedient.

_____

NOTES

[1] As amended by the Law Reform (Miscellaneous Provisions) (Scotland) Act 1985 (c. 73), Sched. 1, Pt. I, para. 12.

[2] Inserted by the Law Reform (Miscellaneous Provisions) (Scotland) Act 1985 (c. 73), Sched. 1, Pt. I, para. 12(b) and (c).

[3] As amended by the Law Reform (Miscellaneous Provisions) (Scotland) Act 1990 (c.40), s.31(3) (effective March 17, 1993 by S.I. 1993/641).

[4] Inserted by the Law Reform (Miscellaneous Provisions) (Scotland) Act 1990 (c.40), s.31(3) (effective March 17, 1993 by S.I. 1993/641).

Accounts rules

Accounts rules

[1] **35.**—[2] (1) The Council shall, subject to section 34(2) and (3), make rules (in this Act referred to as "accounts rules")—

    (a) as to the opening and keeping by solicitors and incorporated practices of accounts and deposits at the banks specified in subsection (2) or with a building society for moneys not belonging to them received by them in the course of their practice;

    (b) as to the opening and keeping by solicitors and incorporated practices of—

        (i) a deposit or share account with a building society, or

        (ii) an account showing sums on loan to a local authority, being in either case for a client whose name is specified in the title of the account;

    (c) as to the keeping by solicitors and incorporated practices of books and accounts containing particulars and information as to money not belonging to them received, held or paid by them in the course of their practice;

    (d) as to the action which the Council may take to enable them to ascertain whether or not the rules are being complied with; and

    (e) as to the recovery from solicitors of fees and other costs incurred by the Council in ascertaining whether or not a solicitor who has failed to comply with the accounts rules has remedied that failure and is complying with the rules.

[3] (2) The banks mentioned in paragraph (a) of subsection (1) are—

    (a) the Bank of England;

    (b) [Repealed by the Trustee Savings Banks Act 1985 (c.58), Sched. 4.]

    (c) the National Savings Bank;

    (d) the Post Office, in the exercise of its powers to provide banking services;

    (e) an institution authorised under the Banking Act 1987;

and the rules may specify the location of the banks' or companies' branches at which the accounts are to be kept.

(3) If any solicitor fails to comply with any rule made under this section that failure may be treated as professional misconduct for the purposes of Part IV.

(4) Rules made under this section shall not apply to a solicitor—

    (a) who is in employment as solicitor to a Minister of the Crown or a Government Department or as an assistant or officer appointed to act under the direction of such solicitor; or

    [4] (b) who is in employment to which Part V of the Legal Aid (Scotland) Act 1986 applies; or

(c) who is in employment in an office connected with the administration of a local authority or a statutory undertaking or a
designated body to which he has been appointed by the authority
or the statutory undertakers or the persons responsible for the
management of that body by reason of his being a solicitor,

so far as regards monies received, held or paid by him in the course of that
employment.

In this subsection—

"local authority" means a local authority within the meaning of the
Local Government (Scotland) Act 1973;

"statutory undertakers" means any persons (including a local
authority) authorised by any enactment or statutory order or any
scheme made under or confirmed by an enactment to construct,
work or carry on any railway, light railway, tramway, road
transport, water transport, canal, inland navigation, dock, harbour,
pier or lighthouse undertaking or any undertaking for the supply of
gas, electricity, hydraulic power or water;

"designated body" means any body whether corporate or unincorporate for the time being designated by the Council for the purposes of
this section.

[THE NEXT PAGE IS F 17]

NOTES

[1] Extended by the Trustee Savings Banks Act 1985, Sched. 1, para. 11(2)(*b*).

[2] As amended by the Law Reform (Miscellaneous Provisions) (Scotland) Act 1985, Sched. 1, Pt. I, para. 13, Pt. II, para. 4 and Sched. 4, and (with effect from 29th January 1989) the Solicitors (Scotland) Act 1988, Sched. 1, para. 9 and Sched. 2.

[3] As amended by the Banking Act 1987, Sched. 6, para. 9.

[4] As amended by the Legal Aid (Scotland) Act 1986, Sched. 3, para. 7.

Interest on client's money

[1] **36.**—[2](1) Accounts rules shall make provision for requiring a solicitor or an incorporated practice, in such cases as may be prescribed by the rules—

  (*a*) to keep in a separate deposit or savings account at a bank or with a building society, or on a separate deposit receipt at a bank, for the benefit of the client money received for or on account of a client; or

  (*aa*) to keep in—

  (i) a deposit or share account with a building society; or

  (ii) an account showing sums on loan to a local authority,

  being in either case an account kept by the solicitor in his or, as the case may be, by the incorporated practice in its own name for a specified client, money so received; or

  (*b*) to make good to the client out of the solicitor's or, as the case may be, the incorporated practice's own money a sum equivalent to the interest which would have accrued if the money so received had been kept as mentioned in paragraph (*a*) or (*aa*).

(2) The cases in which a solicitor or incorporated practice may be required to act as mentioned in subsection (1) may be defined among other things by reference to the amount of any sum received or balance held or the period for which it is or is likely to be retained or held or both; and the rules may include provision for enabling a client (without prejudice to any other remedy) to require that any question arising under the rules in relation to the client's money be referred to and determined by the Society.

(3) Except as provided by the rules, a solicitor or incorporated practice shall not be liable by virtue of the relation between solicitor and client to account to any client for interest received by the solicitor or, as the case may be, the incorporated practice on monies lodged in an account at a bank or with a building society, or on deposit receipt, at a bank, being monies received or held for or on account of his or, as the case may be, its clients generally.

(4) Nothing in this section or in the rules shall affect any arrangement in writing whenever made between a solicitor and his client or an incorporated practice and its client as to the application of the client's money or interest on it.

NOTES

[1] As amended by the Law Reform (Miscellaneous Provisions) (Scotland) Act 1985, Sched. 1, Pt. I, para. 14, and (with effect from 29th January 1989) the Solicitors (Scotland) Act 1988, Sched. 1, para. 10 and Sched. 2.

[2] As amended by the Law Reform (Miscellaneous Provisions) (Scotland) Act 1980, s.25.

Accountant's certificates

[1] **37.**—(1) This section shall have effect for the purpose of securing satisfactory evidence of compliance with the accounts rules.

(2) Subject to the following provisions of this section, every solicitor and incorporated practice to whom the accounts rules apply shall, in accordance with the rules made under subsection (3), deliver to the Council a certificate by an accountant (in this section referred to as an "accountant's certificate").

(3) The council shall make rules (in this Act referred to as "accountant's certificate rules") prescribing—

  (*a*) the qualifications to be held by an accountant by whom an accountant's certificate may be given;

    (*b*) the nature and extent of the examination to be made by an accountant of the books and accounts of a solicitor or his firm or of an incorporated practice and of any other relative documents with a view to the signing of an accountant's certificate;

    (*c*) the intervals at which an accountant's certificate shall be delivered to the Council, not being more frequent than once in each practice year;

    (*d*) the accounting period for which an accountant's certificate shall be delivered or the different accounting periods for which in different circumstances an accountant's certificate shall be delivered;

    (*e*) the period within which an accountant's certificate shall be delivered; and

    (*f*) the form and content of an accountant's certificate.

    (4) The accountant's certificate rules may include such other provisions as the Council consider necessary or proper for the purpose of giving effect to the foregoing provisions of this section and for regulating any incidental, consequential or supplementary matters.

    (5) The delivery of an accountant's certificate in pursuance of subsection (2) shall not be required in the case of—

    (*a*) a solicitor who or incorporated practice which, in agreement with the Council, furnishes to the Council and keeps in force a fidelity bond by an insurance office or other institution accepted by the court as cautioners for a judicial factor appointed by the court for such amount as the Council may determine, guaranteeing the intromissions of the solicitor or his firm or, as the case may be, of the incorporated practice with money held by him or them or, as the case may be, it for or on behalf of clients; or

    (*b*) a solicitor or incorporated practice who satisfies the Council that during the accounting period to which the accountant's certificate would ordinarily relate he has not in the course of his practice or, as the case may be, it has not held or received any money on behalf of clients.

    (6) If the Council are of opinion that satisfactory evidence of compliance with the accounts rules for the time being in force will be secured by some method other than by delivery of an accountant's certificate under subsection (2), they may make rules—

    (*a*) prescribing—

      (i) that other method;

      (ii) the terms and conditions to be observed in connection therewith; and

      (iii) the procedure to be followed by solicitors or incorporated practices desiring to adopt that other method, and

    (*b*) containing such incidental, consequential and supplementary provisions relative thereto as the Council may consider necessary or proper;

and a solicitor who satisfies the Council that he or, as the case may be, an incorporated practice which satisfies the Council that it is complying with rules made under this subsection shall not be required to deliver an accountant's certificate in pursuance of subsection (2).

    (7) A certificate under the hand of the secretary of the Society certifying that a specified solicitor or incorporated practice has or has not, as the case may be, delivered to the Council an accountant's certificate, or supplied any evidence required from him or, as the case may be, it under this section or under the accountant's certificate rules or, as the case may be, under any rules made under subsection (6), shall, unless the contrary is proved, be evidence of the fact so certified.

    (8) Failure by a solicitor to comply with any provision of this section or of the accountant's certificate rules or of any rules made under subsection (6),

so far as applicable to him, may be treated as professional misconduct for the purposes of Part IV.

NOTE
[1] As amended by the Law Reform (Miscellaneous Provisions) (Scotland) Act 1985, Sched. 1, Pt. I, para. 15 (reading the word "substituted" in para. 15(*c*)(i) as "inserted").

Powers of Council to intervene

Powers where dishonesty alleged
[1] **38.**—(1) If the Council have reasonable cause to believe that a solicitor or an employee of his or an incorporated practice or any employee thereof has been guilty of any such dishonesty as is mentioned in section 43(2) they may—

(*a*) require the production or delivery to any person appointed by the Council at a time and place fixed by the Council of the documents to which this section applies;

(*b*) take possession of all such documents; and

(*c*) apply to the court for an order that no payment be made by any banker, building society or other body named in the order out of any banking account or any sum deposited in the name of such solicitor or his firm or, as the case may be, such incorporated practice without the leave of the court and the court may make such order.

(2) This section applies to the following documents—

(*a*) all books, accounts, deeds, securities, papers and other documents in the possession or control of such solicitor or his firm or, as the case may be, such incorporated practice;

[2] (*b*) all books, accounts, deeds, securities, papers and other documents relating to any trust of which he is a sole trustee or is a co-trustee only with one or more of his partners or employees or, as the case may be, of which the incorporated practice or one of its employees is a sole trustee or it is a co-trustee only with one or more of its employees.

(3) Part II of Schedule 3 shall have effect in relation to the powers of the Council under this section.

NOTES
[1] As amended by the Law Reform (Miscellaneous Provisions) (Scotland) Act 1985, Sched. 1, Pt. I, para. 16.
[2] As amended by the Solicitors (Scotland) Act 1988, Sched. 1, para. 11, with effect from 29th January 1989.

Powers where delay alleged
[1] **39.**—(1) If

(*a*) a complaint is made to the Society that there has been undue delay on the part of a solicitor or an incorporated practice in dealing with any matter in which he or his firm or, as the case may be, it is or has been concerned in a professional capacity, or any matter relating to a trust of which he is or was the sole trustee, or a co-trustee only with one or more of his partners or employees or, as the case may be, the incorporated practice or one of its employees was the sole trustee or it was a co-trustee only with one or more of its employees, and

(*b*) the Council are of opinion that the delay ought to be investigated,

the Council may by notice in writing at any time, and from time to time, require the solicitor or, as the case may be, incorporated practice to give an explanation of the delay.

(2) Any notice given by the Council under subsection (1) may specify a period, not being less than 21 days, within which they require an explanation to be furnished; and if within that period the solicitor or, as the case may be, incorporated practice does not reply or fails to furnish an explanation which the Council regard as sufficient and satisfactory, and he or, as

the case may be, it is so informed in writing, section 38 shall apply in relation to that solicitor and his firm or, as the case may be, to that incorporated practice in so far as it relates to documents or payments connected with the matter complained of (but not otherwise) and shall so apply notwithstanding that the Council may not have reasonable cause to believe that the solicitor or, as the case may be, incorporated practice has been guilty of any such dishonesty as is mentioned in section 43(2).

NOTE

[1] As amended by the Law Reform (Miscellaneous Provisions) (Scotland) Act 1985, Sched. 1, Pt. I, para. 17.

Powers where excessive fees etc. charged

[1] **39A.**—(1) This section applies where the Council are satisfied, in the case of any solicitor or incorporated practice, after inquiry and after giving the solicitor or incorporated practice an opportunity of being heard, that the solicitor or incorporated practice has issued an account for professional fees and outlays of an amount which is grossly excessive (whether or not the account has been paid by or on behalf of the client or debited by the solicitor or incorporated practice to the account of any sums held on behalf of the client).

(2) Where this section applies the Council may—

   (a) in the case of a solicitor, withdraw his practising certificate; or

   (b) in the case of an incorporated practice, withdraw the practising certificates of all or any of the solicitors who are directors of the incorporated practice;

and a certificate so withdrawn shall cease to have effect and the solicitor shall be suspended from practice as a solicitor.

(3) On being satisfied by the solicitor or, as the case may be, incorporated practice that he or it has complied with the requirements of subsection (4) the Council, unless they are of the opinion that the solicitor or incorporated practice is liable to disciplinary proceedings under Part IV, shall terminate the suspension from practice of the solicitor or solicitors concerned and shall restore to him or them any practising certificates held by him or them for the practice year then current.

(4) The requirements referred to in subsection (3) are—

   (a) to submit the account to the Auditor of the Court of Session for taxation together with all documents in the possession or control of the solicitor or incorporated practice which relate to the matters in respect of which the account was issued; and

   (b) to refund to the client a sum not less than the relevant amount.

(5) The Council shall be entitled to be represented at a diet for taxation by virtue of subsection (4)(a) and to make representations to the Auditor of Court.

(6) Where, on taxation of an account by virtue of subsection (4)(a), the amount due in respect of the account as taxed is the amount specified in the account as issued, the fee of the Auditor of Court shall be paid by the Council; but in any other case the fee shall be paid by the solicitor or, as the case may be, the incorporated practice.

(7) In subsection (4)(b) "the relevant amount" is the amount (if any) by which the sum received by the solicitor or incorporated practice in respect of the account exceeds the amount due in respect of the account as taxed.

(8) A solicitor may, within 21 days of receiving written notice of a decision of the Council under subsection (2) to withdraw his practising certificate, appeal to the Court against that decision; and on any such appeal the Court may give such directions in the matter, including directions as to the expenses of the proceedings before the Court, as it may think fit; and the order of the Court shall be final.

(9) The withdrawal of a solicitor's practising certificate under subsection (2) shall be without prejudice to the operation of section 35(3) or section 37(8).

NOTE
    [1] Inserted by the Solicitors (Scotland) Act 1988, s.4, with effect from 29th January 1989.

Powers where failure to comply with accounts rules, etc.
    [1] **40.**—[2] (1) Where the Council are satisfied, in the case of any solicitor or incorporated practice, after enquiry and after giving the solicitor or, as the case may be, incorporated practice an opportunity of being heard, that the solicitor or, as the case may be, incorporated practice has failed or is failing to comply with any provisions of—
    (*a*) section 35 or the accounts rules made under that section, or
    (*b*) section 37 or the accountant's certificate rules or other rules made under that section,
so far as applicable in his or, as the case may be, its case (in this section referred to as "the applicable provisions"), the Council may, subject to the provisions of this section,
    (*a*) withdraw the practising certificate held by the solicitor; or as the case may be—
    (*b*) withdraw the practising certificate or certificates or any or all of the solicitors who are directors of the incorporated practice,
and a certificate so withdrawn shall thereupon cease to have effect and the solicitor shall be suspended from practice as a solicitor.
    (2) On being satisfied by the solicitor that he or, as the case may be, by the incorporated practice that it is able and willing to comply with the applicable provisions, the Council, unless they are of opinion that the solicitor or, as the case may be, the incorporated practice is liable to disciplinary proceedings under Part IV, shall terminate the suspension from practice of the solicitor or solicitors concerned and shall restore to him or them any practising certificate or certificates held by him or them for the practice year then current.
    (3) Within 21 days after receiving written notice of a decision of the Council under this section to withdraw his practising certificate, or to refuse to terminate his suspension from practice, a solicitor may appeal to the court against the decision; and on any such appeal the court may give such directions in the matter, including directions as to the expenses of the proceedings before the court, as it may think fit; and the order of the court shall be final.
    (4) Any withdrawal of a solicitor's practising certificate by the Council in exercise of the power conferred by subsection (1) shall be without prejudice to the operation of section 35(3) or section 37(8).

NOTES
    [1] As amended by the Law Reform (Miscellaneous Provisions) (Scotland) Act 1985, Sched. 1, Pt. I, para. 18.
    [2] As amended by the Solicitors (Scotland) Act 1988, Sched. 1, para. 12, with effect from 29th January 1989.

Appointment of judicial factor
    [1] **41.** Where the Council, in exercise of any power conferred on them by the accounts rules, have caused an investigation to be made of the books, accounts and other documents of a solicitor or an incorporated practice, and, on consideration of the report of the investigation, the Council are satisfied—
    (*a*) that the solicitor or, as the case may be the incorporated practice has failed to comply with the provisions of those rules, and
    (*b*) that, in the case of a solicitor, in connection with his practice as such either—
        (i) his liabilities exceed his assets in the business, or
        (ii) his books, accounts and other documents are in such a condition that it is not reasonably practicable to ascertain definitely whether his liabilities exceed his assets, or

      (iii) there is reasonable ground for apprehending that a claim on the Guarantee Fund may arise; or

  (c) that, in the case of an incorporated practice, either—

      (i) its liabilities exceed its assets, or

      (ii) its books, accounts and other documents are in such a condition that it is not reasonably practicable to ascertain definitely whether its liabilities exceed its assets, or

      (iii) there is reasonable ground for apprehending that a claim on the guarantee fund may arise,

the Council may apply to the court for the appointment of a judicial factor on the estate of the solicitor or as the case may be, of the incorporated practice; and the court, on consideration of the said report and after giving the solicitor or as the case may be, the incorporated practice an opportunity of being heard, may appoint a judicial factor on such estate, or do otherwise as seems proper to it.

NOTE

[1] As amended by the Law Reform (Miscellaneous Provisions) (Scotland) Act 1985, Sched. 1, Pt. I, para. 19, and (with effect from 29th January 1989), the Solicitors (Scotland) Act 1988, Sched. 1, para. 13 and Sched. 2.

Distribution of sums in client bank account

[1] **42.**—(1) Subject to the provisions of this section, where, in any of the events mentioned in subsection (2) or (2A), the sum at the credit of any client account kept by a solicitor or an incorporated practice (or where several such accounts are kept by him or, as the case may be, by it the total of the sums at the credit of those accounts) is less than the total of the sums received by him in the course of his practice on behalf of his clients or, as the case may be, by it on behalf of its clients and remaining due by him or, as the case may be, by it to them, then, notwithstanding any rule of law to the contrary, the sum at the credit of the client account (or where several such accounts are kept, the total of the sums at the credit of those accounts) shall be divisible proportionately among the clients of the solicitor or, as the case may be, the incorporated practice according to the respective sums received by him in the course of his practice on their behalf or, as the case may be, by it on their behalf and remaining due by him or as the case may be, by it to them.

    (2) The events to which subsection (1) applies are in relation to any solicitor—

  (a) the sequestration of his estate;

  (b) the granting by him of a trust deed for behoof of creditors;

  (c) the appointment of a judicial factor on his estate.

    (2A) The events to which subsection (1) applies are in relation to any incorporated practice—

  (a) the making of an administration or winding up order or the appointment of a provisional liquidator, liquidator, receiver or judicial factor; or

  (b) the passing of a resolution for voluntary winding up (other than one passed solely for the purposes of reconstruction or amalgamation with another incorporated practice).

    [2] (3) Where a solicitor or an incorporated practice keeps an account at a bank in his or, as the case may be, its own name for a specified client no regard shall be had for the purposes of this section to the sum at the credit of that account or to any sums received by the solicitor in the course of his practice on behalf of that client or, as the case may be, by the incorporated practice on that behalf and remaining due by him or, as the case may be, by it to that client, so far as these are represented by the sum at the credit of that bank account; nor shall any regard be had for such purposes to any—

  (a) deposit or share account with a building society; or

  (b) account showing sums on loan to a local authority,

being in either case an account kept by the solicitor in his own name or, as the case may be, by the incorporated practice in its own name for a specified client.

(4) For the purposes of this section any reference to an account at a bank includes a reference to a deposit receipt at a bank.

NOTES

[1] As amended by the Law Reform (Miscellaneous Provisions) (Scotland) Act 1985, Sched. 1, Pt. I, para. 20.

[2] As amended by the Law Reform (Miscellaneous Provisions) (Scotland) Act 1980, s.25, and the Solicitors (Scotland) Act 1988, Sched. 2.

Powers where inadequate professional services alleged

[1] **42A.**—(1) Where—

   (*a*) the Council receive, from any person having an interest, a complaint that professional services provided by a solicitor in connection with any matter in which he has been instructed by a client were inadequate; and

   (*b*) the Council, after inquiry and after giving the solicitor an opportunity to make representations, uphold the complaint,

they may take such of the steps mentioned in subsection (2) as they think fit.

[2](2) The steps referred to in subsection (1) are—

   (*a*) to determine that the amount of the fees and outlays to which the solicitor shall be entitled for the services shall be—

   (i) nil; or

   (ii) such amount as the Council may specify in the determination, and to direct the solicitor to comply, or secure compliance, with such of the requirements set out in subsection (3) as appear to them to be necessary to give effect to the determination;

   (*b*) to direct the solicitor to secure the rectification at his own expense of any such error, omission or other deficiency arising in connection with the services as the Council may specify;

   (*c*) to direct the solicitor to take, at his own expense, such other action in the interests of the client as the Council may specify;

   (*d*) to direct the solicitor to pay to the client by way of compensation such sum, not exceeding £1,000, as the Council may specify.

(3) The requirements referred to in subsection (2)(*a*) are—

   (*a*) to refund, whether wholly or to any specified extent, any amount already paid by or on behalf of the client in respect of the fees and outlays of the solicitor in connection with the services;

   (*b*) to waive, whether wholly or to any specified extent, the right to recover those fees and outlays.

(4) Before making a determination in accordance with subsection (2)(*a*) the Council may submit the solicitor's account for the fees and outlays to the Auditor of the Court of Session for taxation.

(5) Where a solicitor in respect of whom a complaint of inadequate professional services is made was, at the time when the services were provided, an employee of another solicitor, a direction under this section shall specify and apply to that other solicitor as well as the solicitor in respect of whom the complaint is made.

(6) The Council shall intimate a determination or direction made under this section to every solicitor specified in it by sending a copy of the determination or direction to him.

(7) A solicitor in respect of whom a determination or direction has been made under this section may, within 21 days of the date on which the determination or direction is intimated to him, appeal to the Tribunal against the determination or direction.

(8) In the foregoing provisions of this section—

   "client", in relation to any matter in which a solicitor has been instructed, includes any person on whose behalf the person who gave the instructions was acting;

"complaint" includes a complaint of provision of inadequate professional services remitted to the Council by the Tribunal under paragraph 8A of Schedule 4; and

"solicitor" includes—

(*a*) any solicitor, whether or not he had a practising certificate in force at the time of provision of the professional services which are alleged to be inadequate, and notwithstanding that subsequent to that time he has had his name removed from or struck off the roll, ceased to practise or been suspended from practice;

(*b*) a firm of solicitors, whether or not, since the provision of the professional services which are alleged to be inadequate—
(i) there has been any change in the firm by the addition of a new partner or the death or resignation of an existing partner; or
(ii) the firm has ceased to practise; and

(*c*) an incorporated practice, whether or not, since the provision of the professional services which are alleged to be inadequate—
(i) there has been any change in the persons exercising the management and control of the practice; or
(ii) the practice has ceased to be recognised by virtue of section 34(1A) or has been wound up.

NOTES
[1] Inserted by the Solicitors (Scotland) Act 1988, s.1.
[2] As amended by the Law Reform (Miscellaneous Provisions) (Scotland) Act 1990, Sched. 8, para. 29(8).

Inadequate professional services: Council's powers to monitor compliance with directions
[1] **42B.**—(1) The Council shall, by notice in writing, require every solicitor specified in—

(*a*) a direction made under section 42A; or

(*b*) such a direction as confirmed or varied on appeal by—
(i) the Tribunal; or
(ii) the Court,

to give, within such period being not less than 21 days as the notice may specify, an explanation of the steps which he has taken to comply with the direction.

(2) Where an appeal is made under subsection (7) of section 42A against a direction made under that section, any notice under subsection (1)(*a*) above relating to that direction shall cease to have effect.

(3) Where an appeal is made by virtue of subsection (2) of section 53B against a decision of the Tribunal under subsection (1) of that section, any notice under subsection (1)(*b*)(i) above relating to the direction confirmed or varied by that decision shall cease to have effect.

(4) In this section "solicitor" has the same meaning as in section 42A(8).

NOTE
[1] Inserted by the Solicitors (Scotland) Act 1988, s.1.

Powers to examine documents and demand explanations in connection with complaints
[1] **42C.**—(1) Where the Council are satisfied that it is necessary for them to do so for the purpose of investigating a complaint made to them or remitted to them by the Tribunal alleging—

(*a*) professional misconduct by a solicitor;

(*b*) the failure of an incorporated practice to comply with any provision of this Act or of rules made under this Act applicable to that practice; or

(*c*) the provision by a solicitor or an incorporated practice of inadequate professional services,

the Council may give notice in writing in accordance with subsection (2) to the solicitor or his firm or to the incorporated practice or, where the solicitor is an employee of a firm or of an incorporated practice, to his employer.

(2) A notice under subsection (1) may require—

(*a*) the production or delivery to any person appointed by the Council, at a time and place specified in the notice, of all documents to which this section applies which are in the possession or control of the solicitor, firm or incorporated practice and relate to the matters to which the complaint relates (whether or not they relate also to other matters); and

(*b*) an explanation, within such period, not being less than 21 days, as the notice may specify, from the solicitor, firm or incorporated practice regarding the matters to which the complaint relates.

(3) This section applies to the documents specified in section 38(2).

(4) Part II of Schedule 3 shall have effect in relation to the powers conferred by subsection (1) to require the production or delivery of documents as it has effect in relation to the powers conferred by section 38, but with the following modifications—

(*a*) for the references in that Part to section 38 there shall be substituted references to this section; and

(*b*) for the reference in paragraph 5(1) in that Part to a person failing to produce or deliver documents immediately on being required by the Council to do so there shall be substituted a reference to a person failing to produce or deliver the documents within the time specified in the notice under subsection (1) of this section.

NOTE

[1] Inserted by the Solicitors (Scotland) Act 1988, s.2, with effect from 29th January 1989.

Protection of clients

Guarantee Fund

[1] **43.**—(1) There shall be a fund to be called "The Scottish Solicitors Guarantee Fund" (in this Act referred to as "the Guarantee Fund"), which shall be vested in the Society and shall be under the control and management of the Council.

(2) Subject to the provisions of this section and of Schedule 3 the Guarantee Fund shall be held by the Society for the purpose of making grants in order to compensate persons who in the opinion of the Council suffer pecuniary loss by reason of dishonesty on the part of

(*a*) any solicitor in practice in the United Kingdom, or any employee of such solicitor in connection with the practice of the solicitor, whether or not he had a practising certificate in force when the act of dishonesty was committed, and notwithstanding that subsequent to the commission of that act he may have died or had his name removed from or struck off the roll or may have ceased to practise or been suspended from practice; or

(*b*) any incorporated practice or any director, manager, secretary or other employee of an incorporated practice, notwithstanding that subsequent to the commission of that act it may have ceased to be recognised under section 34(1A) or have been wound up.

(3) No grant may be made under this section—

(*a*) in respect of a loss made good otherwise;

(*b*) in respect of a loss which in the opinion of the Council has arisen while the solicitor was suspended from practice;

(*c*) to a solicitor or his representatives in respect of a loss suffered

[THE NEXT PAGE IS F 23]

by him or them in connection with his practice as a solicitor by reason of dishonesty on the part of a partner or employee of his;

 (*cc*) to an incorporated practice or any director or member thereof in respect of a loss suffered by it or him by reason of dishonesty on the part of any director, manager, secretary or other employee of the incorporated practice in connection with the practice; or

 (*d*) unless an application for a grant is made to the Society in such manner, and within such period after the date on which the loss first came to the knowledge of the applicant, as may be prescribed by rules made under Schedule 3.

(4) The decision of the Council with respect to any application for a grant shall be final.

(5) The Council may refuse to make a grant, or may make a grant only to a limited extent, if they are of opinion that there has been negligence on the part of the applicant or of any person for whom he is responsible which has contributed to the loss in question.

(6) The Council or any committee appointed by them may administer oaths for the purpose of inquiry into any matters which affect the making or refusal of a grant from the Guarantee Fund.

(7) Part I of Schedule 3 shall have effect with respect to the Guarantee Fund, including the making of contributions thereto by solicitors and the administration and management of the Fund by the Council; but nothing in that Schedule shall apply to or in the case of a solicitor—

 (*a*) who is not in practice as a solicitor; or

 (*b*) who is suspended from practice as a solicitor during suspension; or

 (*c*) who is in any such employment as is specified in section 35(4);

but where any solicitor in any such employment as is mentioned in paragraph (*c*) engages in private practice as a solicitor, the said Schedule and the other provisions of this Act relating to the Guarantee Fund shall apply to him and in his case so far as regards such private practice or in the employment of an incorporated practice.

NOTE

[1] As amended by the Law Reform (Miscellaneous Provisions) (Scotland) Act 1985, Sched. 1, Pt. I, para. 21, with effect from 30th December 1985.

Professional indemnity

[1] **44.**—(1) The Council may make rules with the concurrence of the Lord President concerning indemnity for solicitors and incorporated practices and former solicitors against any class of professional liability, and the rules may for the purpose of providing such indemnity do all or any of the following things, namely—

 (*a*) authorise or require the Society to establish and maintain a fund or funds;

 (*b*) authorise or require the Society to take out and maintain insurance with any person permitted under the Insurance Companies Act 1974 to carry on liability insurance business or pecuniary loss insurance business;

 (*c*) require solicitors or any specified class of solicitors and incorporated practices or any specified class thereof to take out and maintain insurance with any person permitted under the Insurance Companies Act 1974 to carry on liability insurance business or pecuniary loss insurance business.

(2) The Society shall have power, without prejudice to any of its other powers, to carry into effect any arrangements which it considers necessary or expedient for the purpose of the rules.

(3) Without prejudice to the generality of subsections (1) and (2) rules made under this section—

(a) may specify the terms and conditions on which indemnity is to be available, and any circumstances in which the right to it is to be excluded or modified;

(b) may provide for the management, administration and protection of any fund maintained by virtue of subsection (1)(a) and require solicitors or any class of solicitors and incorporated practices or any class of incorporated practices to make payments to any such fund;

(c) may require solicitors or any class of solicitors and incorporated practices or any class of incorporated practices to make payments by way of premium on any insurance policy maintained by the Society by virtue of subsection (1)(b);

(d) may prescribe the conditions which an insurance policy must satisfy for the purpose of subsection (1)(c);

(e) may authorise the Society to determine the amount of any payments required by the rules subject to such limits, or in accordance with such provisions, as may be prescribed by the rules;

(f) may specify circumstances in which, where a solicitor or incorporated practice for whom indemnity is provided has failed to comply with the rules, proceedings in respect of sums paid by way of indemnity in connection with a matter in relation to which he or, as the case may be, it has failed to comply may be taken against him or, as the case may be, it by the Society or by insurers;

(g) may specify circumstances in which solicitors and incorporated practices are exempt from the rules;

(h) may empower the Council to take such steps as they consider necessary or expedient to ascertain whether or not the rules are being complied with; and

(i) may contain incidental, procedural or supplementary provisions.

(4) Failure to comply with rules made under this section may be treated as professional misconduct for the purposes of Part IV, and any person may make a complaint in respect of that failure to the Discipline Tribunal.

(5) In this section "professional liability" means any civil liability incurred by a solicitor or former solicitor in connection with his practice or in connection with any trust of which he is or formerly was a trustee and, as respects incorporated practices, means any liability incurred by it which if it had been incurred by a solicitor would constitute such civil liability.

NOTE
[1] As amended by the Law Reform (Miscellaneous Provisions) (Scotland) Act 1985, Sched. 1, Pt. I, para. 22, with effect from 30th December 1985.

Safeguarding interests of clients of solicitor struck off or suspended

[1] **45.**—(1) The following provisions of this section shall have effect in relation to the practice of a solicitor whose name is struck off the roll or who is suspended from practice as a solicitor under any provision of this Act and, in relation to any incorporated practice, the recognition under section 34(1A) of which is revoked.

(2) In the case of a solicitor, the solicitor shall within 21 days of the material date satisfy the Council that he has made suitable arrangements for making available to his clients or to some other solicitor or solicitors or incorporated practice instructed by his clients or by himself—

(a) all deeds, wills, securities, papers, books of accounts, records, vouchers and other documents in his or his firm's possession or control which are held on behalf of his clients or which relate to any trust of which he is sole trustee or co-trustee only with one or more of his partners or employees, and

(b) all sums of money due from him or his firm or held by him or his firm on behalf of his clients or subject to any such trust as aforesaid.

(2A) In the case of an incorporated practice, it shall within 21 days of the material date satisfy the Council that it has made suitable arrangements for making available to its clients or to some other solicitor or solicitors or incorporated practice instructed by its clients or itself—

(*a*) all deeds, wills, securities, papers, books of accounts, records, vouchers and other documents in its possession or control which are held on behalf of its clients or which relate to any trust of which it is sole trustee or co-trustee only with one or more of its employees; and

(*b*) all sums of money due from it or held by it on behalf of its clients or subject to any trust as aforesaid.

(3) If the solicitor or as the case may be, incorporated practice fails so to satisfy the Council the provisions of section 38 shall apply in relation to that solicitor or as the case may be, incorporated practice, notwithstanding that the Council may not have reasonable cause to believe that he or, as the case may be, any director, manager, secretary or other employee of the incorporated practice has been guilty of any such dishonesty as is mentioned in section 43(2).

(4) If the solicitor, immediately before the striking off or, as the case may be, the suspension, was a sole solicitor, the right to operate on, or otherwise deal with, any client account in the name of the solicitor or his firm shall on the occurrence of that event vest in the Society (notwithstanding any enactment or rule of law to the contrary) to the exclusion of any other person.

(5) In this section—

"material date" means whichever is the latest of—

(*a*) the date when the order of the Tribunal or court by or in pursuance of which the solicitor is struck off the roll or suspended from practice or, as the case may be, the recognition under section 34(1A) is revoked is to take effect;

(*b*) the last date on which

(i) an appeal against that order may be lodged or an application may be made to the court under section 54(2), or

(ii) an appeal against a decision of the Council under section 40 may be lodged;

(*c*) the date on which any such appeal is dismissed or abandoned; and

"sole solicitor" means a solicitor practising under his own name or as a single solicitor under a firm name.

NOTE
[1] As amended by the Law Reform (Miscellaneous Provisions) (Scotland) Act 1985, Sched. 1, Pt. I, para. 23, with effect from 30th December 1985.

Safeguarding interests of clients in certain other cases

46.—(1) Where the Council are satisfied that a sole solicitor is incapacitated by illness or accident to such an extent as to be unable to operate on, or otherwise deal with, any client account in the name of the solicitor or his firm, and that no other arrangements acceptable to the Council have been made, the right to operate on, or otherwise deal with, that account shall vest in the Society (notwithstanding any enactment or rule of law to the contrary) to the exclusion of any other person so long, but only so long, as the Council are satisfied that such incapacity and absence of other acceptable arrangements continues.

(2) Where a sole solicitor ceases to practise for any reason other than that his name has been struck off the roll or that he has been suspended from practice, and the Council are not satisfied that suitable arrangements have been made for making available to his clients or to some other solicitor or solicitors instructed by his clients or on their behalf—

(a) all deeds, wills, securities, papers, books of accounts, records, vouchers and other documents in his or his firm's possession or control which are held on behalf of his clients or which relate to any trust of which he is the sole trustee, or a co-trustee only with one or more of his employees, and

(b) all sums of money due from him or his firm or held by him or his firm on behalf of his clients or subject to any such trust as aforesaid,

the provisions of section 38 shall apply in relation to that solicitor, notwithstanding that the Council may not have reasonable cause to believe that he has been guilty of any such dishonesty as is mentioned in section 43(2).

(3) Where a sole solicitor dies—

(a) the right to operate on or otherwise deal with any client account in the name of the solicitor or his firm shall vest in the Society (notwithstanding any enactm ent or rule of law to the contrary) to the exclusion of any personal representatives of the solicitor, and shall be exercisable as from the death of the solicitor; and

(b) if the Council are not satisfied that suitable arrangements have been made for making available to the solicitor's clients or to some other solicitor or solicitors instructed by his clients or on their behalf—

(i) all deeds, wills, securities, papers, books of accounts, records, vouchers and other documents which were in his or his firm's possession or control which were held on behalf of his clients or which relate to any trust of which he was the sole trustee, or a co-trustee only with one or more of his employees, and

(ii) all sums of money which were due from him or his firm or were held by him or his firm on behalf of his clients or subject to any such trust as aforesaid,

the provisions of section 38 shall apply in relation to that solicitor notwithstanding that the Council may not have reasonable cause to believe that he had been guilty of any such dishonesty as is mentioned in section 43(2).

(4) In a case where the Society have operated on or otherwise dealt with a client account by virtue of subsection (3) the Society shall be entitled to recover from the estate of the solicitor who has died such reasonable expenses as the Society have thereby incurred.

(5) In this section "sole solicitor" has the same meaning as in section 45.

Restriction on employing solicitor struck off or suspended

[1] **47.**—(1) Unless he has the written permission of the Council to do so, a solicitor shall not, in connection with his practice as a solicitor and, unless it has such permission, an incorporated practice shall not, employ or remunerate any person who to his or, as the case may be, its knowledge is disqualified from practising as a solicitor by reason of the fact that his name has been struck off the roll or that he is suspended from practice as a solicitor.

(2) Any permission given by the Council for the purposes of subsection (1) may be given for such period and subject to such conditions as the Council think fit.

(3) A solicitor or, as the case may be, incorporated practice aggrieved by the refusal of the Council to grant any such permission as aforesaid, or by any conditions attached by the Council to the grant thereof, may appeal to the court; and on any such appeal the court may give such directions in the matter as it thinks fit.

(4) If any solicitor acts in contravention of this section or of any condition subject to which any permission has been given thereunder, his name shall be struck off the roll or he shall be suspended from practice as a

solicitor for such period as the Tribunal, or, in the case of an appeal, the court, may think fit and if any incorporated practice so acts its recognition under section 34(1A) shall be revoked.

NOTE
[1] As amended by the Law Reform (Miscellaneous Provisions) (Scotland) Act 1985, Sched. 1, Pt. I, para. 24.

48. [Repealed by the Law Reform (Miscellaneous Provisions) (Scotland) Act 1985, Sched. 1, Pt. II, para. 5.]

PART IV

COMPLAINTS AND DISCIPLINARY PROCEEDINGS

Lay Observer

49. [Repealed by the Law Reform (Miscellaneous Provisions) (Scotland) Act 1990, Sched. 9.]

The Scottish Solicitors' Discipline Tribunal

The Tribunal
 50.—(1) For the purposes of this Part of this Act there shall be a tribunal, which shall be known as the Scottish Solicitors' Discipline Tribunal and is in this Act referred to as "the Tribunal".

(2) Part I of Schedule 4 shall have effect in relation to the constitution of the Tribunal.

Complaints to Tribunal
 [1] **51.**—(1) A complaint may be made to the Tribunal by the Council; and, for the purpose of investigating and prosecuting complaints, the Council may appoint a solicitor to act as fiscal.

(2) The persons mentioned in subsection (3) may report to the Tribunal any case where it appears that a solicitor may have been guilty of professional misconduct (including any case where it appears that a solicitor may have been seeking to make extraordinary and apparently unjustified claims against his client or against the Scottish Legal Aid Fund) or an incorporated practice may have failed to comply with any provision of this Act or of rules made under this Act applicable to it or a solicitor or an incorporated practice may have provided inadequate professional services, and any such report shall be treated by the Tribunal as a complaint under subsection (1).

 [2] (3) The persons referred to in subsection (2) are—
 (*a*) the Lord Advocate;
 (*b*) any judge;
 (*ba*) the Dean of the Faculty of Advocates;
 (*c*) the Auditor of the Court of Session;
 (*d*) the Auditor of any sheriff court;
 (*e*) the Scottish Legal Aid Board;
 (*f*) the Scottish legal services ombudsman.

(4) Where a report is made to the Tribunal under subsection (2) the Tribunal may, if it thinks fit, appoint a solicitor to prosecute the complaint and the expenses of the solicitor, so far as not recoverable from the solicitor complained against, shall be paid out of the funds of the Tribunal.

NOTES
[1] As amended by the Law Reform (Miscellaneous Provisions) (Scotland) Act 1985, Sched. 1, Pt. I, para. 26, the Legal Aid (Scotland) Act 1986, Sched. 3, para. 8, and the Solicitors (Scotland) Act 1988, Sched. 1, para. 14.
 [2] As amended by the Law Reform (Miscellaneous Provisions) (Scotland) Act 1990, Sched. 8, para. 29(9).

Procedure on complaints to Tribunal

[1] **52.**—(1) Part II of Schedule 4 shall have effect in relation to the procedure and powers of the Tribunal in relation to any complaint concerning a solicitor or an incorporated practice.

(2) Subject to the other provisions of this Part, and of any rules of court made under this Act, the Tribunal, with the concurrence of the Lord President, may make rules—

(a) for regulating the making, hearing and determining of complaints made to it under this Act; and

(aa) for regulating the making, hearing and determining of appeals made to it under section 42A(7) or 53D(1);

(b) generally as to the procedure of the Tribunal (including provision for hearings taking place in public or wholly or partly in private).

NOTE

[1] As amended by the Law Reform (Miscellaneous Provisions) (Scotland) Act 1985, Sched. 1, Pt. I, para. 27 and the Solicitors (Scotland) Act 1988, Sched. 1, para. 15. Applied by the Legal Aid (Scotland) Act 1986, s.31(10).

Powers of Tribunal

[1] **53.**—(1) Subject to the other provisions of this Part, the powers exercisable by the Tribunal under subsection (2) shall be exercisable if—

(a) after holding an inquiry into a complaint against a solicitor the Tribunal is satisfied that he has been guilty of professional misconduct, or

(b) a solicitor has (whether before or after enrolment as a solicitor), been convicted by any court of an act involving dishonesty or has been sentenced to a term of imprisonment of not less than 2 years, or

(c) an incorporated practice has been convicted by any court of an offence, which conviction the Tribunal is satisfied renders it unsuitable to continue to be recognised under section 34(1A); or

(d) after holding an inquiry into a complaint, the Tribunal is satisfied that an incorporated practice has failed to comply with any provision of this Act or of rules made under this Act applicable to it.

[1a] (2) Subject to subsection (1), the Tribunal may—

(a) order that the name of the solicitor be struck off the roll; or

(b) order that the solicitor be suspended from practice as a solicitor for such time as it may determine; or

(ba) order that any right of audience held by the solicitor by virtue of section 25A be suspended or revoked;

(c) subject to subsection (3), impose on the solicitor or, as the case may be, the incorporated practice a fine not exceeding £10,000; or

(d) censure the solicitor or, as the case may be, the incorporated practice; or

(e) impose such fine and censure him or, as the case may be, it; or

(f) order that the recognition under section 34(1A) of the incorporated practice be revoked; or

(g) order that an investment business certificate issued to a solicitor, a firm of solicitors or an incorporated practice be—

(i) suspended for such time as they may determine; or

(ii) subject to such terms and conditions as it may direct; or

(iii) revoked.

(3) The Tribunal shall not impose a fine under subsection (2)(c) in any of the circumstances mentioned in subsection (1)(b).

(3A) The powers conferred by subsection (2)(c), (d) and (e) may be exercised by the Tribunal—

(a) in relation to a former solicitor, notwithstanding that his name has been struck off the roll or that he has, since the date of the misconduct, conviction or sentence referred to in subsection (1)(*a*) or (*b*), ceased to practise as a solicitor or been suspended from practice;

(*b*) in relation to a body corporate which was formerly an incorporated practice, notwithstanding that the body has, since the date of the conviction or failure referred to in subsection (1)(*c*) or (*d*), ceased to be recognised as an incorporated practice by virtue of section 34(1A).

(3B) The power conferred by subsection (2)(*ba*) may be exercised by the Tribunal either independently of, or in conjunction with, any other power conferred by that subsection.

(4) Any fine imposed by the Tribunal under subsection (2) shall be forfeit to Her Majesty.

(5) Where the Tribunal have exercised the power conferred by subsection (2) to censure, or impose a fine on, a solicitor, or both to censure and impose a fine, the Tribunal may order that the solicitor's practising certificate shall be subject to such terms and conditions as the Tribunal may direct; and the Council shall give effect to any such order of the Tribunal.

[1](6) Where the Tribunal order that the name of a solicitor be struck off the roll, or that the solicitor be suspended from practice as a solicitor, or that any right of audience held by the solicitor by virtue of section 25A be suspended or revoked, the Tribunal may direct that the order shall take effect on the date on which it is intimated to the solicitor; and if any such direction is given the order shall take effect accordingly.

(6A) Where the Tribunal order that the recognition under section 34(1A) of an incorporated practice be revoked, the Tribunal shall direct that the order shall take effect on such date as the Tribunal specifies, being a date not earlier than 60 days after its order is intimated to the incorporated practice, and such an order shall take effect accordingly.

(6B) Where the Tribunal make an order under subsection (2)(*g*), they may direct that the order shall take effect on the date on which it is intimated to the solicitor, firm or incorporated practice; and if any such direction is given the order shall take effect accordingly.

(7) Where in relation to any such order as is mentioned in subsection (6) or (6A) the Tribunal give a direction under subsection (6) or, as the case may be, subsection (6A) and an appeal against the order is taken to the court under section 54, the order shall continue to have effect pending the determination or abandonment of the appeal unless, on an application under subsection (2) of section 54, the court otherwise directs.

[2] (8) The Secretary of State may, by order made by statutory instrument subject to annulment in pursuance of a resolution of either House of Parliament, amend—

(*a*) paragraph (*c*) of subsection (2) by substituting for the amount for the time being specified in that paragraph such other amount as appears to him to be justified by a change in the value of money;

(*b*) the definition of "investment business certificate" in subsection (7A) by substituting for the reference to Rule 2.2 of the Solicitors (Scotland) (Conduct of Investment Business) Practice Rules 1988, or such reference replacing that reference as may for the time being be specified in that subsection, a reference to such Practice Rule as may from time to time replace Rule 2.2.

NOTES
  [1] As amended by the Law Reform (Miscellaneous Provisions) (Scotland) Act 1985, Sched. 1, Pt. I, para. 28, the Solicitors (Scotland) Act 1988, Sched. 1, para. 16, and the Law Reform (Miscellaneous Provisions) (Scotland) Act 1990, Sched. 8, para. 29(10).
  [1a] As amended by the Law Reform (Miscellaneous Provisions) (Scotland) Act 1980, s.24, and S.I. 1987 No. 333.
  [2] Inserted by the Law Reform (Miscellaneous Provisions) (Scotland) Act 1980, s.24 and as amended by the 1988 Act as noted above.

Inadequate professional services: powers of Tribunal

[1] **53A.**—(1) Subject to the other provisions of this Part where—

(a) a complaint is made to the Tribunal that professional services provided by a solicitor in connection with any matter in which he has been instructed by a client were inadequate; and

(b) the Tribunal, after inquiry and after giving the solicitor an opportunity to make representations, upholds the complaint,

it may take such of the steps mentioned in subsection (2) as it thinks fit.

[2] (2) The steps referred to in subsection (1) are—

(a) to determine that the amount of the fees and outlays to which the solicitor shall be entitled for the services shall be—

(i) nil; or

(ii) such amount as the Tribunal may specify in the determination, and by order direct the solicitor to comply, or secure compliance, with such of the requirements set out in subsection (3) as appear to it to be necessary to give effect to the determination;

(b) to direct the solicitor to secure the rectification at his own expense of any such error, omission or other deficiency arising in connection with the services as the Tribunal may specify;

(ba) to order that any right of audience held by the solicitor by virtue of section 25A be suspended or revoked;

(c) to direct the solicitor to take, at his own expense, such other action in the interests of the client as the Tribunal may specify;

(d) to direct the solicitor to pay to the client by way of compensation such sum, not exceeding £1,000, as the Tribunal may specify.

(3) The requirements referred to in subsection (2)(a) are—

(a) to refund, whether wholly or to any specified extent, any amount already paid by or on behalf of the client in respect of the fees and outlays of the solicitor in connection with the services;

(b) to waive, whether wholly or to any specified extent, the right to recover those fees and outlays.

(4) Before making a determination in accordance with subsection (2)(a) the Tribunal may submit the solicitor's account for the fees and outlays to the Auditor of the Court of Session for taxation.

(5) Where a solicitor in respect of whom a complaint of inadequate professional services is made was, at the time when the services were provided, an employee of another solicitor, a direction under this section shall specify and apply to that other solicitor as well as the solicitor in respect of whom the complaint is made.

(6) A direction of the Tribunal under this section shall be enforceable in like manner as an extract registered decree arbitral in favour of the Council bearing a warrant for execution issued by the sheriff court of any sheriffdom in Scotland.

(7) Section 54(1) shall apply to a direction of the Tribunal under this section (but not to a decision to submit an account for taxation under subsection (4)) as it applies to a decision of the Tribunal relating to discipline under this Act.

(8) In the foregoing provisions of this section "solicitor" and "client" have the same meanings as in section 42A(8).

NOTES

[1] Inserted by the Solicitors (Scotland) Act 1988, s.3.

[2] As amended by the Law Reform (Miscellaneous Provisions) (Scotland) Act 1990, Sched. 8, para. 29(11).

Inadequate professional services: appeal to Tribunal against Council determination or direction

[1] **53B.**—(1) On an appeal to the Tribunal under section 42A(7) the Tribunal may quash, confirm or vary the determination or direction being appealed against.

(2) Section 54(1) shall apply to a decision of the Tribunal under subsection (1) as it applies to a decision of the Tribunal relating to discipline under this Act.

NOTE
[1] Inserted by the Solicitors (Scotland) Act 1988, s. 3.

Inadequate professional services: enforcement by Tribunal of Council direction
[1] **53C.**—(1) Where a solicitor fails to comply with a direction given by the Council under section 42A (including, as the case may be, such a direction as confirmed or varied on appeal by the Tribunal or the Court) within the period specified in the notice relating to that direction given to the solicitor under section 42B(1), or such longer period as the Council may allow, the Council shall make a complaint to the Tribunal and may appoint a solicitor to represent them in connection with the complaint.

(2) If after inquiry into a complaint made under subsection (1) the Tribunal is satisfied that the solicitor has failed to comply with the direction the Tribunal may order that the direction, or such part of it as the Tribunal thinks fit, shall be enforceable in like manner as an extract registered decree arbitral in favour of the Council bearing a warrant for execution issued by the sheriff court of any sheriffdom in Scotland.

(3) Paragraph 9 of Schedule 4 shall not apply to a complaint made under subsection (1).

NOTE
[1] Inserted by the Solicitors (Scotland) Act 1988, s.3.

[1] **53D.**—(1) Where, in accordance with rules made under this Act, the Council suspend or withdraw an investment business certificate or impose conditions or restrictions on it the solicitor, firm of solicitors or incorporated practice to whom it was issued may, within 21 days of the date of intimation of the decision of the Council, appeal to the Tribunal against that decision.

(2) On an appeal to the Tribunal under subsection (1) the Tribunal may quash, confirm or vary the decision being appealed against.

(3) Section 54(1) shall apply to a decision of the Tribunal under subsection (2) as it applies to a decision of the Tribunal relating to discipline under this Act.

NOTE
[1] Inserted by the Solicitors (Scotland) Act 1988, Sched. 1, para. 17.

Appeals from decisions of Tribunal
[1] **54.**—(1) Any person aggrieved by a decision of the Tribunal relating to discipline under this Act may within 21 days of the date on which the decision of the Tribunal is intimated to that person, appeal against the decision to the court, and on any such appeal the court may give such directions in the matter as it thinks fit, including directions as to the expenses of the proceedings before the court and as to any order by the Tribunal relating to expenses; and the order of the court shall be final.

(2) Where
(*a*) the Tribunal has exercised the power conferred by section 53(6) to direct that its decision shall take effect on the date on which it is intimated to the solicitor concerned, the solicitor may, within 21 days of that date, apply to the court for an order varying or quashing the direction in so far as it relates to the date of taking effect;
(*b*) the Tribunal has ordered the revocation of the recognition under section 34(1A) of an incorporated practice, the incorporated practice may within 21 days of the date when the order is intimated to it apply to the court for an order varying (subject to the limit of 60

days referred to in subsection (6A) of section 53) the direction under that subsection; and on any such application the court may make the order applied for or such other order with respect to the matter as it thinks fit.

NOTE

[1] As amended by the Law Reform (Miscellaneous Provisions) (Scotland) Act 1985, Sched. 1, Pt. I, para. 29.

The Court

Powers of court

55.—[1] (1) In the case of professional misconduct by any solicitor the court may—

(*a*) cause the name of that solicitor to be struck off the roll; or

(*b*) suspend the solicitor from practice as a solicitor for such period as the court may determine; or

(*ba*) suspend the solicitor from exercising any right of audience held by him by virtue of section 25A for such period as the court may determine; or

(*bb*) revoke any right of audience so acquired by him; or

(*c*) fine the solicitor; or

(*d*) censure him; and in any of those events,

(*e*) find him liable in any expenses which may be involved in the proceedings before the court.

(2) Subject to subsection (3), a decision of the court under this section shall be final.

(3) A solicitor whose name has been struck off the roll in pursuance of an order made by the court under subsection (1), may apply to the court for an order directing his name to be restored to the roll and the court may make such order.

[2] (3A) A solicitor whose rights of audience under section 25A have been revoked in pursuance of an order made by the court under subsection (1) may apply to the court for an order restoring those rights, and the court may make such order.

(4) An application under subsection (3) shall be by way of petition and intimation of any such petition shall be made to the Tribunal who shall be entitled to appear and to be heard in respect of the application.

NOTES

[1] As amended by the Law Reform (Miscellaneous Provisions) (Scotland) Act 1990, Sched. 8, para. 29(12).

[2] Inserted by the Law Reform (Miscellaneous Provisions) (Scotland) Act 1990, Sched. 8, para. 29(12).

Saving for jurisdiction of courts

56. Except as otherwise expressly provided, nothing in this Part shall affect the jurisdiction exercisable by the court, or by any inferior court, over solicitors.

Further provision as to compensation awards

[1] **56A.**—(1) The taking of any steps under section 42A(2) or 53A(2) shall not be founded upon in any proceedings for the purpose of showing that the solicitor in respect of whom the steps were taken was negligent.

(2) A direction under section 42A(2)(*d*) or 53A(2)(*d*) to a solicitor to pay compensation to a client shall not prejudice any right of that client to take proceedings against that solicitor for damages in respect of any loss which he alleges he has suffered as a result of that solicitor's negligence, and any sum directed to be paid to that client under either of those provisions may be taken into account in the computation of any award of damages made to him in any such proceedings.

(3) The Secretary of State may by order made by statutory instrument amend subsection (2)(*d*) of sections 42A and 53A by substituting for the sum for the time being specified in those provisions such other sum as he considers appropriate.

(4) Before making any such order the Secretary of State shall consult the Council.

(5) An order made under this section shall be subject to annulment in pursuance of a resolution of either House of Parliament.

NOTE

[1] Inserted by the Law Reform (Miscellaneous Provisions) (Scotland) Act 1990 (c. 40), Sched. 8, para. 29(13).

PART V

NOTARIES PUBLIC

Admission and enrolment of solicitors as notaries public

[1] **57.**—(1) The offices and functions of—

(*a*) the clerk to the admission of notaries public; and

(*b*) the keeper of the register of notaries public,

are hereby transferred to the Council.

(2) Any solicitor may apply to the court to be admitted as a notary public; and on any such application the court may so admit the applicant and may direct the Council to register him in the register of notaries public.

(2A) A petition by the Council under section 6(3A) for the admission of a person as a solicitor may, if the person so requests, include an application for the person's admission as a notary public; and an order on any such petition admitting that person as a solicitor may admit him as a notary public and direct the Council to register him in the register of notaries public.

(2B) A petition by a person under section 6(2) for his admission as a solicitor may include an application for his admission as a notary public; and an order on any such petition admitting that person as a solicitor may admit him as a notary public and direct the Council to register him in the register of notaries public.

(3) It shall not be necessary for any person to find caution on his admission as a notary public.

[2] (4) The procedure to be followed on any application by a person to be admitted a notary public may be prescribed by rules of court.

(5) The Council may charge such reasonable fees as they consider appropriate in respect of the admission of any person as a notary public.

NOTES

[1] As amended by the Law Reform (Miscellaneous Provisions) (Scotland) Act 1990 (c. 40), s. 37(2) (effective 20th July 1992: S.I. 1992 No. 1599).

[2] As amended by the Solicitors (Scotland) Act 1988 (c. 42), Sched. 1, para. 18 and Sched. 2.

Removal from and restoration to register of names of notaries public

[1] **58.**—(1) In the case of any person who is both a solicitor and a notary public, if his name is struck off the roll of solicitors or is removed from that roll in pursuance of an order under any provision of this Act, the Council shall forthwith strike off or, as the case may be, remove his name from the register of notaries public.

(2) If the name of any such person, having been struck off or removed from the roll as aforesaid, is subsequently restored thereto in pursuance of an order under any provision of this Act, the Council shall forthwith restore the name to the register of notaries public.

(3) Where a person who is both a solicitor and a notary public is suspended from practising as a solicitor under this Act the Council shall forthwith remove the person's name from the register of notaries public.

(4) If the suspension of such a person as is mentioned in subsection (3) is terminated or otherwise comes to an end the Council shall restore the person's name to the register.

NOTE
[1] As amended by the Law Reform (Miscellaneous Provisions) (Scotland) Act 1990 (c. 40), s. 37(3) (effective 20th July 1992: S.I. 1992 No. 1599).

Authority of notaries public to administer oaths, etc.
   59.—(1) Subject to subsection (2), in any case where the administration of an oath, or the receipt of an affidavit or solemn affirmation, is authorised by or under any enactment, it shall be lawful for the oath to be administered, or, as the case may be, for the affidavit or affirmation to be received, by a notary public.
   (2) Nothing in this section applies to an oath or affirmation relating to any matter or thing relating to the preservation of the peace or to the prosecution, trial or punishment of an offence, or to any proceedings before either House of Parliament or any committee thereof.
   (3) This section is without prejudice to any other statutory provision relating to the administration of oaths by notaries public.

Offence for notaries public to act for unqualified persons
   60. [Repealed by the Solicitors (Scotland) Act 1988 (c. 42), Sched. 2.]

PART VI

MISCELLANEOUS AND GENERAL

Miscellaneous

Multi-national practices
   [1] **60A.**—(1) Subject to the provisions of this section, solicitors and incorporated practices may enter into multi-national practices with registered foreign lawyers.
   (2) The Council shall maintain a register of foreign lawyers, and may make rules with regard to registration; and, without prejudice to the generality of the foregoing, such rules may include provision as to—
   (*a*) the manner in which applications for registration are to be made;
   (*b*) the fees payable in respect of such applications;
   (*c*) conditions which may be imposed in respect of registration; and
   (*d*) the period for which any such registration is to run.
   (3) Section 34(2) and (3) apply to rules made under subsection (2) as they apply to rules made under that section.
   (4) Any foreign lawyer may apply to the Council to be registered as such for the purposes of this section and the Council shall, if they are satisfied that the legal profession of which the applicant is a member is so regulated as to make it appropriate for him to be allowed to enter into a multi-national practice with solicitors or incorporated practices, enter his name on the register.
   (5) Subject to subsection (6), the Secretary of State may by order made by statutory instrument provide that any enactment or instrument—
   (*a*) passed or made before the commencement of this section;
   (*b*) having effect in relation to solicitors; and
   (*c*) specified in the order,
shall have effect with respect to registered foreign lawyers as it has effect with respect to solicitors.

(6) Before making any order under subsection (5), the Secretary of State shall consult the Council.

(7) An order under subsection (5) may provide for an enactment or instrument to have effect with respect to registered foreign lawyers subject to such additions, omissions or other modifications as the Secretary of State specifies in the order.

(8) No order shall be made under subsection (5) unless a draft of the order has been approved by both Houses of Parliament.

NOTE

[1] Inserted by the Law Reform (Miscellaneous Provisions) (Scotland) Act 1990 (c. 40), s. 32 (in force 17th March 1993, only in respect of the provisions relating to the making of rules and orders in s. 60A(2), (3) and (5)–(8): S.I. 1993 No. 641).

Protection of banks

[1] **61.**—(1) Subject to the provisions of this section, no bank or building society shall, in connection with any transaction on any account of a solicitor or an incorporated practice kept with it or with any other bank or building society—

(*a*) incur any liability, or

(*b*) be under any obligation to make any inquiry, or

(*c*) be deemed to have any knowledge of any right of any person to any money paid or credited to the account,

which it would not incur, or be under, or be deemed to have (as the case may be) in the case of an account kept by a person entitled absolutely to all money paid or credited to it; but nothing in this subsection shall relieve the bank or building society from any liability or obligation under which it would be apart from this Act.

(2) In subsection (1) "account" does not include an account kept by a solicitor or an incorporated practice as trustee for a specified beneficiary.

(3) Notwithstanding anything in the preceding provisions of this section a bank or building society at which a solicitor or an incorporated practice keeps a special account for clients' money shall not, in respect of any liability of the solicitor or, as the case may be, the incorporated practice to the bank or building society (not being a liability in connection with that account) have or obtain any recourse or right, whether by way of set-off, counter-claim, charge or otherwise, against money standing to the credit of that account.

NOTE

[1] As amended by the Law Reform (Miscellaneous Provisions) (Scotland) Act 1985 (c. 73), Sched. 1, Pt. I, para. 31, and the Solicitors (Scotland) Act 1988 (c. 42), Sched. 1, para. 19.

Solicitors' fees

[1] **61A.**—(1) Subject to the provisions of this section, and without prejudice to—

(*a*) section 32(1)(*i*) of the Sheriff Courts (Scotland) Act 1971; or

(*b*) section 5(*h*) of the Court of Session Act 1988,

where a solicitor and his client have reached an agreement in writing as to the solicitor's fees in respect of any work done or to be done by him for his client it shall not be competent, in any litigation arising out of any dispute as to the amount due to be paid under any such agreement, for the court to remit the solicitor's account for taxation.

(2) Subsection (1) is without prejudice to the court's power to remit a solicitor's account for taxation in a case where there has been no written agreement as to the fees to be charged.

(3) A solicitor and his client may agree, in relation to a litigation undertaken on a speculative basis, that, in the event of the litigation being successful, the solicitor's fee shall be increased by such a percentage as may, subject to subsection (4), be agreed.

(4) The percentage increase which may be agreed under subsection (3) shall not exceed such limit as the court may, after consultation with the Council, prescribe by act of sederunt.

NOTE
[1] Inserted by the Law Reform (Miscellaneous Provisions) (Scotland) Act 1990 (c. 40), s. 36(3) (effective 4th July 1992: S.I. 1992 No. 1599).

Charge for expenses out of property recovered
62.—(1) Where a solicitor has been employed by a client to pursue or defend any action or proceeding, the court before which the action or proceeding has been heard or is depending may declare the solicitor entitled, in respect of the taxed expenses of or in reference to the action or proceeding, to a charge upon, and a right to payment out of, any property (of whatsoever nature, tenure or kind it may be) which has been recovered or preserved on behalf of the client by the solicitor in the action or proceeding; and the court may make such order for the taxation of, and for the raising and payment of, those expenses out of the said property as the court thinks just.

(2) Where a declaration has been made under subsection (1) any act done or deed granted by the client after the date of the declaration except an act or deed in favour of a *bona fide* purchaser or lender, shall be absolutely void as against the charge or right.

Council's power to recover expenses incurred under section 38, 45 or 46
[1] **62A.**—(1) Without prejudice to the Society's entitlement under section 46(4) to recover expenses, the Council shall be entitled to recover from a solicitor or incorporated practice in respect of whom it has taken action under section 38, 45, or 46, any expenditure reasonably incurred by it in so doing.

(2) Expenditure incurred in taking action under section 38 is recoverable under subsection (1) above only where notice has been served under paragraph 5(2) of Schedule 3 in connection with that action and—
  (*a*) no application has been made in consequence under paragraph 5(4) of that Schedule; or
  (*b*) the Court, on such an application, has made a direction under paragraph 5(5) of that Schedule.

NOTE
[1] Inserted by the Law Reform (Miscellaneous Provisions) (Scotland) Act 1985 (c. 73), Sched. 1, Pt. II, para. 6.

General

Penalties and time limit for prosecution of offences
[1] **63.**—(1) Any person guilty of an offence under this Act shall be liable on summary conviction to a fine not exceeding level 4 on the standard scale.

(2) Notwithstanding any provision of the Criminal Procedure (Scotland) Act 1975, the prosecution of any offence under this Act shall be commenced within 6 months of its first discovery by the prosecutor or in any event within 2 years after the commission of that offence.

(3) Where an offence under this Act is committed by a body corporate and is proved to have been committed with the consent or connivance of or to be attributable to any neglect on the part of—

(*a*) any director, secretary or other similar officer of the body corporate; or

(*b*) any person who was purporting to act in any such capacity,

he (as well as the body corporate) shall be guilty of the offence and shall be liable to be proceeded against and punished accordingly.

(4) Where an offence under this Act is committed by a partnership or by an unincorporated association (other than a partnership) and is proved to have been committed with the consent or connivance of a partner in the partnership or, as the case may be, a person concerned in the management or control of the association, he (as well as the partnership or association) shall be guilty of the offence and shall be liable to be proceeded against and punished accordingly.

NOTE
[1] As amended by virtue of the Criminal Procedure (Scotland) Act 1975 (c. 21), ss. 289F and 289G, and by the Law Reform (Miscellaneous Provisions) (Scotland) Act 1990 (c. 40), Sched. 8, para. 29(14) and Sched. 9.

Service of notices, etc.
[1] **64.** Any notice or other document which is required or authorised under this Act to be given to, or served on, any person shall be taken to be duly given or served if it is delivered to him or left at, or sent by post to, his last-known place of business or residence or, in the case of an incorporated practice, if it is left at, or delivered or sent by post to, its registered office.

NOTE
[1] As amended by the Law Reform (Miscellaneous Provisions) (Scotland) Act 1985 (c. 73), Sched. 1, Pt. I, para. 32.

Advisory and supervisory functions of the Director General of Fair Trading
[1] **64A.**—(1) Before considering any rule—
(*a*) made under section 25A(4) or (5); or
(*b*) such as is mentioned in section 34(3A),
the Secretary of State shall send a copy of the proposed rule in question to the Director.

(2) The Director shall consider whether the rule in question would have, or would be likely to have, the effect of restricting, distorting or preventing competition to any significant extent.

(3) When the Director has completed his consideration he shall give such advice to the Secretary of State as he thinks fit.

(4) The Director may publish any advice given by him under subsection (3).

(5) The Director shall, so far as practicable, exclude from anything published under subsection (4) any matter—
(*a*) which relates to the affairs of a particular person; and
(*b*) the publication of which would, or might in the Director's opinion, seriously and prejudicially affect the interests of that person.

(6) For the purposes of the law of defamation, the publication of any advice or report by the Director under this section shall be absolutely privileged.

NOTE
[1] Inserted by the Law Reform (Miscellaneous Provisions) (Scotland) Act 1990 (c. 40), s. 43.

Duty of Secretary of State
[1] **64B.** When he has received advice under section 64A(3) in relation to a rule made under section 25A(4) or (5) or such as is mentioned in section 34(3A), the Secretary of State may, having considered—

(*a*) that advice;
(*b*) whether the interests of justice require that there should be such a rule; and
(*c*) in relation to a rule made under section 25A(5), any relevant practice obtaining in the sheriff court,

approve or refuse to approve the rule.

NOTE
[1] Inserted by the Law Reform (Miscellaneous Provisions) (Scotland) Act 1990 (c. 40), s. 43.

Investigatory powers of the Director

[1] **64C.**—(1) For the purpose of investigating any matter under section 64A, the Director may by notice in writing—
(*a*) require any person to produce to him or to any person appointed by him for the purpose, at a time and place specified in the notice, any documents which are specified or described in the notice and which—
(i) are in that person's custody or under that person's control; and
(ii) relate to any matter relevant to the investigation; or
(*b*) require any person carrying on any business to furnish to him (within such time and in such manner and form as the notice may specify) such information as may be specified or described in the notice.

(2) A person shall not be required under this section to produce any document or disclose any information which he would be entitled to refuse to produce or disclose on the grounds of confidentiality between a client and his professional legal adviser in any civil proceedings.

(3) Subsections (5) to (8) of section 85 of the Fair Trading Act 1973 shall apply in relation to a notice under this section as they apply in relation to a notice under subsection (1) of that section.

NOTE
[1] Inserted by the Law Reform (Miscellaneous Provisions) (Scotland) Act 1990 (c. 40), s. 43.

Review of rules approved by the Secretary of State

[1] **64D.**—(1) Without prejudice to the power of the Council to review any rule made by them, where the Secretary of State has approved a rule under section 64B he may, and if so requested by the Lord President shall, require the Council to review its terms.

(2) When they have reviewed a rule following a requirement made under subsection (1), the Council may revise the rule in the light of that review, and shall then submit the rule as revised or, if they have not revised it, as previously approved to the Lord President and the Secretary of State.

(3) Where the Lord President and the Secretary of State are agreed that the terms of [any] rule as submitted to them are satisfactory, the Secretary of State shall approve the rule, and may direct the Council to bring it into force as soon as is practicable.

(4) Where either the Secretary of State or the Lord President is of the view that any rule, as submitted to them, is not satisfactory, but they do not agree as to what the terms of the rule should be, the rule shall continue to have effect as previously approved.

(5) Where the Secretary of State and the Lord President agree both that any rule submitted to them under subsection (2) is not satisfactory, and as to what the terms of the rule should be, the Secretary of State may direct the Council—
(*a*) to amend the rule in such manner as he and the Lord President consider appropriate; and
(*b*) to bring the rule, as so amended, into force as soon as is practicable.

(6) The provisions of sections 64A and 64B apply to rules submitted to the Secretary of State under this section as they apply to rules submitted to him under sections 25A(9) or (10) and 34(3A).

NOTE
[1] Inserted by the Law Reform (Miscellaneous Provisions) (Scotland) Act 1990 (c. 40), s. 43.

[THE NEXT PAGE IS F 35]

Interpretation
65.—[1] (1) In this Act, except in so far as the context otherwise requires—
"accounts rules" has the meaning given by section 35;
"accountant's certificate rules" has the meaning given by section 37(3);
"advocate" means a member of the Faculty of Advocates;
"building society" means a building society within the meaning of the Building Societies Act 1986;
"client account" means a current or deposit or savings account at a bank or with a building society, or a deposit receipt, at a bank, being an account or, as the case may be, a deposit receipt in the title of which the word "client", "trustee", "trust" or other fiducial term appears, including—
    (*a*) an account or deposit receipt for a client whose name is specified in the title of the account on deposit receipt, and
    (*b*) an account such as is mentioned in paragraphs (*a*) and (*b*) of section 35(1);
"the Council" has the meaning given by section 3;
"the court" means the Court of Session;
"the Director" means the Director General of Fair Trading;
"foreign lawyer" means a person who is not a solicitor or an advocate but who is a member, and entitled to practise as such, of a legal profession regulated within a jurisdiction outwith Scotland;
"functions" includes powers and duties;
"inadequate professional services" means professional services which are in any respect not of the quality which could reasonably be expected of a competent solicitor, and cognate expressions shall be construed accordingly; and references to the provision of inadequate professional services shall be construed as including references to not providing professional services which such a solicitor ought to have provided;
"incorporated practice" has the meaning given by section 34(1A)(*c*);
"judge" includes sheriff;
"law centre" means a body—
    (*a*) established for the purpose of providing legal services to the public generally as well as to individual members of the public; and
    (*b*) which does not distribute any profits made either to its members or otherwise, but reinvests any such profits for the purposes of the law centre;
"Lord President" means the Lord President of the Court of Session;
"multi-disciplinary practice" means a body corporate or a partnership—
    (*a*) having as one of its directors or, as the case may be, partners, a solicitor or an incorporated practice; and
    (*b*) which offers services, including professional services such as are provided by individual solicitors, to the public; and
    (*c*) where that solicitor or incorporated practice carries out, or supervises the carrying out of, any such professional services as may lawfully be carried out only by a solicitor;
"multi-national practice" means—
    (*a*) a partnership whose members are solicitors or incorporated practices and registered foreign lawyers; or
    (*b*) a body corporate whose members include registered foreign lawyers, and membership of which is restricted to solicitors, incorporated practices, registered foreign lawyers and other multi-national practices;
"notary public" means a notary public duly admitted in Scotland;
"practice year" means the year ending on 31st October;

"practising certificate" has the meaning given by section 4;

"property" includes property, whether heritable or moveable, and rights and interests in, to or over such property;

"registered foreign lawyer" means a foreign lawyer who is registered under section 60A;

"the roll" has the meaning given by section 7;

"the Society" has the meaning given by section 1;

"Scottish legal services ombudsman" means the ombudsman appointed under section 34 of the Law Reform (Miscellaneous Provisions) (Scotland) Act 1990;

"solicitor" means any person enrolled or deemed to have been enrolled as a solicitor in pursuance of this Act;

"the Tribunal" has the meaning given by section 50;

"unqualified person" means a person, other than a multi-disciplinary practice, who is not qualified under section 4 to act as a solicitor.

(2) Unless the context otherwise requires a reference—

(*a*) in any enactment to law agents includes solicitors;

(*b*) in any enactment to the register of law agents kept in pursuance of the Law Agents (Scotland) Act 1873 includes the roll;

(*c*) in any enactment or instrument to the Solicitors Discipline (Scotland) Committee shall be construed as a reference to the Tribunal.

(*d*) in any enactment or instrument or other document to the General Council of Solicitors in Scotland shall be construed as a reference to the Council.

(*e*) in any enactment to a solicitor's being entitled to practise in the court, or in any other court, or to act in any matter, by reason of his being enrolled in, or of his having subscribed, the list of solicitors practising in that court, shall be construed as a reference to his being entitled so to practise or act by reason of his name being included in the appropriate list provided under section 20.

(3) In this Act references to any enactment shall, except in so far as the context otherwise requires, be construed as references to that enactment as amended, extended or applied by or under any other enactment, including any enactment contained in this Act.

(4) In this Act, except in so far as the context otherwise requires—

(*a*) any reference to a numbered Part, section or Schedule is a reference to the Part or section of, or the Schedule to, this Act so numbered;

(*b*) a reference in a section to a numbered subsection is a reference to the subsection of that section so numbered;

(*c*) a reference in a section, subsection or Schedule to a numbered or lettered paragraph is a reference to the paragraph of that section, subsection or Schedule so numbered or lettered; and

(*d*) a reference to any provision of an Act (including this Act) includes a reference to any Schedule incorporated in the Act by that provision.

NOTE

[1] As amended by the Law Reform (Miscellaneous Provisions) (Scotland) Act 1985 (c. 73), Sched. 1, Pt. I, para. 33, the Solicitors (Scotland) Act 1988 (c. 42), s.5(1), Sched. 1, para. 20 and Sched. 2, and the Law Reform (Miscellaneous Provisions) (Scotland) Act 1990 (c. 40), Sched. 8, para. 29(15) and Sched. 9 (all in force by 17th March 1993: S.I. 1993 No. 641).

Transitional and savings provisions, and repeals

66.—(1) Schedule 6 (transitional and savings provisions) shall have effect, but the provisions of that Schedule shall not be taken as prejudicing the operation of section 16 of the Interpretation Act 1978 (general savings in respect of repeals).

(2) The enactments specified in Schedule 7 are hereby repealed to the extent shown in column 3 of that Schedule.

Citation, extent and commencement
67.—(1) This Act may be cited as the Solicitors (Scotland) Act 1980.
(2) This Act extends to Scotland only.
(3) This Act shall come into operation on the expiration of one month from the date on which it is passed.

SCHEDULES

Section 1   SCHEDULE 1

THE LAW SOCIETY OF SCOTLAND

Constitution and Proceedings

1. The Society shall be a body corporate with a common seal and may sue and be sued in its own name.

2. The Council shall prepare a scheme providing for—
    (*a*) the constitution, election, and proceedings of the Council;
    (*b*) the meetings of the Society;
    (*c*) the appointment of a chairman, vice-chairman, secretary and other officers and employees of the Society;
    (*d*) the appointment and constitution of committees.

[THE NEXT PAGE IS F 37]

3. The scheme prepared under paragraph 2—

   (*a*) may make provision enabling the Council to admit as honorary members of the Society persons who have ceased to be practising solicitors, no such honorary member being entitled to vote at meetings of the Society or liable to pay an annual subscription;

   (*b*) shall make provision for the admission on application made in that behalf and on payment of the annual subscription as a member of the Society of any solicitor who by virtue of the provisions of section 24 is exempted from taking out a practising certificate;

   (*c*) may contain such other provisions with respect to the administration, management and proceedings of the Society as are considered necessary or proper and are consistent with the provisions of this Act.

4. A scheme prepared under paragraph 2 shall have effect on being approved by a resolution passed by a majority of the members present in person or by proxy at a general meeting of the Society, or at an adjournment of such meeting.

5. The Society may by a resolution passed by a majority consisting of not less than two-thirds of the members of the Society present in person or by proxy at a meeting of the Society of which due notice specifying the intention to propose the resolution has been given, or at any adjournment of such meeting, rescind, add to or amend any of the provisions of the scheme so approved.

Revenue

[1] 6. Subject to paragraph 7, every member of the Society shall, for each year, pay to the Society such subscription as may be fixed from time to time by the Society in general meeting.

NOTE

[1] Substituted by the Law Reform (Miscellaneous Provisions) (Scotland) Act 1985, Sched. 1, Pt. II, para. 7.

---

[1] 6A. The subscription payable under paragraph 6 by a practising member (or the proportion of it so payable, calculated by reference to the number of months remaining in the practice year) shall be paid at the time of submission of his application for a practising certificate.

NOTE

[1] Inserted by the Law Reform (Miscellaneous Provisions) (Scotland) Act 1985, Sched. 1, Pt. II, para. 7.

---

[1] 7. The subscription payable by a solicitor in respect of the year or part thereof in which he is first included in the roll of solicitors and in respect of each of the two years immediately following shall be one half of the amount of the subscription fixed under paragraph 6 (reduced, in the case of a solicitor first included in the roll for only part of a year, in that year proportionately).

NOTE

[1] As amended by the Law Reform (Miscellaneous Provisions) (Scotland) Act 1985, Sched. 1, Pt. II, para. 7 and Sched. 4.

---

[1] 7A. The Society shall have power, subject to paragraphs 7B to 7D, to impose in respect of any year a special subscription on all members of the Society of such amount and payable at such time and for such specified purpose as it may determine.

[1] 7B. The Society may determine that an imposition under paragraph 7A shall not be payable by any category of member or shall be abated as respects any category of member.

[1] 7C. An imposition under paragraph 7A or a determination under that paragraph or paragraph 7B may be made only in general meeting.

[1] 7D. No imposition may be made under paragraph 7A above unless a majority of those members voting at the general meeting at which it is proposed has, whether by proxy or otherwise, voted in favour of its being made.

NOTE

[1] Paras. 7A to 7D inserted by the Law Reform (Miscellaneous Provisions) (Scotland) Act 1985, Sched. 1, Pt. II, para. 7. Para. 7D amended by the Solicitors (Scotland) Act 1988, Sched. 1, para. 21.

---

8. Except as otherwise provided in this Act, the expenses of the Society shall be defrayed out of the subscriptions and other income received by the Society or the Council and out of other property belonging to the Society.

In this paragraph "expenses of the Society" includes the expenses of the Tribunal so far as not otherwise defrayed and any expenses incurred by the Council in exercise of their functions under this Act, and the reasonable travelling and maintenance expenses of members of the Council or committees of the Council incurred in attending meetings of the Council or committees, or otherwise incurred in the business of the Society.

9. Paragraph 8 does not affect any trust constituted for a special purpose.

Powers

10. The Society may—
    (a) purchase or otherwise acquire land for any of the purposes of this Act;
    (b) sell, lease or otherwise dispose of land so acquired;
    (c) borrow for any of the purposes of this Act in such manner and on such security as they may determine;
    (d) invest any monies not immediately required to meet expenses and other outlays of the Society in any investment in which trustees in Scotland are by law authorised to invest (but nothing in this sub-paragraph prevents the investment of any monies forming any part of any property held in trust for a special purpose in any class of investment authorised by the deed constituting the trust);
    (e) accept any gift of property for the purposes of the Society;
    (f) accept, hold and administer any gift of property or hold as trustees any property for any purpose which the Society consider to be for the benefit of solicitors in Scotland or their dependants or employees or any substantial body of such solicitors or dependants or employees; and
    (g) subject to the provisions of this Act exercise the functions formerly exercised by the General Council of Solicitors in Scotland.

11. The Council may—
    (a) act for and in the name of the Society in any matter other than a matter which in accordance with the provisions of this Schedule is to be determined by the Society in general meeting;
    (b) without prejudice to any other powers they may have, take into consideration and make recommendations or representations with regard to any matters which are in their opinion of importance to solicitors in Scotland.

Exemption from liability for damages

[1] 11A. Neither the Society nor any of its officers or servants shall be liable in damages for anything done or omitted in the discharge or purported discharge of its functions unless the act or omission is shown to have been in bad faith.

NOTE

[1] Inserted by the Law Reform (Miscellaneous Provisions) (Scotland) Act 1990, Sched. 8, para. 29(16).

Attestation

12. [Repealed by the Requirements of Writing (Scotland) Act 1995 (c. 7), Sched. 5 (effective 1st August 1995: s. 15(2)). On 21 September 1995 the Council passed a resolution in the following terms:

"Any deed or document to which the Society is a party shall be held to be validly executed on behalf of the Society if it is subscribed on behalf of the Society by any two of the following:—
The President,
Vice-President,
Past President,
The Secretary."]

Section 11   [1] SCHEDULE 2

NOTE
[1] As amended by the Solicitors (Scotland) Act 1988 (c. 42), Sched. 1, para. 22 and Sched. 2.

THE ROLL: POWERS OF THE COUNCIL
AND ANCILLARY PROVISIONS

1. The Council (as registrar of solicitors) for the purpose of maintaining the roll as correctly as is reasonably practicable shall have power—
   (*a*) to remove from the roll the name of any solicitor who has died;
   (*b*) to send to any solicitor at his address as shown in the roll a letter enquiring whether he wishes to continue to have his name included in the roll and intimating that if no reply is made within the period of 6 months beginning with the date of the posting of the letter his name may be removed from the roll;

[THE NEXT PAGE IS F39]

(c) to send any solicitor on the roll who has for at least 3 years been so enrolled in pursuance of regulations made by the Council under section 5 on an undertaking by him to serve a post qualifying year for practical training which the Council are not satisfied that he has implemented, a letter enquiring whether he intends to fulfil that undertaking and intimating that unless a reply which the Council regard as satisfactory is received within the period of 6 months beginning with the date of the posting of the letter his name may be removed from the roll; and

(d) if a reply indicating that he does not wish that his name shall continue to be included in the roll is returned by any solicitor to whom a letter has been so sent, or if no reply or in a case of a letter sent under subparagraph (c) a reply which the Council do not regard as satisfactory is returned within the period mentioned in subparagraph (b) or (c), as the case may be, by any such solicitor, to remove the name of that solicitor from the roll.

2. The Council may, on the application of a solicitor whose name has been removed from the roll in pursuance of paragraph 1(d), and on payment by him to the Council of such reasonable fee in respect of restoration as the Council may fix, order that his name shall be restored to the roll.

3. Any person aggrieved by a decision of the Council under paragraph 2 may appeal against the decision to the Court, and the provisions of section 40(3) shall, subject to any necessary modifications, apply to any such appeal.

4. Subject to section 7(3), the Council may charge such reasonable fees (including an annual fee payable by enrolled solicitors) as they may fix in connection with the keeping of the roll.

Section 43   SCHEDULE 3

PART I

THE SCOTTISH SOLICITORS GUARANTEE FUND

Contributions by Solicitors

[1] 1.—(1) Subject to the provisions of this Act, there shall be paid to the Society on behalf of the Guarantee Fund by every solicitor in respect of each year during which, or part of which, he is in practice as a solicitor, along with his application for a practising certificate, a contribution (hereafter referred to as an "annual contribution").

(2) The sum payable by a solicitor in respect of the year in which he first commences to practise after admission and in respect of each of the two years immediately following shall be one half of the annual contribution.

(2A) Sub-paragraphs (1) and (2) do not apply to solicitors who are directors of incorporated practices.

(2B) Subject to the provisions of this Act, there shall be paid to the Society on behalf of the Guarantee Fund by every incorporated practice in respect of each year during which, or part of which, it is recognised under section 34(1A) a contribution (hereafter referred to as an "annual corporate contribution") in accordance with the scale of such contributions referred to in sub-paragraph (3).

(3) The Council shall not later than 30th September in each year fix the amount, if any, of the annual contribution to be paid in respect of the following year and the scale of the annual corporate contributions to be so paid, which scale be fixed by reference to factors which shall include the number of solicitors who are directors or employees of each of the incorporated practices to which the scale relates.

(4) No annual contribution shall be payable by a solicitor and no annual corporate contribution by an incorporated practice so long as the amount of the Guarantee Fund including the value of all investments forming part of the Fund and after providing for all outstanding liabilities, is in the opinion of the Council not less than £2 million[2] or such other sum as the Council may from time to time determine.

(5) If at any time the Council are of opinion that the liabilities of the Guarantee Fund render it expedient in order to secure the financial stability of the Fund, the Council may, by resolution of which not less than 10 days' previous notice in writing has been given to each member of the Council, impose upon every solicitor a contribution (hereafter referred to as a "special contribution") of the amount specified in the resolution, and upon every incorporated practice a contribution (hereafter referred to as a "special corporate contribution") in accordance with a scale of such contributions fixed by the Council as under sub-paragraph (3), and a special or special corporate contribution shall be payable to the Society in one sum or, if the Council so

determine, by instalments on or before such date or dates as may be specified in the resolution.

(6) No special contribution shall be payable by a solicitor in the year in which he first commences to practice after admission nor in either of the 2 years immediately following.

(7) [Repealed by the Law Reform (Miscellaneous Provisions) (Scotland) Act 1985], Sched. 1, Pt. II. para. 8(c), with effect from 30th December 1985.

(8) No annual contribution and no special contribution shall be payable by any solicitor who is in the employment of another solicitor or of a firm of solicitors or of an incorporated practice and who does not engage in practice as a solicitor on his own account.

(9) Without prejudice to any other method of recovering contributions payable to the Society under this Schedule whether annual or special a practising certificate shall not be issued to a solicitor except on production of evidence of payment of the contributions (if any) due by him to the Fund on or before the issue of the certificate.

(10) In this Schedule the expression "year" means the period of 12 months commencing on 1st November or such other day as may be fixed by the Council.

NOTE

[1] As amended by the Law Reform (Miscellaneous Provisions) (Scotland) Act 1985, Sched. 1, Pt. I, para. 34, Pt. II, para. 8, and Sched. 4.

[2] As amended by Council at its meeting on July 26, 1996.

Investment etc.

2.—(1) Monies not immediately required to meet sums payable out of the Guarantee Fund may be invested by the Society in any investments in which trustees in Scotland are by law authorised to invest.

(2) The Society may borrow money for the purposes of the Guarantee Fund in such manner and on such security as they may determine but the total sum due at any time in respect of any such loans shall not exceed £20,000.

(3) The accounts of the Guarantee Fund shall be made up annually for the year ending 31st October or on such other day as may be fixed by the Council and shall be audited by an auditor appointed by the Society.

(4) As soon as the audit is completed the audited accounts and the auditor's report on the accounts shall be submitted to the Council and a copy of the audited accounts and the auditor's report shall be sent to the Lord Advocate and to every solicitor who is contributing to the Fund.

(5) All investments and other monies forming part of the Guarantee Fund and the books and accounts relating to that Fund shall be kept separate from the other investments and monies, books and accounts of the Society, and the investments and other monies forming part of the Guarantee Fund shall not be liable for any obligations, debts or liabilities incurred by the Society or the Council in relation to any business of the Society other than the business of the Guarantee Fund, nor shall the investments and other monies of the Society held for the purposes other than those relating to the Guarantee Fund be liable for any obligations, debts or liabilities incurred by the Society or the Council in relation to the Guarantee Fund.

Insurance

3.—(1) The Society may enter into a contract of insurance with any person, body of persons or corporation authorised by law to carry on insurance business for guaranteeing the sufficiency of the Guarantee Fund or for any other purpose in relation to the Fund.

[1] (2) Any such contract of insurance may be entered into in relation to solicitors and incorporated practices generally or in relation to any solicitor or solicitors or incorporated practice or practices named therein.

(3) No person other than the Society shall have any right of action against a person, body or corporation with whom any such contract of insurance was entered into or have any right to any monies payable under that contract.

NOTE

[1] As amended by the Law Reform (Miscellaneous Provisions) (Scotland) Act 1985, Sched. 1, Pt. I, para. 34.

Grants

4.—(1) Every application for a grant from the Guarantee Fund shall be in such form as may be prescribed by rules made under this Schedule and shall be accompanied, if so required by the Council, by a statutory declaration and the applicant shall produce to the Council such documents and other evidence as they demand.

[1] (2) The Council may, as a condition of making a grant out of the Guarantee Fund, require the person to whom the grant is made to assign to the Society at the expense of the Society any rights and remedies competent to him against the solicitor in question, his partner or employee or the incorporated practice in question or its employee or any other person in respect of the loss.

(3) A grant from the Guarantee Fund may at the discretion of the Council be paid in one sum or in such instalments as the Council may determine.

(4) The Council may make rules with regard to the procedure to be followed in giving effect to the provisions of this Act relating to the Guarantee Fund, including matters to be prescribed thereunder, and also with respect to any matters incidental, ancillary or supplemental to those provisions or concerning the administration, management or protection of the Guarantee Fund.

NOTE
[1] As amended by the Law Reform (Miscellaneous Provisions) (Scotland) Act 1985, Sched. 1, Pt. I, para. 34.

Section 38   PART II

Power of Council to investigate

5.—(1) If under section 38 any person (whether a solicitor or not) having possession or control of any documents mentioned in that section refuses or fails to produce or deliver them immediately on being required by the Council to do so or cause them to be so produced or delivered, the Council may apply to the court for an order requiring that person to produce or deliver the documents or to cause them to be produced or delivered to the person appointed at the place fixed by the Council within such time as the court may order.

[1] (2) Upon taking possession of any such documents which have been produced or delivered to the Council, the Council shall serve upon the solicitor or incorporated practice mentioned in section 38, and every such person, a notice giving particulars and the date on which they took possession.

(3) Every requirement made or notice given under section 38 or under this Part of this Schedule shall be in writing under the hand of such person as may be appointed by the Council for the purpose and may be served either personally or by registered letter or by a letter sent by recorded delivery service addressed to the last known place of business or residence of the person to whom the requirement is made or notice given.

(4) Within 14 days after service of a notice under sub-paragraph (2) the person upon whom such notice has been served may apply to the court for an order directing the Council to return such documents to the person from whom they were received by the Council or to such other person as the applicant may request and on the hearing of any such application the court may make the order applied for or such other order as they think fit.

(5) If no application is made to the court under sub-paragraph (4) or if the court on any such application directs that the documents in question remain in the custody or control of the Council, the Council may make enquiries to ascertain the person to whom they belong and may deal with the documents in accordance with the directions of that person.

NOTE
[1] As amended by the Law Reform (Miscellaneous Provisions) (Scotland) Act 1985, Sched. 1, Pt. I, para. 34.

CONSTITUTION, PROCEDURE AND POWERS OF TRIBUNAL

PART I

Constitution

[1] 1. The Tribunal shall consist of—
  (*a*) not less than 10 and not more than 14 members (in this Part referred to as "solicitor members") who are solicitors recommended by the Council as representatives of the solicitors' profession throughout Scotland, appointed by the Lord President; and
  (*b*) 8 members (in this Part referred to as "lay members") who are neither solicitors nor advocates, appointed by the Lord President after consultation with the Secretary of State.

———

NOTE
  [1] As amended by the Law Reform (Miscellaneous Provisions) (Scotland) Act 1980 (c. 55), s. 24, and the Law Reform (Miscellaneous Provisions) (Scotland) Act 1990 (c. 40), Scheds. 8, para. 29(17), and 9.

———

[1] 2. Each member of the Tribunal shall retire from office on the expiry of 5 years from the date of his appointment, but in the case
  (*a*) of a lay member, may be re-appointed by the Lord President after consultation with the Secretary of State; and
  (*b*) of a solicitor member, may be re-appointed by the Lord President on the recommendation of the Council.

———

NOTE
  [1] As amended by the Law Reform (Miscellaneous Provisions) (Scotland) Act 1980, s. 24, and the Law Reform (Miscellaneous Provisions) (Scotland) Act 1990 (c. 40), Sched. 8, para. 29(17) (effective 20th July 1992: S.I. 1992 No. 1599).

———

[1] 3. The Lord President may from time to time terminate the appointment of any member of the Tribunal, and may fill any vacancy therein by the appointment of a solicitor recommended by the Council or, as the case may be, after consultation with the Secretary of State, by the appointment of a lay member.

———

NOTE
  [1] As amended by the Law Reform (Miscellaneous Provisions) (Scotland) Act 1990 (c. 40), Sched. 8, para. 29(17) (effective 20th July 1992: S.I. 1992 No. 1599).

———

4. The Tribunal may appoint one of their number to be chairman, and may also appoint a clerk, who shall not be a member of the Tribunal, and, subject to the provisions of this Act, may regulate their procedure in such way as they may think fit.

5. The Tribunal shall be deemed to be properly constituted if—
  (*a*) at least 4 members are present, and
  (*b*) at least 1 lay member is present, and
  (*c*) the number of solicitor members present exceeds the number of lay members present, and
  [1] (*d*) there are present not more than three solicitor members for every lay member.

NOTE
[1] Added by the Solicitors (Scotland) Act 1988, Sched. 1, para. 23.

6. There shall be paid to the lay members of the Tribunal out of money provided by Parliament such fees and allowances as the Secretary of State may, with the approval of the Minister for the Civil Service, determine.

[1] PART II

PROCEDURE AND POWERS OF TRIBUNAL

NOTE
[1] Applied by the Legal Aid (Scotland) Act 1986, s. 31(10).

Complaints

7. The making of a complaint to the Tribunal or the giving of any information in connection with a complaint shall confer qualified privilege.

8. A complaint made to the Tribunal shall not be withdrawn except with the Tribunal's leave and subject to such conditions with respect to expenses or otherwise as the Tribunal thinks fit.

[1] 8A. Where a complaint is made to the Tribunal by a person other than—
(*a*) the Council; or
(*b*) a person mentioned in section 51(3),
the Tribunal may remit the complaint to the Council.

NOTE
[1] Inserted by the Solicitors (Scotland) Act 1988, Sched. 1, para. 23.

[1] 9. Subject to Part IV, the Tribunal may dismiss a complaint against a solicitor or an incorporated practice—
(*a*) without requiring the solicitor or the incorporated practice to answer the allegations made against him or, as the case may be, it or without holding any inquiry if—
(i) they are of the opinion that the complaint discloses no *prima facie* case of professional misconduct on the part of the solicitor or, of failure on the part of the incorporated practice to comply with any provision of this Act or of rules made under this Act or, as the case may be, of provision of inadequate professional services; or
(ii) the complainer fails to comply with any rule made under section 52; or
(*b*) without hearing parties if they are of the opinion upon consideration of the complaint and other documents that they disclose no case of professional misconduct on the part of the solicitor or, of failure on the part of the incorporated practice to comply with any provision of this Act or of rules made under this Act or, as the case may be, of provision of inadequate professional services.

NOTE
[1] As amended by the Law Reform (Miscellaneous Provisions) (Scotland) Act 1985, Sched. 1, Pt. I, para. 35, and the Solicitors (Scotland) Act 1988, Sched. 1, para. 23.

[1] 10. The Tribunal shall give notice of the complaint to the solicitor or incorporated practice against whom the complaint is made ("the respondent") and shall inquire into the complaint, giving him or, as the case may be, it reasonable opportunity of making his or, as the case may be, its defence.

NOTE
[1] As amended by the Law Reform (Miscellaneous Provisions) (Scotland) Act 1985, Sched. 1, Pt. I, para. 35.

11. For the purpose of inquiring into the complaint the Tribunal may administer oaths and receive affirmations; and the complainer and respondent shall each be entitled—
   (*a*) to require the evidence of parties, witnesses and others interested, and
   (*b*) to call for and recover such evidence and documents, and examine such witnesses, as they think proper, but no person shall be compelled to produce any document which he could not be compelled to produce in an action.

12. On a petition by the complainer or the respondent to the court, or to the sheriff having jurisdiction in any place in which the respondent carries on business, the court or, as the case may be, the sheriff, on production of copies (certified by the clerk of the Tribunal) of the complaint and answers, if lodged, together with a statement signed by the clerk specifying the place and date of the hearing of the complaint and certifying that notice to that effect has been given to the complainer and to the respondent, and on being satisfied that it would be proper to compel the giving of evidence by any witness or the production of documents by any haver, may—
   (*a*) grant warrant for the citation of witnesses and havers to give evidence or to produce documents before the Tribunal, and for the issue of letters of second diligence against any witness or haver failing to appear after due citation;
   (*b*) grant warrant for the recovery of documents; and
   (*c*) appoint commissioners to take the evidence of witnesses, to examine havers, and to receive exhibits and productions.

Decisions
13. The Tribunal shall set out in their decision—
   (*a*) in the case of a complaint, the facts proved, and
   (*b*) in the case of a conviction, particulars of the conviction and sentence,
and shall in the case of a complaint add to their decision a note stating the grounds on which the decision has been arrived at.
[1] 14. Every decision of the Tribunal shall be signed by the chairman or other person presiding and shall, subject to paragraph 14A, be published in full.

NOTE
[1] As amended by the Law Reform (Miscellaneous Provisions) (Scotland) Act 1990 (c. 40), Sched. 8, para. 29(17) (effective 20th July 1992: S.I. 1992 No. 1599).

14A In carrying out their duty under paragraph 14, the Tribunal may refrain from publishing any names, places or other facts the publication of which would, in their opinion, damage, or be likely to damage, the interests of persons other than—
   (*a*) the solicitor against whom the complaint was made; or
   (*b*) his partners; or
   (*c*) his or their families,
but where they so refrain they shall publish their reasons for so doing.

NOTE
[1] Inserted by the Law Reform (Miscellaneous Provisions) (Scotland) Act 1990 (c. 40), Sched. 8, para. 29(17) (effective 20th July 1992: S.I. 1992 No. 1599).

15. A copy of every decision by the Tribunal certified by the clerk shall be sent forthwith by the clerk to the respondent and to the complainer intimating the right of appeal available from that decision under this Act.
[1] 16. In the case of a decision by the Tribunal—
   (*a*) ordering a solicitor to be struck off the roll; or

(*b*) ordering a solicitor to be suspended from practice; or

(*c*) censuring a solicitor or an incorporated practice; or

(*d*) fining a solicitor or an incorporated practice; or,

(*e*) ordering that the recognition under section 34(1A) of an incorporated practice be revoked; or,

(*f*) containing a direction under section 53A or an order under section 53C(2); or

(*g*) confirming or varying a determination or direction of the Council on an appeal under section 42A(7); or

(*h*) ordering that an investment business certificate issued to a solicitor, a firm of solicitors or an incorporated practice be—

  (i) suspended; or

  (ii) subject to such terms and conditions as they may direct; or

  (iii) revoked,

on the expiration of the days of appeal if any without an appeal being lodged or, where an appeal has been lodged, if and as soon as the appeal is withdrawn or a decision by the court is given in terms of subparagraphs (*a*) to (*h*) or in the case of a decision of the Tribunal under section 53(6) or (6B) which has not been varied or quashed by the court or under section 53(6A) which has not been varied by the court, the clerk of the Tribunal shall immediately send to the Council a copy of the decision of the Tribunal certified by him and a copy of the decision by the court in any appeal, and the Council shall forthwith give effect to any order as to striking the solicitor off the roll or as to revoking the recognition under section 34(1A) of an incorporated practice and to any terms and conditions directed by the Tribunal under section 53(5); and in any other case shall cause a note of the effect of the decision to be entered against the name of the solicitor in the roll.

NOTE

[1] As amended by the Law Reform (Miscellaneous Provisions) (Scotland) Act 1985, Sched. 1, Pt. I, para. 35, the Solicitors (Scotland) Act 1988, Sched. 1, para. 23, and the Law Reform (Miscellaneous Provisions) (Scotland) Act 1990, Sched. 8.

---

[1] 17. The Council shall forthwith intimate any order striking a solicitor off the roll or suspending a solicitor from practice to each sheriff clerk and to the Principal Clerk of Session, and shall, without prejudice to paragraph 14, cause a notice of the operative part of the order to be published in the *Edinburgh Gazette.*

NOTE

[1] As amended by the Law Reform (Miscellaneous Provisions) (Scotland) Act 1990 (c. 40), Sched. 8, para. 29(17), and 9.

---

18. The file of orders under this Act striking solicitors off the roll, suspending solicitors from practice, or restoring persons to the roll shall be open for inspection at the office of the Society at any reasonable hour by any person without payment of any fee.

[1] 18A. Without prejudice to paragraph 18, the Council shall ensure that a copy of every decision published under paragraph 14 is open for inspection at the office of the Society during office hours by any person without payment of any fee.

NOTE

[1] Inserted by the Law Reform (Miscellaneous Provisions) (Scotland) Act 1990 (c. 40), Sched. 8, para. 29(17) (effective 20th July 1992: S.I. 1992 No. 1599).

Expenses

19. Subject to the provisions of Part IV, the Tribunal may make in relation to any complaint against a solicitor such order as it thinks fit as to the payment by the complainer or by the respondent of the expenses incurred by the other party and by the Tribunal or a reasonable contribution towards those expenses.

20. On the application of the person in whose favour an order for expenses under paragraph 19 is made and on production of a certificate by the clerk of the Tribunal that the days of appeal against the order have expired without an appeal being lodged or, where such an appeal has been lodged, that the appeal has been dismissed or withdrawn, the court may grant warrant authorising that person to recover those expenses from the person against whom the order was made.

21. Such warrant shall have effect for execution and for all other purposes as if it were an extracted decree of court awarded against the person against whom the order of the Tribunal was made.

22. The expenses of the Tribunal so far as not otherwise defrayed shall be paid by the Society as part of the expenses of the Society.

[1] *Appeals*

NOTE
[1] Paras. 23–25 added by the Solicitors (Scotland) Act 1988, Sched.1, para. 23.

23. The foregoing provisions of Part II of this Schedule shall apply in relation to an appeal to the Tribunal under section 42A(7) or section 53D(1) as they apply in relation to a complaint, but with the following modifications—
   (a) for references to a complaint there shall be substituted references to an appeal;
   (b) for references to the respondent there shall be substituted references to the appellant;
   (c) paragraphs 8A, 9 and 10 shall not apply; and
   (d) in paragraph 19 the words "against a solicitor" shall be omitted.

24. Subject to Part IV, the Tribunal may dismiss an appeal without holding an inquiry if—
   (a) they are of the opinion that the appeal is manifestly ill-founded; or
   (b) the appellant fails to comply with any rule made under section 52.

25. The Tribunal shall give notice of the appeal to the person by whom the original complaint was made (referred to in this Schedule as "the complainer") and to the Council and shall enquire into the matter, giving the appellant and the complainer reasonable opportunity to make representations to the Tribunal.

SCHEDULE 5

[Repealed by the Law Reform (Miscellaneous Provisions) (Scotland) Act 1990, Sched. 9].

Section 66 SCHEDULE 6

TRANSITIONAL AND SAVINGS PROVISIONS

General

1.—(1) In so far as—
   (a) any agreement, appointment, operation, authorisation, determination, scheme, instrument, order or regulation made by virtue of an enactment repealed by this Act, or
   (b) any approval, consent, direction or notice given by virtue of such an enactment, or
   (c) any complaint made or investigation begun by virtue of such enactment, or
   (d) any other proceedings begun by virtue of such an enactment, or
   (e) anything done or having effect as if done,
could, if a corresponding enactment in this Act were in force at the relevant time, have been made, given, begun or done by virtue of the corresponding enactment, it shall, if effective immediately before the corresponding enactment comes into force, continue to have effect thereafter as if made, given, begun or done by virtue of that corresponding enactment.
   (2) Where—
   (a) there is any reference in this Act (whether expressed or implied) to a thing done or required or authorised to be done, or a thing omitted, or to an event which has occurred, under or for the purposes of or by reference to or in contravention of this Act, then
   (b) that reference shall be construed (subject to its context) as including a reference to the corresponding thing, done or required or authorised to be done, or omitted, or to the corresponding events which occurred, as the case may be, under

Powers of societies

or for the purposes of or by reference to or in contravention of any of the corresponding provisions of the repealed enactments.

2. Where any enactment passed before this Act or any instrument or document refers either expressly or by implication to an enactment repealed by this Act, the reference shall (subject to its context) be construed as or as including a reference to the corresponding provision of this Act.

3. Where any period of time specified in an enactment repealed by this Act is current at the commencement of this Act, this Act has effect as if its corresponding provision has been in force when that period began to run.

Admission of enrolled law agent

4. Notwithstanding the repeal by this Act of section 15 of the Solicitors (Scotland) Act 1933, the court may grant an application to be admitted as a solicitor to any applicant who was on 28th June 1933 entitled to be admitted as an enrolled law agent according to the regulations for admission then ii force under the Law Agents (Scotland) Act 1873.

Restriction of grant under Guarantee Fund

5. Notwithstanding the repeal by this Act of section 22(2)(*b*) of the Legal Aid and Solicitors (Scotland) Act 1949, no grant shall be made by the Council under section 43 in respect of a loss which in the opinion of the Council arose before 1st November 1951.

Rights of banks

6. Nothing in section 61(3) shall deprive a bank of any right existing on 1st November 1949.

Admission to societies

7. Notwithstanding the repeal by this Act of sections 44 and 45 of the Solicitors (Scotland) Act 1933 any society may—
   (*a*) admit a solicitor as a member on such conditions as it thinks fit;
   (*b*) accept as a qualification for admission an apprenticeship served under the provisions of this Act with a solicitor who is not a member.

8. The repeal of Section 35 of the Solicitors (Scotland) Act 1933 is without prejudice to powers of control exercisable by any society over its members, being powers the society were entitled to exercise immediately before 1st March 1934.

In this paragraph and in paragraph 7, "society" means a faculty or society of solicitors in Scotland, incorporated by Royal Charter or otherwise formed in accordance with law, other than the Law Society of Scotland.

[THE NEXT PAGE IS F 47]

Saving for non-qualified person to conduct certain proceedings

[1] 9. Nothing in this Act shall affect any enactment empowering any person, not being a person qualified to act as a solicitor, to conduct, defend or otherwise act in relation to any action or proceedings in any court.

NOTE
[1] As amended by the Solicitors (Scotland) Act 1988, Sched. 1, para. 24.

Register of law agents

10. Notwithstanding the repeal by this Act of section 18(1) of the Solicitors (Scotland) Act 1933, the Council shall continue to keep in their custody the Register of Law Agents kept under the Law Agents (Scotland) Act 1873 and any relative documents transferred to their custody by virtue of section 18(4) of the Solicitors (Scotland) Act 1949.

Certificate of admission

11. Notwithstanding the repeal by this Act of section 14 of the Solicitors (Scotland) Act 1933, the certificate of admission of a solicitor shall be in writing and signed by a judge of the court.

Law Reform (Miscellaneous Provisions) (Scotland) Act 1990

(1990 c. 40)

An Act, as respects Scotland, … to provide as to rights of audience in courts of law, legal services and judicial appointments, and for the establishment and functions of an ombudsman in relation to legal services; … and to make certain other miscellaneous reforms of the law.   [November 1, 1990]

. . . . . .

PART I

CHARITIES

1.–15. [Not printed.]

[1] PART II

LEGAL SERVICES

NOTE
[1] Pt. II is to come into force on a day or days to be appointed: s. 75(2): see notes to each section, *infra*.

Conveyancing and Executry Services

16.–19. [Not printed.]

Professional misconduct, inadequate professional services, etc.
[1] **20.**—(1) Where, after such inquiry as they consider appropriate (whether or not following a complaint to them) and after giving the practitioner concerned an opportunity to make representations, the Board are satisfied that a practitioner—

(a) is guilty of professional misconduct;
(b) has provided inadequate professional services;
(c) has failed to comply with regulations made under section 17(11) or 18(10) of this Act; or
(d) has been convicted of a criminal offence rendering him no longer a fit and proper person to provide conveyancing services as a qualified conveyancer or, as the case may be, executry services as an executry practitioner,

they may take such of the steps out in subsection (2) below as they think fit and shall, without prejudice to subsection (6) below, intimate their decision to the practitioner by notice in writing.

(2) The steps referred to in subsection (1) above are—
(a) to determine that the amount of fees and outlays which the practitioner may charge in respect of such services as the Board may specify shall be—
(i) nil; or
(ii) such amount as the Board may specify in the determination,
and to direct the practitioner to comply, or secure compliance, with such of the requirements set out in subsection (5) below as appear to them to be necessary to give effect to the determination;
(b) to direct the practitioner to secure the rectification at his or its own expense of any such error, omission or other deficiency arising in connection with the services as the Board may specify;
(c) to attach conditions (or, as the case may be, further conditions) to the registration of the practitioner or to vary any condition so attached;
(d) to suspend or revoke that registration;
(e) subject to subsection (3) below, to impose on the practitioner a fine not exceeding £10,000;
(f) in a case where the practitioner has provided inadequate professional services, to direct the practitioner to pay to the client by way of compensation such sum, not exceeding £1,000, as the Board may specify;
(g) to censure the practitioner; and
(h) to make a report of the Board's findings to any other person exercising functions with respect to—
(i) the practitioner; or
(ii) any person employed by or acting on behalf of the practitioner in connection with the provision of the services.

(3) The Board shall not impose a fine under subsection (2)(e) above where, in relation to the subject matter of the Board's inquiry, the practitioner has been convicted by any court of an offence involving dishonesty and sentenced to a term of imprisonment of not less than two years.

(4) Any fine imposed under subsection (2)(e) above shall be treated for the purposes of section 203 of the Criminal Procedure (Scotland) Act 1975 (fines payable to HM Exchequer) as if it were a fine imposed in the High Court.

(5) The requirements referred to in subsection (2)(a) above are—
(a) to refund, whether in whole or to any specified extent, any amount already paid by or on behalf of the client in respect of the fees and outlays of the practitioner in connection with the services; and
(b) to waive, whether wholly or to any specified extent, the right to recover those fees and outlays.

(6) Where the Board make a direction under subsection (2)(a), (b) or (f) above they shall, by notice in writing, require the practitioner to which the direction relates to give, within such period being not less than 21 days as the notice may specify, an explanation of the steps which he or it has taken to comply with the direction.

(7) Where a practitioner—

(a) fails to comply with a notice under subsection (6) above; or
(b) complies with such a notice but the Board are not satisfied as to the steps taken by the practitioner to comply with the direction to which the notice relates,

the Board may apply to the Court of Session for an order requiring the practitioner to comply with the direction to which the notice relates within such time as the court may order.

(8) Where the Board take a step set out in subsection (2)(c) or (d) above and—
(a) the period specified in subsection (11)(a) or (b) below has expired without an application for review or, as the case may be, an application to the Court of Session having been made, or
(b) where such an application is made, the matter is finally determined in favour of the Board's decision or the application is withdrawn,

they shall amend the register of executry practitioners or, as the case may be, the register of qualified conveyancers accordingly.

(9) The Board shall—
(a) subject to subsection (10) below, publish every decision taken by them under subsection (1) above (including a decision that they are not satisfied as to the matters mentioned in subsection (1)(a) to (d)); and
(b) make available a copy of every decision published under paragraph (a) above for inspection by any person without charge.

(10) In carrying out their duty under subsection (9) above, the Board may refrain from publishing any names or other information which would, in their opinion, damage or be likely to damage the interest of persons other than—
(a) the practitioner to whom the decision relates; or
(b) where the practitioner is an individual, his partners; or
(c) his or their families,

but where they so refrain, they shall publish their reasons for so doing.

(11) Where the Board take a step set out in subsection (2)(a) to (g) above, the practitioner concerned may—
(a) within 21 days of the date on which the Board's decision is intimated to it or him, apply to the Board to review their decision; and
(b) within 21 days of the date on which the outcome of such review is intimated to it or him, apply to the Court of Session, which may make such order in the matter as it thinks fit.

(12) Part II of Schedule 1 to this Act (Board's powers of investigation for the purposes of this section and section 21) shall have effect.

(13) The Secretary of State, after consulting the Board, may by order made by statutory instrument subject to annulment in pursuance of a resolution of either House of Parliament, amend subsection (2)(f) above by substituting for the sum for the time being specified in that provision such other sum as he considers appropriate.

(14) The taking of any steps under subsection (2) above shall not be founded upon in any proceedings for the purpose of showing that the practitioner in respect of whom the steps were taken was negligent.

(15) A direction under subsection (2)(f) above to a practitioner to pay compensation to a client shall not prejudice any right of that client to take proceedings against that practitioner for damages in respect of any loss which he alleges he has suffered as a result of that practitioner's negligence, and any sum directed to be paid to that client under that provision may be taken into account in the computation of any award of damages made to him in any such proceedings.

(16) The Secretary of State may, by order made by statutory instrument subject to annulment in pursuance of a resolution of either House of Parliament, amend subsection (2)(e) above by substituting for the amount

for the time being specified in that provision such other amount as appears to him to be justified by a change in the value of money.

(17) In this section "executry practitioner" and "qualified conveyancer" respectively include any executry practitioner or qualified conveyancer whether or not it or he was registered as such at the time when the subject matter of the Board's inquiry occurred and notwithstanding that subsequent to that time it or he has ceased to be so registered.

NOTE

[1] Brought into force on March 1, 1997 by S.I. 1996 No. 2894, as amended by S.I. 1996 No. 2966.

Board's intervention powers

[1] **21.**—(1) The powers conferred on the Board by this section may be exercised if, after such inquiry (if any) as the Board consider appropriate, it appears to them to be desirable to do so for the purpose of protecting the interests of the clients, or prospective clients, of an independent qualified conveyancer or an executry practitioner (each of which is in this section referred to as a "relevant practitioner").

(2) The Board may, in particular, exercise any such power where it appears to them that a relevant practitioner—

    (a) is no longer a fit and proper person to provide conveyancing services or, as the case may be, executry services;

    (b) has ceased, for whatever reason, to provide such services; or

    (c) has failed, or is likely to fail, to comply with regulations made under section 17(11) or, as the case may be, section 18(10) of this Act.

(3) The Board may direct the relevant practitioner not to dispose of, or otherwise deal with, except in accordance with the terms of the direction—

    (a) any assets belonging to any client of the practitioner and held by or under the control of the practitioner in connection with his business as an independent qualified conveyancer or, as the case may be, an executry practitioner; or

    (b) any assets of the practitioner which are specified, or of a kind specified, in the direction.

(4) The Board may direct the relevant practitioner to transfer to the Board, or to such persons (in this section referred to as "the trustees") as may be specified in the direction—

    (a) all assets belonging to any client of the practitioner and held by or under the control of the practitioner in connection with his business as an independent qualified conveyancer or, as the case may be, an executry practitioner; or

    (b) any assets of the practitioner which are specified, or of a kind specified, in the direction.

(5) A relevant practitioner to whom a direction is given may, within 21 days of the date on which the direction is received by him, apply to the Court of Session, which may make such order in the matter as it thinks fit.

(6) A relevant practitioner to whom a direction is given shall comply with it as soon as it takes effect (and whether or not he proposes to apply to the Court of Session under subsection (5) above).

(7) If, on an application to the Court of Session by the Board, the court is satisfied—

    (a) that a relevant practitioner has failed, within a reasonable time, to comply with any direction given to him; or

    (b) that there is a reasonable likelihood that a relevant practitioner will so fail,

the court may make an order requiring the practitioner, and any other person whom the court considers it appropriate to subject to its order, to take such steps as the court may direct with a view to securing compliance with the direction.

(8) Any assets which have been transferred as a result of a direction given

under subsection (4) above shall be held by the Board, or by the trustees, on trust for the client or, as the case may be, the practitioner concerned.

(9) The trustees may deal with any assets which have been transferred to them only in accordance with directions given to them by the Board.

(10) If the Board have reasonable cause to believe that a relevant practitioner or an employee of a relevant practitioner has been guilty of dishonesty resulting in pecuniary loss to a client of the relevant practitioner, they may apply to the Court of Session for an order that no payment be made by any bank, building society or other body named in the order out of any bank, building society or other account or any sum deposited in the name of the relevant practitioner without the leave of the court and the court may make such an order.

(11) Any direction under this section—

(a) shall be given in writing;

(b) shall state the reason why it is being given;

(c) shall take effect on such date as may be specified in the direction (which may be the date on which it is served on the relevant practitioner); and

(d) may be varied or revoked by a further direction given by the Board.

(12) In this section—

"assets" includes any sum of money (in whatever form and whether or not in any bank, building society or other account) and any book, account, deed or other document held by the relevant practitioner on his own behalf in connection with his business as a relevant practitioner or on behalf of the client concerned; and

"independent qualified conveyancer" and "executry practitioner" respectively include any independent qualified conveyancer or executry practitioner whether or not he was registered as such at the time when the matter in relation to which the Board exercise or propose to exercise their powers under this section arose and notwithstanding that subsequent to that time he has ceased to be so registered.

NOTE

[1] Brought into force on March 1, 1997 by S.I. 1996 No. 2894, as amended by S.I. 1996 No. 2966.

Disclosure of documents etc.

[1] **22.**—(1) Any communication made to or by—

(a) an independent qualified conveyancer or an executry practitioner in the course of his or its acting as such for a client; or

[(b) a recognised financial institution in the course of providing executry services for a client],

shall in any action or proceedings in any court be protected from disclosure on the ground of confidentiality between client and professional legal adviser in like manner as if the conveyancer, practitioner or institution had at all material times been a solicitor acting for the client.

(2) Any enactment or instrument making special provision in relation to a solicitor or other legal representative as to the disclosure of information, or as to the production, seizure or removal of documents, with respect to which a claim to confidentiality between client and professional legal adviser could be maintained, shall, with any necessary modifications, have effect in relation to—

(a) an independent qualified conveyancer;

(b) an executry practitioner; and

[(c) a recognised financial institution in relation to the provision of executry services],

as it has effect in relation to a solicitor.

NOTE
[1] Brought into force on March 1, 1997 by S.I. 1996 No. 2894, as amended by S.I. 1996 No. 2966, except subsection (1)(b) and (2)(c) [in square brackets].

Interpretation of sections 16 to 22
[1] **23.** In sections 16 to 22 of this Act and this section, except where the context otherwise requires—
    "the Board" means the Scottish Conveyancing and Executry Services Board;
    "conveyancing services" means the preparation of writs, contracts and other documents in connection with the transfer of heritable property and loans secured over such property, and services ancillary thereto, but does not include any services—
        (a) relating to the arranging of loans; or
        (b) falling within section 1(1)(a) of the Estate Agents Act 1979;
    "executry practitioner" means a person registered under section 18 in the register of executry practitioners;
    "executry services" means the drawing and preparation of papers on which to found or oppose an application for a grant of confirmation of executors and services in connection with the administration, ingathering, distribution and winding up of the estate of a deceased person by executors, but does not include anything which constitutes investment business within the meaning of the Financial Services Act 1986;
    "inadequate professional services" means professional services which are in any respect not of the quality which could reasonably be expected of a competent practitioner; and references to the provision of inadequate professional services shall be construed as including references to not providing professional services which such a practitioner ought to have provided;
    "independent qualified conveyancer" means a person registered as such under section 17(7) in the register of qualified conveyancers;
    "practitioner" means an executry practitioner or a qualified conveyancer;
    "qualified conveyancer" means a person registered under section 17 in the register of qualified conveyancers; and
    "recognised financial institution" has the meaning given to it in section 19(2).

NOTE
[1] Brought into force on April 1, 1991 by S.I. 1991 No. 822.

Rights of audience

Rights of audience in the Court of Session, the House of Lords, the Judicial Committee of the Privy Council and the High Court of Justiciary
24. [Inserts s.25A in the Solicitors (Scotland) Act 1980 (c. 46), *supra.*]

Rights to conduct litigation and rights of audience
[1] **25.**—(1) Any professional or other body may, for the purpose of enabling any of their members who is a natural person to acquire—
    (a) rights to conduct litigation on behalf of members of the public; and
    (b) rights of audience,
make an application in that regard to the Lord President and the Secretary of State.
    (2) An application under subsection (1) above shall include a draft scheme—
    (a) specifying—
        (i) the courts;
        (ii) the categories of proceedings;

    (iii) the nature of the business; and
    (iv) the rights to conduct litigation and the rights of audience,
  in relation to which the application is made;
  (b) describing—
    (i) the training requirements which the body would impose upon any of their members who sought to acquire any right such as is mentioned in subsection (1) above; and
    (ii) the code of practice which they would impose upon their members in relation to the exercise by those members of any rights acquired by them by virtue of this section,
  in the event of the application being granted; and
  (c) proposing arrangements for—
    (i) the indemnification of members of the public against loss suffered by them through the actings of the body's members in the exercise by those members of any rights acquired by them by virtue of this section; and
    (ii) the treatment by the body of complaints made to them by members of the public in relation to the actings of members of the body exercising rights acquired by virtue of this section,
and shall state that the body have complied with the provisions of Schedule 2 to this Act.

  (3) A code of practice such as is mentioned in subsection (2)(b)(ii) above shall include provision with regard to revoking, suspending or attaching conditions to the exercise of any right acquired by a member of the body by virtue of this section in consequence of a breach by that member of that code of practice; and shall in particular include provision enabling the body to comply with the provisions of section 27(4) of this Act.

  (4) A draft scheme submitted under this section shall also include the proposals of the body in relation to such other matters as may be prescribed by the Secretary of State in regulations made under this section.

  (5) Regulations under this section shall be made by statutory instrument subject to annulment in pursuance of a resolution of either House of Parliament.

  (6) Schedule 2 shall have effect in relation to the publication of applications made under subsection (1) above.]

NOTE
[1] Not yet in force.

Consideration of applications made under section 25
 [1] **26.**—(1) The Lord President shall consider the provision made in any draft scheme submitted to him under section 25(1) of this Act in relation to the matters mentioned in section 25(2); and the Secretary of State shall, subject to subsection (5) below and to section 40 of this Act, consider the provision so made in section 25(2)(b) and (c).

  (2) In considering the code of practice included in the draft scheme by virtue of section 25(2)(b)(ii), the Lord President shall have regard to the desirability of there being common principles applying in relation to the exercising of rights to conduct litigation and rights of

audience by all practitioners in relation to the court or, as the case may be, the courts, mentioned in the application.

(3) The Lord President and the Secretary of State shall—

(*a*) consult each other in considering a draft scheme submitted to them under section 25(1); and

(*b*) consider any written representations timeously made to them under Schedule 2 to this Act,

and may, either jointly or severally, make preliminary observations to the body concerned in relation to that draft; and the body may make such adjustments to the draft as appear to them to be appropriate, and the Lord President and the Secretary of State (who shall, in accordance with section 40, consult the Director in respect of any adjustments made in relation to the matters mentioned in section 25(2)(*b*) or (*c*)) shall thereafter consider the draft scheme as so adjusted.

(4) In considering a draft scheme under subsection (1) or (3) above, the Lord President and the Secretary of State shall have regard to whether the provisions of the draft scheme are such as—

(*a*) to achieve; and

(*b*) to ensure the maintenance of,

appropriate standards of conduct and practice by persons who may acquire rights to conduct litigation or rights of audience in the event of the draft scheme being approved.

(5) In relation to any code of practice such as is mentioned in section 25(2)(*b*)(ii), the duty of the Secretary of State under subsection (1) above is limited to a consideration of any provision of such a code as would, in his view, directly or indirectly inhibit the freedom of a member of the body concerned to undertake all the work necessary for the preparation of a case or for the presentation of a case before the court, other than such a provision which has that effect only by reason of the provision made in the draft scheme with respect to the matters mentioned in section 25(2)(*a*).

(6) After they have considered a draft scheme under subsections (1) and (3) above, if the Lord President and the Secretary of State—

(*a*) are satisfied with the draft scheme, the Lord President shall grant the application, and shall so inform the body;

(*b*) are not satisfied with the scheme, the Lord President shall refuse the application, and shall so inform the body, giving written reasons for the refusal,

and the Lord President shall send a copy of the letter granting or refusing the application to any person who has made representations in relation to the draft scheme under Schedule 2 to this Act.

(7) Where the Lord President has granted an application under subsection (6)(*a*) above, in relation to—

(*a*) civil proceedings, the Court of Session may by act of sederunt; and

(*b*) criminal proceedings, the High Court of Justiciary may by act of adjournal,

make such provision for giving effect to the scheme as appears to it to be appropriate.]

NOTE
[1] Section 26 remains prospective.

Exercise of rights to conduct litigation and rights of audience
[1] [**27.**—(1) Where an application made under section 25 of this Act has been granted under section 26 of this Act, any member of the body concerned who has complied with the terms of the scheme in relation to the matters mentioned in section 25(2)(*b*)(i), and who appears to the body to be a fit and proper person, shall have the right to conduct litigation or rights of audience to which that compliance entitles him.

(2) Where a function is, whether expressly or by implication, conferred on any person or body by section 26 or this section he or, as the case may be, they shall exercise that function as soon as is reasonably practicable.

(3) Nothing in subsection (1) above affects the power of any court in relation to any proceedings—

(*a*) to hear a person who would not otherwise have a right of audience before that court in relation to those proceedings; or

(*b*) to refuse to hear a person (for reasons which apply to him as an individual) who would otherwise have a right of audience before that court in relation to those proceedings, and where a court so refuses it shall give its reasons for that decision.

(4) Where a complaint has been made that a person has been guilty of professional misconduct in the exercise of any right to conduct litigation or right of audience held by him by virtue of this section, the body of which he is a member may, or if so requested by the Lord President shall, suspend that person from exercising that right pending determination of that complaint by the body.

(5) Where a person holding a right of audience in any court by virtue of this section is instructed to appear in that court, those instructions shall take precedence before any of his other professional or business obligations, and the code of practice mentioned in section 25(2)(*b*)(ii) shall include rules—

   (*a*) stating the order of precedence of courts for the purposes of this subsection;

   (*b*) stating general criteria to which members of the body should have regard in determining whether to accept instructions in particular circumstances; and

   (*c*) securing, through such of their officers as they think appropriate, that, where reasonably practicable, any person wishing to be represented before any court by one of their members holding an appropriate right of audience is so represented,

and, for the purposes of such rules, the Inner and Outer Houses of the Court of Session, and the High Court of Justiciary exercising its appellate jurisdiction, may be treated as separate courts.

(6) A person exercising any right of audience held by virtue of this section shall have the same immunity from liability for negligence in respect of his acts or omissions as if he were an advocate, and no act or omission on the part of any such person shall give rise to an action for breach of contract in relation to the exercise by him of such a right of audience.

(7) Any person who wilfully and falsely—

   (*a*) pretends to have any right to conduct litigation or right of audience by virtue of this section; or

   (*b*) where he has any such right, pretends to have any further such right which he does not have; or

   (*c*) takes or uses any name, title, addition or description implying that he has any such right or, as the case may be, any further such right,

shall be guilty of an offence and liable on summary conviction to a fine not exceeding level 4 on the standard scale.

(8) For the purposes of section 25, section 26 and this section—

"right of audience" includes, in relation to any court, any such right exercisable by an advocate; and

"right to conduct litigation" means the right to exercise on behalf of a client all or any of the functions, other than any right of audience, which may be exercised by a solicitor in relation to litigation.]

NOTE
[1] Section 27 remains prospective.

Surrender of rights to conduct litigation and rights of audience

[1] [**28.**—(1) Subject to the provisions of this section, where an application made under section 25 of this Act has been granted under section 26(6) of this Act, the body concerned may apply to the Lord President and the Secretary of State for permission to surrender any entitlement of their members to acquire rights to conduct litigation or rights of audience.

(2) The Lord President and the Secretary of State shall jointly issue directions as to the requirements with which any body wishing to surrender their members' entitlement will have to comply, and, without prejudice to the generality of the foregoing, any such directions may include provision—

   (*a*) where members of a body have acquired rights to conduct litigation or rights of audience, as to the arrangements to be made for the completion of any work outstanding at the time the application is made; and

   (*b*) relating to the particular circumstances of a particular body.

(3) An application under subsection (1) above shall describe the manner in which the body have complied, or will comply, with the directions issued under subsection (2) above.

(4) Where the Lord President and the Secretary of State are satisfied that the body concerned have complied, or will comply, with the directions issued under subsection (2) above, the Lord President shall grant the application, and shall so inform the body.

(5) With effect from the date on which an application under subsection (1) above is granted, any member of the body concerned who has acquired rights to conduct litigation or rights of audience by virtue of the scheme shall cease to hold those rights.]

NOTE
[1] Section 28 remains prospective.

Revocation of rights granted under section 26
[1] [**29.**—(1) Where it appears to the Secretary of State that a body has failed to comply with a direction under section 42(6) of this Act, he may by order made by statutory instrument revoke the grant of the application made by that body under section 25 of this Act.

(2) No instrument shall be made under subsection (1) above unless a draft of the instrument has been laid before and approved by each House of Parliament.

(3) With effect from the date on which an order under subsection (1) above takes effect, any member of the body concerned who has acquired rights to conduct litigation or rights of audience by virtue of the scheme shall cease to hold those rights.]

NOTE
[1] Section 29 remains prospective.

Regulation of right of English, Welsh and Northern Irish practitioners to practise in Scotland
[1] **30.**—(1) The Secretary of State, after consulting the Lord President, may by regulations prescribe circumstances in which, and conditions subject to which, practitioners who are qualified to practise in England and Wales or Northern Ireland may, in such capacity as may be prescribed, exercise in Scotland—

(a) prescribed rights of audience; or
(b) prescribed rights to conduct litigation,

without being entitled to do so apart from the regulations.

(2) The Secretary of State, after consulting the Lord President, may by regulations make provision for the purpose of enabling practitioners who are entitled to practise in England and Wales or Northern Ireland to become qualified to practise in Scotland on terms, and subject to conditions, corresponding or similar to those on which practitioners who are entitled to practise in member States may become qualified to practise in Scotland.

(3) Regulations made under subsection (1) above may, in particular—

(a) prescribe any right of audience which may not be exercised by a person in Scotland unless he is instructed to act together with a person who has that right of audience there;

(b) prescribe legal services which may not be provided by any person practising by virtue of the regulations;

(c) prescribe the title or description which must be used by any person practising by virtue of the regulations;

(d) provide for the body by whom and the means by which the qualification of any person claiming to be entitled to practise by virtue of the regulations is to be verified; and

(e) provide for such professional or other body as may be prescribed to have power to investigate and deal with any complaint made against a person practising by virtue of the regulations.

(4) Regulations made under subsection (1) or (2) above may modify any rule of law or practice which the Secretary of State considers should be modified in order to give effect to the regulations.

F 52   *Solicitors: Statutes*

(5) Regulations under this section shall be made by statutory instrument subject to annulment in pursuance of a resolution of either House of Parliament.

(6) In this section "practitioner" means, in relation to England and Wales and Northern Ireland—

(a) a barrister or solicitor; and

(b) any person falling within such category as may be prescribed in regulations made by the Secretary of State after consultation with the Lord President.

NOTE
[1] In force June 3, 1991: S.I. 1991 No. 1252.

Rules of Conduct

Rules of conduct etc.
[1] **31.**—(1) Any rule, whether made before or after the coming into force of this section, whereby an advocate is prohibited from forming a legal relationship with another advocate or with any other person for the purpose of their jointly offering professional services to the public shall have no effect unless it is approved by the Lord President and the Secretary of State; and before approving any such rule the Secretary of State shall consult the Director in accordance with section 40 of this Act.

(2) Where it appears to the Faculty of Advocates that any rule of conduct in relation to the exercise of an advocate's right of audience in the Court of Session is more restrictive than the equivalent rule in relation to the exercise of the equivalent right in the sheriff court, they may submit that rule to the Secretary of State for his approval, and the Secretary of State shall consult the Director in accordance with section 40 of this Act, and thereafter, having—

(a) considered any advice tendered to him by the Director;

(b) compared the rule applicable in the Court of Session with the equivalent rule applicable in the sheriff court; and

(c) considered whether the interests of justice require that there should be such a rule in the Court of Session,

he may approve or refuse to approve the rule.

(3) In section 34 of the 1980 Act (rules as to professional practice, conduct and discipline)—

(a) at the end of subsection (1A) there shall be inserted—
"and
(f) make such additional or different provision as the Council think fit in relation to solicitors who, or incorporated practices which, are partners in or directors of multi-disciplinary practices."; and

(b) after subsection (3) there shall be inserted—
"(3A) Without prejudice to subsection (3), any rule made, whether before or after the coming into force of this subsection, by the Council under this section or section 35 which has the effect of prohibiting the formation of multi-disciplinary practices shall not have effect unless the Secretary of State, after consulting the Director in accordance with section 64A, has approved it.".

NOTE
[1] In force March 17, 1993: S.I. 1993 No. 641.

Multi-national practices

Multi-national practices
32. [Inserts s.60A in Solicitors (Scotland) Act 1980 (c. 46), *above.*]

Release 44: 28 April 1997

Complaints in relation to legal services

Complaints in relation to legal services
[1] **33.**—(1) Where any person with an interest has made a complaint (a "conduct complaint") to a professional organisation that a practitioner has—
(a) been guilty of professional misconduct; or
(b) provided inadequate professional services,
the organisation shall investigate the matter, and shall thereafter make a written report to the complainer and the practitioner concerned of—
(i) the facts of the matter as found by the organisation; and
(ii) what action the organisation propose to take, or have taken, in the matter.
(2) [2] The organisation shall ensure that their procedures for dealing with conduct complaints do not conflict with the duty imposed by section 34A of this Act in relation to any report sent to them under that section.
(3)–(4) [Repealed by the Scottish Legal Services Ombudsman and Commissioner for Local Administration in Scotland Act 1997 (c. 35), s.5(1)(b) and Sched.[3]]
(5) For the purposes of this section and sections 34, 34A and 34B of this Act[4]—
    "professional organisation" means—
        (a) the Faculty of Advocates;
        (b) the Council of the Law Society of Scotland;
        (c) the Scottish Conveyancing and Executry Services Board established under section 16 of this Act; and
        (d) a body which has made a successful application under section 25 of this Act; and
    "practitioner" means, in relation to—
        (a) the Faculty of Advocates, an advocate;
        (b) the Council, a solicitor;
        (c) the Scottish Conveyancing and Executry Services Board, a practitioner within the meaning of section 23 of this Act; and
        (d) a body which has made a successful application under section 25 of this Act, any person exercising—
            (i) a right to conduct litigation; or
            (ii) a right of audience;
        acquired by virtue of section 27 of this Act.

NOTES
[1] In force June 3, 1991: S.I. 1991 No. 1252.
[2] As amended by 1997 (c. 35), s.5(1)(a), effective July 22, 1997.
[3] Effective two months following royal assent (May 21, 1997), *i.e.* July 22, 1997.
[4] Inserted by 1997 (c. 35), s.5(1)(c), effective July 22, 1997.

Scottish legal services ombudsman

Scottish legal services ombudsman
[1] **34.**—(1) The Secretary of State may, after consultation with the Lord President, and subject to subsection (9) below, appoint a person, to be known as the Scottish legal services ombudsman, for the purpose of conducting investigations under this Act.[2]
(1A)[3] Subject to subsection (1E) below, the ombudsman may investigate any written complaint (a "handling complaint") made to him by or on behalf of any person which relates to the manner in which a conduct complaint made by or on behalf of that person has been dealt with by the professional organisation concerned.
(1B)[3] Subsection (1A) above applies whether or not the professional organisation concerned have treated the conduct complaint as a conduct complaint.

(1C)[3] The ombudsman may decide—
   (a) not to investigate a handling complaint; or
   (b) to discontinue his investigation of a handling complaint.
   (1D)[3] If the ombudsman decides not to investigate a handling complaint or decides to discontinue his investigation of such a complaint he shall notify—
   (a) the person who made the handling complaint; and
   (b) the professional organisation concerned,
of his decision and the reason for it.
   (1E)[3] The ombudsman shall not investigate a handling complaint where—
   (a) the professional organisation concerned have not completed their investigation of the conduct complaint to which it relates; or
   (b) it is made after the expiry of such period of time as may be specified for the purpose of this subsection in directions given by the Secretary of State by virtue of paragraph 2 of Schedule 3 to this Act.
   (1F)[3] Paragraph (a) of subsection (1E) above does not apply if—
   (a) the handling complaint is that the professional organisation concerned—
     (i) have acted unreasonably in failing to start an investigation into the complaint; or
     (ii) having started such an investigation, have failed to complete it within a reasonable time; or
   (b) the ombudsman considers that, even though the complaint is being investigated by that organisation, an investigation by him is justified.
   (2) The ombudsman shall make such investigation of any handling complaint as seems to him to be appropriate.[4]
   (2A)[3] Where the ombudsman is conducting an investigation under this Act, he may require the professional organisation concerned—
   (a) to provide him with such information, being information which is within the knowledge of the professional organisation, as he considers relevant to his investigation; or
   (b) to produce to him such documents, being documents which are within the possession or control of the organisation, as he considers relevant to his investigation,
(including any information or, as the case may be, documents obtained by the organisation from the practitioner concerned while investigating the conduct complaint to which the handling complaint relates); and, notwithstanding any duty of confidentiality owed to any person by the professional organisation as respects any such information or, as the case may be, documents, the organisation shall comply with such a requirement.
   (2B)[3] Where any information requested by the ombudsman under subsection (2A) above is not within the knowledge of the professional organisation concerned, or any documents so requested are not within their possession or control, the ombudsman may require the practitioner concerned in the conduct complaint to which the handling complaint relates—
   (a) to provide him with that information, in so far as it is within the knowledge of the practitioner; or
   (b) to produce to him those documents, if they are within the possession or control of the practitioner;
and, notwithstanding any duty of confidentiality owed to any person by the practitioner as respects any such information or, as the case may be, documents, the practitioner shall comply with such a requirement.
   (3) [Repealed by 1997 (c. 35), s.1(6), effective July 22, 1997.]
   (4)[2] Where the ombudsman is conducting an investigation under this Act, he may at any time make a written interim report in relation to the investigation and shall send a copy of any such report to—
   (a) the person who made the handling complaint; and
   (b) the professional organisation concerned.

(5) The ombudsman may—

(a) if so requested by any person appointed to carry out equivalent functions in relation to the provision of legal services in England and Wales, investigate a complaint against a professional body in England and Wales on that person's behalf; and

(b) request any person appointed as mentioned in paragraph (a) above to investigate a complaint against an organisation in Scotland on his behalf.

(6) The Secretary of State may by regulations extend the jurisdiction of the ombudsman by providing for this section to apply, with such modifications (if any) as he thinks fit, in relation to the investigation by the ombudsman of such categories of handling complaints as may be specified in the regulations with respect to the provision of executry services by persons other than executry practitioners within the meaning of section 23 of this Act.

(7) Without prejudice to the generality of subsection (6) above, regulations under that subsection may make provision for the investigation of handling complaints with respect to particular persons or categories of person.

(8) Regulations under subsection (6) above shall be made by statutory instrument subject to annulment in pursuance of a resolution of either House of Parliament.

(9) The following shall not be eligible to be appointed as the ombudsman—

(a) advocates;

(b) solicitors;

(c) members and officers of the Scottish Conveyancing and Executry Services Board established by section 16 of this Act;

(d) subject to paragraph (e) below, executry practitioners within the meaning of section 23 of this Act;

(e) where any such executry practitioner is a partnership or a body corporate, the partners or, as the case may be, the directors, secretary or other similar officers;

(f) the directors, secretary or other similar officers of any recognised financial institution within the meaning of section 19(2) of this Act;

(g) qualified conveyancers within the meaning of section 23 of this Act; or

(h) any member or employee of a professional or other body any of whose members has acquired any right to conduct litigation or right of audience by virtue of section 27 of this Act.

(10) Schedule 3 to this Act shall have effect in relation to the ombudsman.

NOTES

[1] In force April 1, 1991 (subss. (1), (9)(a)–(c), 10 and Sched. 3: S.I. 1991 No. 822); June 3, 1991 (subss. (2)–(8): S.I. 1991 No. 1252). Subsections (9)(d)–(h) remain prospective.

[2] Substituted by Scottish Legal Services Ombudsman and Commissioner for Local Administration in Scotland Act 1997 (c. 35), s.1(2), effective two months following Royal Assent on May 21, *i.e.* July 22, 1997.

[3] Inserted by *ibid.*

[4] Part repealed by *ibid.*

Ombudsman's final report and recommendations

34A.[1]—(1) Where the Scottish legal services ombudsman has completed an investigation under this Act he shall make a written report of his conclusions and shall send a copy of the report to—

(a) the person who made the handling complaint;

(b) the professional organisation concerned; and

(c) the practitioner concerned in the conduct complaint to which the handling complaint relates.

(2) If the ombudsman decides to make a complaint about the practitioner concerned to the appropriate disciplinary body he may include in the report under this section a statement to that effect.

(3) A report under this section may include one or more of the following recommendations—

(a) that the professional organisation concerned provide to the person making the handling complaint such information about the conduct complaint to which the handling complaint relates, and how it was dealt with, as the ombudsman considers appropriate;

(b) that the conduct complaint be investigated further by the professional organisation concerned;

(c) that the conduct complaint be reconsidered by the professional organisation concerned;

(d) that the professional organisation concerned consider exercising their powers in relation to the practitioner concerned;

(e) that the professional organisation concerned pay compensation of the stated amount to the person making the handling complaint for loss suffered by him, or inconvenience or distress caused to him, as a result of the way in which the conduct complaint was handled by that organisation;

(f) that the professional organisation to whom a recommendation under paragraph (e) above applies pay to the person making the handling complaint an amount specified by the ombudsman by way of reimbursement of the cost, or part of the cost, of making the handling complaint.

(4) Where a report under this section includes any recommendation, the report shall state the ombudsman's reasons for making the recommendation.

(5) For the purposes of the law of defamation the publication of any report of the ombudsman under this section and any publicity given under subsection (8) below shall be privileged unless the publication is proved to be made with malice.

(6) It shall be the duty of any professional organisation to whom a report is sent by the ombudsman under this section to have regard to the conclusions and recommendations set out in the report so far as relating to that organisation.

(7) Where a report sent to a professional organisation under this section includes a recommendation relating to them, the organisation shall, before the end of the period of three months beginning with the date on which the report was sent, notify the ombudsman, and the person who made the handling complaint, of—

(a) the action which they have taken to comply with the recommendation or in consequence of further consideration of the matter by them; or

(b) their decision not to comply wholly with a recommendation and any reason for that decision.

(8) Where, at the end of the period of three months mentioned in subsection (7) above, a professional organisation have not wholly complied with a recommendation relating to them in a report under this section, the ombudsman may take such steps as he considers reasonable to publicise that fact; but shall in so publicising it state any reason given to the ombudsman by the organisation for their not having so complied (or a summary by the ombudsman of any such reason).

(9) Any reasonable expenses incurred by the ombudsman under subsection (8) above may be recovered by him (as a civil debt) from the professional organisation concerned.

(10) In this section—

"the stated amount" means such amount as may be specified by the ombudsman, being an amount which does not exceed the prescribed amount; and

"the prescribed amount" means £1000 or such greater amount as may from time to time be specified by order made by the Secretary of State by statutory instrument subject to annulment in pursuance of a resolution of either House of Parliament.

NOTE
   [1] Inserted by Scottish Legal Services Ombudsman and Commissioner for Local Administration in Scotland Act 1997 (c. 35), s.2, effective July 22, 1997, and applied by s.6 of that Act.

Advisory functions of ombudsman
   34B.[1]—(1) The Scottish legal services ombudsman may make recommendations to any professional organisation about their procedures for,
and methods of, dealing with conduct complaints.
   (2) It shall be the duty of a professional organisation to whom a
recommendation is made under this section—
   (a) to consider the recommendation; and
   (b) to notify the ombudsman of the results of that consideration and any
         action which they have taken, or propose to take, in consequence of
         the recommendation.

NOTE
   [1] Inserted by Scottish Legal Services Ombudsman and Commissioner for Local Administration in Scotland Act 1997 (c. 35), s.3, effective July 22, 1997.

Judicial appointments

   35. [See Division B.]

Solicitors' and counsel's fees

Solicitors' and counsel's fees
   36. [Inserts new section 61A into the Solicitors (Scotland) Act 1980 (c. 46),
above.]

Miscellaneous and supplementary

Admission of solicitors and notaries public
   [1] **37.**—(1) [amends s.6(2) of the Solicitors (Scotland) Act 1980 (c. 46),
above].
   (2) [amends s.57 of the Solicitors (Scotland) Act 1980 (c. 46), *above*].
   (3) [amends s.58 of the Solicitors (Scotland) Act 1980 (c. 46), *above*].

NOTE
   [1] In force July 20, 1992: S.I. 1992 No. 1599.

Availability of legal aid in relation to services provided under this Act
   38. [Inserts new section 43A in the Legal Aid (Scotland) Act 1986 (c. 47):
Div. G *below*.]

   [1] **39.** [Repeals s.29 of the Solicitors (Scotland) Act 1980 (c. 46), *above*].

NOTE
   [1] In force September 30, 1991: S.I. 1991 No. 2151.

Advisory and supervisory functions of the Director
   [1] **40.**—(1) Before—
   (a) making any regulations under section 17(11) or 18(10) of this Act; or
   (b) approving any rules—
         (i) made under section 17(3); or
         (ii) such as are mentioned in section 31(1) or (2),
         of this Act; or
   (c) considering any provisions of a draft scheme under section 26(1) or
         (3) of this Act,
the Secretary of State shall first send a copy of the proposed regulations,
rules or provisions to the Director.

(2) The Director shall consider whether any such regulations, rules or provisions as are mentioned in subsection (1) above would have, or would be likely to have, the effect of restricting, distorting or preventing competition to any significant extent.

(3) When the Director has completed his consideration he shall give such advice to the Secretary of State as he thinks fit.

(4) The Director may publish any advice given by him under subsection (3) above.

(5) The Director shall, so far as practicable, exclude from anything published under subsection (4) above any matter—

(a) which relates to the affairs of a particular person; and

(b) the publication of which would, or might in the Director's opinion, seriously and prejudicially affect the interests of that person.

(6) For the purposes of the law of defamation, the publication of any advice by the Director under this section shall be absolutely privileged.

NOTE
[1] Section 40 remains prospective.

Investigatory powers of the Director
[1] **41.**—(1) For the purpose of investigating any matter under section 40 of this Act, the Director may by notice in writing—

(a) require any person to produce to him or to any person appointed by him for the purpose, at a time and place specified in the notice, any documents which are specified or described in the notice and which—

(i) are in that person's custody or under that person's control; and

(ii) relate to any matter relevant to the investigation; or

(b) require any person carrying on any business to furnish to him (within such time and in such manner and form as the notice may specify) such information as may be specified or described in the notice.

(2) A person shall not be required under this section to produce any document or disclose any information which he would be entitled to refuse to produce or disclose on the grounds of confidentiality between a client and his professional legal adviser in any civil proceedings.

(3) Subsections (5) to (8) of section 85 of the Fair Trading Act 1973 shall apply in relation to a notice under this section as they apply in relation to a notice under subsection (1) of that section.

NOTE
[1] Section 41 remains prospective.

Review of rules approved by the Secretary of State
[1] **42.**—(1) Where the Secretary of State has approved—

(a) a rule under section 17(15) or 31(2) of this Act; or

(b) a draft scheme under section 26(6) of this Act,

he may and, where the Lord President, in the case of a draft scheme such as is mentioned in paragraph (b), so requests shall, require the body which made the rule or, as the case may be, the scheme to review its terms.

(2) When they have reviewed a rule or, as the case may be, a scheme, following a requirement made under subsection (1) above, the body concerned may revise the rule or scheme in the light of that review, and shall then submit the rule or scheme as revised or, if they have not revised it, as previously approved—

(a) in the case of a rule such as is mentioned in subsection (1)(a) above, to the Secretary of State; or

(b) in the case of a draft scheme such as is mentioned in subsection (1)(b) above, to the Secretary of State and the Lord President.

(3) Where a rule, whether revised or as previously approved, is submitted to the Secretary of State under subsection (2)(a) above, he may—

(a) approve the rule as submitted to him; or

(b) amend the rule in such manner as he considers appropriate,

and (except where the rule remains in the form previously approved) he may direct the body concerned to bring it into operation as soon as is practicable.

(4) Where the Lord President and the Secretary of State are agreed that the terms of a draft scheme submitted to them under subsection (2)(b) above are satisfactory, the Secretary of State may—

(a) approve the scheme; and

(b) (except where the scheme remains in the form previously approved) direct the body concerned to bring the scheme, as so amended, into force as soon as is practicable.

(5) Where either the Secretary of State or the Lord President is of the view that the terms of any such scheme so submitted to them are not satisfactory, but they do not agree as to what the terms of the scheme should be, the scheme shall continue to have effect as previously approved.

(6) Where the Secretary of State and the Lord President agree both that the terms of a scheme so submitted to them are not satisfactory, and as to what the terms of the scheme should be, the Secretary of State may amend the scheme in such manner as he and the Lord President consider appropriate; and may direct the body concerned to bring the scheme, as so amended, into force as soon as is practicable.

(7) The provisions of section 40(1)(b) and (c) of this Act shall apply to rules and schemes submitted under subsection (2) of this section as they apply to rules submitted under sections 17(15) and 31(2) and schemes submitted under section 25(1) of this Act.

NOTE
[1] Section 42 remains prospective.

Functions of Director in relation to certain rules made under the 1980 Act

   43. [New ss. 64A–64D of the Solicitors (Scotland) Act 1980 (c. 46) appear in the print of that Act, *above*.]

Interpretation of Part II

[1] **44.** In this Part of this Act, unless the context otherwise requires—

   "advocate" means a member of the Faculty of Advocates practising as such;

   "the Director" means the Director General of Fair Trading;

   "Lord President" means the Lord President of the Court of Session;

   "solicitor" has the same meaning as in section 65(1) of the 1980 Act; and

   "the 1980 Act" means the Solicitors (Scotland) Act 1980.

NOTE
[1] In force April 1, 1991: S.I. 1991 No. 822.

PART III

THE LICENSING (SCOTLAND) ACT 1976

   45.–55. [See Division E, *above*.]

PART IV

56.–72. [See Divs. B, I and M.]

PART V

GENERAL

Finance
   73. [Not printed.]

Amendments and repeals
   74.—(1) The enactments mentioned in Schedule 8 to this Act shall have effect subject to the amendments specified in that Schedule.
   (2) The enactments mentioned in Schedule 9 to this Act are hereby repealed to the extent specified in the third column of that Schedule.

Citation, commencement and extent
   75.—(1) This Act may be cited as the Law Reform (Miscellaneous Provisions) (Scotland) Act 1990.
   (2) Subject to subsections (3) and (4) below, this Act shall come into force on such day as the Secretary of State may appoint by order made by statutory instrument and different days may be appointed for different provisions and for different purposes.
   (3) The provisions of—
    (a) Part III and section 66 of this Act and so much of section 74 as relates to those provisions; and
    (b) sections 67, 70 and 71 of this Act and paragraphs 21 and 34 of Schedule 8 to this Act,
shall come into force at the end of the period of two months beginning with the day on which this Act is passed.
   (4) Paragraph 27(3) of Schedule 8 to this Act shall come into force on the day on which this Act is passed.
   (5) Subject to subsections (6) and (7) below, this Act extends to Scotland only.
   (6) Section 72 of this Act, paragraph 33 of Schedule 8 to this Act and Schedule 9 to this Act so far as relating to the Companies Act 1985 and the Companies Act 1989 extend also to England and Wales.
   (7) Paragraph 17 of Schedule 1 to this Act, paragraph 11 of Schedule 3 to this Act and Schedule 9 to this Act so far as relating to the House of Commons Disqualification Act 1975 extend also to England and Wales and Northern Ireland.

SCHEDULES

SCHEDULE 1

SCOTTISH CONVEYANCING AND EXECUTRY SERVICES BOARD

   [Not printed.]

[1] SCHEDULE 2

PUBLICATION OF APPLICATIONS MADE UNDER SECTION 25

   1. Any professional or other body making an application under section 25 of this Act shall, for a period of six weeks beginning with the date on which the application is submitted to the Lord President and the Secretary of State—

(a) make a copy of the draft scheme referred to in section 25(2) of this Act available for public inspection at a specified place; and
(b) on a request from any person—
    (i) send him a copy of the draft scheme; or
    (ii) make a copy of the draft scheme available for public inspection at a suitable place in his locality.

2. Any person may make written representations concerning any draft scheme submitted under section 25 of this Act, and such representations shall—
(a) be made to both the Lord President and the Secretary of State; and
(b) be delivered to both the Lord President and the Secretary of State before the expiry of the period of six weeks beginning with the date on which the application is made.

3. At the same time as an application under section 25 is submitted to the Lord President and the Secretary of State, the body making the application shall place an advertisement mentioning the matters referred to in paragraph 4 below in the *Edinburgh Gazette* and in a daily newspaper circulating throughout Scotland.

4. An advertisement such as referred to in paragraph 3 above shall state that—
(a) a copy of the draft scheme referred to in section 25(2) of this Act will be available for public inspection at a specified place for a period of six weeks beginning with the date on which the advertisement appears;
(b) a copy of the draft scheme will be—
    (i) sent, free of charge, to any person on request; or
    (ii) made available for public inspection at a suitable place in that person's locality;
(c) any person may make written representations concerning the draft scheme to the Lord President and the Secretary of State; and
(d) any such representations are to be delivered within the period of six weeks beginning with the date on which the application is made.

NOTE
[1] Schedule 2 remains prospective.

SCHEDULE 3

SCOTTISH LEGAL SERVICES OMBUDSMAN

1.[1] The Scottish legal services ombudsman shall hold and vacate his office in accordance with the terms of his appointment and shall, on ceasing to hold office, be eligible for re-appointment.

2. The Secretary of State may give general directions to the ombudsman about the scope and discharge of his functions, and shall publish any such directions.

3.—(1) The Secretary of State may with the consent of the Treasury determine the terms and conditions of service, including remuneration, of the ombudsman.

(2) Where a person appointed to the office of ombudsman ceases to hold that office otherwise than on the expiry of the term of office specified in his appointment, and it appears to the Secretary of State that there are special circumstances which make it right for that person to receive compensation, the Secretary of State may, with the consent of the Treasury, make a payment to that person of such amount as the Secretary of State may, with the consent of the Treasury, determine.

4. The Secretary of State may appoint staff for the ombudsman of such number, and on such terms and conditions of service, as he may with the consent of the Treasury determine; and such terms and conditions may include provision as to remuneration, and as to compensation for loss of employment (which may take the form of pensions, allowances or gratuities).

5. Neither the ombudsman nor his staff are, in such capacity, Crown servants.

6. The Secretary of State shall pay the expenses of the ombudsman and of his staff.

7.–8. [Repealed by 1997 (c. 35), s.5(2), effective July 22, 1997.]

9. The ombudsman shall make an annual report of the discharge of the functions conferred on him under this Act to the Secretary of State.

9A.[2] The ombudsman may, in addition to making a report under paragraph 9 above, report to the Secretary of State at any time on any matter relating to the discharge of the ombudsman's functions.

9B.[2] The ombudsman shall provide the Secretary of State with such information relating to the discharge of the ombudsman's functions as the Secretary of State may see fit to require.

10. The Secretary of State shall lay any report made to him under paragraph 9 above before each House of Parliament.

11. In Part III of Schedule 1 to the House of Commons Disqualification Act 1975 (offices disqualifying for membership) there shall be inserted at the appropriate place in alphabetical order the entry "Scottish legal services ombudsman appointed under section 34 of the Law Reform (Miscellaneous Provisions) (Scotland) Act 1990".

NOTES
¹ Amended by Scottish Legal Services Ombudsman and Commissioner for Local Administration in Scotland Act 1997 (c. 35), s.5(2), effective July 22, 1997.
² Inserted by *ibid.*, s.4.

SCHEDULES 4–7

[Not printed.]

Property Misdescriptions Act 1991

(1991 c. 29)

ARRANGEMENT OF SECTIONS

An Act to prohibit the making of false or misleading statements about property matters in the course of estate agency business and property development business.   [27th June 1991]

Offence of property misdescription
   1.—(1) Where a false or misleading statement about a prescribed matter is made in the course of an estate agency business or a property development business, otherwise than in providing conveyancing services, the person by whom the business is carried on shall be guilty of an offence under this section.
   (2) Where the making of the statement is due to the act or default of an employee the employee shall be guilty of an offence under this section; and the employee may be proceeded against and punished whether or not proceedings are also taken against his employer.
   (3) A person guilty of an offence under this section shall be liable—
   (a) on summary conviction, to a fine not exceeding the statutory maximum, and
   (b) on conviction on indictment, to a fine.
   (4) No contract shall be void or unenforceable, and no right of action in civil proceedings in respect of any loss shall arise, by reason only of the commission of an offence under this section.
   (5) For the purposes of this section—
   (a) "false" means false to a material degree,
   (b) a statement is misleading if (though not false) what a reasonable person may be expected to infer from it, or from any omission from it, is false,

(c) a statement may be made by pictures or any other method of signifying meaning as well as by words and, if made by words, may be made orally or in writing,

(d) a prescribed matter is any matter relating to land which is specified in an order made by the Secretary of State,

(e) a statement is made in the course of an estate agency business if (but only if) the making of the statement is a thing done as mentioned in subsection (1) of section 1 of the Estate Agents Act 1979 and that Act either applies to it or would apply to it but for subsection (2)(a) of that section (exception for things done in course of profession by practising solicitor or employee),

(f) a statement is made in the course of a property development business if (but only if) it is made—

(i) in the course of a business (including a business in which the person making the statement is employed) concerned wholly or substantially with the development of land, and

(ii) for the purpose of, or with a view to, disposing of an interest in land consisting of or including a building, or a part of a building, constructed or renovated in the course of the business, and

(g) "conveyancing services" means the preparation of any transfer, conveyance, writ, contract or other document in connection with the disposal or acquisition of an interest in land, and services ancillary to that, but does not include anything done as mentioned in section 1(1)(a) of the Estate Agents Act 1979.

(6) For the purposes of this section any reference in this section or section 1 of the Estate Agents Act 1979 to disposing of or acquiring an interest in land—

(a) in England and Wales and Northern Ireland shall be construed in accordance with section 2 of that Act, and

(b) in Scotland is a reference to the transfer or creation of an "interest in land" as defined in section 28(1) of the Land Registration (Scotland) Act 1979.

(7) An order under this section may—

(a) make different provision for different cases, and

(b) include such supplemental, consequential and transitional provisions as the Secretary of State considers appropriate;

[THE NEXT PAGE IS F 63]

and the power to make such an order shall be exercisable by statutory instrument which shall be subject to annulment in pursuance of a resolution of either House of Parliament.

Due diligence defence
  2.—(1) In proceedings against a person for an offence under section 1 above it shall be a defence for him to show that he took all reasonable steps and exercised all due diligence to avoid committing the offence.
  (2) A person shall not be entitled to rely on the defence provided by subsection (1) above by reason of his reliance on information given by another unless he shows that it was reasonable in all the circumstances for him to have relied on the information, having regard in particular—
  (a) to the steps which he took, and those which might reasonably have been taken, for the purpose of verifying the information, and
  (b) to whether he had any reason to disbelieve the information.
  (3) Where in any proceedings against a person for an offence under section 1 above the defence provided by subsection (1) above involves an allegation that the commission of the offence was due—
  (a) to the act or default of another, or
  (b) to reliance on information given by another,
the person shall not, without the leave of the court, be entitled to rely on the defence unless he has served a notice under subsection (4) below on the person bringing the proceedings not less than seven clear days before the hearing of the proceedings or, in Scotland, the diet of trial.
  (4) A notice under this subsection shall give such information identifying or assisting in the identification of the person who committed the act or default, or gave the information, as is in the possession of the person serving the notice at the time he serves it.

Enforcement
  3. The Schedule to this Act (which makes provision about the enforcement of this Act) shall have effect.

Bodies corporate and Scottish partnerships
  4.—(1) Where an offence under this Act committed by a body corporate is proved to have been committed with the consent or connivance of, or to be attributable to neglect on the part of, a director, manager, secretary or other similar officer of the body corporate or a person who was purporting to act in such a capacity, he (as well as the body corporate) is guilty of the offence and liable to be proceeded against and punished accordingly.
  (2) Where the affairs of a body corporate are managed by its members, subsection (1) above applies in relation to the acts and defaults of a member in connection with his functions of management as if he were a director of the body corporate.
  (3) Where an offence under this Act committed in Scotland by a Scottish partnership is proved to have been committed with the consent or connivance of, or to be attributable to neglect on the part of, a partner, he (as well as the partnership) is guilty of the offence and liable to be proceeded against and punished accordingly.

Prosecution time limit
  5.—(1) No proceedings for an offence under section 1 above or paragraph 5(3), 6 or 7 of the Schedule to this Act shall be commenced after—
  (a) the end of the period of three years beginning with the date of the commission of the offence, or
  (b) the end of the period of one year beginning with the date of the discovery of the offence by the prosecutor,
whichever is the earlier.

(2) For the purposes of this section a certificate signed by or on behalf of the prosecutor and stating the date on which the offence was discovered by him shall be conclusive evidence of that fact; and a certificate stating that matter and purporting to be so signed shall be treated as so signed unless the contrary is proved.

Financial provision

6. There shall be paid out of money provided by Parliament any increase attributable to this Act in the sums payable out of such money under any other Act.

Short title and extent

7.—(1) This Act may be cited as the Property Misdescriptions Act 1991.

(2) This Act extends to Northern Ireland.

Section 3   SCHEDULE

ENFORCEMENT

Enforcement authority

1.—(1) Every local weights and measures authority in Great Britain shall be an enforcement authority for the purposes of this Act, and it shall be the duty of each such authority to enforce the provisions of this Act within their area.

(2) The Department of Economic Development in Northern Ireland shall be an enforcement authority for the purposes of this Act, and it shall be the duty of the Department to enforce the provisions of this Act within Northern Ireland.

Prosecutions

2.—(1) In section 130(1) of the Fair Trading Act 1973 (notice to Director General of Fair Trading of intended prosecution by local weights and measures authority in England and Wales), after the words "the Consumer Protection Act 1987," there shall be inserted the words "or for an offence under section 1 of, or paragraph 6 of the Schedule to, the Property Misdescriptions Act 1991,".

(2) Nothing in paragraph 1 above shall authorise a local weights and measures authority to bring proceedings in Scotland for an offence.

Powers of officers of enforcement authority

3.—(1) If a duly authorised officer of an enforcement authority has reasonable grounds for suspecting that an offence under section 1 of this Act has been committed, he may—

(*a*) require a person carrying on or employed in a business to produce any book or document relating to the business, and take copies of it or any entry in it, or

(*b*) require such a person to produce in a visible and legible documentary form any information so relating which is contained in a computer, and take copies of it,

for the purpose of ascertaining whether such an offence has been committed.

(2) Such an officer may inspect any goods for the purpose of ascertaining whether such an offence has been committed.

(3) If such an officer has reasonable grounds for believing that any documents or goods may be required as evidence in proceedings for such an offence, he may seize and detain them.

(4) An officer seizing any documents or goods in the exercise of his power under sub-paragraph (3) above shall inform the person from whom they are seized.

(5) The powers of an officer under this paragraph may be exercised by him only at a reasonable hour and on production (if required) of his credentials.

(6) Nothing in this paragraph—

(*a*) requires a person to produce a document if he would be entitled to refuse to produce it in proceedings in a court on the ground that it is the subject of legal professional privilege or, in Scotland, that it contains a confidential communication made by or to an advocate or a solicitor in that capacity, or

(*b*) authorises the taking possession of a document which is in the possession of a person who would be so entitled.

4.—(1) A duly authorised officer of an enforcement authority may, at a reasonable hour and on production (if required) of his credentials, enter any premises for the purpose of ascertaining whether an offence under section 1 of this Act has been committed.

(2) If a justice of the peace, or in Scotland a justice of the peace or a sheriff, is satisfied—

(a) that any relevant books, documents or goods are on, or that any relevant information contained in a computer is available from, any premises, and that production or inspection is likely to disclose the commission of an offence under section 1 of this Act, or

(b) that such an offence has been, is being or is about to be committed on any premises,

and that any of the conditions specified in sub-paragraph (3) below is met, he may by warrant under his hand authorise an officer of an enforcement authority to enter the premises, if need be ·by force.

(3) The conditions referred to in sub-paragraph (2) above are—

(a) that admission to the premises has been or is likely to be refused and that notice of intention to apply for a warrant under that sub-paragraph has been given to the occupier,

(b) that an application for admission, or the giving of such a notice, would defeat the object of the entry,

(c) that the premises are unoccupied, and

(d) that the occupier is temporarily absent and it might defeat the object of the entry to await his return.

(4) In sub-paragraph (2) above "relevant", in relation to books, documents, goods or information, means books, documents, goods or information which, under paragraph 3 above, a duly authorised officer may require to be produced or may inspect.

(5) A warrant under sub-paragraph (2) above may be issued only if—

(a) in England and Wales, the justice of the peace is satisfied as required by that sub-paragraph by written information on oath,

(b) in Scotland, the justice of the peace or sheriff is so satisfied by evidence on oath, or

(c) in Northern Ireland, the justice of the peace is so satisfied by complaint on oath.

(6) A warrant under sub-paragraph (2) above shall continue in force for a period of one month.

(7) An officer entering any premises by virtue of this paragraph may take with him such other persons as may appear to him necessary.

(8) On leaving premises which he has entered by virtue of a warrant under sub-paragraph (2) above, an officer shall, if the premises are unoccupied or the occupier is temporarily absent, leave the premises as effectively secured against trespassers as he found them.

(9) In this paragraph "premises" includes any place (including any vehicle, ship or aircraft) except premises used only as a dwelling.

Obstruction of officers

5.—(1) A person who—

(a) intentionally obstructs an officer of an enforcement authority acting in pursuance of this Schedule,

(b) without reasonable excuse fails to comply with a requirement made of him by such an officer under paragraph 3(1) above, or

(c) without reasonable excuse fails to give an officer of an enforcement authority acting in pursuance of this Schedule any other assistance or information which the officer may reasonably require of him for the purpose of the performance of the officer's functions under this Schedule,

shall be guilty of an offence.

(2) A person guilty of an offence under sub-paragraph (1) above shall be liable on summary conviction to a fine not exceeding level 5 on the standard scale.

(3) If a person, in giving any such information as is mentioned in sub-paragraph (1)(c) above,—

(a) makes a statement which he knows is false in a material particular, or

(b) recklessly makes a statement which is false in a material particular,

he shall be guilty of an offence.

(4) A person guilty of an offence under sub-paragraph (3) above shall be liable—

(a) on summary conviction, to a fine not exceeding the statutory maximum, and

(b) on conviction on indictment, to a fine.

Impersonation of officers

6.—(1) If a person who is not a duly authorised officer of an enforcement authority purports to act as such under this Schedule he shall be guilty of an offence.

(2) A person guilty of an offence under sub-paragraph (1) above shall be liable—
(a) on summary conviction, to a fine not exceeding the statutory maximum, and
(b) on conviction on indictment, to a fine.

Disclosure of information

7.—(1) If a person discloses to another any information obtained by him by virtue of this Schedule he shall be guilty of an offence unless the disclosure was made—
(a) in or for the purpose of the performance by him or any other person of any function under this Act, or
(b) for a purpose specified in section 38(2)(a), (b) or (c) of the Consumer Protection Act 1987.
(2) A person guilty of an offence under sub-paragraph (1) above shall be liable—
(a) on summary conviction, to a fine not exceeding the statutory maximum, and
(b) on conviction on indictment, to a fine.

Privilege against self-incrimination

8. Nothing in this Schedule requires a person to answer any question or give any information if to do so might incriminate him.

Statutory Instruments

Money Laundering Regulations 1993

(S.I. 1993 No. 1933)

ARRANGEMENT OF REGULATIONS

GENERAL

The Treasury being a government department designated for the purposes of section 2(2) of the European Communities Act 1972 in relation to measures relating to preventing the use of the financial system for the purpose of money laundering, in exercise of the powers conferred by that section hereby make the following regulations:—

General

Citation and commencement

1.—(1) These Regulations may be cited as the Money Laundering Regulations 1993.

(2) These Regulations shall come into force on 1st April 1994.

Interpretation

2.—(1) In these Regulations—

"applicant for business" means a person seeking to form a business relationship, or carry out a one-off transaction, with a person who is carrying out relevant financial business in the United Kingdom;

"business relationship" has the meaning given by regulation 3 below;

"Case 1", "Case 2", "Case 3" and "Case 4" have the meanings given in regulation 7 below;

"constable" includes a person commissioned by the Commissioners of Customs and Excise;

"European institution" has the same meaning as in Banking Coordination (Second Council Directive) Regulations 1992;

"insurance business" means long term business within the meaning of the Insurance Companies Act 1982;

"the Money Laundering Directive" means the Council Directive on prevention of the use of the financial system for the purpose of money laundering (No. 91/308/EEC);

"one-off transaction" means any transaction other than a transaction carried out in the course of an established business relationship formed by a person acting in the course of relevant financial business;

"relevant financial business" has the meaning given by regulation 4 below; and

"supervisory authority" has the meaning given by regulation 15 below.

(2) In these Regulations "ecu" means the european currency unit as defined in article 1 of Council Regulation No. 3180/78/EEC; and the exchange rates as between the ecu and the currencies of the member States to be applied for each year beginning on 31st December shall be the rates applicable on the last day of the preceding October for which rates for the currencies of all the member States were published in the Official Journal of the Communities.

(3) In these Regulations, except in so far as the context otherwise requires, "money laundering" means doing any act which constitutes an offence under—

(a) section 23A or 24 of the Drug Trafficking Offences Act 1986 (which relate to the handling etc. of proceeds of drug trafficking);

(b) section 42A or 43 of the Criminal Justice (Scotland) Act 1987 (which relate to the handling etc. of proceeds of drug trafficking);

(c) section 93A, 93B or 93C of the Criminal Justice Act 1988 (which relate to the handling etc. of proceeds of certain other criminal conduct);

(d) section 11 of the Prevention of Terrorism (Temporary Provisions) Act 1989 (which relates to financial assistance for terrorism);

(e) section 14 of the Criminal Justice (International Co-operation) Act 1990 (concealing or transferring proceeds of drug trafficking);

(f) Article 29 or 30 of the Criminal Justice (Confiscation) (Northern Ireland) Order 1990 (which relate to the handling etc. of proceeds of drug trafficking);

(g) section 53 or 54 of the Northern Ireland (Emergency Provisions) Act 1991 (which relate to the handling etc. of proceeds of terrorist-related activities); or

(h) any provision, whenever made, which has effect in Northern Ireland and corresponds to any of the provisions mentioned in sub-paragraph (a) or (c) above;

or, in the case of an act done otherwise than in England and Wales, Scotland or, as the case may be, Northern Ireland would constitute such an offence if done in England and Wales, Scotland or Northern Ireland.

(4) The reference in paragraph (3) above to doing any act which would constitute an offence under the provisions mentioned in sub-paragraph (c) of that paragraph shall, for the purposes of these Regulations, be construed as a reference to doing any act which would constitute an offence under those provisions if, for the definition of "criminal conduct" in section 93A(7) of the Criminal Justice Act 1988, there were substituted—

"(7) In this Part of this Act "criminal conduct" means—
(a) conduct which constitutes an offence to which this Part of this Act applies; or
(b) conduct which—
  (i)   would constitute such an offence if it had occurred in England and Wales or (as the case may be) Scotland; and
  (ii) contravenes the law of the country in which it occurred."

(5) For the purposes of these Regulations, any provision having effect in Northern Ireland which corresponds to the provisions referred to in paragraph 3(c) above shall be construed as if it had been amended by a provision which corresponds to paragraph (4) above, with appropriate modifications.

(6) For the purposes of this regulation, a business relationship formed by any person acting in the course of relevant financial business is an established business relationship where that person has obtained, under procedures maintained by him in accordance with regulation 7 below, satisfactory evidence of the identity of the person who, in relation to the formation of that business relationship, was the applicant for business.

Business relationships
3.—(1) Any reference in this regulation to an arrangement between two or more persons is a reference to an arrangement in which at least one person is acting in the course of a business.

(2) For the purposes of these Regulations, "business relationship" means any arrangement between two or more persons where—
(a) the purpose of the arrangement is to facilitate the carrying out of transactions between the persons concerned on a frequent, habitual or regular basis; and
(b) the total amount of any payment or payments to be made by any person to any other in the course of that arrangement is not known or capable of being ascertained at the time the arrangement is made.

Relevant financial business
4.—(1) For the purposes of these Regulations, "relevant financial business" means, subject to paragraph (2) below, the business of engaging in one or more of the following—
(a) deposit-taking business carried on by a person who is for the time being authorised under the Banking Act 1987;
(b) acceptance by a building society of deposits made by any person (including the raising of money from members of the society by the issue of shares);
(c) business of the National Savings Bank;
(d) business carried on by a credit union within the meaning of the Credit Unions Act 1979 or the Credit Unions (Northern Ireland) Order 1985;
(e) any home regulated activity carried on by a European institution in respect of which the requirements of paragraph 1 of Schedule 2 to the Banking Coordination (Second Council Directive) Regulations 1992 have been complied with;
(f) investment business within the meaning of the Financial Services Act 1986;
(g) any activity carried on for the purpose of raising money authorised to be raised under the National Loans Act 1968 under the auspices of the Director of National Savings;
(h) any of the activities in points 1 to 12, or 14, of the Annex to the Second Banking Coordination Directive (the text of which is, for convenience of reference, set out in the Schedule to these Regulations), other than an activity falling within sub-paragraphs (a) to (g) above;

(i) insurance business carried on by a person who has received official authorisation pursuant to Article 6 or 27 of the First Life Directive.

(2) A business is not relevant financial business in so far as it consists of—

(a) any of the following activities carried on by a society registered under the Industrial and Provident Societies Act 1965—
  (i) the issue of withdrawable share capital within the limit set by section 6 of that Act; or
  (ii) the acceptance of deposits from the public within the limit set by section 7(3) of that Act;

(b) the issue of withdrawable share capital within the limit set by section 6 of the Industrial and Provident Societies Act (Northern Ireland) 1969 by a society registered under that Act;

(c) activities carried on by the Bank of England;

(d) in relation to any person who is an exempted person for the purposes of section 45 of the Financial Services Act 1986 (miscellaneous exemptions for holders of certain judicial and other offices), such of the activities as are specified in that section in relation to that person; or

(e) in relation to any person who is an exempted person for the purposes of any order made under section 46 of the Financial Services Act 1986 which was made before the date on which these Regulations come into force, any activities carried on by him or, as the case may be, such of the activities as are specified in such an order in relation to him.

(3) For the purposes of paragraph (1)(f) above, any reference in these Regulations to the carrying on of relevant financial business in the United Kingdom shall be construed in accordance with section 1(3) of the Financial Services Act 1986.

(4) In this regulation—

"building society" has the same meaning as in the Building Societies Act 1986;

"deposit-taking business" has the same meaning as in the Banking Act 1987;

"the First Life Directive" means the First Council Directive on the coordination of laws, regulations and administrative provisions relating to the taking up and pursuit of the business of direct life assurance (No. 79/267/EEC); and

"the Second Banking Coordination Directive" means the Second Council Directive on the coordination of laws, regulations and administrative provisions relating to the taking up and pursuit of the business of credit institutions (No. 89/646/EEC).

Systems and training to prevent money laundering

Systems and training to prevent money laundering

5.—(1) No person shall, in the course of relevant financial business carried on by him in the United Kingdom, form a business relationship, or carry out a one-off transaction, with or for another unless that person—

(a) maintains the following procedures established in relation to that business—
  (i) identification procedures in accordance with regulations 7 and 9 below;
  (ii) record-keeping procedure in accordance with regulation 12 below;
  (iii) except where the person concerned is an individual who in the course of relevant financial business does not employ or act in association with any other person, internal reporting procedures in accordance with regulation 14 below; and
  (iv) such other procedures of internal control and communication as may be appropriate for the purposes of forestalling and preventing money laundering;

(b) takes appropriate measures from time to time for the purposes of making employees whose duties include the handling of relevant financial business aware of—
  (i) the procedures under sub-paragraph (a) above which are maintained by him and which relate to the relevant financial business in question, and
  (ii) the enactments relating to money laundering; and

(c) provides such employees from time to time with training in the recognition and handling of transactions carried out by, or on behalf of, any person who is, or appears to be, engaged in money laundering.

(2) Any person who contravenes this regulation shall be guilty of an offence and liable—

(a) on conviction on indictment, to imprisonment not exceeding a term of two years or a fine or both,

(b) on summary conviction, to a fine not exceeding the statutory maximum.

(3) In determining whether a person has complied with any of the requirements of paragraph (1) above, a court may take account of—

(a) any relevant supervisory or regulatory guidance which applies to that person;

(b) in a case where no guidance falling within sub-paragraph (a) above applies, any other relevant guidance issued by a body that regulates, or is representative of, any trade, profession, business or employment carried on by that person.

(4) In proceedings against any person for an offence under this regulation, it shall be a defence for that person to show that he took all reasonable steps and exercised all due diligence to avoid committing the offence.

(5) In this regulation—
  "enactments relating to money laundering" means the enactments referred to in regulation 2(3) above and the provisions of these Regulations; and
  "supervisory or regulatory guidance" means guidance issued, adopted or approved by a supervisory authority.

Offences by bodies corporate, partnerships and unincorporated associations
6.—(1) Where an offence under regulation 5 above committed by a body corporate is proved to have been committed with the consent or connivance of, or to be attributable to any neglect on the part of, any director, manager, secretary or other similar officer of the body corporate or any person who was purporting to act in any such capacity he, as well as the body corporate, shall be guilty of that offence and shall be liable to be proceeded against and punished accordingly.

(2) Where the affairs of a body corporate are managed by the members, paragraph (1) above shall apply in relation to the acts and defaults of a member in connection with his functions of management as if he were a director of a body corporate.

(3) Where an offence under regulation 5 above committed by a partnership, or by an unincorporated association other than a partnership, is proved to have been committed with the consent or connivance of, or is attributable to any neglect on the part of, a partner in the partnership or (as the case may be) a person concerned in the management or control of the association, he, as well as the partnership or association, shall be guilty of that offence and shall be liable to be proceeded against and punished accordingly.

Identification procedures

Identification procedures; business relationships and transactions
7.—(1) Subject to regulations 8 and 10 below, identification procedures maintained by a person are in accordance with this regulation if in Cases 1 to

4 set out below they require, as soon as is reasonably practicable after contact is first made between that person and an applicant for business concerning any particular business relationship or one-off transaction—

    (a) the production by the applicant for business of satisfactory evidence of his identity; or

    (b) the taking of such measures specified in the procedures as will produce satisfactory evidence of his identity;

and the procedures are, subject to paragraph (6) below, in accordance with this regulation if they require that where that evidence is not obtained the business relationship or one-off transaction in question shall not proceed any further.

(2) Case 1 is any case where the parties form or resolve to form a business relationship between them.

(3) Case 2 is any case where, in respect of any one-off transaction, any person handling the transaction knows or suspects that the applicant for business is engaged in money laundering, or that the transaction is carried out on behalf of another person engaged in money laundering.

(4) Case 3 is any case where, in respect of any one-off transaction, payment is to be made by or to the applicant for business of the amount of ecu 15,000 or more.

(5) Case 4 is any case where, in respect of two or more one-off transactions—

    (a) it appears at the outset to a person handling any of the transactions—

        (i) that the transactions are linked, and

       (ii) that the total amount, in respect of all of the transactions, which is payable by or to the applicant for business is ecu 15,000 or more; or

    (b) at any later stage, it comes to the attention of such a person that paragraphs (i) and (ii) of sub-paragraph (a) above are satisfied.

(6) The procedures referred to in paragraph (1) above are in accordance with this regulation if, when a report is made in circumstances falling within Case 2 (whether in accordance with regulation 14 or directly to a constable), they provided for steps to be taken in relation to the one-off transaction in question in accordance with any directions that may be given by a constable.

(7) In these Regulations references to satisfactory evidence of a person's identity shall be construed in accordance with regulation 11(1) below.

Payment by post etc.

8.—(1) Where satisfactory evidence of the identity of an applicant for business would, apart from this paragraph, be required under identification procedures in accordance with regulation 7 above but—

    (a) the circumstances are such that a payment is to be made by the applicant for business; and

    (b) it is reasonable in all the circumstances—

        (i) for the payment to be sent by post or by any electronic means which is effective to transfer funds; or

       (ii) for the details of the payment to be sent by post, to be given on the telephone or to be given by any other electronic means;

then, subject to paragraph (2) below, the fact that the payment is debited from an account held in the applicant's name at an institution mentioned in paragraph (4) below (whether the account is held by the applicant alone or jointly with one or more other persons) shall be capable of constituting the required evidence of identity.

(2) Paragraph (1) above shall not have effect to the extent that—

    (a) the circumstances of the payment fall within Case 2; or

    (b) the payment is made by any person for the purpose of opening a relevant account with an institution falling within paragraph (4)(a) or (b) below.

(3) For the purposes of paragraph (1)(b) above, it shall be immaterial whether the payment or its details are sent or given to a person who is bound by regulation 5(1) above or to some other person acting in his behalf.

(4) The institutions referred to in paragraph (1) above are—

[1] (a) an institution which is for the time being authorised by the Financial Services Authority under the Banking Act 1987 or by the Building Societies Commission under the Building Societies Act 1986;

(b) a European authorised institution within the meaning of the Banking Coordination (Second Council Directive) Regulations 1992; or

(c) any other institution which is an authorised credit institution.

(5) For the purposes of this regulation—

"authorised credit institution" means a credit institution, as defined in Article 1 of the First Council Directive on the coordination of laws, regulations and administrative provisions relating to the taking up and pursuit of the business of credit institutions (77/780/EEC), which is authorised to carry on the business of a credit institution by a competent authority of a member state; and

"relevant account" means an account from which a payment may be made by any means to a person other than the applicant for business, whether such a payment—

(a) may be made directly to such a person from the account by or on behalf of the applicant for business; or

(b) may be made to such a person indirectly as a result of—

(i) a direct transfer of funds from an account from which no such direct payment may be made to another account, or

(ii) a change in any of the characteristics of the account.

NOTE
[1] As amended by the Bank of England Act 1998 (Consequential Amendments of Subordinate Legislation Order 1998 (S.I. 1998 No. 1129), Art. 2, Sched. 1, para. 15.

Identification procedures; transactions on behalf of another

9.—(1) This regulation applies where, in relation to a person who is bound by regulation 5(1) above, an applicant for business is or appears to be acting otherwise than as principal.

(2) Subject to regulation 10 below, identification procedures maintained by a person are in accordance with this regulation if, in a case to which this regulation applies, they require reasonable measures to be taken for the purpose of establishing the identity of any person on whose behalf the applicant for business is acting.

(3) In determining, for the purposes of paragraph (2) above, what constitutes reasonable measures in any particular case regard shall be had to all the circumstances of the case and, in particular, to best practice which, for the time being, is followed in the relevant field of business and which is applicable to those circumstances.

(4) Without prejudice to the generality of paragraph (3) above, if the conditions mentioned in paragraph (5) below are fulfilled in relation to an applicant for business who is, or appears to be, acting as an agent for a principal (whether undisclosed or disclosed for reference purposes only) it shall be reasonable for a person bound by regulation 5(1) above to accept a written assurance from the applicant for business to the effect that evidence of the identity of any principal on whose behalf the applicant for business may act in relation to that person will have been obtained and recorded under procedures maintained by the applicant for business.

(5) The conditions referred to in paragraph (4) above are that, in relation to the business relationship or transaction in question, there are reasonable grounds for believing that the applicant for business—

(a) acts in the course of a business in relation to which an overseas regulatory authority exercises regulatory functions; and

(b) is based or incorporated in, or formed under the law of, a country other than a member State in which there are in force provisions at least equivalent to those required by the Money Laundering Directive.

(6) In paragraph (5) above, "overseas regulatory authority" and "regulatory functions" have the same meaning as in section 82 of the Companies Act 1989.

Identification procedures; exemptions

10.—(1) Subject to paragraph (2) below, identification procedures under regulations 7 and 9 above shall not require any steps to be taken to obtain evidence of any person's identity—

(a) where there are reasonable grounds for believing that the applicant for business is a person who is bound by the provisions of regulation 5(1) above;

(b) where there are reasonable grounds for believing that the applicant for business is otherwise a person who is covered by the Money Laundering Directive;

(c) where any one-off transaction is carried out with or for a third party pursuant to an introduction effected by a person who has provided an assurance that evidence of the identity of all third parties introduced by him will have been obtained and recorded under procedures maintained by him, where that person identifies the third party and where—

(i) that person falls within sub-paragraph (a) or (b) above; or

(ii) there are reasonable grounds for believing that the conditions mentioned in regulation 9(5)(a) and (b) above are fulfilled in relation to him;

(d) where the person who would otherwise be required to be identified, in relation to a one-off transaction, is the person to whom the proceeds of that transaction are payable but to whom no payment is made because all of those proceeds are directly reinvested on this behalf in another transaction—

(i) of which a record is kept, and

(ii) which can result only in another reinvestment made on that person's behalf or in a payment made directly to that person;

(e) in relation to insurance business consisting of a policy of insurance in connection with a pension scheme taken out by virtue of a person's contract of employment or occupation where the policy—

(i) contains no surrender clause, and

(ii) may not be used as collateral for a loan;

(f) in relation to insurance business in respect of which a premium is payable in one instalment of an amount not exceeding ecu 2,500; or

(g) in relation to insurance business in respect of which a periodic premium is payable and where the total payable in respect of any calendar year does not exceed ecu 1,000.

(2) Nothing in this regulation shall apply in circumstances falling within Case 2.

(3) In this regulation "calendar year" means a period of twelve months beginning on 31st December.

Identification procedures; supplementary provisions

11.—(1) For the purposes of these regulations, evidence of identity is satisfactory if—

(a) it is reasonably capable of establishing that the applicant is the person he claims to be; and

(b) the person who obtains the evidence is satisfied, in accordance with the procedures maintained under these Regulations in relation to the relevant financial business concerned, that it does establish that fact.

(2) In determining for the purposes of regulation 7(1) above the time span in which satisfactory evidence of a person's identity has to be obtained, in relation to any particular business relationship or one-off transaction, all the circumstances shall be taken into account including, in particular—

(a) the nature of the business relationship or one-off transaction concerned;

(b) the geographical locations of the parties;

(c) whether it is practical to obtain the evidence before commitments are entered into between the parties or before money passes;

(d) in relation to Case 3 or 4, the earliest stage at which there are reasonable grounds for believing that the total amount payable by an applicant for business is ecu 15,000 or more.

Record-keeping procedures

Record-keeping procedures

12.—(1) Record-keeping procedures maintained by a person are in accordance with this regulation if they require the keeping, for the prescribed period, of the following records—

(a) in any case where, in relation to any business relationship that is formed or one-off transaction that is carried out, evidence of a person's identity is obtained under procedures maintained in accordance with regulation 7 or 9 above, a record that indicates the nature of the evidence and—

(i) comprises a copy of the evidence;

(ii) provides such information as would enable a copy of it to be obtained; or

(iii) in a case where it is not reasonably practicable to comply with paragraph (i) or (ii) above, provides sufficient information to enable the details as to a person's identity contained in the relevant evidence to be re-obtained; and

(b) a record containing details relating to all transactions carried out by that person in the course of relevant financial business.

(2) For the purposes of paragraph (1) above, the prescribed period is, subject to paragraph (3) below, the period of at least five years commencing with—

(a) in relation to such records as are described in sub-paragraph (a), the date on which the relevant business was completed within the meaning of paragraph (4) below; and

(b) in relation to such records as are described in sub-paragraph (b), the date on which all activities taking place in the course of the transaction in question were completed.

(3) Where a person who is bound by the provisions of regulation 5(1) above—

(a) forms a business relationship or carries out a one-off transaction with another person;

(b) has reasonable grounds for believing that that person has become insolvent; and

(c) after forming that belief, takes any step for the purpose of recovering all or part of the amount of any debt payable to him by that person which has fallen due;

the prescribed period for the purposes of paragraph (1) above is the period of at least five years commencing with the date on which the first such step is taken.

(4) For the purposes of paragraph (2)(a) above, the date on which relevant business is completed is, as the case may be—

(a) in circumstances falling within Case 1, the date of the ending of the business relationship in respect of whose formation the record under paragraph (1)(a) above was compiled;

    (b) in circumstances falling within Case 2 or 3, the date of the completion of all activities taking place in the course of the one-off transaction in respect of which the record under paragraph (1)(a) above was compiled;

    (c) in circumstances falling within Case 4, the date of the completion of all activities taking place in the course of the last one-off transaction in respect of which the record under paragraph (1)(a) above was compiled:

and where the formalities necessary to end a business relationship have not been observed, but a period of five years has elapsed since the date on which the last transaction was carried out in the course of that relationship, then the date of the completion of all activities taking place in the course of that last transaction shall be treated as the date on which the relevant business was completed.

Record-keeping procedures; supplementary provisions

    13.—(1) For the purposes of regulation 12(3)(b) above, a person shall be taken to be insolvent if, but only if, in England and Wales—

    (a) he has been adjudged bankrupt or has made a composition or arrangement with his creditors;

    (b) an order has been made with respect to him under section 112, 112A or 112B of the County Courts Act 1984 (administration orders, orders restricting enforcement and administration orders with composition provisions);

    (c) he has died and his estate falls to be administered in accordance with an order under section 421 of the Insolvency Act 1986 (insolvent estates of deceased persons); or

    (d) where that person is a company, a winding up order or an administration order has been made or a resolution for voluntary winding up has been passed with respect to it, or a receiver or manager of its undertaking has been duly appointed, or possession has been taken, by or on behalf of the holders of any debentures secured by a floating charge, of any property of the company comprised in or subject to the charge, or a voluntary arrangement proposed for the purpose of Part I of the Insolvency Act 1986 has been approved under that Part, or a compromise or arrangement in accordance with section 425 of the Companies Act 1985 has taken effect.

    (2) For the purposes of regulation 12(3)(b) above, a person shall be taken to be insolvent if, but only if, in Scotland—

    (a) his estate has been sequestrated, he has granted a trust deed for the benefit of his creditors or he has made a composition or arrangement for the benefit of his creditors; or

    (b) where that person is a company, a winding up order or an administration order has been made or a resolution for voluntary winding up has been passed with respect to it, or a receiver has been appointed under a floating charge over any property of the company, or a voluntary arrangement proposed for the purpose of Part I of the Insolvency Act 1986 has been approved under that Part, or a compromise or arrangement in accordance with section 425 of the Companies Act 1985 has taken effect.

    (3) For the purposes of regulation 12(3)(b) above, a person shall be taken to be insolvent if, but only if, in Northern Ireland—

    (a) he has been adjudged bankrupt or has made a composition or arrangement with his creditors;

    (b) an administration order has been made with respect to him under Article 80 of the Judgements Enforcement (Northern Ireland) Order 1981 (power to make administration order on application of debtor);

(c) he has died and his estate falls to be administered in accordance with an order under Article 365 of the Insolvency (Northern Ireland) Order 1989 (insolvent estates of deceased persons); or

(d) where that person is a company, a winding up order or an administration order has been made or a resolution for voluntary winding up has been passed with respect to it, or a receiver or manager of its undertaking has been duly appointed, or possession has been taken, by or on behalf of the holders of any debentures secured by a floating charge, of any property of the company comprised in or subject to the charge, or a voluntary arrangement proposed for the purpose of Part II of the Insolvency (Northern Ireland) Order 1988 has been approved under that Part, or a compromise or arrangement in accordance with Article 418 of the Companies (Northern Ireland) Order 1986 has taken effect.

(4) Where a person bound by regulation 5(1) above—

(a) is an appointed representative; and

(b) is not—

   (i) an authorised person within the meaning of the Financial Services Act 1986,

   (ii) authorised under the Building Societies Act 1986 or the Banking Act 1987, or

   (iii) a European institution;

it shall be the responsibility of the appointed representative's principal to ensure that record-keeping procedures in accordance with regulation 12 above are maintained in respect of any relevant financial business carried out by the appointed representative which is investment business carried on by him for which the principal has accepted responsibility in writing under section 44 of the Financial Services Act 1986.

(5) Where record-keeping procedures in accordance with regulation 12 above are not maintained in respect of business relationships formed, and one-off transactions carried out, in the course of such relevant financial business as is referred to in paragraph (4) above, an appointed representative's principal shall be regarded as having contravened regulation 5 in respect of those procedures and he, as well as the appointed representative, shall be guilty of an offence and shall be liable to be proceeded against and punished accordingly.

(6) Section 44(2) of the Financial Services Act 1986 (construction of references to appointed representative, his principal and investment business carried out by an appointed representative) shall for the purposes of paragraphs (4) and (5) above as it applies for the purposes of that Act.

Internal reporting procedures
.

Internal reporting procedures

14. Internal reporting procedures maintained by a person are in accordance with this regulation if they include provision—

(a) identifying a person ("the appropriate person") to whom a report is to be made of any information or other matter which comes to the attention of a person handling relevant financial business and which, in the opinion of the person handling that business, gives rise to a knowledge or suspicion that another person is engaged in money laundering;

(b) requiring that any such report be considered in the light of all other relevant information by the appropriate person, or by another designated person, for the purpose of determining whether or not the information or other matter contained in the report does give rise to such a knowledge or suspicion;

(c) for any person charged with considering a report in accordance with sub-paragraph (b) above to have reasonable access to other information which may be of assistance to him and which is available to the person responsible for maintaining the internal reporting procedures concerned; and

(d) for securing that the information or other matter contained in a report is disclosed to a constable where the person who has considered the report under the procedures maintained in accordance with the preceding provisions of this regulation knows or suspects that another person is engaged in money laundering.

Duty of supervisory authorities to report evidence of money laundering

Supervisory authorities

15.—(1) References in these Regulations to supervisory authorities shall be construed in accordance with the following provisions.

(2) For the purposes of these Regulations, each of the following is a supervisory authority—

(a) the Bank of England;

[1] (aa) the Financial Services Authority;

(b) the Building Societies Commission;

(c) a designated agency within the meaning of the Financial Services Act 1986;

(d) a recognised self-regulating organisation within the meaning of the Financial Services Act 1986;

(e) a recognised professional body within the meaning of the Financial Services Act 1986;

(f) a transferee body within the meaning of the Financial Services Act 1986;

(g) a recognised self-regulating organisation for friendly societies within the meaning of the Financial Services Act 1986;

(h) the Secretary of State;

(i) the Treasury;

(j) the Council of Lloyd's;

(k) the Director General of Fair Trading;

(l) the Friendly Societies Commission;

(m) the Chief Registrar of Friendly Societies;

(n) the Central Office of the Registry of Friendly Societies;

(o) the Registrar of Friendly Societies for Northern Ireland;

(p) the Assistant Registrar of Friendly Societies for Scotland.

(3) These Regulations apply to the Secretary of State in the exercise, in relation to any person carrying on relevant financial business, of his functions under the enactments relating to insurance companies, companies or insolvency or under the Financial Services Act 1986.

NOTE

[1] Inserted by the Bank of England Act 1998 (Consequential Amendments of Subordinate Legislation Order 1998 (S.I. 1998 No. 1129), Art. 2, Sched. 1, para. 13.

Supervisors etc. to report evidence of money laundering

16.—(1) Subject to paragraph (2) below, where a supervisory authority—

(a) obtains any information; and

(b) is of the opinion that the information indicates that any person has or may have been engaged in money laundering,

the authority shall, as soon as is reasonably practicable, disclose that information to a constable.

(2) Where any person is a secondary recipient of information obtained by a supervisory authority, and that person forms such an opinion as is mentioned in paragraph (1)(b) above, that person may disclose the information to a constable.

(3) Where any person within paragraph (6) below—

(a) obtains any information whilst acting in the course of any investigation, or discharging any functions, to which his appointment or authorisation relates; and

(b) is of the opinion that the information indicates that any person has or may have been engaged in money laundering,

that person shall, as soon as is reasonably practicable, either disclose that information to a constable or disclose that information to the supervisory authority by whom he was appointed or authorised.

(4) Any disclosure made by virtue of the preceding provisions of this regulation shall not be treated as a breach of any restriction imposed by statute or otherwise.

(5) Any information—

(a) which has been disclosed to a constable by virtue of the preceding provisions of this regulation; and

(b) which would, apart from the provisions of paragraph (4) above, be subject to such a restriction as is mentioned in that paragraph;

may be disclosed by the constable, or any person obtaining the information directly or indirectly from him, in connection with the investigation of any criminal offence or for the purposes of any criminal proceedings, but not otherwise.

(6) Persons falling within this paragraph are—

(a) a person or inspector appointed under section 17 of the Industrial Assurance Act 1923 or section 65 or 66 of the Friendly Societies Act 1992;

(b) an inspector appointed under section 49 of the Industrial and Provident Societies Act 1965 or section 18 of the Credit Unions Act 1979;

(c) an inspector appointed under section 431, 432, 442 or 446 of the Companies Act 1985 or under Article 424, 425, 435 or 439 of the Companies (Northern Ireland) Order 1986;

(d) a person or inspector appointed under section 55 or 56 of the Building Societies Act 1986;

(e) an inspector appointed under section 94 or 177 of the Financial Services Act 1986;

(f) a person appointed under section 41 of the Banking Act 1987; and

(g) a person authorised to require the production of documents under section 44 of the Insurance Companies Act 1982, section 447 of the Companies Act 1985, section 106 of the Financial Services Act 1986, Article 440 of the Companies (Northern Ireland) Order 1986 or section 84 of the Companies Act 1989.

(7) In this regulation "secondary recipient", in relation to information obtained by a supervisory authority, means any person to whom that information has been passed by the authority.

Transitional provisions

Transitional provisions
17.—(1) Nothing in these Regulations shall require a person who is bound by regulation 5(1) above to maintain procedures in accordance with regulations 7 and 9 which require evidence to be obtained, in respect of any business relationship formed by him before the date on which these Regulations come into force, as to the identity of the person with whom that relationship has been formed.

(2) For the purposes of regulation 2(6) above, any business relationship referred to in paragraph (1) above shall be treated as if it were an established business relationship.

(3) In regulation 10(1)(g), the reference to the total payable in respect of any calendar year not exceeding ecu 1,000 shall, for the period commencing with the coming into force of these regulations and ending with 30th December 1994, be construed as a reference to the total payable in respect of that period not exceeding ecu 750.

Regulation 4(1)   SCHEDULE

"ANNEX

LIST OF ACTIVITIES SUBJECT TO MUTUAL RECOGNITION

1. Acceptance of deposits and other repayable funds from the public.
2. Lending.
3. Financial leasing.
4. Money transmission services.
5. Issuing and administering means of payment (*e.g.* credit cards, travellers' cheques and bankers' drafts).
6. Guarantees and commitments.
7. Trading for own account or for account of customers in:
   (a) money market instruments (cheques, bills, CDs, etc.);
   (b) foreign exchange;
   (c) financial futures and options;
   (d) exchange and interest rate instruments;
   (e) transferable securities.
8. Participation in securities issues and the provision of services related to such issues.
9. Advice to undertakings on capital structure, industrial strategy and related questions and advice and services relating to mergers and the purchase of undertakings.
10. Money broking.
11. Portfolio management and advice.
12. Safekeeping and administration of securities.
13. Credit reference services.
14. Safe custody services."

[NEXT TEXT PAGE IS F 201]

Subordinate Legislation

Solicitors' (Scotland) Practice (Rules) 1975

Rules dated 24th October 1975, made by the Council of The Law Society of Scotland and approved by the Lord President of the Court of Session under section 20 of the Solicitors (Scotland) Act 1949.

Citation
1.—(1) These Rules may be cited as the Solicitors' (Scotland) Practice Rules 1975;
(2) These Rules shall come into operation on the 1st day of November 1975.

Interpretation
2.—(1) In these Rules, unless the context otherwise requires, "solicitor" means a solicitor holding a practising certificate under the Act and includes a firm of solicitors.
(2) The Interpretation Act 1889 applies to the interpretation of these Rules as it applies to the interpretation of an Act of Parliament.

3. No solicitor shall, in connection with his practice as a solicitor, without the prior written permission of the Council of the Law Society of Scotland, which may be given for such period and subject to such conditions as the Council thinks fit, employ, remunerate, associate in business with or provide facilities for any person who is disqualified from practising as a solicitor by reason of the fact that his name has been struck off the Roll of Solicitors or that he is suspended from practising as a solicitor.

[THE NEXT PAGE IS F 279]

Solicitors (Scotland) Practice Rules 1981

Rules dated 24th April 1981, made by the Council of The Law Society
of Scotland and approved by the Lord President of the Court of
Session under section 34 of the Solicitors (Scotland) Act 1980.

1.—(1) These rules should be cited as the Solicitors (Scotland) Practice
Rules 1981.
(2) These rules shall come into operation on 1st June 1981.

2.—(1) "Courts" means the civil and criminal courts in Scotland, the
House of Lords, the Court of Justice of the European Communities and the
European Court of Human Rights.
(2) "A dispute" means a "trade dispute" as defined in section 29 of the
Trade Union and Labour Relations Act 1974.
(3) "Industrial action" means an act done or taken by a solicitor in
contemplation or furtherance of a dispute.

3. Subject to rule 4 hereof, a solicitor may take industrial action.

4.—(1) Notwithstanding that a solicitor is taking or has taken industrial
action, he will (a) fulfil his professional duties to the courts or to the
Parliament of the United Kingdom of Great Britain and Northern Ireland,
and (b) fulfil any personal obligation undertaken by him other than an
obligation which is imposed upon him under the terms and conditions of his
employment.
(2) Notwithstanding that a solicitor is about to take, is taking or has taken
industrial action, he will take all reasonable steps open to him to secure the
consent of the appropriate body organising such industrial action to his
acting as a solicitor (a) where a failure to do so could result in danger to any
member or members of the public and (b) where a failure to do so would
cause serious damage to a party other than his employer.

[THE NEXT PAGE IS F 313]

Admission as Solicitor (Scotland) Regulations 1986

Regulations dated 18th July 1986, made by the Council of the Law Society of Scotland with the concurrence of the Lord President of the Court of Session under section 5 of the Solicitors (Scotland) Act 1980.

ARRANGEMENT OF REGULATIONS

PART I—INTRODUCTORY

Title and commencement
1. These Regulations may be cited as the Admission as Solicitor
(Scotland) Regulations 1986 and shall come into operation on 1st August
1986.

Interpretation
2.—(1) In these Regulations, unless the context otherwise requires—
"the Act" means the Solicitors (Scotland) Act 1980 (as amended);
"certificate of fitness" means a certificate granted by the Council that
the person to whom the certificate applies has fulfilled all the
conditions and requirements prescribed in these Regulations and
in any enactment for admission as a solicitor in Scotland;
"the Council" means the Council of the Society;
"degree" means a degree, other than an honorary degree, granted by a
university;

"degree in law of a Scottish university" means the degree of Bachelor of Laws (LL.B.) granted by one of the Universities of Aberdeen, Dundee, Edinburgh, Glasgow and Strathclyde;

"Diploma" means a Diploma in Legal Practice granted by one of the Universities of Aberdeen, Dundee, Edinburgh, Glasgow and Strathclyde;

"employer" shall mean an employing solicitor who is a party to a pre-Diploma, post-Diploma, or non-Diploma training contract;

"employing solicitor" means, but subject always to the provisions of reg. 14 of these Regulations, a solicitor who holds a practising certificate issued under section 14 of the Act and who—

   (i) is engaged in private practice as a solicitor in Scotland, or

   (ii) is employed as a solicitor by a regional council, islands council or district council in Scotland, or

   (iii) is in such other employment as a solicitor in Scotland as the Council may approve,

and the expression "employing solicitor" shall include a firm or an incorporated practice of solicitors as defined in the Act;

"entrance certificate" means a certificate issued by the Council under the hand of the Secretary that the person to whom the certificate applies has fulfilled all the conditions and requirements prescribed in these Regulations to entitle him to enter into a post-Diploma or a non-Diploma training contract;

"examiner" means an examiner appointed under reg. 20 of these Regulations;

"intrant" means a person seeking to become a solicitor in Scotland;

"non-Diploma training contract" has the meaning assigned by reg. 11 of these Regulations;

"post-Diploma training contract" means a contract which is entered into between an employing solicitor and an intrant who is qualified under the provisions of reg. 8 of these Regulations;

"pre-Diploma training contract" means a contract which is entered into between an employing solicitor and an intrant who is qualified under the provisions of reg. 6 and Schedule 2 of these Regulations;

"preliminary entrance certificate" means a certificate issued by the Council under the hand of the Secretary that the person to whom the certificate applies has fulfilled all the conditions and requirements prescribed in these Regulations to entitle him to enter into a pre-Diploma training contract;

"the 1976 Regulations" means the Admission as Solicitor (Scotland) Regulations 1976 as amended by the Admission as Solicitor (Scotland) (Amendment) Regulations 1979, the Admission as Solicitor (Scotland) Regulations 1981, and these Regulations;

"the Secretary" means the Secretary of the Society and includes any person authorised by the Council to act on behalf of the Secretary;

"the Society" means the Law Society of Scotland;

"trainee" means an intrant who is a party to a pre-Diploma, post-Diploma, or non-Diploma training contract;

"university" means—

   (i) any university in Great Britain, or

   (ii) the Council of National Academic Awards, or

   (iii) any other university or institute recognised by the Council for the purposes of these Regulations.

(2) The provisions of the Interpretation Act 1978 shall apply for the interpretation of these Regulations as they apply for the interpretation of an Act of Parliament.

Conditions precedent to admission
3. Subject to the provisions of section 6 of the Act and of these
Regulations, every intrant shall as a condition precedent to his admission as
a solicitor, comply with these Regulations so far as applicable to him, and the
Council may require any intrant to satisfy it by such means as it considers
necessary as to such compliance.

Application of these regulations
4. These Regulations shall apply to all intrants who are not in any of the
classes of intrant specified in Schedule 1 to these Regulations. The 1976
Regulations, as amended, shall apply to all intrants who fall within the
classes specified in said Schedule 1.

PART II—ENTRANCE QUALIFICATIONS

(A) Pre-Diploma training contracts

Service under a pre-Diploma training contract
5.—(1) Any intrant who for the purpose of qualifying for an entrance
certificate proposes to meet the requirements of reg. 8(2)(iii)(*a*) of these
Regulations without obtaining a degree in law of a Scottish university shall
be required to enter into a pre-Diploma training contract with an employing
solicitor.
    (2) The period of a pre-Diploma training contract shall be three years.
    (3) Every pre-Diploma training contract shall be in or as nearly as may be
in such a form as the Council may from time to time prescribe and shall,
subject to the provisions of reg. 18(1) of these Regulations, contain an
obligation on the employing solicitor to provide training for the intrant in—
    (*a*) conveyancing;
    (*b*) litigation; and
    (*c*) either
        (i) trusts and executries, or
        (ii) the legal work of a public authority.
    (4) Subject to the consent of the employer and the Council an intrant who
is a party to a pre-Diploma training contract may be permitted to attend,
during office hours, classes in law at a university or elsewhere.

Preliminary entrance certificate
6.—(1) An intrant may not enter into a pre-Diploma training contract
unless he holds a preliminary entrance certificate issued by the Council.
    (2) An intrant shall be entitled to a preliminary entrance certificate if he
satisfies the Council that—
    (*a*) he is a fit and proper person to be a solicitor; and
    (*b*) he is qualified under the provisions of Schedule 2 to these
        Regulations.
    (3) The Council shall have power, in the case of an intrant who, being not
less than 23 years of age, satisfies the Council both that he is a fit and proper
person to be a solicitor, and having regard to evidence of recent academic
attainment and to his experience of legal work, as to his fitness to enter into a
pre-Diploma training contract, to grant such an intrant's preliminary
entrance certificate without compliance with paragraph (2)(*b*) of this
Regulation.

(B) Post-Diploma training contract

Service under a post-Diploma training contract
7.—(1) Subject to the provisions of these Regulations it shall be a

requirement for admission as a solicitor in Scotland that an intrant shall serve for an appropriate period as prescribed in Schedule 4 to these Regulations under a post-Diploma training contract entered into with an employing solicitor.

(2) Every such post-Diploma training contract shall be in or as nearly as may be in such a form as the Council may from time to time prescribe.

Entrance certificate

8.—(1) An intrant may not enter into a post-Diploma training contract unless he holds an entrance certificate issued by the Council.

(2) An intrant shall be entitled to an entrance certificate if he satisfies the Council that—

(i)   he is a fit and proper person to be a solicitor;

(ii) he has obtained a Diploma; and

(iii)   (*a*) he has served for a period of three years under a pre-Diploma training contract and, within three years of the commencement of such contract has passed or has obtained exemption from any of the Society's examinations in accordance with the provisions of Part III of these Regulations; or

(*b*) he holds a degree in law of a Scottish University or a certificate from such a university that he is entitled to graduate in such a degree notwithstanding that he has not so graduated; or

(*c*) he is or has recently ceased to be a member of the Faculty of Advocates; or

[1] (*d*) he has been called to the bar in England and Wales or Northern Ireland, or the Republic of Ireland and has passed such of the Society's examinations as the Council may require in accordance with regs. 26 and 27 of these Regulations; or

[1] (*e*) he has been admitted as a solicitor in England and Wales or Northern Ireland, or the Republic of Ireland, and has passed such of the Society's examinations as the council may require, in accordance with regs. 26 and 27 of these Regulations.

NOTE

[1] By the EC Qualified Lawyers Transfer (Scotland) Regulations 1990, reg. 7, references to the Republic of Ireland shall be of no effect.

Commencement of post-Diploma training contract

9. In the case of an intrant who is required to hold a Diploma, the commencement of his post-Diploma training contract shall be within a period of two years of the date of 1st January first occurring after the date when the intrant became eligible for the award of the Diploma provided that the Council may in its discretion extend such period and may, in granting such extension, impose such conditions as it thinks fit, including a condition extending the period of service as prescribed in Schedule 4 to these Regulations which the intrant will require to serve under such a contract.

Service elsewhere in Scotland, UK and EEC

10. Subject to the prior approval of the employer and the Council in each case, a trainee under a post-Diploma training contract may be permitted—

(*a*) in order to extend the range of his training, to undertake legal work under appropriate supervision within Scotland on secondment to another employing solicitor, or

(*b*) to undertake legal work under appropriate supervision or on an approved course of attachment outwith Scotland but only elsewhere in the United Kingdom or in any country which is a member of the European Economic Community,

in each case for a period of not more than six months, and such period may, with the Council's approval be reckoned as part of the period of service under a post-Diploma training contract.

(C) Non-Diploma training contracts

Service under a non-Diploma training contract

11.—(1) A non-Diploma training contract shall be a contract which is entered into with an employing solicitor and an intrant who is exempt from holding a Diploma under the provisions of Schedule 3(i), (ii) and (v) to these Regulations and who holds an entrance certificate in terms of sub-paragraph (2) hereof. The non-Diploma training contract shall be in similar terms to a post-Diploma training contract and shall be subject to the same conditions and requirements as are specified in these Regulations in relation to post-Diploma training contracts; provided that the minimum period of time which an intrant is required to serve under a non-Diploma training contract shall be the period appropriate to the class of intrant to which he belongs as specified in the said Schedule 3 or reg. 31 of these Regulations as the case may be.

(2) An intrant who is exempt from holding a Diploma under the provisions of Schedule 3 to these Regulations and who is required to enter into a non-Diploma training contract in terms of sub-paragraph (1) above shall be entitled to an entrance certificate if he satisfies the Council that he is a fit and proper person to be a solicitor, and has passed such examinations and has agreed to undergo such training as the Council may require.

(D) General provisions affecting training contracts

Fitness of intrants

12.—(1) In determining whether an intrant is a fit and proper person for the purposes of these Regulations, the Council may if it thinks fit—

(*a*) require an intrant to attend before it or an interviewing panel appointed by it, and to furnish such additional evidence as to character, fitness and suitability for service as a trainee as it may consider necessary;

(*b*) make such investigations on its own initiative as may seem proper and necessary, always providing that in any circumstances where an intrant is called for interview as provided in sub-paragraph (1) above, any information obtained as a result of such investigations shall be disclosed to the intrant in advance of such interview.

(2) In determining whether a trainee is a fit and proper person to be admitted as a solicitor an employer shall have regard not only to the moral character of the trainee but also to his aptitude for and application to his duties and his conduct generally.

(3) Subject to the provisions of reg. 35 of these Regulations, the Council may withhold a certificate of fitness from an intrant until satisfied by him of his fitness and competence to be admitted as a solicitor.

Service under training contracts

13. For the purposes of these Regulations and subject to reg. 5(4) hereof an intrant during the term of his training contract shall be employed full-time as a trainee solicitor and shall not during office hours engage in any other gainful employment or otherwise absent himself from his employer's business without the prior consent of his employer and of the Council.

Provisions as to employing solicitors, and intrants

14.—(1) An employing solicitor shall not, without the special consent in writing of the Council take any trainee, unless he is in practice as a solicitor in Scotland at the time and has been in continuous practice for a period of at least three years immediately prior to his taking the trainee or where the employing solicitor is a firm or incorporated practice, at least one of the partners or directors thereof, as the case may be, has been in such continuous practice.

(2) An employing solicitor shall not take any trainee who is his near relative, or, where the employing solicitor is a firm or incorporated practice, who is a near relative of any of the partners or directors thereof as the case may be. For the purposes of this Regulation, a "near relative" shall be the following:— son/daughter; grandson/granddaughter; father/mother; brother/sister; nephew/niece; uncle/aunt; first cousin; husband/wife; son-in-law/daughter-in-law; father-in-law/mother-in-law; brother-in-law/sister-in-law; stepson/stepdaughter; stepfather/stepmother; stepbrother/stepsister.

(3) If the Council after such inquiry as it may think fit as regards the practice of an employing solicitor decides that he would be unable to fulfil or is not fulfilling the proper obligations of an employer under a training contract either in relation to a particular application to take a trainee or in relation to a particular contract or generally, it shall intimate its decision to the solicitor and the solicitor notwithstanding that he satisfies the provisions of sub-paragraph (1) of this paragraph shall not thereafter engage or retain the services of any trainee without the special consent in writing of the Council.

(4) The total number of intrants employed at any time under pre-Diploma, post-Diploma and non-Diploma training contracts shall not, except with the special consent of the Council exceed—
   (i) in the case of a solicitor practising in Scotland on his own under his own name or as a sole solicitor under a firm name, one;
   (ii) in the case of a firm or an incorporated practice of solicitors practising in Scotland, twice the number of partners in the firm, or twice the number of directors of the incorporated practice, as the case may be;
   (iii) in the case of a solicitor employed by a regional council, islands council or district council in Scotland, the number of solicitors employed by the said regional, island or district council in each case, or such larger number as the Council may in special circumstances allow; and
   (iv) in the case of any other solicitor practising in Scotland such number as the Council may in each case determine.

(5) Contravention of the foregoing provisions of this Regulation on the part of an employer may be treated as an act of professional misconduct for the purposes of the provisions of the Act relating to discipline.

(6) Any person aggrieved by a decision of the Council under sub-paragraph (3) of this Regulation, may within 21 days of the date of intimation of the decision, appeal to the Court of Session and on any such appeal the said court may give such directions, including directions as to the expenses of the proceedings before it, as it thinks fit.

(7) If—
   (a) during the term of any training contract either the trainee or the employer has been continuously absent from the employer's place of business for a period of three months or longer without reasonable cause; or
   (b) the Council is for any other reason of the opinion that the training contract ought to be discharged or assigned;
the Council may require the parties to discharge or assign the training contract upon such terms, if any, as it thinks fit, and may determine what period, if any, of service under the training contract shall be deemed to be good service.

Registration of training contracts
   15.—(1) For the purposes of these Regulations the Council shall establish and maintain a register of pre-Diploma training contracts, a register of post-Diploma training contracts and a register of non-Diploma training contracts each of which shall be open to the inspection of any person

during office hours without payment and in which there shall be recorded the names and addresses of the parties to any such contract, and the date and commencement date of the contract.

(2) Every such contract shall be produced by the intrant to the Council for registration within three months of its commencement and thereafter shall be presented for registration in the Books of Council and Session by the Society at the expense of the intrant.

(3) When an intrant produces his contract to the Council he shall at the same time lodge with the Council his Preliminary Entrance Certificate or his Entrance Certificate as the case may be and pay such registration fees as the Council may from time to time prescribe.

(4) If his contract, and where appropriate, the relevant preliminary entrance certificate or entrance certificate, as the case may be, and the prescribed registration fee are not presented to the Council within three months from the date of the commencement of the contract, the period of service under the contract shall for the purposes of these Regulations be reckoned, unless the Council otherwise directs, as commencing from the date of production of the contract to the Council.

Power to disregard irregularities
16. Service by a trainee under any type of training contract shall be continuous, provided however that in exceptional circumstances, the Council may, in considering whether or not such service has been continuous, disregard short periods of absence by the trainee from employment, not exceeding six months in aggregate; but always providing that the total period of service shall not be less than three years in the case of a pre-Diploma training contract, and subject always to the provisions of Schedule 4 to these Regulations, shall not be less than two years in the case of a post-Diploma training contract.

Further training contracts
17.—(1) Where before the expiration of the period of service under a pre-Diploma, post-Diploma or non-Diploma training contract the employer ceases to practise as a solicitor or dies, or such contract is terminated, an intrant may enter into a further pre-Diploma, post-Diploma or non-Diploma training contract as the case may be with another employing solicitor approved by the Council for the residue of the said period.

(2) Where an employer ceases to practise as a solicitor or dies before the expiration of the period of service under a pre-Diploma, post-Diploma or non-Diploma training contract and the intrant enters into a further pre-Diploma, post-Diploma or non-Diploma training contract, if the Council are satisfied that there has been no undue delay before the intrant has entered into such further training contract and that during the period between the date of cessation of practice or death of the employer and the date of entry into the further contract the intrant has been *bona fide* employed by a practising solicitor in such a way as would, had the intrant entered into such a pre-Diploma, post-Diploma or non-Diploma training contract with such a solicitor, have been in compliance with the provision of these Regulations, they may allow such period to be reckoned as service under such training contract for the purposes of these Regulations.

(3) If an intrant does not enter into a new pre-Diploma, post-Diploma or non-Diploma training contract within two years of the termination of his original pre-Diploma, post-Diploma or non-Diploma training contract as the case may be, he shall be required to obtain the consent of the Council in writing before entering into any further training contract and the period of service under such further training contract shall be such as the Council may prescribe.

(4) The provisions of reg. 15 of these Regulations shall apply to any further pre-Diploma, post-Diploma or non-Diploma training contract and

an intrant who produces to the Council such a contract for registration shall at the same time produce his original and any other training contract to which he was a party.

Consent to transfer of a pre-Diploma training contract
    18.—(1) Subject to the provisions of reg. 5(3) of these Regulations every employer under a pre-Diploma training contract shall (1) if requested by his trainee, and (2) if called upon to do so by the Council, assign such pre-Diploma training contract to another employing solicitor approved by the Council, to enable the trainee either to complete his training in the three prescribed areas of practice or to extend the range of his training generally, or on any other ground which the Council shall consider reasonable.
    (2) Every such assignation shall, together with the relevant supporting documents, be produced to the Council within six weeks of the date of assignation for registration in the Register of pre-Diploma training contracts kept in accordance with the provisions of reg. 15 of these Regulations and service prior to such registration under the training contract so assigned which has not been produced as aforesaid within six weeks of the assignation shall be reckoned as part of the trainee's service under the training contract only to such extent as the Council may in its discretion determine.
    (3) Any person producing to the Council for registration an assignation of a pre-Diploma training contract shall pay to the Council such fee as it may from time to time determine.

Consent to transfer of post-Diploma training contract
    19.—(1) Subject to the provisions of reg. 16 of these Regulations a post-Diploma or non-Diploma training contract shall not be assigned by the employer without the consent in writing of the Council; and an employer shall be obliged to assign a post-Diploma or non-Diploma training contract if called upon to do so by the Council.
    (2) The provisions of reg. 18(2) and (3) above shall also apply in the case of the assignation of a post-Diploma or non-Diploma training contract as they apply to the assignation of a pre-Diploma training contract.

PART III—QUALIFICATIONS AND EXAMINATIONS

Appointment of examiners
    20.—(1) In order to test the suitability and qualifications of intrants the Council shall from time to time nominate and appoint fit and proper persons to be examiners and hold examinations in accordance with this Part of these Regulations, which examinations shall be under the management and control of the Council.
    (2) The examiners shall comply with all directions that may be given by the Council with respect to the number of papers to be set on any subject, the number of questions to be set and to be answered and the percentage mark to be attained to qualify for a pass and any other matters in connection with the examinations.
    (3) The examiners shall be appointed for such period of time and be paid such remuneration as the Council may from time to time determine.

Eligibility for examinations
    21. An intrant shall not be entitled, except with the special permission of the Council, to present himself for any of the Society's examinations unless he—
    (i) holds a preliminary entrance certificate and is serving under a pre-Diploma training contract, or that contract having terminated, has already presented himself for one or more of the Society's examinations; or
    (ii) holds, or is entitled to hold, a degree in law of a Scottish university.

Examinations
  22.—(1) The Society's examinations shall normally consist of examinations in the law of Scotland, conveyancing, evidence and taxation law in accordance, in each case, with the syllabus prescribed by the Council from time to time, and such other examinations as the Council may from time to time prescribe.
  (2) An intrant who has failed to pass in any one of the Society's examinations on four separate occasions or within the period of three years from the date on which he first presented himself for that examination, notwithstanding that during that period he has failed to pass the said examination on fewer than four separate occasions, shall not be allowed again to present himself for any of the Society's examinations: provided that the examiners may, at their discretion and subject to such conditions, if any, as to the examiners seem proper, waive this prohibition if they are satisfied that in any particular case it is appropriate for them to do so.
  (3) In addition to the provisions of sub-paragraph (2) above, an intrant shall be required to obtain passes in such of the Society's examinations as he is required to take within a period of not more than three years commencing from the first examination diet at which he presents himself.

Award of distinction
  23. A certificate of distinction in any subject may be awarded to an intrant at the discretion of the examiners.

Conduct, dates and places of examinations
  24.—(1) Diets for the Society's examinations shall be held in Edinburgh not less than twice each year and additional diets may be held as considered necessary by the examiners.
  (2) Every candidate shall be examined in writing, and may be required by the examiners to present himself for oral examination.
  (3) Intrants intending to present themselves at any of the Society's examinations shall give three weeks' notice of their intention to the Secretary provided that the examiners may at their discretion allow an intrant who has not given such notice to present himself for any examination.

Exemptions for Faculty of Advocates examinations
  25. The Council may exempt from any of the Society's examinations an intrant who has obtained a pass in the corresponding examination in the examinations for admission to the Faculty of Advocates.

Exemption from taxation examination
  26.—(1) In the case of an intrant who has passed the revenue law portion of Pt. II of the qualifying examinations or the equivalent thereof under the Qualifying Regulations 1979, or any subsequent Regulations made by the Law Society of England and Wales, or is entitled under the said Qualifying Regulations to obtain exemption therefrom, the Council may, if it thinks fit, exempt such intrant from the Society's examination in taxation law.
  (2) The Council may, in the case of an intrant who (*a*) holds a certificate that he has passed an examination in taxation at a Scottish university on a standard approved by the Council, or (*b*) is a member of the Institute of Chartered Accountants of Scotland, or of the Institute of Chartered Accountants in England and Wales, or of the Association of Certified and Corporate Accountants, exempt such intrant from the Society's examination in taxation law.

Further exemption of intrants from outwith Scotland
  27.—(1) The Council may, on application by an intrant who has qualified as a solicitor or barrister in England and Wales, Northern Ireland or the Republic of Ireland, or has passed the examinations required for

admission as such solicitor or barrister in any of the said jurisdictions, in either case within a reasonable time prior to such application, determine which of the Society's examinations, if any, such intrant shall be required to pass for the purposes of regs. 8 and 11 of these Regulations, and grant special permission in terms of reg. 21 hereof accordingly, subject always to such conditions as the Council may impose, including conditions as to the period of time during which the examinations must be passed.

(2) The decision of the Council on any question arising under this Regulation shall be final.

NOTE

By the EC Qualified Lawyers Transfer (Scotland) Regulations 1990, reg. 7, references to the Republic of Ireland shall be of no effect.

Fees
28. An intrant shall together with his application to sit any examination tender such fee as may be prescribed by the Council from time to time.

Provision for purposes of Order in Council under Colonial Solicitors Act 1900
29. Where, in any Order in Council made in pursuance of the Colonial Solicitors Act 1900, it is provided that an intrant shall undergo the examination in law prescribed for the time being for the admission of solicitors in Scotland, the examinations prescribed under Pt. III of these Regulations shall be the examinations in law for the purposes of such Order in Council.

PART IV—PROCEDURE FOR ADMISSION AS SOLICITOR

Eligibility for certificate of fitness
30. Subject to the provisions of section 6 of the Act and of these Regulations, an intrant shall be entitled to apply for a certificate of fitness for the purposes of section 6 of the Act if—
(1) (*a*) he has passed or obtained exemption from the Society's examinations, or
(*b*) he has obtained, or is entitled to obtain a degree in law of a Scottish university which includes passes in subjects corresponding to all the subjects examined by the Society's examiners, as required by the Council from time to time, unless otherwise exempt, or where such degree does not include passes in all such subjects, he obtains passes therein in the Society's examinations, or otherwise passes corresponding subjects at the standard required for a degree in law of a Scottish university, and
(2) he holds a Diploma, unless he is exempted from doing so in terms of these Regulations, and
(3) (*a*) he has completed not less than one year of his two-year period of service under a post-Diploma training contract and has submitted to the Council an undertaking in such form as the Council may prescribe that he will complete the remaining period of service under such contract in fulfilment of his obligation under that contract, or
(*b*) he has completed the full period of service under a post-Diploma training contract appropriate in his case in accordance with the provisions of Sched. 4 to these Regulations, or
(*c*) he has completed the full period of service under a non-Diploma training contract as is prescribed for his class of intrant under Sched. 3 to these Regulations, or as may be prescribed by the Council under reg. 31 hereof as the case may be, or
(*d*) he is otherwise entitled to apply for a certificate of fitness on commencement of his post-Diploma, or non-Diploma training contract, in accordance with the provisions of Scheds. 3 and 4 to these Regulations.

Exemption from Diploma

31.—(1) An intrant who seeks to obtain a certificate of fitness under these Regulations and who satisfies the Council that there are exceptional circumstances which justify his being exempted from obtaining a Diploma may be granted a certificate of fitness on such conditions, including the passing of examinations, as the Council may in its discretion prescribe; provided that an intrant who receives such exemption shall be required to grant an undertaking that he will serve for a period of not less than three years under a non-Diploma training contract with an employing solicitor, in terms similar to those of a post-Diploma training contract.

(2) The categories of intrant specified in Sched. 3 shall not be required to hold a Diploma in order to obtain a certificate of fitness.

Applications for admission on completion of first year of post-Diploma training contract

32. In the case of an intrant to whom para. 30(3)(*a*) of these Regulations applies—

(*a*) the Council shall not grant a certificate of fitness to him unless he submits to the Council a certificate by his employer that during the first year of his post-Diploma training contract he has fulfilled his obligations under such contract and is, in the opinion of his employer a fit and proper person to be admitted as a solicitor in Scotland, and

(*b*) he shall, on completion of his full period of service under his post-Diploma training contract submit to the Council a declaration by his employer in such form as the Council may prescribe certifying that in his opinion the intrant continues to be a fit and proper person to be admitted as a solicitor in Scotland.

Applications for admission on completion of post-Diploma training contract

33. In the case of an intrant to whom para. 30(3)(*a*), (*b*) or (*c*) applies, the Council shall not grant a certificate of fitness to him unless he submits to the Council a declaration by his employer in such form as the Council may prescribe certifying in his opinion that the intrant has fulfilled his obligation to date under the training contract and is a fit and proper person to be admitted as a solicitor in Scotland; always provided however that in any case where the employer of an intrant has declined to provide any such certificate, the Council may after due inquiry and where it appears that the employer has acted unreasonably in withholding such certificate, grant a declaration as aforesaid which shall be deemed for all purposes to have the same effect as if granted by the employer.

Application for admission after seven years

34. If an application for a certificate of fitness is made by an intrant under these Regulations more than seven years after the date on which he became entitled to apply therefor, he shall be required to submit along with his application an affidavit certifying his occupation and employment since that date and shall provide the Council with such other information as it in its discretion shall require.

PART V—GENERAL

Arbitration and conciliation

35.—(1) If a complaint is made to the Council in writing by an employer or an intrant in respect of any matter arising out of a pre-Diploma, post-Diploma or non-Diploma training contract, the Council shall take such steps to enquire into the matter that it may deem necessary and proper, including where the Council considers it appropriate submission of the complaint to the arbitration of a person nominated by the Council, provided always that such submission shall expressly exclude the application of section 3 of the Administration of Justice (Scotland) Act 1972, and the decision of such person shall be final, provided that in any case where an intrant is aggrieved by the Council's decision to refuse to grant him a preliminary entrance certificate, entrance certificate or certificate of fitness, or by the Council's decision to take such action as is specified in reg. 35(2) herein, on the ground that in reaching its decision the Council acted in a manner contrary to the rules of natural justice, and in the event of the arbiter finding that the Council did so act, the whole matter shall be considered by the Council having regard to the arbiter's findings and to any guidance or instruction provided by the arbiter as to its procedure in the matter.

(2) After such enquiry or arbitration, the Council may require the parties to discharge or assign the intrant's pre-Diploma, post-Diploma or non-Diploma training contract, as the case may be, upon such terms and conditions, if any as it thinks fit and may determine what part if any of the period of service of the intrant under such contract shall be reckoned as part of his period of service under such contract for the purposes of these Regulations.

General discretion of the Council

36. The Council may in what it deems to be exceptional circumstances and taking into account the merits of a particular case, vary, waive, modify or otherwise alter any provision of these Regulations, provided that a motion to do so is supported by two-thirds of the members voting thereon; provided that this Regulation shall not apply to any application for exemption from the Diploma under reg. 31(1) of these Regulations.

Amendment of 1976 Regulations

37. The 1976 Regulations shall be amended as set out in Sched. 5 to these Regulations.

Revocation of 1979 and 1981 Regulations

38. The Admission as Solicitor (Scotland) (Amendment) (No. 2) Regulations 1979 and Admission as Solicitor (Scotland) Regulations 1981 are hereby revoked.

Regulation 4   SCHEDULE 1

Classes of intrant to whom these Regulations shall not apply

These Regulations shall not apply to—

(1) any intrant who entered into an apprenticeship under the 1976 Regulations prior to 1st January 1984 having satisfied the Council that he—

  (*a*) obtained a degree in law of a Scottish University prior to 1st January 1980 or was entitled to graduate in such a degree prior to that date notwithstanding that he has not so graduated; or

  (*b*) obtained a degree of any university other than a law degree of a Scottish University, prior to 1st January 1980 and a degree in law of a Scottish University, prior to 1st January 1981 or was entitled to graduate in such a degree in law prior to the latter date notwithstanding that he has not so graduated; or

  (*c*) obtained a degree in law, with Honours, of a Scottish University prior to 1st January 1981 or was entitled to graduate in such a degree notwithstanding that he has not so graduated;

(2) any intrant who obtained an entrance certificate under the 1976 Regulations prior to 1st January 1980 and completes his term of apprenticeship and passes all of the

Society's examinations prior to 1st January 1987, or obtains exemption from some or all of them prior to that last mentioned date.

Regulation 6   SCHEDULE 2

Provisions with respect to minimum qualifications for intrants applying for a preliminary entrance certificate, with a view to entering into a pre-Diploma training contract and to qualifying for admission by means of the Society's examinations

1. An intrant offering United Kingdom school qualifications must have passed in the necessary subjects either of the Scottish Certificate of Education or the General Certificate of Education as specified in para. 2 of this Schedule.

2. An intrant may qualify for a preliminary entrance certificate by one or other of the following methods designated A, B or C below.

(A) *Scottish Certificate of Education.* If he
(1) passes in at least five of the approved subjects, as provided from time to time by the Scottish Universities Council on Entrance at no more than two sittings;
(2) amasses a total of such points as the Council may from time to time determine in respect of the subjects passed, calculated as follows:—
a pass at Higher grade at—
"A" being valued at three points,
"B" being valued at two points, and
"C" being valued at one point;
(3)(i) obtains a pass at Higher grade in English at not less than "B",
(ii) obtains a pass at Higher grade in a subject chosen from one of the following groups.
(*a*) a group comprising mathematics or an approved science, or
(*b*) a group comprising an approved language other than English, and
(iii) obtains a pass at Higher, Ordinary or Standard grade in a subject chosen from the other group, provided that if at Ordinary or Standard grade, such pass is at not less than grade 3 or grade C as the case may be.
Provided that if he is deficient in pointage or subject passes from the minimum standard as set out above, either may be made up from an equivalent number of passes at A level in the General Certificate of Education, to the value of points attributed in (B) below, or

(B) *General Certificate of Education.* If he
(1) passes in at least five of the approved subjects, as provided from time to time by the Scottish Universities Council on Entrance, at no more than two sittings;
(2) amasses a total of such points in respect of the subjects passed, as the Council may from time to time determine, calculated as follows:—
a pass at the Advanced level at—
"A" being valued at four points,
"B" being valued at three points,
"C" being valued at two points, and
"D" being valued at one point;
(3)(i) obtains a pass at the Advanced level in English, at not less than "C" standard,
(ii) obtains a pass at the Advanced level in a subject chosen from one of the following groups.
(*a*) a group comprising mathematics or an approved science, or
(*b*) a group comprising an approved language other than English, and
(iii) obtains a pass at the Advanced or Ordinary level in a subject chosen from the other group.
Provided that if he is deficient in pointage or subject passes from the minimum standard as set out above, either may be made up from an equivalent number of passes at Higher grade in the Scottish Certificate of Education to the value of the points attributed to (A) above, or

(C) If he
(*a*) has graduated in a degree of any university, other than an honorary degree or a degree in law of a Scottish University, or is entitled to graduate in such a degree notwithstanding that he has not so graduated, or
(*b*) is a member of the Institute of Chartered Accountants of Scotland or of the Institute of Chartered Accountants in England and Wales or of the Association of Certified and Corporate Accountants, or
(*c*) is a commissioned officer in one of the British armed services where his commission has been obtained following study at a Royal Naval, Army or Royal Air Force college.

Regulation 31   SCHEDULE 3

INTRANTS EXEMPT FROM HOLDING A DIPLOMA

The following intrants shall be entitled, subject to any conditions specified, to apply for a certificate of fitness under section 6 of the Act without being required to hold a Diploma—

  (i) a member of the Faculty of Advocates of not less than five years standing, on condition that he grants an undertaking to serve for a period of not less than six months under a non-Diploma training contract, in terms similar to those of the second year of a post-Diploma training contract, with an employing solicitor;

[1] (ii) a person who has been called to the bar in England and Wales, Northern Ireland or the Republic of Ireland and who is of not less than five years standing as a barrister, on condition that he grants an undertaking to serve for a period of two years, or such lesser period as the Council shall require, under a non-Diploma training contract, in terms similar to those of a post-Diploma training contract, with an employing solicitor;

[1] (iii) an admitted solicitor of not less than three years standing in England and Wales, Northern Ireland or the Republic of Ireland;

  (iv) an admitted solicitor of not less than three years standing to whom the Colonial Solicitors Act 1900 applies; and

  (v) an intrant who has been exempted from holding the Diploma in terms of reg. 31(1) of these Regulations.

———

NOTE
  [1] By the EC Qualified Lawyers Transfer (Scotland) Regulations 1990, reg. 7, references to the Republic of Ireland shall be of no effect.

———

Regulations 7 and 9   SCHEDULE 4

PROVISIONS WITH RESPECT TO THE PERIOD OF SERVICE UNDER A POST-DIPLOMA TRAINING CONTRACT

  1. In the case of an intrant who has obtained a degree in law of a Scottish university his period of service under a post-Diploma training contract shall be two years.

  2. In the case of an intrant who has passed or obtained exemption from some or all of the Society's examinations and has served for the required period under a pre-Diploma training contract in accordance with these Regulations his period of service under a post-Diploma training contract shall be two years.

  3. In the case of an intrant who is a member of the Faculty of Advocates, his period of service under a post-Diploma training contract shall be one year, subject to the provisions of para. 7 below.

  [1] 4. In the case of an intrant who is a solicitor admitted in England and Wales, Northern Ireland or the Republic of Ireland, his period of service under a post-Diploma training contract shall be one year, subject to the provisions of para. 7 below.

———

NOTE
  [1] By the EC Qualified Lawyers Transfer (Scotland) Regulations 1990, reg. 7, references to the Republic of Ireland shall be of no effect.

———

  [1] 5. In the case of an intrant who has been called to the bar in England and Wales or Northern Ireland or the Republic of Ireland his period of service under a post-Diploma training contract shall be two years provided that in special circumstances this period may be reduced by the Council to such period as it at its discretion, thinks fit.

———

NOTE
  [1] By the EC Qualified Lawyers Transfer (Scotland) Regulations 1990, reg. 7, references to the Republic of Ireland shall be of no effect.

———

[1] 6. In the case of a solicitor admitted elsewhere than in the United Kingdom or the Republic of Ireland and to whom the provisions of the Colonial Solicitors Act 1900 do not apply his period of service under a post-Diploma training contract shall be one year, subject to the provision of para. 7 below.

―――――

NOTE
[1] By the EC Qualified Lawyers Transfer (Scotland) Regulations 1990, reg. 7, references to the Republic of Ireland shall be of no effect.

―――――

7. An intrant in categories 3, 4 and 6 above shall be required to submit a written undertaking to the Council prior to the commencement of his post-Diploma training contract that during his year of service he will not engage in practice on his own account, but will remain in the service of his employer.

SCHEDULE 5

AMENDMENTS TO 1976 REGULATIONS

[These amendments re-enact amendments made by the Admission as Solicitor (Scotland) Regulations 1981 and are given effect to in the print of the 1976 Regulations, *supra*.]

Solicitors (Scotland) Practice Rules 1986

Rules made by the Council of the Law Society of Scotland and approved by the Lord President of the Court of Session pursuant to section 34 of the Solicitors (Scotland) Act 1980.

1.—(1) These rules may be cited as the Solicitors (Scotland) Practice Rules 1986.
(2) These rules shall come into operation with respect to transactions commenced on or after 1st January 1987.

2.—(1) In these rules, unless the context otherwise requires:—
"the Act" means the Solicitors (Scotland) Act 1980;
"client" includes prospective client;
"Council" means the Council of the Society;
"established client" means a person for whom a solicitor or his firm has acted on at least one previous occasion;
"employed solicitor" means a solicitor employed by his employer for the purpose, wholly or partly, of offering legal services to the public whether or not for a fee;
"firm" includes any office at which that firm carries on practice and any firm in which that firm has a direct interest through one or more of its partners, or members;
"the Society" means the Law Society of Scotland established under the Act;
"solicitor" means a solicitor holding a practising certificate under the Act, or an incorporated practice;
"transaction" includes a contract and any negotiations leading thereto.
(2) The Interpretation Act 1978 applies to the interpretation of these rules as it applies to the interpretation of an Act of Parliament.

3. A solicitor shall not act for two or more parties whose interests conflict.

4. Without prejudice to the generality of rule 3 hereof an employed solicitor whose only or principal employer is one of the parties to a transaction shall not act for any other party to that transaction; provided always that such solicitor may, where no dispute arises or appears likely to arise between the parties to that transaction, act for more than one party thereto, if and only if:—

(a) the parties are associated companies, public authorities, public bodies, or government departments or agencies;

(b) the parties are connected one with the other within the meaning of section 533 Income and Corporation Taxes Act 1970.

5.—(1) Without prejudice to the generality of rule 3 hereof, a solicitor, or two or more solicitors practising either as principal or employee in the same firm or in the employment of the same employer, shall not at any stage, act for both seller and purchaser in the sale or purchase or conveyance of heritable property, or for both landlord and tenant, or assignor and assignee in a lease of heritable property for value or for lender and borrower in a loan to be secured over heritable property; provided, however, that where no dispute arises or might reasonably be expected to arise between the parties and that, other than in the case of exception (a) hereto, the seller or landlord of residential property is not a builder or developer, this rule shall not apply if:—

(a) the parties are associated companies, public authorities, public bodies, or government departments or agencies;

(b) the parties are connected one with the other within the meaning of section 533 Income and Corporation Taxes Act 1970;

(c) the parties are related by blood, adoption or marriage, one to the other, or the purchaser, tenant, assignee or borrower is so related to an established client, or

(d) both parties are established clients or the prospective purchaser, tenant, assignee or borrower is an established client; or

(e) there is no other solicitor in the vicinity whom the client could reasonably be expected to consult; or

(f) in the case of a loan to be secured over heritable property, the terms of the loan have been agreed between the parties before the solicitor has been instructed to act for the lender, and the granting of the security is only to give effect to such agreement.

(2) In all cases falling within exceptions (c), (d) and (e) both parties shall be advised by the solicitor at the earliest practicable opportunity that the solicitor, or his firm, has been requested to act for both parties, and that if a dispute arises, they or one of them will require to consult an independent solicitor or solicitors, which advice shall be confirmed by the solicitor in writing as soon as may be practicable thereafter.

6. A solicitor shall unless the contrary be proved be presumed for the purposes of rules 4 and 5 hereof to be acting for a party for whom he prepares an offer whether complete or not, in connection with a transaction of any kind specified in these rules, for execution by that party.

7. A solicitor acting on behalf of a party or prospective party to a transaction of any kind specified in rule 5 hereof shall not issue any deed, writ, missive or other document requiring the signature of another party or prospective party to him without informing that party in writing that:—

(a) such signature may have certain legal consequences, and

(b) he should seek independent legal advice before signature.

8. Where a solicitor, or two or more solicitors practising as principal or employee in the same firm or in the employment of the same employer, knowingly intends or intend to act on behalf of two or more prospective purchasers or tenants (other than prospective joint purchasers or tenants) of heritable property (in this rule referred to as "the clients"), the clients shall be informed of such intention, and a single solicitor shall not, where he has given any advice to one of the clients with respect to the price or rent to be offered, or with respect to any other material condition of the prospective bargain, give advice to another of the clients in respect of such matters.

9. The Council shall have power to waive any of the provisions of these rules in any particular circumstances or case.

10. Breach of any of these rules may be treated as professional misconduct for the purposes of Part IV of the Act (complaints and disciplinary proceedings).

[THE NEXT PAGE IS F 385]

Solicitors' (Scotland) Practising Certificate Rules 1988

Rules dated 29th July, 1988 made by the Council of The Law Society of Scotland under section 13 of the Solicitors (Scotland) Act 1980.

Citation
  1.—(1) These Rules may be cited as the Solicitors (Scotland) Practising Certificate Rules 1988.
  (2) These Rules shall come into operation on the 20th day of September, 1988.

Interpretation
  2.—(1) In these Rules unless the context otherwise requires:—
  "the Act" means the Solicitors (Scotland) Act 1980;
  "the Council" means the Council of the Law Society of Scotland established under the Act;
  "practising certificate" means a practising certificate issued in accordance with the provisions of the Act;
  "application" means an application for a practising certificate;
  "year" means the period of twelve months ending on the 31st day of October;
  "principal" means a solicitor who is a sole practitioner or a partner in a firm of solicitors or a member of an incorporated practice.
  (2) The Interpretation Act 1978 applies to these Rules as it applies to an Act of Parliament.

[THE NEXT PAGE IS F 409]

Application for practising certificate
   3. A solicitor who wishes to obtain a practising certificate shall make application therefor by completing (so far as applicable to him) and signing a form in or substantially in the form set out in Part I of the Schedule to these Rules.

Issue of practising certificate
   4.—(1) Subject always to the provisions of Rule 5 the Council on receipt of an application which has been duly completed and signed shall cause a practising certificate to be issued to the applicant without delay.
   (2) A practising certificate shall be in or substantially in the form set out in Part II of the Schedule to these Rules.

Professional indemnity insurance
   5. The Council shall not issue a practising certificate to any solicitor making an application unless he provides, along with his application either:—
     (*a*) evidence that a certificate of insurance has been issued to the practice unit of which he is a principal in terms of the Master Policy for Professional Indemnity Insurance taken out and maintained by the Council in terms of Rule 4 of the Solicitors (Scotland) Professional Indemnity Insurance Rules 1988; or
     (*b*) a declaration that he is not a principal.

Register of applications and practising certificates issued
   6.—(1) The Council shall cause to be kept in respect of each year a register of applications for practising certificates and of certificates issued.
   (2) The register shall be in or substantially in the form set out in Part III of the Schedule to these Rules and may be divided into parts according to the districts in which the solicitors practise as the Council may determine.
   (3) The register shall be open for inspection by any person having an interest therein at any time during office hours without payment.

Repeals
   7. The Solicitors (Scotland) Practising Certificate Rules 1966 are hereby revoked, but such revocation shall not affect the validity of any application made, certificate granted or other thing done under the said regulations and such application, certificate or thing shall have effect as if it were made, granted or done under these regulations.

SCHEDULE

PART I

Form of Application for a Practising Certificate

19

   I(*a*)

> TELEPHONE No.

hereby apply for a practising certificate for the year ending 31st October 19
Please also state whether admitted as N.P.
   I was admitted as a solicitor on the (*b*)
day of   19   and commenced to practise on the
day of   19   (see note (*b*))
Please state any other places of business (*c*)

Name of firm (if any) of which applicant is a partner

Employee applicants (please give name of employer(s))

If the applicant's place of business has changed since his last practising certificate was issued, address which appeared on last practising certificate to be stated here

(*d*) The provisions of section 15 of the Solicitors (Scotland) Act, 1980 (which relate to a discretion to the Registrar in special cases to refuse a practising certificate or to issue a certificate subject to conditions), do not apply to me.

Or,

(*d*) The provisions of section 15 of the Solicitors (Scotland) Act, 1980 apply to me and I have given notice required by that paragraph.
    I enclose remittance in payment of:—

(i) Annual subscription to the Society (*e*) £

(ii) Annual contribution to the Scottish Solicitor's guarantee Fund (*f*)

(iii) Fee payable under Act of Sederunt (Rules of court Amendment No. 5) 1979 (retention Fee)

£

(*g*) I have struck out sub-paragraph (ii) above as I am exempt from payment of any contribution to the Scottish Solicitors' Guarantee Fund on the following ground (*h*)

Declaration in regard to the Solicitors (Scotland) Accounts Rules.
    1. I have complied with the Solicitors (Scotland) Accounts Rules.
    2. I have not held or received clients' money during the practice year ended 31st October 19 .
        (Delete line 1 or 2 whichever is inapplicable.)

Declarations in regard to the Solicitors (Scotland) Professional Indemnity Insurance Rules 1988.
    1. I herewith provide evidence of insurance in terms of the Solicitors Professional Indemnity Insurance Rules 1988.
    2. I declare in terms of Rule 4 that I am not a principal in private practice in Scotland and I am exempt from providing evidence of insurance in terms of the Solicitors (Scotland) Professional Indemnity Insurance Rules 1988.
    (Delete whichever of 1 or 2 is inapplicable and if 2 is inapplicable then evidence of insurance must be provided.)

Dated this   day of   19

(Signature)

To the Council of the Law Society of Scotland.

Notes
    (*a*) Please give full name and principal business address.
    (*b*) This information may be omitted if more than three years have expired since the date of commencing practice.
    (*c*) All other places of business, excluding principal address, must be stated.
    (*d*) Strike out whichever of the two alternative paragraphs does not apply.
    (*e*) The annual subscription is £   in the case of (i) a solicitor who has been admitted and enrolled for less than three years prior to 1st November 19   and (ii) £   in the case of a solicitor who does not require to take out a Practising Certificate. In all other cases the annual subscription is £

(f) The annual contribution is £   . The sum payable by a solicitor in respect of the year in which he first commences to practise after admission and in respect of each of the two years immediately following shall be one half of the annual contribution.

(h) If exemption from payment of any contribution to the Scottish Solicitors' Guarantee Fund is claimed, state here the ground of exemption—e.g., employed as solicitor to a Government Department or as assistant to a Government Department solicitor, or employed as an officer of a local authority or statutory undertakers or a designated body by reason of being a solicitor, and not engaged in private practice; or employed by another solicitor, and not engaged in private practice; or employed by another solicitor and not engaged in practice as a solicitor on own account; and not engaged in practice as a solicitor. A solicitor participating in the Legal Aid and Legal Advice Schemes is regarded as engaging in private practice on his own account. See section 43(7) of, and paragraph 1(8) of the Third Schedule to, the Solicitors (Scotland) Act, 1980.

This form, when completed and signed, should be forwarded, along with the firm remittance advice and a remittance for the appropriate amount in the enclosed envelope. Remittances should be made payable to "The Law Society of Scotland" and should be crossed "& Co."

The making of a false statement by a solicitor in an application for a practising certificate may be treated as professional misconduct for the purposes of the Solicitors (Scotland) Act 1980.

Part II

Form of Practising Certificate

No.

PURSUANT to the Solicitors (Scotland) Act, 1980

THE COUNCIL OF THE LAW SOCIETY OF SCOTLAND as the Registrar of Solicitors, HEREBY CERTIFIES, that

has lodged with the Council an application in writing pursuant to the said Act, is entitled to practise as a Solicitor *until the thirty-first day of October, nineteen hundred and* and is a member of The Law Society of Scotland.

GIVEN under the hand of the
Secretary of THE LAW SOCIETY OF SCOTLAND
this   day
of   19

Secretary

Entered

PART III

Form of Register of Applications for and of Issue of Practising Certificates for year to 31st October 19

Name		Designation	Place(s) of Business	Date of Admission	No. of Certificate	Certificate Issued	Remarks
Surname	Christian Names						

[THE NEXT PAGE IS F 415]

Constitution of the Law Society of Scotland

Scheme under the Solicitors (Scotland) Act 1980, approved at a General Meeting of the Society held on 23rd September 1988 and having, by virtue of section 1 of, and Schedule 1 to, the said Act, effect as if enacted in that Act.

TITLE AND INTERPRETATION

Title
  1.—(1) This Scheme may be cited as the Constitution of the Law Society of Scotland.
  (2) This constitution shall come into operation on 1st November 1988.

Interpretation
  2.—(1) In this Constitution unless the context otherwise requires:—
  "the Act" means the Solicitors (Scotland) Act 1980;
  "the Society" means The Law Society of Scotland established by the Solicitors (Scotland) Act 1949;
  "the Council" means the Council of the Society;
  "a member of the Society" means a solicitor who in terms of Section 2(1) of the Act has in force a practising certificate, and any other solicitor who has paid the current annual membership subscription to the Society and whose name appears upon the Roll of Solicitors kept by the Council;
  "the Secretary" means the Secretary of the Society and includes any person authorised by the Council to act on behalf of the Secretary;
  "the President" means the President of the Society and includes, in the case of the absence of the President, or of his inability to act, the Vice-President of the Society;
  "place of business", in relation to a member of the Society means the member's place of business, or if the member has more than one place of business, the member's principal place of business, as specified in the member's practising certificate, if the member has one, or in a notice of change of place of business given by the member to the Society after the issue of the member's practising certificate, if the member has given such a notice, or if the member does not have a place of business, his residence, and references to the constituency in which a member practises shall be construed as a reference to the constituency in which such member has his place of business;
  "financial year" means the period of twelve months ending on 31st October.
  (2) The Interpretation Act 1978 applies to the interpretation of this Constitution as it applies to the interpretation of an Act of Parliament.

CONSTITUTION AND ELECTION OF MEMBERS OF COUNCIL

Constitution of the Council
  [1] **3.** The Council shall consist of 44 members of the Society elected in accordance with the provisions in this Constitution, together with such *ex officiis* members as there may be from time to time in terms hereof and such number of members, not exceeding nine, as may be co-opted by the Council in terms of Article 4 hereof.

NOTE
  [1] As amended, 27th September 1991.

Election of members of Council by constituencies
   4.—(1) For the election of members of Council, Scotland shall be divided into constituencies as set out in the first column of Part I of the First Schedule to this Constitution, and there shall be a separate election in each constituency. For the purposes of this Article and of the said Schedule, a member of the Society having a place of business outwith Scotland shall be treated as having a place of business within such constituency as such member may select.
   (2) A member of the Society shall be entitled to vote in the constituency in which such member's place of business is situated and in that constituency only.
   (3) The members of the Society in each of the several constituencies shall elect the number of members of Council as set out in the second column of the said Part of the said Schedule opposite to the constituency.
   (4) Constituencies shall be arranged in three groups as set out in Part II of the said Schedule and the Council shall arrange that in each year there will be an annual election in one of such groups taken in rotation.
   (5) The Council may co-opt as full members of Council such number of members of the Society not exceeding nine in all as the Council may determine. Such persons shall hold office for such term not exceeding three years as the Council may fix and different terms may be fixed for different persons. There shall be no limitation upon the number of terms for which such a person may be co-opted.
   (6) Only a member of the Society may be elected or co-opted or continue to be a member of Council.

Term of office of members of Council
   5. A member of Council shall retire from office on the day immediately before the day fixed by the Council for the annual election of members of the Council in the third year after such member's election. A retiring member shall be eligible for re-election.

Date of election of members of Council
   6. The annual election of members of Council in terms of Article 4(4) hereof shall be held in the month of May in each year on a date to be fixed by the Council.

Returning officer
   7. The Secretary shall act as returning officer for the election in each constituency.

Conduct of election
   8.—(1) Subject to the provisions of this Constitution the election of members of Council for a constituency shall be conducted in accordance with the provisions of the Second Schedule hereto and of any regulations made thereunder.
   (2) No election held under this Constitution shall be invalidated by reason of any misdescription or non-compliance with the provisions thereof or of any regulations thereunder or by reason of any miscount or of the non-delivery, loss or miscarriage of any document required to be sent under this Constitution or regulations thereunder, if it appears to the Returning Officer that the election was conducted substantially in accordance with this Constitution and the regulations and that the result of such misdescription, non-compliance, miscount, non-delivery, loss or miscarriage does not affect the return of any candidate at the election.

Expenses of election
   9. All expenses properly incurred by the returning officer or by the Society in relation to the holding of an election of members of Council shall be paid by the Society.

Failure of constituency to elect members of Council
   10. If the members of the Society in a constituency fail to elect the number of members of Council for the constituency as herein prescribed, the Council shall fill the vacancy by appointing a member of the Society to be a member of Council representing the constituency. Such member of the Society shall have his place of business within such constituency or as close thereto as may be reasonably practicable.

Casual vacancies in Council
   11.—(1) A member of Council may at any time resign from office by a notice in writing signed by such member and delivered to the Secretary. The resignation shall take effect upon the delivery of the notice or on a date not later than such member's date of retiral from office in terms of Article 5 hereof specified by such member in such notice, whichever is the later.
   (2) The office of a member of Council shall be vacated if such member is absent, without leave of the President, from three consecutive meetings of the Council, with effect from the conclusion of that third meeting of Council. Such leave may be given retrospectively.
   (3) Council may by a majority of three-quarters of members present and voting, suspend a member of Council from attendance at meetings of Council and its committees.
   (4) If the office of a member of Council becomes vacant before the expiration of such member's term of office whether by death, resignation or otherwise, an election by the electors in the constituency shall be held as soon as practicable in order to fill the vacancy on a date to be fixed by the Council and shall be conducted in the same manner as an election in ordinary course; and the provisions of this Constitution including the Second Schedule hereto relating to elections shall apply subject to any necessary modifications: provided that if the vacancy arises within three months before the date on which the vacating member would have retired in ordinary course the vacancy shall not be filled until the next election in the constituency. A person elected to fill a casual vacancy under this provision shall hold office only for the unexpired period of office of the member in whose place such person is elected and shall be eligible for re-election.

MEETINGS OF SOCIETY

Meetings of Society
   12.—(1) General Meetings of the Society shall comprise the Annual General Meeting and Special General Meetings.
   (2) An Annual General Meeting shall be held each year at such time on such date and at such place as the Council may appoint but not more than 15 months after the last preceding Annual General Meeting.
   (3) Special General Meetings of the Society shall be convened by the Secretary on the instructions of the President or of the Council or on a requisition signed by not less than 20 members of the Society. The requisition must state the objects of the meeting. It must be deposited with the Secretary and may consist of several documents in like form each signed by one or more requisitionists. A Special General Meeting required by requisition shall be held within 28 days of receipt of the requisition at such time on such date and at such place as the President, whom failing the Vice-President, may appoint.
   (4) Fourteen days' notice at least (exclusive of the day on which the notice is sent but inclusive of the day for which the notice is given), specifying the place, day, and hour of any General Meeting and the business to be considered shall be given to each member of the Society. A notice of a General Meeting shall be deemed to have been effected at the expiration of 24 hours after the letter containing the notice is sent. The accidental

omission to give notice of a meeting to, or the non-receipt of notice of a
meeting by any member shall not invalidate the proceedings at the meeting.

Proceedings at General Meetings of the Society
    13.—(1) The President, whom failing the Vice-President, shall preside at a
General Meeting, and if at any meeting neither the President nor the
Vice-President is present, the members present shall choose one of their
number who is a member of Council to preside.
    (2) The business of the Annual General Meeting shall be to receive and
consider the Report of the Council (a copy of which shall be sent to each
member of the Society at least 14 days before the date of the meeting), the
statement of accounts of the Society and the report of the auditors thereon,
to elect auditors, and any other business specified in the notice of the
meeting.
    (3) The Council shall include in the notice of the Annual General Meeting
any item relating to the business of the Society specified in a requisition
made by not less than 10 members of the Society and received by the
Secretary not less than 42 days before the meeting. The business of any
Special General Meeting shall be to consider only the business specified in
the notice of meeting.
    (4) No business shall be transacted at any General Meeting unless a
quorum of members of the Society is present within half an hour after the
time appointed for the meeting. Twenty members personally present shall
be a quorum. A meeting at which a quorum is not present, if not convened on
a requisition shall stand adjourned to a day and hour to be fixed by the
majority of the members present, and if convened on a requisition shall fail
and not be held.
    (5) Subject to the provisions of this Constitution and to any directions
given by the Society in General Meeting, the Council may make standing
orders with regard to the conduct of the business at meetings of the Society,
including the adjournment of meetings.
    (6) Subject to the provisions of paragraph 5 of Schedule 1 to the Act, no
resolution passed at a General Meeting shall be binding on the Society until
it has been adopted by the Council or has been confirmed at the next
General Meeting, and it shall be the duty of the Council, if it does not adopt
the resolution, to bring the same before the next General Meeting
accordingly, but this provision shall not apply to a resolution proposed by
the Council and passed at the meeting at which it has been proposed.

Voting at General Meetings
    14.—(1) At any General Meeting a resolution put to the vote of the
meeting shall be decided by a show of hands unless a poll is (before or on the
declaration of the result of the show of hands) demanded by at least three
members present in person and unless a poll is so demanded a declaration by
the chairman of the meeting that a resolution has, on a show of hands, been
carried or carried unanimously or by a particular majority or lost, and an
entry to that effect in the minutes of the proceedings of the Society shall be
conclusive evidence of the fact, without proof of the number or proportion
of the votes recorded in favour of, or against, that resolution: always
provided that a poll may not be demanded in the case of a resolution with
regard to the appointment of a chairman of the meeting or the adjournment
of the meeting or in the case of a motion that the question be now put or that
the meeting move to the next business.
    (2) If a poll is demanded, it shall be taken at once in such manner as the
chairman directs, and the result of the poll shall be deemed to be the
resolution of the meeting at which the poll was demanded.
    (3) In the case of an equality of votes, whether on a show of hands or on a
poll, the chairman of the meeting at which the show of hands takes place or
at which the poll is taken shall be entitled to a second or casting vote.

(4) On a show of hands every member present in person shall have one vote.

(5) On a poll, votes may be given either personally or by proxy.

(6) The instrument appointing a proxy shall be deposited with the Secretary at any time after the notice is sent calling the General Meeting and not less than 48 hours before the time for holding the meeting or adjourned meeting at which the person named in the instrument proposes to vote, and in default the instrument of proxy shall not be treated as valid. A proxy must be a member of the Society.

PRESIDENT, VICE-PRESIDENT, PAST PRESIDENT AND HONORARY VICE-PRESIDENT OF THE SOCIETY

President, Vice-President, Past President and Honorary Vice-President

15.—(1) The Council shall at its first meeting after the 1st day of November in each year, receive nominations for the office of President and Vice-President and shall thereafter elect at its first meeting after the 1st day of December in each year one of its number who has been a member of Council for at least three years to be President of the Society, and another of its number who has also been a member of Council for at least three years to be Vice-President of the Society, to hold office as from the date of the first meeting of the Council held after the next annual election of members of the Council; provided always that if at or prior to the latter date the President elect or Vice-President elect ceases to be a member of Council, his election as President or Vice-President shall be void as at the date of such cessation, and the Council shall at its first meeting held not less than four weeks after the date of such cessation, proceed to a new election of President or Vice-President as the case may be. Provided that if there are two or more nominations for either office the resulting competition shall be decided by postal ballot. If there are three or more nominations for either office the election shall be conducted by the single transferable vote method.

(2) Notwithstanding Article 5 hereof, the President and Vice-President shall hold office until the date from which their respective successors take office. A President or Vice-President shall cease to hold office if he ceases to be a member of the Society. The President shall be eligible for re-election to that office for each of the two succeeding years, but shall not again be eligible to be President until a period of at least two years has elapsed since he last held that office.

(3) The Vice-President shall not again be eligible to be Vice-President until at least one year has elapsed since he last held that office.

(4) The President or Vice-President may resign at any time from office as such by a signed notice in writing delivered to the Secretary, and the resignation shall take effect upon the delivery of the notice or on a date not later than the date on which he would otherwise have demitted office specified in the said notice, whichever is the later.

(5) (*a*) On a casual vacancy occurring in the office of President or Vice-President at a time when there is a President elect or Vice-President elect as the case may be appointed to take up office in the ensuing month of May, the President elect or Vice-President elect shall immediately assume office as President or Vice-President as the case may be; and the resulting additional period of office, which will terminate at the first meeting of the Council held after the next annual election of members of the Council, shall be disregarded in applying the provisions of Articles 15(2) and 15(3) hereof.

(*b*) On a casual vacancy occurring in the office of President at a time when there is no President elect, the Vice-President shall assume the additional office of Interim President until the next meeting of the Council held less than four weeks after the date of the occurrence of the said vacancy, when the Council shall elect a new President.

(*c*) On a casual vacancy occurring in the office of Vice-President at a time when there is no Vice-President elect, the Council shall as soon as practicable appoint one of its number to fill the vacancy until the date of the first meeting of the Council held after the next annual election of members of the Council.

(6) From the date upon which the President ceases to hold office as such except when he has resigned in terms of Article 15(4) hereof he shall serve as Past President of the Society for a period of one year. If the Past President is not or if during his period of office he should cease to be a member of Council, he shall *ex officio* be a member of Council until the expiry of his period of office. The Past President may resign as provided in Article 15(4) hereof and shall cease to hold office if he ceases to be a member of the Society.

(7) The Council may at any meeting elect one of its number or a former one of its number to be Honorary Vice-President of the Society to hold office until the next annual election of members of Council and to carry out such duties as may from time to time be prescribed by the Council. If the Honorary Vice-President is not a member of Council or if during his period of office he should cease to be a member of Council, he shall *ex officio* be a member of Council until the expiry of his period of office. An Honorary Vice-President shall not be eligible for re-election as such. An Honorary Vice-President may resign as provided in Article 15(4) hereof and shall cease to hold office if he ceases to be a member of the Society.

ADMISSION OF HONORARY AND OTHER MEMBERS OF SOCIETY

Honorary members of Society
16.—(1) The Council may admit as an honorary member of the Society any person of distinction in the legal profession whether or not such person is or has been a member of the Society.

(2) Unless he is a member of the Society an honorary member shall have no right to vote at meetings of the Society or in elections of members of Council and shall not be liable in payment of any annual subscription to the Society.

Admission as members of solicitors exempt from holding practising certificates
17. The Council shall, on application and on payment of the annual subscription, admit as a member of the Society any solicitor who is exempt from taking out a practising certificate.

HONORARY PRESIDENTS OF SOCIETY

Honorary Presidents
18. The Society in General Meeting may elect one or more persons of distinction in the legal profession to be the Honorary President or Honorary Presidents of the Society, and every such person shall continue to hold that office until the Society in General Meeting otherwise determine. Honorary Presidents shall have no right as such to vote at meetings of the Society or in the election of members of Council.

SECRETARY AND STAFF

Secretary and staff
   19.—(1) The Council shall appoint a Secretary of the Society who shall be chief executive officer of the Council and it shall pay a suitable remuneration for his services and may make such provision for pension or other rights for his benefit as it thinks proper. The Secretary shall perform such duties as the Council may from time to time determine.
   (2) The Council shall appoint such other staff as it thinks necessary for the efficient discharge of the functions of the Society and of the Council, and shall pay to every member of staff appointed under this Article suitable remuneration and may make such provision for pension or other rights for his benefit as it thinks proper.

ACCOUNTS

Accounts
   20.—(1) The Council shall keep proper books of accounts with regard to all sums of money received and expended by the Society, the Council and staff of the Society, and the matters in respect of which the receipt and expenditure take place.
   (2) The Council shall keep such bank accounts in name of the Society as the Council may determine, and, save as otherwise directed by the Council, there shall be paid into the said bank accounts all sums received by the Society or the Council or staff of the Society or otherwise all payments due to be met by the Society or the Council or otherwise payable out of the funds of the Society. The Council may give directions with respect to keeping, paying money into, and operating on the several bank accounts

Accounts to be made up yearly and submitted for audit
   21.—(1) Immediately after the end of each financial year the Council shall cause the accounts of the Society for that year to be brought to a balance and a balance sheet prepared.
   (2) The Council shall cause the accounts for the financial year to be audited as soon as practicable after the end of the year by the auditors appointed by the Society at the Annual General Meeting. A copy of the accounts or an abstract thereof and of the auditors' certificate thereon shall be sent to each member of the Society at least 14 days before the date of the Annual General Meeting.
   (3) If a vacancy arises in the office of auditor of the accounts of the Society between Annual General Meetings, the Council may appoint an auditor to fill the vacancy until the next Annual General Meeting and fix the remuneration.

MISCELLANEOUS

Committees
   22. The Council shall establish such Committees as it considers necessary. The President's Committee, the Guarantee Fund Committee and the Professional Practice Committee shall consist of such members of the Council as the Council may appoint.

Notice to members of Society
   23. Any notice or other document required by or under this Constitution to be sent to a member of the Society shall be sent to such member at his place of business.

Release 44: 28 April 1997

Council may hold referendum of members of the Society
24. The Council may if it thinks fit and shall on a requisition signed by not fewer than 50 members of the Society and deposited with the Secretary ascertain the views of the members of the Society at any time on any question affecting the Society or the members thereof by holding a referendum of its members and the Council shall make such arrangements as it considers proper for that purpose, including issuing to every member of the Society a voting paper and arranging for the scrutiny of voting papers. The Council shall include in its annual report a report of any referendum taken during the year.

Standing orders
25.—(1) Subject to the provisions of this Constitution, the Council may by standing orders make provision with respect to—
    (a) keeping minutes of General Meetings of the Society; and
    (b) any other matters which the Council considers would facilitate the conduct of business of meetings of the Society, and of the Council.
    (2) Standing orders made under this Article or under any other provision of this Constitution may be varied or revoked at any time by the Council.

Validity of acts of Council
26. The acts and proceedings of the Council shall not be invalidated by any vacancy among its members or by any defect in the election or qualification of any member.

Expenses of members of Council and committees
27. There shall be paid to the members of the Council and of committees thereof such travelling and other expenses in respect of attendance at meetings as may be approved by the Council.

COMMON SEAL OF SOCIETY

Common seal of Society
28. The Secretary shall be responsible for the custody of the common seal of the Society. The seal shall not be affixed to any instrument except by order of the Council or of a committee of the Council specifically authorised for the purpose.

FIRST SCHEDULE

[1] *PART I*

———

NOTE
  [1] As amended, March 22, 1996.

———

Constituencies for election of members of Council of the Law Society of Scotland.

Constituencies	Number of members of Council to be elected by constituency
Sheriff Court District of Aberdeen	2
Sheriff Court Districts of Stonehaven, Peterhead and Banff	1
Sheriff Court Districts of Airdrie and Lanark	1
Sheriff Court District of Hamilton	1

Constituencies	Number of members of Council to be elected by constituency
Sheriff Court Districts of Arbroath and Forfar	1
Sheriff Court District of Ayr	1
Sheriff Court District of Kilmarnock	2
Sheriff Court Districts of Campbeltown, Dunoon, Oban, Rothesay and Fort William	1
Sheriff Court District of Greenock	1
Sheriff Court District of Paisley	1
Sheriff Court Districts of Dumfries, Kirkcudbright and Stranraer	2
Sheriff Court District of Dundee	2
Sheriff Court District of Dunfermline	1
Sheriff Court District of Kirkcaldy	1
Sheriff Court District of Cupar	1
Sheriff Court District of Edinburgh	7
Sheriff Court Districts of Elgin and Nairn	1
Sheriff Court Districts of Haddington, Peebles, Jedburgh, Duns and Selkirk	2
Sheriffdom of Glasgow and Strathkelvin	7
Sheriff Court District of Perth	1
Sheriff Court District of Stirling, Falkirk and Alloa	2
Sheriff Court Districts of Kirkwall, Lerwick, Portree, Lochmaddy and Stornoway	1
Sheriff Court District of Dumbarton	1
Sheriff Court District of Linlithgow	1
Sheriff Court Districts of Inverness, Dingwall, Tain, Dornoch and Wick	1
England and Wales	1
	44

PART II

Grouping of constituencies for purposes of Article 4 so as to determine the rotation of the retiral of members of Council and of elections.

[1]*First Group*

Sheriffdom of Glasgow and Strathkelvin	7
Sheriff Court Districts of Campbeltown, Dunoon, Oban, Rothesay and Fort William	1
Sheriff Court District of Greenock	1
Sheriff Court District of Paisley	1
Sheriff Court District of Dunfermline	1
Sheriff Court District of Kirkcaldy	1
Sheriff Court District of Cupar	1
Sheriff Court District of Perth	1
Sheriff Court Districts of Arbroath and Forfar	1
England and Wales	1
	16

NOTE
[1] As amended, March 22, 1996.

Second Group

Sheriff Court District of Edinburgh	7
Sheriff Court District of Aberdeen	2
Sheriff Court Districts of Stonehaven, Peterhead and Banff	1

Sheriff Court Districts of Dumfries, Kirkcudbright and Stranraer	2
Sheriff Court Districts of Airdrie and Lanark	1
Sheriff Court District of Hamilton	1
	14

Third Group

Sheriff Court District of Dundee	2
Sheriff Court District of Ayr	1
Sheriff Court District of Kilmarnock	2
Sheriff Court Districts of Stirling, Falkirk and Alloa	2
Sheriff Court Districts of Haddington, Peebles, Jedburgh, Duns and Selkirk	2
Sheriff Court Districts of Elgin and Nairn	1
Sheriff Court Districts of Kirkwall, Lerwick, Portree, Lochmaddy and Stornoway	1
Sheriff Court District of Dumbarton	1
Sheriff Court District of Linlithgow	1
Sheriff Court Districts of Inverness, Dingwall, Tain, Dornoch and Wick	1
	14

SECOND SCHEDULE

PART I

RULES WITH REGARD TO THE ELECTION OF MEMBERS OF COUNCIL

Roll of electors

1. The Council shall cause to be prepared by a date not later than six weeks before the day of election in a constituency a roll of electors for each constituency in which an election is to be held, according to their respective places of business as at the first day of November last preceding.

Notice of election

2. The returning officer shall on or before a date not later than five weeks before the day of the elections in the various constituencies concerned cause a notice of election of the members of Council for the various constituencies to be published in the Journal issued by the Society or in such other manner as the Council may determine. The notice of election shall be in the appropriate form set out in Part II of this Schedule or in a form substantially to the like effect.

Nominations

3. No person may be elected a member of Council unless a nomination paper in respect of such person is lodged with the returning officer at the place stated in the notice of election on or before a date specified in the notice of election, not less than three weeks before the day of election. No person may be nominated as a candidate for election by a constituency unless he is a member of the Society. A nomination paper in respect of a candidate shall be signed by two proposers being electors within the constituency, and shall contain a signed statement by the candidate that he consents to be nominated and that, if elected, he will act as a member of Council. The nomination paper shall be in the appropriate form set out in Part II of this Schedule or in a form substantially to the like effect. No person may sign more nomination papers in respect of candidates than there are members of Council to be elected by the constituency; and if he signs more than is permitted, his signature shall be inoperative in all but those papers up to the permitted number which are first delivered. The returning officer shall treat as null and void any nomination paper which does not comply with any of the foregoing provisions.

A nomination may be withdrawn at any time before the latest date for lodging nomination papers.

Uncontested elections

4. If on the latest date for lodging nomination papers the number of persons remaining validly nominated for a constituency does not exceed the number of persons to be elected by the constituency, the returning officer shall cause a notice to be published in the Journal of the Society or in such other manner as the Council may determine intimating the election of the persons nominated as members of Council and that no voting will take place in the constituency.

Voting in contested elections

5.—(1) If the number of persons remaining validly nominated for a constituency exceeds the number of members to be elected by the constituency, the members of Council shall be elected in accordance with the following provision of this Schedule and with the provisions of any regulations made thereunder.

(2) The returning officer shall immediately after the latest date for lodging nomination papers cause voting papers and identification envelopes to be prepared in respect of each constituency in which the election is taking place. Voting papers prepared by the returning officer shall contain the names, places of business, date of birth, professional degrees, diplomas or qualifications, date of admission as a solicitor, date of joining practice or employer, date of assumption as a partner or position now held with employer, and (where appropriate) service to local Faculty or the Society and service on Council and committees of the Society, of the persons nominated for the constituency and state the place to which voting papers are to be returned and the latest date (being the date of election) and time by which they may be received, and the identification envelope shall bear a declaration of identity. Each voting paper and identification envelope shall be in the appropriate form set out in Part II of this Schedule or in a form substantially to the like effect.

(3) The returning officer shall on or before a date to be fixed by the Council, being not less than 10 days before the day of election, send a voting paper to each elector in the various constituencies concerned at such elector's place of business together with an identification envelope

[THE NEXT PAGE IS F 425]

and a covering envelope. Each elector shall be entitled to receive one voting paper, an identification envelope, and a covering envelope and no more; and votes may not be given except upon the voting paper provided by the returning officer.

(4) An elector in recording his vote (a) shall place a cross (thus X) on the right-hand side of the voting paper opposite the name of each candidate for whom he votes; and (b) shall sign the declaration upon the identification envelope. Each elector shall have as many votes as there are members to be elected from the constituency.

(5) The returning officer shall in the case of each constituency immediately after the last day fixed for the return of voting papers cause the validity of the votes to be ascertained by an examination of the identification envelopes and by such other relevant evidence (if any) as there may be, and shall cause the identification envelopes found to be valid to be opened and the voting papers withdrawn, kept folded face inwards, and placed apart. An identification envelope which has not been signed by the voter shall, together with the voting paper therein contained, be treated as invalid.

(6) The returning officer shall then examine the voting papers for each constituency and shall reject as invalid any voting paper (a) on which votes are given for more candidates than the elector is entitled to vote for, or (b) on which anything is written or marked by which the elector can be identified, except the number on the back, or (c) which is unmarked or void for uncertainty, or (d) which is defaced.

Any voting paper which the returning officer has rejected shall be marked with the word "Rejected".

(7) The returning officer shall, in the case of each constituency, cause the votes found to be valid to be counted in his presence and shall declare the result of the election. The returning officer shall forthwith give to every person elected on a vote notice of his election, and shall furnish to the Society and also publish in the journal of the Society, or in such other manner as the Council may determine, a list of the persons certified by him to have been duly elected, whether as a result of an uncontested election or a contested election.

Power to returning officer to cancel election

6. Notwithstanding anything in this Schedule, if after the latest date for lodging nomination papers a candidate withdraws with the result that the number of the remaining candidates does not exceed the number of persons to be elected by the constituency, the returning officer may cancel the election and declare the remaining candidates to be the elected members for the constituency.

Provisions in case of death of candidate

7. If a candidate remaining validly nominated dies before the last day fixed for lodging nomination papers his nomination shall be treated as having been withdrawn, but if such a candidate dies after that day, but before the day of election, the returning officer shall order a fresh election to be held.

Power to make regulations varying for certain purposes provisions of schedule

8. Notwithstanding anything in this Schedule, the Council may make regulations varying the provisions of this Schedule by prescribing a method of voting otherwise than by means of the combination of the voting paper and the identification envelope as herein before provided, and by prescribing another form of voting paper and making such other consequential amendments of the provisions of this Schedule as appear to the Council to be necessary.

Decision of returning officer final

9. Any question arising with regard to the validity of a nomination paper, a voting paper, or otherwise in connection with an election held under this Constitution shall be determined by the returning officer, whose decision shall be final.

PART II

[1] NOTICE OF ELECTION

THE LAW SOCIETY OF SCOTLAND

Election of Members of Council

NOTICE IS HEREBY GIVEN that, pursuant to the Solicitors (Scotland) Act 1980 and the Constitution of the Law Society of Scotland, an election of   members of Council representing the solicitors having places of business in the several constituencies undernoted is about to be held. Every member of the Society having a place of business as defined in Article 2 of the Constitution of the Society in a constituency at 1st November, 19   is entitled to one vote for each candidate up to the number of members of Council to be elected by that constituency. A member of the Society cannot vote in more than one constituency.

Constituencies	Number of members of Council to be elected by constituency

The returning officer for the purposes of this election is

(Name and Address).

No person may be elected a member of Council unless he or she is a member of the Society and unless a nomination paper in respect of such person is sent or delivered by hand so as to reach the office of the returning officer at or before noon on the   day of   19

Forms of nomination papers may be obtained from the returning officer on application. Every person proposed for election for a constituency must be nominated by a separate nomination paper in the appropriate form contained in Part II of the Second Schedule to the said Constitution, and every nomination paper must be subscribed by two proposers, being electors in the constituency, and shall contain a statement subscribed by the candidate that he or she consents to be nominated and that, if elected, he or she accepts office as a member of the Council.

No person may sign more nomination papers than the number of members to be elected by the constituency.

Dated   19   *Returning Officer*

NOTE
[1] As amended by the Council, July 1995.

FORM OF NOMINATION PAPER

THE LAW SOCIETY OF SCOTLAND

Election of Members of Council

Constituency

We, A.B. and C.D. (*here insert names of proposers and places of business*), being electors in this constituency, hereby nominate E.F. (*here insert name and place of business of candidate*), being a member of the Society, for election as a member of the Council of the Society at the next ensuing election.

Given under our hand this   (*insert date*) 19
                                                                A.B.
                                                                C.D.

I, the nominee for election, consent to be nominated as a candidate, and if elected agree to accept office as a member of the Council of the Society. I am a member of the Society.

E.F.

To the Returning Officer
(*Name and Address*).

[1] FORM OF VOTING PAPER

THE LAW SOCIETY OF SCOTLAND

Election of Members of Council

Constituency

Election of   members of Council by the constituency.

Names and Places of business of
candidates

DIRECTIONS FOR THE GUIDANCE OF ELECTORS

The elector may vote for   candidates.

If the elector votes for more than the number of candidates referred to in the previous line his voting paper will be treated as invalid.

The elector will place a cross on the right-hand side of the voting paper opposite the name of each candidate for whom the elector votes, thus X, and will not sign or otherwise mark this voting paper.

If the elector inadvertently spoils a voting paper the elector may return it to the returning officer, who will, if satisfied of such inadvertence, if time permits, forward another paper.

This paper must be folded *face inwards* and placed in the "Identification Envelope", which must be securely fastened and signed and then placed in the covering envelope, which must be sent or delivered by hand to the returning officer   (*Name and Address*), and must be received there before noon on the   day of   19

(Back of voting paper)

Official
Stamp and
Number

Note: The number on the voting paper should be the same as that on the identification envelope issued with it.

(Form of Declaration of Identification Envelope)

To

Place of business

I, the undersigned, hereby declare that I am the person to whom the enclosed voting paper was addressed as above and that I have not marked any other voting paper in this election.

Signature

NOTE
[1] As amended by the Council, July 1995.

Release 43: 31 January 1997

Rules for the Conduct of Meetings of the Council of the Law Society of Scotland approved by the Council on September 23, 1988

Meetings of the Council

1. Meetings of the Council shall be held at the office of the Society or at such other place and at such time as the Council may determine.

2. The Council shall hold not less than 10 meetings in each year for the transaction of Council business.

3. The Secretary shall call a meeting of the Council at any time on being required so to do by the President (whom failing in the absence of the President, the Vice-President) or on receiving a requisition in writing for that purpose specifying the business proposed to be transacted at the meeting signed by not less than nine members of the Council, which meeting shall be held within 14 days of receipt of the requisition.

4. The Secretary shall give at least seven days' written notice of the time and place of every meeting of Council to every member of Council at his place of business or to such other address as specified in writing by that member. The notice shall specify the business proposed to be transacted at the meeting, but the Chairman may, if it appears to him that any additional item of business should receive consideration include it in the business of the meeting although not mentioned in the notice. A notice of a meeting of the Council shall be deemed to have been received on the expiration of twenty-four hours after the notice is sent.

5. Notwithstanding anything in Rule 4 the President may require the Secretary to convene a meeting of the Council to consider any item of business demanding urgency to be held on giving not less than three days' notice.

Proceeding at meetings of the Council

6. The President whom failing the Vice-President shall preside at each meeting of the Council, but if both be not present the members present shall choose one of their number to preside. The person presiding shall be entitled to a second or casting vote.

7. No business shall be transacted at a meeting of the Council unless at least nine members are present.

8. The decision of the Chairman of a meeting of the Council on any question relating to procedure or order at the meeting shall be final.

9. So far as not inconsistent with these Rules, the Rules relating to the conduct of business shall be those applicable to the conduct of business at General Meetings of the Society as provided by the Constitution and Standing Orders of the Society.

10. Questions coming and arising before the Council shall be decided by a majority of the members present and voting at the meeting, except in so far as may be otherwise provided by Rule 15.

11. No business shall be transacted at a meeting of the Council other than that specified in the notice of the meeting or permitted by the Chairman as a matter of urgency.

12. The Council may adjourn a meeting of the Council to any other day, hour and place.

13. Notice by a member of Council of business which he wishes to be considered at a meeting of the Council shall be in writing and shall be deposited with the Secretary at least ten days before the date fixed for the meeting. Such business shall be included in the agenda for the meeting and intimated to the members.

14. A motion, the purport of which in the opinion of the Chairman of a meeting of the Council is to alter or rescind a resolution of the Council, shall not be competent within three months from the date of the passing of that resolution.

15. The provisions of Rules 13 and 14 may be suspended at a meeting of

the Council as regards any business at the meeting, provided the motion for suspension is supported by two-thirds of the members present and voting. Any motion for suspension of any such Rule must be seconded. It shall not be necessary to suspend any such provision with a view to adoption of an alteration of mere detail.

16. The Secretary shall keep or cause to be kept Minutes of Meetings of the Council recording (i) the names of members attending and (ii) all resolutions and proceedings at meetings of Council.

17. The Minute of each meeting of the Council shall be submitted to the following meeting of the Council. At each meeting of Council the Minutes of meetings of Committees held since the last meeting of Council shall be submitted for approval by the Council.

Rules for the Constitution of Committees of the Council and for the Conduct of Committee Business approved by the Council on September 23, 1988

Committees and their Constitution

1. The Council shall constitute such Committees and Sub-Committees as are necessary to fulfil the work of the Council and shall specify their remit, functions and duties.

2. The Council may delegate to Committees such powers and authority as it deems appropriate from time to time. Such delegated powers shall be set out in a Schedule which Council may change from time to time.

(1) The committees shall consist of such members of Council and/or such other persons as the Council may in each case appoint.

(2) The President and Vice-President shall *ex officiis* be members of all Committees.

Terms of Office of Members of Committees

3. Members of all Committees shall hold office until the day immediately before the day fixed by the Council for the annual election of members of Council, and the Council shall in each year at their first meeting after the annual election of members of Council appoint members to the various Committees.

Meetings of Committees

4.(1) Meetings of Committees shall be held as required, provided that in the case of the President's Committee it will meet at least once in each month, except in the month of August.

(2) The Committee Secretary shall call a meeting of a Committee at any time on being required to do so by the President or by the Convener of that Committee or on receiving a request in writing for that purpose specifying the business proposed to be transacted at the meeting signed by not less than one-fourth of the members of the Committee which meeting shall be held within ten days of the receipt of the request. Normally seven days written notice of a meeting will be given.

Conveners and Vice-Conveners of Committees

5. The President shall be Convener and the Vice-President Vice-Convener of the President's Committee and of the President's Sub-Committee. The Council shall, in the case of any other Committee, appoint a member of the Committee to be Convener thereof and if appropriate a further member to be Vice-Convener provided that the Council shall not normally appoint as Convener of a Committee a member of the Committee

who has already served for three consecutive years as Convener of that Committee, nor as Vice-Convener of a Committee a member who has already served for two consecutive years as Vice-Convener of the Committee.

Quorum of Committees
6. Three members or a majority of members or such other number as the Council may determine, shall be a quorum for meetings of Committees other than the President's Committee where five members shall constitute a quorum.

The Convener whom failing the Vice-Convener shall preside at each meeting of the Committee but if both be not present the members present shall choose one of their members to preside. The person presiding shall have a second or casting vote.

The decision of the Chairman of a meeting of a Committee on any question as to procedure or order of a meeting shall be final.

The Committee Secretary shall keep or cause to be kept Minutes of all meetings of Committees and Sub-Committees recording (i) the names of members attending and (ii) all resolutions, recommendations and proceedings.

So far as not inconsistent with these Rules the Rules relating to the conduct of business shall be those applicable to the conduct of business at General Meetings of the Society as provided by the Constitution and Standing Orders of the Society.

Standing Orders of The Law Society of Scotland

Standing Orders made by the Council of the Law Society of Scotland for the Conduct of Business at General Meetings of the Society in terms of Article 25 of the Constitution of the Society (as approved by the Council on September 23, 1988).

Interpretation
1.—(1) "the Act" means the Solicitors (Scotland) Act 1980; and other expressions used in these Orders shall have the same respective meanings as in the Constitution of the Society.

(2) The Interpretation Act 1978 applies to the interpretation of these Standing Orders as it applies to the interpretation of an Act of Parliament.

(3) These Standing Orders shall come into force on 1st November 1988.

CONDUCT OF BUSINESS AT GENERAL MEETINGS OF SOCIETY

Authority of the Chair
2. The decision of the Chairman of a General Meeting of the Society on any question relating to procedure or order at the meeting shall be final and conclusive.

Motions and Amendments at Meetings of Society
3.—(a) Every motion submitted to a General Meeting, except those relating to routine matters or the conduct or procedure of the meeting, shall be in writing and signed by the mover, who shall be a member, and shall relate to business specified in the notice calling the meeting.

(b) In the case of any motion, any member may propose—
    (i) an amendment of the motion by substitution, deletion and/or addition.
    (ii) the direct negative.
    (iii) that the debate be adjourned, or
    (iv) that the question be now put or that the meeting move to the next business.

(c) All proposals under 3(b)(i), (iii) and (iv) but not (ii) shall require a seconder.

(d) Movers of motions and of proposals under 3(b)(i), (ii) or (iii) shall be allowed five minutes to speak and other speakers shall be allowed three minutes. The Chairman may, at his discretion, allow a specified extension of time to any speaker.

(e) Without the permission of the Chairman, no member shall be entitled to speak more than once on any motion or on any proposal under 3(b)(i), (ii) or (iii) (unless on a point of order or information) except that movers of motions and of proposals under 3(b)(i), (ii) or (iii) may reply, and shall be allowed three minutes therefor. In replying, members shall confine themselves to answering previous speakers and shall not introduce new matter. Movers of motions shall have the opportunity of closing the debate.

(f) Proposers and seconders of a proposal, under 3(b)(iv) shall not be permitted initially to speak in support of the proposal. When the proposal has been proposed and seconded, the Chairman will ask the meeting whether any member wishes to move the direct negative and, if he does,

F 428/4

whether he has the support of one other member. If no member and supporting member wishes so to do, the proposal will be stated by the Chairman to have been carried unanimously. If the direct negative is moved and supported as aforesaid the proposer of the proposal will be allowed three minutes to speak to the proposal and the seconder two minutes to speak to it. The mover of the direct negative will be allowed three minutes to speak in support of the negative and the said supporting member two minutes to speak to it. No other member will be allowed to speak and, at the conclusion of the four speeches herein referred to, the proposal will forthwith be put to the meeting.

(*g*) Points of order shall be confined strictly to the conduct or procedure of the meeting.

(*h*) No motion or proposal may be withdrawn except with the concurrence of its seconder and, in the case of a motion, by permission of the meeting.

(*i*) No member shall unless with the permission of the Chairman move more than once that any one motion be amended.

Adjournment of General Meetings of the Society and suspension of standing orders
   4.—(*a*) The Chairman may with the consent of any General Meeting of the Society at which a quorum is present, and shall, if so instructed by the meeting, adjourn the meeting from time to time and from place to place, but no business shall be transacted at any adjourned meeting other than the business left unfinished at the meeting at which the adjournment took place. When a meeting is adjourned for more than 14 days, seven days' notice of the adjourned meeting shall be given to each member but, save as aforesaid, it shall not be necessary to give any notice of an adjournment. It shall not be necessary in any case to give notice of the business to be transacted at an adjourned meeting.

(*b*) At any General Meeting of the Society a motion to suspend standing orders may be made and may be spoken to only by the mover who shall be allowed five minutes for that purpose. Such a motion if seconded shall be put forthwith to the meeting and shall not be passed unless it be supported by two-thirds of the members voting thereon. Any such suspension shall relate to one item of business only, or shall be for a fixed period of time not extending beyond the conclusion of that General Meeting.

Minutes of General Meetings of the Society
   5.—(1) Minutes shall be kept by or on behalf of the Secretary recording—
   (*a*) the names and places of business of the members present at each meeting; and
   (*b*) all resolutions and proceedings at such meetings of the Society.
   (2) The minutes of each General Meeting of the Society shall be submitted to the following Annual General Meeting of the Society and if approved as a true record shall be signed by the Chairman of the meeting to which it relates or the Chairman of the meeting at which the minute is approved.

REPEAL OF STANDING ORDERS

   The Standing Orders approved by the Council on 26th September, 1980 are hereby repealed.

NOTE:
Procedure for consideration of draft Rules submitted in terms of section 34 or section 35 of the Act to a General Meeting of the Society

Draft Rules to be submitted to a General Meeting of the Society in terms of sections 34 or 35 of the Act shall be sent, wherever practicable, at least 28 days before the date of the General Meeting. Any member who wishes to submit proposals for amendments to such Rules to be considered at the General Meeting shall submit such amendments supported by six members of the Society to the Secretary not later than 14 days before said General Meeting and the Secretary shall send notice of such duly submitted and supported amendments to each member of the Society not later than 72 hours before the said General Meeting.

Scottish Solicitors' Discipline Tribunal Procedure Rules 1989

Rules made by the Scottish Solicitors' Discipline Tribunal with the concurrence of the Lord President of the Court of Session under section 52 of the Solicitors (Scotland) Act 1980

PART I

INTRODUCTORY

1.—(1) These rules may be cited as the Scottish Solicitors' Discipline Tribunal Procedure Rules 1989.

(2) The Interpretation Act, 1978, shall apply to the interpretation of these rules as it applies to the interpretation of an Act of Parliament.

PART II

COMPLAINTS AGAINST SOLICITORS

2.—(1) Save as hereinafter provided, any complaint against a solicitor or a former solicitor for professional misconduct or in respect of inadequate professional services or any complaint against an incorporated practice of failure to comply with any relevant statutory provisions or rules, shall be in writing under the hand of the complainer in the Form No. I set out in the Schedule annexed to these rules, and shall be sent to or lodged with the clerk to the Tribunal. Along with the complaint the complainer shall also send to or lodge with the clerk an affidavit by the complainer stating in concise numbered paragraphs the matters of fact on which he bases his complaint, and that the same to the best of his knowledge and belief are true, which affidavit shall be in the Form No. II set out in the said Schedule to these rules.

Where the complainer is the Council of the Law Society of Scotland (hereinafter referred to as "the Society") it shall not be necessary that the complaint be supported by an affidavit, but the complaint shall contain a statement setting forth in concise numbered paragraphs the matters of fact on which the Society base their complaint.

Where a solicitor or former solicitor in respect of whom a complaint of inadequate professional services is made was, at the time when the services were provided, an employee of another solicitor or solicitors, the instance of the complaint shall contain the name of that other solicitor or those other solicitors.

Where a complaint may result in an order affecting the Investment Business Certificate of a firm, the instance of the complaint shall contain the names of all the solicitors who are partners in that firm.

Where the respondent is an incorporated practice, the instance of the complaint shall contain the names of all the solicitors who are or at the time when the services were provided were members of that incorporated practice and any associated incorporated practice.

If a report is made to the Tribunal by the Lord Advocate or by any judge of the Court of Session or sheriff principal or sheriff or by the auditor of the Court of Session or of any sheriff court or the Scottish Legal Aid Board or the Lay Observer under section 51 of the Solicitors (Scotland) Act 1980 as amended ("the Act of 1980"), it shall not be necessary that such report be supported by an affidavit, and the report shall be dealt with as if it were a complaint and affidavit.

3. Where a complaint is made to the Tribunal by a person other than the Society or a person mentioned in section 51(3) of the Act of 1980, the Tribunal may remit the complaint to the Society whether or not the complaint is made in accordance with rule 2.

4. On receiving a complaint which in the opinion of the Tribunal is not made in accordance with rule 2, the Tribunal, if it thinks fit, may appoint a solicitor to represent the complainer, and the solicitor shall make a report thereon for the information of the Tribunal, who may, if they are of the opinion that further inquiry is necessary, instruct the solicitor for the complainer to formulate and lodge a complaint and affidavit by the complainer in terms of rule 2. The expenses of such solicitor, so far as not recoverable from the solicitor, or former solicitor, or incorporated practice complained against, shall be paid out of the funds of the Tribunal.

5. On receiving a complaint made, in the opinion of the Tribunal, in accordance with rule 2 the Tribunal shall consider the same, and they may from time to time and either before or after fixing a day for the hearing require the complainer to supply such further information and documents in support of the complaint as they think fit. In any case where, in the opinion of the Tribunal, no prima facie case against the solicitor, or former solicitor, or the incorporated practice and all solicitors whose names appear in the instance of the complaint is disclosed the Tribunal may, without further procedure and whether or not an opportunity to supply further information and documents may have been given to the complainer as aforesaid, make an order in writing dismissing the complaint.

6. If, in the opinion of the Tribunal, any complaint as originally lodged with the clerk to the Tribunal or as supplemented in accordance with the procedure in rule 5 discloses a prima facie case the Tribunal shall serve a full copy of the complaint and affidavit as lodged or of the complaint if made by the Society and (in the appropriate case) as supplemented and shall allow answers to be lodged within such time as the Tribunal may appoint. If answers are lodged, a full copy thereof shall be sent by the party lodging said answers to the complainer, and a certificate that this has been done shall be sent to the clerk of the Tribunal. On the expiry of the date appointed for lodging answers and whether answers have been lodged or not, the Tribunal may, if on considering the documents lodged they are of opinion that no further action by them is called for, make an order dismissing the complaint; but otherwise the Tribunal shall fix a day for hearing the complaint and shall serve a notice thereof on the complainer and on the solicitor, or former solicitor, or the incorporated practice and all solicitors whose names appear in the instance of the complaint. The day, time and place to be fixed for the hearing shall be in the discretion of the Tribunal, but parties concerned shall receive at least twenty-one days' notice thereof, unless all parties and the Tribunal agree to proceed on shorter notice.

7. The notice to be given to the parties under rule 6 may be in the Forms Nos. III, IV and V set out in the Schedule to these rules, and shall be sent by recorded delivery post to the solicitor or former solicitor or the incorporated practice and all solicitors whose names appear in the instance of the complaint and to the complainer at the respective addresses given in the complaint; said notice shall require the complainer and the respondents respectively to furnish to the clerk to the Tribunal and also each to the other a list of all documents on which they respectively propose to rely, and also a list of all witnesses whom they respectively propose to examine. Such lists shall, unless otherwise ordered by the Tribunal, be furnished by the complainer and by the respondents respectively in the case of lists of documents at least fourteen days, and in the case of lists of witnesses at least four days, before the day fixed for the hearing and so far as practicable each list of documents sent to the other party shall be accompanied by a copy of the documents referred to therein provided that if such lists are not furnished as aforesaid, the Tribunal at the hearing may have regard to any prejudice which may have been occasioned to the party not receiving the list or lists timeously.

8. Any party may inspect the documents contained in the list to be furnished by another party in terms of rule 7; the said documents shall be lodged with the clerk to the Tribunal at least ten days before the date fixed for the hearing. If any party desires production of any documents, he may not later than seven days before the date fixed for the hearing send a list of such documents to the other party with a request that the same shall be lodged forthwith. In the event of the other party declining or failing to comply with the said request, the party requiring production shall be entitled to apply for and to obtain from the Tribunal an order on the other party to produce the said documents, if after hearing the parties the Tribunal are of opinion that it is necessary for the proper consideration of the complaint that production should be made.

9. Each of the parties shall be in attendance and any incorporated practice shall be represented on the day and at the time and place fixed for the hearing and shall then be prepared to lead all competent evidence. If any party fails to appear or any incorporated practice fails to be represented at the hearing the Tribunal may, upon formal proof that the notice of the day fixed for the hearing has been duly posted to that party or incorporated practice as the case may be in terms of rule 7, proceed to hear and determine the complaint in the absence of the party who failed to appear or incorporated practice which has failed to be represented.

10. In any case in which the solicitor or former solicitor does not appear or any incorporated practice is not represented and the Tribunal under rule 9 determine to proceed in the absence of such solicitor or former solicitor or representative of an incorporated practice, as the case may be, and in any other case with the consent in writing of all the parties the Tribunal may, either as to the whole case or as to any particular fact or facts, proceed and act upon evidence given by affidavit.

11. The Tribunal shall announce their decision as soon as reasonably possible after the complaint has been considered by them. If the decision of the Tribunal is not pronounced on the day of hearing it shall not be necessary to hold a hearing for the purpose of announcing the decision, but whether such a hearing be held or not, a copy of the decision certified by the clerk to the Tribunal shall in accordance with the provisions of paragraph 15 of the Fourth Schedule to the Act of 1980 be sent forthwith to each party with an intimation of the right of appeal competent under the provisions of section 54 of the Act of 1980.

12. At any stage of the proceedings the Tribunal may, if they think fit, appoint a solicitor to represent the complainer, and the expenses of such solicitor, so far as not recoverable from the solicitor or former solicitor or any incorporated practice complained against, shall be paid out of the funds of the Tribunal.

Where any report is made to the Tribunal in pursuance of section 51 of the Act of 1980, the Tribunal, if they think fit, may appoint a solicitor to act as prosecutor in the complaint, and the expenses of such a solicitor, so far as not recoverable from the solicitor or former solicitor or any incorporated practice complained against, shall be paid out of the funds of the Tribunal.

13. No complaint shall be withdrawn after it has been received by the clerk to the Tribunal, except by the special leave of the Tribunal. Application for leave to withdraw shall be made not later than the day fixed for the hearing, unless the Tribunal otherwise direct. In granting leave to withdraw the Tribunal may attach such terms as to expenses or otherwise as they shall think fit.

PART III

CONVICTIONS

14. Where information is received by the Society from which it appears that a solicitor or former solicitor has, whether before or after enrolment, been convicted by any court of an act involving dishonesty, or sentenced to a term of imprisonment of not less than two years or an incorporated practice has been convicted by any court of an offence which may render it unsuitable to continue to be recognised under section 34(1A) of the Act of 1980, the Society shall as soon as may be, submit the information to the Tribunal so that they may take such action, if any, as they think proper under section 53(1)(*b*) of the Act of 1980.

15. The Tribunal shall cause to be sent to the solicitor, former solicitor or incorporated practice concerned particulars of the information submitted by the Society and shall invite the respondent to submit in writing to the Tribunal within such period as they may determine any explanations or observations which the respondent may wish to offer.

16. After the expiration of that period, whether such explanations or observations have been lodged or not, the Tribunal shall fix a date for the hearing of the case, and shall give not less than twenty-one days' notice thereof in writing to the respondent. The day, time and place of the hearing shall be in the discretion of the Tribunal.

17. The Tribunal shall announce their decision as soon as reasonably possible after the hearing. It shall not be necessary to hold a hearing for the purpose of announcing their decision. A copy of the decision certified by the clerk to the Tribunal shall in accordance with the provision of paragraph 15 of the Fourth Schedule to the Act of 1980 be sent forthwith to the respondent with an intimation of the right to appeal competent under the provisions of Section 54 of the Act of 1980.

PART IV

APPEALS BY SOLICITORS

18. Every appeal to the Tribunal shall be in writing in the Form No. VI set out in the Schedule annexed to these rules and shall be accompanied by a copy of the determination or direction appealed against, and shall be sent to or lodged with the clerk to the Tribunal within twenty-one days of the date on which the decision of the Society was sent to the appellant.

19. The respondents to an appeal shall be the Society and such other party, if any, who may have complained to the Society under section 42A(1)(*a*) of the Act of 1980.

20. On receiving a notice of appeal made, in the opinion of the Tribunal, in accordance with rule 18 the Tribunal shall consider the same, and they may from time to time and either before or after fixing a date for the hearing require the appellant to supply such further information and documents in support of the appeal as they think fit. In any case where in the opinion of the Tribunal the appeal is manifestly illfounded or if the appellant fails to comply with any of these rules, the Tribunal may, without further procedure and whether or not an opportunity to supply further information and documents may have been given to the appellant as aforesaid, make an order in writing dismissing the appeal.

21. If in the opinion of the Tribunal, any appeal as originally lodged with the clerk to the Tribunal or as supplemented does not fall to be dismissed under rule 20, the Tribunal shall serve upon each of the respondents a full copy of the statement of appeal and (in the appropriate case) as supplemented and shall allow answers to be lodged within such time as the Tribunal may appoint. In addition the Society shall lodge with the Tribunal all the documents which were before the Society in making their decision which is the subject of appeal. If answers are lodged, a full copy shall be sent by each respondent lodging answers to the appellant, and a certificate that this has been done shall be sent by such respondents to the clerk to the Tribunal. On the expiry of the date appointed for lodging answers and whether answers have been lodged or not, the Tribunal may, if on considering the documents lodged they are of the opinion that no further action by them is called for, make an order dismissing the appeal; but otherwise the Tribunal shall fix a date for hearing the appeal and shall serve a notice thereof on the appellant and on each respondent. The day, time and place to be fixed for the hearing shall be in the discretion of the Tribunal, but the parties concerned shall receive at least twenty-one days' notice thereof, unless all parties and the Tribunal agree to proceed on shorter notice.

22. The notices to be given to parties under Rule 21 may be in the Forms Nos. VII, VIII and IX set out in the Schedule to these rules and shall be sent by recorded delivery post to the appellant and to each of the respondents.

23. The Tribunal may on the application of a party or ex proprio motu require any party to produce any document within such period as the Tribunal may determine.

24. Each of the parties shall be in attendance on the day and at the time and place fixed for the hearing. If any party fails to appear at the hearing the Tribunal may, upon formal proof that the notice of the day fixed for the hearing has been duly posted to that party in terms of rule 21, proceed to hear and determine the appeal in the absence of that party.

25. The Tribunal shall announce their decision as soon as reasonably possible after the appeal has been considered by them. If the decision of the Tribunal is not pronounced on the day of hearing it shall not be necessary to hold a hearing for the purpose of announcing the decision but whether such a hearing be held or not, a copy of the decision certified by the clerk to the Tribunal shall, in accordance with the provisions of paragraph 15 of the Fourth Schedule to the Act of 1980 be sent forthwith to the appellant and each respondent with an intimation of the right of appeal competent under the provisions of section 54 of the Act of 1980.

26. No appeal shall be withdrawn after it has been received by the clerk to the Tribunal except by the special leave of the Tribunal. In granting leave to withdraw, the Tribunal may attach such terms as to expenses or otherwise as they shall think fit.

PART V

RESTORATION TO ROLL OF SOLICITORS

27. An application to the Tribunal for restoration to the Roll of Solicitors under section 10 of the Act of 1980 by a person who has been struck off the Roll by order of the Tribunal shall be in writing in the Form No. X set out in the Schedule to these rules and shall be verified by affidavit in the Form No. XI set out in the said Schedule. The application shall set forth the occupation or occupations of the applicant since his name was struck off the Roll. The application and affidavit shall be sent to or lodged with the clerk to the Tribunal and shall be supported by letters from two solicitors who at the date of application are in practice and who declare that they know the applicant.

28. The Tribunal may if they think fit, require the applicant to give notice by advertisement or otherwise as they may direct that application for restoration to the Roll has been made by the applicant and that the same will be disposed of by the Tribunal on a date appointed for the hearing.
If any person desires to object to the application he shall give notice in writing to the solicitor and to the clerk to the Tribunal at least ten days before the day fixed for the hearing, specifying the grounds of his objection. Styles of notice for such objection are in Form No. XII Nos. 1 and 2, set out in the Schedule to these rules.

29. The Tribunal shall afford to the applicant an opportunity of being heard by the Tribunal and of adducing evidence. The Tribunal may require such evidence as they think necessary concerning the identity and character of the applicant, his conduct since his name was struck off the Roll and his suitability for restoration to the Roll and for this purpose may receive written or oral evidence.

30. If the objector appears on the day fixed for the hearing and if the Tribunal are of opinion, after considering the notice of objection and after hearing the solicitor (if they think fit to do so) that the notice discloses a prima facie case for inquiry, the Tribunal shall afford to the objector an opportunity of being heard by the Tribunal and of adducing evidence.

31. Subject to the foregoing provisions, the procedure of the Tribunal in connection with applications for restoration to the Roll shall be such as the Tribunal may determine.

32. A copy of the decision of the Tribunal in the application, certified by the clerk to the Tribunal shall, in accordance with the provision of paragraph 15 of the Fourth Schedule to the Act of 1980, be sent forthwith to the applicant with an intimation of the right of appeal competent under the provisions of section 54 of that Act.

33. In all cases in which the final decision whether by the Tribunal or by the court is to order restoration to the Roll, such decision shall be intimated to the Registrar of Solicitors who shall forthwith give effect thereto.

34. An applicant shall as a condition of having his name restored to the Roll of Solicitors pay to the Registrar of Solicitors where the name of the applicant was struck off the Roll by Order of the Discipline Tribunal a fee of £100 or such other sum as may be fixed from time to time by the Tribunal.

PART VI

GENERAL

35. The Tribunal may hear all proceedings in public or in private as they think fit and may pronounce their decision in public or in private as they think fit.

36. The Tribunal may of their own motion, or upon the application of any party, adjourn the hearing upon such terms as to expenses or otherwise, as to the Tribunal shall appear just.

37. If, upon a hearing, it shall appear to the Tribunal that the allegation contained in an affidavit, statement or report should be amended or added to, the Tribunal may permit such amendment or addition, and they may also require the same to be embodied in a further affidavit, statement or report, if in the judgment of the Tribunal such amendment or addition is not within the scope of the original affidavit, statement or report, provided always that if, in consequence of such amendment or addition, any party applies for an adjournment, the Tribunal may at their discretion grant an adjournment of the hearing, upon such terms as to the Tribunal shall appear just. On the application of any party, or ex proprio motu, the Tribunal shall order the attendance for cross-examination of the person making the affidavit. Upon a hearing, the Tribunal may permit an appellant to amend his statement of appeal or a respondent to amend or withdraw his answers, provided always that if in consequence of such amendment or withdrawal any party applies for an adjournment the Tribunal may at their discretion grant an adjournment of the hearing, upon such terms as to the Tribunal shall appear just.

38. Shorthand notes of proceedings before the Tribunal may be taken by a shorthand writer appointed by the Tribunal; the notes may be transcribed if the Tribunal think fit, and if transcribed any party to the proceedings shall be entitled to inspect the transcript thereof. The shorthand writer shall, if required, supply to the Tribunal and to any person entitled to be heard upon an appeal against a decision of the Tribunal, but to no other person, a copy of the transcript if made, on payment of his charges. If no shorthand notes be taken, the Chairman shall take note of the proceedings, and the provisions of this rule as to inspection and taking copies shall apply to such note accordingly.

39. The Tribunal may from time to time dispense with any requirements of these rules respecting notices, affidavits, documents, service or time, where it appears to the Tribunal to be just to do so.

40. The Tribunal may extend, and with consent of parties may at their discretion reduce, the time for doing anything under these rules.

41. All complaints, reports, affidavits and statements of appeal shall be filed by the clerk to the Tribunal. The Tribunal may order that any books, papers or other exhibits produced or used at a hearing before them shall be retained by the clerk to the Tribunal until the time for appealing has expired, or if notice of appeal is given, until the appeal is heard or otherwise disposed of.

42. All Orders, determinations, directions and decisions of the Tribunal shall be signed on behalf of the Tribunal by their Chairman or other member presiding and a copy of such orders or decisions purporting to be signed by the Chairman or other presiding member shall be prima facie evidence of the due making thereof.

43. The Scottish Solicitors Discipline Tribunal Procedure Rules, 1981 are hereby revoked without prejudice to any order, reference or appointment made or instruction given or finding pronounced or other thing done thereunder and such order, reference, appointment, instruction, finding or other thing so far as the same could have been made, given, pronounced or done under these rules shall have effect as if made, given, pronounced or done under these rules.

SCHEDULE

Form 1

Form of Complaint

To the Scottish Solicitors' Discipline Tribunal, constituted under the Solicitors (Scotland) Act, 1980

COMPLAINT by A.B. against C.D.

I, the undersigned A.B. hereby request that C.D. of
                be required to answer the allegations contained in the affidavit which accompanies this application, and that the Tribunal issue such Order under section 53 of the Solicitors (Scotland) Act, 1980, in the matter as they may think right.

Dated...

....*Signature*

....*Address*

....*Designation*

Form II

Form of Affidavit by Complainer

At   the   day of   in presence of   , one of Her Majesty's Justices of the Peace for   , compeared A.B. of   , who being solemnly sworn and interrogated, depones as follows, viz.:—

1. C.D.   has been employed by him in a professional capacity for the last ten years (or as the case may be).

2. (*Here state the facts concisely in numbered paragraphs, and show the Deponent's means of knowledge.*)

All which is truth as the Deponent shall answer to God.

FORM III

Notice of Complaint

COMPLAINT by A.B. against C.D.

To C.D. of

TAKE NOTICE that a complaint has been made by A.B. of   to the Scottish Solicitors' Discipline Tribunal, constituted under the Solicitors (Scotland) Act 1980, requesting that you be required to answer the allegations contained in the affidavit whereof a copy accompanies this notice, and that the Tribunal may issue such Order under section 53 of the Solicitors (Scotland) Act, 1980, in the matter as they think right.

    The Tribunal have appointed that answers to the complaint shall be lodged with the Clerk at within   days from the date hereof, and that a copy of such answers shall, at the same time, be intimated to

                         Dated this   day of   19   .

                                    ....
                                     Clerk to the Tribunal

    (*N.B.*—A print of the Rules made under the said Act is sent herewith for your information and guidance.)

FORM IV

Notice to Respondent of Date Fixed for the Hearing

COMPLAINT by A.B. against C.D.

To C.D. of

TAKE NOTICE that the Scottish Solicitors' Discipline Tribunal have fixed the   day of   at   noon within   for the hearing of this complaint, and if you fail then to appear the Tribunal may in accordance with the Rules made under the Solicitors (Scotland) Act, 1980, proceed in your absence.

    You are required by the said Rules to furnish to the said A.B. and to the Clerk to the Tribunal at   at least fourteen days before the said   day of   , a list of all the documents on which you propose to rely. So far as practicable said list of documents sent to A.B. shall be accompanied by a copy of the documents referred to therein. Under the said Rules the said A.B. is also required to furnish you with a list of documents on which he proposes to rely. The said documents must be lodged with the Clerk to the Tribunal at least ten days before the date fixed for the hearing.

    Either party may inspect the documents included in the list furnished by the other.

    If either party desires productions of any documents he may, not later than seven days before the date fixed for the hearing, send a list of such documents to the other party with a request that the same shall be lodged forthwith. In the event of the other party declining or failing to comply with the said request, the party requiring production shall be entitled to apply for and to obtain from the Tribunal an order on the other party to produce the said documents, if after hearing the parties the Tribunal is of the opinion that it is necessary for the proper consideration of the complaint that production should be made.

Dated this   day of   19   .

....
Clerk to the Tribunal

Form V

Notice to the Complainer of the Date Fixed for the Hearing

To A.B. of

TAKE NOTICE that answers to your complaint have been lodged by C.D. (if such is that case) and that the   day of   has been fixed by the Scottish Solicitors' Discipline Tribunal for the hearing of your complaint against C.D., Solicitor. The Tribunal will sit at   at   o'clock in the   noon.

You are required by the Rules made under the Solicitors (Scotland) Act, 1980, to furnish to the said C.D. and to the Clerk to the Tribunal at   at least fourteen days before the said   ·   day of   a list of all the documents on which you propose to rely, and at least four days before the said date a list of the witnesses whom you propose to examine. So far as practicable said list of documents sent to C.D. shall be accompanied by a copy of the documents referred to therein. The said documents must be lodged with the Clerk to the Tribunal at least ten days before the date fixed for the hearing. Under the Rules of the Tribunal the said C.D. is also required to furnish, within the said respective periods, a list of the documents (if any) on which he proposes to rely, and a list of the witnesses (if any) whom he proposes to examine.

Either party may inspect the documents included in the list furnished by the other. If either party desires production of any documents he may not later than seven days before the date fixed for the hearing send a list of such documents to the other party with a request that the same shall be lodged forthwith. In the event of the other party declining or failing to comply with the said request, the party requiring production shall be entitled to apply for and to obtain from the Tribunal an order on the other party to produce the said documents, if after hearing the parties the Tribunal is of opinion that it is necessary for the proper consideration of the complaint that production should be made.

In the event of a party complained of not appearing or any incorporated practice complained of not being represented, and of the Tribunal being asked to proceed in the absence of such party or representation of any incorporated practice you must be prepared to prove that any notice on which you rely was duly served on that party or incorporated practice as the case may be in accordance with the Rules issued under the said Act.

Dated this   day of   19   .

....
Clerk to the Tribunal

(*N.B.*—A print of the Rules is sent herewith for your information and guidance.)

Form VI

Form of Appeal to the Tribunal

To the Scottish Solicitors' Discipline Tribunal constituted under the Solicitors (Scotland) Act 1980

APPEAL by A.B. against a determination/direction/
order of the Council of the Law Society of Scotland
dated

I, the undersigned A.B., hereby appeal against the determination/direction/order of the Council of the Law Society of Scotland dated   and intimated to me on   a copy of which is produced herewith.

The grounds of my appeal are as follows (*here state concisely in numbered paragraphs, the grounds of the appeal*).

I hereby request the Tribunal (*here state the Order which you wish the Tribunal to pronounce in your favour*).

[*Release 17: 26 - v - 89.*]

In the consideration of the matter by the Council of the Law Society, the complainer was (*name and address of the party or parties whose complaint to the Law Society resulted in the decision appealed against.*)

Dated...

.... *Signature*

.... { *Address and place or places of business*

FORM VII

Form of Intimation of Appeal

APPEAL by A.B. against a determination/direction/
order of the Council of the Law Society of Scotland
dated

To: *The Secretary*
The Law Society of Scotland

    or

    C.D. of

TAKE NOTICE that an appeal has been lodged with the Scottish Solicitors' Discipline Tribunal by A.B. against a determination/direction/order of the Council of the Law Society of Scotland dated   . A copy of the statement of appeal accompanies this notice.
  The Tribunal have appointed that answers to the statement of appeal shall be lodged with the Clerk at   within   days from the date hereof, and that a copy of such answers shall, at the same time, be intimated to

Dated this   day of   19   .

....
Clerk to the Tribunal

  (*N.B.*—A print of the Rules made under the said Act is sent herewith for your information and guidance.)

FORM VIII

Form of Notice to an Appellant of Date Fixed for the Hearing of an Appeal
To A.B. of

TAKE NOTICE that answers to your statement of appeal have been lodged by   and   and that the   day of   has been fixed for the hearing of your appeal. The Tribunal will sit at   at   'clock in the   noon, and if you fail then to appear the Tribunal may in accordance with the Rules made under the Solicitors (Scotland) Act 1980 proceed in your absence.
You are required by the said rules to furnish to   and to   and to the Clerk to the Tribunal at   at least fourteen days before the said   day of   a list of all the documents on which you propose to rely. The said documents must be lodged with the Clerk to the Tribunal at least seven days before the date fixed for the hearing.

Dated this   day of   19   .

....
Clerk to the Tribunal

[*Release 17: 26 - v - 89.*]

FORM IX

Form of Notice to the Respondent of Date Fixed for the Hearing of an Appeal

APPEAL by   against a determination/direction/
order of the Council of the Law Society of Scotland
dated

TAKE NOTICE that the Scottish Solicitors' Discipline Tribunal have fixed the
day of   at   noon within   for the hearing of
this appeal, and if you fail then to appear, the Tribunal may in accordance with the Rules made
under the Solicitors (Scotland) Act 1980 proceed in your absence.

You are required by the said Rules to furnish to   and to   and to the
Clerk to the Tribunal at   at least fourteen days before the said   day
of   a list of all the documents on which you propose to rely. The said documents
must be lodged with the Clerk to the Tribunal at least seven days before the date fixed for the
hearing.

Dated this   day of   19   .

....
Clerk to the Tribunal

FORM X

Form of Application by a Solicitor for Restoration to Roll of Solicitors

To the Scottish Solicitors' Discipline Tribunal constituted under the Solicitors (Scotland) Act 1980.

1. I, the undersigned A.B. hereby apply to the Discipline Tribunal under Section 10 of the
Solicitors (Scotland) Act, 1980, for an order restoring my name to the Roll of Solicitors.

2. I was admitted a Solicitor on the   day of   19   .

3. On   19   , I was struck off the Roll of Solicitors by order of the Discipline
Committee/Tribunal.

4. Since then my occupations have been as follows:—

(*Here specify in the case of each employment the name and address of the employer, the nature
of the work on which the applicant was employed and the period of employment.*)

5. The following persons are prepared on request to testify to the Discipline Tribunal
concerning my identity and character, my conduct since my name was struck off from the Roll
and my suitability for restoration to the Roll.
(*Here state the names and addresses of the persons prepared to testify.*)

.... *Signature*

.... *Address*

FORM XI

Form of Affidavit by Applicant for Restoration to Roll of Solicitors

At   the   day of   in presence of   , one of Her
Majesty's Justices of the Peace for   compeared A.B. of   who being
solemnly sworn and interrogated, depones as follows, viz.:—

1. The Deponent was admitted as a Solicitor on the   day of   19   ,
and on the   day of 19   , was struck off the Roll of Solicitors by order of the
Solicitors' Discipline (Scotland) Committee/the Scottish Solicitors' Discipline Tribunal.

2. The particulars of his occupations since then as set forth in the application for restoration to the Roll now produced, and marked "A", are true.

3. The Deponent is not aware and does not know of any cause of complaint or proceedings which might have arisen out of his conduct since his name was struck off the Roll.

All which is truth as the Deponent shall answer to God.

FORM XII

Forms of Notice of Objection to an Application by a Solicitor for the Restoration of his Name to the Roll of Solicitors

No. 1

FORM OF NOTICE TO BE GIVEN TO THE SOLICITOR

To C.D. of   , Solicitor.

TAKE NOTICE that I object to the application made by you to the Scottish Solicitors' Discipline Tribunal for restoration of your name to the Roll of Solicitors, on the following grounds viz.:—

(The grounds of objection to be stated in articulate numbered paragraphs.)

Dated ....

.... *Signature*

.... *Address*

.... *Designation*

No. 2

FORM OF NOTICE TO BE GIVEN TO THE TRIBUNAL

To the Scottish Solicitors' Discipline Tribunal.

TAKE NOTICE that I object to the application made by C.D. of   to the Scottish Solicitors' Discipline Tribunal for restoration of his name to the Roll of Solicitors, on the following grounds, viz.:—

(The grounds of objection to be stated in articulate numbered paragraphs.)

Dated ....

.... *Signature*

.... *Address*

.... *Designation*

[THE NEXT PAGE IS F 453]

Solicitors (Scotland) (Cross-border Code of Conduct) Practice Rules 1989

Rules dated 29th September 1989, made by the Council of the Law Society of Scotland and approved by the Lord President of the Court of Session in terms of section 34 of the Solicitors (Scotland) Act 1980.

Citation and commencement
1. These rules may be cited as the Solicitors (Scotland) (Cross-border Code of Conduct) Practice Rules 1989 and shall come into force on 16th October 1989.

Interpretation
2. In these rules, unless the context otherwise requires:—
"the Code" means the Code of Conduct for lawyers in the European Community adopted by the Bars and Law Societies of the European Community on 28th October 1988 and reproduced as the Schedule to these rules;
"the Act" means the Solicitors (Scotland) Act 1980 as amended;
"solicitor" means a solicitor holding a practising certificate under the Act and includes a firm of solicitors and an incorporated practice;
"Council" means the Council of the Society;
"the Society" means the Law Society of Scotland, established under the Act;
"cross-border practice" means:
(a) all professional contacts with lawyers of Member States of the European Community other than the United Kingdom; and
(b) the professional activities of a solicitor in a Member State of the European Community other than the United Kingdom, whether or not the solicitor is physically present in that Member State.

3. The Interpretation Act 1978 applies to the interpretation of these rules as it applies to the interpretation of an Act of Parliament.

4. A solicitor conducting cross-border practice shall observe and be bound by the terms of the Code at all times.

5. The Council shall have power to waive or modify any of the provisions of these rules as they apply to a solicitor in any particular case.

6. Breach of these rules may be treated as professional misconduct for the purposes of Part IV of the Act (Complaints and Disciplinary Proceedings).

SCHEDULE

CODE OF CONDUCT FOR LAWYERS IN THE EUROPEAN COMMUNITY ADOPTED BY THE BARS AND LAW SOCIETIES OF THE EUROPEAN COMMUNITY ON 28TH OCTOBER 1988

CONTENTS

1. PREAMBLE

[THE NEXT PAGE IS F 455]

1. PREAMBLE

1.1. The function of the lawyer in society

In a society founded on respect for the rule of law the lawyer fulfils a special role. His duties do not begin and end with the faithful performance of what he is instructed to do so far as the law permits. A lawyer must serve the interests of justice as well as those whose rights and liberties he is trusted to assert and defend and it is his duty not only to plead his client's cause but to be his adviser.

A lawyer's function therefore lays on him a variety of legal and moral obligations (sometimes appearing to be in conflict with each other) towards:

the client;

the courts and other authorities before whom the lawyer pleads his client's cause or acts on his behalf;

the legal profession in general and each fellow member of it in particular; and

the public for whom the existence of a free and independent profession, bound together by respect for rules made by the profession itself, is an essential means of safeguarding human rights in face of the power of the state and other interests in society.

1.2. The nature of rules of professional conduct

1.2.1. Rules of professional conduct are designed through their willing acceptance by those to whom they apply to ensure the proper performance by the lawyer of a function which is recognised as essential in all civilised societies. The failure of the lawyer to observe these rules must in the last resort result in a disciplinary sanction.

1.2.2. The particular rules of each Bar or Law Society arise from its own traditions. They are adapted to the organisation and sphere of activity of the profession in the Member State concerned and to its judicial and administrative procedures and to its national legislation. It is neither possible nor desirable that they should be taken out of their context nor that an attempt should be made to give general application to rules which are inherently incapable of such application.

The particular rules of each Bar and Law Society nevertheless are based on the same values and in most cases demonstrate a common foundation.

1.3. The purpose of the common code

1.3.1. The continued integration of the European Community and the increasing frequency of the cross border activities of lawyers within the Community have made necessary in the public interest the statement of common rules which apply to all lawyers from the Community whatever Bar or Law Society they belong to in relation to their cross border practice. A particular purpose of the statement of those rules is to mitigate the difficulties which result from the application of "double deontology" as set out in article 4 of the E.C. Directive 77/249 of 22nd March 1977.

1.3.2. The organisations representing the legal profession through the CCBE propose that the rules codified in the following articles:

> be recognised at the present time as the expression of a consensus of all the Bars and Law Societies of the European Community;
>
> be adopted as enforceable rules as soon as possible in accordance with national or Community procedures in relation to the cross border activities of the lawyer in the European Community;
>
> be taken into account in all revisions of national rules of deontology or professional practice with a view to their progressive harmonisation.

They further express the wish that the national rules of deontology or professional practice be interpreted and applied whenever possible in a way consistent with the rules in this code.

After the rules in this code have been adopted as enforceable rules in relation to his cross border activities the lawyer will remain bound to observe the rules of the Bar or Law Society to which he belongs to the extent that they are consistent with the rules in this code.

1.4. Field of application ratione personae

The following rules shall apply to lawyers of the European Community as they are defined by the Directive 77/249 of 22nd March 1977.

1.5. Field of application ratione materiae

Without prejudice to the pursuit of a progressive harmonisation of rules of deontology or professional practice which apply only internally within a Member State, the following rules shall apply to the cross border activities of the lawyer within the European Community. Cross border activities shall mean:

> (*a*) all professional contacts with lawyers of Member States other than his own; and
> (*b*) the professional activities of the lawyer in a Member State other than his own, whether or not the lawyer is physically present in that Member State.

1.6. Definitions

In these rules:

> "home Member State" means the Member State of the Bar or Law Society to which the lawyer belongs;
>
> "host Member State" means any other Member State where the lawyer carries on cross border activities;
>
> "competent authority" means the professional organisation(s) or authority(ies) of the Member State concerned responsible for the laying down of rules of professional conduct and the administration of discipline of lawyers.

2. GENERAL PRINCIPLES

2.1. Independence

2.1.1. The many duties to which a lawyer is subject require his absolute independence, free from all other influence, especially such as may arise from his personal interests or external pressure. Such independence is as necessary to trust in the process of justice as the impartiality of the judge. A lawyer must therefore avoid any impairment of his independence and be careful not to compromise his professional standards in order to please his client, the court or third parties.

2.1.2. This independence is necessary in non-contentious matters as well as in litigation. Advice given by a lawyer to his client has no value if it is given only to ingratiate himself, to serve his personal interests or in response to outside pressure.

2.2. Trust and personal integrity

Relationships of trust can only exist if a lawyer's personal honour, honesty and integrity are beyond doubt. For the lawyer these traditional virtues are professional obligations.

2.3. Confidentiality

2.3.1. It is of the essence of a lawyer's function that he should be told by his client things which the client would not tell to others, and that he should be the recipient of other information on a basis of confidence. Without the certainty of confidentiality there cannot be trust. Confidentiality is therefore a primary and fundamental right and duty of the lawyer.

2.3.2. A lawyer shall accordingly respect the confidentiality of all information given to him by his client, or received by him about his client or others in the course of rendering services to his client.

2.3.3. The obligation of confidentiality is not limited in time.

2.3.4. A lawyer shall require his associates and staff and anyone engaged by him in the course of providing professional services to observe the same obligation of confidentiality.

2.4. Respect for the rules of other Bars and Law Societies

Under Community law (in particular under the Directive 77/249 of 22nd March 1977) a lawyer from another Member State may be bound to comply with the rules of the Bar or Law Society of the host Member State. Lawyers have a duty to inform themselves as to the rules which will affect them in the performance of any particular activity.

2.5. Incompatible occupations

2.5.1. In order to perform his functions with due independence and in a manner which is consistent with his duty to participate in the administration of justice a lawyer is excluded from some occupations.

2.5.2. A lawyer who acts in the representation or the defence of a client in legal proceedings or before any public authorities in a host Member State shall there observe the rules regarding incompatible occupations as they are applied to lawyers of the host Member State.

2.5.3. A lawyer established in a host Member State in which he wishes to participate directly in commercial or other activities not connected with the practice of the law shall respect the rules regarding forbidden or incompatible occupations as they are applied to lawyers of that Member State.

2.6. Personal publicity

2.6.1. A lawyer should not advertise or seek personal publicity where this is not permitted. In other cases a lawyer should only advertise or seek personal publicity to the extent and in the manner permitted by the rules to which he is subject.

2.6.2. Advertising and personal publicity shall be regarded as taking place where it is permitted, if the lawyer concerned shows that it was placed for the purpose of reaching clients or potential clients located where such advertising or personal publicity is permitted and its communication elsewhere is incidental.

2.7. The client's interests

Subject to due observance of all rules of law and professional conduct, a lawyer must always act in the best interests of his client and must put those interests before his own interests or those of fellow members of the legal profession.

3. RELATIONS WITH CLIENTS

3.1. Acceptance and termination of instructions

3.1.1. A lawyer shall not handle a case for a party except on his instructions. He may, however, act in a case in which he has been instructed by another lawyer who himself acts for the party or where the case has been assigned to him by a competent body.

3.1.2. A lawyer shall advise and represent his client promptly, conscientiously and diligently. He shall undertake personal responsibility for the discharge of the instructions given to him. He shall keep his client informed as to the progress of the matter entrusted to him.

3.1.3. A lawyer shall not handle a matter which he knows or ought to know he is not competent to handle, without co-operating with a lawyer who is competent to handle it.
A lawyer shall not accept instructions unless he can discharge those instructions promptly having regard to the pressure of other work.

3.1.4. A lawyer shall not be entitled to exercise his right to withdraw from a case in such a way or in such circumstances that the client may be unable to find other legal assistance in time to prevent prejudice being suffered by the client.

3.2. Conflict of interest

3.2.1. A lawyer may not advise, represent or act on behalf of two or more clients in the same matter if there is a conflict, or a significant risk of a conflict, between the interests of those clients.

3.2.2. A lawyer must cease to act for both clients when a conflict of interests arises between those clients and also whenever there is a risk of a breach of confidence or where his independence may be impaired.

3.2.3. A lawyer must also refrain from acting for a new client if there is a risk of a breach of confidences entrusted to the lawyer by a former client or if the knowledge which the lawyer possesses of the affairs of the former client would give an undue advantage to the new client.

3.2.4. Where lawyers are practising in association, paragraphs 3.2.1 to 3.2.3 above shall apply to the association and all its members.

3.3. Pactum de quota litis

3.3.1. A lawyer shall not be entitled to make a *pactum de quota litis.*

3.3.2. By "*pactum de quota litis*" is meant an agreement between a lawyer and his client entered into prior to the final conclusion of a matter to which the client is a party, by virtue of which the client undertakes to pay the lawyer a share of the result regardless of whether this is represented by a sum of money or by any other benefit achieved by the client upon the conclusion of the matter.

3.3.3. The *pactum de quota litis* does not include an agreement that fees be charged in proportion to the value of a matter handled by the lawyer if this is in accordance with an officially approved fee scale or under the control of the competent authority having jurisdiction over the lawyer.

3.4. Regulation of fees

3.4.1. A fee charged by a lawyer shall be fully disclosed to his client and shall be fair and reasonable.

3.4.2. Subject to any proper agreement to the contrary between a lawyer and his client fees charged by a lawyer shall be subject to regulation in accordance with the rules applied to members of the Bar or Law Society to which he belongs. If he belongs to more than one Bar or Law Society the rules applied shall be those with the closest connection to the contract between the lawyer and his client.

3.5. Payment on account

If a lawyer requires a payment on account of his fees and/or disbursements such payment should not exceed a reasonable estimate of the fees and probable disbursements involved. Failing such payment, a lawyer may withdraw from the case or refuse to handle it, but subject always to paragraph 3.1.4 above.

3.6. Fee sharing with non-lawyers

3.6.1. Subject as aftermentioned a lawyer may not share his fees with a person who is not a lawyer.

3.6.2. The provisions of paragraph 3.6.1 above shall not preclude a lawyer from paying a fee, commission or other compensation to a deceased lawyer's heirs or to a retired lawyer in respect of taking over the deceased or retired lawyer's practice.

3.7. Legal aid

A lawyer shall inform his client of the availability of legal aid where applicable.

3.8. Clients' funds

3.8.1. When lawyers at any time in the course of their practice come into possession of funds on behalf of their clients or third parties (hereinafter called "clients' funds") it shall be obligatory:

> **3.8.1.1.** That clients' funds shall always be held in an account in a bank or similar institution subject to supervision of public authority and that all clients' funds received by a lawyer should be paid into such an account unless the client explicitly or by implication agrees that the funds should be dealt with otherwise.

> **3.8.1.2.** That any account in which the clients' funds are held in the name of the lawyer should indicate in the title or designation that the funds are held on behalf of the client or clients of the lawyer.

> **3.8.1.3.** That any account or accounts in which clients' funds are held in the name of the lawyer should at all times contain a sum which is not less than the total of the clients' funds held by the lawyer.

> **3.8.1.4.** That all clients' funds should be available for payment to clients on demand or upon such conditions as the client may authorise.

> **3.8.1.5.** That payments made from clients' funds on behalf of a client to any other person, including (a) payments made to or for one client from funds held for another client, and (b) payment of the lawyer's fees, be prohibited except to the extent that they are permitted by law or have the express or implied authority of the client for whom the payment is being made.

> **3.8.1.6.** That the lawyer shall maintain full and accurate records, available to each client on request, showing all his dealings with his clients' funds and distinguishing clients' funds from other funds held by him.

> **3.8.1.7.** That the competent authorities in all Member States should have powers to allow them to examine and investigate on a confidential basis the financial records of lawyers' clients' funds to ascertain whether or not the rules which they make are being complied with and to impose sanctions upon lawyers who fail to comply with those rules.

3.8.2. Subject as aftermentioned, and without prejudice to the rules set out in 3.8.1 above, a lawyer who holds clients' funds in the course of carrying on practice in any Member State must comply with the rules relating to holding and accounting for clients' funds which are applied by the competent authorities of the home Member State.

3.8.3. A lawyer who carries on practice or provides services in a host Member State may with the agreement of the competent authorities of the home and host Member States concerned comply with the requirements of the host Member State to the exclusion of the requirements of the home Member State. In that event he shall take reasonable steps to inform his clients that he complies with the requirements in force in the host Member State.

3.9. Professional indemnity insurance

3.9.1. Lawyers shall be insured at all times against claims based on professional negligence to an extent which is reasonable having regard to the nature and extent of the risks which lawyers incur in practice.

3.9.2.

3.9.2.1. Subject as aftermentioned, a lawyer who provides services or carries on practice in a Member State must comply with any rules relating to his obligation to insure against his professional liability as a lawyer which are in force in his home Member State.

3.9.2.2. A lawyer who is obliged so to insure in his home Member State and who provides services or carries on practice in any host Member State shall use his best endeavours to obtain insurance cover on the basis required in his home Member State extended to services which he provides or practice which he carries on in a host Member State.

3.9.2.3. A lawyer who fails to obtain the extended insurance cover referred to in paragraph 3.9.2.2 above or who is not obliged so to insure in his home Member State and who provides services or carries on practice in a host Member State shall in so far as possible obtain insurance cover against his professional liability as a lawyer whilst acting for clients in that host Member State on at least an equivalent basis to that required of lawyers in the host Member State.

3.9.2.4. To the extent that a lawyer is unable to obtain the insurance cover required by the foregoing rules, he shall take reasonable steps to draw that fact to the attention of such of his clients as might be affected in the event of a claim against him.

3.9.2.5. A lawyer who carries on practice or provides services in a host Member State may with the agreement of the competent authorities of the home and host Member States concerned comply with such insurance requirements as are in force in the host Member State to the exclusion of the insurance requirements of the home Member State. In this event he shall take reasonable steps to inform his clients that he is insured according to the requirements in force in the host Member State.

4. RELATIONS WITH THE COURT

4.1. Applicable rules of conduct in court

A lawyer who appears, or takes part in a case, before a court or tribunal in a Member State must comply with the rules of conduct applied before that court or tribunal.

4.2. Fair conduct of proceedings

A lawyer must always have due regard for the fair conduct of proceedings. He must not, for example, make contact with the judge without first informing the lawyer acting for the opposing party or submit exhibits, notes or documents to the judge without communicating them in good time to the lawyer on the other side unless such steps are permitted under the relevant rules of procedure.

4.3. Demeanour in court

A lawyer shall while maintaining due respect and courtesy towards the court defend the interests of his client honourably and in a way which he considers wil be to the client's best advantage within the limits of the law.

4.4. False or misleading information

A lawyer shall never knowingly give false or misleading information to the court.

4.5. Extension to arbitrators etc.

The rules governing a lawyer's relations with the courts apply also to his relations with arbitrators and any other persons exercising judicial or quasi-judicial functions, even on an occasional basis.

5. RELATIONS BETWEEN LAWYERS

5.1. Corporate spirit of the profession

5.1.1. The corporate spirit of the profession requires a relationship of trust and co-operation between lawyers for the benefit of their clients and in order to avoid unnecessary litigation. It can never justify setting the interests of the profession against those of justice or of those who seek it.

5.1.2. A lawyer should recognise all other lawyers of Member States as professional colleagues and act fairly and courteously towards them.

5.2. Co-operation among lawyers of different Member States

5.2.1. It is the duty of a lawyer who is approached by a colleague from another Member State not to accept instructions in a matter which he is not competent to undertake. He should be prepared to help his colleague to obtain the information necessary to enable him to instruct a lawyer who is capable of providing the service asked for.

5.2.2. Where a lawyer of a Member State co-operates with a lawyer from another Member State, both have a general duty to take into account the differences which may exist between their respective legal systems and the professional organisations, competences and obligations of lawyers in the Member States concerned.

5.3. Correspondence between lawyers

5.3.1. If a lawyer sending a communication to a lawyer in another Member State wishes it to remain confidential or without prejudice he should clearly express this intention when communicating the document.

5.3.2. If the recipient of the communication is unable to ensure its status as confidential or without prejudice he should return it to the sender without revealing the contents to others.

5.4. Referral fees

5.4.1. A lawyer may not demand or accept from another lawyer or any other person a fee, commission or any other compensation for referring or recommending a client.

5.4.2. A lawyer may not pay anyone a fee, commission or any other compensation as a consideration for referring a client to himself.

5.5. Communication with opposing parties

A lawyer shall not communicate about a particular case or matter directly with any person whom he knows to be represented or advised in the case or matter by another lawyer, without the consent of that other lawyer (and shall keep the other lawyer informed of any such communications).

5.6. Change of lawyer

5.6.1. A lawyer who is instructed to represent a client in substitution for another lawyer in relation to a particular matter should inform that other lawyer and, subject to 5.6.2 below, should not begin to act until he has ascertained that arrangements have been made for the settlement of the other lawyer's fees and disbursements. This duty does not, however, make the new lawyer personally responsible for the former lawyer's fees and disbursements.

5.6.2. If urgent steps have to be taken in the interests of the client before the conditions in 5.6.1 above can be complied with, the lawyer may take such steps provided he informs the other lawyer immediately.

5.7. Responsibility for fees

In professional relations between members of Bars of different Member States, where a lawyer does not confine himself to recommending another lawyer or introducing him to the client but himself entrusts a correspondent with a particular matter or seeks his advice, he is personally bound, even if the client is insolvent, to pay the fees, costs and outlays which are due to the foreign correspondent. The lawyers concerned may, however, at the outset of the relationship between them make special arrangements on this matter. Further, the instructing lawyer may at any time limit his personal responsibility to the amount of fees, costs and outlays incurred before intimation to the foreign lawyer of his disclaimer of responsibility for the future.

[Release 18: 17 - xi - 89.]

5.8. Training young lawyers

In order to improve trust and co-operation amongst lawyers of different Member States for the clients' benefit there is a need to encourage a better knowledge of the laws and procedures in different Member States. Therefore when considering the need for the profession to give good training to young lawyers, lawyers should take into account the need to give training to young lawyers from other Member States.

5.9. Disputes amongst lawyers in different Member States

5.9.1. If a lawyer considers that a colleague in another Member State has acted in breach of a rule of professional conduct he shall draw the matter to the attention of his colleague.

5.9.2. If any personal dispute of a professional nature arises amongst lawyers in different Member States they should if possible first try to settle it in a friendly way.

5.9.3. A lawyer shall not commence any form of proceedings against a colleague in another Member State on matters referred to in 5.9.1 or 5.9.2 above without first informing the Bars or Law Societies to which they both belong for the purpose of allowing both Bars or Law Societies concerned an opportunity to assist in reaching a settlement.

EXPLANATORY MEMORANDUM AND COMMENTARY ON THE CCBE CODE OF CONDUCT

This Explanatory Memorandum and Commentary is prepared at the request of the CCBE Standing Committee by the CCBE's deontology working party, who were responsible for the drafting of the Code of Conduct itself. It seeks to explain the origin of the provisions of the code, to illustrate the problems which they are designed to resolve, particularly in relation to cross border activities, and to provide assistance to the competent authorities in the Member States in the application of the code. It is not intended to have any binding force in the interpretation of the code.

The original versions of the code are in the French and English languages. Translations into other Community languages are being prepared under the authority of the national delegations concerned.

1. PREAMBLE

1.1 The function of the lawyer in society

The Declaration of Perugia, adopted by the CCBE in 1977, laid down the fundamental principles of professional conduct applicable to lawyers throughout the European Community. The provisions of article 1.1 reaffirm the statement in the Declaration of Perugia of the function of the lawyer in society which forms the basis for the rules governing the performance of that function.

1.2 The nature of rules of professional conduct

These provisions substantially restate the explanation in the Declaration of Perugia of the nature of rules of professional conduct and how particular rules depend on particular local circumstances but are nevertheless based on common values.

1.3 The purpose of the common code

These provisions introduce the development of the principles in the Declaration of Perugia into a specific Code of Conduct for Lawyers throughout the European Community, with particular reference to their cross border activities (defined in 1.5 below).

The provisions of article 1.3.2 lay down the specific intentions of the CCBE with regard to the substantive provisions in the code.

1.4 Field of application ratione personae

The rules are here stated to apply to all the lawyers of the European Community as defined in the Lawyers Services Directive of 1977. This includes lawyers of the Member States which subsequently acceded to the Treaty, whose names have been added by amendment to the directive. It accordingly applies to all the lawyers represented on the CCBE, namely:

Belgium	Avocat/Advocaat/Rechtsanwalt
Denmark	Advokat
France	Avocat
Germany	Rechtsanwalt
Greece	Dikigoros
Ireland	Barrister
	Solicitor
Italy	Avvocato
	Procuratore
Luxembourg	Avocat-Avoué/Rechtsanwalt
Netherlands	Advocaat
Portugal	Advogado
Spain	Abogado
United Kingdom	Advocate
	Barrister
	Solicitor

Although the competence of the CCBE extends only to Member States, representatives of the observer delegations to the CCBE from European states which are not members of the Community (Austria, Norway, Sweden, Switzerland, Finland and Cyprus) have participated in the work on the code. It is believed that its provisions are acceptable in those states and it is hoped that the code can be applied as between them and the Member States by appropriate Conventions. It is also hoped that the code will be acceptable to the legal professions of other non-Member States in Europe and elsewhere so that it could also be applied in the same way between them and the Member States.

1.5 *Field of application* ratione materiae

The rules are here given direct application only to "cross border activities", as defined, of lawyers within the European Community. (See also on 1.4 above as to possible extensions in the future to lawyers of other states.) The definition of cross border activities would, for example, include contacts in state A even on a matter of law internal to state A between a lawyer of state A and a lawyer of state B; it would exclude contacts between lawyers of state A in state A on a matter arising in state B, provided that none of their professional activities takes place in state B; it would include any activities of lawyers of state A in state B, even if only in the form of communication sent from state A to state B.

1.6 *Definitions*

This provision defines three terms used in the code, "home Member State", "host Member State" and "competent authority". The references to "Member State" include, where appropriate, separate jurisdictions within a single Member State. The reference to "the Bar or Law Society to which the lawyer belongs" includes the Bar or Law Society responsible for exercising authority over the lawyer. The reference to "where the lawyer carries on cross border activities" should be interpreted in the light of the definition of "cross border activities" in article 1.5, in particular 1.5(*b*).

2. GENERAL PRINCIPLES

2.1 *Independence*

This provision substantially reaffirms the general statement of principle in the Declaration of Perugia.

2.2 *Trust and personal integrity*

This provision also restates a general principle contained in the Declaration of Perugia.

2.3 *Confidentiality*

This provision first restates, in article 2.3.1, general principles laid down in the Declaration of Perugia and recognised by the European Court of Justice in the *A.M. & S.* case (157/79). It then, in articles 2.3.2–2.3.4, developes them into a specific rule relating to the protection of confidentiality. Article 2.3.2 contains the basic rule requiring respect for confidentiality. Article 2.3.3 confirms that the obligation remains binding on the lawyer even if he ceases to act for the client in question. Article 2.3.4 confirms that the lawyer must not only respect the obligation of confidentiality himself but must require all members and employees of his firm to do likewise.

2.4 Respect for the rules of other Bars and Law Societies

Article 4 of the Lawyers Services Directive of 1977 contains the provisions with regard to the rules to be observed by a lawyer from one Member State providing services by virtue of article 59 of the Treaty in another Member State as follows:

(1) Activities relating to the representation of a client in legal proceedings or before public authorities shall be pursued in each host Member State under the conditions laid down for lawyers established in that state, with the exception of any conditions requiring residence, or registration with a professional organisation, in that state.

(2) A lawyer pursuing these activities shall observe the rules of professional conduct of the host Member State, without prejudice to his obligations in the Member State from which he comes.

(3) When these activities are pursued in the United Kingdom, "rules of professional conduct of the host Member State" means the rules of professional conduct applicable to solicitors, where such activities are not reserved for barristers and advocates. Otherwise the rules of professional conduct applicable to the latter shall apply. However, barristers from Ireland shall always be subject to the rules of professional conduct applicable in the United Kingdom to barristers and advocates.

(4) A lawyer pursuing activities other than those referred to in paragraph (1) shall remain subject to the conditions and rules of professional conduct of the Member State from which he comes without prejudice to respect for the rules, whatever their source, which govern the profession in the host Member State, especially those concerning the incompatibility of the exercise of the activities of a lawyer with the exercise of other activities in that state, professional secrecy, relations with other lawyers, the prohibition on the same lawyer acting for parties with mutually conflicting interests, and publicity. The latter rules are applicable only if they are capable of being observed by a lawyer who is not established in the host Member State and to the extent to which their observance is objectively justified to ensure, in that state, the proper exercise of a lawyer's activities, the standing of the profession and respect for the rules concerning incompatibility.

In cases not covered by this directive, the obligations of a lawyer under Community law to observe the rules of other Bars and Law Societies are a matter of interpretation of the applicable provisions of the Treaty or any other relevant directive. A major purpose of the code is to minimise, and if possible eliminate altogether, the problems which may arise from "double deontology", that is the application of more than one set of potentially conflicting national rules to a particular situation (see article 1.3.1.).

2.5 Incompatible occupations

There are differences both between and within Member States on the extent to which lawyers are permitted to engage in other occupations, for example in commercial activities. The general purpose of rules excluding a lawyer from other occupations is to protect him from influences which might impair his independence or his role in the administration of justice. The variations in these rules reflect different local conditions, different perceptions of the proper function of lawyers and different techniques of rule making. For instance in some cases there is a complete prohibition of engagement in certain named occupations, whereas in other cases engagement in other occupations is generally permitted, subject to observance of specific safeguards for the lawyer's independence.

Articles 2.5.2 and 2.5.3 make provision for different circumstances in which a lawyer of one Member State is engaging in cross border activities (as defined in article 1.5) in a host Member State when he is not a member of the host state legal profession.

Article 2.5.2 imposes full observation of host state rules regarding incompatible occupations on the lawyer acting in national legal proceedings or before national public authorities in the host state. This applies whether the lawyer is established in the host state or not.

Article 2.5.3, on the other hand, imposes "respect" for the rules of the host state regarding forbidden or incompatible occupations in other cases, but only where the lawyer who is established in the host Member State wishes to participate directly in commercial or other activities not connected with the practice of the law.

2.6 Personal publicity

The term "personal publicity" covers publicity by firms of lawyers, as well as individual lawyers, as opposed to corporate publicity organised by Bars and Law Societies for their members as a whole. The rules governing personal publicity by lawyers vary considerably in the Member States. In some there is a complete prohibition of personal publicity by lawyers; in others this prohibition has been (or is in the process of being) relaxed substantially. Article 2.6 does not therefore attempt to lay down a general standard on personal publicity.

Article 2.6.1 requires a lawyer not to advertise or seek personal publicity in a territory where this is not permitted to local lawyers. Otherwise he is required to observe the rules on publicity laid down by his own Bar or Law Society.

Article 2.6.2 contains provisions clarifying the question of the place in which advertising and personal publicity is deemed to take place. For example, a lawyer who is permitted to advertise in his home Member State may place an advertisement in a newspaper published there which circulates primarily in that Member State, even though some issues may circulate in other Member States where lawyers are not permitted to advertise. He may not, however, place an advertisement in a newspaper whose circulation is directed wholly or mainly at a territory where lawyers are not permitted to advertise in that way.

2.7 The client's interests

This provision emphasises the general principle that the lawyer must always place the client's interests before his own interests or those of fellow members of the legal profession.

3. RELATIONS WITH CLIENTS

3.1 Acceptance and termination of instructions

The provisions of article 3.1.1 are designed to ensure that a relationship is maintained between lawyer and client and that the lawyer in fact receives instructions from the client, even though these may be transmitted through a duly authorised intermediary. It is the responsibility of the lawyer to satisfy himself as to the authority of the intermediary and the wishes of the client.

Article 3.1.2 deals with the manner in which the lawyer should carry out his duties. The provision that he shall undertake personal responsibility for the discharge of the instructions given to him means that he cannot avoid responsibility by delegation to others. It does not prevent him from seeking to limit his legal liability to the extent that this is permitted by the relevant law or professional rules.

Article 3.1.3 states a principle which is of particular relevance in cross border activities, for example when a lawyer is asked to handle a matter on behalf of a lawyer or client from another state who may be unfamiliar with the relevant law and practice, or when a lawyer is asked to handle a matter relating to the law of another state with which he is unfamiliar.

A lawyer generally has the right to refuse to accept instructions in the first place, but article 3.1.4 states that, having once accepted them, he has an obligation not to withdraw without ensuring that the client's interests are safeguarded.

3.2 Conflict of interest

The provisions of article 3.2.1 do not prevent a lawyer acting for two or more clients in the same matter provided that their interests are not in fact in conflict and that there is no significant risk of such a conflict arising. Where a lawyer is already acting for two or more clients in this way and subsequently there arises a conflict of interests between those clients or a risk of a breach of confidence or other circumstances where his independence may be impaired, then the lawyer must cease to act for both or all of them.

There may, however, be circumstances in which differences arise between two or more clients for whom the same lawyer is acting where it may be appropriate for him to attempt to act as a mediator. It is for the lawyer in such cases to use his own judgment on whether or not there is such a conflict of interest between them as to require him to cease to act. If not, he may consider whether it would be appropriate for him to explain the position to the clients, obtain their agreement and attempt to act as mediator to resolve the difference between them, and only if this attempt to mediate should fail, to cease to act for them.

Article 3.2.4 applies the foregoing provisions of article 3 to lawyers practising in association. For example a firm of lawyers should cease to act when there is a conflict of interest between two clients of the firm, even if different lawyers in the firm are acting for each client. On the other hand, exceptionally, in the "chambers" form of association used by English barristers, where each lawyer acts for clients individually, it is possible for different lawyers in the association to act for clients with opposing interests.

3.3 Pactum de quota litis

These provisions reflect the common position in all Member States that an unregulated agreement for contingency fees (*pactum de quota litis*) is contrary to the proper administration of justice because it encourages speculative litigation and is liable to be abused. The provisions are not, however, intended to prevent the maintenance or introduction of arrangements under which lawyers are paid according to results or only if the action or matter is successful, provided that these arrangements are under sufficient regulation and control for the protection of the client and the proper administration of justice.

3.4 Regulation of fees

Article 3.4.1 lays down a general standard of disclosure of a lawyer's fees to the client and a requirement that they should be fair and reasonable in amount. Article 3.4.2 deals with the question of the machinery for regulating the lawyer's fees. In many Member States such machinery exists under national law or rules of conduct, whether by reference to a power of adjudication by the "bâtonnier" or otherwise. Article 3.4.1 applies the rules of the Bar or Law Society to which the lawyer belongs (see on article 1.6 above) unless this has been varied by an agreement between lawyer and client which is in accordance with the relevant law or rules of conduct. It goes on to provide a "choice of law" rule to deal with cases when the lawyer belongs to more than one Bar or Law Society.

3.5 Payment on account

Article 3.5 assumes that a lawyer may require a payment on account of his fees and/or disbursements, but sets a limit by reference to a reasonable estimate of them. See also on article 3.1.4 regarding the right to withdraw.

3.6 Fee sharing with non-lawyers

In some Member States lawyers are permitted to practise in association with members of certain other approved professions, whether legal professions or not. The provisions of article 3.6.1 are not designed to prevent fee sharing within such an approved form of association. Nor are the provisions designed to prevent fee sharing by the lawyers to whom the code applies (see on article 1.4 above) with other "lawyers", for example lawyers from non-Member States or members of other legal professions in the Member States such as notaries or conseils juridiques.

3.7 Legal aid

Article 3.7 requires a lawyer to inform his client of the availability of legal aid where applicable. There are widely differing provisions in the Member States on the availability of legal aid. In cross border activities a lawyer should have in mind the possibility that the legal aid provisions of a national law with which he is unfamiliar may be applicable.

3.8 Clients' funds

The provisions of article 3.8.1 reflect the recommendation adopted by the CCBE in Brussels in November 1985 on the need for minimum regulations to be made and enforced governing the proper control and disposal of clients' funds held by lawyers within the Community. In some Member States such regulations have not yet been introduced for internal purposes. Article 3.8.1.2–3.8.1.7 lays down minimum standards to be observed, while not interfering with the details of national systems which provide fuller or more stringent protection for clients' funds.

The provisions of articles 3.8.2 and 3.8.3 deal with questions which arise where the rules on clients' funds of more than one Member State may be applicable.

3.9 Professional indemnity insurance

Article 3.9.1 reflects a recommendation, also adopted by the CCBE in Brussels in November 1985, on the need for all lawyers in the Community to be insured against the risks arising from professional negligence claims against them. Again in some Member States such an obligation has not yet been introduced for internal purposes. Article 3.9.2 deals with questions which arise when the risks to be insured relate to more than one Member State.

4. RELATIONS WITH THE COURT

4.1 Applicable rules of conduct in court

This provision applies the principle that a lawyer is bound to comply with the rules of the court or tribunal before which he practises or appears.

4.2 Fair conduct of proceedings

This provision applies the general principle that in adversarial proceedings a lawyer must not attempt to take unfair advantage of his opponent, in particular by unilateral communications with the judge. An exception however is made for any steps permitted under the relevant rules of the court in question (see also on 4.5 below).

4.3 Demeanour in court

This provision reflects the necessary balance between respect for the court and for the law on the one hand and the pursuit of the client's best interests on the other.

4.4 False or misleading information

This provision applies the principle that the lawyer must never knowingly mislead the court. This is necessary if there is to be trust between the courts and the legal profession.

4.5 Extension to arbitrators etc.

This provision extends the preceding provisions relating to courts to other bodies exercising judicial or quasi-judicial functions.

5. RELATIONS BETWEEN LAWYERS

5.1 Corporate spirit of the profession

These provisions, which are based on statements in the Declaration of Perugia, emphasise that it is in the public interest for the legal profession to maintain a relationship of trust and co-operation between its members. However this cannot be used to justify setting the interests of the profession against those of justice or of clients (see also on article 2.7 above).

5.2 Co-operation among lawyers of different Member States

This provision also develops a principle stated in the Declaration of Perugia with a view to avoiding misunderstandings in dealings between lawyers of different Member States.

5.3 Correspondence between lawyers

In certain Member States communications between lawyers (written or by word of mouth) are normally regarded as confidential. This means that lawyers accept that those communications may not be disclosed to others and copies may not be sent to the lawyer's own client. This principle is recognised in Belgium, France, Greece, Italy, Luxembourg, Portugal and Spain. Such communications if in writing are often marked as "confidential" or "sous la foi du Palais".

In the United Kingdom and Ireland the notion of "confidentiality" is different in that it refers not to such communications between lawyers but to the lawyer's right and duty to keep his client's affairs confidential. However communications between lawyers made in order to attempt to settle a dispute are normally not regarded by a court as admissible evidence and the lawyer should not attempt to use them as evidence. If a lawyer wishes to indicate that he regards a document as such a communication he should indicate that it is sent "without prejudice". This means that the letter is sent without prejudice to and under reservation of the client's rights in the dispute.

In Denmark as a general rule, a lawyer has a right and duty to keep his client informed about all important correspondence from a lawyer acting from an opposing party, in practice normally by sending photocopies. This rule applies whether or not the letter is marked "without prejudice" or "confidential". As an exception, lawyers may exchange views—normally by word of mouth only—on a case with a view to finding an amicable settlement, on the mutual understanding that such communications should be kept confidential and not disclosed to the clients. A lawyer is not legally bound by such a confidence, but to break it would prejudice his future participation in such confidential exchanges. Some lawyers do not wish to receive such communication in any form without having the right to inform their clients; in that event they should inform the other lawyer before he makes such a confidential communication to them. As a general rule also, all correspondence between lawyers may be freely produced in court. Normally, however, if such correspondence is marked "without prejudice" or, even if not so marked, it is clearly of a "without prejudice" nature, the court will disregard it and the lawyer producing it will be treated as being in contravention of the rules of professional conduct.

In the Netherlands legal recourse based on communications between lawyers may not be sought, unless the interest of the client requires it and only after prior consultation with the lawyer for the other party. If such consultation does not lead to a solution, the advice of the Dean should be sought before recourse to law. The content of settlement negotiations between lawyers may not be communicated to the court without the permission of the lawyer for the other party, unless the right to do so was expressly reserved when the settlement proposal in question was made. There is however no general rule preventing a lawyer from sending copies of such communications to his client.

In Germany communications between lawyers are not confidential. The lawyer has an obligation to communicate them to his client and they may be admitted as evidence in court.

These differences often give rise to misunderstandings between lawyers of different Member States who correspond with each other. For this reason lawyers should be particularly careful to clarify the basis upon which correspondence with lawyers in other Member States is sent and received. In particular a lawyer who wishes to make a confidential or "without prejudice" communication to a colleague in a Member State where the rules may be different should ask in advance whether it can be accepted as such.

5.4 Referral fees

This provision reflects the principle that a lawyer should not pay or receive payment purely for the reference of a client, which would risk impairing the client's free choice of lawyer or his interest in being referred to the best available service. It does not prevent fee sharing arrangements between lawyers on a proper basis (see also on article 3.6 above).

In some Member States lawyers are permitted to accept and retain commissions in certain cases provided the client's best interests are served, there is full disclosure to him and he has consented to the retention of the commission. In such cases the retention of the commission by the lawyer represents part of his remuneration for the service provided to the client and is not within the scope of the prohibition on referral fees which is designed to prevent lawyers making a secret profit.

5.5 Communication with opposing parties

This provision reflects a generally accepted principle, and is designed both to promote the smooth conduct of business between lawyers and to prevent any attempt to take advantage of the client of another lawyer.

5.6 Change of lawyer

This provision is designed to promote the orderly handing over of the business when there is a change of lawyer. It also reflects the commonly accepted principle in Member States that there is some duty on the new lawyer in respect of the settlement of the former lawyer's account. This duty is not, however, generally accepted as being more than a duty to ascertain that arrangements have been made for the settlement.

5.7 Responsibility for fees

These provisions substantially reaffirm provisions contained in the Declaration of Perugia. Since misunderstandings about responsibility for unpaid fees are a common cause of difference between lawyers of different Member States, it is important that a lawyer who wishes to exclude or limit his personal obligation to be responsible for the fees of his foreign colleague should reach a clear agreement on this at the outset of the transaction.

5.8 Training young lawyers

This provision is by way of an exhortation emphasising the general obligation of the members of the legal profession in the European Community to ensure that future generations of lawyers in each Member State have knowledge of the laws and procedures in other Member States.

5.9 Disputes amongst lawyers in different Member States

A lawyer has the right to pursue any legal or other remedy to which he is entitled against a colleague in another Member State. Nevertheless it is desirable that, where a breach of a rule of professional conduct or a dispute of a professional nature is involved, the possibilities of friendly settlement should be exhausted, if necessary with the assistance of the Bars or Law Societies concerned, before such remedies are exercised.

Solicitors (Scotland) Practice Rules 1991

Rules dated 3rd May 1991, made by the Council of The Law Society of Scotland and approved by the Lord President of the Court of Session under section 34 of the Solicitors (Scotland) Act 1980 as amended.

1.—(1) These rules may be cited as the Solicitors (Scotland) Practice Rules 1991.

(2) These rules shall come into operation on 3rd May 1991.

2.—(1) In these rules unless the context otherwise requires:—

"the Act" means the Solicitors (Scotland) Act 1980 as amended;

"the Council" means the Council of the Law Society of Scotland established under the Act;

"lawyer" means a member of the Faculty of Advocates in Scotland or a legal practitioner offering legal services to the public, who is qualified and licensed to practise in accordance with the law of a legal jurisdiction other than that of Scotland, and includes a firm of lawyers, a law centre, a European Economic Interest Group the membership of which is exclusively lawyers, an incorporated practice of lawyers and any association (whether corporate or unincorporate) consisting exclusively of lawyers or exclusively of lawyers and solicitors;

"solicitor" means any person enrolled as a solicitor in pursuance of the Act and includes a firm of solicitors, an incorporated practice and any association of solicitors;

(2) The Interpretation Act 1978 applies to these rules as it applies to an Act of Parliament.

3. Rules 2, 4, 5 and 6 of the Solicitors (Scotland) Practice Rules 1964 are hereby repealed.

4. A solicitor shall not share with any unqualified person any profits or fees or fee derived from any business transacted by the solicitor of a kind which is commonly carried on by solicitors in Scotland in the course of or in connection with their practice; provided always that the provisions of this rule shall not apply to the sharing of profits or fees where:—

   (i) a person who has ceased to practise as a solicitor shall receive from any solicitor a share of the profits or fees of the latter, as a price or value of the business which he has transferred to the latter or shall receive a share of such profits as a voluntary or other allowance out of the profits or fees of a business in which he had been a partner; or

  (ii) the widow, heirs, executors, representatives, next of kin or dependants of any deceased solicitor receive from any solicitor who has purchased or succeeded to the business of such deceased solicitor or from any firm of solicitors of which such deceased solicitor was a partner at his death any share of the profits of such business; or

 (iii) the salary of any clerk or assistant of a solicitor who is wholly employed by such solicitor is partly or wholly paid in the form of a percentage on the profits of such solicitor's business or any part thereof; or

 (iv) such profits or fees are received by any public officer in respect of work done in the course of his duty; or

  (v) an agreement for sharing such profits or fees is made between a solicitor and a lawyer;

(vi) such profits or fees are received by an officer of a public body who is a solicitor or by the public body and are dealt with in accordance with Statutory Provisions.

5. The Council shall have power to waive any of the provisions of these rules in any particular case or cases.

6. Breach of these rules may be treated as professional misconduct for the purposes of Part IV of the Act (Complaints and Disciplinary Proceedings).

Solicitors (Scotland) (Multi-Disciplinary Practices) Practice Rules 1991

Rules dated 3rd May 1991, made by the Council of The Law Society of Scotland and approved by the Lord President of the Court of Session in terms of section 34 of the Solicitors (Scotland) Act 1980.

1.—(1) These rules may be cited as the Solicitors (Scotland) (Multi-Disciplinary Practices) Practice Rules 1991.
(2) These rules shall come into operation on 3rd May 1991.

2.—(1) In these rules unless the context otherwise requires:—
"the Act" means the Solicitors (Scotland) Act 1980;
"the Council" means the Council of the Society;
"legal relationship" means membership of a partnership or a joint venture which is not a partnership, or membership or directorship of a corporate body;
"multi-disciplinary practice" means a body corporate or partnership:—
    (a) having as one of its directors, or as the case may be, partners, a solicitor or an incorporated practice; and
    (b) which offers services, including professional services, such as are provided by individual solicitors, to the public; and
    (c) where a solicitor or incorporated practice carries out, or supervises the carrying out, or makes provision of legal services;
"the Society" means the Law Society of Scotland;
"solicitor" means any person enrolled as a solicitor in pursuance of the Act, and includes a firm of solicitors or incorporated practice and any association of solicitors.
(2) The Interpretation Act 1978 applies to these rules as it applies to an Act of Parliament.

3. Rule 3 of the Solicitors (Scotland) Practice Rules 1964 is hereby repealed.

4. A solicitor shall not form a legal relationship with a person or body who is not a solicitor with a view to their jointly offering professional services as a multi-disciplinary practice to any person or body.

5. The Council shall have power to waive any of the provisions of these rules in any particular case or cases.

6. Breach of these rules may be treated as professional misconduct for the purposes of Part IV of the Act (Complaints and Disciplinary Proceedings).

[THE NEXT PAGE IS F 499]

Admission as Solicitor (Scotland) Regulations 1991

Rules dated 20th November 1991, made by the Council of The Law Society of Scotland with the concurrence of the Lord President of the Court of Session under section 5 of the Solicitors (Scotland) Act 1980.

ARRANGEMENT OF REGULATIONS

PART I—INTRODUCTORY

PART II—ENTRANCE QUALIFICATIONS

PART III—QUALIFICATIONS AND EXAMINATIONS

PART IV—EXEMPTIONS FROM EXAMINATIONS AND DIPLOMA

PART V—REQUIREMENTS FOR SPECIAL INTRANTS

PART VI—PROCEDURE FOR ADMISSION AS SOLICITOR

[THE NEXT PAGE IS F 501]

PART I—INTRODUCTORY

Title and commencement
1. These Regulations may be cited as the Admission as Solicitor (Scotland) Regulations 1991 and shall come into operation on 1st January 1992.

Interpretation
2.—(1) In these Regulations, unless the context otherwise requires—
"the Act" means the Solicitors (Scotland) Act 1980 (as amended);
"Certificate of Fitness" means a certificate issued by the Council under the hand of the Secretary that the person to whom the certificate applies has fulfilled the applicable conditions and requirements prescribed in these Regulations and in any enactment for admission as a solicitor in Scotland;
"the Council" means the Council of the Society or, where the Council has delegated powers for the consideration of applications under the Regulations, a Committee of the Council or such other body or individual to whom such powers have been delegated;
"degree" means a degree, other than an honorary degree, granted by a University;
"Degree in Law" means the degree of Bachelor of Laws (LL.B.) granted by one of the Universities of Aberdeen, Dundee, Edinburgh, Glasgow and Strathclyde;
"Diploma" means a Diploma in Legal Practice granted by one of the Universities of Aberdeen, Dundee, Edinburgh, Glasgow and Strathclyde;
"employer" means an employing solicitor who is a party to a pre-Diploma, post-Diploma or non-Diploma training contract;
"employing solicitor" means a solicitor who holds a practising certificate issued under section 14 of the Act and who—
    (i) is engaged as a principal in private practice in Scotland, or
    (ii) is employed as a solicitor by a regional council, islands area council or district council in Scotland, or
    (iii) is in such other employment as a solicitor in Scotland as the Council may approve,
        and the expression "employing solicitor" shall include a firm or an incorporated practice of solicitors as defined in the Act;
"Entrance Certificate" means a certificate issued by the Council under the hand of the Secretary to the effect that the person to whom the certificate applies has fulfilled the applicable conditions and

requirements prescribed in these Regulations and in any enactment for admission as a solicitor in Scotland to entitle him to enter
into a post-Diploma or a non-Diploma training contract;

"Examiner" means an examiner appointed under regulation 18 of these
Regulations;

"intrant" means a person seeking to become a solicitor in Scotland;

"non-Diploma training contract" has the meaning assigned by regulation 12 of these Regulations;

"post-Diploma training contract" means a contract under regulation 9
of these Regulations which is entered into between an employing
solicitor and an intrant who holds an Entrance Certificate;

"pre-Diploma training contract" means a contract which is entered into
between an employing solicitor and an intrant who is qualified
under the provisions of regulation 6 of and the Schedule to these
Regulations;

"Preliminary Entrance Certificate" means a certificate issued by the
Council under the hand of the Secretary to the effect that the
person to whom the certificate applies has fulfilled all the
conditions and requirements prescribed in these Regulations and
in any enactment for admission as a solicitor in Scotland to entitle
him to enter into a pre-Diploma training contract;

"the 1986 Regulations" means the Admission as Solicitor (Scotland)
Regulations 1986;

"the Secretary" means the Secretary of the Society and includes any
person authorised by the Council to act on behalf of the Secretary
for the purpose of these Regulations;

"the Society" means the Law Society of Scotland;

"the Society's examinations" means examinations set under regulation
20(1) of these Regulations;

"trainee" means an intrant who is a party to a pre-Diploma, post-
Diploma or non-Diploma training contract;

"University" means—
  (i) any University in Great Britain, or
  (ii) the Council for National Academic Awards, or
  (iii) any other University or Institute recognised by the Council for
       the purposes of these Regulations.

(2) The provisions of the Interpretation Act 1978 shall apply for the
interpretation of these Regulations as they apply to the interpretation of an
Act of Parliament.

Conditions precedent to admission
3. Subject to the provisions of section 6 of the Act and of these
Regulations, every intrant shall, as a condition precedent to his admission as
a solicitor, comply with these Regulations so far as applicable to him and the
Council may require any intrant to satisfy it by such means as it considers
necessary as to such compliance.

Application of these Regulations
4. These Regulations shall apply to all intrants other than
  (a) intrants (hereinafter referred to as "1986 intrants") who have
      presented themselves for any of the Society's Examinations, obtained
      a Preliminary Entrance Certificate or obtained an Entrance Certifi-
      cate under the 1986 Regulations and
  (b) intrants eligible under the EC Qualified Lawyers Transfer (Scotland)
      Regulations 1990. Any 1986 intrants who wish to do so may, by notice
      in writing to the Council, elect to proceed to admission under these
      Regulations but such election, once made, shall be irrevocable.

PART II—ENTRANCE QUALIFICATIONS

(A) *Pre-Diploma training contracts*

Service under a pre-Diploma training contract
    5.—(1) Any intrant who for the purpose of qualifying for an Entrance Certificate proposes to meet the requirements of regulation 7(2)(ii)(b) of these Regulations without obtaining a Degree in Law shall be required to enter into a pre-Diploma training contract with an employing solicitor.
    (2) The period of training under a pre-Diploma training contract shall comprise three years of full-time training, provided always that any intrant may, with the written consent of the Council, undergo training on a part-time basis provided that the Council is satisfied that the total time spent working under such a training contract shall equate to three years of full-time training.
    (3) Every pre-Diploma training contract shall be in or as nearly as may be in such form as the Council may from time to time prescribe and shall, subject to the provisions of regulation 17(1) of these Regulations, contain an obligation on the employing solicitor to provide training for the intrant in—
    (a) conveyancing;
    (b) litigation; and
    (c) either
        (i) trusts and executries, or
        (ii) the legal work of a public authority.
    (4) Subject to the consent of the employer, an intrant who is a party to a pre-Diploma training contract may be permitted to attend, during office hours, classes in law at a University or elsewhere.

Preliminary Entrance Certificate
    6.—(1) An intrant may not enter into a pre-Diploma training contract unless he holds a Preliminary Entrance Certificate issued by the Council.
    (2) An intrant shall be entitled to a Preliminary Entrance Certificate if he satisfies the Council that—
    (a) he is a fit and proper person to be a solicitor; and
    [1](b) he is qualified under the provisions of the First Schedule to these Regulations or such other requirement as may be approved by the Council from time to time.
    (3) The Council shall have power, in the case of an intrant who, being at least 23 years of age, satisfies the Council both that he is a fit and proper person to be a solicitor and, having regard to evidence of academic attainment and to any experience of legal work, as to his fitness to enter into a pre-Diploma training contract, to grant to such an intrant a Preliminary Entrance Certificate without requiring compliance with sub-paragraph (2)(b) of this regulation.

NOTE
    [1] As amended by the Admission as a Solicitor (Scotland) (Amendment) Regulations 1996 (effective August 1, 1996).

(B) *Entrance Certificates*

Issue of Entrance Certificate
    7.—(1) An intrant may not enter into either a post-Diploma or a non-Diploma training contract unless he holds an Entrance Certificate.
    (2) An intrant shall be entitled to an Entrance Certificate if he satisfies the Council that—
        (i) he is a fit and proper person to be a solicitor; and
        (ii) either (a) he holds a Degree in Law or a certificate that he is entitled to graduate in such a Degree notwithstanding that he has not so graduated; or (b) he has served for a period of three years under a pre-Diploma training contract and has passed or

obtained exemption from the Society's examinations; or (c) he is
an intrant to whom the provisions of any of regulations 28, 30, 31
or 32 of these Regulations apply; and
   (iii) unless exempt in terms of regulation 27 or Part V of these
   Regulations, he has obtained a Diploma.

Withdrawal of Entrance Certificate
   8. An intrant's Entrance Certificate may be withdrawn by the Council in
such exceptional circumstances as the Council may in its sole discretion
determine and, in any event, an intrant's Entrance Certificate shall
automatically lapse if a trainee does not enter into a training contract within
two years of the date of said Entrance Certificate or such extended period as
the Council may in its discretion determine.

(C) *Post-Diploma training contracts*

Service under a post-Diploma training contract
   9.—(1) Subject to regulation 27 or Part V of these Regulations, it shall be a
requirement for admission as a solicitor in Scotland that an intrant shall
serve under a post-Diploma training contract entered into with an employing solicitor.
   (2) The period of training under a post-Diploma training contract shall
comprise two years of full-time training, provided always that any intrant
may, with the written consent of the Council, undergo training on a part-time
basis provided that the Council is satisfied that the total time spent working
under such a training contract shall equate to two years of full-time training.
   (3) Every post-Diploma training contract shall be in or as nearly as may be
in such a form as the Council may from time to time prescribe.

Commencement of post-Diploma training contract
   10. In the case of an intrant who is required to hold a Diploma, the
commencement of his post-Diploma training contract shall be within a
period of two years of the date of 1st January first occurring after the date
when the intrant became eligible for the award of the Diploma provided that
the Council may in its discretion extend such period but may, in granting
such extension, impose such conditions as it thinks fit.

Service elsewhere in Scotland, UK and EC
   11. Subject to the prior approval of the employer and the Council in each
case, a trainee under a post-Diploma training contract may be permitted in
order to extend the range of his training—
   (a) to undertake legal work under appropriate supervision within
       Scotland on secondment to one or more solicitors, or
   (b) to undertake legal work for a period or periods not exceeding in the
       aggregate six months in any other part of the United Kingdom or any
       country which is a member of the European Community,
and such period or periods of legal work shall be reckoned as part of the
trainee's period of service under his post-Diploma training contract.

(D) *Non-Diploma training contracts*

Service under a non-Diploma training contract
   12.—(1) An intrant who is exempt from holding a Diploma under
regulation 27 or Part V of these Regulations shall serve under a non-
Diploma training contract entered into with an employing solicitor.
   (2) The non-Diploma training contract shall be in similar terms to a
post-Diploma training contract and shall be subject to the same conditions
and requirements as are specified in these Regulations in relation to
post-Diploma training contracts; provided that the minimum period of time
which an intrant is required to serve under a non-Diploma training contract
shall be the appropriate period specified in these Regulations or such other
period as the Council may in its discretion determine.

(E) *General provisions affecting training contracts*

Provisions as to employing solicitors and intrants

13.—(1) An employing solicitor shall not, without consent in writing of the Council, employ any trainee, unless he is in practice as a solicitor in Scotland at the time and has been in continuous practice for a period of at least three years immediately prior to his employing the trainee or where the employing solicitor is a firm or incorporated practice, at least one of the partners or directors thereof, as the case may be, has been in such continuous practice.

¹ (2)(a) An employing solicitor who—
    (i) is engaged in practice as a sole principal, or
    (ii) is a firm or an incorporated practice with two or three partners or directors, shall not employ any trainee related to the employing solicitor or any of the partners, directors or members of the employing solicitor within any of the categories of relationship specified in the Second Schedule to these Regulations.

(b) An employing solicitor who is a firm or an incorporated practice with no less than four partners or directors shall not employ any trainee related to any of the partners, directors or members of the employing solicitor within any of the categories of relationship specified in the Third Schedule to these Regulations.

(c) A pre-Diploma or non-Diploma training contract entered into between an employing solicitor and a trainee in breach of paragraphs (a) or (b) of this Regulation shall be of no effect for the purposes of the compliance with these Regulations.

(d) Notwithstanding the provisions of Regulation 40, the Council shall have power, in what it deems to be exceptional circumstances and taking into account the merits of a particular case, to waive the provisions of paragraphs (a) and (b) of this Regulation, subject to the imposition of such conditions as it may reasonably require, and a decision to grant such a waiver shall be taken by a simple majority of the members voting thereon.

(3) If the Council after due inquiry decides that an employing solicitor would be unable to fulfil or is not fulfilling the proper obligations of an employer under a training contract either in relation to a particular application to employ a trainee or in relation to a particular contract or generally, it shall intimate its decision to the solicitor and the solicitor, notwithstanding that he satisfies the provisions of paragraph (1) of this regulation, shall not thereafter engage or retain the services of any trainee without the consent in writing of the Council.

(4) Any person aggrieved by a decision of the Council under paragraph (3) of this regulation may, within 21 days of the date of written intimation of the decision, appeal to the Court of Session.

(5) The total number of intrants employed at any time under pre-Diploma, post-Diploma and non-Diploma training contracts shall not, except with the consent of the Council, exceed:—
    (i) in the case of a solicitor practising on his own under his own name or as a sole solicitor under a firm name, one;
    (ii) in the case of a firm or an incorporated practice of solicitors, twice the number of partners in the firm, or twice the number of directors of the incorporated practice, as the case may be;
    (iii) in the case of a firm or an incorporated practice of solicitors having more than one office, within each such office, twice the number of solicitors having their principal place of business within that office;
    (iv) in the case of a solicitor employed by a regional council, islands area council or district council in Scotland, the number of solicitors employed by the said regional, islands area or district council in each case, or such larger number as the Council may in special circumstances allow; and

(v) in the case of any other solicitor practising in Scotland, such number as the Council may in each case determine.

NOTE
[1] As amended by the Admission as a Solicitor (Scotland) (Amendment) Regulations 1996 (effective August 1, 1996).

Registration of training contracts
14.—(1) For the purposes of these Regulations, the Council shall establish and maintain a register of pre-Diploma training contracts, a register of post-Diploma training contracts and a register of non-Diploma training contracts.
(2) Every such contract shall be produced by the intrant to the Council for registration within three months from its commencement and thereafter shall be presented for registration in the Books of Council and Session by the Society at the expense of the intrant.
(3) When an intrant produces his contract to the Council, he shall pay such registration fee as the Council may from time to time prescribe.
(4) If an intrant's contract and the prescribed registration fee are not presented to the Council within three months from the date of the commencement of the contract, the period of service under the contract shall for the purposes of these Regulations be reckoned, if the Council so directs, as commencing only from the date of production of the contract to the Council or such earlier date as the Council may determine.

Service under training contracts
15. For the purposes of these Regulations and subject to regulations 5, 9 and 11 hereof,
(1) a trainee during the term of his training contract shall not during office hours engage in any other gainful employment or otherwise absent himself from his employer's business without the prior consent of his employer and of the Council;
(2) service by a trainee under any type of training contract shall be continuous, provided however that in exceptional circumstances, the Council may, in considering whether or not such service has been continuous and provided that the employer is prepared to certify the trainee's fitness to become a solicitor in due course or to continue as a solicitor as the case may be, disregard short periods of absence by the trainee from employment, not exceeding an aggregate of six months;
(3) if
(a) during the term of any training contract either the trainee or the employer has been continuously absent from the employer's place of business for an aggregate period of at least three months within any period of six months without reasonable cause, or
(b) the Council, after due and diligent enquiry and after affording the parties the opportunity to make representations, is of the reasonable opinion that the training contract ought to be terminated, assigned or extended,
it may by notice in writing to the parties terminate the training contract with effect from such date as may be specified in the notice or may require an assignation of the training contract or an extension to it as the case may be or may take such other action as it thinks fit.

Further training contracts or extension of training contracts
16.—(1) Where, before the expiration of the period of service under a pre-Diploma, post-Diploma or non-Diploma training contract, such contract is terminated for any reason, an intrant shall be entitled and may be required, subject to such conditions as the Council may impose, to enter into a further pre-Diploma, post-Diploma or non-Diploma training contract as the case may be with another employing solicitor.

(2) Where there is a dispute between the parties to a pre-Diploma, post-Diploma or non-Diploma training contract, the Council may require an assignation of the training contract or an extension to it as the case may be or may take such other action as it thinks fit.

Consent to transfer of training contracts
17.—(1) Subject to the provisions of regulation 5(3) of these Regulations, an employer under a pre-Diploma training contract shall, if requested by his trainee or if called upon to do so by the Council, assign such pre-Diploma training contract to another employing solicitor approved by the Council, to enable the trainee either to complete his training in the three prescribed areas of practice or to extend the range of his training generally, or for any other reason which the Council shall consider reasonable.

(2) A post-Diploma or non-Diploma training contract shall not be assigned by the employer without the consent in writing of the Council; and an employer shall be obliged to assign a post-Diploma or non-Diploma training contract if called upon to do so by the Council.

(3) Every such assignation shall, together with the relevant supporting documents, be produced to the Council within six weeks from the date of assignation for registration in the relevant Register of Training Contracts kept in accordance with the provisions of regulation 14 of these Regulations and, where the assignation has not been registered within said period, service prior to its registration shall be reckoned as part of the trainee's service under the training contract only to such extent as the Council may in its discretion determine.

(4) Any person seeking registration of an assignation of a training contract shall pay to the Council such fee as it may from time to time determine.

PART III—QUALIFICATIONS AND EXAMINATIONS

Appointment of examiners
18.—(1) In order to test the suitability and qualifications of intrants, the Council shall from time to time nominate and appoint fit and proper persons to be Examiners and hold examinations in accordance with this part of these Regulations, which examinations shall be under the management and control of the Council.

(2) The Examiners shall comply with all directions that may be given by the Council with respect to the number of papers to be set on any subject, the number of questions to be set and to be answered and the percentage mark to be attained to qualify for a pass and any other matters in connection with the examinations.

(3) The Examiners shall be appointed for such period of time and be paid such remuneration as the Council may from time to time determine.

Eligibility of intrants
19. An intrant shall not be entitled, except with the consent of the Council, to present himself for any of the Society's examinations unless he—
    (i)   holds a Preliminary Entrance Certificate and is serving under a pre-Diploma training contract or, that contract having terminated, has already presented himself for one or more of the Society's examinations; or
    (ii) holds, or is entitled to graduate with, a Degree in Law which does not include passes in all the subjects prescribed by Regulation 20(1) of these Regulations.

Examinations
20.—(1) The Society's examinations shall consist of examinations in the laws of Scotland in accordance with the syllabus prescribed by the Council from time to time.

(2) An intrant shall not be permitted to sit any one examination on more than four occasions or later than four years from the date of the first of the Society's examinations for which he presented himself except with the consent of the Council following on a recommendation by the Society's Examiners, which consent may be given subject to such conditions as are deemed appropriate.

Award of distinction
21. A certificate of distinction in any subject may be awarded to an intrant at the discretion of the Examiners.

Conduct, dates and places of examinations
22.—(1) Diets for the Society's examinations shall be held in Edinburgh not less than twice each year and additional diets may be held as considered necessary by the Examiners.

(2) Intrants intending to present themselves as candidates at any of the Society's examinations shall give three weeks' notice in writing of their intention to the Secretary, provided that the Examiners may at their discretion allow an intrant who has not given such notice to present himself for any examination.

(3) Every candidate shall be examined in writing and may be required by the Examiners to present himself for oral examination.

(4) Every candidate shall be required to advise the Society of any permanent change of address.

Fees
23. A candidate shall tender with his application to sit any examination such fee as may be prescribed by the Council from time to time.

PART IV—EXEMPTIONS FROM EXAMINATIONS AND DIPLOMA

Faculty of Advocates' examinees
24. The Council may exempt from any of the Society's examinations an intrant who has obtained a pass in the corresponding examination in the examinations for admission to the Faculty of Advocates.

Equivalent passes
25. Where an intrant seeks exemption from any of the Society's examinations, the Examiner in the appropriate subject shall be consulted and, provided such Examiner is satisfied that the intrant has passed an equivalent examination in the laws of Scotland to a standard approved by the Council, then the Council may grant such exemption.

Further exemptions for intrants from elsewhere in UK
26. Where the terms of regulation 29 or 30 of these Regulations do not apply, the Council may, on application by an intrant who has passed the examinations required for admission as a solicitor or barrister in England and Wales or Northern Ireland, in any such case within a reasonable time prior to such application, determine which of the Society's examinations, if any, such intrant shall be required to pass for the purposes of regulation 7 of these Regulations, and grant consent in terms of regulation 19 hereof accordingly, subject always to such conditions as the Council may impose, including conditions as to the period of time during which the examinations must be passed.

Exemptions from Diploma
27. An intrant who seeks to obtain a Certificate of Fitness under these Regulations and who satisfies the Council that there are exceptional

circumstances which justify his being exempted from obtaining a Diploma may be granted a Certificate of Fitness on such conditions, including the passing of examinations, as the Council may in its discretion prescribe; provided that an intrant who receives such exemption shall be required to serve for a period of not less than three years under a non-Diploma training contract with an employing solicitor, in terms similar to those of a post-Diploma training contract.

PART V—REQUIREMENTS FOR SPECIAL INTRANTS

Scottish advocates
28. Notwithstanding any other provisions herein contained and unless the Council otherwise determines, an intrant who is a member of the Faculty of Advocates shall be exempt from
  (a) pre-Diploma training,
  (b) the Society's examinations and
  (c) the Diploma, but he shall be required to undergo six months of non-Diploma training prior to applying for admission in terms of regulation 33 of these Regulations.

English/Welsh and Northern Irish solicitors
29. Notwithstanding any other provisions herein contained and unless the Council otherwise determines, an intrant who has been admitted as a solicitor in England and Wales or Northern Ireland and who provides such evidence as the Council may require that he is a fit and proper person to be admitted as a solicitor in Scotland shall be exempt from (a) the Society's examinations, (b) the Diploma and (c) any period of training, but he shall be required to pass in such manner as the Council may require an intra-UK transfer test comprising examinations in conveyancing, trusts and succession, Scots criminal law, with civil and criminal evidence and procedure and (unless admitted as aforesaid prior to 1st January 1992) European Community law and institutions or such other examinations as may be prescribed by the Council from time to time prior to applying for admission in terms of regulation 33 of these Regulations.

English/Welsh and Northern Irish barristers
30. Notwithstanding any other provisions herein contained, an intrant who is a member of the Bar in England and Wales or Northern Ireland who (i) provides such evidence as the Council may require that he is a fit and proper person to be admitted as a solicitor in Scotland and (ii) can demonstrate that he has had five years of recent active practice since his call to the Bar shall be exempt from (a) pre-Diploma training, (b) the Society's examinations and (c) the Diploma, but he shall be required to pass in such manner as the Council may require an intra-UK transfer test comprising examinations in conveyancing, trusts and succession, Scots criminal law, with civil and criminal evidence and procedure and (unless called as aforesaid prior to 1st January 1992) European Community law and institutions and such other examinations and undergo a period of six months of non-Diploma training or such longer period as the Council may in its discretion determine prior to applying for admission in terms of regulation 33 of these Regulations.

Colonial solicitors
31. Notwithstanding any other provisions herein contained, an intrant to whom the Colonial Solicitors Act 1900 and any Order in Council made thereunder apply shall be required to pass the Society's examinations and

undergo one year of non-Diploma training prior to applying for admission in terms of regulation 33 of these Regulations but such intrant shall be exempt from pre-Diploma training and the Diploma.

Other overseas lawyers
32. Notwithstanding any other provisions herein contained and unless the Council otherwise determines, a practising lawyer from outwith the United Kingdom to whom the Colonial Solicitors Act 1900 and the E.C. Qualified Lawyers Transfer (Scotland) Regulations 1990 do not apply shall require (i) to satisfy the Council that he is qualified to undertake within the jurisdiction in which he qualified or practises, professional work equivalent in its nature to that of a solicitor or advocate in Scotland, (ii) to provide such evidence as the Council may require that he is a fit and proper person to be admitted as a solicitor in Scotland and (iii) to pass the Society's examinations, gain the Diploma and complete one year of post-Diploma training prior to applying for admission in terms of regulation 33 of these Regulations but such intrant shall be exempt from pre-Diploma training.

PART VI—PROCEDURE FOR ADMISSION AS SOLICITOR

Eligibility for Certificate of Fitness
33. Subject to the provisions of section 6 of the Act and of these Regulations, an intrant shall be entitled to apply for a Certificate of Fitness for the purposes of section 6 of the Act if—
(1) (a) he has passed or obtained exemption from any or all of the required examinations, or
     (b) he has obtained or is entitled to obtain a Degree in Law which includes passes in subjects corresponding to all the subjects prescribed in the syllabus referred to in regulation 20(1) of these Regulations, unless otherwise exempt, or, where such Degree does not include passes in all such subjects, he obtains passes therein in the Society's examinations, or otherwise passes corresponding subjects at the standard required for a Degree in Law; and
(2) he holds a Diploma, unless he is exempted from doing so in terms of these Regulations; and
(3) (a) he has completed not less than one year of his two-year period of service under a post-Diploma training contract and has submitted to the Council
         (i) a declaration in conformity with regulation 34(1)(a) of these Regulations and
         (ii) an undertaking in such form as the Council may prescribe that he will complete the remaining period of service under such contract in fulfilment of his obligation under that contract, or
     (b) he has completed the full period of service under a post-Diploma training contract and has submitted to the Council a declaration in conformity with regulation 35 of these Regulations, or
     (c) he has completed the full period of service under a non-Diploma training contract as is prescribed for him by the Council and has submitted to the Council a declaration in conformity with regulation 35 of these Regulations, and
     (d) in the event that any such declaration is dated more than 12 months prior to its submission to the Council or if, for any other reason the Council so requires, he has submitted to the Council

such further evidence as it may require that he continues to be a fit and proper person to be admitted as a solicitor in Scotland; and

(4) being an intrant to whom regulation 29 of these Regulations applies, he has submitted to the Council such further evidence as it may require that he continues to be a fit and proper person to be admitted as a solicitor in Scotland.

Applicants admitted after one year of post-Diploma training—employer's declaration

34.—(1) In the case of an intrant to whom regulation 33(3)(a) of these Regulations applies, he shall (a) submit to the Council a declaration by his employer in such form as the Council may prescribe certifying that, during the first year of his post-Diploma training contract, he has fulfilled his obligations under such contract and is, in the opinion of his employer, a fit and proper person to be admitted as a solicitor in Scotland and (b) on completion of his full period of service under his post-Diploma training contract, submit to the Council a declaration by his employer in such form as the Council may prescribe certifying that in his opinion the intrant continues to be a fit and proper person to be a solicitor in Scotland, provided always that, in any case where the employer of an intrant has declined to provide any such declaration, the Council may, after due enquiry and where it appears reasonable to do so, waive the requirement for such declaration from the employer, subject to such conditions as it may in its discretion determine.

(2) In determining whether the intrant is a fit and proper person to be admitted as a solicitor, the employer shall have regard not only to the moral character of the intrant but also to his aptitude for and application to his duties and his conduct generally.

Applicants admitted after two years of post-Diploma training—employer's declaration

35.—(1) In the case of an intrant to whom regulation 33(3)(b) or (c) of these Regulations applies, the Council shall not grant a Certificate of Fitness to him unless he submits to the Council a declaration by his employer in such form as the Council may prescribe certifying that in his opinion the intrant has fulfilled his obligations under the training contract and is a fit and proper person to be admitted as a solicitor in Scotland, provided always that, in any case where the employer of an intrant has declined to provide any such declaration, the Council may, after due inquiry and where it appears reasonable to do so, waive the requirement for such declaration from the employer.

(2) In determining whether the intrant is a fit and proper person to be admitted as a solicitor, the employer shall have regard not only to the moral character of the intrant but also to his aptitude for and application to his duties and his conduct generally.

Qualified Practising Certificates

36. Where an intrant is admitted as a solicitor by virtue of regulation 33(3)(a) of these Regulations or otherwise while still undergoing post-Diploma training and applies for a Practising Certificate, the Council may in its discretion issue such Certificate subject to such qualifications as it may see fit, provided that such qualifications shall apply only until the grant of an employer's declaration pursuant to regulation 34(1)(b) of these Regulations or until the requirement for such a declaration is waived by the Council in terms of regulation 34(1)(b) of these Regulations.

Applicants for admission after five years
37. Where an application for a Certificate of Fitness is made by an intrant under these Regulations more than five years after the date on which he became entitled to apply therefor, the Council may, after due enquiry and where it appears reasonable to do so, refuse the application or grant the application subject to such conditions as it may reasonably require.

PART VII—GENERAL

Revocations
38. The Admission as Solicitor (Scotland) Regulations 1976 are hereby revoked.

Breaches of the Regulations
39. Contravention of any of the foregoing Regulations may be treated as professional misconduct for the purposes of Part IV of the Act (Complaints and Disciplinary Proceedings).

General Council discretion
[1] **40.** Subject to Regulation 13(2)(d), the Council may, in what it deems to be exceptional circumstances and taking into account the merits of a particular case, vary, waive, modify or otherwise alter any provision of these Regulations, provided that a motion to do so is supported by two-thirds of the members voting thereon.

NOTE
[1] As amended by the Admission as a Solicitor (Scotland) (Amendment) Regulations 1996 (effective November 1, 1996).

FIRST SCHEDULE

An intrant will be deemed to be duly qualified for the purposes of regulation 6(2)(b) of these Regulations if he complies with any of paragraphs (a) to (f) below—

Scottish Certificate of Education
  (a) (1) passes in at least five of the Approved Subjects in the Scottish Certificate of Education, as provided from time to time by the Universities Central Council on Admissions, at no more than two sittings, said passes to include:—
  (i) a pass at Higher grade in English at not less than "B",
  (ii) a pass at Higher grade in a subject chosen from one of the following groups—
     (a) a group comprising mathematics or an approved science, or
     (b) a group comprising an approved language other than English, and
  (iii) a pass at Higher, Ordinary or Standard grade in a subject chosen from the group not chosen under sub-paragraph (ii) above, provided that if at Ordinary or Standard grade, such pass is at not less than grade 3 and
  (2) a total of such points as the Council may from time to time determine in respect of the subjects passed, calculated as follows:—
a pass at Higher grade at—
"A" being valued at three points,
"B" being valued at two points, and
"C" being valued at one point.
Provided that if he has insufficient points or subject passes, he may add to these equivalent passes and points under (b)(1) and (2) below.

General Certificate of Education
  (b) (1) passes in at least five of the Approved Subjects in the General Certificate of Education, as provided from time to time by the Universities Central Council on Admissions, at no more than two sittings, said passes to include:—
  (i) a pass at the Advanced level in English, at not less than "C" standard,
  (ii) a pass at the Advanced level in a subject chosen from one of the following groups—
     (a) a group comprising mathematics or an approved science, or
     (b) a group comprising an approved language other than English, and
  (iii) a pass at the Advanced or Ordinary level or GCSE in a subject chosen from the group not chosen under sub-paragraph (ii) above; and

(2) a total of such points as the Council may from time to time determine in respect of the subjects passed, calculated as follows:—
a pass at the Advanced level at—
"A" being valued at four points,
"B" being valued at three points,
"C" being valued at two points, and
"D" being valued at one point.
Provided that if he has insufficient points or subject passes, he may add to these equivalent passes and points under (a)(1) and (2) above.

HND in Legal Studies
(c) a Scottish Higher National Diploma in Legal Studies from any College of Further Education approved by the Council offering such Diploma and also a pass in English at Higher grade in the Scottish Certificate of Education at not less than "B" or its equivalent.

University Degree
(d) a degree of any University, other than an honorary degree or a Degree in Law, or is entitled to graduate in such a degree notwithstanding that he has not so graduated.

Chartered Accountant
(e) membership of the Institute of Chartered Accountants of Scotland or of the Institute of Chartered Accountants in England and Wales or of the Association of Certified and Corporate Accountants.

Commissioned Officer
(f) a commission as a commissioned officer in one of the British armed services, where his commission has been obtained following study at a Royal Naval, Army or Royal Air Force college.

[1]SECOND SCHEDULE

son/daughter	husband/wife
grandson/granddaughter	son-in-law/daughter-in-law
father/mother	father-in-law/mother-in-law
brother/sister	brother-in-law/sister-in-law
nephew/niece	stepson/stepdaughter
uncle/aunt	stepfather/stepmother
first cousins	stepbrother/stepsister

[1]THIRD SCHEDULE

son/daughter	husband/wife
grandson/granddaughter	stepson/stepdaughter
father/mother	stepfather/stepmother
brother/sister	stepbrother/stepsister

NOTE
[1]As inserted by the Admission as a Solicitor (Scotland) (Amendment) Regulations 1996 (effective August 1, 1996).

Property Misdescriptions (Specified Matters) Order 1992

(S.I. 1992 No. 2834)

[11th November 1992]

The Secretary of State, in exercise of the powers conferred upon him by section 1 of the Property Misdescriptions Act 1991, hereby makes the following Order:

1. This Order may be cited as the Property Misdescriptions (Specified Matters) Order 1992 and shall come into force on 4th April 1993.

2. The matters contained in the Schedule to this Order are hereby specified to the extent described in that Schedule for the purposes of section 1(1) of the Property Misdescriptions Act 1991.

Article 2   SCHEDULE

SPECIFIED MATTERS

1. Location or address.

2. Aspect, view, outlook or environment.

3. Availability and nature of services, facilities or amenities.

4. Proximity to any services, places, facilities or amenities.

5. Accommodation, measurements or sizes.

6. Fixtures and fittings.

7. Physical or structural characteristics, form of construction or condition.

8. Fitness for any purpose or strength of any buildings or other structures on land or of land itself.

9. Treatments, processes, repairs or improvements or the effects thereof.

10. Conformity or compliance with any scheme, standard, test or regulations or the existence of any guarantee.

11. Survey, inspection, investigation, valuation or appraisal by any person or the results thereof.

12. The grant or giving of any award or prize for design or construction.

13. History, including the age, ownership or use of land or any building or fixture and the date of any alterations thereto.

14. Person by whom any building, (or part of any building), fixture or component was designed, constructed, built, produced, treated, processed, repaired, reconditioned or tested.

15. The length of time during which land has been available for sale either generally or by or through a particular person.

16. Price (other than the price at which accommodation or facilities are available and are to be provided by means of the creation or disposal of an interest in land in the circumstances specified in section 23(1)(a) and (b) of the Consumer Protection Act 1987 or Article 16(1)(a) and (b) of the Consumer Protection (NI) Order 1987 (which relate to the creation or disposal of certain interests in new dwellings)) and previous price.

17. Tenure or estate.

18. Length of any lease or of the unexpired term of any lease and the terms and conditions of a lease (and, in relation to land in Northern Ireland, any fee farm grant creating the relation of landlord and tenant shall be treated as a lease).

19. Amount of any ground-rent, rent or premium and frequency of any review.

20. Amount of any rent-charge.

21. Where all or any part of any land is let to a tenant or is subject to a licence, particulars of the tenancy or licence, including any rent, premium or other payment due and frequency of any review.

22. Amount of any service or maintenance charge or liability for common repairs.

23. Council tax payable in respect of a dwelling within the meaning of section 3, or in Scotland section 72, of the Local Government Finance Act 1992 or the basis or any part of the basis on which that tax is calculated.

24. Rates payable in respect of a non-domestic hereditament within the meaning of section 64 of the Local Government Finance Act 1988 or, in Scotland, in respect of lands and heritages shown on a valuation roll or the basis or any part of the basis on which those rates are calculated.

25. Rates payable in respect of a hereditament within the meaning of the Rates (Northern Ireland) Order 1977 or the basis or any part of the basis on which those rates are calculated.

26. Existence or nature of any planning permission or proposals for development, construction or change of use.

27. In relation to land in England and Wales, the passing or rejection of any plans of proposed building work in accordance with section 16 of the Building Act 1984 and the giving of any completion certificate in accordance with regulation 15 of the Building Regulations 1991.

28. In relation to land in Scotland, the granting of a warrant under section 6 of the Building (Scotland) Act 1959 or the granting of a certificate of completion under section 9 of that Act.

29. In relation to land in Northern Ireland, the passing or rejection of any plans of proposed building work in accordance with Article 13 of the Building Regulations (Northern Ireland) Order 1979 and the giving of any completion certificate in accordance with building regulations made under that Order.

30. Application of any statutory provision which restricts the use of land or which requires it to be preserved or maintained in a specified manner.

31. Existence or nature of any restrictive covenants, or of any restrictions on resale, restrictions on use, or pre-emption rights and, in relation to land in Scotland, (in addition to the matters mentioned previously in this paragraph) the existence or nature of any reservations or real conditions.

32. Easements, servitudes or wayleaves.

33. Existence and extent of any public or private right of way.

[THE NEXT PAGE IS F 533]

**Solicitors (Scotland) Order of Precedence, Instructions and
Representation Rules 1992**

Rules made by the Council of the Law Society of Scotland and
approved by the Lord President of the Court of Session pursuant
to section 25A of the Solicitors (Scotland) Act 1980.

Title and commencement
1. These Rules may be cited as the Solicitors (Scotland) Order of
Precedence, Instructions and Representation Rules 1992 and shall come
into force on 31st October 1992.

Interpretation
2.—(1) In these Rules, unless the context otherwise requires—
"the Society" means the Law Society of Scotland;
"the Council" means the Council of the Society;
"the Secretary" means the Secretary of the Society and includes any
person authorised by the Council to act on behalf of the Secretary
for the purposes of these Rules;
"Courts" means the Court of Session, the House of Lords, the Judicial
Committee of the Privy Council and the High Court of Justiciary
and the expression "court" shall be construed accordingly;
"extended rights" means a right of audience in the Court of Session, the
House of Lords and the Judicial Committee of the Privy Council
or, as the case may be, the High Court of Justiciary;
"instructions" means for the purpose of rule 5—
    (a) where a solicitor has on behalf of his firm arranged with
        another firm for the representation of his client before a court
        by a solicitor-advocate, the agreement for representation
        between the two firms; and
    (b) where a client has arranged on his own behalf with a firm of
        solicitors his representation before a court by a solicitor-
        advocate, the agreement for representation between him and
        the firm;
"a solicitor-advocate" means a solicitor who has been granted extended
rights.
(2) Any reference in these Rules to a firm of solicitors shall be deemed to
include a solicitor practising solely on his own account.
(3) The provisions of the Interpretation Act 1978 shall apply to these
Rules as they apply to an Act of Parliament.

Order of precedence of court
3. Where a solicitor-advocate accepts instructions to appear in a court,
those instructions shall:—
    (i) take precedence before any other professional obligation;
    (ii) themselves be in the following order of precedence—
        (a) where the solicitor-advocate has extended rights in the civil
        courts only—
        House of Lords

[THE NEXT PAGE IS F 535]

Inner House of the Court of Session
Outer House of the Court of Session;
  (*b*) where the solicitor-advocate has extended rights in the High
Court of Justiciary only—
High Court of Justiciary exercising its appellate jurisdiction
High Court of Justiciary;
  (*c*) where the solicitor-advocate has extended rights in all courts—
House of Lords
High Court of Justiciary exercising its appellate jurisdiction
High Court of Justiciary
Inner House of the Court of Session
Outer House of the Court of Session.
Subject to the above order of precedence instructions shall take priority
according to the date, or, if on the same date, the time when they are
delivered, or, if orally transmitted, when they have been accepted by the
solicitor-advocate.

Priority of instructions

4. Notwithstanding the general rule stated in rule 3 the solicitor-advocate
shall have regard to the following considerations in determining which
instructions are to be accepted:—
  (*a*) the seriousness, importance or value of the case;
  (*b*) in the case of an appeal, that the solicitor-advocate has appeared for
the client in the lower court;
  (*c*) in the case of an adjourned diet or continued hearing, that the
solicitor-advocate appeared at the previous diet or hearing;
  (*d*) in the case of a debate on the pleadings, that the solicitor-advocate
was responsible for drafting or revising the pleadings, particularly
where a difficult or delicate point of law is involved to which the
solicitor-advocate has already devoted a substantial amount of time
and research;
  (*e*) in the case of a proof or trial, that the solicitor-advocate was involved
to a substantial extent in drafting the pleadings, debating the
pleadings, consulting with the client or advising on the pre-trial or
pre-proof preparations;
  (*f*) that the client has, for the purposes of the case, come to rely on the
advice and guidance of the solicitor-advocate to an unusual extent;
  (*g*) that because of the nature or circumstances of the case, or because of
the limited time available, it would be unusually difficult for either
counsel or another solicitor-advocate adequately to prepare for
appearance;
  (*h*) that a suitable fee has been tendered with instructions or conversely
that the instructions were given on the basis of an agreement with the
client that no fee or only a modified fee will be paid.
If in doubt as to what his decision should be, the solicitor-advocate should
consult the Secretary.

Cancellation of instructions

5.—(1) Acceptance of instructions involves a professional commitment on
which the client and the court are entitled to rely. A solicitor-advocate is not
entitled without good cause to cancel instructions once accepted so as to
relieve himself of that professional commitment.
  (2) In considering whether, and if so when, to cancel instructions after
having accepted them, a solicitor-advocate should have in mind the
following considerations—
  (*a*) so long as instructions to do so have been accepted and not cancelled a
solicitor-advocate owes a duty to the client and the court to attend in
court when the case is called;

(*b*) a solicitor-advocate owes a duty to the client and the court to ensure, as far as he can, that the case is properly prepared and properly presented;

(*c*) a solicitor-advocate owes a duty to the client and the court to remain in attendance until the trial or hearing has been completed;

(*d*) a solicitor-advocate owes a duty to his fellow solicitor-advocates to avoid placing them unnecessarily in a position where they have to take over his cases at short notice and face the client and the court without adequate time for preparation.

It may also be appropriate to take into account the considerations mentioned in rule 4 above.

(3) Where a solicitor-advocate has been instructed by a solicitor and has:—

(*a*) an actual clash of commitments he shall, subject to rule 6(1), without delay intimate the cancellation of the instructions with which he cannot comply and return the relevant papers; or

(*b*) a foreseeable clash of commitments he shall, subject to rule 6(1), immediately inform the instructing solicitor of the situation and comply with any subsequent instructions as to alternative arrangements in the event of his being unable to appear.

(4) Where a solicitor-advocate has been instructed directly by a client and has:—

(*a*) an actual clash of commitments; or

(*b*) a foreseeable clash of commitments;

he shall, subject to rule 6(1) immediately inform the client of the situation, and comply with any subsequent instructions as to alternative arrangements in the event of his being unable to appear.

(5) In the case of proceedings before the High Court of Justiciary on appeal, there is a particular obligation on the solicitor-advocate who represented the appellant at the trial and has recommended an appeal to present that appeal.

Securing representation

6.—(1) Where a solicitor or a solicitor-advocate is unable, in a difficult or urgent situation, to secure representation for a person wishing to be represented by a solicitor-advocate before any court he shall inform the Secretary of the situation.

(2) Where the Secretary is informed under paragraph (1) he shall:—

(*a*) nominate and appoint an appropriate solicitor-advocate to represent the client; or if this is not reasonably practicable,

(*b*) consult the Dean of the Faculty of Advocates.

7. These Rules do not apply to an employed solicitor-advocate whose contract of employment prevents him from acting for persons other than his employer.

FORM OF UNDERTAKING

Rule

1. Name and address of instructed firm: ....

....

2. Name and address of instructing party (if solicitor, insert firm name and reference)

....

....

3. Case name and number: ....

4. Name of solicitor-advocate: ....

5. I/We* the instructing party have arranged my/our client's* representation in the above case with the instructed firm by the above solicitor-advocate. It has been explained that the above solicitor-advocate may cancel the arrangement to appear if he receives other instructions which have priority. If he receives such instructions in a difficult or urgent situation, he may not be able to consult me/us* as to an alternative representative.

6. I/We*, the instructing party, authorise the instructed firm, in the above situation, to contact the Law Society of Scotland in order that they may on my/our* behalf make alternative arrangements for representation by any other solicitor-advocate or if there is no such person who can appear, by counsel; and I/We* undertake to pay the charges due for such representation.

.... (Signature of instructing party)

.... (Date)

....(Signature   ....(Signature
of witness)   of witness)

.... (Occupation)   .... (Occupation)

.... (Address)   .... (Address)

....

....

*delete as appropriate

Code of Conduct (Scotland) Rules 1992

Rules made by the Council of the Law Society of Scotland and approved by the Lord President of the Court of Session pursuant to section 25A of the Solicitors (Scotland) Act 1980.

Title and commencement
   1. These Rules may be cited as the Code of Conduct (Scotland) Rules 1992 and shall come into force on 31st October 1992.

Interpretation
   2.—(1) In these Rules, unless the context otherwise requires:—
   "the Society" means the Law Society of Scotland;
   "the Council" means the Council of the Society;
   "the Secretary" means the Secretary of the Society and includes any person authorised by the Council to act on behalf of the Secretary for the purposes of these Rules;
   "court" means the Court of Session, the House of Lords, the Judicial Committee of the Privy Council and the High Court of Justiciary;
   "extended rights" means a right of audience in the Court of Session, the House of Lords and the Judicial Committee of the Privy Council or, as the case may be, the High Court of Justiciary;
   "rules of conduct" means—
      (a) Code of Conduct for Scottish Solicitors set out in Schedule 1 to these Rules; and
      (b) Supplementary Code of Conduct for Solicitors Exercising Extended Rights of Audience set out in Schedule 2 to these Rules;
   "a solicitor" means a solicitor enrolled with the Society and who holds a full practising certificate;
   "a solicitor-advocate" means a solicitor who has been granted extended rights.

(2) The provisions of the Interpretation Act 1978 shall apply to these Rules as they apply to an Act of Parliament.

3. Where in the course of advising a client a solicitor identifies a situation which may require appearance in a court, he shall advise his client:—

   (a) that appearance before a particular court is restricted to a solicitor-advocate and counsel;

   (b) the advantages and disadvantages of instructing appearance by a solicitor-advocate and by counsel respectively, which advice, subject to the foregoing generality, shall cover—

     (i) the gravity and complexity of the case;

     (ii) the nature of practice, including specialisation, and experience of the solicitor-advocate;

     (iii) the likely cost of instructing the solicitor-advocate and of instructing counsel;

   (c) that the decision of whether the solicitor-advocate or counsel should be instructed is entirely that of the client.

4. A solicitor-advocate shall observe and comply with the rules of conduct.

5. Where a solicitor-advocate is in any doubt as to the propriety of any course of conduct he should:—

   (a) seek the advice of the Secretary;

   (b) explain the position to the Secretary including anything which may be relevant to the advice sought.

6. The Council may, at its discretion, waive compliance with any of these Rules.

7. Breach of any of these Rules may be treated as professional misconduct for the purposes of Part IV of the Solicitors (Scotland) Act 1980 (Complaints and Disciplinary Proceedings).

SCHEDULE 1

Code of Conduct for Solicitors Holding Practising Certificates Issued by the Law Society of Scotland

[See page F 825]

SCHEDULE 2

Supplementary Code of Conduct for Solicitors exercising extended Rights of Audience

1. The acceptance of instructions by a solicitor-advocate

   (1) A solicitor-advocate accepts that it is the responsibility of the Council of the Society to make rules to secure, through the Secretary whom failing such of their officers as they think appropriate, that, where reasonably practicable, any person wishing to be represented before a court by a solicitor-advocate is so represented.

   (2) A solicitor-advocate shall not accept instructions as a solicitor-advocate (as opposed to a solicitor) without satisfying himself that it is proper for him to accept them. A solicitor-advocate shall be entitled at all stages of the case at his sole discretion to decide whether he requires the assistance of a solicitor or other representative of his firm or of the instructing firm in connection with the preparation of the case and also at consultations with the client and at the presentation of the case in court.

(3) There are circumstances in which a solicitor-advocate is entitled and indeed bound to refuse instructions.

(4) A solicitor-advocate may not allow his personal interests to affect the performance of his professional duty. Accordingly, he should not accept instructions to act in his professional capacity in circumstances where he has a direct personal interest in the outcome. Where he has, or may have, an indirect personal interest in the outcome (*e.g.* where he is asked to act for a company in which he is a major shareholder or for an organisation in which he holds office although unremunerated), he should consult the Secretary before accepting instructions. Where a conflict of personal interest arises later, he should inform the instructing solicitor or client and cancel instructions.

(5) A solicitor-advocate may not accept instructions on any basis which would deprive him of the responsibility for the conduct of the case or fetter his discretion to act in consultation with the client in accordance with his professional judgment and public duty.

(6) A solicitor-advocate must not accept instructions to act in circumstances where, in his professional opinion, the case is unstateable in law or where the case is only stateable if facts known to him are misrepresented to, or concealed from, the court. If such circumstances arise after he has accepted instructions, he should decline to act further. There may, however, be exceptional circumstances in which it is proper for a solicitor-advocate, in order to assist the court, to present a case which he believes to be unstateable in law. In such circumstances, the solicitor-advocate must explain to the client that he cannot do more than explain the client's position to the court, and that he will be bound to draw the court's attention to such statutory provisions or binding precedents as have led him to the conclusion that the case is unstateable.

2. Duty in relation to other members of the legal profession

(1) A solicitor-advocate has a duty of loyalty to professional colleagues.

(2) The efficient conduct of litigation under the adversarial system depends on mutual trust between those acting for different parties. Discussion and negotiation between professional colleagues may achieve settlement of a case or at least dispose of incidental points which would otherwise take up time and cause unnecessary expense. It is therefore essential that counsel and solicitor-advocates should be able to discuss cases with each other on the basis that confidence will be respected and that agreements and undertakings will be honoured.

(3) It must, however, also be remembered that all have a duty to act in the best interests of the respective clients. Solicitor-advocates cannot assume that everything said to opposing professional colleagues will be treated in confidence and not disclosed to the solicitor-advocate or the client. It is therefore desirable, at the outset of such discussions that the basis of the discussion be clarified. If it is intended to disclose information on a basis of confidence, this should be stated. Correspondingly, if one party to the discussion is not prepared to treat information as confidential he should say so before the information is disclosed.

(4) Where an agreement is reached following such discussions or an undertaking is given by counsel or solicitor-advocate to another it is binding in honour between them and should be reported as soon as possible so that it can, if necessary, be incorporated in a formal exchange of letters. Alternatively, a joint minute should be drafted and initialled by counsel or solicitor-advocate who should also bear in mind that once recorded in writing the written agreement supersedes the verbal agreement.

3. Duties in relation to an instructing solicitor

(1) A solicitor-advocate when instructed by a solicitor must respect the fact that the solicitor's relationship is different from, and likely to be more

continuing than, his own. He should do nothing, beyond what his professional duty requires, to upset the solicitor-client relationship or destroy the trust which the client has in the solicitor.

(2) When a solicitor-advocate has reason to believe that a solicitor has been guilty of professional misconduct (as opposed to professional negligence) he has a duty to the client, the court and the profession to take appropriate action.

If the matter comes to his knowledge in the course of proceedings in court, it may be necessary to take immediate action, and if an adjournment is necessary for this purpose, it should be asked for. If the matter does not call for immediate action, the solicitor-advocate should consult the Secretary before making any formal complaint or report.

(3) If a solicitor-advocate feels compelled to criticise the conduct of a solicitor in respect of something falling short of professional misconduct, he should avoid doing so in the presence of the client and should in any event ask the solicitor to explain what he has done and why before criticising his conduct.

(4) A solicitor-advocate where instructed by a solicitor or directly by a client should consider carefully whether he should attend a consultation without his instructing solicitor or another representative of his firm or of the instructing firm being present. The presence of the solicitor or representative will protect both the solicitor-advocate and the solicitor should a dispute arise later as to what advice the solicitor-advocate gave or what instructions he was given by the client.

(5) In exceptional circumstances, it may be unavoidable that a solicitor-advocate instructed by a solicitor has to speak to the client without the solicitor being present. Such an occasion will however be rare, and when it arises the solicitor should be told as soon as possible what transpired.

4. Duties in relation to the client

(1) *Confidentiality*. It is a fundamental duty of the solicitor-advocate not to disclose or use any information communicated to him in his professional capacity other than for the purpose of which it was communicated to him, so long as it remains in confidence and has not otherwise been made public. Any conversations relating to a case which take place between solicitor-advocate and those representing the other side, including Crown counsel, are confidential and should not be revealed to anyone other than the client or those who are professionally concerned with the case. If he wishes to discuss a case with a colleague, for example, for the purpose of seeking his advice about law, he should do so only in terms which do not disclose, or risk disclosure of, the identity of client or other parties involved.

This applies equally where a solicitor-advocate is asked to give a written opinion or to advise in consultation. There may be good reasons, unknown to him, why the client or instructing solicitor would not even wish it to be known that his advice has been sought. Idle gossip about cases and clients, even if the facts are publicly known, is damaging to the reputation of the solicitor-advocate and of the profession.

(2) *Duty to uphold the interests of the client*. A solicitor-advocate should remember that the client relies on him to exercise his professional skill and judgment in the client's best interests. He must at all times do, and be seen to do, his best for the client and he must be fearless in defending his client's interests, regardless of the consequences to himself (including, if necessary, incurring the displeasure of the bench). But he must also remember that his client's best interests require him to give honest advice however unwelcome that advice may be to the client and that duty to the client is only one of several duties which he must strive to reconcile.

(3) *Conflict between client and instructing solicitor* (e.g. *where the client may have a claim for professional negligence against his solicitor*). Where it appears to a solicitor-advocate who is instructed by a solicitor that a conflict

of interest has arisen or may arise between the client and the instructing solicitor, it is his duty to take steps to ensure that the client is so advised in order that he can get the advice of another solicitor. It will depend on the circumstances how this can be done. The great majority of instructing solicitors can be relied upon, when the conflict has been pointed out, to take the necessary steps themselves. It will therefore normally be inappropriate to mention the matter in the presence of the client. But it may be necessary to record the solicitor-advocate's advice as to the existence of a conflict in a formal note and to ask the instructing solicitor to send it to the client, or to deal with the matter at consultation with the client. In extreme cases, it may be the duty of the solicitor-advocate to refuse to act further on the instructions of the solicitor concerned, but before doing so he should where practicable intimate in writing to the instructing solicitor that it is his intention to refuse to act further.

(4) *Cancellation of instructions.* In any case where the solicitor-advocate feels obliged to cancel instructions, he must do so without delay and take such steps as are necessary to ensure that the client, and where appropriate the instructing solicitor, knows why he has withdrawn. Where he feels obliged to cancel in the course of a trial or other hearing, he must formally intimate to the court that he has cancelled instructions and is withdrawing from acting and must protect the interests of the client by moving for an adjournment so that the client can get other advice. He is under no obligation to explain in detail to the court or tribunal his reasons for cancellation, since to do so may prejudice his client, and he should not yield to pressure to do so. If in doubt as to whether he is entitled or bound to cancel he should seek the advice of the Secretary, and if necessary obtain an adjournment to do so.

5. Special duties in criminal cases

(1) *Pleas.* Where the Crown offers to accept a reduced or restricted plea, the defending solicitor-advocate has a duty to advise the accused of that offer and to obtain his instructions about it. Likewise, where any limited offer to plead is made by an accused, it should (if considered in law to be appropriate) be conveyed to the Crown for consideration, without delay. For avoidance of doubt, it is prudent to obtain written instructions from the accused, for the tendering of a plea. In no circumstances should the solicitor-advocate tender any plea on behalf of the accused unless instructions to do so have been obtained.

(2) In advising as to the possible consequences of a plea of guilty, a solicitor-advocate should refrain from making any positive forecast of the possible sentence beyond drawing the attention of the accused to the normally anticipated range of sentences in the circumstances of that particular case.

(3) *Confessions.* Where an accused person makes a confession to a solicitor-advocate and the solicitor-advocate is satisfied in law that such confession amounts to guilt, the solicitor-advocate must explain to the accused (if he is not pleading guilty) that the conduct of his defence will be limited by that confession. It must be emphasised to the accused that no substantive defence involving an assertion or a suggestion of innocence will be put forward on his behalf and that, if he is not satisfied with this, he should seek other advice. A solicitor-advocate should consider whether it is advisable to obtain confirmation in writing from the accused that he has been so advised and that he accepts such an approach to the conduct of his defence.

(4) So long as an accused maintains his innocence, the solicitor-advocate's duty lies in advising him on the law appropriate to his case and the conduct thereof. The solicitor-advocate may not put pressure on him to tender a plea of guilty, whether to a restricted charge or not, so long as he maintains his innocence. Nor should the solicitor-advocate accept instructions to tender a

plea in mitigation on a basis inconsistent with the plea of guilty. The solicitor-advocate should always consider very carefully whether it is proper, in the interests of justice, to accept instructions to tender a plea of guilty. He should ensure that the accused is fully aware of the consequences and should insist that the instructions to plead guilty are recorded in writing.

(5) *Acting for co-accused.* Save in the most exceptional circumstances, a solicitor-advocate should not accept instructions to act for more than one accused or appellant.

6. The duty to the court

(1) *Duties in relation to matters of law.* Where a solicitor-advocate is aware of a previous decision binding on the court, or of a statutory provision relevant to a point of law in issue, it is his duty to draw that decision or provision to the attention of the court whether or not it supports his argument and whether or not it has been referred to by his opponent.

(2) Where there is no contradictor, a solicitor-advocate should inform the court of authorities relevant to that case, even when such authority may be against his interest.

(3) In proceedings before the House of Lords, a solicitor-advocate should have in mind the observations of Lord Chancellor Birkenhead in *Glebe Sugar Refining Co. v. Greenock Harbour Trustees* 1921 S.C.(H.L.) 72, 73–74.

7. Duties in relation to matters of fact

(1) In relation to matters of fact, a solicitor-advocate should have two principles in mind:—

   (a) It is for the court, not for a solicitor-advocate, to assess the credibility of witnesses; and

   (b) a solicitor-advocate must not, directly or indirectly, deceive or mislead the court.

(2) *In court.* When conducting a case in court, a solicitor-advocate should base his questions upon his instructions, the precognitions and the productions supplemented by information obtained at consultation and, after evidence has been led, upon the evidence.

(3) A solicitor-advocate should not state his personal opinion on matters of fact. It is particularly important to observe this rule when addressing a jury. A solicitor-advocate must not make observations on matters of fact which are not based on, or justified by, the evidence. In a criminal trial, he should not under any circumstances express either directly or indirectly a personal belief in the innocence of the accused.

(4) A solicitor-advocate may not be a party to the giving of evidence which he knows to be perjured evidence, or to any other course that would enable a case to be put forward on behalf of a client which the client has informed him is unfounded in fact.

(5) A solicitor-advocate may not put to a witness any question suggesting that the witness has been guilty of a crime, fraud or other illegal or improper conduct unless he has personally satisfied himself that there is evidence which could, if necessary, be led in support of the suggestion.

(6) *Interviewing witnesses.* There is no general rule that a solicitor-advocate may not discuss the case with a potential witness, but a solicitor-advocate when instructed by a solicitor, is entitled to insist that he accepts instructions on the basis that he, the solicitor-advocate, will not do so.

(7) In cases where a solicitor-advocate has not accepted instructions on such a basis he must avoid doing or saying anything which could have the effect of, or could be construed as, inducing the client or skilled witness to "tailor" his evidence to suit the case.

(8) Once a proof or trial has begun, a solicitor-advocate must not interview any potential witness in relation to what has been said in court in the absence of that witness.

(9) Some cases cannot be properly prepared or conducted if the foregoing rules against interviewing potential witnesses are followed strictly according to the letter. The client may be accompanied at consultation by a relative or friend who is also a potential witness. Where the client is a corporate persona, those who can speak for the corporation may also be potential witnesses, although in that case it is usually better to discuss the case with someone who is not personally involved and can take a more objective view of it. Some witnesses may be witnesses to fact as to part of their evidence and expert witnesses giving opinion evidence as to another part. It may be essential in a case raising technical issues to discuss points arising from the evidence with a skilled witness who has not yet given evidence. In such cases, a solicitor-advocate must use his discretion. But he should always act according to the spirit of the rule—namely, that a solicitor-advocate should not under any circumstances do or say anything which might suggest to the witness that he should give evidence otherwise than in accordance with his honest recollection or opinion.

(10) A solicitor-advocate may not, except with the consent of his opponent and of the court, communicate with any witness, including his client, once that witness has begun to give evidence until that evidence is concluded.

(11) As to interviewing the client or witnesses in the absence of an instructing solicitor, see paragraphs 3(4) and 3(5) above.

(12) *Confessions to a solicitor-advocate by accused persons.* It follows from the rules stated in paragraphs 5(3) and 5(4) that, where an accused person has admitted that he committed the act with which he is charged (whether or not the admission is an explicit admission of guilt in law), a solicitor-advocate may not conduct the defence on a basis inconsistent with that admission. Thus, he may not put to a witness any question suggesting, or tending to suggest, that the accused did not commit the act. *A fortiori*, he may not seek to set up a special defence of alibi or incrimination.

(13) Subject to the rule stated in the previous paragraph, a solicitor-advocate may—

(a) take any proper objection to the jurisdiction of the court, to the competency or relevancy of the indictment, or to the admissibility of evidence;
(b) test the evidence for the prosecution by cross-examination;
(c) cross-examine or lead evidence in support of a special defence of insanity or (depending on the tenor of the accused's admission) self-defence;
(d) cross-examine or lead evidence for the purpose of explaining the actings of the accused or supporting a plea in mitigation;
(e) make submissions as to the sufficiency in law of the evidence to support a verdict of guilty.

(14) *Ex parte statements of fact by a solicitor-advocate at the bar.* The court frequently must rely on statements as to matters of fact made at the bar, for example, in the motion roll and certain types of petition procedure. Such statements are made on the responsibility of the solicitor-advocate as an officer of the court and a solicitor-advocate must therefore be scrupulously careful that anything stated as fact is justified by the information in his possession. If the court asks a question which a solicitor-advocate cannot answer on the information in his possession, he must say that he cannot answer it and, if necessary, ask leave to take instructions on the matter. This rule applies whether or not the opposing party is represented in court.

(15) *Pleadings.* A solicitor-advocate must have a proper basis on precognition or in the light of consultation with the client for stating a fact in any pleadings.

8. The duty of courtesy
(1) Discourtesy is as offensive in court as it is outside, and is detrimental to the reputation of a solicitor-advocate and of the bench, to the interests of the

client and to public confidence in the administration of justice.

(2) In the examination of witnesses,and particularly in the cross-examination of hostile witnesses, a solicitor-advocate must remember that the law places him in a privileged position which he should not abuse, for example, by bullying or insulting behaviour or by making offensive or personal remarks.

(3) A solicitor-advocate should seek to uphold a relationship of mutual trust and courtesy with the bench.

(4) A failure to appear in court on time should always, as a matter of courtesy, be the subject of an apology. If the court is still sitting, and has not yet passed on to other business, the proper time to make the apology is at once on arrival in court.

The apology should always be in open court to the bench. It is not sufficient to offer an apology through the macer or clerk of court.

9. The duty to attend court

(1) It is the duty of the solicitor-advocate to arrange his affairs so as to avoid a reasonably foreseeable clash of commitments.

(2) Having accepted instructions to appear, it is the solicitor-advocate's responsibility to ensure, unless (in a civil case only) other arrangements have been made with an instructing solicitor, that he is present in court on the day and at the time appointed and thereafter until the trial or hearing is concluded. Where unforeseen circumstances make it impossible for him to be present and he is unable to contact the Secretary, he must ensure that someone else is present at or before the time appointed to explain his absence and, if necessary, to move for an adjournment.

(3) Since instructions to appear in the High Court of Justiciary and the Inner House take precedence over instructions to appear in the Outer House, it follows that if a solicitor-advocate has accepted instructions to appear in the High Court or the Inner House, including instructions for the single bills, it is his duty to ensure that he is present there at the appointed time, even although he also has instructions to appear in the Outer House. If a clash of commitments appears likely, and he is unable to contact the Secretary, he should ensure that someone else is present to appear in the Outer House in his place and, if necessary, to move for an adjournment until he is free to appear there. If a conflict arises due to unforeseen circumstances and he finds himself still detained in the Outer House when he must appear in the High Court or the Inner House, he should inform the Lord Ordinary that he requires to go to the High Court or the Inner House as the case may be and ask for an adjournment so that he can do so.

(4) If a solicitor-advocate engaged in a proof or other hearing in the Outer House expects to be in difficulty because he is required to attend elsewhere in the Outer House to deal with an important matter on the motion roll on the same day, he or a representative from his firm should inform the clerk of court as soon as possible so that the judge concerned may be alerted to the problem and take such action as is appropriate. It has been accepted that in such circumstances the start of the proof might reasonably be delayed until the solicitor-advocate's business in the other court has been completed.

(5) Where a senior solicitor-advocate appears with a junior solicitor-advocate he should only be absent from court if he is satisfied that his junior will be present and will be able to deal properly with any matter which may arise.

10. Responsibility for pleadings and presentation in civil actions

(1) A solicitor-advocate who signs any pleadings accepts personal responsibility to the court for their contents. He has a professional responsibility for any other pleadings drafted by him, except where his draft has been altered without his knowledge and consent. Where a solicitor-advocate finds that pleadings drafted by him have been altered without his

knowledge and consent, it is his professional duty to consider whether he can support the case on the basis of the pleadings so altered.

(2) Since a solicitor-advocate accepts responsibility for pleadings or documents he has signed, he should not sign in his own name pleadings drafted by someone else save in exceptional circumstances. Papers may be signed in that way provided the solicitor-advocate concerned is satisfied that the solicitor-advocate for whom he signs cannot reasonably be found and he is also satisfied that the paper is in proper form for submission to the court.

(3) The presentation of a case in court is a matter for the sole professional responsibility and discretion of the solicitor-advocate.

11. Speculative actions

In speculative actions, a solicitor-advocate has a particular responsibility to the court both with regard to his own assessment of the merits of the case and with regard to the advice which he gives. The nature of the responsibility undertaken by counsel and solicitor was stated thus by Lord President Normand (*X Insurance Co. v. A & B* 1936 S.C. 225, 239)—

"It has long been recognised by the Courts that this is a perfectly legitimate basis on which to carry on litigation and a reasonable indulgence to people who while they are not qualified for admission to [legal aid] are nevertheless unable to finance a costly litigation.

"But it is equally recognised that there is involved in such business a grave risk of abuse unless it is carried out with strict regard to honour by all who are professionally concerned in it. Before acting in business of this kind it is the imperative duty of the solicitor and of the counsel to consider whether the party for whom they are to act has a reasonable prospect of success.

"The reasons for this are obvious, and need no discussion. If a solicitor, when asked to conduct the case on a speculative footing, is, after consideration, unable to advise that there is a reasonable prospect of success, he should refuse to conduct the case. But, if he has reasonable doubts about the prospects of success, he is justified in consulting counsel. If counsel advises that the action may properly be raised, the solicitor is entitled to follow his advice, and in the future conduct of the action he is bound to act in accordance with counsel's instructions. If he does this after having fairly disclosed to counsel all the information at his disposal, he will not be exposed to a charge of professional misconduct. In order that the prospects of success may be fairly estimated by the solicitor and by counsel in their turn, it is in most cases, where questions of fact are involved, a necessary precaution that fair and honest precognitions of the chief witnesses who will be relied on should be taken at the outset." (See also the opinion of Lord Fleming, 250–251.)

12. Criminal appeals

(1) In advising on criminal appeals, a solicitor-advocate has a duty, first, to consider whether there are grounds for an appeal which he is prepared to state to the court and, second, if in his opinion there are none, to refuse to act further in the case: *Scott v. H.M. Advocate*, 1946 J.C. 68, *per* Lord President Normand at 69.

(2) Having advised that an appeal is stateable, a solicitor-advocate may later come to the view that it is not. If so, he must promptly inform his client that he can no longer act in the case.

13. Opposing a party litigant

Where a solicitor-advocate appears against a party litigant, he must avoid taking unfair advantage of the party litigant and must, consistently with his duty to the client, co-operate with the court in enabling the party litigant's case to be fairly stated and justice to be done. But he must not sacrifice the interests of the client to those of the party litigant.

ANNEX

Solicitors (Scotland) (Continuing Professional Development) Regulations 1993

Regulations dated 29th July 1993 made by the Council of the Law Society of Scotland with the concurrence of the Lord President of the Court of Session under section 5 of the Solicitors (Scotland) Act 1980.

1.—(1) These Regulations may be cited as the Solicitors (Scotland) (Continuing Professional Development) Regulations 1993.
(2) These Regulations shall come into operation on 1st November 1993.

2.—(1) In these Regulations unless the context otherwise requires:—
  "the Act" means the Solicitors (Scotland) Act 1980;
  "the Council" means the Council of the Law Society of Scotland;
  "solicitor" means a solicitor holding a practising certificate under the Act;
  "continuing professional development" means relevant education and study by a solicitor to develop his or her professional knowledge, skills and abilities.
(2) The Interpretation Act 1978 applies to the interpretation of these Regulations as it applies to the interpretation of an Act of Parliament.

3. From 1st November 1993 every solicitor shall undertake continuing professional development the nature and timing of which shall be prescribed by the Council from time to time.

4. Every solicitor shall keep a record of continuing professional development undertaken to comply with these Regulations and produce that record to the Council on demand.

5. The Council shall have power to waive any of the provisions of these Regulations in any particular circumstances or case and to revoke such a waiver.

6. Breach of any of these Regulations may be treated as professional misconduct for the purposes of Part IV of the Act (Complaints and Disciplinary Proceedings).

Solicitors (Scotland) (Written Fee Charging Agreements) Practice Rules 1993

Rules dated 29th July 1993 made by the Council of the Law Society of Scotland and approved by the Lord President of the Court of Session in terms of section 34 of the Solicitors (Scotland) Act 1980.

1. These Rules may be cited as the Solicitors (Scotland) (Written Fee Charging Agreements) Practice Rules 1993.

2. These Rules shall come into operation on 1st August 1993.

3. In these Rules unless the context otherwise requires:—
"the Act" means the Solicitors (Scotland) Act 1980;
"the Council" means the Council of the Law Society of Scotland;
"solicitor" means a solicitor holding a practising certificate under the Act and includes a firm of solicitors and an incorporated practice;
"written fee charging agreement" means an agreement in writing between a solicitor and his client as to the solicitor's fees in respect of any work done or to be done by the solicitor for his client entered into in terms of section 61(A)(1) of the Act.

4. A written fee charging agreement shall not contain a consent to registration for preservation and execution.

5. The Council shall have power on cause shown to waive the provisions of these Rules in any particular case, and to revoke such a waiver.

6. Breach of any of these Rules may be treated as professional misconduct for the purposes of Part IV of the Act (Complaints and Disciplinary Proceedings).

Solicitors (Scotland) Investment Business Training Regulations 1994

Regulations dated 25th March 1994, made by the Council of the Law
Society of Scotland with the concurrence of the Lord President
of the Court of Session under section 5 of the Solicitors
(Scotland) Act 1980 and rule 4.1 of the CBRs (as defined in
regulation 2(1)).

Citation and Commencement
1. These regulations may be cited as the Solicitors (Scotland) Investment
Business Training Regulations 1994 and shall, with the exception of
regulation 7 (Transitional Provisions) (which shall come into force on the
date hereof), come into operation on 1st July 1994.

Definitions and interpretation
2.—(1) In these regulations unless the context otherwise requires:—
  "the Act" means the Solicitors (Scotland) Act 1980;
  "the CBRs" means the Solicitors (Scotland) (Conduct of Investment
      Business) Practice Rules 1994 or any amendment thereof or any
      other rules which may be substituted therefor;
  "certified person" has the meaning ascribed to it by rule 1.4(1) of the
      CBRs;
  "the Council" means the Council of the Society or any Committee or
      Sub-Committee of the Council or panel of examiners to which the
      Council may delegate its powers in terms of these regulations;
  "employee" has the meaning ascribed to it by rule 1.4(1) of the CBRs;
  "the FSA" means the Financial Services Act 1986;
  "officer" has the meaning ascribed to it by rule 1.4(1) of the CBRs;
  "the Society" means the Law Society of Scotland under the Act;
  "solicitor" means a solicitor holding a practising certificate under the
      Act.
  (2) The Interpretation Act 1978 applies to these regulations as it applies to
an Act of Parliament.
  (3) Words defined in the FSA:—
  unless the context requires, words and expressions defined in the FSA
  have the same meanings when used in these regulations.

Applicability
3. These regulations apply to every certified person which wishes to
continue to be a certified person from and after 1st November 1995.

Obligations on a certified person
4.—(a) With effect from 1st November 1995 and on 1st November in every
subsequent year a certified person shall—
      (i) identify those officers and employees of the certified person who
          will conduct investment business in the practice year ending on
          31st October following, and notify the Council in writing
          accordingly; and
      (ii) similarly notify the Council of the identity of any other officer or
          employee who becomes qualified in terms of these regulations
          and will conduct investment business in the said practice year,
          within one month of such qualification.
  (b) With effect from 1st November 1995, a certified person shall:—
      (i) ensure that at all times at least one officer of the certified person
          is, and all other officers and employees who will conduct
          investment business are, qualified to do so or exempt in terms of
          these regulations.

(ii) ensure that all solicitors to whom the Continuing Professional Development Practice Regulations apply who are officers or employees of the certified person and have been identified in terms of regulation 4(a) above comply with the requirements of the Solicitors (Scotland) (Continuing Professional Development) Practice Regulations 1993 to the effect that not less than one third of non-management time spent by such solicitors on continuing professional development is so spent on education and training in investment business; or

that all solicitors admitted before 1st November 1983 who are officers or employees of the certified person and have been identified in terms of regulation 4(a) above shall spend in the practice year 1st November 1995 to 31st October 1996 not less than five hours per annum on education and training in investment business, and

(iii) ensure that all non-solicitor employees who conduct investment business on behalf of the certified person by way of giving investment advice to clients of the certified person undertake continuing professional development in investment business in each practice year for the same period of time as applies to solicitors conducting investment business as required by regulation 4(*b*)(ii).

Qualifications to conduct investment business
5.—(1) Every solicitor and every employee who will conduct investment business on behalf of a certified person from and after 1st November 1995 shall, unless otherwise exempt in terms of these regulations, be required to have sat and passed the Society's Investment Business Examination ("the Exam");
(2) The Exam shall consist of examinations in the law and practice of investment business to assess a candidate's knowledge and understanding of financial services generally, investments, savings and protection products and financial advice, in accordance with the syllabus prescribed or approved by the Council from time to time, which syllabus may contain different requirements for solicitors and non-solicitor employees respectively;
(3) The Council may from time to time appoint a panel of not less than three nor more than five suitably qualified and experienced persons to be examiners of candidates for the Exam at such remuneration as the Council may determine, or the Council may delegate the power of examination to a body approved by it;
(4) The diets of the Exam shall be held at such times and in such places as the Council may determine;
(5) A candidate shall tender with his application to sit the Exam, such fees as may be prescribed by the Council from time to time.

Recognition of other qualifications
6. A solicitor or employee who has satisfied the Council that he is the possessor of a qualification to conduct investment business which is of a standard equivalent to that of the Exam shall not be required to sit the Exam.

Transitional provisions—exemptions from the Exam
7.—(1) A solicitor who—
   (*a*) will conduct investment business after 1st November 1995 in terms of regulation 4(*a*); and
   (*b*) has held a full and unrestricted practising certificate under the Act for a continuous period of not less than five years ending on 31st October 1994; and
   (*c*) satisfies the Council that he has had sufficient experience of the conduct of investment business in the three years prior to 31st October 1994;
may apply, not later than 30th November 1994, to the Council for exemption from the requirement to sit the Exam, on a form to be prescribed by the Council whose decision on whether or not to grant such exemption, or to grant such exemption subject to conditions, shall be final.
(2) A non-solicitor employee who—
   (*a*) will conduct investment business after 1st November 1995 in terms of regulation 4(*a*); and
   (*b*) satisfies the Council that he has had sufficient experience of the conduct of investment business in the three years prior to 31st October 1994;
may apply, not later than 30th November 1994, to the Council for exemption from the requirement to sit the Exam, on a form to be prescribed by the Council whose decision on whether or not to grant such exemption, or to grant such exemption subject to conditions, shall be final.

8. The Council shall have power to waive or modify any of the requirements of these regulations in any particular case.

9. Breach of or failure to comply with these regulations may be treated as professional misconduct for the purposes of Part IV of the Act (Complaints and Disciplinary Proceedings).

EC Qualified Lawyers Transfer (Scotland) Regulations 1994

EC Qualified Lawyers Transfer (Scotland) Regulations 1994 made by the Council of the Law Society of Scotland in June 1994 with the concurrence of the Lord President of the Court of Session under section 5 of the Solicitors (Scotland) Act 1980.

Title and commencement
1. These regulations may be cited as the EC Qualified Lawyers Transfer (Scotland) Regulations 1994 and shall come into operation on 1st July 1994.

Definitions and interpretation
2.—(1) In these Regulations, unless the context otherwise requires—
    "the Act" means the Solicitors (Scotland) Act 1980;
    "the Society" means The Law Society of Scotland;
    "the Council" means the Council of the Society;
    "the Directive" means the Directive of the Council of the European Communities for recognition of Higher Education Diplomas dated 21st December 1988 and numbered 89/48/EEC;
    "applicant" means a person seeking admission as a solicitor in Scotland under these Regulations;
    "the Test" means the qualified lawyers transfer test being the aptitude test defined in Article 1(*g*) of the Directive and being an assessment of competence in the subjects specified in these Regulations;
    "the court" means the Court of Session.
    (2) The provisions of the Interpretation Act 1978 shall apply to the interpretation of these Regulations as they apply to the interpretation of an Act of Parliament.
    (3) The headings to these Regulations do not form part of these Regulations.

Scope of regulations
3. These Regulations shall apply to any lawyer making application for admission as a solicitor in Scotland pursuant to the Directive or legislation implementing the Directive in the United Kingdom.

Eligibility
4.—(1) An applicant shall submit his application in writing to the Society and shall—
    (i) make payment of such fee for assessment of his application by the Society as the Council shall from time to time prescribe; and
    (ii) provide such evidence as the Society may require that he
        (*a*) is a person to whom the Directive and in consequence these Regulations may apply; and
        (*b*) is a fit and proper person to be a solicitor.
    (2) The Council shall within a period of four months after presentation by the applicant of all relevant documentation, issue a written statement giving its decision as to whether or not the applicant is eligible to seek admission as a solicitor in Scotland.

(3) Where it is established that an applicant is eligible to seek admission in terms of regulation 4(2), the Council shall specify those subjects (if any) in the Test which the applicant shall be required to pass and any other conditions which the applicant must satisfy, having regard to the nature and extent of the applicant's experience (if any) of legal practice in Scotland and any academic or other qualification in the law of Scotland.

The Test
5.—(1) An applicant who has established his eligibility conform to regulation 4 shall be required to pass the Test in such subjects as are specified in the written statement referred to in regulation 4(2).

(2) The Test shall be an assessment by written and oral examination of an applicant's competence in the following subjects—
   (a) the Scottish law of Property including for this purpose the law of trusts and succession and family law;
   (b) the Scottish Legal System including for this purpose the law of evidence and civil and criminal procedure;
   (c) European Community Law and Institutions;
   (d) Professional Conduct including for this purpose a knowledge of the Solicitors' (Scotland) Accounts Rules in force from time to time; and
   (e) such other subjects as the Council may from time to time reasonably prescribe.

(3) The Council may delegate to appropriately qualified persons the examination of applicants taking the Test and the Test will be held at such times as the Council may determine.

(4) An applicant shall be required to give such notice of his intention to sit the Test and pay to the Society such fee for the Test as the Council shall from time to time prescribe.

(5) An applicant who has failed to pass the Test on four separate occasions shall not be again entitled to present himself for the Test.

(6) Unless the Council in exceptional circumstances otherwise determines, an applicant shall require to pass the Test at a single diet.

(7) The Council may at its sole discretion and subject to such reasonable conditions as it may impose, in what it deems to be appropriate circumstances, and taking into account the particular merits of an applicant, exempt him from all or any part of the Test or from the provisions of regulation 5(5).

Certificate of fitness
6. Where an applicant has
   (a) passed or gained exemption from the Test or any part thereof; and
   (b) complied with any conditions imposed upon him by the Council in terms of these Regulations; and
   (c) satisfied the Council that he remains a fit and proper person to be a solicitor
he shall be entitled to obtain from the Council a certificate in terms of section 6(1)(b)(ii) of the Act and thereafter to call upon the Council to apply to the court on his behalf for admission as a solicitor in terms of section 6(3A) of the Act.

Application of these regulations
7. These Regulations shall have effect in relation to applications for admission as a solicitor in Scotland received by the Society from applicants on or after 1st January 1994.

Revocation of 1990 regulations
8. The EC Qualified Lawyers Transfer (Scotland) Regulations 1990 are hereby revoked.

Solicitors (Scotland) Professional Indemnity Insurance Rules 1995

Rules dated 31st March 1995 made by the Council of the Law Society of Scotland with the concurrence of the Lord President of the Court of Session under section 44 of the Solicitors (Scotland) Act 1980.

Citation
   1.—(1) These Rules may be cited as the Solicitors (Scotland) Professional Indemnity Insurance Rules 1995.
   (2) These Rules shall come into operation on the 1st day of May 1995.

   2.—(1) In these Rules, unless the context otherwise requires:—
      "the Act" means the Solicitors (Scotland) Act 1980;
      "authorised insurers" means any person permitted under the Insurance Companies Act 1974 to carry on liability insurance business or pecuniary loss insurance business;
      "brokers" means the brokers from time to time appointed by the Council to act on behalf of the Society and its members in relation to any Master Policy entered into by the Society in terms of these Rules;
      "the Society" means the Law Society of Scotland established under the Act;
      "the Council" means the Council of the Society;
      "practice unit" means where a practice is carried on by a sole practitioner that practitioner and where a practice is carried on by solicitors in partnership that partnership and where the practice is carried on by an incorporated practice that incorporated practice;
      "solicitor" means a solicitor holding a practising certificate under the Act and includes a firm of solicitors and an incorporated practice.
   (2) The Interpretation Act 1978 applies to the interpretation of these Rules as it applies to the interpretation of an Act of Parliament.

   3. The Solicitors (Scotland) Professional Indemnity Insurance Rules 1988 are hereby repealed.

To whom the Rules apply
   4.—(*a*) These Rules apply to every solicitor who is, or is held out to the public as, a principal in private practice in Scotland.
      (*b*) A solicitor shall not be deemed to be a principal in private practice or to be held out as such by reason only:—
         (i)   that he practises only as consultant or associate to another solicitor provided that if his name appears on the name-plate or letter paper of such other solicitor it is accompanied by the designation "Consultant" or "Associate"; or
         (ii) in the case of a solicitor employed by another solicitor that the former in carrying out work for his employer uses his own name.

Master policy
   5.—(1) The Society shall take out and maintain with authorised insurers to be determined from time to time by the Council a master policy in terms to be approved by the Council to provide indemnity against such classes of professional liability as the Council may decide. The Council at its discretion may amend the terms of the master policy from time to time.
   (2) The master policy shall provide indemnity for all solicitors to whom these Rules apply and for such former solicitors and other parties as may be mentioned in the master policy.

(3) The limits of indemnity and the self-insured amounts under the master policy shall be as may be determined from time to time by the Council.

Provided that nothing in these Rules shall prohibit any solicitor from arranging with the insurers to extend the cover provided by the master policy if and on such terms as the insurers may agree.

Contingency fund
6.—(1) The master policy may provide for the intimation to the brokers of circumstances affecting a practice unit which have not given rise to a claim under the master policy but which may reasonably be expected to do so, and the terms of the master policy may provide for such circumstances to be taken into account in calculating the premium payable by practice units.

(2) The Society may establish a fund (in these Rules referred to as the "contingency fund") for the purpose of refunding to practice units such portion of the premiums paid by them as may be attributable to circumstances intimated in accordance with the master policy if and when the brokers are satisfied that no claim will result from such circumstances. The terms and conditions upon which such refund shall be made shall be determined from time to time by the Council.

(3) Every solicitor to whom these Rules apply shall contribute such sum (if any) as may be required by the Council to establish and maintain the contingency fund. Every such solicitor shall produce along with each application for a practising certificate such evidence as the Council may require that he has paid such contribution as aforesaid.

Commencement
7. On and after the 1st day of November 1994, every solicitor to whom these Rules apply shall be obliged to be insured under the master policy and:—
  (i) to comply with the terms of the master policy and of any certificate of insurance issued to him thereunder; and
  (ii) to produce along with each application for a practising certificate a certificate from the brokers certifying that the solicitor in question is insured under the master policy for the practice year then commencing or the part thereof still to run as the case may be, or such other evidence as may be acceptable to the Council.

Waiver
8. The Council shall have power in any case or class of case to waive in writing any of the provisions of these Rules and to revoke any such waiver.

Additional powers
9.—(1) The Council is hereby empowered to take such steps as it may consider expedient in order to:—
  (a) ascertain whether or not these Rules are being complied with; or
  (b) satisfy itself with regard to any matters arising out of the master policy.
(2) The powers conferred on the Council under this Rule shall include:—
  (a) power to inspect files and any information or documents recorded whether by paper, electronic or other means in the hands of the authorised insurers and to obtain such further information from the authorised insurers or those instructed by them as the Council may from time to time consider necessary;
  (b) power, by written notice to require a practice unit to produce, in order to carry out inspections at a time to be fixed by the Council or in the option of the practice unit at its place of business, files and any information recorded whether by paper, electronic or other means within the offices or within the control of the accountants of any practice unit; and

    (c) power to give advice and guidance to the practice unit in order that it may secure compliance with the provisions of the master policy or these Rules.

    (3) A practice unit duly required to do so under this rule shall produce such files and any other information or documents at the time and place fixed.

    (4) A written notice given by the Council to a practice unit under paragraph (2)(b) of this rule shall be signed by the Secretary or a Deputy Secretary of the Society and shall be sent by Recorded Delivery service to the practice unit at its place of business as defined in the Constitution of the Society. Such written notice shall be given to each person who is known to the Council to be a principal of the practice unit.

    (5) Where following an inspection in terms of this rule it appears to the Council that the practice unit has not complied with the provisions of these Rules and the guidance given thereunder, the Council may, after giving written notice, carry out such further inspections and examinations as it may consider necessary to require the said practice unit to secure compliance with these Rules.

Professional practice

10. Failure to comply with these Rules may be treated as professional misconduct for the purposes of Part IV of the Solicitors (Scotland) Act 1980.

[THE NEXT PAGE IS F 607]

Solicitors (Scotland) (Admission with Extended Rights of Audience) Rules 1995

Rules made by the Council of the Law Society of Scotland and approved by the Lord President of the Court of Session pursuant to section 25A of the Solicitors (Scotland) Act 1980.

PART I—INTRODUCTORY

Title and commencement
1. These Rules may be cited as the Solicitors (Scotland) (Admission with Extended Rights of Audience) Rules 1995 and shall come into force on 1st May 1995. These Rules apply to any application for extended rights whether made before or after the coming into force of these Rules.

Interpretation
2.—(1) In these Rules, unless the context otherwise requires:—
    "the Act" means the Solicitors (Scotland) Act 1980;
    "the Society" means the Law Society of Scotland;
    "the Council" means the Council of the Society;
    "the Secretary" means the Secretary of the Society and includes any person authorised by the Council to act on behalf of the Secretary for the purposes of these Rules;
    "applicant" means a solicitor seeking extended rights;
    "extended rights" means a right of audience in the Court of Session, the House of Lords and the Judicial Committee of the Privy Council or, as the case may be, the High Court of Justiciary;
    "a solicitor" means a solicitor enrolled with the Law Society of Scotland and who holds a full practising certificate;
    "examiners" means examiners appointed under Part IV of these Rules;
    "the Panel" means a body constituted for the purposes of these Rules consisting of six members, each of whom is a solicitor appointed by the Council with the approval of the Lord President, of which three members shall represent a quorum. The Panel shall exercise such functions as may be properly delegated to it by the Council from time to time;
    "the Register" means the register of solicitors with extended rights kept in accordance with rule 28;
    "sitting-in" means attendance at court at the hearing of a case or cases in which the applicant or his firm or (with the exception of solicitors in the Procurator Fiscal Service) his employer does not act for any of the parties.
(2) The provisions of the Interpretation Act 1978 shall apply to these Rules as they apply to an Act of Parliament.

Compliance
3. Every applicant shall as a condition precedent to being granted extended rights comply with these Rules and the Council may require any applicant to satisfy them of such compliance by such means as they may consider necessary.

Qualifications for applying for extended rights
4.—(1) Every applicant shall at the date of his application:—
    (a) be a solicitor; and
    (b) have had relevant experience of court work for a continuous period of not less than five years immediately prior to that date.

(2) For the purposes of sub-paragraph (1)(b) above, "relevant experience of court work" means experience of both:—

    (a) advocacy as a solicitor or as an advocate; and

    (b) acting either as a local correspondent or as an instructing solicitor in the court or courts for which extended rights are sought.

(3) The provisions of paragraph (2) above shall not apply to an applicant who satisfies the Council that, for a continuous period of not less than five years prior to the date of his application:—

    (a) he has been a practising member of the Faculty of Advocates; or

    (b) he has been a practising member of the Bar of England and Wales or Northern Ireland; or

    (c) he, having been admitted or enrolled as a solicitor in England and Wales or Northern Ireland, has had relevant experience of court work there as a solicitor; or

    (d) he has relevant experience of court work as a practising member of a bar or law society in any other member state of the European Community.

(4) The Council shall have power in exceptional cases to exempt an applicant from complying with the requirements of sub-paragraph (1)(b) above and their decision on any question arising under this sub-paragraph shall be final.

The application

    5.—(1) Every applicant shall lodge with the Society:—

    (a) an application in the prescribed form;

(b) such additional documents as the applicant thinks fit to demonstrate his experience under rule 4(1);

(c) such fee as the Council may from time to time determine.

(2) The application will be remitted to the Panel who shall have power:—

(a) to call for further references; or

(b) to interview the applicant.

(3) The Panel, having considered the application with such additional information as may have been made available shall make a recommendation to the Council who shall have power:—

(a) to allow the application to proceed;

(b) to reject the application; or

(c) to deal with the application in such other way as they think fit.

(4) On rejection of an application by the Council the Secretary shall within 14 days issue to the applicant in writing the Council's reasons for the rejection.

Record of applications

6. The Secretary shall keep a record of solicitors who have applied for extended rights.

Order of procedure

7. Every applicant shall, in the following order:—

(1) Subject to rule 10(2), complete a course of induction training in accordance with Part II of these Rules;

(2) Subject to rule 11(6), undertake sitting-in in accordance with Part III of these Rules;

(3) Subject to rule 16, pass the examinations required in accordance with Part IV of these Rules; and

(4) Subject to rule 23, complete to the satisfaction of the Council a Supreme Courts Training and Assessment Course in accordance with Part V of these Rules.

Fitness

8. Every applicant shall satisfy the Council that he is a fit and proper person to have extended rights.

Time limit

9.—(1) Each applicant must complete the requirements for qualification set out in rules 7 and 8 within three years from the date his application is allowed to proceed by the Council.

(2) The Council shall have power on cause shown to extend the foregoing period and their decision on any question arising under this sub-paragraph shall be final.

PART II—INDUCTION TRAINING

10.—(1) The applicant shall attend a course of induction training at Parliament House to be provided by the Society's Administration Officer in order to familiarise the applicant with procedural rules and practices and administrative arrangements in the transaction of business in the court or courts for which extended rights are sought. The form and content of the course shall be as prescribed by the Council from time to time.

(2) The Council may, on the recommendation of the Panel, where they are satisfied that the applicant has sufficient experience and knowledge of the matters to be covered in the course, exempt an applicant from complying with this rule and their decision on any question arising under this sub-paragraph shall be final.

PART III—SITTING-IN

11.—(1) The Secretary, once the Council is satisfied that the application can proceed, shall issue the applicant with a record card unless the applicant is granted exemption from the requirements of this part of the Rules.

(2) Within nine months of the record card being issued to the applicant he shall:—

(a) as regards civil applications undertake sitting-in for at least 12 court days (of which at least four days shall be spent sitting-in in the Inner House) at the Court of Session; or

(b) as regards criminal applications undertake sitting-in for at least six court days at the High Court of Justiciary in Edinburgh, of which at least four days shall be when it is exercising its appellate jurisdiction.

(3) After giving a minimum of 48 hours' notice of his intention to present himself at Parliament House for each day of sitting-in, the applicant shall attend the Society's Administration Officer not later than 9.40 a.m. in order to collect a set of papers for the relevant case or cases to be heard that day.

(4) The applicant shall note on his record card the names of the cases and dates and the times of the hearings he has attended for sitting-in.

(5) On completion of the prescribed period of sitting-in the applicant shall transmit his record card to the Secretary who shall mark the record referred to in rule 6 accordingly.

(6) The Council, on the recommendation of the Panel, may at their discretion exempt an applicant from complying with any part of sitting-in where they are satisfied:—

(a) with regard to civil applications that the applicant has sufficient experience as an instructing solicitor in the Court of Session;

(b) with regard to criminal applications that the applicant has sufficient experience of advocacy in solemn procedure and as an instructing solicitor in the High Court of Justiciary exercising its appellate jurisdiction.

PART IV—EXAMINATIONS

Appointment of examiners

12.—(1) In order to test the suitability and qualifications of applicants the Council shall from time to time nominate and appoint fit and proper persons to be examiners and hold examinations in accordance with this Part of these Rules, which examinations shall be under the management and control of the Council.

(2) The examiners shall comply with all directions that may be given by the Council with respect to the number of papers to be set on any subject, the number of questions to be set and answered and the percentage mark to be attained to qualify for a pass and any other matters in connection with the examinations.

(3) The examiners shall be appointed for such period of time and be paid such remuneration as the Council may from time to time determine.

Eligibility for examinations

13. An applicant shall not be entitled to present himself for any of the Society's examinations unless he has completed induction training and sitting-in or has been exempted from doing so all as prescribed in rules 10 and 11.

Examinations
    14.—(1) The examinations shall:—
    (*a*) make separate provision with regard to civil and criminal appli-
        cations, and
    (*b*) include questions on evidence, pleading, practice, procedure and
        professional conduct in accordance with the syllabus prescribed by
        the Council from time to time.
    (2) An applicant shall be required to pass all of the appropriate
examinations under paragraph (1) above:—
    (*a*) within two years of the first examination diet at which he presents
        himself; and
    (*b*) in any event in not more than two attempts.
    (3) Failure to comply with paragraph (2) above shall result in:—
    (*a*) the refusal of the application; and
    (*b*) prohibition of any renewed application whether civil or criminal for a
        period of three years following intimation by the Council to the
        applicant of refusal under this sub-paragraph.

Conduct, dates and places of examinations
    15.—(1) A diet for the Society's examinations shall be held at such place as
the Council may decide not less than once each year and additional diets may
be held as considered necessary by the Council.
    (2) Every candidate shall be examined in writing.
    (3) Applicants intending to present themselves at any of the Society's
examinations shall give three weeks' notice of their intention to the
Secretary provided that the Secretary may at his discretion allow an
applicant who has not given such notice to present himself for any
examination.
    (4) At the time of giving notice under paragraph (3) above an applicant
shall tender such fee as may be prescribed by the Council from time to time.

Exemptions
    16. An applicant who has obtained a pass in an examination for admission
to the Faculty of Advocates shall be exempt from the corresponding
examination under rule 14.

PART V—TRAINING AND ASSESSMENT COURSES

The courses
    17. The Council shall arrange and organise a Supreme Courts Training
and Assessment Course for solicitors seeking extended rights. There shall be
separate courses for applicants seeking civil and criminal extended rights
respectively.

Form, locus, duration and content
    18. The form, locus, duration and content of the courses shall be
prescribed by the Council from time to time, and shall include lectures by
solicitors or advocates of at least five years' standing or persons who have
been employed for at least five years in the full-time teaching of law at any of
the Scottish universities who are suitably experienced in the opinion of the
Council in the subject of the lecture. The courses shall include practical
sessions involving participation by applicants.

Administration
    19. Each course shall have a Convener who shall be responsible to the
Council for the administration and content of the course. The Convener
shall be suitably qualified in the opinion of the Council to conduct the
course. The Secretary shall with the Convener supervise the organisation
and running of the course.

Assessment
20. The performance of each applicant attending each element of the Training and Assessment Course will be appropriately assessed.

Notice
21. Applicants intending to present themselves at the course shall give three weeks' notice of their intention to the Secretary (who may at his sole discretion allow an applicant who has not given such notice to attend the course).

Fees
22. An applicant shall together with his notice of intention to attend the course tender such fee as may be prescribed by the Council from time to time.

Exemptions
23. The Council, on the recommendation of the Panel, may exempt any applicant from any part of the course but, save in exceptional circumstances, no such exemption shall be granted to applicants who have:—
    (*a*) with regard to civil applications less than 10 years' immediately prior experience both of advocacy and of being an instructing solicitor in the Court of Session;
    (*b*) with regard to criminal applications less than 10 years' immediately prior experience of advocacy in solemn procedure and as an instructing solicitor in the High Court of Justiciary exercising its appellate jurisdiction.

Completion
24.—(1) The applicant shall be required to satisfactorily complete the Training and Assessment Course in not more than two attempts.
    (2) Failure to comply with paragraph (1) above shall result in:—
    (*a*) the refusal of the application; and
    (*b*) prohibition of any renewed application whether civil or criminal for a period of three years from the date of intimation of the refusal.

The report
25. After the course the Convener shall prepare a report on the performance of each participating applicant and provide such other information as the Panel may require.

The Panel
26.—(1) The Panel, having considered the report, the applicant's performance in the examinations and a statement of any relevant exemptions shall recommend to the Council that:—
    (*a*) the applicant be allowed a further opportunity to satisfactorily complete the course which must be exercised at the next available course; or
    (*b*) the application be granted; or
    (*c*) the application be refused.

PART VI—DECISION OF COUNCIL

27.—(1) The Council shall determine the application not later than three months after the Panel has issued a recommendation.
    (2) The Council shall consider:—
    (*a*) a statement by the Panel that the applicant has passed the examinations;
    (*b*) the report on the applicant under rule 25;

(c) the recommendation of the Panel;
(d) any other evidence, including performance at an interview, which is relevant to the question whether the applicant is a fit and proper person to have extended rights.

(3) If the Council is satisfied that the applicant has satisfied the requirements of section 25A(2) of the Act and the provisions of these Rules, they shall grant the application.

(4) Where the Council refuse the application the Secretary shall within 14 days issue to the applicant written reasons for the decision.

(5) Where the application has been granted the Secretary shall intimate the grant to the Lord President or the Lord Justice General as the case may be and The Scottish Legal Aid Board. The Secretary shall also make an appropriate annotation on the Roll of Solicitors in terms of section 25A(3) of the Act and in the Register to be kept for the purposes of Part VII hereof.

PART VII—THE REGISTER

28.—(1) The Council as Registrar of Solicitors shall keep at the office of the Secretary a register of solicitors who have been granted extended rights.

(2) The register shall have separate sections covering extended rights in civil and criminal courts respectively.

(3) Any person may inspect the register during office hours without payment.

(4) For the purpose of maintaining the register as correctly as is reasonably practicable the Council shall have power:—
(a) to remove from the register the name of any solicitor who has died;
(b) to send to any solicitor with extended rights at his address as shown in the register a letter enquiring whether he wishes to continue to have his name included in the register and intimating that if no reply is received within the period of six months beginning with the date of posting of the letter his name may be removed from the register.

(5) The Council may, on the application of a solicitor whose name has been removed from the register in pursuance of paragraph (4)(b), after such enquiry and on such conditions as they think proper (including payment by the solicitor to the Council of such reasonable fee in respect of restoration as the Council may fix) order that his name shall be restored to the register.

(6) Subject to rule 27(3) the Council may charge such reasonable fees (including an annual fee payable by solicitors with extended rights) as they may fix in connection with the keeping of the register.

(7) Solicitors with extended rights shall intimate the following to the Secretary within one month of occurrence of the same:—
(a) any change of business address;
(b) if they become a consultant; or
(c) if they cease to practise.

PART VIII—REPEALS

29. The Admission as a Solicitor with Extended Rights (Scotland) Rules 1992 are hereby revoked, but such revocation shall not affect the validity of any application granted under the said Rules and such application shall have effect as if it were granted under these Rules.

Solicitors (Scotland) (Advertising and Promotion) Practice Rules 1995

Rules dated 21st September 1995 made by the Council of the Law Society of Scotland and approved by the Lord President of the Court of Session in terms of section 34 of the Solicitors (Scotland) Act 1980.

1.—(1) These Rules may be cited as the Solicitors (Scotland) (Advertising and Promotion) Practice Rules 1995.
(2) These Rules shall come into operation on 1st November 1995.

2.—(1) In these Rules unless the context otherwise requires:—
"the Act" means the Solicitors (Scotland) Act 1980;
"the Council" means the Council of the Society;
"established client" means a person for whom a solicitor has acted on at least one previous occasion, but does not include a person:—
   (a) whom the solicitor knows or ought reasonably to know to be exclusively a client of another solicitor; or
   (b) for whom the solicitor has acted only on the instructions of another solicitor;
"practice" means professional practice of the solicitor and includes any area of practice;
"the Secretary" means the Secretary of the Society and includes any person authorised by the Council to act on behalf of the Secretary;
"services" means services provided by a solicitor and includes any part of such services;
"the Society" means the Law Society of Scotland;
"solicitor" means any person enrolled as a solicitor in pursuance of the Act and includes a firm of solicitors, an incorporated practice and any association of solicitors;
"specialist" means an individual solicitor who possesses knowledge of and expertise in a particular branch or area of law or legal practice significantly greater than that which might reasonably be expected to be possessed by a solicitor who is not a specialist in that branch or area of law or legal practice.
(2) The Interpretation Act 1978 applies to the interpretation of these Rules as it applies to the interpretation of an Act of Parliament.

3. The Solicitors (Scotland) (Advertising and Promotion) Practice Rules 1991 are hereby repealed.

4. Subject to Rules 5 and 8 hereof a solicitor shall be entitled to promote his services in any way he thinks fit.

5. A solicitor shall not make a direct or indirect approach whether verbal or written to any person whom he knows or ought reasonably to know to be the client of another solicitor with the intention to solicit business from that person.

6. Rule 5 shall not preclude the general circulation by a solicitor of material promoting that solicitor's services whether or not the persons to whom it is directed are established clients.

7. A solicitor shall not be in breach of these rules by reason only of his claim to be a specialist in any particular field of law or legal practice, provided that:—
   (a) the onus of proof that any such claim is justified shall be on the solicitor making it; and

(b) an advertisement of or by a solicitor or other material issued by or on behalf of a solicitor making any such claim shall conform otherwise to the requirements of rule 8.

8. An advertisement of or by a solicitor or promotional material issued by or on behalf of a solicitor or any promotional activity by or on behalf of a solicitor shall be decent and shall not:—
(1) claim superiority for his services or practice over those of or offered by another solicitor; or
(2) compare his fees with those of any other solicitor; or
(3) contain any inaccuracy or misleading statement; or
(4) be of such nature or character or be issued or done by such means as may reasonably be regarded as bringing the profession of solicitors into disrepute; or
(5) identify any client or item of his business without the prior written consent of the client; or
(6) be defamatory or illegal.

9. Any advertisement, promotional material or promotional activity of or by a solicitor (whether or not he be named or referred to therein) and any advertisement, promotional material or promotional activity of or by a third party which relates to the services of a solicitor shall be presumed to have been issued or promoted with the authority of the solicitor.

10.—(1) Where an advertisement or promotional material or activity by a solicitor, or by a third party which relates to the services of a solicitor is deemed by the Council to contravene any of these Rules, the Council may by way of written notice duly given to him require the solicitor forthwith, or from such date as the notice may stipulate, to withdraw, terminate or cancel the advertisement or promotional material or activity as the case may require and not to repeat the same during the currency of the notice.
(2) A notice given by the Council to a solicitor under paragraph 1 of this rule, shall be signed by the Secretary and shall be deemed to have been duly given if it is delivered to him or left or sent by recorded delivery post to his last known place of business.
(3) It shall be the duty of a solicitor to obtemper any notice duly given to him under this rule. A solicitor aggrieved by the terms of any such notice may, within 14 days of the date thereof, make written representations thereanent to the Council, which shall, within two calendar months of the receipt of such representations, either confirm or withdraw said notice; provided that should the Council neither confirm nor withdraw said notice within said period said notice shall be deemed to have been withdrawn at the expiry thereof.

11. The Council shall have power to waive any of the provisions of these Rules in any particular case.

12. Breach of any of these Rules may be treated as professional misconduct for the purposes of Part IV of the Act (Complaints and Disciplinary Proceedings).

PROFESSIONAL PRACTICE GUIDELINE

In addition to the foregoing Rules the Council have also approved the following guideline on the advertising of solicitors' fees, whether that is done by the solicitor or by another party such as an estate agent.

Guideline on Advertising Fees

Where a solicitor's fees for his services are advertised either by the solicitor or by a third party whether or not the solicitor is named in such an advertisement the advertisement must show the full range of fees chargeable for such work and not simply the cheapest end of the range. The advertisement must also include mention of outlays and VAT with no less prominence than the fees. Failure to show the full range of fees or failure to mention outlays and VAT with no less prominence than the fees may be regarded as misleading and inaccurate and therefore in breach of rule 8(3) of the Solicitors (Scotland) (Advertising and Promotion) Practice Rules 1995. In terms of rule 12 of those rules, breach of any of the rules may be treated as professional misconduct.

Scottish Solicitors' Guarantee Fund Rules 1995

Rules dated 21st September 1995 made by the Council of the Law Society of Scotland in terms of section 43 of, and Schedule 3 to, the Solicitors (Scotland) Act 1980.

Citation
   1. These Rules may be cited as the Scottish Solicitors' Guarantee Fund Rules 1995, and shall come into operation on the first day of November 1995, and from that date the Scottish Solicitors' Guarantee Fund Rules 1985 shall cease to have effect.

Interpretation
   2.—(1) In these Rules, unless the context otherwise requires:—
   "the Act" means the Solicitors (Scotland) Act, 1980;
   "the Fund" means the Scottish Solicitors' Guarantee Fund;
   "the Society" means the Law Society of Scotland the establishment of
      which is confirmed under the Act;
   "the Council" means the Council of the Society;
   "the Secretary" means the Secretary of the Society and includes a
      Deputy Secretary of the Society and the Chief Accountant;
   "loss" means pecuniary loss by reason of dishonesty on the part of a
      solicitor in practice in the United Kingdom or any employee of
      such solicitor in connection with the practice of the solicitor, and
      whether or not he had a practising certificate in force when the act
      of dishonesty was committed, and notwithstanding that sub-
      sequent to the commission of that act he may have died or had his
      name removed from or struck off the Roll of Solicitors or may have
      ceased to practise or been suspended from practice.
   (2) The Interpretation Act 1978 applies to these Rules as it applies to an Act of Parliament.

Payments into and out of the Fund
   3.—(1) There shall be carried to the credit of the Fund:—
   (a) All contributions paid by solicitors under section 43 of, and the Third
        Schedule to, the Act;
   (b) All interest, dividends and other income, and accretions of capital
        arising from investments of the Fund;
   (c) All moneys borrowed for the purposes of the Fund;
   (d) All sums received by the Society in respect of contracts of insurance
        entered into under paragraph 3 of the Third Schedule to the Act;
   (e) All sums recovered by the Society in consequence of the provisions of
        sub-paragraph (2) of paragraph 4 of the Third Schedule to the Act;
        and

(f) Any other moneys which may belong or accrue to the Fund or be received by the Society in respect of the Fund.

(2) There shall from time to time be paid out of the Fund:—

(a) The expenses of constituting and administering the Fund, including the remuneration of officers and employees of, and other expenses incurred by, the Society in relation to the Fund under or in the exercise of powers conferred by the Act;

(b) All grants made by the Society under section 43 of the Act;

(c) All premiums payable by the Society under contracts of insurance entered into under paragraph 3 of the Third Schedule to the Act;

(d) All interest and other sums payable in respect of sums borrowed by the Society for the purposes of the Fund; and

(e) Any other moneys payable out of the Fund in accordance with the Act or any Rules relating to the Fund made thereunder.

Intimation of loss

4. Any person proposing to apply to the Society for a grant from the Fund in respect of a loss shall, as soon as is reasonably practicable, write to the Secretary giving such particulars of the loss as he or she is at the time able to furnish. Failure to intimate such loss timeously may restrict in whole or in part the amount of any grant that may be awarded.

Application for grant from Fund

5.—(1) An application for a grant from the Fund in respect of a loss shall be made by the applicant in or substantially in the form set out in Form in the Schedule hereto and shall be delivered to the Secretary within 12 months of the date on which the loss was first intimated to the Secretary.

(2) The Council may require an application to be supported by oral evidence to be tendered and documents to be produced to it or to any Committee appointed by it for the purpose and for this purpose the Council or any Committee appointed by it may administer oaths.

Council may require institution of proceedings

6. The Council before deciding whether or not to make a grant out of the Fund may require in respect of any application the pursuit by the applicant of any civil remedy which may be available in respect of the loss or the taking by him of steps with a view to the institution of criminal proceedings in respect of the dishonesty leading to the loss or the making of a complaint to the Scottish Solicitors Discipline Tribunal.

Council may waive requirements

7. The Council may on cause shown waive any of the provisions of these Rules as regards the time limit within which a notice may be given or an application made.

Notice by Council

8. Any requirement of the Council under these Rules may be communicated by a notice in writing which may be delivered personally or sent by post to the addressee at his last known address. Any such notice sent by post shall be deemed to have been received by the addressee within forty-eight hours of the time of posting.

SCHEDULE

THE LAW SOCIETY OF SCOTLAND
THE SCOTTISH SOLICITORS' GUARANTEE FUND

Application Form for a Grant out of the Scottish Solicitors' Guarantee Fund

To: The Law Society of Scotland
     The Law Society's Hall
     26 Drumsheugh Gardens
     Edinburgh EH3 7YR

I, (*Full name of applicant*) ....

Designation ....

Address ....

....

Post Code ....

Telephone Number ....
hereby apply to the Council of The Law Society of Scotland that in the exercise of the
absolute discretion conferred upon them by the Solicitors (Scotland) Act 1980, they make
to me a grant of £ ....
or such other sum as they may think proper out of the Scottish Solicitors' Guarantee Fund
by way of compensation for a pecuniary loss sustained by me by reason of the dishonesty of

Name ....

Designation ....

Address ....

....

Firm ....

Status in firm if known ....

Date the original notice of claim was sent to the Secretary ....

Schedule of Particulars

Please state as clearly and concisely as you can the answers to the following questions:—

   1. Please give the date or dates upon which the money or other property in respect of
       which your loss has been sustained came into the possession of the solicitor, or his or
       her employee.

       ....

   2. Please give full particulars of such money or property.

       ....

       ....

       ....

       ....

       ....

   3. Please explain why you allege dishonesty.

       ....

       ....

       ....

       ....

       ....

4. State the date [on] which your loss first came to your attention :...............................

5. Explain briefly how this happened.

....

....

....

....

....

6. If you have any documents which you think would help your claim, please list them here and enclose a copy of each.

....

....

....

....

....

7. Are you aware of any other application that may be made in respect of this loss? Yes/no*   *Please delete as appropriate. If yes, please give name and address of other applicant.

....

....

....

....

....

8. Are you aware of any civil, criminal or disciplinary hearings arising out of this matter? Yes/no*   *Please delete as appropriate. If yes, please give details including the result if known.

....

....

....

....

....

9. Have you taken court or other proceedings in respect of your loss? Yes/no*   *Please delete as appropriate. (a) If yes, please give brief details.

....

....

....

....

....

(b) If no, are you considering taking court or other proceedings in respect of your loss? Yes/no*   *Please delete as appropriate.

10. Do you have a solicitor acting on your behalf?
Yes/no* *Please delete as appropriate.
If yes, please give his name, firm, address and telephone number

Name ....

Firm ....

Address ....

....

Post Code ....

Telephone Number ....

11. Is there **any other relevant information** which you think would be of assistance to the Guarantee Fund Committee in considering your application?
If so, please detail.

....

....

....

....

....

....

....

....

I solemnly and sincerely declare that the information given by me in this application is true to the best of my knowledge and belief, and I make this solemn declaration conscientiously believing the same to be true, and by virtue of the Statutory Declarations Act 1835.

.... Claimant

Declared at ....

on (*date*) ....

before me ....

(This application should be signed in the presence of a Notary Public, Commissioner for Oaths, Justice of the Peace or other person authorised to administer oaths.)

Solicitors (Scotland) (Restriction on Practice as a Principal) Practice Rules 1996

Rules dated 26th April 1996 made by the Council of the Law Society of Scotland and approved by the Lord President of the Court of Session in terms of sections 1(3) and 34 of the Solicitors (Scotland) Act 1980.

1.—(1) These Rules may be cited as the Solicitors (Scotland) (Restriction on Practice as a Principal) Practice Rules 1996.
(2) These Rules shall come into operation on 1st July 1997.

2.—(1) In these Rules, unless the context otherwise requires:
"the Act" means the Solicitors (Scotland) Act 1980;
"the Council" means the Council of the Society;
"solicitor" means any person enrolled as a solicitor in pursuance of the Act;

"principal" means a solicitor who is a sole practitioner or is a partner in a firm of two or more solicitors or is a director of an incorporated practice;

"unrestricted practising certificate" means a practising certificate held by a solicitor free of conditions imposed in terms of section 15 or other relevant sections of the Act or any Regulations made thereunder, or by the Scottish Solicitors' Discipline Tribunal or by the Court of Session;

"the Society" means the Law Society of Scotland established under the Act;

(2) The Interpretation Act 1978 applies to these Rules as it applies to an Act of Parliament.

3.—(1) A solicitor shall not practise as a principal unless:
   (a) he has had issued to him his fourth consecutive unrestricted practising certificate; and
   (b) he has been employed as a solicitor for three years immediately preceding commencing practice as a principal, during each of which he has held an unrestricted practising certificate;

(2) Rule 3(1) shall not apply if the solicitor, who commences practice as a principal:
   (a) is assumed into and remains in partnership with at least one other solicitor who had practised as a principal for a period of not less than three years prior to the assumption into partnership of the solicitor; or
   (b) is appointed and remains a director of an incorporated practice having as one of its principals a solicitor who had practised as a principal for a period of not less than three years prior to the appointment of the solicitor as such director.

(3) The provisions of paragraphs (1) and (2) of this Rule shall not apply to any solicitor who commenced practice as a principal before the coming into operation of these Rules.

4. The Council shall have power to waive any of the provisions of these Rules in any particular case or cases on cause shown and subject to such conditions as they may impose.

[THE NEXT PAGE IS F 635]

**Solicitors (Scotland) (Associates, Consultants and Employees) Practice
Rules 1996**

Rules dated 29th March 1996, made by the Council of the Law
   Society of Scotland and approved by the Lord President of the
   Court of Session in terms of Section 34 of the Solicitors
   (Scotland) Act 1980.

   1.—(1) These Rules may be cited as the Solicitors (Scotland) (Associates,
Consultants and Employees) Practice Rules 1996.
   (2) These Rules shall come into operation on 1st August 1996.
   2. In these Rules, unless the context otherwise requires:
      "the Act" means the Solicitors (Scotland) Act 1980;
      "solicitor" means a solicitor holding a practising certificate under the
         Act and includes a firm of solicitors and an incorporated practice;
      "Council" means the Council of the Society;
      "the Society" means the Law Society of Scotland, established under the
         Act;
      "consultant" means a solicitor whose practising certificate is held by
         him free of conditions imposed in terms of Section 15 or other
         relevant Sections of the Act or any Regulations made thereunder
         or by the Scottish Solicitors' Discipline Tribunal or by the Court of
         Session and who, not being in partnership with a solicitor or a
         director of an incorporated practice, makes his services and advice
         available to that solicitor or incorporated practice.
      "private practice" means practice by a solicitor acting on his own
         account (whether as an individual or as a partner or as an
         incorporated practice);
      "associate" means a solicitor, whose practising certificate is held by him
         free of conditions imposed in terms of Section 15 or other relevant
         Sections of the Act or any Regulations made thereunder, or by the
         Scottish Solicitors' Discipline Tribunal, or by the Court of Session
         who is in the employment of another solicitor whether full-time or
         part-time and who has been afforded the status of "associate" of
         that other solicitor;
      "employee" means a bona fide employee of a solicitor, whether
         full-time or part-time, and includes a solicitor in the employment of
         that other solicitor who has been afforded the status of consultant
         to or associate of that other solicitor;
      "the Secretary" means the Secretary of the Society and includes any
         person authorised by the Council to act on behalf of the Secretary.

   3. The Interpretation Act 1978 applies to the interpretation of these Rules
as it applies to the interpretation of an Act of Parliament.

   4. The Solicitors (Scotland) (Associates, Consultants and Employees)
Practice Rules 1989 are hereby repealed.

   5. No solicitor engaged in private practice shall cause or permit the name
of any person to appear on his nameplate or professional stationery unless
that person is:
   (a) a partner of that solicitor,
   (b) if the solicitor is an incorporated practice, a director of that
         incorporated practice,
   (c) a consultant to that solicitor,
   (d) an associate of that solicitor, or
   (e) an employee of that solicitor.

   6. Where a solicitor in terms of Rule 5 hereof causes or permits the name
of a consultant, associate or employee to appear on his nameplate or
professional stationery, the status and designation of such consultant,
associate or employee shall be unambiguously stated in such a manner as to

distinguish clearly such consultant, associate or employee from a principal solicitor, the partners of a firm of solicitors or the directors of an incorporated practice as the case may be.

7.—(1) Where a solicitor is deemed by the Council to have contravened these Rules, the Council may, by written notice duly given to him, require that solicitor from such date as the notice may stipulate, to amend that solicitor's nameplate or professional stationery in such a manner as shall comply with these Rules.

(2) A notice given by the Council to a solicitor under paragraph (1) hereof shall be signed by the Secretary and shall be deemed to have been duly given if it is delivered to him or left at or sent by recorded delivery post to his last known place of business.

8. The Council shall have power to waive any of the provisions of these Rules in any particular case.

[1] Solicitors (Scotland) Accounts Rules 1997

Rules made by the Council of the Law Society of Scotland under sections 34, 35 & 36 of the Solicitors (Scotland) Act 1980 on 25th April 1997.

NOTE
[1] See also the Simple Guide to the Solicitors (Scotland) Accounts Rules 1997, Solicitors' (Scotland) Accounts Certificate Rules 1997, Money Laundering Regulations 1993 at pp. F 946 *et seq.*

Citation, commencement and repeal
1.—(1) These Rules may be cited as the Solicitors (Scotland) Accounts Rules 1997.

(2) These Rules shall come into operation on the 1st January 1998 and from that date the Solicitors (Scotland) Accounts Rules 1996 shall cease to have effect.

Interpretation
2.—(1) In these Rules, unless the context otherwise requires—
"the Act" means the Solicitors (Scotland) Act 1980;
"Certificate" and "accounting period" shall have the meanings respectively assigned to them in the Solicitors (Scotland) Accounts Certificate Rules in force from time to time.
"balance his books" means to prepare and bring to a balance a Trial Balance being a schedule or list of balances both debit and credit extracted from the accounts in both firm and client ledgers and including the cash and bank balances from the cash book;
"bank" means the Bank of England, the National Savings Bank, the Post Office in the exercise of its powers to provide banking services and an authorised institution within the meaning of the Banking Act 1987 and which operates within the bankers automated clearing system provided however that a recognised bank not operating within the bankers automated clearing system may be approved by the Council for the purposes of this subsection;
"client account" means a current, deposit, or savings account or other form of account or a deposit receipt at a branch of a bank in the United Kingdom in the name of the solicitor in the title of which the word "client", "trustee", "trust", or other fiduciary term appears and includes an account or a deposit receipt with a bank, a deposit, share or other account with a Building Society authorised

under the Building Societies Act 1986, a current or general account with a building society operating such an account within the bankers automated clearing system or an account showing sums on loan to a local authority being in such cases in name of the solicitor for a client whose name is specified in the title of the account or receipt;

"clients' money" means money (not belonging to him) received by a solicitor whether as a solicitor or as a trustee in the course of his practice;

"the Council" means the Council of the Society;

"Faculty" means a faculty or society of solicitors in Scotland incorporated by Royal Charter or otherwise formed in accordance with law, but does not include the Society;

"the Keeper" means the Keeper of the Registers of Scotland;

"local authority" means a local authority within the meaning of the Local Government etc. (Scotland) Act 1994;

"Money Laundering Regulations" means Money Laundering Regulations 1993 (S.I. 1993 No. 1933), and

> "Regulation" means a regulation on the Money Laundering Regulations,
>
> "relevant financial business" has the meaning given by Regulation 4, and
>
> "other business" means any business which is not relevant financial business;

"partner" means a member of a firm of solicitors or a director or member of an incorporated practice;

"print out" means a printed or typewritten copy of any account or other information stored in a computer;

"the Society" means the Law Society of Scotland, established under the Act;

"solicitor" means a solicitor holding a practising certificate under the Act and includes a firm of solicitors and an incorporated practice under section 34(1)(a) of the Act.

(2) The Interpretation Act 1978 applies to the interpretation of these Rules as it applies to the interpretation of an Act of Parliament.

Rules not to apply to solicitors in certain employments
3. These Rules shall not apply to a solicitor who is in any of the employments mentioned in sub-section (4)(a), (b) and (c) of section 35(1) of the Act so far as regards monies received, held or paid by him in the course of that employment.

Clients' money to be paid into Client Account
4.—(1) Subject to the provisions of Rule 7 every solicitor shall—
(a) ensure that at all times the sum at the credit of the client account, or where there are more such accounts than one, the total of the sums at the credit of those accounts, shall not be less than the total of the clients' money held by the solicitor; and
(b) pay into a client account without delay any sum of money exceeding £50 held for or received from or on behalf of a client.

(2) Where money is held by the solicitor in a client account in which the name of the client is specified and where no money is due to that client by the solicitor or the amount due is less than the amount in the specified client account, the sum in that account or, as the case may be, the excess, shall not be treated as clients' money for the purposes of paragraph (1)(a) of this Rule.

(3) Nothing herein contained shall—

(a) empower a solicitor, without the express written authority of the client, to deposit any money held by the solicitor for that client with a bank or on share, deposit or other account with a building society or on loan account with a local authority in name of the solicitor for that client, except on such terms as will enable the amount of the share or deposit or loan or any part thereof to be uplifted or withdrawn on notice not exceeding one calendar month;

(b) relieve a solicitor of his responsibilities to the client to ensure that all sums belonging to that client and held in a client account in terms of these Rules are available when required for that client or for that client's purpose; and

(c) preclude the overdrawing by a solicitor of a client account in which the name of the client for whom it is held is specified where that client has given written authority to overdraw, and an overdraft on such account shall not be taken into account to ensure compliance with paragraph (1)(a) of this Rule.

Other payments to client accounts

5. There may be paid into a client account—

(a) such money belonging to the solicitor as may be necessary for the purpose of opening the account or required to ensure compliance with Rule 4(1)(a); and

(b) money to replace any sum which may by mistake or accident have been withdrawn from the account.

Drawings from client account

6.—(1) So long as money belonging to one client is not withdrawn without his written authority for the purpose of meeting a payment to or on behalf of another client, there may be drawn from a client account—

(a) money required for payment to or on behalf of a client;

(b) money required for or to account of payment of a debt due to the solicitor by a client or in or to account of repayment of money expended by the solicitor on behalf of a client;

(c) money drawn on a client's authority;

(d) money properly required for or to account of payment of the solicitor's professional account against a client which has been debited to the ledger account of the client in the solicitor's books and where a copy of said account has been rendered;

(e) money for transfer to a separate client account kept or to be kept for the client only;

(f) money which may have been paid into the account under paragraph (a) of Rule 5 and which is no longer required to ensure compliance with Rule 4(1)(a); and

(g) money which may be mistaken or accident have been paid into the account.

(2) For the purposes of paragraph (1)(b) of this Rule and of Rule (7)(e) hereof a debt due to the solicitor by the client shall not include dues payable in respect of deeds which have been sent to the Keeper for recording or registration until receipt by the solicitor of the Keeper's invoice in respect thereof.

(3) Where money drawn from a client account by cheque is payable to a person's account with any bank or building society, the cash book and ledger entries relating thereto and said cheque shall include the name or account number of the person whose account is to be credited with the payment.

Exceptions from Rule 4

7. Notwithstanding any of the provisions of these Rules, a solicitor shall not be obliged to pay into a client account, but shall be required to record in his books, clients' money held or received by him—

    (a) in the form of cash which is without delay paid in cash to the client or a third party on the client's behalf;

    (b) in the form of a cheque or draft or other bill of exchange which is endorsed over to the client or to a third party on the client's behalf and which is not passed by the solicitor through a bank account;

    (c) which he pays without delay into a separate bank, building society or local authority deposit account opened or to be opened in name of the client or of some person named by the client;

    (d) which the client for his own convenience has requested the solicitor in writing to withhold from such account;

    (e) for or to account of payment of a debt due to the solicitor from the client or in repayment in whole or in part of money expended by the solicitor on behalf of the client;

    (f) expressly on account of a professional account incurred by the client, or as an agreed fee or to account of an agreed fee for business done for the client where a copy of said account has been rendered; or

    (g) in the form of a cheque, draft or other bill of exchange payable to a third party on behalf of a client which relates to the consideration in relation to a transaction involving heritable property.

Bridging Loans

8. A solicitor shall not enter into or maintain any contract or arrangement with a bank or other lender in terms of which the solicitor may draw down loan or overdraft facilities in his name for behoof of clients unless—

    (1) the solicitor shall, in every case before drawing down any sums in terms of such contract or arrangement, have intimated in writing to the bank or other lender—

    (a) the name and present address of the client for whom the loan or overdraft facilities are required; and

    (b) the arrangements for repayment of the loan or overdraft facilities; and

    (2) the contract or arrangement does not impose personal liability for repayment of any such loan or overdraft facilities on the solicitor.

Borrowing from clients

9. A solicitor shall not borrow money from his client unless his client is in the business of lending money or his client has been independently advised in regard to the making of the loan.

Prohibition on solicitor acting for lender to the solicitor or connected persons

10.—(1) A solicitor shall not act for a lender in the constitution, variation, assignation or discharge of a standard security securing a loan which has been advanced or is to be advanced to—

    (a) the solicitor,

    (b) the spouse of the solicitor,

    (c) any partner of the solicitor,

    (d) any incorporated practice of which the solicitor or his spouse is a member,

    (e) the spouse or any such partner,

    (f) any company in which any person specified in sub-paragraphs (a) to (e) inclusive and (g) of this paragraph holds shares, whether directly or indirectly, other than a holding amounting to not more than 5% of the issued shares in a public company quoted on a recognised stock exchange, or

(g) any partnership of which any of the persons specified in subparagraphs (a) to (e) inclusive of this paragraph is a partner, and, for the avoidance of doubt, rule 5(1)(f) of the Solicitors (Scotland) Practice Rules 1986 shall not apply to any such loan.

(2) For the purposes of this Rule "loan" shall include an obligation ad factum praestandum or any obligation to pay money and "lender" shall include any person to whom said obligation is owned.

(3) This Rule shall not apply if—

(a) the lender to any of the persons specified in paragraph (1) is the solicitor, or

(b) the borrower's obligations under the Standard Security have been fully implemented before a discharge is obtained from the lender.

(4) The Council shall have power to waive the provisions of paragraph 1(f) and (g) of this Rule in any particular circumstances or case.

Powers of Attorney

11.—(1) This Rule shall, subject to paragraph (2) below, apply to monies received or payments made by a solicitor by virtue of any Power of Attorney in his favour.

(2) In the event of any Power of Attorney granted in favour of a solicitor continuing to have effect by virtue of section 71 of the Law Reform (Miscellaneous Provisions) (Scotland) Act 1990 any money of the granter held or received by the solicitor shall be clients' money.

(3) Every solicitor shall deliver to the Council a list of any Powers of Attorney in the solicitor's favour held or granted during an accounting period, the list to be as set out in the Certificate set out in the Solicitors (Scotland) Accounts Certificate Rules 1997 or such other terms as the Council may from time to time prescribe.

Accounts required to be kept in books of solicitor

12.—(1) A solicitor shall at all times keep properly written up such books and accounts as are necessary—

(a) to show all his dealing with—

  (i) clients' money held or received or paid or in any way intromitted with by him;

  (ii) any other money dealt with by him through a client account;

  (iii) any bank overdrafts or loans procured by him in his own name for behoof of a client or clients; and

  (iv) any other money held by the solicitor in a separate account in the title of which the client's name is specified; and

(b) (i) to show separately in respect of each client all money of the categories specified in sub-paragraph (a) of this paragraph which is received, held or paid by him on account of that client; and

  (ii) to distinguish all money of the said categories received, held or paid by him from any other money received, held or paid by him.

(2) Without prejudice to paragraph (1) above, this Rule shall apply to money received or payments made by a solicitor by virtue of any Power of Attorney in his favour.

(3) All dealings referred to in paragraph (1) of this Rule shall be recorded—

(a) in a clients' cash book, or a clients' column of a cash book, or

(b) in a record of sums transferred from the ledger account of one client to that of another;

as may be appropriate, and in addition in a clients' ledger or a clients' column of a ledger.

(4) Every solicitor shall—

(a) at all times keep properly written up such books and accounts as are necessary to show the true financial position of his practice; and

(b) balance his books monthly and on the last day of the accounting period.

(5) The "books", "accounts", "ledger" and "records" referred to in these Rules shall be deemed to include loose-leaf books and such cards or other permanent records as are necessary for the operation of any system of book-keeping, mechanical or computerised.

(6) Where a solicitor maintains the accounts required by these Rules on a computerised system which does not rely on a visible ledger card for its operation such system must be such that—

(a) an immediate printout can be obtained of any account notwithstanding that immediate visual access is available; and

(b) all accounts which for any reason may require to be removed from the working store of the system must before removal be copied on to a storage medium which will enable a visual record of the detailed entries therein to be produced and be filed in alphabetical or other suitable order, indexed and retained for the period set out in paragraph (7) of this Rule.

(7) A solicitor shall preserve for at least ten years from the date of the last entry therein all books and accounts kept by him under this Rule or a copy thereof in a form which will enable a visible record of the detailed entries therein to be produced from such a copy.

Client bank statements to be regularly reconciled
    13.—(1) Every solicitor shall within one month of the coming into force of these Rules or of his commencing practice on his own account (either alone or in partnership or as an incorporated practice), and thereafter at intervals not exceeding one month, cause the balance between the client bank lodged and drawn columns of his cash book or the balance of his client bank ledger account as the case may be to be agreed with his client bank statements and shall retain such reconciliation statements showing this agreement for a period of three years from the dates they were respectively carried out.

(2) On the same date or dates specified in paragraph (1) of this Rule every solicitor shall extract from his clients' ledger a list of balances due by him to clients and prepare a statement comparing the total of the said balances with the reconciled balance in the client bank account and retain such lists of balances and statements for a period of three years from the dates they were respectively carried out.

Client funds invested in specified accounts
    14.—(1) Every solicitor shall within three months of the coming into force of these Rules or of his commencing practice on his own account (either alone or in partnership or as an incorporated practice), and thereafter at intervals not exceeding three months and coinciding with the date of a reconciliation in terms of Rule 13 hereof, cause the balance between the client deposited and withdrawn columns of his cash book or the balance on his client invested funds ledger account as the case may be to be agreed with his client passbooks, building society printouts, special deposit accounts, Local Authority deposits, joint deposits or other statements or certificates and shall retain such reconciliation statements showing this agreement for a period of three years from the dates they were respectively carried out.

(2) On the same date or dates specified in paragraph (1) of this Rule every solicitor shall extract from his client ledger a list of funds invested by him in his name for specified clients and prepare a statement comparing the total of the said balances with the reconciled investment funds and retain such lists of balances and statements for a period of three years from the dates they were respectively carried out.

Interest to be earned for a client
    15.—(1) Where a solicitor holds money for or on account of a client and, having regard to the amount of such money and the length of time for which it or any part of it is likely to be held, it is reasonable that interest should be

earned for the client, the solicitor shall so soon as practicable place money or, as the case may be, such part thereof, in a separate interest bearing client account in the title of which the client's name is specified and shall account to the client for any interest earned thereon, failing which the solicitor shall pay to the client out of his own money a sum equivalent to the interest which would have accrued for the benefit of the client if the sum he ought to have placed in such an interest bearing client account under this Rule had been so placed.

(2) Without prejudice to the generality of paragraph (1) of this Rule it shall be deemed reasonable that interest should be earned for a client from the date on which a solicitor receives for or on account of the client a sum of money not less than £500 which at the time of its receipt is unlikely within two months thereafter to be either wholly disbursed or reduced by payments to a sum less than £500.

(3) Without prejudice to any other remedy which may be available, any client who feels aggrieved that interest has not been paid under this Rule shall be entitled to require the solicitor to obtain a certificate from the Society as to whether or not interest ought to have been earned and, if so, the amount of such interest, and upon the issue of such certificate any interest certified to be due shall be payable by the solicitor to the client.

(4) Nothing in this Rule shall affect any arrangement in writing, whenever made, between a solicitor and his client as to the application of a client's money or interest thereon provided such arrangement was made prior to the said application.

(5) For the purposes of this Rule only, money held by a solicitor for or on account of a client—

(a) for the purpose of paying dues in respect of deeds which have been sent to the Keeper for recording or registration; or

(b) for or to account of the solicitor's professional account where said account has been rendered shall not be regarded as clients' money.

Money Laundering

16.—(1) Every solicitor shall in respect of all other business carried on by the solicitor comply with the provisions of the Money Laundering Regulations as if such other business constituted relevant financial business, but as if—

(a) for the figure "1" where it appears in the second line of Regulation 7(1) there were substituted the figure "2"; and

(b) Regulation 12(4)(a) were deleted.

(2) For the avoidance of doubt, this Rule is without prejudice to the application of the Money Laundering Regulations to relevant financial business.

Investigation of accounts on behalf of Council

17.—(1) To enable them to ascertain whether or not these Rules are being complied with, the Council may by written notice require any solicitor to produce at a time to be fixed by the Council and at a place to be fixed by the Council, or in the option of the solicitor at his place of business, his books of account, bank passbooks, loose-leaf bank statements, deposit receipts, documents of joint deposit, building society passbooks, local authority deposits, separate statements of bank overdrafts or loans procured by him in his own name for behoof of a client or clients, statements of account, vouchers and any other necessary documents including magnetic storage disks and microfilm records and any Powers of Attorney in his favour (in this Rule referred to as "books and other documents") for the inspection of a person appointed by the Council being a professional accountant.

(2) A solicitor duly required to do so under paragraph (1) of this Rule shall produce such books and other documents at the time and place fixed.

(3) The person appointed by the Council to make the inspection shall investigate the solicitor's books and other documents with the object of

ascertaining whether or not these Rules are being complied with by the solicitor, and thereafter shall report to the Council upon the result of his inspection.

(4) In any case in which a Faculty request that an inspection should be made under this Rule of the books and other documents of a solicitor, such Faculty shall transmit to the Council a statement containing all relevant information in their possession and a request that such an inspection be made.

(5) A written notice given by the Council to a solicitor under paragraph (1) and where appropriate paragraph (6) of this Rule shall be signed by the Secretary, a Deputy Secretary or the Chief Accountant of the Society and sent by recorded delivery service to the solicitor at his place of business as defined in the Constitution of the Society or in the case of a solicitor who has ceased to hold a practising certificate at his last known address, and shall be deemed to have been received by the solicitor within forty-eight hours of the time of posting. In the case of a firm or incorporated practice the written notice shall be given to each person who is known to the Council to be a partner of the firm or director of the incorporated practice and it shall not be necessary to give notice to the firm or incorporated practice also.

(6) Where following an inspection of the books and other documents of a solicitor in terms of paragraph (1) of this Rule it appears to the Council that the solicitor has not complied with these Rules and the Council instructs a further inspection of the books and other documents of the solicitor, the Council may by written notice require the solicitor to pay to the Council such sum as may be required to meet the fees and costs incurred by the Council in carrying out such further inspection, provided always that such written notice is given to the solicitor not more than one year after the date of the inspection first referred to in this paragraph. The amount of such sum shall be fixed by the Council and intimated to the solicitor following such inspection.

(7) It shall be the duty of a solicitor upon whom a notice in terms of paragraph (6) of this Rule has been served to make payment forthwith of the amounts so intimated.

(8) Any sum paid to the Council in terms of paragraph (7) hereof shall accrue to the Guarantee Fund.

Application of Rules in case of firm of solicitors or incorporated practice
18.—(1) Each partner of a firm of solicitors or member of an incorporated practice shall be responsible for securing compliance by the firm with the provisions of these Rules.

(2) Without prejudice to paragraph (1) of this Rule within one month of the coming into force of these Rules or of its commencing practice on its own account every firm of solicitors or incorporated practice shall designate one or more of the partners of the firm or the members of the incorporated practice as Designated Cashroom Partner or Partners who will be responsible for the supervision of the staff and systems employed by the firm or incorporated practice to carry out the provisions of these Rules and for securing compliance by the firm or incorporated practice with the provisions of these Rules.

(3) Every firm of solicitors or incorporated practice shall deliver to the Council a Certificate in the form as set out in the Solicitors (Scotland) Accounts Certificate Rules 1997 or in such terms as Council may prescribe listing the name or names of the Designated Cashroom Partner or Partners and the period or periods in respect of which he was, or they were, designated during the accounting period in respect of which the Certificate is delivered.

Savings of right of solicitor against client
19. Nothing in these Rules shall deprive a solicitor of or prejudice him with reference to any recourse or right in law, whether by way of lien, set-off, counter-claim, charge or otherwise, against monies standing to the credit of a client account or against monies due to a client by a third party.

Solicitors (Scotland) Accounts Certificate Rules 1997

Rules made by the Council of the Law Society of Scotland under
   section 37(6) of the Solicitors (Scotland) Act 1980 on 25th April
   1997.

Citation, commencement and repeal
   1.—(1) These Rules may be cited as the Solicitors (Scotland) Accounts
Certificate Rules 1997.
   (2) These Rules shall come into operation on the 1st January 1998 and the
Solicitors (Scotland) Accountant's Certificate Rules 1996 are hereby
revoked but such revocation shall not affect any outstanding obligation to
deliver an Accountant's Certificate in terms thereof nor the rights of the
Society against any solicitor in respect of his failure to do so.

Interpretation
   2.—(1) In these Rules, unless the context otherwise requires—
      "The Accounts Rules" shall mean the Solicitor (Scotland) Accounts
         Rules 1997 and "solicitor", "clients' money", "client account",
         "balance his books", "bank", "the Society", "the Council", "Build-
         ing Society", "local authority" and "Money Laundering Regu-
         lations" shall have the meanings respectively assigned to them
         therein;
      "practice year" shall have the meaning assigned to it by the Solicitors
         (Scotland) Act 1980;
      "accounting period" shall mean—
         (a)   a period not exceeding six months in duration commencing
               with the expiry of the immediately preceding accounting
               period after the commencement of these Rules; or
         (b)   where there is no immediately preceding accounting period
               a period commencing with the date on which the Accounts
               Rules apply to the solicitor or, having ceased to apply,
               apply again to that solicitor; or
         (c)   a period not exceeding 12 months which includes the date
               of commencement of these Rules;
      "Certificate" shall mean a certificate in the form set out in the Schedule
         to these Rules, or in such other form as the Council may from time
         to time approve.
   (2) The Interpretation Act 1978 applies to the interpretation of these
Rules as it applies to the interpretation of an Act of Parliament.

Obligation to deliver a Certificate
   3.—(1) A solicitor shall deliver to the Council within one calendar month
of the completion of each accounting period a Certificate in respect of that
period.
   (2) The Council may, in any case on cause satisfactory to them being
shown, extend the period of one calendar month within which a Certificate is
required following a balancing of books, but such extension shall in no case
exceed three months from the date on which the Certificate should have
been delivered.
   (3) If appropriate, the solicitor may deliver an interim style of Certificate
in respect of the accounting period which includes the date of the
introduction of these Rules. The period covered by the interim Certificate
shall not exceed twelve months.

Who may sign a Certificate

4. The Certificate under these Rules must be signed by two partners, one of whom must be the current Designated Cashroom Partner, unless the solicitor is a sole practitioner.

Where solicitor practises in two or more places

5. In the case of a solicitor who has two or more places of business and where separate books and accounts are maintained for each office a separate Certificate shall be submitted in respect of each such place of business. In any such case the client account balance shall be struck on the same date in respect of each place of business.

Notice to a solicitor under these Rules

6. Every notice to be given by the Council under these Rules to a solicitor shall be in writing under the hand of the Secretary or a Deputy Secretary or the Chief Accountant of the Society and sent by the recorded delivery service to the solicitor at his place of business as defined in the Constitution of the Society and shall be deemed to have been received by the solicitor within forty-eight hours of the time of posting. In the case of a firm or incorporated practice the written notice shall be given to each person who is known to the Council to be a partner of the firm or director of the incorporated practice and it shall not be necessary to give notice to the firm or incorporated practice also.

Reservation of power of Council to require inspection of a solicitor's books

7.—(1) The delivery of a Certificate to the Council in terms of these Rules shall not prejudice the power of the Council to require the inspection of a solicitor's books as provided for in Rule 17 of the Accounts Rules.

(2) In the event of a solicitor failing to produce a Certificate timeously, the Council may instruct an inspection of the solicitor's accounting records and other documents. The inspection to be carried out by a suitably qualified accountant with the costs being borne by the solicitor and a copy of the report to be sent to the Society.

SCHEDULE

FORM OF INTERIM CERTIFICATE

(In respect of an accounting period commencing before the coming into operation of the Solicitors (Scotland) Accounts Certificate Rules 1997)

The Secretary,
The Law Society of Scotland,
26 Drumsheugh Gardens,
Edinburgh EH3 7YR

Dear Sir

I/We confirm that, within the premises at (Note (a)) ....

....

being the address at which I/we carry on practice as solicitor(s) I/we have maintained the necessary books of account, bank passbooks, bank statements, deposit receipts including building society or local authority deposits, statements, deposit receipts and other accounting records required by the Solicitors (Scotland) Accounts Rules 1997 for the accounting period from .... to .... and I/we certify, subject to points referred to under item 4 of additional matters noted overleaf:—

Note (b)

(1) That the accounting records are up to date and balanced as at the last day of the accounting period, and

(2) That the accounting records, to the best of my/our knowledge and belief, are in accordance with the terms of the Solicitors (Scotland) Accounts Rules 1997, and

(3) That all outstanding reconciling entries noted as at the balance dates disclosed overleaf under Rules 13 and 14 have been entered in the records or confirmed as correct.

(4) That the following Powers of Attorney were held by the undernoted or granted in favour of the undernoted during the accounting period:—

GRANTER   ATTORNEY   DATE GRANTED

and

(5) That during the said accounting period the Designated Cashroom Partner(s) in terms of Rule 18 of the Solicitors (Scotland) Accounts Rules 1997 was/were as follows:—

NAME   DATE DESIGNATED   DATE DESIGNATION CEASED

I solemnly and sincerely declare that the information given by me in this Certificate is true to the best of my knowledge and belief.

CURRENT DESIGNATED CASHROOM PARTNER ....

PARTNER ....

DATE ....

ADDITIONAL MATTERS

1.   Client account reconciliations as at   ....

      Note (c)

   (i)   (a) Monies held on general client account £   £   £   £
         (b) Monies due to clients
         (c) Surplus or deficit   £   £   £   £

  (ii)   (a) Funds held for named clients   £   £   £   £

         (b) Monies due to named clients   £   £   £   £

2.   Firm's account balances

      Due to the firm   £   £   £   £
      Due by the firm   £   £   £   £

3.   If the assistance of an external accountant was needed to prepare this Certificate please indicate the scope of the assistance here (If none, state NONE):—

      Note (d)

4.   Other matters which require to be reported:—

      (If no other matters state NONE)

NOTES

(a) State addresses of all places of business of the solicitor or firm of solicitors in respect of whom the Certificate is granted.
(b) This balance is to be a balance of the whole books covering client and non-client accounts.
(c) These dates are those quarterly dates required to be reconciled under the terms of Rule 14.
(d) It is anticipated that many solicitors will instruct an external accountant to assist them in the checking of the accounting records and/or the preparation of the Certificate in respect of Investment Business. If the services of an external accountant are required you should indicate the extent of the help offered. The following tasks are examples of the assistance which may be obtained from the accountant:—

   (a) The preparation of day books, ledgers and other records for clients or firm's accounting records; or
   (b) Reconciling the funds position under Rules 13 and 14; or
   (c) Testing for compliance with aspects of the Accounts Rules as agreed per a letter of engagement; or
   (d) Balancing the client or firm's accounting records; or
   (e) Conducting a review of compliance with all aspects of the Accounts Rules in support of the solicitor's certification of compliance with the Rules.

SCHEDULE

FORM OF CERTIFICATE

(In respect of an accounting period commencing on or after the coming into operation of the Solicitors (Scotland) Accounts Certificate Rules 1997)

The Secretary,
The Law Society of Scotland,
26 Drumsheugh Gardens,
Edinburgh EH3 7YR

Dear Sir

I/We confirm that, within the premises at (Note (a)) ....
....
being the address at which I/we carry on practice as solicitor(s) I/we have maintained the necessary books of account, bank passbooks, bank statements, deposit receipts including building society or local authority deposits, statements, deposit receipts and other accounting records required by the Solicitors (Scotland) Accounts Rules 1997 for the accounting period from .... to .... and I/we certify, subject to points referred to under item 4 of additional matters noted overleaf:—

Note (b)
(1) That the accounting records are up to date and balanced as at the last day of the accounting period, and
(2) That the accounting records, to the best of my/our knowledge and belief, are in accordance with the terms of the Solicitors (Scotland) Accounts Rules 1997, and
(3) That all outstanding reconciling entries noted as at the balance dates disclosed overleaf under Rules 13 and 14 have been entered in the records or confirmed as correct.
(4) That the following Powers of Attorney were held by the undernoted or granted in favour of the undernoted during the accounting period:—

GRANTER	ATTORNEY	DATE GRANTED

and

(5) That during the said accounting period the Designated Cashroom Partner(s) in terms of Rule 18 of the Solicitors (Scotland) Accounts Rules 1997 was/were as follows:—

NAME	DATE DESIGNATED	DATE DESIGNATION CEASED

I solemnly and sincerely declare that the information given by me in this Certificate is true to the best of my knowledge and belief.

CURRENT DESIGNATED CASHROOM PARTNER ....

PARTNER ....

DATE ....

ADDITIONAL MATTERS

1. Client account reconciliations as at   ....

   Note (c)

   (i) (a) Monies held on general client account   £   £
        (b) Monies due to clients
        (c) Surplus or deficit   £   £

   (ii) (a) Funds held for named clients   £   £

        (b) Monies due to named clients   £   £

2. Firm's account balances

   Due to the firm   £   £

   Due by the firm   £   £

3. If the assistance of an external accountant was needed to prepare this Certificate please indicate the scope of the assistance here (If none, state NONE):—

   Note (d)

4. Other matters which require to be reported:—

   (If no other matters state NONE)

NOTES

(a) State addresses of all places of business of the solicitor or firm of solicitors in respect of whom the Certificate is granted.

(b) This balance is to be a balance of the whole books covering client and non-client accounts.

(c) These dates are those quarterly dates required to be reconciled under the terms of Rule 14.

(d) It is anticipated that many solicitors will instruct an external accountant to assist them in the checking of the accounting records and/or the preparation of the Certificate in respect of Investment Business. If the services of an external accountant are required you should indicate the extent of the help offered. The following tasks are examples of the assistance which may be obtained from the accountant:—

   (a) The preparation of day books, ledgers and other records for clients or firm's accounting records; or

   (b) Reconciling the funds position under Rules 13 and 14; or

   (c) Testing for compliance with aspects of the Accounts Rules as agreed per a letter of engagement; or

   (d) Balancing the client or firm's accounting records; or

   (e) Conducting a review of compliance with all aspects of the Accounts Rules in support of the solicitors certification of compliance with the Rules.

SCHEDULE

FORM OF CERTIFICATE

(In respect of an Accounting Period for which no client monies have been held)

NAME: ....

BUSINESS ADDRESS: HOME ADDRESS:

....

....

....

Tel No: .... Tel No: ....

Fax No: .... Fax No: ....

I hereby confirm to the Council of the Law Society of Scotland that:

(Note 1) (a) I have contributed to the Guarantee Fund in respect of the practice year commencing 1st November 199 ;

(b) I do/do not submit accounts to the Scottish Legal Aid Board for payment to my own account;

(c) I do/do not accept instructions directly from clients;

(Note 2) (d) I have not handled client monies during the accounting period from: .... to: ....

(e) I keep up to date records of fees earned and expenses incurred in my practice and have balanced my books as required by Rule 12(4) of the Solicitors (Scotland) Accounts Rules 1997.

(f) If circumstances change with the result that I require to hold or intromit with client monies, I shall immediately advise the Council.

I solemnly and sincerely declare that the information given by me in this Certificate is true to the best of my knowledge and belief.

Yours faithfully

.... (Sign Full Name)

.... (Print Full Name)

.... (Date)

Note 1. The current practice year for this purpose commences on 1st November within the accounting year which includes the six month period shown at item (d).

Note 2. The accounting period must be six months or less and follow immediately on from the previous accounting period without a gap or overlap in the dates covered.

INDEX FOR THE SOLICITORS (SCOTLAND) ACCOUNTS CERTIFICATE RULES 1997

Solicitors (Scotland) (Incorporated Practices) Practice Rules 1997

Rules dated 27th March 1997, made by the Council of the Law
Society of Scotland and approved by the Lord President of the
Court of Session in terms of section 34 of the Solicitors
(Scotland) Act 1980 (as amended).

Preamble
   1.—(1) These rules may be cited as the Solicitors (Scotland) (Incorporated Practices) Practice Rules 1997 and they are made under section 34(1A)
of the Solicitors (Scotland) Act 1980 (as amended).
   (2) These rules shall come into operation on 1st June 1997.
   (3) The Solicitors (Scotland) (Incorporated Practices) Practice Rules 1987
are hereby repealed with effect from the date of commencement of these
rules.

Definitions
   2.—(1) In these rules, unless the context otherwise requires:—
      "the Act" means the Solicitors (Scotland) Act 1980 (as amended);
      "the Society" means the Law Society of Scotland established under the
         Act;
      "the Secretary" means the Secretary of the Society and includes any
         person authorised by the Council to act on his behalf;
      "the Council" means the Council of the Society;
      "solicitor" means any person enrolled as a solicitor in pursuance of the
         Act and who holds a Practising Certificate under the Act free of
         conditions imposed in terms of section 15 or other sections of the
         Act, or any regulations made thereunder or by the Scottish
         Solicitors Discipline Tribunal; and shall include a firm of solicitors
         and an association of solicitors.
      "incorporated practice" means a body corporate recognised by the
         Council in terms of section 34(1A) of the Act and these rules as
         being suitable to undertake the provision of professional services
         such as are provided by solicitors.
   (2) The Interpretation Act 1978 applies to the interpretation of these rules
as it applies to the interpretation of an Act of Parliament.

Permission
   3. Subject to the provisions of these rules, a solicitor or an incorporated
practice may trade as a body corporate in terms of section 34(1A) of the Act
provided:—
      (a) any such body corporate has been recognised by the Council as an
         incorporated practice;
      (b) the control of any such body corporate is exclusively by solicitors or
         other incorporated practices; and
      (c) the membership of any such body corporate is restricted to solicitors
         or other incorporated practices.

Application
   4. Any person wishing to form an incorporated practice shall, prior to the
anticipated date of commencement of business as such incorporated
practice, submit to the Council:—
      (a) the names, designations and business addresses of all solicitors who
         will be members of the incorporated practice;
      (b) the names and addresses of the registered offices of all incorporated
         practices which will be members of the incorporated practice;
      (c) the names, designations and business addresses of all solicitors who
         will be directors of the incorporated practice;

(d) the proposed name and address of the registered office of the incorporated practice;

(e) a draft of the memorandum and articles of association of the proposed incorporated practice;

(f) a completed form of application for recognition as an incorporated practice in terms of the schedule to these rules;

(g) the fee to be prescribed from time to time by the Council in connection with such application; and

(h) in the case of an incorporated practice to be incorporated with limited liability, an irrevocable undertaking to the Council by each of the solicitors and incorporated practices who will be members of the incorporated practice that he or it or they will jointly and severally along with the other members of the incorporated practice reimburse to the Society grants paid out of the Scottish Solicitors' Guarantee Fund in terms of section 43 of the Act to a person who has suffered pecuniary loss by reason of dishonesty on the part of the incorporated practice or any director, manager, secretary or other employee thereof and that to any extent to which the Society shall have been unable to recover the amount of said grants from the incorporated practice or any liquidator thereof.

Memorandum and Articles of Association

5.—(1) The memorandum and articles of association of an incorporated practice shall contain provisions which show that it complies and will continue to comply with these rules (as in force from time to time) including, without prejudice to the foregoing generality, provisions to the following effect:—

(a) that no person shall be appointed or re-appointed or act as a director unless he is a member of the company duly qualified within the meaning of sub-paragraph (d) hereof;

(b) that no person other than a person duly qualified to act as a director may be appointed as an alternate director;

(c) that a director or alternate director shall vacate office if he ceases to be a member of the company or to be qualified to act as a director;

(d) that no person shall be capable of being a member of the company or (subject to rule 8(2)) enjoy any of the rights of members unless he or it is a solicitor or an incorporated practice; and

(e) that (subject to rule 9(7)) any member who ceases to be a solicitor or incorporated practice shall forthwith transfer his or its share or other interest in the company to another solicitor or incorporated practice, or otherwise cease to be a member of the company.

(2) The memorandum and articles of association of an incorporated practice shall contain provisions to anticipate and to deal with the situation where for whatever reason there is no longer a solicitor, or other validly constituted incorporated practice, exercising the day to day management and control of the incorporated practice. Without prejudice to the foregoing, the memorandum and articles of association shall contain specific provisions for:—

(a) the operation in the situation aforesaid of all client accounts in the name of the incorporated practice; and

(b) suitable arrangements in the situation aforesaid for making available to its clients or to some other solicitor or incorporated practice instructed by its clients or itself, (i) all deeds, wills, securities, papers, books of account, records, vouchers and other documents in its possession or control which are held on behalf of its clients or which relate to any trust of which it is sole trustee or co-trustee only with one or more of its employees and (ii) all sums of money due from it or held by it on behalf of its clients or subject to any trust as aforesaid.

(3) The memorandum and articles of association of an incorporated practice shall be only in terms previously approved by the Council, following submission of a draft thereof in terms of rule 4(e), and thereafter no incorporated practice shall alter its memorandum or articles of association without the prior consent of the Council.

(4) The Council may charge a fee in respect of its examination and, if thought fit, its approval of the memorandum and articles of association of an incorporated practice or any alteration thereof and such fee shall be in addition to the fee referred to in rule 4(g).

Financial soundness

6. No proposed body corporate shall be afforded recognition by the Council as an incorporated practice with limited liability unless the Council shall, after such enquiry as it deems necessary, be satisfied as to the financial soundness of the proposed body corporate and as to the arrangements to be made by the directors and members, by means of personal guarantees or otherwise, for discharging the liabilities to creditors of such body corporate. The Council may charge a fee in respect of such enquiries.

Minimum contributions

7. The Council may by resolution impose any requirement as to the minimum contributions to be made by the members of an incorporated practice having limited liability by way of guarantee on a winding up or by way of contribution in the form of uncalled share capital.

Undertaking to Council

8. Every solicitor who and every incorporated practice which becomes a member of an incorporated practice which is incorporated with limited liability shall grant an undertaking to the Council on the same terms as the undertaking described in rule 4(h).

Ongoing provisions

9.—(1) The members and directors of an incorporated practice shall ensure that the conditions of its memorandum and articles are given effect to all times and without delay.

(2) The Council may at any time require an incorporated practice to demonstrate that the requirements of rule 5 are being complied with.

(3) Incorporated practices shall notify the Council within fourteen days of such change of:—

    (a) any change in the address of the registered office of the incorporated practice; and

    (b) any change in the members or directors of an incorporated practice.

(4) Incorporated practices shall send to the Secretary a copy of all documents which require to be filed with the registrar of companies contemporaneously with the despatch of such documents to the registrar of companies.

(5) Incorporated practices shall send to the Secretary a copy of all certificates issued by the registrar of companies forthwith upon the receipt by the incorporated practice thereof.

(6) No person shall be a registered member of an incorporated practice unless he is a solicitor or an incorporated practice.

(7) No person not being a registered member of an incorporated practice shall enjoy any of the rights of membership except an executor of a deceased member of the incorporated practice *qua* executor of that member; provided always that such an executor shall have no voting rights in respect of his membership of the incorporated practice.

(8) No person against whom a disqualification order under sections 6 or 8 of the Company Directors Disqualification Act 1986 is in force shall be permitted to become or remain a member of an incorporated practice, except with the consent of the Council.

(9) Where a member of an incorporated practice:—

(a) dies or for any other reason ceases to hold a current practising certificate or, as the case may be, has its certificate of recognition revoked under rule 11 hereof; or

(b) becomes subject to a disqualification order under sections 6 or 8 of the Company Directors Disqualification Act 1986,

the incorporated practice shall, unless the Council has exercised its discretion under paragraph (8) of this rule, immediately take the necessary steps in terms of its articles of association to ensure compliance with paragraphs (7) and (8) of this rule.

(10) No person shall be appointed or shall act as a director of an incorporated practice unless he is a member thereof.

(11) Every incorporated practice to which these rules apply shall require to be insured against such classes of professional liability as are indemnified by the Master Policy (as defined by the Solicitors (Scotland) Professional Indemnity Insurance Rules 1995) and the Council shall prescribe from time to time the limits of indemnity and self-insured amounts applicable to incorporated practices and may prescribe different limits for different incorporated practices or classes of incorporated practices.

(12) The Council shall maintain a list containing the names and places of business of all incorporated practices, which list shall be open for inspection at the office of the Society during office hours by any person without payment of any fee.

Recognition
10.—(1) The Council shall consider every application made to it in terms of these rules, and, if the Council is satisfied by the applying solicitors that a body corporate has complied in all respects with the requirements of these rules, the Council shall issue to the applying solicitors a certificate recognising the proposed body corporate as an incorporated practice which certificate shall state:—

(a) the name and registered number of the incorporated practice;

(b) whether the incorporated practice will carry on business with liability which is unlimited or limited by guarantee or limited by share capital; and

(c) the date of the certificate of recognition.

(2) The certificate of recognition or a true copy of it shall at all times be displayed at every place of business of the incorporated practice.

(3) An incorporated practice which proposes to re-register as unlimited under section 49 or as limited under section 51 of the Companies Act 1985 shall, before applying for re-registration under section 49 or passing a resolution under section 51 submit to the Council an application to be allowed to re-register accordingly. Such application shall be in the form *mutatis mutandis* required by rule 4 for the recognition of an incorporated practice in the form proposed after re-registration. If the Council is satisfied by the applying incorporated practice that it has complied in all respects with the requirements of these rules, the Council shall issue to the applying incorporated practice a certificate entitling it to apply for or to resolve to be re-registered as aforesaid and containing the information specified in paragraph (1) of this rule. The incorporated practice shall not apply for or resolve to be re-registered as aforesaid until such certificate has been issued and shall so apply or resolve within one month of the date of such certificate. The certificate of authorisation for re-registration or a true copy of it shall at all times be displayed at every place of business of the incorporated practice along with the certificate of recognition.

Revocation

11. A certificate of recognition of an incorporated practice may be revoked by the Council if:—

(a) recognition of the incorporated practice was granted by the Council by reason of error or fraud; or

(b) an incorporated practice goes into liquidation (other than members' voluntary liquidation approved by the Council for the purpose of amalgamation or reconstruction) or if a provisional liquidator, receiver or judicial factor is appointed to such incorporated practice or if an administrator within the meaning of the Insolvency Act 1986 is appointed to such incorporated practice or if the incorporated practice enters into a voluntary arrangement under Part I of the Insolvency Act 1986, or if such incorporated practice is struck off the register of companies; or

(c) control of an incorporated practice ceases for any reason, or however temporarily, to be other than exclusively by solicitors or other incorporated practices; or

(d) any solicitor who is a director or member of the incorporated practice has been excluded in terms of section 31 of the Legal Aid (Scotland) Act 1986 or any statutory re-enactment thereof; or

(e) such incorporated practice has failed to comply with any of the provisions of these rules.

Other practice rules

12. All rules made under the Act shall apply in all respects *mutatis mutandis* to incorporated practices.

Power of waiver

13. The Council shall have power to waive any of the provisions of these rules in any particular circumstances or case.

Breach of rules

14. Breach of any of these rules may be treated as professional misconduct for the purposes of Part IV of the Act (Complaints and Disciplinary Proceedings).

SCHEDULE

FORM OF APPLICATION FOR RECOGNITION AS AN INCORPORATED PRACTICE

No.   19

We the undernoted hereby apply for a certificate of recognition by the Council as an incorporated practice

....

name of body corporate (a)

....

registered office of body corporate (a)

....

registered number of body corporate (a)

....

date of incorporation of body corporate (a)

SOLICITORS WHO WILL BE MEMBERS OF THE INCORPORATED PRACTICE (b)

Name	Designation (c)	Place(s) of business (d)	Place of business as at date of last practising certificate (if applicable) (e)	Date and number of last practising certificate (if applicable)
1.	....	(1)	....	....
			....	
			....	
		(2)		
2.	....	(1)	....	....
			....	
			....	
		(2)		

INCORPORATED PRACTICES WHICH WILL BE MEMBERS OF THE INCORPORATED PRACTICE (b)

Name	Address of registered office	Date and number of certificate of recognition
....	....	....
	....	
	....	
....	....	....
	....	
	....	
....	....	....
	....	
	....	

SOLICITORS WHO WILL BE DIRECTORS OF THE INCORPORATED PRACTICE (f)

Name	Designation (c)	Place(s) of business (d)	Place of business as at date of last practising certificate (if applicable) (e)	Date and number of last practising certificate (if applicable)
1.	....	(1)	....	....
			....	
			....	
		(2)		
2.	....	(1)	....	....
			....	
			....	
		(2)		

etc.

Dated·this   day of   19

(g)

(signatures)   ....

....

....

FORM OF INCORPORATION

To assist the Council in its duties under rules 5(7) and 7(1)(b) state here:—
  (a) Whether the incorporated practice will carry on business with unlimited unliability, or
  (b) Whether the incorporated practice will carry on business limited by guarantee and, if so, the extent of the guarantee, or
  (c) Whether the incorporated practice will carry on business limited by share capital, and, if so, the amounts of the authorised and issued share capital of the company.

ASSETS AND LIABILITIES

To assist the Council in its duties under rule 5(6), set out here or attach a statement of the assets and liabilities of the incorporated practice as at the proposed date of commencement of business of the incorporated practice.

Notes:
  (a) If the company has not yet been incorporated insert the proposed company name and the address of the proposed registered office and explain the circumstances in a covering letter.
  (b) Details of **all** proposed members of the incorporated practice must be given.
  (c) *i.e.* W.S., S.S.C., Advocate in Aberdeen, or solicitor.
  (d) All places of business if more than one should be stated. The principal place of business should be given first.
  (e) If the applicant's place of business has changed since his last practising certificate was issued, the address which appeared on his practising certificate should be stated.
  (f) All proposed directors must be members of the incorporated practice.
  (g) All proposed solicitor members of the incorporated practice must sign. In the case of proposed incorporated practice members, a director of the incorporated practice must sign.

Further Notes
  1. This form when completed and signed should be forwarded along with the proposed memorandum and articles of association of the incorporated practice and a remittance for the appropriate fee in the enclosed envelope. Remittance should be made payable to "The Law Society of Scotland" and should be crossed "account payee only".
  2. To permit the Council adequate time to carry out its duties in terms of these rules, any person wishing to form an incorporated practice should, at least three months prior to the anticipated date of commencement of business as such incorporated practice, submit to the Council the documentation required under these rules.
  3. The making of a false statement by a solicitor in an application for recognition as an incorporated practice may be treated as professional misconduct for the purposes of the Solicitors (Scotland) Act 1980.

Solicitors (Scotland) Investment Business Compliance Certificate Rules 1997

Rules dated 25th April 1997, made by the Council of the Law Society of Scotland and approved by the Lord President of the Court of Session in terms of section 34 of the Solicitors (Scotland) Act 1980.

Citation and commencement
  1.—(1) These rules may be cited as the Solicitors (Scotland) Investment Business Compliance Certificate Rules 1997 and shall come into operation on 1st January 1998.
  (2) The Solicitors (Scotland) Compliance Certificate Rules 1994 are revoked with effect from the date of commencement of these rules.

Interpretation
   2. In these Rules unless the context otherwise requires:
      "accounting period" shall have the meaning given in the Solicitors
         (Scotland) Accounts Certificate Rules in force from time to time;
      "the CBRs" means the Solicitors (Scotland) (Conduct of Investment
         Business) Practice Rules in force from time to time;
      "certified person", "the Council" and "officer" shall have the meaning
         ascribed to them in the CBRs; and
      "Investment Business Compliance Certificate" means a certificate in
         the form set out in the Schedule to these rules or in such other form
         as the Council may from time to time prescribe.

Obligation to deliver Investment Business Compliance Certificate
   3.—(1) Subject to the provisions of rule 7 hereof, every certified person
shall deliver to the Council within one calendar month of the completion of
each accounting period an Investment Business Compliance Certificate in
respect of that period.
   (2) If appropriate, a certified person may deliver an Investment Business
Compliance Certificate in respect of the accounting period which includes
the date of the introduction of these Rules. The period covered by this
Certificate shall not exceed twelve months.

Who may sign certificates
   4. An Investment Business Compliance Certificate shall be signed by two
officers, at least one of whom has passed, or is exempt from the Society's
Investment Business Examination, unless the certified person is a sole
practitioner in which case the Certificate shall be signed by him.

Where a certified person practises in two or more places
   5. In the case of a certified person which has two or more places of business
and where separate records are maintained for each place of business, a
separate Investment Business Compliance Certificate shall be delivered in
respect of each place of business.

Power to Council to extend period of time referred to in rule 3
   6. The Council may, in any case on satisfactory cause shown, extend the
period of one calendar month within which an Investment Business
Compliance Certificate requires to be delivered provided that such extension shall in no case exceed three months from the date of completion of the
relevant accounting period.

*Reservation of power to Council to require inspection of a certified person's
   records etc.*
   7.—(1) The delivery of an Investment Business Compliance Certificate to
the Council in terms of these rules shall not prejudice the power of the
Council to require the inspection of a certified person's files and records.
   (2) In the event of a certified person failing to produce an Investment
Business Compliance Certificate timeously, the Council may instruct an
inspection of the certified person's accounting and other client investment
records and documents. Such inspection shall be carried out by a suitably
qualified accountant with the costs being met by the certified person and a
copy of the accountant's report shall be sent to the Council.

SCHEDULE

To be Printed on the Certified Person's Letter Paper

To: The Secretary,
The Law Society of Scotland,
26 Drumsheugh Gardens,
EDINBURGH,
EH3 7YR.

Dear Sir,

INVESTMENT BUSINESS COMPLIANCE CERTIFICATE

The accounting period to which the undernoted declarations relate ("the relevant period") is:
from .... to ....

1. EXTENT OF INVESTMENT BUSINESS

I/We certify that, in the relevant period, I was/we were carrying on the practice of a Scottish solicitor and that my/our gross income did not derive wholly or mainly from investment business.

The total income arising from investment business amounted to ....% of the total income.

2. SCOPE OF INVESTMENT BUSINESS

I/We certify that, in the relevant period, I/we engaged in the following categories of investment business:

(*Delete as applicable)

 1. Discretionary investment management .... *Yes/No
 2. Non-discretionary investment management .... *Yes/No
 3. Advising on investments .... *Yes/No
 4. Arranging transactions in securities .... *Yes/No
 5. Advising on and/or arranging life policies .... *Yes/No
 6. Advising on and/or arranging pensions .... *Yes/No
 7. Advising on and/or arranging transfers or opt-outs
    from occupational pensions schemes .... *Yes/No
 8. Advising on and/or arranging other packaged products
    (*e.g.* unit trusts, OEICs and investment trust savings schemes) .... *Yes/No
 9. Advising on and/or arranging corporate finance activities .... *Yes/No
10. Operating a nominee company .... *Yes/No
11. Other investment areas (please specify) .... *Yes/No

3. SCALE OF SECURITIES TRANSACTIONS AND DISCRETIONARY MANAGEMENT

(a) I/We certify that I/we maintained records of all purchases, sales and transfers in securities undertaken during the relevant period;

(b) I was/We were party to .... statements of terms of business provided or issued to clients or written contracts/client agreements referred to in the CBRs (See note 1);

(c) I/We managed on a discretionary basis .... portfolios of a value in excess of £100,000 (See note 2);

(d) I/We effected or arranged for the effecting of .... individual transactions for discretionary managed portfolios of a value in excess of £100,000 (See note 3); and

(e) I/We managed on a discretionary basis portfolios to a total value of £.......... (See note 4).

4. LIFE POLICIES AND UNITS IN COLLECTIVE INVESTMENTS

I/We certify that in the relevant period the following number of life policies and transactions in units in regulated collective investment schemes were placed (both directly or indirectly through another intermediary) with the undernoted life offices and operators of regulated collective investment schemes.

A   <u>Name of Life Office</u>   <u>No of Policies</u>

B   <u>Name of Operator</u>   <u>No of Transactions</u>
    <u>of Collective Investment</u>
    <u>Scheme</u>

5. INDIVIDUALS AUTHORISED TO CONDUCT INVESTMENT BUSINESS

I/We certify that in the relevant period the following individuals were authorised to conduct investment business:

Name	Status	Conducted Business?	CPD for Investment Business. Undertaken?
Solicitors	Exempt/Qualified	(YES/NO)	(YES/NO)

Name	Status	Conducted Business?	Training for Investment Business. Undertaken?
Non solicitors	Exempt/Qualified	(YES/NO)	(YES/NO)

6. INVESTMENT BUSINESS RECORDS

I/We confirm that proper records were maintained in respect of all investment business conducted on behalf of clients, all necessary information was provided to clients and the documents of title were held and transferred in accordance with the CBRs.

7. ASSISTANCE OF AN EXTERNAL ACCOUNTANT

If the services of an external accountant were employed to assist in the preparation of this Investment Business Compliance Certificate, indicate the scope and extent of that assistance.

(See note 5)

(If none state NONE).

8. OTHER MATTERS WHICH REQUIRE TO BE REPORTED

(See note 6)

(If none state NONE).

9. COMPLIANCE

I/We certify that, to the best of my/our knowledge and belief I/we have in the relevant period complied with the requirements of the Financial Services Act 1986, the CBRs and the Solicitors (Scotland) Investment Business Training Regulations 1994.

Dated this   day of   19

Officer ....

Officer ....

Name of firm: (in block capitals)

....

Address ....

....

NOTES
1. The number of statements of terms of business provided or issued to clients or written contracts/client agreements in force at the date of the Investment Business Compliance Certificate must be shown.

2. The number of portfolios managed on a discretionary basis in excess of £100,000 at the date of the Investment Business Compliance Certificate must be shown.

3. The number of individual securities transactions in excess of £100,000 effected or arranged on a discretionary basis in the relevant period must be shown.

4. The total value of the funds comprised in the portfolio(s) at the date of the Investment Business Compliance Certificate must be shown.

5. It is anticipated that many solicitors will instruct an external accountant to assist them in the checking of the accounting records and/or the preparation of the Investment Business Compliance Certificate. If the services of an external accountant are required you should indicate the extent of the help offered. The following tasks are examples of the assistance which may be obtained from an accountant:—

(a) The preparation of the list of investment business transactions which are required to be disclosed in the Investment Business Compliance Certificate;

(b) Checking your records to confirm the contents of the Investment Business Compliance Certificate;

(c) A test check of terms of business letters and client agreement records;

(d) A test check of the client accounting records to identify the categories of investment business which are disclosed as having been conducted during the accounting period;

(e) Calculation of the percentage income which is attributable to the conduct of investment business as a percentage of the total income during the accounting period;

(f) Confirmation of individual records of continuing professional development in respect of investment business; and

(g) A complete review of all aspects of the investment business activity including the production of the Investment Business Compliance Certificate as submitted.

6. The solicitor should only make entries at this note if there are matters which are relevant to the firm's failure to comply with the CBRs during the current accounting period. Examples might include a delay in preparing the investment business records during the accounting period which may be rectified during the period, receipt of a complaint in connection with the investment business dealings of the firm which is acknowledged and resolved during the accounting period, or any other event which the solicitor feels should be drawn to the attention of the Council in respect of their failing to comply with the CBRs.

Solicitors (Scotland) (Practice Management Course) Practice Rules 1997

Rules dated 27th March 1997 made by the Council of the Law Society of Scotland and approved by the Lord President of the Court of Session in terms of section 34 of the Solicitors (Scotland) Act 1980.

1.—(1) These rules may be cited as the Solicitors (Scotland) (Practice Management Course) Practice Rules 1997.

(2) These rules shall come into operation on 1st June 1997.

2.—(1) In these rules, unless the context otherwise requires:—

"the Act" means the Solicitors (Scotland) Act 1980;

"the Council" means the Council of the Society;

"solicitor" means any person enrolled as a solicitor in pursuance of the Act and who holds a practising certificate free of conditions imposed in terms of section 15 or other sections of the Act, or any Regulations made thereunder or by the Scottish Solicitors Discipline Tribunal;

"Practice Management Course" means a course of practical training in the management of solicitors' practices, the duration, form and content of which shall be prescribed by the Council from time to time;

"principal" means a solicitor who is a sole practitioner or is a partner in a firm of two or more solicitors or is a director of an incorporated practice;

"practice unit" means the business of a sole practitioner, a firm of two or more solicitors or an incorporated practice;

"the Society" means The Law Society of Scotland established under the
Act.

(2) The Interpretation Act 1978 applies to these rules as it applies to an
Act of Parliament.

3. The Solicitors (Scotland) (Attendance at Courses on Practice Management) Practice Rules 1989 are hereby repealed.

4. Subject to rule 5 hereof a solicitor who becomes a principal of a practice
unit shall be obliged to attend a Practice Management Course within a
period not exceeding twelve months after the date on which he becomes
such a principal, or such other period as may be determined by the Council in
any particular case.

5. Rule 4 shall not apply to a solicitor who (a) has attended a Practice
Management Course within the year preceding the date on which he
becomes a principal or (b) has been a principal for a continuous period of at
least twelve months within the twenty four month period before that date.

6. The Council shall have power to waive any of the provisions of these
rules in any particular circumstances or case.

7. Breach of these rules may be treated as professional misconduct for the
purposes of Part IV of the Act (Complaints and Disciplinary Proceedings).

Solicitors (Scotland)
(Conduct of Investment Business) Practice Rules 1997

Rules dated 26th September 1997, made by the Council of the Law Society of Scotland and approved by the Lord President of the Court of Session in terms of section 34 of the Solicitors (Scotland) Act 1980.

CONTENTS

PART 1

CITATION, COMMENCEMENT, APPLICATION AND INTERPRETATION

PART 2

INVESTMENT BUSINESS CERTIFICATES

PART 3

SCOPE

PART 4

OBLIGATIONS ON A CERTIFIED PERSON

SCHEDULE 1

TERMS OF BUSINESS

1.   Contents
2.   Discretionary managed portfolios
3.   PEPs

SCHEDULE 2

INVESTMENT ADVERTISEMENTS

1.   Approval of investment advertisements
2.   PEPs

PART 1

CITATION, COMMENCEMENT, APPLICATION AND INTERPRETATION

Citation and commencement
    1.1.—(1) These rules may be cited as the Solicitors (Scotland) (Conduct of Investment Business) Practice Rules 1997 and shall come into operation on 1st January 1998.
    (2) The Solicitors (Scotland) (Conduct of Investment Business) Practice Rules 1994 are revoked with effect from the date of commencement of these rules.

Applications
    1.2. The following do not apply to the corporate finance activities of a certified person:—
rule 3.2(1)(c), rule 3.4, rule 3.6(1); Part 4 (Obligations on a certified person) except rules 4.1 to 4.4, 4.14 (Unsolicited calls) and 4.15 (Insider dealing); Part 6 except rules 6.4 (Record of investment business income) and 6.7 (Compliance procedures and review); Schedule 1 (Terms of business); Schedule 2 (Investment advertisements).

Practice notes
    1.3. A practice note appended to a rule or a paragraph of a rule gives guidance as to how the Council considers the rule or paragraph would operate in particular circumstances. It is not part of the rule.

Interpretation
    1.4.—(1) In these rules, unless the context otherwise requires:—
    "accounting period" has the meaning given in rule 2 of the Solicitors (Scotland) Accounts Certificate Rules 1997;
    "the Act" means the Financial Services Act 1986 as amended;
    "the 1980 Act" means the Solicitors (Scotland) Act 1980 as amended;
    "associate" has the meaning given by section 435 of the Insolvency Act 1986 as though the same were amended as follows:—
        (a)   by the insertion at the end of subsection (6) of the words "or (c) if both companies are members of the same group, group having for this purpose the meaning assigned to it in paragraph 30 of Schedule 1 to the Financial Services Act 1986";
        (b)   by the substitution of the words "fifteen per cent" for the words "one-third" in subsection 10(b);
        (c)   by the insertion after the words "or elsewhere)" in subsection (11) of the words "or unincorporated association"; and

    (d)   by the insertion of the following additional subsection:
> "(12) A person is an associate of an appointed represen-
> tative of his, and a company is an associate of an
> appointed representative of a company in the same
> group as the first company, group having for this purpose
> the meaning assigned to it in paragraph 30 of Schedule 1
> to the Financial Services Act 1986.";

"authorised person" means a person authorised to conduct investment
    business in terms of the Act as a member of a RPB or a SRO;

"the Board" means the Securities and Investments Board;

"the Brokers" means the Society's Brokers for the time being under the
    Master Policy for Professional Indemnity Insurance effected by the
    Society in terms of the Solicitors (Scotland) Professional Indem-
    nity Insurance Rules 1995;

"broker funds arrangement" means an arrangement whereby a life
    office issues policies to the clients of a certified person the benefits
    under which are linked to the performance of a fund of the life
    office, and the certified person has authority from the life office to
    determine any of the matters by reference to which the perform-
    ance of the fund is from time to time to be measured (whether by
    determining the assets in which the fund is invested or otherwise);

"certified person" means a firm or incorporated practice holding a
    current investment business certificate of which at least one officer
    is either exempt from or has passed the Society's Investment
    Business Exam as determined by the Council or has an equivalent
    investment qualification; and

"certification" shall be construed accordingly;

"cold call" means:
    (a)   a personal visit or oral communication made without express
        invitation to a person in the United Kingdom; or
    (b)   an oral communication made without express invitation from
        the United Kingdom to a person elsewhere;
        and, where the context permits, the act of making any such visit
        or communication;

"compliance officer" means an officer who has responsibility for
    securing compliance with the provisions of these rules;

"corporate finance activities" means any service provided in the course
    of carrying on investment business to—
    (a)   an issuer, holder or owner of investments with regard to the
        offer, issue, underwriting, repurchase, exchange or redemp-
        tion of, or the variation or abrogation of the terms of, the
        investments, or any related matter;
    (b)   an ordinary business investor, any other body corporate,
        partnership or an unincorporated association, or an inter-
        national or supranational organisation, which relate to the
        manner in which, or the terms on which, or the persons by
        whom, any business, activities or undertakings relating to it, or
        any associate, are to be financed, structured, managed, con-
        trolled, regulated or reported upon;
    (c)   any body corporate in connection with
        (i)   a proposed or actual takeover or related operation by or
           on behalf of, or involving investments issued by, that body
           corporate or its associate; or
        (ii)   a merger, de-merger, re-organisation or reconstruction
           involving any investments issued by that body corporate
           or its associate;
    (d)   any shareholder or prospective shareholder of a body corpor-
        ate to be established for the purpose of effecting a takeover or
        related operation in connection with that takeover or related
        operation;

(e) a person who, acting as a principal for his own account,
- (i) is involved in negotiations or decisions relating to the commercial, financial or strategic intentions or requirements of a business or prospective business; or
- (ii) (provided he is acting otherwise than solely in his capacity as an investor) assists the interests of another person by himself undertaking all or part of any transactions involved in business falling within (a), b), (c) or (d) above;

(f) a person who is undertaking business with or for a person falling within (a), (b), (c), (d) or (e) above in respect of activities described in those sub-paragraphs;

"the Council" means the Council of the Society;

"derivatives" means options, futures and contracts for differences;

"direct offer advertisement" means a specific investment advertisement (including a pre-printed or off-the-screen advertisement) which:
(a) contains:
- (i) an offer by the certified person or another offeror to enter into an investment agreement with anyone who responds to the advertisement; or
- (ii) an invitation to anyone to respond to the advertisement by making an offer to the certified person or another offeree to enter into an investment agreement; and
(b) specifies the manner or indicates a form in which any response is to be made.

PRACTICE NOTE

An example of a direct offer advertisement is one which requires a reply by a tear-off slip.

"documents of title", for the purposes of Part 7 of these rules, means share certificates, statements relating to certificated or uncertificated securities, life policies, statements relating to regulated collective investment schemes and entitlements to other investments as defined in the Act;

"employee" means an individual who is employed in connection with a certified person's investment business whether under a contract of service or for services or otherwise and includes a "consultant" which has the meaning given in rule 2 of the Solicitors (Scotland) (Associates, Consultants and Employees) Practice Rules 1996.

PRACTICE NOTE

This definition covers all full time, part time and temporary staff but not brokers or other "outside" intermediaries having a contract for services with the certified person.

"execution-only client" means a client for whom a transaction is effected in circumstances in which the certified person can reasonably assume that the client is not relying upon the certified person to advise him on or to exercise any judgment on his behalf as to the merits or the suitability for him of that transaction.

PRACTICE NOTE

The certified person should maintain a record to show that the client is an "execution-only client".

"firm" means a partnership or association of solicitors and includes a sole practitioner;

"incorporated practice" has the meaning given in rule 2 of the Solicitors (Scotland) (Incorporated Practices) Practice Rules 1997;

"investment business certificate" means a certificate issued by the Council under rule 2.2 below;

"investment manager" means a person who, on behalf of a client, either:
- (a) manages a portfolio in the exercise of discretion (discretionary portfolio management); or
- (b) has assumed responsibility for advising or commenting upon the investments comprised in a client's portfolio (portfolio management);

and "discretionary managed portfolio" and "managed portfolio" shall be construed accordingly.

PRACTICE NOTE
A certified person who communicates a stockbroker's report on a portfolio to its client(s) without commenting upon the investments comprised therein is not an investment manager for the purposes of these rules.

"life office" means a person who carries on a long term business within the meaning of section 1 of the Insurance Companies Act 1982;

"life policy" means an investment of the description set out in paragraph 10 of Schedule 1 to the Act and includes a pension policy where contributions are paid to a life office;

"market maker", in relation to an investment of any description, means a person who (otherwise than in his capacity as the operator of a regulated collective investment scheme) holds himself out as able and willing to enter into transactions of sale and purchase in investments of that description at prices determined by him generally and continuously rather than in respect of each particular transaction; and

"making markets" shall be construed accordingly;

"officer", in relation to a body corporate, means a director, manager or secretary and, in relation to a firm, means a partner or a sole practitioner and, in relation to an incorporated practice, means a member of an incorporated practice;

"ordinary business investor" means:
- (a) a government, local authority or public authority within the meaning of Schedule 1 to the Act;
- (b) a body corporate, partnership or unincorporated association which satisfies any of the following size requirements:
  - (i) that it is a body corporate which has more that 20 members (or is the subsidiary of a body corporate which has more than 20 members) and it (or any of its holding companies or subsidiaries) has a paid up share capital or net assets of £500,000 or more;
  - (ii) that it is a body corporate and it (or any of its holding companies or subsidiaries) has a paid up share capital or net assets of £5 million or more; or
  - (iii) that, if it is not a body corporate, it has net assets of £5 million or more; or
- (c) a trustee of a trust which satisfies either of the following size requirements:
  - (i) that the aggregate value of the cash and investments which form part of the trust's assets (before deducting the amount of its liabilities) is £10 million or more; or
  - (ii) that the aggregate value has been £10 million or more at any time during the previous two years;

"PEP" means a scheme of investment which is a plan satisfying the conditions prescribed in the Personal Equity Plan Regulations 1989 and in relation to which the certified person is the plan manager and the client is the plan investor within the meaning of those regulations;

"PIA" means the Personal Investment Authority Ltd;

"packaged product" means a life policy, a share in an open-ended
investment company (OEIC), a unit of a regulated collective
investment scheme, or an investment trust savings scheme;

"pension fund withdrawal" is where a certified person advises a client to
delay the purchase of a compulsory purchase annuity and instead
take income withdrawals;

"prescribed disclosure" is a written statement which must make clear:

(a) that all or most of the protections provided by the UK
regulatory system do not apply; and

(b) where the business is excluded from the Investors Compensation Scheme by its territorial scope (or would be so excluded
if the person carrying it on were a participant firm), a statement
that compensation under that scheme will not be available; and

(c) where the introduction is to any person carrying on investment
business outwith the UK, a statement that compensation
under schemes established by the Law Society of Scotland may
not be available;

and which may also indicate the protections or compensation
available under another system of regulation;

"RPB" means a recognised professional body;

"readily realisable investment" means a unit in a regulated collective
investment scheme, a life policy or any investment which is traded
on or under the rules of a recognised investment exchange other
than one traded so infrequently or irregularly that it cannot be
certain that a price will be quoted at all times or that it may be
difficult to effect transactions at any price which may be quoted;

"recognised investment exchange" means any investment exchange
which may be recognised from time to time by the Board;

"regulated business" means investment business which is:

(a) business carried on from a permanent place of business
maintained by a certified person in the United Kingdom; and

(b) other business carried on with or for clients in the United
Kingdom, unless that business is business carried on from an
office of a certified person outside the United Kingdom which
would not be treated as carried on in the United Kingdom if
that office was not the office of the certified person;

"regulated collective investment scheme" means an authorised unit
trust scheme, an OEIC or a recognised scheme;

"SRO" means a self regulating organisation;

"the Secretary" means the Secretary of the Society and includes any
person authorised by the Council to act on behalf of the Secretary;

"the Society" means the Law Society of Scotland under the 1980 Act;

"solicitor" means a solicitor holding a practising certificate under the
1980 Act;

"specific investment advertisement" means an investment advertisement which identifies and promotes a particular investment;

"stabilising bid" means an offer by the person responsible for making
allotments in the course of managing an issue, to purchase
securities with a view to stabilising or maintaining the market price
of the securities; and

"stabilising transactions" means the purchase of securities under a
stabilising bid:

"takeover or related operation" means:

(a) any offer to which the Takeover Code applies and any
transaction or arrangement which is of such a nature that the
Takeover Code would have applied to it had it concerned a
company whose shares are listed under Part IV of the Act and
whose head office and place of central management are in the
United Kingdom;

(b) any offer, transaction or arrangement relating to the purchase of securities with a view to establishing or increasing a strategic holding of a person, or of a person together with his associates, in the securities concerned;

(c) any transaction or arrangement entered into in contemplation or furtherance of any offer, transaction or arrangement falling within (a) or (b) above; and

(d) any transaction or arrangement entered into by way of defence or protection against any offer, transaction or arrangement falling within (a), (b) or (c) above which has taken place or which is contemplated.

(2) In these rules, unless the context otherwise requires, references to the effecting of a transaction by a certified person on behalf of another person include references to the certified person's arranging for a transaction to be effected by a third party on behalf of that person.

(3) A person for whom services are provided by a certified person for reward may be regarded as being a client of the certified person notwithstanding that the certified person is remunerated by a third party for the performance of those services and not by that person.

Words defined in the Act
1.5. Unless the context otherwise requires, words and expressions defined in the Act have the same meanings when used in these rules.

Interpretation Act 1978
1.6. The Interpretation Act 1978 applies to the interpretation of these rules as it applies to the interpretation of an Act of Parliament.

PART 2

INVESTMENT BUSINESS CERTIFICATES

Investment business certificates (application)
2.1.—(1) An application for an investment business certificate may be made by a firm or incorporated practice by submitting to the Council:
(a) a completed form of application for an investment business certificate in the form from time to time prescribed by the Council; and
(b) the fee to be prescribed from time to time by the Council in connection with such application; and
(c) such information as the Council may specify in connection with such application.

(2) At any time after receiving an application and before determining it, the Council may require the applicant to furnish additional information and such additional information shall be in such form or verified in such manner as the Council may specify.

Investment business certificates (issue and refusal)
2.2.—(1) Subject to paragraph (2) below, the Council may, on an application duly made in accordance with rule 2.1 above, issue or refuse to issue an investment business certificate or may issue such certificate subject to such conditions or restrictions as it considers appropriate.

(2) The Council shall refuse to issue an investment business certificate unless it is satisfied that:—
(a) the applicant is a firm or incorporated practice; and
(b) the main business of the applicant is the practice of the profession of a Scottish solicitor; and
(c) the applicant's business does not consist wholly or mainly of investment business; and

(d) the applicant has at least one officer who has passed, or is exempt from the Society's Investment Business Examination or possesses another qualification to conduct investment business all in terms of the Solicitors (Scotland) Investment Business Training Regulations 1994.

(3) The Council may refuse to issue an investment business certificate unless it is satisfied that all non-solicitor employees of a firm or incorporated practice who are to conduct investment business in the course of their employment in that firm or incorporated practice are fit and proper persons and are qualified to conduct such investment business.

Investment business certificates (compliance certificates and annual fee)
2.3.—(1) A firm or incorporated practice which has been issued an investment business certificate shall submit to the Council within one calendar month of the completion of each accounting period an Investment Business Compliance Certificate in accordance with the Solicitors (Scotland) Investment Business Compliance Certificate Rules 1997. The prescribed fee for the retention of the investment business certificate shall be payable annually in November.

(2) The amount of the fee referred to in paragraph (1) above shall be such as the Council may from time to time prescribe and the Council may prescribe different amounts for different certified persons or classes of certified persons.

Investment business certificates (withdrawal, suspension, restriction and qualification)
2.4.—(1) An investment business certificate shall be withdrawn immediately on the certified person ceasing to practise as solicitors or ceasing to be managed and controlled by solicitors.

(2) An investment business certificate issued to an incorporated practice shall be withdrawn immediately on the revocation of the recognition of that incorporated practice.

(3) An investment business certificate shall be withdrawn immediately if the certified person ceases to comply with the requirements of the Solicitors (Scotland) Investment Business Training Regulations 1994.

(4) The Council may suspend or withdraw an investment business certificate if after due enquiry it is satisfied that a non-solicitor employee who is conducting investment business is not a fit and proper person or is not qualified to conduct such investment business.

(5) An investment business certificate issued to a sole practitioner shall be suspended immediately on the occurrence in relation to that solicitor of any of the circumstances mentioned in section 18(1) of the 1980 Act and an investment business certificate granted to a firm comprising two or more solicitors shall be suspended immediately on the occurrence in relation to that firm of any of the circumstances mentioned in section 18(1)(c)–(e) of the 1980 Act inclusive; provided that, in either case, such suspension shall cease to have effect on the occurrence of the events specified in section 19(4) or (5) of the 1980 Act.

(6) An investment business certificate issued to an incorporated practice shall be suspended immediately on the occurrence in relation to that incorporated practice of any of the circumstances mentioned in section 18(1 A) of the 1980 Act.

(7) An investment business certificate shall be suspended immediately if, within 30 days of the due date for payment of any fee required under rules 2.3 above or 9.1 below, payment has not been received, provided that such suspension shall cease to have effect immediately on payment being received.

(8) An investment business certificate shall be suspended immediately if the certified person has not, within one month of the completion of its accounting period, delivered to the Council an Investment Business Compliance Certificate in accordance with the Solicitors (Scotland) Invest-

ment Business Compliance Certificate Rules 1997; provided that such suspension shall cease to have effect on the date of production to the Council of an Investment Business Compliance Certificate.

(9) The Council may, by written notice to a certified person, suspend or restrict its investment business certificate or attach such conditions as it thinks fit thereto if, after reasonable enquiry, it is satisfied that investors would not otherwise be adequately protected. Any such suspension, restriction or qualification shall take effect on the date specified in the written notice ("the effective date") and shall cease to have effect on the date, if any, determined by the Council. A certified person shall be entitled at any time after the effective date to represent either orally or in writing to the Council that such suspension, restriction or condition should be terminated or removed and may require the Council to confirm or terminate or remove the suspension, restriction or condition within seven days of the hearing or receipt of representations.

(10) An investment business certificate shall be suspended if the Council after due enquiry ceases to be satisfied that the certified person's gross income does not derive wholly or mainly from investment business. Any such suspension shall take effect from the date on which the certified person is given written notice thereof and shall cease to have effect only if and when the Council is satisfied that the certified person's gross income no longer consists wholly or mainly of investment business and the certified person is given written notice by the Council that the suspension has ceased to have effect.

(11) Where an investment business certificate has been or is to be suspended, restricted, qualified or withdrawn, the Council may direct the certified person whose investment business certificate has been or is to be suspended, restricted, qualified or withdrawn to take such action and make such arrangements as are necessary, in the view of the Council, to ensure the speedy and satisfactory completion and/or transfer to another authorised person of clients' outstanding investment business.

(12) It shall be a condition of every investment business certificate issued under this rule that neither the Society nor any of its officers, employees or agents nor any member of the Council shall be liable in damages or otherwise for anything done or omitted to be done in the exercise of its certifying, disciplinary or investigatory functions under the 1980 Act or these rules, unless the act or omission is shown to have been in bad faith.

PART 3

SCOPE

Scope of permitted investment business
3.1. Subject to rule 3.2 below, a certified person may, in the course of or in conjunction with its practice, engage in any activity constituting investment business.

Activities specifically excluded
3.2.—(1) Neither a certified person nor any officer or employee of that certified person shall:—
   (a) as principal on its or his own account, buy an investment from or sell an investment to a client or offer or agree to do so; or
   (b) make markets; or
   (c) undertake or effect or arrange for the effecting of a transaction in derivatives otherwise than by way of introducing a client to an appropriately authorised person, who is responsible to the client for the obligations imposed by rules 4.4 and 4.5 (Know your client and the market ("best advice") and best execution); or

(d) act as manager or trustee of a regulated collective investment scheme or an unregulated collective investment scheme which has been established or created specifically to permit the pooling of funds for investment purposes; or
(e) enter into a broker funds arrangement; or
(f) give advice or make arrangements for a client in relation to a transfer or opt-out from an occupational pension scheme.

PRACTICE NOTES
Paragraph (1)(a) is not breached where a certified person discloses that it is acting on behalf of clients, where the identification of those clients is not necessarily disclosed.
Paragraph (1)(c) above would prevent certified persons dealing or arranging deals for clients in derivatives except by introducing clients to an appropriately authorised person. It would not prevent certified persons from advising on such transactions or from e.g. negotiating a sale and purchase agreement for the shares of a private company where such an agreement included options to acquire or dispose of shares. Paragraph (1)(c) does not apply where the prohibited activity forms part of a corporate finance activity.

(2) A certified person may engage in any of the activities referred to in paragraph (1) above if it:—
(a) is authorised in respect of that activity by another SRO or another RPB other than the Society; or
(b) is an exempted person in respect of that activity; or
(c) in respect of rule 3.2(1)(f) above obtains authorisation from the Society to give such advice or make such arrangements.

Securities transactions
3.3.— (1) No certified person shall instruct another person to effect a transaction (other than the sale of units in a regulated collective investment scheme or a transaction relating to a life policy) on behalf of a client unless that other person is advised that the transaction is to be effected on behalf of a client or clients of the certified person and that this fact is to be stated in the contract note containing the essential details of the transaction.

PRACTICE NOTE
Under the rules of the Securities & Futures Authority (SFA) where an agent identifies his principal to an SFA-authorised firm, the identified principal will be an indirect customer of the SFA-authorised firm unless there is an agreement in writing between the SFA-authorised firm and the agent to the contrary. To the extent that the agent 's identified principal is an indirect customer, the principal (and not his agent) is the customer of the SFA-authorised firm. In all other respects, the agent (and not his principal) is the customer of the SFA authorised firm.

(2) Paragraph (2) of rule 3.2 above applies to paragraph (1) of this rule.

Allocation
3.4.—(1) No certified person shall arrange for an investment transaction to be effected collectively for a client and for itself.
(2) Where an investment transaction has been effected collectively for more than one client and all cannot be satisfied, the transaction shall be allocated fairly.
(3) Allocations shall be effected promptly and be fair and reasonable in the interests of each client.
(4) Allocations shall not conflict with any instructions which a client has given to the certified person or with any limitations placed on the firm's discretion under the terms of business agreed with the client.

Appointed representatives

3.5.—(1) Subject to paragraph (3) below no solicitor or certified person nor any officer or employee thereof, shall be or hold himself or itself out to be an appointed representative.

(2) No certified person shall be the principal of an appointed representative.

(3) Paragraph (1) above does not apply to a solicitor who is in any such employment as is specified in section 35(4) of the 1980 Act in relation to activities in the course of that employment.

Dual agency

3.6.—(1) Subject to paragraph (2) below a certified person shall not act as an agent for a client in relation to an investment transaction in which the certified person is also acting as an agent for another party to the transaction, unless both parties have, with full knowledge of the circumstances, given their express agreement to the certified person's effecting that particular transaction in that particular way and rule 4.5 (best execution) is complied with.

(2) No certified person who effects on behalf of a client a transaction relating to the issue of a life policy shall thereafter act as agent of the life office in connection with any matter arising in relation to the policy other than in receiving premiums paid by the client or relaying communications to and from him.

PRACTICE NOTE

This rule is without prejudice to rule 3 of the Solicitors (Scotland) Practice Rules 1986.

Independence

3.7.—(1) No certified person or officer or employee thereof shall have any association or arrangement with any other person under which it or he will be constrained to recommend to clients or effect for them (or refrain from doing so) transactions:—

(a) in some investments but not others; or
(b) with some persons but not with others; or
(c) through the agency of some persons but not of others.

(2) A certified person shall not recommend to any client, or effect for a discretionary managed portfolio, transactions of excessive size or of unnecessary frequency.

(3) A certified person shall not recommend to any client, or effect for a discretionary managed portfolio, a switch between or within a packaged product unless it believes on reasonable grounds that the switch is justifiable.

(4) A certified person shall not give or receive directly or indirectly any gifts, services or any other benefits or inducements which might reasonably be regarded as likely improperly to influence the recommendation of particular investments or the investment services of particular persons.

PRACTICE NOTE

Paragraph (4) does not prohibit e.g. commission sharing agreements with brokers.

(5) A certified person on or before recommending to a client the investment services of any person shall make full disclosure to that client of the fact and nature of any material association, arrangement or relationship existing between the certified person and the person whose services are recommended.

(6) A certified person shall not recommend to nor effect for a client an investment transaction in respect of which the certified person or any person associated with it has any material interest without first disclosing to the client the fact and nature of that interest and, in the case of effecting a transaction, receiving that client's consent thereto.

PRACTICE NOTES

1. Any significant pecuniary interest (other than a commission or similar remuneration receivable in the ordinary course of business for effecting a transaction) which might reasonably be expected to influence a person to recommend an investment transaction or to effect such a transaction for a client would be regarded as a disclosable material interest.

2. A certified person would be regarded as having a material interest in a transaction if the transaction relates to securities the issue or offer for sale of which it or any person associated with it has underwritten within the past 12 months.

3. Failure to disclose when prohibited from doing so by the law relating to confidentiality would not be regarded as a breach of this rule —see rule 4.8 (2) (b).

4. Where a certified person does recommend to a client the investment services of any person attention is drawn to rule 3 of the Solicitors (Scotland) Practice Rules 1986 and the Code of Conduct in so far as they relate to disclosure of material interests.

Disclosure of certification
3.8. A certified person shall state on all its stationery, terms of business and other publications relating to its investment business the following (or words to the same effect):

"Authorised by the Law Society of Scotland to conduct investment business".

Introduction to any persons conducting investment business outwith the UK
3.9. No certified person or officer or employee thereof, shall introduce a client to a person who is not authorised to conduct investment business or give advice or make arrangements with a view to any person carrying on investment business outwith the UK for the client unless there is no reason to doubt that the client will be dealt with in an honest and reliable way and the prescribed disclosure has been made.

Overseas business for UK clients
3.10. A certified person shall not carry on investment business:—
(a) which is not regulated business; and
(b) with or for a client who is in the UK;
unless it has made the prescribed disclosure to the client.

PART 4

OBLIGATIONS ON A CERTIFIED PERSON

Investment Business Training Regulations
4.1.—(1) Every officer of a certified person shall be responsible for ensuring compliance with these rules and the Solicitors (Scotland) Investment Business Training Regulations 1994.

(2) Without prejudice to paragraph (1) of this rule every certified person shall designate one officer as designated Compliance Officer.

Clients' rights
4.2. Except in so far as permitted in terms of the Act or these rules a certified person shall not, in any written communication or agreement, seek to exclude or restrict any duty or liability to a client which the certified person has under the Act or under these rules, or under the rules and practices of professional conduct to which the certified person is subject in the course of carrying on investment business.

Client order priority
4.3. A certified person should deal with client transactions in priority to any other transactions.

PRACTICE NOTE
This rule means that a certified person shall at all times effect investment transactions for clients in priority to investment transactions for itself.

Know your client and the market ("best advice")
4.4.—(1) Except when acting for an execution-only client, a certified person shall take all reasonable steps to ensure that:
  (a) any investment recommendation or any exercise of discretion on behalf of a client is suitable for that client, having regard to the facts disclosed by that client and other relevant facts about the client, of which the certified person is or should reasonably be aware;
  (b) the client understands the nature of the risks involved in any investment transaction or the exercise of discretionary powers conferred upon the certified person; and
  (c) where the recommendation is to acquire a packaged product or where a packaged product is acquired for a client in the exercise of discretion, there is no other investment which would be likely to secure the client's investment objectives more advantageously, and the client has information which is adequate to enable him to make an informed investment decision.

PRACTICE NOTE
When providing investment services for a client who is acting in his capacity as attorney, a certified person will be expected to make due enquiry as to the scope of the attorney's powers.

(2) Before or as soon as practicable after a certified person recommends a packaged product to a client and in any event before effecting or arranging such a product, a certified person must provide the client with appropriate information about the product which is adequate to enable the client to make an informed investment decision and provide the client in particular with general information about the key features of the product unless:—
  (a) the certified person buys the packaged product as a discretionary investment manager in which case the written contract as defined in rule 4.6(2) shall provide for the provision of general information about the key features of the product to be despatched to the client as soon as practicable after the contract or change is made; or
  (b) the transaction is effected or arranged on an execution-only basis, in which case the general information about the key features of the product shall be despatched as soon as practicable after the contract or change is made.

(3) Before or as soon as practicable after a certified person recommends to a client that the client should:—
  (a) take on a long term commitment which is or appears to be acceptable to the client; or
  (b) relinquish a long term commitment; or
  (c) elect to make pension fund withdrawals from a personal pension fund;
the certified person shall explain in writing to the client the reasons why on the basis of the facts about the client of which it is aware it believes the commitment or relinquishment or pension fund withdrawal to be suitable for the client.

(4) A certified person shall maintain records adequate to demonstrate compliance with this rule.

PRACTICE NOTE
Under the rules of PIA (or other regulatory body), life offices and operators of regulated collective investment schemes are required to produce a written

statement disclosing certain particulars about their products, which will include notice of any cancellation rights. Certified persons should ensure that a copy of the relevant written statement is given to any client to whom a recommendation to acquire such investments is made. The duty will generally be discharged by the life office or the operator of a regulated collective investment scheme.

Best execution
4.5.—(1) A certified person shall take all reasonable steps to ensure that any investment transaction effected for a client, whether by the certified person or a person instructed by the certified person, is effected or arranged with due timeliness and on terms that may reasonably be regarded as the best available at the time in the interests of the client in all the circumstances; but for this purpose any fees payable by the client to the certified person and which are payable however the transaction is effected shall be disregarded.

(2) A certified person shall maintain records adequate to demonstrate compliance with this rule.

PRACTICE NOTE
Where a certified person instructs another authorised person to effect a transaction, the certified person will be regarded as having taken sufficient steps to discharge the obligation contained in this rule provided the certified person effects the transaction with due timeliness and provided the authorised person does not contract out of the obligation to provide best execution.

Client terms of business
4.6.—(1) If a certified person has assumed responsibility for portfolio management that certified person shall provide to a client a statement of the terms of business for so acting, which must comply with Schedule 1(1) to these rules.

(2) Where a certified person manages a portfolio in the exercise of discretion, the certified person shall do so under a written contract complying with Schedule 1(2) to these rules, unless the client is ordinarily resident outside the United Kingdom and the certified person believes on reasonable grounds that the client does not wish a contract to be used.

(3) The existing client agreements, statements of terms of business and written contracts for a certified person entered into in terms of the Solicitors (Scotland) (Conduct of Investment Business) Practice Rules 1989 and 1994 shall continue to have effect in all respects unless or until determined otherwise for any reason.

Client terms of business records
4.7. A certified person shall retain a copy of all statements of terms of business provided and written contracts entered into under rule 4.6 and any client agreement, statement of terms of business and written contracts entered into in terms of the Solicitors (Scotland) (Conduct of Investment Business) Practice Rules 1989 and 1994 until the expiry of ten years from the time when the terms of business provided, written contracts or client agreement ceases to be effective.

Disclosures
4.8.—(1) Any statement of disclosure required to be made under these rules shall be so expressed as to be readily understood by the person to whom it is addressed and shall not be accompanied by any other statement which negates, qualifies or otherwise reduces the impact of the disclosure.

(2) Nothing in these rules shall require the disclosure of:—
(a) any information which (by reason of arrangements whereby information held by certain individuals will be withheld from other individuals), the officer or employee making the relevant recommendation or effecting the relevant transaction neither knew nor was in a position to have known; or

(b) any information which the certified person is prohibited from disclosing by the law, rules or principles relating to confidentiality.

Disclosures (remuneration)

4.9. A certified person shall not recommend to or effect for a client an investment transaction without disclosing to that client, in the client terms of business or otherwise, the basis on which the remuneration of the certified person payable by the client in respect of the transaction will be determined.

Disclosures (commissions-packaged products)

4.10.—(1) A certified person shall not recommend to or effect for a client a transaction relating to a packaged product without first disclosing:—
  (a) if the transaction is one in respect of which the certified person will receive commission, that fact; and
  (b) the fact that written details of such commission will be forthcoming from the provider of the packaged product in due course; and
  (c) the amount of such commission unless the commission relates to the purchase of a non-life packaged product effected or arranged by a certified person acting as a discretionary investment manager or effected or arranged on an execution-only basis.

(2) Where a non-life packaged product is effected or arranged by a certified person acting as a discretionary investment manager or is effected or arranged on an execution-only basis, the amount of commission shall be disclosed as soon as practicable after the transaction is so effected or arranged.

Disclosures (stabilisation)

4.11. A certified person shall take all reasonable steps to ensure that it does not recommend to a client or effect for a client (other than an execution-only client) a transaction in securities in relation to which stabilising bids or transactions are being made or effected or have recently been made or effected unless the terms of business or client agreements contemplate that the client's funds may be invested in such securities without prior disclosure and contain an appropriate risk warning.

Valuation of investments

4.12. Where a certified person is a portfolio manager and the amount of any remuneration of the certified person is dependent on the value of the investments which are not traded on or under the rules of a recognised investment exchange, such valuation shall be prepared by a person, other than the certified person or any person associated with the certified person, whom it reasonably believes to be competent to undertake such a valuation.

Communication via third parties

4.13. Any communication required under these rules to be sent to a client may be sent to the order of the client, so long as the recipient is independent of the certified person; and there is no need for a certified person to send a communication itself where it believes on reasonable grounds that this has been or will be supplied direct by another person.

Unsolicited calls

4.14. A certified person may only enter into an investment agreement with any person or procure or endeavour to procure that person to enter into an investment agreement in the course of or in consequence of a cold call if the certified person observes the requirements of the Common Unsolicited Calls Regulations issued by the Board.

Insider dealing

4.15.—(1) The conviction of an officer or employee of a certified person of an offence under Part V of the Criminal Justice Act 1993 as may be amended from time to time will be deemed to be a breach of these rules by that certified person.

(2) A certified person must use its best endeavours to ensure that it does not knowingly effect (either in the course of regulated business or otherwise) a transaction it knows it is prohibited from effecting by the statutory restrictions on insider dealing.

(3) This rule does not apply to a certified person or an associate, or an officer or employee of a certified person or associate, who is a trustee or executor acting on the advice of a third party, where the third party appears to be an appropriate adviser who is not subject to a prohibition from effecting the transaction in question by the statutory restrictions on insider dealing.

PART 5

ADVERTISEMENTS

Advertisements
5.1.—(1) Where a certified person issues or approves an investment advertisement, it shall:—
  (a) apply appropriate expertise;
  (b) be able to show that it believes on reasonable grounds that the advertisement is fair and not misleading;
  (c) ensure that the advertisement identifies it as issuer or approver; and
  (d) ensure that the advertisement identifies the Society as the certified person's regulator.

(2) A certified person shall not issue a specific investment advertisement except one which:
  (a) relates to a PEP of which the certified person is plan manager; or
  (b) is issued in the course of corporate finance activities; or
  (c) is issued to an established investment business client.

(3) A certified person shall not issue or approve a specific investment advertisement which is calculated to lead directly or indirectly to an overseas person carrying on investment business:—
  (a) which is not regulated business; or
  (b) with or for a client who is in the United Kingdom;
unless both the advertisement contains the prescribed disclosure and the certified person has no reason to doubt that the overseas person will deal with investors in the United Kingdom in an honest and reliable way.

(4) A certified person shall not approve a specific investment advertisement if it relates to units in an unregulated collective investment scheme.

(5) Unless a direct offer advertisement is issued in the course of corporate finance activities, a certified person may only issue such an advertisement for the sale of investments or the provision of investment services:—
  (a) if the recipient is an established client; or
  (b) where the advertisement relates to a PEP of which the certified person is a plan manager;
provided always that such an advertisement may not relate to a packaged product.

(6) An advertisement covered by paragraph (5) above shall give information about the investments or investment services, the terms of the offer, and the risks involved, which is adequate and fair having regard to the regulatory protections (UK or overseas) which apply and the market to which the advertisement is directed.

(7) A certified person shall keep copies of all investment advertisements issued or approved by it for at least five years.

(8) Any advertisement approved or issued by a certified person shall comply with the relevant parts of Schedule 2 to these rules.

(9) A certified person shall not publish, or cause to be published, to any person:—

(a) any forecast of what any benefit under a life policy is likely to be unless the amount thereof is fixed at the outset; or

(b) any forecast of the realisable value of an investment in units in a collective investment scheme; or

(c) any illustration of what such a benefit or realisable value might be on any particular assumption;

unless such forecast or illustration has been supplied to it by an appropriately authorised person.

(10) The above rules on advertisements do not apply to the reissue of an investment advertisement which has been prepared and issued by another person and which the certified person believes on reasonable grounds is already issued or approved by a person authorised to conduct investment business and is issued to a market for which it was intended at the time of its issue or approval by the person authorised to conduct investment business.

PART 6

TRANSACTION RECORDS

Transaction records

6.1.—(1) Immediately upon receiving instructions to effect a transaction, or, in the case of a discretionary managed portfolio, making a decision to effect a transaction, a certified person shall make a record of:—

(a) the investment which is the subject of the instructions or the decision and the number of units involved;

(b) the nature of the proposed transaction; and

(c) the date on which the instructions were received or the decision made.

(2) Where a certified person gives instructions to another person to effect a transaction, the certified person shall, as soon as reasonably practicable, make a record of:—

(a) the name of the other person so instructed;

(b) the terms of the instructions; and

(c) the date on which the instructions were given.

(3) When a transaction has been effected by or on the instructions of a certified person, the certified person shall make a record of:—

(a) the date on which the transaction was effected;

(b) the investment involved and the number of units;

(c) the price and other terms on which the transaction was effected (including, where any conversion between currencies was involved, the rate of exchange); and

(d) the name of the client on whose behalf the transaction has been effected.

(4) The records required under paragraphs (1)–(3) above shall be retained for a period of at least ten years.

PRACTICE NOTE

The requirements of paragraph (3) above can be complied with by keeping a copy of the relevant contract note.

Client notification

6.2.—A certified person which effects a sale or purchase of an investment shall, as soon as is practicable in the circumstances, send to the client a note containing the essential details of the transaction.

PRACTICE NOTE

The essential details in a stock exchange transaction are contained in a contract note. The essential details in a transaction relating to a life policy or

units in a regulated collective investment scheme are contained in the
information supplied by the life office or the operator of a regulated collective
investment scheme.

Managed portfolios—reports
6.3. A certified person which acts as an investment manager for a client
shall ensure that the client is sent at suitable intervals a report stating the
value of the portfolio at the beginning and end of the period to which the
report relates, its composition at the end, and, in the case of a discretionary
portfolio, changes in the composition between those dates.

Record of investment business income
6.4. A certified person shall maintain such records as are necessary to
ascertain whether or not the gross income of its practice is wholly or mainly
derived from investment business.

Life policies and units
6.5. A certified person shall maintain a separate record of the number of
life policies placed directly with each individual life office and those placed
indirectly through another intermediary and the number of units in
regulated collective investment schemes acquired directly or through
another intermediary from each individual operator of such schemes.

Transactions other than on a recognised investment exchange
6.6. A certified person shall maintain a record of transactions in securities
which it effects other than on a recognised investment exchange.

Compliance procedures and review
6.7.—(1) A certified person shall establish and maintain rules and
procedures ("compliance procedures") by reference to which each officer
and employee of the certified person can ensure that he complies with these
rules.
(2) A certified person's compliance procedures shall be in writing except
where the number of individuals within the certified person who are engaged
in investment business does not exceed ten, and, if in writing, the compliance
procedures shall be available to each such individual.
(3) A certified person shall periodically and in any event not less than once
in every 12 months carry out a review of its compliance procedures to ensure
that they are effective and that the Act and these rules have been complied
with.

PART 7

SAFEKEEPING OF CLIENTS' DOCUMENTS OF TITLE

Application of rules
7.1. Where a certified person either on its own account or through the
intermediary of a third party custodian (a) holds documents of title of
investments for safe-keeping on behalf of clients and (b) administers such
investments, the certified person shall comply with Part 7 of these rules.

PRACTICE NOTE
*The mere safekeeping of documents of title of investments is not covered by
this Part.*

Holding of client investments
7.2.—(1) Where a certified person has custody of a client's investments it
shall keep safe, or arrange for the safekeeping of any documents of title
relating to such investments and shall ensure that at all times such

documents of title are readily accessible and are separately identifiable from the certified person's own investments.

(2) Where a certified person has custody of a client's investments it shall not part with any documents of title relating to such investments other than to the client or on the client's instructions.

(3) Where a certified person holds a registrable investment for a client it shall ensure that the registrable investment is properly registered in the client's name or in the name of a nominee approved by the client.

(4) Where a certified person itself acts as a custodian it shall clarify with each client the services which are to be provided and the respective responsibilities of the certified person and of the client in relation to:—

(a) arrangements for recording, registering and separately identifying the client's investments;

(b) procedures for the giving and receiving of clear instructions;

(c) losses of clients' investments; and

(d) the appointment of sub-custodians, the review, as appropriate, of their performance and the extent (if any) of the certified person's responsibility for losses caused by their fraud, wilful default or negligence.

(5) A certified person shall notify its clients of any different settlement, legal and regulatory requirements in overseas jurisdictions from those applying in the UK where investments are held overseas.

(6) A certified person shall identify in its records, investments held as collateral from its own investments and from other investments held in custody.

(7) A certified person shall at least once a year, provide each client with a statement of investments held on the client's behalf and separately identify which investments (if any) have been lent or which are held as collateral and which are not free to be delivered.

PRACTICE NOTE

The requirement to keep investments safe includes the need to ensure that access to systems for the electronic recording and transmission of shares is controlled and kept secure.

Holding and registration of client documents of title by the certified person's nominee

7.3.—(1) Where client documents of title are registered in the name of the certified person's own nominee, the certified person shall ensure that the nominee acts, in relation to each client's investments, only in accordance with the certified person's instructions.

(2) The certified person shall accept responsibility to its clients for the actings of its nominee.

(3) A client shall agree to the holding of his investments in a certified person's nominee.

(4) A certified person in respect of its nominee:

(a) shall register the client's investments in the name of the nominee and ensure that the certified person's own investments are separately identifiable from those of the certified person's clients;

(b) shall not use for the certified person's account the investments of a client;

(c) shall not pool the investments of different clients except where those clients have been given notification of the intention to pool and of its implications;

(d) shall engage in stocklending of clients' pooled investments only where each client whose investments are lent has given consent;

(e) shall advise the client of any lien, charge or other incumbrance over the investments of which it has knowledge; and

(f) shall provide to each client at least once a year, a statement of investments held on that client's behalf.

(5) A nominee company for the holding and registration of client documents of title established after the commencement of these rules, shall be dedicated solely to the holding and to activities related to the holding of such documents of title.

Holding and registration of client documents of title by a third party custodian or sub-custodian

7.4.—(1) A certified person shall not recommend to a client that a person other than the certified person, a bank (as defined in the Solicitors (Scotland) Accounts Rules 1997), an authorised person or a custodian located overseas subject to regulation or supervision by a regulatory body shall act as registered holder of a client's investments or custodian of a client's documents of title and the certified person, after due enquiry, shall ensure and be satisfied that that person is suitable so to act.

(2) A certified person shall not employ another person to act as custodian of a client's documents of title unless:

  (a) the certified person has that person's written undertaking to comply where applicable with the requirements of rules 7.2, 7.3 and 7.7 in relation to clients' investments, and

  (b) the certified person has that person's written acknowledgement that he will not have or claim any lien or right of retention over the documents of title placed in his custody or any right to sell or convert any of these investments except in relation to any unpaid sum due to the custodian for or in connection with services rendered in relation to any of these investments or on the express instructions of a client;

and a certified person shall maintain such records as are necessary to demonstrate compliance with sub-paragraphs (a) and (b) above.

(3) Where a certified person appoints a third party custodian, it shall ensure that the agreement between it and its clients defines the respective responsibilities of the certified person and of the custodian as to, where relevant:

  (a) the losses of clients' investments; and

  (b) the appointment of sub-custodians, the review, as appropriate, of their performance and the extent, if any, of the certified person's responsibility for losses caused by their fraud, wilful default or negligence.

Client acting as or appointing their custodian

7.5. Where a client of a certified person acts as or appoints his own custodian, the certified person shall agree in writing the necessary consequential arrangements (for example, for settlement) with the client and his custodian.

Safekeeping facilities

7.6. A certified person shall ensure that:—

  (a) storage facilities are appropriate to the value and risk of loss of the investments to be safeguarded, and are adequate to protect documents of title from damage, misappropriation or other loss; and

  (b) records relating to documents of title are appropriately stored.

PRACTICE NOTE

The records of the documents of title held by a firm or its nominee should be stored separately from the actual documents of title.

Record keeping

7.7. Where a certified person or its nominee has custody of a client's investments it shall record:—

  (a) the nature and identity of the client's documents of title and the place where these documents of title are kept;

(b) the nature and, where appropriate, the amount and nominal value of the investments to which the client's documents of title relate;

(c) the date on which each client's documents of title came into or left the custody of the certified person; and

(d) if the client's documents of title have left the possession of the certified person the identity of the person to whom possession has passed.

PRACTICE NOTE
Records of client documents of title may be maintained either manually or on a computer system. The record should include a note of:—
(a) the receipt and disposal of client documents of title;
(b) the purchase or sale of the investments to which the documents of title relate; and
(c) the transfer of the documents of title to another beneficiary.
The record should disclose the titles held for each client, from time to time. The chronological record may consist of a file of copy contract notes or file notes indicating the effect of the individual movement. The client's own portfolio record need not disclose the individual movements but should be an up to date record of the portfolio holdings from time to time.

Checking of client documents of title
7.8.—(1) Where a certified person or its nominee acts as custodian of investments it shall, at least once a year, carry out a check of each client's documents of title and reconcile the same with the certified person's investment records relating to that client.

(2) Where a certified person identifies a discrepancy revealed by the reconciliation in paragraph (1) above for a registrable investment it shall make good and correct the difference as soon as reasonably practicable.

(3) Where a certified person appoints a third party custodian it shall ensure that such third party custodian carries out the checking and, if appropriate, correction referred to in paragraphs (1) and (2) above.

PART 8

COMPLIANCE, COMPLAINTS AND DISCIPLINE

Complaints
8.1. A certified person shall ensure in relation to each complaint relating to the conduct of its investment business or to that of any officer or employee:—

(a) that the complaint is investigated promptly and thoroughly, where practicable by an officer not concerned in the action or inaction complained of; and

(b) that appropriate action is taken promptly; and

(c) that the complainer is reminded that it is open to him to report the matter to the Council which may investigate the complaint.

Disciplinary action
8.2. A certified person shall make a record of any disciplinary action taken against any officer or employee in respect of an investment business matter and shall keep such records for at least five years from the date the action was taken.

Professional misconduct
8.3. Breach of any of these rules may be treated as professional misconduct for the purposes of Part IV of the 1980 Act (Complaints and Disciplinary Proceedings).

PART 9

NOTIFICATION

Insolvency and allied situations
9.1. A certified person shall notify the Council forthwith of the occurrence of any of the following:—
    (a) the appointment of a trustee in sequestration, judicial factor, liquidator, receiver or administrator of the certified person;
    (b) the making of a composition or arrangement by the certified person with its creditors;
    (c) the presentation of a petition for the winding up or sequestration of the certified person or any officer or, in the case of an incorporated practice, member thereof.

Investigations, offences and disciplinary action
9.2. A certified person shall notify the Council forthwith of the occurrence of any of the following:—
    (a) the grant or refusal of any application by the certified person for, or the suspension, restriction or withdrawal of the certified person's membership of any SRO, recognised investment exchange or clearing house;
    (b) the appointment of inspectors by a statutory or other regulatory authority to investigate the affairs of the certified person;
    (c) the imposition of disciplinary measures or sanctions by any regulatory authority on the certified person or any of the certified person's officers or employees in relation to its investment business;
    (d) the bringing of any action against the certified person under sections 61 or 62 of the Act;
    (e) the conviction of any officer or employee of the certified person for any offence involving fraud or dishonesty.

Change of name, address, partners or directors and cessation of business
9.3.—(1) A certified person shall notify the Council of:
    (a) any change of name, registered name or business name of the certified person, and
    (b) any change of address of the certified person's principal place of business not more than 28 days after such change.
    (2) A certified person shall notify the Council forthwith if any person has:—
    (a) become, or
    (b) ceased to be
an officer of the certified person (including in the case of (b) a statement of the reasons for the change).
    (3) A certified person which is a sole practitioner shall notify the Council forthwith if it ceases to practise as a solicitor.
    (4) Where two or more certified persons amalgamate their practices, and all hold current unconditional investment business certificates which have not been suspended or revoked, they may continue to carry on investment business under the existing investment business certificates for up to 28 days.

Volume of investment business
9.4. A certified person shall notify the Council forthwith if the gross income of its practice is wholly or mainly derived from investment business or if it expects or intends that the gross income of its practice will become wholly or mainly derived from investment business.

Qualification of officers or employees
9.5.—(1) A certified person shall notify the Secretary in writing of the identity of an officer or employee who becomes qualified in terms of the Solicitor (Scotland) Investment Business Training Regulations 1994, within two months of such qualification.

(2) A certified person shall notify the Secretary in writing if a non-solicitor employee qualified in terms of the Solicitors (Scotland) Investment Training Regulations 1994 commences or ceases to be an employee of the certified person, within one month of such commencement or cessation.

PART 10

INSPECTIONS

Inspections
10.1.—(1) To enable it to ascertain whether or not the Act or these rules are being complied with, the Council may:
  (a) on its own motion, or
  (b) on a written complaint lodged with it by a third party,
by written notice require any certified person to produce at a time to be fixed by the Council and at a place to be fixed by the Council, or in the option of the certified person at its place of business, its files and records and any other necessary documents for inspection by a person appointed by the Council.

(2) A certified person duly required to do so under paragraph (1) of this rule shall produce such files, records and other necessary documents at the time and place fixed.

(3) The person appointed by the Council to make the inspection shall investigate the certified person's files, records and other necessary documents with the object of ascertaining whether or not the Act or these rules are being complied with by the certified person and thereafter shall report to the Council upon the result of his inspection.

(4) A written notice given by the Council to a certified person under paragraph (1) of this rule shall be signed by the Secretary, a Deputy Secretary or the Chief Accountant of the Society and sent by the Recorded Delivery service to the certified person at its place of business as defined in the Constitution of the Society or in the case of a certified person who has ceased to practise as a solicitor, at its last known address, and shall be deemed to have been received by the certified person within 48 hours of the time of posting. In the case of a firm or incorporated practice, the written notice shall be given to each person who is known to the Council to be a partner of the firm or a director of the incorporated practice and it shall not be necessary to give notice to the firm or, as the case may be, the incorporated practice also.

(5) Where, following an inspection in terms of paragraph (1) of this rule, it appears to the Council that the certified person has not complied with these rules and the Council instructs a further inspection of the files, records and other necessary documents of the certified person, the Council may, by written notice, require the certified person to pay to the Council such sum as may be required to meet the fees and costs incurred by the Council in carrying out such further inspection. The amount of such sum shall be fixed by the Council and intimated to the certified person following such inspection provided always that such written notice shall be given to the certified person not more than one year after the date of the inspection first referred to in this paragraph.

(6) It shall be the duty of a certified person on whom a notice in terms of paragraph (5) of this rule has been served to make payment forthwith of the amount so intimated.

PART 11

MISCELLANEOUS

Discretionary Investment Management

11.1. A certified person shall not act as a discretionary portfolio manager to a significant extent (as to which the Council shall be the sole judge) without having first obtained authorisation from the Council which may be given subject to such conditions as the Council may from time to time prescribe.

Force majeure

11.2. If any event happens or any circumstances arise which are outwith the control of a certified person and which make it impossible or impracticable for a certified person to comply with any obligation imposed on it by these rules, the certified person shall forthwith inform the Council of what has happened and the steps (if any can be taken) which the certified person proposes to take to deal with it, and the certified person shall not, so long as the event or circumstances subsist and the certified person is expeditiously taking all practicable steps available to it to relieve the situation, be regarded as in breach of any of these rules to the extent that in consequence thereof it has become impossible or impracticable to comply with that rule.

Good market practice

11.3. A certified person shall comply with generally accepted standards as to what constitutes good market practice in respect of the provision of financial services and the conduct of investment business and shall advise its clients as to what constitutes, and the consequences of failing to comply with, good market practice.

PRACTICE NOTE

Examples of what are regarded as good market practice may be found in the Conduct of Business Rules published by the Board, and the Takeover Code and the practice rules and ethical codes applying to solicitors generally.

Reliance on others

11.4. A certified person shall not be regarded as having breached any of these rules to the extent that it can show that it reasonably relied on information provided to it in writing by a third party whom it believed on reasonable grounds to be independent and competent to provide the information.

Waiver

11.5. The Council may, by resolution, waive or modify any of the provisions of these rules in any particular case provided that the Council is satisfied that adequate investor protection will be maintained and that compliance with the rule in question would be unduly burdensome for the certified person as compared with the benefit which compliance would confer on investors.

SCHEDULE 1

TERMS OF BUSINESS

CONTENTS

1.—Where a certified person acts as an investment manager for a client, the terms of business (and for the purposes of this Schedule the words "client agreement" may be substituted for the words "terms of business" in respect of client agreements entered into in terms of the Solicitors

(Scotland) (Conduct of Investment Business) Practice Rules 1989 and 1994) are to be reduced
to writing and those terms shall:—
  (a) state the nature of the services to be provided by the certified person and shall in
      particular:—
        (i) if the client's funds may be invested in investments which are not readily realisable,
            contain the warning that such an investment may be difficult to dispose of and that
            proper information for determining its current value may not be available;
       (ii) state any restrictions on the markets on which transactions are to be effected;
      (iii) state if transactions may be effected in investments in which the certified person or
            any person associated with it has a material interest, or with or through persons
            associated with the certified person;
  (b) state the arrangements for accounting to the client in respect of transactions arranged on
      his behalf and the basis on which any fees payable to the certified person are to be
      calculated;
  (c) state the frequency with which the client will be supplied with a report and valuation of
      the cash and investments comprised in the portfolio;
  (d) where the services to be provided by the certified person relate to transactions in
      investments which are single premium life policies issued by regulated life offices or units
      in regulated collective investment schemes, contain a prominent statement that the client
      will not have any right under regulations made by the Board under section 51 of the Act
      to cancel any such transaction;
  (e) state the circumstances (if any) in which the certified person may make an unsolicited call
      on the client and that the client, in relation to investment agreements entered into in the
      course of or in consequence of such calls will forfeit the rights conferred by section 56 of
      the Act to treat the agreement as unenforceable;
   (f) if it is the case, state whether a person other than the certified person is to hold money on
      the client's behalf or is to be the nominal holder of the client's registered investments or
      the custodian of the client's documents of title and that such a person shall comply where
      applicable with the relevant requirements of Part 7 of these Rules and, if that person is
      associated with the certified person, that fact and the nature of the association;
  (g) if income is received from or voting or other rights attach to investments held on the
      client's behalf, state the arrangements for accounting to the client for income received or
      for determining how those rights are to be exercised;
  (h) state how the terms of business may be terminated, and that, unless it is for a PEP, it may
      be terminated without penalty on written notice by or on behalf of the client to the
      certified person and, if it is for a PEP, state the costs payable by the client on termination
      or transfer to another plan manager;
   (i) if the certified person's fees are to be deducted from income or capital belonging to the
      client in the hands of the certified person, state the notice (if any) which must be given
      before such deductions can be made;
   (j) state how the client is to give instructions to the certified person and the circumstances (if
      any) in which the certified person may refuse instructions;
  (k) state the investment objectives of the client.

DISCRETIONARY MANAGED PORTFOLIOS

2.—In the case of a discretionary managed portfolio, the terms on which the certified person
carries on investment business for a client, must be signed by the client and shall, in addition to
the requirements of paragraph 1 above, state:
  (a) whether the certified person has authority to commit the client to a financial obligation to
      supplement the funds in the portfolio, to commit the client to an obligation as an
      underwriter or to delegate the exercise of its discretion to another person and detail any
      restrictions on such authority including restrictions on the persons or category of persons
      to whom discretion may be delegated; and
  (b) the fact, if it be the case, that the certified person has an arrangement with a third party
      under which the certified person will receive investment advice from that third party as to
      how the client's funds ought to or might be invested, with particulars of that
      arrangement; and
  (c) the frequency with which the client will be supplied with a report and valuation of the
      cash and investments comprised in the portfolio, which may not be less often than once in
      every year; and
  (d) whether or not the reports referred to in paragraph (c) above are to include a measure of
      portfolio performance and, if so, the basis on which it is to be measured; and

(e) whether or not the client wishes to specify any restriction on the amount of any one investment or the proportion of the portfolio which any one investment may constitute; and

(f) the frequency with which the client will be provided with general information relating to the key features of packaged products, as detailed in Rule 4.4(2)(a).

PEPs

3.—Any PEP agreement shall include, in addition to any other regulatory requirements, the terms set out in paragraph 1 and, if relevant, paragraph 2.

SCHEDULE 2

INVESTMENT ADVERTISEMENTS

Approval of investment advertisements

1.—A certified person shall not approve the contents of an investment advertisement to be issued by a person who is not authorised to conduct investment business unless the contents and the circumstances of issue comply with the requirements of Part 7 of the Financial Services (Conduct of Business) Rules 1990 issued by the Board.

PRACTICE NOTE
Where a certified person issued, or causes to be issued, any publication which will or may contain an investment recommendation, the certified person shall take all reasonable steps to ensure that such publication, together with any document attached to it if it contains a recommendation relating to an investment in the case of which deductions for charges and expenses are not made uniformly throughout the life of the investment but are loaded disproportionately on to the early years, draws attention to that fact

PEPs

2.—Any advertisement of a PEP issued by a certified person which is the plan manager of that PEP shall:—

(a) state that the certified person is regulated in the conduct of its investment business by the Society;

(b) give a fair view of the nature of the PEP, the financial commitment and the risks involved and state how a full written statement of the rights, obligations, terms and conditions attaching to the PEP can be obtained;

(c) not contain any quotations from a statement made by any person commending the PEP;

(d) not state or imply that the PEP has the approval of any government department or the Board provided that the advertisement may refer to the fact that the PEP has been recognised by the Inland Revenue for the purpose of reliefs from taxation;

(e) if it refers to taxation, contain a warning that the levels and bases of taxation may change and if it refers to reliefs from taxation, state that the reliefs are those which currently apply and that the value of such reliefs depends upon the circumstances of the taxpayer, and state any assumed rate of taxation on which the advertisement is based;

(f) if it contains a statement that the investor may cancel the PEP agreement, state the period during which the investor will have that right and when that period will begin;

(g) if it contains information about the past performance of the PEP, state the source of that information and contain a warning that the past is not necessarily a guide to the future.

[THE NEXT PAGE IS F 801]

Codes, etc.

Securities and Investments Board Statement of Principle

Statement of principle issued by the Securities and Investments Board on March 15, 1990 under section 47A of (and, in relation to friendly societies, paragraph 13A of Schedule 11 to) the Financial Services Act 1986.

© Securities and Investments Board 1990. Reproduced with permission.

INTRODUCTION

1. These principles are intended to form a universal statement of the standards expected. They apply directly to the conduct of investment business and financial standing of all authorised persons ("firms"), including members of recognised self-regulating organisations and firms certified by recognised professional bodies.

2. The principles are not exhaustive of the standards expected. Conformity with the principles does not absolve a failure to observe other requirements, while the observance of other requirements does not necessarily amount to conformity with the principles.

3. The principles do not give rise to actions for damages, but will be available for purposes of discipline and intervention.

4. Where the principles refer to customers, they should be taken to refer also to clients and to potential customers, and where they refer to a firm's regulator, they mean SIB, or a self-regulating organisation or professional body which regulates the firm.

5. Although the principles may be taken as expressing existing standards, they come into force formally, with additional sanctions resulting, on 30th April 1990.

THE PRINCIPLES

Integrity
1. A firm should observe high standards of integrity and fair dealing.

Skill, care and diligence
2. A firm should act with due skill, care and diligence.

Market practice
3. A firm should observe high standards of market conduct. It should also, to the extent endorsed for the purpose of this principle, comply with any code or standard as in force from time to time and as it applies to the firm either according to its terms or by rulings made under it.

Information about customers
4. A firm should seek from customers it advises or for whom it exercises discretion any information about their circumstances and investment objectives which might reasonably be expected to be relevant in enabling it to fulfil its responsibilities to them.

Information for customers

5. A firm should take reasonable steps to give a customer it advises, in a comprehensible and timely way, any information needed to enable him to make a balanced and informed decision. A firm should similarly be ready to provide a customer with a full and fair account of the fulfilment of its responsibilities to him.

Conflicts of interest

6. A firm should either avoid any conflict of interest arising or, where conflicts arise, should ensure fair treatment to all its customers by disclosure, internal rules of confidentiality, declining to act, or otherwise. A firm should not unfairly place its interests above those of its customers and, where a properly informed customer would reasonably expect that the firm would place his interests above its own, the firm should live up to that expectation.

Customer assets

7. Where a firm has control of or is otherwise responsible for assets belonging to a customer which it is required to safeguard, it should arrange proper protection for them, by way of segregation and identification of those assets or otherwise, in accordance with the responsibility it has accepted.

Financial resources

8. A firm should ensure that it maintains adequate financial resources to meet its investment business commitments and to withstand the risks to which its business is subject.

Internal organisation

9. A firm should organise and control its internal affairs in a responsible manner, keeping proper records, and where the firm employs staff or is responsible for the conduct of investment business by others, should have adequate arrangements to ensure that they are suitable, adequately trained and properly supervised and that it has well-defined compliance procedures.

Relations with regulators

10. A firm should deal with its regulator in an open and cooperative manner and keep the regulator properly informed of anything concerning the firm which might reasonably be expected to be disclosed to it.

Securities and Investments Board Rules

© Securities and Investments Board. Reproduced with permission. "The Act" in these rules is the Financial Services Act 1986.

. . . . . .

CHAPTER III

. . . . . .

PART 7—ADVERTISEMENTS

Application
   7.01.—(1) This Part of these rules applies to advertisements in respect of investment business other than:
   (*a*)   an advertisement which is excluded from paragraph (*e*) of section 48(2) of the Act by virtue of section 48(5) of the Act, and
   (*b*)   an advertisement which contains matter required or permitted to be published:
      (i)   by or under any enactment, or
      (ia)   by or under any provision of the law of a member State other than the United Kingdom corresponding to section 85 of the Act, or
      (ii)   by an exchange which is:
         (A)   a recognised investment exchange, or
         (B)   a designated investment exchange, or
         (C)   an approved exchange under Part V of the Act,
      and contains no other matter, and
   (*c*)   an advertisement offering any securities within the meaning of section 159(1) of the Act, an advertisement offering securities which is a primary or secondary offer within the meaning of section 160 of the Act and an advertisement offering securities which is exempted from sections 159 and 160 of the Act by virtue of section 161 of the Act, and
   (*d*)   an advertisement issued in such circumstances that it is unlikely that it will be communicated to persons who are neither business investors nor persons who carry on investment business.

PRACTICE NOTE
   The Board considers that a person within subparagraph (d) *who by way of business passes on an advertisement which he receives as such will be issuing an advertisement and so is subject to section 57 of the Act and, if a firm, this Part of these rules.*

   (2) Except where the context otherwise requires references in this Part of these rules to an advertisement are references to an advertisement to which this Part of these rules applies.

   7.02. [Not used]

Issue of advertisements by a firm
   7.03. A firm shall not issue an advertisement unless the requirements of this Part of these rules are complied with in relation to that advertisement.

Approval by a firm of advertisements issued by unauthorised persons
7.04.—(1) [Not used]

(2) A firm shall not approve for the purposes of section 57 of the Act the contents of an investment advertisement to be issued or caused to be issued by a person who is not an authorised person unless the requirements of this rule are complied with in relation to that advertisement.

(3) In the case of an advertisement which relates to a collective investment scheme the requirements of this rule are that:

(a) all the requirements of this Part of these rules are complied with in relation to the advertisement as if the unauthorised person were a firm, and

(b) if the approval is required for the purpose of the advertisement's being issued by an overseas person, that person is the operator of a regulated collective investment scheme and the advertisement relates to units in that scheme.

(4) In the case of an advertisement which relates to a life policy the requirements of this rule are that:

(a) all the requirements of rule 5.11 (if applicable) and of this Part of these rules are complied with in relation to the advertisement as if the unauthorised person were a firm and,

(b) if the life policy is to be issued by a life office which is an overseas person:

(i) that life office is one referred to in section 130(2)(c) or (d) of the Act, or

(ii) that life office is one referred to in section 130(3)(a) of the Act and the requirements of section 130(3) of the Act have been fulfilled.

(5) In the case of an advertisement which does not relate to a collective investment scheme or to a life policy and is an image advertisement or a short form advertisement, the requirements of this rule are that all the requirements of this Part of these rules are complied with in relation to the advertisement as if the unauthorised person were a firm.

(6) In the case of an advertisement which does not relate to a collective investment scheme or to a life policy and is not an image advertisement or a short form advertisement and is not an advertisement to which rule 7.23 applies, the requirements of this rule are:

(a) if the approval is required for the purpose of the advertisement's being issued by an overseas person who is an associate of the firm in circumstances in which the advertisement is not likely to be received by anyone other than an established customer with whom the firm or the associate has a continuing relationship governed by a written agreement, that the firm has no reason to believe that any matter in the advertisement is inaccurate, unfair or misleading, or

(b) if the approval is not required for the purpose and in the circumstances mentioned in subparagraph (a):

(i) that all the requirements of this Part of these rules are complied with in relation to the advertisement as if the unauthorised person were a firm, and

(ii) if the approval is required for the purpose of the advertisement's being issued by an overseas person:

(A) that the firm carries on in the United Kingdom in compliance with rule 2.01 (business plan) investment business which relates to investments of the same description as the investment the subject of the advertisement, and

(B) if the advertisement is a relevant publication within the meaning of Part 8 of these rules which will or may include recommendations to acquire investments which are not readily realisable, that the firm has reasonable grounds for believing that the issuer will not:

(I)   give or send that publication to any person in the United Kingdom, or

(II)   enter into any arrangement with any person in the United Kingdom or procure any such person to enter into any arrangement under which that person will be regularly given or sent issues of that publication,

unless that person is a person whom the issuer believes, on the basis of such facts about his financial situation and competence in financial matters as may be expected to be relevant, to be a person for whom investments which are not readily realisable are suitable, and

(C)   that the firm has no reason to believe that the issuer of the advertisement will not treat responders to the advertisement honestly and fairly, and

(D)   that the advertisement contains warnings that rules and regulations. made under the Act for the protection of investors do not apply to the issuer of the advertisement and that the Board's compensation scheme will not apply in relation to the investment the subject of the advertisement, and

(E)   except in the case of a tombstone, that the advertisement contains statements that the advertisement has been approved by the firm and that the firm is regulated in the conduct of its business by the Board.

Overseas insurers

7.04A.—(1) This rule applies in the case of an advertisement which relates to life policies which is issued at a time when the insurer who is to issue the life policies is not authorised to carry on long term business in the United Kingdom of the class to which the advertisement relates by or under sections 3 or 4 of the Insurance Companies Act 1982 and is not otherwise permitted to carry on long term business of that class in the United Kingdom.

(2) A firm shall not issue an advertisement to which this rule applies unless the contents of the advertisement and the manner of its presentation are such that the advertisement would have complied with regulations 65 to 65C of the Insurance Companies Regulations 1981 (S.I. 1981 No. 1654) as amended by the Insurance Companies (Advertisements) (Amendment) (No. 2) Regulations 1983 (S.I. 1983 No. 396) as those regulations had effect on 20 September 1990 as if they applied to the advertisement but subject to the amendment that, in regulation 65B there be inserted at the beginning of subparagraph (*f*) of paragraph (3) the following:

"except in a case where the insurer is authorised to effect or carry out contracts of insurance to which the advertisement relates in any country or territory which is for the time being designated for the purposes of section 130 of the Financial Services Act 1986 by an order made by the Secretary of State and where any conditions imposed by the order designating the country or territory have been satisfied".

Prominence of required statements

7.05. The significance of any statement or other matter required by these rules to be included in an advertisement shall not be disguised either through lack of prominence in relation to the other matter in the advertisement or by the inclusion of matter calculated to minimise the significance of the statement.

Approval

7.06.—(1) A firm which issues an advertisement shall ensure that the advertisement is approved prior to its issue by an individual within the firm, or within a group of which the firm is a member, appointed for the purpose of this rule.

(2) A firm shall not approve the contents of an advertisement in pursuance of rules 7.03 or 7.04 except through the agency of an individual within the firm, or within a group of which the firm is a member, appointed for the purpose of this rule.

PRACTICE NOTE
    In relation to a short form advertisement in the form of a screen price quotation service, the Board considers that an individual empowered by his firm to input its prices to the system might properly also be empowered to approve short form advertisements of that type.

Advertisements to be clear and not misleading

7.07.—(1) The content of an advertisement and the manner of its presentation shall be such that the advertisement is not likely to be misunderstood by those to whom it is addressed including, if it be the case, persons who cannot be expected to have any special understanding of the matter in the advertisement.

(2) An advertisement shall not contain any statement, promise or forecast unless the firm issuing or approving the advertisement has taken all reasonable steps to satisfy itself that each such statement, promise or forecast is not misleading in the form or context in which it appears.

(3) An advertisement shall not contain any statement purporting to be a statement of fact which the firm issuing it does not reasonably believe at the time of issue, on the basis of evidence of which it has a record in its possession, to be true.

(4) An advertisement shall not contain any statement of fact which, although true when the advertisement is issued, the firm has reason to believe is likely to become untrue before the advertisement ceases to be current.

(5) An advertisement shall not state that any person is of any particular opinion unless the firm issuing or approving the advertisement has taken all reasonable steps to satisfy itself that the advertiser or other person, as the case may be, is of that opinion when the advertisement is issued.

(6) If the investment or service to which an advertisement relates is available in limited quantities, for a limited period or on special terms for a limited period the advertisement may say so but, if that is not the case, the advertisement shall not contain any statement or matter which implies that it is so.

Advertisements to be distinguished from other matter

7.08.—(1) The terms of an advertisement and the manner of its presentation shall be such that it appears to be an advertisement issued with the object of promoting the investment, service or firm to which it relates.

(2) Where the medium in which the advertisement is carried contains or presents other matter the advertisement shall be distinguished from that other matter so that what is an advertisement does not appear to be or to form part of a news item, report, bulletin, entertainment, instruction, story, drama, performance or other such means of communication.

PRACTICE NOTE
    The Board takes the view that an advertisement on a hoarding at a football ground would not contravene this rule but that an advertisement forming part of a dialogue of a televised drama would do so.

Advertisements to identify the investments or services to which they relate

7.09. Except in the case of a short form advertisement or an image advertisement, the nature of the investment or the services to which an advertisement relates shall be clearly described.

Promotions to be genuine
7.10. An advertisement shall not be issued with the intention not of persuading persons who respond to the advertisement to pursue the subject matter of the advertisement but instead of persuading them to enter into an investment agreement, or use financial services, of a description not mentioned in the advertisement.

Disclosure of advertiser's capacity
7.11. An advertisement which invites those to whom it is addressed to enter into an investment agreement with a named person shall:
  (*a*) disclose, by statement or by necessary implication, whether it is proposed that the named person will enter into the agreement as a principal on his own account or as an agent for another person, and
  (*b*) if the named person is to enter into the agreement as an agent for another person and that person can be identified when the advertisement is issued, state the name of that other person.

Identity of regulators
7.12.—(1) An advertisement which is not a short form advertisement or an image advertisement shall state:
  (*a*) if the advertisement has been issued by a firm, that the person who has issued it is a person regulated by the Board, or
  (*b*) if the advertisement has not been issued by an authorised person but has been approved by a firm, that the advertisement has been approved by a person regulated by the Board.
(2) Where an advertisement offers the product or the services of a person other than the firm which has issued or approved it, the advertisement shall state:
  (*a*) whether or not that other person is an authorised person, and
  (*b*) if he is an authorised person:
    (i) the name of the body responsible for regulating his conduct of business, and
    (ii) the fact that the body is so responsible or, if it be the case, that that person is a member of that body, and
    (iii) if it be the case that that body regulates the conduct of that person on an interim basis only that that person has applied to that body:
And any statement in an advertisement that that person has applied to a body responsible for regulating the conduct of that person's business shall be accompanied by the words "Not covered by The Investors' Compensation Scheme" and may be accompanied by a statement that that person is interim authorised.
(3) An advertisement which is not an advertisement in respect of investment business shall not contain any matter referring to the Board.

Advertisements not to imply government approval
7.13.—(1) Subject to paragraphs (2) and (3) an advertisement shall not contain any matter which states or implies that the investment the subject of the advertisement or any matter in the advertisement has the approval of any Government department or of the Board.
(2) This rule does not prohibit the issue of an advertisement which contains or advertises an offer for sale of investments owned by Her Majesty's Government.
(3) Where the investment the subject of an advertisement is recognised by the Inland Revenue for the purpose of qualifying those who acquire the investment for any reliefs from taxation, the advertisement may refer to that recognition.

Synopses to be fair

7.14. An advertisement which states some only of the rights and obligations attaching to an investment or some only of the terms and conditions of an investment agreement shall:

(*a*) state sufficient of them to give a fair view of the nature of the investment or of the investment agreement, of the financial commitment undertaken by an investor in acquiring the investment or in entering into the agreement and of the risks involved, and

(*b*) state how a written statement of all of them can be obtained.

Commendations

7.15. An advertisement may include a quotation from a statement made by any person commending an investment or service if and only if:

(*a*) where that person is an employee or associate of the firm, that fact is disclosed in the advertisement, and

(*b*) the quotation is included with that person's consent, and

(*c*) the statement is relevant to the investment or service which is the subject of the advertisement, and

(*d*) where the whole of the statement is not quoted, what is quoted represents fairly the message contained in the whole of the statement, and

(*e*) the statement has not become inaccurate or misleading through the passage of time since it was made.

Comparison with other investments

7.16.—(1) An advertisement shall not compare or contrast:

(*a*) an investment with an alternative application of an investor's funds, or

(*b*) a service or a provider of a service or of an investment with an alternative service or provider,

unless the comparisons and contrasts are fair in relation to what is promoted and to the alternative having regard to what is not stated as well as to what is stated.

PRACTICE NOTE

The Board considers that it would be a breach of this rule:

(*a*) *to omit a feature of possible comparison or contrast so as to exaggerate the significance of what is included, or*

(*b*) *to misrepresent or unfairly to criticise the alternative or the person who offers it.*

(1A) An advertisement of units in a regulated collective investment scheme shall not compare or contrast the performance or the likely performance of an investment in units of the scheme with an investment in a collective investment scheme which is not a regulated collective investment scheme.

(2) Without prejudice to the generality of paragraph (1) if, in the case of an advertisement of units in a collective investment scheme or in a unit linked life policy, comparison is made between the performance of an investment in those units over a period of time with the performance of an alternative application of the investor's funds over the same period of time, the comparison shall be on an offer to bid basis, that is to say, on the basis of what it would have cost to acquire an amount of the investment and the alternative at the beginning of the period and what a disposal of that amount of the investment and the alternative would have realised at the end of the period, and the fact that that is the basis of the comparison shall be stated.

(3) Without prejudice to the generality of paragraph (1) if, in the case of an advertisement of units in a collective investment scheme or in a unit

linked life policy, comparison is made between the performance of an investment in those units over a period of time with the performance of an index over the same period of time, the comparison shall be on whatever basis is consistent with the basis on which the index is constructed, and the fact that that is the basis of the comparison shall be stated.

Life policies
7.17.—(1) The requirements of this Part of these rules apply to an advertisement relating to a life policy in addition to the requirements of rule 5.11 which rule applies in the case of an advertisement as it applies in the case of publications generally.

(2) An advertisement relating to a life policy which gives particulars of any of the benefits payable under the policy shall state:
- (*a*) which of the benefits under the contract (if any) are of fixed amounts and what those amounts are, and
- (*b*) which of them (if any) are not of fixed amounts.

(3) Such an advertisement may describe a benefit of a fixed amount or a minimum amount of a variable benefit as a "guaranteed" amount but, if it does so and the advertisement refers to the participation of a third party and that third party will not stand as surety for the life office should the life office not meet its obligations, the advertisement shall not contain any matter which implies that the third party will so stand as surety.

PRACTICE NOTE
An example of a breach of this rule would be the following: an advertisement of a life policy, the benefits under which are linked to the performance of a fund held by a third party as trustee but not as a guarantor, states that certain benefits are "guaranteed" without also stating that the trustee is not the guarantor of the obligations of the insurance company.

Taxation
7.18.—(1) An advertisement which refers to taxation shall contain a warning that the levels and bases of taxation can change.

(2) An advertisement which contains any matter based on an assumed rate of taxation shall state what that rate is.

(3) An advertisement which refers to reliefs from taxation:
- (*a*) shall state that the reliefs are those which currently apply, and
- (*b*) shall contain a statement that the value of a relief from taxation depends upon the circumstances of the taxpayer.

(4) An advertisement which relates to an investment the income from which:
- (*a*) is payable out of a fund the income of which has already been taxed, and
- (*b*) is not or may not be subject to income tax in the hands of the investor,

shall not describe the investment as one free from liability to income tax unless the fact that the income is payable out of a fund from which income tax has already been paid is stated with equal prominence.

(5) An advertisement which relates to an investment in whose case:
- (*a*) an investor will not be liable to taxation on realised capital gains in the investment, and
- (*b*) any realised capital gains of the assets of a fund to which the value of the investments is linked are subject to taxation,

shall not describe the investment as one free from liability to capital gains taxation unless the fact that the value of the investment is linked to a fund which will be liable to taxation on realised capital gains in the assets of which it is comprised is stated with equal prominence.

(6) An advertisement which refers to reliefs from taxation shall distinguish between reliefs which apply directly to investors and those which

apply to the issuer of the investment or to a fund in which the investor participates.

Cancellation rights

7.19. An advertisement may state (if it be the case) that an investor who enters into an investment agreement to which the advertisement relates will be given an opportunity to cancel the agreement but, if it does so, the advertisement shall state:
- (*a*) the period during which the investor will have that right and the time when that period will begin, and
- (*b*) (if it be the case) that the right to cancel is conferred by law, and
- (*c*) if upon cancellation the investor will not recover his investment in full should the market have fallen since the investment was acquired:
  - (i) that fact, and
  - (ii) if the advertisement is an advertisement of a higher volatility investment, notice that the shortfall in what he recovers should the market have fallen could be very high because of the possibility of sudden and large falls in the value of the units.

Past performance

7.20. An advertisement shall not contain information about the past performance of investments of any description unless:
- (*a*) it is relevant to the performance of the investment the subject of the advertisement, and
- (*b*) except where the source of the information is the advertiser itself, the source of the information is stated, and
- (*bb*) in the case of an advertisement of a higher volatility investment, information is given for the period of five years ending with the date on which the advertisement is approved for issue and beginning five years before that date or, if the fund came into existence less than five years before that date, beginning when the fund came into existence, and
- (*c*) if the whole of the information is not set out:
  - (i) what is included is not unrepresentative, unfair or otherwise misleading, and
  - (ii) the exclusion of what is excluded does not have the effect of exaggerating the success of performance over the period to which the information which is included relates, and
- (*d*) if the information is presented in the form of a graph or chart, no part of the information is omitted so as to give a misleading impression of the rate at which variable quantities have changed, and
- (*e*) in the case of an advertisement of units in a collective investment scheme or in a unit linked life policy, any comparison made between the value of an investment in those units at different times is on an offer to bid basis, that is to say, on the basis of what it would have cost to acquire an amount of the units at the earlier time and what a disposal of that amount of those units would have realised at the later time, and the fact that that is the basis of the comparison is stated, and
- (*f*) the advertisement contains a warning that the past is not necessarily a guide to the future.

PRACTICE NOTE

The Board considers that a unit trust manager could commit a breach of this rule if it were to issue an advertisement which:
- (*a*) *advertised all or a number of its funds, and*
- (*b*) *either:*
  - (i) *claimed notable successes for some of those funds without indicating that it was some only of those funds which had attained those levels of success, or*

(*ii*) chose to show only an unrepresentative few months of performance.

Indications of the scale of business activities

7.21. An advertisement shall not contain any statement indicating the scale of the activities or the extent of the resources of a person who carries on investment business, or of any group of which such a person is a member, so as to imply that the resources available to support performance of the firm's obligations are greater than they are.

PRACTICE NOTE

The Board would regard the following as breaches of this rule:

(*1*) An advertisement which states the amount of the authorised share capital of a company but does not also state the amount of the issued share capital of that company.

(*2*) An advertisement which states the amount of a company's issued share capital but does not also state how much of that capital has been paid up.

(*3*) An advertisement which states the amount of a company's total assets but does not also state the amount of the company's liabilities.

(*4*) An advertisement which states the amount of a company's income or turnover but does not state the period to which that amount relates.

(*5*) An advertisement which refers to a subsidiary in a group and which mentions the amount of the capital or of the assets of the group as a whole so as to imply that they are resources on which the subsidiary can draw when that is not the case.

(*6*) An advertisement which states the amount of funds under a firm's management in such a way as to imply that those funds are assets of the firm.

Risk warnings

7.22.—(1) This rule applies to any advertisement which is not:

(*a*) a short form advertisement, or

(*b*) an image advertisement.

(2) An advertisement to which this rule applies shall contain a statement or statements in accordance with this rule warning of the risks involved in acquiring or holding the investment the subject of the advertisement.

(3) Where the advertisement relates to an investment in the case of which deductions for charges and expenses are not made uniformly throughout the life of the investment but are loaded disproportionately onto the early years, the advertisement shall draw attention to that fact and that accordingly, if the investor withdraws from the investment in the early years, he may not get back the amount he has invested.

(4) Where the advertisement relates to an investment which can fluctuate in value in money terms, the statement shall draw attention to that fact and to the fact that the investor may not get back the whole of what he has invested and, where the advertisement is an advertisement of a higher volatility investment, the statement shall draw attention to the possibility of sudden and large falls in the value of the units and to the fact that the investor may lose the whole of his investment.

(5) Where the advertisement offers an investment as likely to yield a high income or as suitable for an investor particularly seeking income from his investment, the statement shall draw attention to the fact that income from the investment may fluctuate in value in money terms.

(6) Where the advertisement relates to an investment denominated in a currency other than that of the country in which the advertisement is issued, the advertisement shall draw attention to the fact that changes in rates of exchange between currencies may cause the value of the investment to diminish or to increase.

(7) Where the advertisement relates to a with profits life policy, that statement shall draw attention to the fact that the return on the investment depends on what profits are made and on what decisions are made by the life office as to their distribution.

(8) Where the advertisement contemplates the customer entering into a transaction the nature of which is such that the customer may not only lose what he pays at the outset but may incur a liability to pay unspecified additional amounts later, the statement shall draw attention to the fact that the investor may or, as the case may be, will have to pay more money later and that accordingly a transaction in that investment can lose the investor more than his first payment.

(9) Where the advertisement relates to a margined transaction which is not a limited liability transaction and which will or may be effected otherwise than on a recognised or designated investment exchange and in a contract of a type traded thereon, the advertisement shall draw attention to the fact that the transaction is only suitable for a person who has experience in transactions of that description:

But this does not apply in the case of an advertisement which advertises the services of an execution-only dealer.

PRACTICE NOTE
This rule should be read in conjunction with rule 9.11(1)(b)(iii) below.

(10) Where the advertisement relates to an investment which is not readily realisable:
  (*a*) if the investment is not traded on a recognised or designated investment exchange, the statement shall draw attention to the fact that there is no recognised market for the investment so that it may be difficult for the investor to sell the investment or for him to obtain reliable information about its value or the extent of the risks to which it is exposed, or
  (*b*) if the investment is traded on a recognised or designated investment exchange but is dealt in so irregularly or infrequently:
     (i) that it cannot be certain that a price for that investment will be quoted at all times, or
     (ii) that it may be difficult to effect transactions at any price which may be quoted, and
  the statement shall draw attention to that fact or those facts, as the case may be, and, if there are less than three market makers in that investment or the firm which has issued the advertisement is the only market maker in that investment, the statement shall draw attention to that or to those facts, as the case may be.

PRACTICE NOTE
Examples of investments contemplated by paragraph (10)(b) of this rule might be investments which are classified by The Stock Exchange as "delta" or "gamma" stocks and "off-the-run" bonds which have been in issue for a long time.

(11) Where the advertisement relates to units:
  (*a*) in a property fund, or
  (*b*) in a constituent part of an umbrella fund which, if that part were a separate fund, would be a property fund, or
  (*c*) in a fund of funds in the case of which one of the schemes to which it is dedicated is a property fund,
the statement shall draw attention:
  (i) to the fact that land and buildings may at times be difficult to sell so that there may be periods during which the operator will have the right to refuse to repurchase units offered to him for redemption, and

(ii) to the fact that a valuation of land and buildings has to be the judgment of an individual valuer.

(12) Where the advertisement is of a life policy and refers to benefits under the policy which are measured by reference to the value of, to fluctuations in the value of or to income from land or any interest in land, the statement shall draw attention:

    (i) to the fact that the assets to which the benefits under the policy are linked may at times be difficult to sell so that there may be periods during which the life office will be unable to accept surrenders of the policy, and

    (ii) to the fact that a valuation of land and buildings has to be the judgment of an individual valuer.

(13) Where the advertisement relates to units in a regulated collective investment scheme, and at the time when the advertisement is prepared for issue, the property of the scheme consists, or there is an expectation that the property of the scheme may consist, as to more than 35% thereof in Government and other public securities issued by one issuer, the statement shall include reference to that fact or, as the case may be, to that expectation and shall identify that issuer.

7.22A. [Revoked.]

General duty of disclosure in "off-the-page" and "off-the-screen" advertisements

7.23.—(1) Subject to paragraph (1A) this rule applies to an advertisement containing:

    (*a*) an offer to enter into an investment agreement with a person who responds to the advertisement, or

    (*b*) an invitation to a person to respond to the advertisement by making an offer to enter into an investment agreement, and

in either case, specifying the manner in which that response is invited to be made.

(1A) This rule does not apply to an advertisement if:

    (*a*) the investment agreement the subject of the advertisement is an agreement for the supply of a publication to which Part 8 of these rules applies, or

    (*b*) the investment agreement the subject of the advertisement is an agreement for the acquisition or disposal of shares, debentures, warrants, options or other securities of a company or of an interest in the securities of a company and the advertisement contains:

        (i) all such information as investors and their professional advisers would reasonably require, and reasonably expect to find there, for the purpose of making an informed assessment of:

           (A) the assets and liabilities, financial position, profits and losses, and prospects of the issuer of the securities, and

           (B) the rights attaching to those securities, and

        (ii) no other matter.

(2) An advertisement to which this rule applies may not be issued if the investment agreement the subject of the advertisement is an agreement for the provision of the services of a portfolio manager or investor broker fund adviser or if it relates to an investment other than:

    (*a*) a life policy, or

    (*b*) units in a regulated collective investment scheme, or

    (*c*) a type A or a type B PEP.

(3) A firm shall not issue an advertisement to which this rule applies if the advertisement contains any matter likely to lead to the supposition that the investment agreement the subject of the advertisement is or is thought to be suitable for a particular individual who is the recipient of the advertisement.

PRACTICE NOTE
This rule constrains the issuer of personalised circulars to refrain from implying that he knows a recipient sufficiently well to be sure that the investment is suitable. The rule is not intended to constrain the content of letters to individuals whom the firm writing the letter does know.

(4) A firm shall not issue an advertisement to which this rule applies unless the advertisement is contained in a printed document or is otherwise capable of being examined continuously for a reasonable period of time.

"Off-the-page" advertisements for life policies
7.24. A firm shall not issue an advertisement to which rule 7.23 applies which relates to a life policy unless the advertisement contains statements of the matters specified for the purpose in relation to the investment agreement the subject of the advertisement in Appendix D to Part 5 of these rules and gives information about the following matters:
  (*a*) any minimum to the amount which may be invested or paid regularly, and
  (*b*) if regular amounts are invited to be invested, what those amounts may be, and
  (*c*) how and where full details of the policy may be obtained, and
  (*d*) if any of the benefits under the policy are "linked benefits" within the meaning of Appendix D to this Part of these rules:
       (i) where prices of the units to which the benefits are linked and the yields of those units may be obtained, and
       (ii) the most recent difference between the bid and offer prices of the units as a percentage of the maximum offer price and the maximum permitted such differences or, if there is no such maximum, the discretion available to the life office to vary the difference, and
       (iii) the current price at which units will be allocated to the policy and the basis on which units will be allocated on payment of premiums, and
       (iv) any arrangements under which the investor may make regular withdrawals from the amount of his investment, and
       (v) what periodic information will be sent to the investor and at what intervals, and
  (*e*) what rights the investor will have to cancel any agreement he enters into in response to the advertisement and whether those rights derive from rules made by the Board under section 51 of the Act or are granted by the life office voluntarily.

"Off-the-page" advertisements for regulated collective investment schemes
7.25.—(1) A firm shall not issue an advertisement to which rule 7.23 applies which relates to units in a regulated collective investment scheme (including a type C PEP) unless:
  (*a*) the advertisement contains information about the following matters:
       (i) any minimum amount below which any one person may not invest in the scheme, and
       (ii) if regular amounts are invited to be invested in the scheme, what those amounts may be, and
       (iii) a statement of the investment objectives of the scheme and of any policies which the operator of the scheme proposes to adopt in selecting the investments in which the funds of the scheme will be invested, and

PRACTICE NOTE
The Board considers that sub-paragraph (iii) requires the advertisement to disclose any sectoral, geographical or other restric-

tions on the investments which may be made, for example, that the trust will be invested as to X per cent in Japanese high technology small companies.

   (iv) the most recent difference between the bid and offer prices of the units expressed as a percentage of the maximum offer price and the maximum permitted such difference or, if there is no such maximum, the discretion available to the operator of the scheme to vary the difference, and

   (v) in the case of a lump sum investment, the price at which units will be issued or, if this price is not fixed at the time of the issue of the advertisement, the basis for determining that price, and

   (vi) in the case of a series of payments, the basis for determining the price at which the units will be issued, and

   (vii) the nature and amount or rate of the charges which will be made to the customer and what discretion the operator of the scheme has to vary these (including charges which are included in the price at which units are issued), and

   (viii) what the annual gross yield is expected to be in the future on the basis of the most recent price or the price at which units are to be issued, and

   (ix) where information about current prices of units and the most recent yield or the anticipated future yields may be seen or obtained, and

   (x) if an investor may authorise the income due to him to be reinvested in the scheme, that fact and how the income will or may be reinvested, and

   (xi) the name of the trustee or custodian (if any), and

   (xii) if an application will not be acknowledged, that fact, and

   (xiii) when certificates will be sent to the investor, and

   (xiv) the frequency with which the property of the scheme is valued for the purposes of determining the issue and redemption prices of units and when the operator of the scheme will be available and willing to deal in those units, and

   (xv) how units may be redeemed and when payments on redemption will be made, and

   (xvi) details of any arrangements under which an investor may make regular withdrawals from the amount of his investment in the scheme, and

   (xvii) when statements of the value of a person's investment in the scheme will be sent to him, and

   (xviii) where and how copies of the scheme particulars may be obtained, and

  (b) except where it relates to a type C PEP, the advertisement contains a statement that a person entering into an investment agreement in consequence of a response to the advertisement will not have a right to cancel the agreement under rules made by the Board under section 51 of the Act, and

  (bb) if any commission is or will be payable by or on behalf of the operator of the scheme or an associate of the operator (assuming for the purpose of this reference to an associate that the operator, if not a firm, is a firm) in connection with the transaction to any person other than a person who is not independent of the operator:

   (i) the fact that commission will be so paid, and

   (ii) the identity of the person to whom commission will be paid to the extent that that identity is known when the advertisement is issued, and

   (iii) particulars of the amounts of the commission in accordance with paragraph (2)(b) of item 15 (Commissions) in Section 2 of

Appendix D to this Part of these rules in the appropriate form referred to in paragraph (3) of that item:

but any of the matter specified above under (iii) may be omitted, and

(c) in the case of a type C PEP, its terms do not give authority to anyone to make unsolicited calls upon the investor:

But the statement required by paragraph (b) may be omitted if the firm provides such a right as is referred to therein voluntarily.

(2) The requirements of paragraph (1) in the case of a type C PEP are in addition to the requirements of Part 4 of these rules as to the contents of a customer agreement.

(2A) Paragraph (2B) applies in the case of an advertisement:

(a) to which rule 7.23 applies, and

(b) which relates to a type C PEP under the terms of which the plan investor's cash subscriptions will or may be invested in the units of four or more authorised unit trust schemes, and

(c) which contains no offer which a responder may accept but only an invitation to make an offer.

(2B) An advertisement to which this paragraph applies need comply with sub-subparagraphs (iii), (vii) and (viii) of subparagraph (a) of paragraph (1).

(2C) Before a firm accepts any offer which it receives in response to an advertisement to which paragraph (2B) applies and which complies with sub-subparagraphs (iii), (vii) and (viii) only of subparagraph (a) of paragraph (1), the firm shall carry out the procedures specified in (A) of rule 4.12(2)(b)(ii).

(3) In the case of an advertisement of units in an umbrella fund within the meaning of the Authorised Unit Trust Scheme (Investment and Borrowing Powers) Regulations 1988 (S.I. 1988 No. 284) which contains an offer or an invitation to make an offer which is confined to a particular constituent part of the umbrella fund, it shall be a sufficient compliance with the requirements of heads (iii) to (viii) and (xiv) of subparagraph (a) of paragraph (1) if particulars are given only in relation to that constituent part.

"Off-the-page" advertisements for type B PEPs

7.26.—(1) A firm shall not issue an advertisement to which rule 7.23 applies which relates to a type B PEP unless the terms of the type B PEP the subject of the advertisement do not give any authority to anyone to make unsolicited calls upon the investor.

(2) The requirements of paragraph (1) are in addition to the requirements of Part 4 of these rules as to the contents of a customer agreement.

Restrictions on promotion of unregulated collective investment schemes

7.27. A firm shall not issue or cause to be issued an advertisement containing any matter which invites any person to become or offer to become a participant in a collective investment scheme which is not a regulated collective investment scheme or contains information calculated to lead directly or indirectly to any person becoming or offering to become a participant in such a scheme unless the issue of the advertisement does not contravene subsection (1) of section 76 of the Act by virtue of subsection (2), (3) or (4) of that section.

PRACTICE NOTE

In relation to an advertisement issued or caused to be issued by a firm, this rule merely restates what is already an obligation under section 76(1) of the Act, but the rule has effect, by virtue of section 58(1)(c) of the Act, in relation to advertisements issued or caused to be issued by a national of a member State other than the United Kingdom in the course of investment business lawfully carried on by him in such a State.

Release 32: 6 May 1994

Advertisements by appointed representatives

7.28.—(1) A firm which is a collective investment marketing firm shall ensure that an advertisement issued by an appointed representative of the firm (other than an image advertisement or a short form advertisement):

(a) does not contain any statement commending the principal or its services or products in such a way as to suggest or imply that the appointed representative was free to exercise independent judgment in deciding to make the commendation, and

(b) contains a prominent statement, no less prominent than any other statement describing the relationship between the advertiser and the firm which draws attention to:

(i) the fact that the advertiser is an appointed representative of the firm, and

(ii) the fact that the advertiser has entered into arrangements with the firm which preclude the advertiser from selling or recommending any products other than those of the firm, and

(c) if the advertisement relates to a product of the firm, is not cast in terms which suggest or imply that the product is that of the appointed representative and not that of the firm.

(2) A firm which is a collective investment marketing firm shall ensure that, in an advertisement issued by an appointed representative of the firm which relates to any activity of the appointed representative which is not investment business as well as to an activity of the appointed representative which is investment business, any claim made to independence in respect of the activity which is not investment business does not appear with such prominence relative to the matter in the advertisement which relates to investment business as to create a likelihood that a person reasonably attentive to the advertisement might suppose that the claim to independence applied to the activity of the appointed representative which is investment business.

(3) A firm which is a collective investment marketing firm shall ensure that an advertisement issued by an appointed representative of the firm which is not an advertisement in respect of investment business does not contain any matter referring to the Board or to the fact that the advertiser is connected with a person who is regulated by the Board.

Advertisements not to disguise lack of independence

7.29.—(1) A firm which is not a collective investment marketing firm and which has an associate which is:

(a) a collective investment marketing firm, or

(b) an appointed representative of a collective investment marketing firm,

shall not issue an advertisement of the products or services of the firm in such manner or containing such matter as is likely to cause a reader of the advertisement in its context to suppose that the associate has the same independence as that of the firm.

(2) A firm which is a collective investment marketing firm and which has an appointed representative which is an associate of a person who is not a collective investment marketing firm shall ensure that no advertisement of the products or services of the firm is issued by the appointed representative in such manner or containing such matter as is likely to cause a reader of the advertisement in its context to suppose that the firm has the same independence as that of the said person who is not a collective investment marketing firm.

(3) A firm which is a collective investment marketing firm and which has an associate which is not a collective investment marketing firm shall not issue an advertisement of the products or services of the firm in such manner or containing such matter as is likely to cause a reader of the advertisement in its context to suppose that the firm has the same independence as that of the associate.

PRACTICE NOTE
The Board considers the following to be an example of a breach of this rule. The issue of an advertisement of the services of financial adviser X (the appointed representative of life office Y) in a brochure which advertises the services generally of firm Z (an independent financial adviser) without special mention of the status of X and so to give the impression that X has the same independence as Z. This would be particularly so if X and Z, being associates, have similar names.

. . . . . .

CHAPTER IV

. . . . . .

Common Unsolicited Calls Regulations

Introduction
1. In principle, the effect of section 56 of the Financial Services Act 1986 is that
"no person shall in the course of or in consequence of an unsolicited call:
(*a*) made on a person in the United Kingdom, or
(*b*) made from the United Kingdom on a person elsewhere,
by way of business enter into an investment agreement with the person on whom the call is made or procure or endeavour to procure that person to enter into such an agreement."

2. Those restrictions may be lifted by regulations made by SIB, which is the purpose of these regulations.

3. These regulations do not apply to anything done by a person certified by a recognised professional body in carrying on investment business for which he is subject to its rules.

PART I—NON-PRIVATE INVESTORS

Non-private investors
1.—(1) Unless the call is an overseas person call:
(*a*) the marketing restriction is lifted to the extent that the call is made with a view to the investor entering into the investment agreement as a non-private investor; and
(*b*) the dealing restriction is lifted to the extent that the investor enters into the investment agreement as a non-private investor.
(2) Where the call is an overseas person call:
(*a*) the marketing restriction is lifted to the extent that the call is made with a view to the investor entering into the agreement as a non-private customer; and
(*b*) the dealing restriction is lifted to the extent that the investor enters into the investment agreement as a non-private customer.

PART II—PRIVATE INVESTORS

Sale of non-geared packaged products
2.—(1) In principle, the restrictions are lifted to the extent that the investment agreement concerns the provision of investment services relat-

ing to the sale to the investor of a generally marketable non-geared packaged product.

(2) Where the call is an overseas person call, the restrictions are so lifted from the overseas person only to the extent that the call is made by an unauthorised or exempted person.

Supply of callable investment services

3. The restrictions are lifted to the extent that the investment agreement relates to the provision by an authorised or exempted person to the investor of callable investment services and either:

    (*a*) the agreement is otherwise subject to (or is exempted from) a cancellation or delayed entry procedure under the regulatory system; or

    (*b*) the services are provided under a cancellable customer agreement and it is made clear to the investor in that agreement and in any accompanying letter or promotional material that he has a seven day cooling off period.

Existing customers

4.—(1) In principle, the restrictions are lifted where:

    (*a*) the investor has a legitimately established existing customer relationship with the caller, the dealer, or an associate of either; and

    (*b*) the customer relationship is such that the investor envisages unsolicited calls of the kind concerned.

(2) Where the investment agreement relates to a geared packaged product, the restrictions are lifted by this regulation only where the call is made by the investor's investment manager.

(3) Where the call is an overseas person call, the restrictions are lifted by this regulation only where:

    (*a*) the customer relationship existed while the investor was resident outside the United Kingdom; and

    (*b*) the investor has been given the prescribed disclosure.

(4) Where:

    (*a*) the investment agreement relates to investment services which involve contingent liability transactions or the discretionary management of the customer's assets and which the dealer may provide to the customer only under a two-way customer agreement; or

    (*b*) the call is an overseas person call;

the restrictions are lifted by this regulation only where the investor has indicated in writing before the call is made that he envisages receiving such calls.

Acquisition of investment business

5. Where one person acquires the whole or part of a business from another person, the restrictions are lifted to the extent necessary for the purposes of enabling the acquiror to invite the customers of the business acquired to establish a customer relationship with him, so long as that relationship does not envisage unsolicited calls of any kind not envisaged by the investor in his relationship with the person from whom the business was acquired.

Public takeovers

6. The restrictions are lifted to the extent that the call (including an overseas person call) is made by or under the supervision of an authorised person and in connection with or for the purposes of a takeover or substantial acquisition which is subject to the Takeover Code or to requirements in another member state which afford equivalent protection to investors in the United Kingdom.

Corporate acquisitions
    7.—(1) The marketing restriction is lifted to the extent that:
    (*a*) the call is made on an employee for the purposes of arranging a management buy-out relating to the whole or part of the business of his employer or of one or more other undertakings in the same group;
    (*b*) the call is made on an employee for the purposes of arranging a management buy-in relating to a business in which he would fulfil management functions; or
    (*c*) the call is made in connection with or for the purpose of a corporate acquisition or disposal which fulfils the requirements set out in paragraph 21 of Schedule 1 to the Act.
    (2) The dealing restriction is also lifted to that extent, so long as:
    (*a*) the investor has been provided with a written statement containing information which is adequate to enable him to make an informed investment decision; and
    (*b*) the investor has an adequate opportunity to seek independent advice before entering into the investment agreement.

Connected individuals
    8.—(1) The restrictions are lifted for calls between business partners, fellow directors or close relatives.
    (2) The restrictions are lifted for calls between the settlor of a trust (other than a unit trust scheme), its trustees, beneficiaries and the agents of any of them, to the extent that they relate to the settlement, management or distribution of the trust fund.
    (3) The restrictions are lifted for calls between personal representatives, beneficiaries under a will or intestacy and the agents of any of them, to the extent that they relate to the management or distribution of the estate.

Employee share schemes
    9.—(1) The restrictions are lifted to the extent that the call is made:
    (*a*) by or on behalf of a body corporate, an undertaking in the same group, or the trustee of an employee share scheme; and
    (*b*) for the purpose of enabling or facilitating either:
       (i) transactions in shares or debentures in an undertaking in the group between or for the benefit of existing or former employees of such an undertaking and their close relatives; or
      (ii) the holding of such shares or debentures by or for the benefit of any such persons.
    (2) For this purpose, shares and debentures include share and debenture warrants, certificates representing shares or debentures, and ancillaries on any of them.

Occupational pension schemes
    10. The restrictions are lifted to the extent that the investment agreement is a contract to manage the assets of an occupational pension scheme.

Calls made in non-commercial contexts
    11. The restrictions are lifted to the extent that they apply because of a call made by a person:
    (*a*) who was not acting by way of business; and
    (*b*) who has been provided with no incentive to make the call.

Calls made in the course of a profession or non-investment business
    12.—(1) The restrictions are lifted to the extent that they apply because of a call:
    (*a*) made in the course of the carrying on of any profession or of a business not constituting investment business; and

(b) giving investment advice, or making arrangements, the giving or making of which is a necessary part of other advice or services given in the course of carrying on that profession or business.

(2) For this purpose, the giving of advice or making of arrangements is not to be regarded as a necessary part of other advice or services if it is separately remunerated.

Exempted persons
13. The restrictions are lifted in any case where the investment agreement is to be, or is, entered into with an exempted person (other than an appointed representative) in the course of investment business covered by the exemption.

PART III—LIMITS ON PERMISSIONS PROVIDED

Overseas persons
14.—(1) Where a regulation or any paragraph of a regulation in Part I or Part II above contains a reference to an overseas person call, that regulation lifts the restrictions for such calls only to the extent it specifies.

(2) Where a regulation in Part I or Part II above contains no reference to an overseas person call, that regulation lifts the restrictions for such calls:
(a) in the case of the marketing restriction, only to the extent that the marketing is done through an authorised or exempted person; and
(b) in the case of the dealing restriction, only to the extent that the dealing is done through an authorised or exempted person.

Calls prohibited by telecommunications licence
15. Where the call is made with a view to the provision of investment services and is prohibited by the terms of a telecommunications licence relating to unsolicited calls, the restrictions are lifted only by the permission for calls relating to public takeovers.

Unlawful business
16. The only one of these regulations which lifts a restriction from anything said or done by a person in the course of carrying on investment business in contravention of section 3 of the Act is the permission for calls relating to public takeovers.

PART IV—SUPPLEMENTARY

Reasonable belief
17.—(1) The marketing restriction is lifted to the extent that the caller can demonstrate that he believes on reasonable grounds at the time of the call in the existence of circumstances which would mean that the restriction is lifted from him.

(2) The dealing restriction is lifted to the extent that the dealer can demonstrate that he believes on reasonable grounds at the time of the deal in the existence of circumstances which would mean that the restriction is lifted from him.

Reliance on guidance
18. A person is to be taken to act in conformity with the Common Unsolicited Calls Regulations to the extent that:
(a) the relevant regulator has issued formal guidance on compliance with them; and

(b) in reliance on standards set in that guidance, the person concerned believes on reasonable grounds that he is acting in conformity with the regulations.

Calls made before commencement

19. The restrictions are lifted to the extent that:

(a) they apply because the investment agreement is entered into in consequence of an unsolicited call made before the general commencement date of these regulations; and

(b) the restrictions would not have applied if the investment agreement had been entered into at the time of the call.

General

20.—(1) The Financial Services Glossary 1991 (Second Edition) applies, unless the context otherwise requires, for the interpretation of these regulations.

(2) Any other expression defined for the purposes of the Act or in the Interpretation Act 1978 has the same meanings in these regulations.

(3) These regulations may be cited as the Common Unsolicited Calls Regulations. They are made under section 56 of, and paragraph 20 of Schedule 11 to, the Act and designated so as to apply to members of recognised self-regulating organisations under section 63A of and paragraph 22B of Schedule 11 to, the Act.

(4) The general commencement date of these regulations is 1st September 1991. For investment agreements relating to geared packaged products, they supersede existing permissions on that date. In other cases they supersede existing permissions on 1st January 1992.

(5) Until these regulations supersede existing permissions:

(a) these regulations apply to the members of an SRO subject to further permissions contained in the rules of that SRO; and

(b) the provisions of the Financial Services (Unsolicited Calls) Regulations 1987 and those of the Financial Services (Interim) Rules and Regulations 1990 relating to unsolicited calls remain in full effect.

(6) Where these regulations supersede existing permissions either for calls relating to geared packaged products or generally, then, either for such calls or generally, these regulations no longer apply subject to further permissions contained in SRO rules and the provisions mentioned in (5)(b) of this regulation are revoked.

Code of Conduct for Scottish Solicitors

INTRODUCTION

In common with lawyers in most parts of the world, solicitors in Scotland have always been expected, by the general public and by their professional colleagues and others, to observe certain standards of professional conduct. The standards are required in order to establish the essential relationship of trust between lawyer and client, between lawyer and court, and between lawyer and other members of the legal profession.

All solicitors in Scotland require to be members of the Law Society of Scotland and for many years specific practice rules have been promulgated by the Society as a self-regulatory organisation for solicitors. Some of these rules have been included in Acts of Parliament and the Society's authority for promulgating additional practice rules comes from Parliament itself and the rules are subject to the consent of the Lord President of the Court of Session. These rules are binding upon solicitors. They stem from and have the force of statutory authority.

The Law of Scotland was and is founded upon principles which have the same validity and authority as Acts of Parliament. In the same way, in addition to the written rules governing solicitors in Scotland, there are other commonly accepted standards of conduct which solicitors are expected to meet.

The CCBE (Conseil des Barreaux de la Communauté Européenne), comprising representatives of all the governing bodies of lawyers in the European Community, adopted in 1988 a Code of Conduct for lawyers within the community which governs conduct of lawyers in relation to activities crossing over from one country to another.

In addition, the CCBE Code is to be taken into account in all revisions of national rules with a view to the progressive harmonisation of codes and regulations governing lawyers within the European Community.

All the standards of professional conduct, whether contained in Acts of Parliament or in practice rules (written or unwritten) which are binding upon solicitors in Scotland are based upon certain values and principles which form the foundation of the profession and reflect the legal, moral and professional obligations of the solicitor to:
  (a) the clients;
  (b) the courts and other authorities before whom a lawyer pleads his client's cause or acts on his behalf;
  (c) the public; and
  (d) the legal profession in general and each fellow member of it in particular.

Should any solicitor transgress any of these rules, then such transgression may give rise to disciplinary proceedings and amount to professional misconduct or some lesser finding.

The following Code contains a statement of the basic values and principles which form the foundation of the solicitor profession. It is not intended to be an exhaustive list of all the detailed practice rules and detailed obligations of solicitors, but it is the foundation for those rules and may be referred to for guidance in assessing whether or not a solicitor's conduct meets the standard required of a member of the profession.

Code of Conduct for Solicitors holding Practising Certificates issued by the Law Society of Scotland

PREAMBLE

I. The function of the lawyer in society

In a society founded on respect for the rule of law lawyers fulfil a special role. Their duties do not begin and end with the faithful performance of what they are instructed to do so far as the law permits. Lawyers must serve the interests of justice as well as those whose rights and liberties they are trusted to assert and defend and it is their duty not only to plead their clients' cause but also to be their adviser.

The function of lawyers therefore imposes on them a variety of legal and moral obligations (sometimes appearing to be in conflict with each other) towards:—

(a) the clients;
(b) the courts and other authorities before whom the lawyers plead their clients' cause or act on their behalf;
(c) the public for whom the existence of a free and independent profession, bound together by respect for rules made by the profession itself, is an essential means of safeguarding human rights in face of the power of the state and other interests in society.
(d) the legal profession in general and each fellow member of it in particular.

II. The nature of rules of professional conduct

Rules of professional conduct are designed to ensure the proper performance by the lawyer of a function which is recognised as essential in all civilised societies. The failure of the lawyer to observe these rules must in the last resort result in a disciplinary sanction. The willing acceptance of those rules and of the need for disciplinary sanction ensures the highest possible standards.

The particular rules of all the Bar Associations and Law Societies in the European Community are based on identical values and in most cases demonstrate a common foundation which is also reflected in Bar Associations and Law Societies throughout the world.

THE CODE

1. Independence

Independence is essential to the function of solicitors in their relationships with all parties and it is the duty of all solicitors that they do not allow their independence to be impaired irrespective of whether or not the matter in which they are acting involves litigation

Independence means that solicitors must not allow themselves to be restricted in their actings on behalf of or in giving advice to their clients, nor must they allow themselves to be influenced by motives inconsistent with the principles of this Code. For example, solicitors must not compromise their professional standards in order to promote their own interests or the interests of parties other than their clients. Advice must not be given simply to ingratiate solicitors with their clients, courts or third parties. Non-independent advice may be worse than useless in that it may actively encourage someone to undertake a course of action which is not in his or her best interests.

When representing clients in court solicitors appear as agents and speak for their clients, but this does not mean that they are permitted to put forward statements or arguments which they know to be untruthful or misleading. Similarly, in relation to other services solicitors, although acting as agents, must remain independent for their advice and actings to be of value.

2. The interests of the client

Solicitors must always act in the best interests of their clients subject to preserving their independence as solicitors and to the due observance of the law, professional practice rules and the principles of good professional conduct. Solicitors must not permit their own personal interests or those of the legal profession in general to influence their actings on behalf of clients; further, their actings must be free of all political considerations

Solicitors in advising clients must not allow their advice to be influenced by the fact that a particular course of action would result in the solicitor being able to charge a higher fee. Solicitors are not permitted to "buy" or pay for business introductions, although commission may be paid to a fellow lawyer.

Solicitors should not allow themselves to be persuaded by clients to pursue matters or courses of action which the solicitors consider not to be in the clients' interests. It may be appropriate for solicitors to refuse to act where clients are not prepared to follow the advice given.

Where solicitors are consulted about matters in which they have a personal or a financial interest the position should be made clear to the clients and where appropriate solicitors should insist that the clients consult other solicitors. For example, neither a solicitor, nor a partner of that solicitor, is generally permitted to prepare a will for a client where the solicitor is to receive a significant legacy or share of the estate.

Solicitors are the agents of their clients and as such are not permitted to conceal any profit deriving from their actings for clients and must make known to their clients the source of any commission so arising.

3. Conflict

Solicitors (including firms of solicitors) shall not act for two or more clients in matters where there is a conflict of interest between the clients or for any client where there is a conflict between the interest of the client and that of the solicitor or the solicitor's firm

In considering whether or not to accept instructions from more than one party and where there is potential for a conflict arising at a later date, solicitors must have regard to any possible risk of breaches of confidentiality and impairment of independence. If, having decided to proceed, a conflict should later arise solicitors must not continue to act for all the parties and in most cases they will require to withdraw from acting for all of the parties. There may, however, be certain circumstances which would result in a significant disadvantage to one party were the solicitor not to continue to act for that party and there is no danger of any breach of confidentiality in relation to the other party. In these very special cases, the solicitor may continue to act for one party.

Solicitors must accept instructions only from clients or recognised agents authorised to give instructions on behalf of the clients; for example, persons authorised by a power of attorney or another lawyer. Where a solicitor is requested to act for more than one party in respect of the same matter, the solicitor must be reasonably satisfied that there is no apparent conflict among the interests of all the parties and that each party is indeed authorising the solicitor to act.

4. Confidentiality

The observance of client confidentiality is a fundamental duty of solicitors
    This duty applies not only to the solicitors but also to their partners and
staff, and the obligation is not terminated by the passage of time. This
principle is so important that it is recognised by the courts as being essential
to the administration of justice and to the relationship of trust which must
exist between solicitor and client. Only in special circumstances may a court
require a solicitor to break the obligation of confidentiality.

5. Provision of a professional service

Solicitors must provide adequate professional services
    Solicitors are under a professional obligation to provide adequate
professional services to their clients. An adequate professional service
requires the legal knowledge, skill, thoroughness and preparation necessary
to the matter in hand. Solicitors should not accept instructions unless they
can adequately discharge these. This means that as well as being liable for
damages assessable by a court of law for any act of negligence in dealing with
a client's affairs, a solicitor may face disciplinary action by the Law Society in
respect of a service to a client which is held to be an inadequate professional
service.

(a) *Solicitors must act on the basis of their clients' proper instructions or on the
        instructions of another solicitor who acts for the client*
    Solicitors act as the agents of the clients and must have the authority of the
clients for their actions.
    A client may withdraw authority at any time by giving due notification to
the solicitor. However, such withdrawal cannot act retrospectively.
    Solicitors require to discuss with and advise their clients on the objectives
of the work carried out on behalf of the clients and the means by which the
objectives are to be pursued. Acceptance of instructions from clients does
not constitute an endorsement or approval of the clients' political, social or
moral views, activities or motivations. With the agreement of the client a
solicitor may restrict the objectives and the steps to be taken consistent with
the provision of an adequate professional service. A solicitor may not accept
an improper instruction; for example, to assist a client in a matter which the
solicitor knows to be criminal or fraudulent, but a solicitor may advise on the
legal consequences of any proposed course of conduct or assist a client in
determining the validity, scope or application of the law.
    Solicitors are free to refuse to undertake instructions, but once acting
should withdraw from a case or transaction only for good cause and where
possible in such a manner that the clients' interests are not adversely
affected. This obligation will not, however, prevent solicitors from exercising their rights at law to recover their justified fees and outlays incurred on
behalf of their clients.

(b) *A solicitor shall act only in those matters where the solicitor is competent to
        do so*
    Where a solicitor considers that the service to a client would be
inadequate owing to the solicitor's lack of knowledge or experience it would
be improper for the solicitor to accept instructions and agree to act.

(c) *Solicitors shall accept instructions only where the matter can be carried out
        with due expedition and solicitors shall maintain appropriate systems in
        order to ensure that the matter is dealt with effectively*
    Where a solicitor considers, for example, that the service to a client would
be inadequate, owing to pressure of work or the like so that the matter would
not be dealt with within a reasonable period of time, it would be improper
for the solicitor to accept instructions and agree to act.

(d) *Solicitors are required to exercise the level of skill appropriate to the matter*

In deciding whether or not to accept instructions from a client, and in the carrying out of those instructions, a solicitor must have regard to the nature and complexity of the matter in hand and apply to the work the appropriate level of professional skills.

(e) *Solicitors shall communicate effectively with their clients and others*

Solicitors are required to try to ensure that their communications with their clients and others on behalf of their clients are effective. This includes providing clients with relevant information regarding the matter in hand and the actions taken on their behalf. Solicitors should advise their clients of any significant development in relation to their case or transaction and explain matters to the extent reasonably necessary to permit informed decisions by clients regarding the instructions which require to be given by them. Information should be clear and comprehensive and where necessary or appropriate confirmed in writing.

The duty to communicate effectively extends to include the obligation on solicitors to account to their clients in respect of all relevant monies passing through the solicitor's hands.

(f) *Solicitors shall not act, nor shall they cease to act for clients summarily or without just cause, in a manner which would prejudice the course of justice*

Where the matter in issue involves the courts or otherwise involves the administration of justice, a solicitor must have regard to the course of justice in considering whether or not to cease acting on behalf of a client. The solicitor may not simply and suddenly decide that it would no longer be appropriate to act for the client and in most cases the solicitor will require to seek the agreement of the court to the withdrawal of the solicitor's services.

(g) *Solicitors shall comply with the specific rules issued from time to time by the Law Society of Scotland*

Subject to the consent of the Lord President of the Court of Session the Law Society is empowered to issue specific practice rules regarding the conduct of solicitors and other matters affecting the affairs of clients. All solicitors must comply with these rules. A list of the titles of such rules currently in force is annexed to this Code.

6. Professional fees

The fees charged by solicitors shall be fair and reasonable in all the circumstances

Factors to be considered in relation to the reasonableness of the fee include:—
- (a) the importance of the matter to the client;
- (b) the amount or value of any money, property or transaction involved;
- (c) the complexity of the matter or the difficulty or novelty of the question raised;
- (d) the skill, labour, specialised knowledge and responsibility involved on the part of the solicitor;
- (e) the time expended;
- (f) the length, number and importance of any documents or other papers prepared or perused; and
- (g) the place where and the circumstances in which the services or any part thereof are rendered and the degree of urgency involved.

7. Trust and personal integrity

Solicitors must act honestly at all times and in such a way as to put their
*   personal integrity beyond question*

Solicitors' actions and personal behaviour must be consistent with the
need for mutual trust and confidence among clients, the courts, the public
and fellow lawyers. For example, solicitors must observe the Accounts Rules
which govern the manner in which clients' funds may be held by solicitors
and which are designed to ensure that clients' monies are safeguarded.
Solicitors who are dishonest in a matter not directly affecting their clients are
nonetheless guilty of professional misconduct.

8. Relations with the courts

Solicitors must never knowingly give false or misleading information to the
*   court and must maintain due respect and courtesy towards the court while*
*   honourably pursuing the interests of their clients*

For example, it would be improper for a solicitor to put forward on behalf
of a client a statement of events or a legal argument which the solicitor knew
to be false or misleading. Accordingly, if a client requests a solicitor to put
forward a false story the solicitor must refuse to do so.

In the course of investigation a solicitor must not do or say anything which
could affect evidence or induce a witness, a party to an action, or an accused
person to do otherwise than give in evidence a truthful and honest statement
of that person's recollections.

9. Relations between lawyers

Solicitors shall not knowingly mislead colleagues or where they have given
*   their word go back on it*

A solicitor must act with fellow solicitors in a manner consistent with
persons having mutual trust and confidence in each other.

It is in the public interest and for the benefit of clients and the
administration of justice that there be a corporate professional spirit based
upon relationships of trust and co-operation between solicitors. For
example, the settlement of property transactions in Scotland is facilitated by
the underlying trust between solicitors. A specific example of this is the
payment of the price by a cheque drawn by the purchaser's solicitor on a
joint stock bank in favour of the seller's solicitor. Were the purchaser's
solicitor to instruct the bank to stop payment of the cheque such action could
amount to professional misconduct.

It is not permissible for a solicitor to communicate about any item of
business with a person whom the solicitor knows to be represented by
another solicitor. A solicitor in such circumstances must always communicate with the solicitor acting for that person and not go behind the solicitor's
back.

The rules governing the advertising of solicitors' services take into
account the need to maintain mutual trust and confidence, while permitting
solicitors to market their services effectively and to compete with one
another.

10. Civic professionalism

Solicitors have a duty not only to act as guardians of national liberties, but also
*   to seek improvements in the law and the legal system*

It is the striving by solicitors for improvement both in general terms and in
relation to the individual needs of a particular client that prevents the law
and legal services "from degenerating into a trade or mere mechanical act"
(Lord Cooper, *Selected Papers*, Edinburgh 1957, p. 77). Many solicitors fulfil

this obligation through working on the many committees of the Law Society of Scotland, including those not only commenting and advising on proposed legislative changes and areas of law reform but also recommending and promoting new ideas for reform. Others are involved at the highest level with other reforming bodies and many seek public appointment, both locally and at a national level.

This duty extends beyond the issues of freedom and liberty, through the entire system of law, to the day-to-day legal services provided by solicitors.

11. Discrimination

Solicitors must not discriminate on grounds of race, sex, religion or disability in their professional dealings with clients, employees or other lawyers

Legislation already provides that it is unlawful to discriminate against individuals either directly or indirectly in respect of their race, sex or marital status. However, solicitors should be prepared to observe not only the letter but also the spirit of the anti-discrimination legislation in dealings with clients, employees and others. In particular, solicitors should ensure that within their own firms, there is no discrimination in employment policy and that opportunities for promotion and advancement are open on an equal basis to all employees. In addition, solicitors should give active consideration to opportunities for the disabled.

[1] **Code of Conduct for Criminal Work**

NOTE
[1] Reproduced with kind permission of the Law Society of Scotland.

1. Seeking Business
A solicitor shall seek or accept only those instructions which emanate from the client and which are not given as a result of an inducement.

GUIDANCE NOTE
   This Statement of good practice emphasises that a solicitor is an officer of the court. This must always be remembered when dealing with criminal law work.
   It is essential that a solicitor should at all times remain independent of the client and that the solicitor should be free to give appropriate legal advice. Accordingly, no instructions should be accepted which are or can be tainted by allegations that inducements have been offered in exchange for instructions. The offering of an inducement compromises the solicitor's freedom to give appropriate independent legal advice. It follows that the client should not be considered as a "friend" and that the solicitor must always remain at "arm's length" from the client. This will ensure that the client and the court can be confident that the advice tendered by the solicitor is both impartial and independent.
   Instructions which are given as a result of an inducement by a third party on the solicitor's behalf must not be accepted. The solicitor is considered to be strictly liable for the actions of third parties who contact potential clients and any third party who contacts a potential client shall be deemed to have acted on the instructions of the solicitor whether or not the solicitor is instructed as a result of the third party's approach. When instructed by a client a solicitor may contact (a) an accused person or (b) the accused person's solicitor in relation to a criminal matter. If the client's co-accused is instructing a solicitor contact must be made through the solicitor. All reasonable steps must be taken to ascertain the identity of the co-accused's solicitor.
   It is emphasised that any contract of agency between a solicitor and a client which is based upon an inducement to contract may be illegal both in terms of the criminal law and may also contravene the civil law. Such contracts can be made the subject of a complaint of professional misconduct and may lead to disqualification in terms of Section 31 of Legal Aid (Scotland) Act 1986.

2. Conflict of Interest
A solicitor should not accept instructions from more than one accused in the same matter.

GUIDANCE NOTE
   This Statement reflects the awareness which solicitors have always had of the obvious potential conflict of interest that will arise when instructions are accepted from more than one accused person in the same case, even though that conflict may not arise and the defence is common to all accused. Nevertheless, solicitors should not place themselves in the position whereby they may obtain information confidential to the defence of one accused which at the same time may be detrimental to the defence of another.
   Accordingly when it becomes apparent to the solicitor that he has received instructions from two or more parties in the same case a solicitor may accept instructions from one of the accused and any others must be told immediately that separate representation must be sought.

Under no circumstances should a solicitor apply for a Legal Aid
Certificate for more than one accused person in any matter. However, a duty
solicitor should responsibly carry out his duties under the Legal Aid scheme
and be aware of the terms of this Statement.

However the choice of a solicitor always lies with the accused person and a
solicitor must always ask an accused if he wishes a particular solicitor to be
instructed before a recommendation can be made. A solicitor may suggest
that an accused seeks representation from a particular solicitor but that
alternative solicitor must be based within the same jurisdiction as the
accused.

3. Legal Aid
*A solicitor is under a duty to prepare and conduct criminal legal aid cases by
carrying out work which is actually and reasonably necessary and having due
regard to economy.*

GUIDANCE NOTE
This Statement is declaratory of Regulation 7.1 of the Criminal Legal Aid
(Scotland) (Fees) Regulations 1989. The solicitor's primary duties are to the
court and to a client. Every solicitor should carry out these duties in a
responsible and professional manner. With these duties uppermost in mind
the solicitor must not abuse the Legal Aid system and view criminal cases
only as a means of financial enrichment.

The terms of Regulation 7.1 are—"Subject to the provisions of Regulations 4, 5, 6 and 9, and paragraph (2) of this Regulation, a solicitor shall be
allowed such amount of fees as shall be determined to be reasonable
remuneration for work actually and reasonably done, and travel and waiting
time actually and reasonably undertaken or incurred, due regard being had
to economy".

Where requested, files and information should be provided to SLAB.

Abuse of the Legal Aid system may be fraudulent and may be considered
as professional misconduct and may lead to disqualification under Section 31
of the Legal Aid (Scotland) Act 1986.

Any complaints can be dealt with in terms of Section 31 of the Legal Aid
(Scotland) Act 1986.

4. Identification of solicitor
*A solicitor who seeks access to any party who is in custody should have in his
possession an identification card provided by the Law Society of Scotland and
should exhibit this upon request.*

GUIDANCE NOTE
This Statement is designed to prohibit unqualified employees or individuals from attending meetings with persons in custody. It will ensure not only
that impersonation of solicitors or trainees is made more difficult but also
that only those persons qualified to provide independent legal advice are
granted access.

As a corollary of this Statement those instructed by solicitors to obtain
precognitions from any witness should carry identification and a letter of
authority from the instructing solicitor. It is good practice to write to all
civilian witnesses advising them that an agent will contact them with a view
to obtaining a statement. Where possible, multiple precognitions of civilian
witnesses by each accused should be avoided unless this is absolutely
essential in the interests of justice and of the accused.

5. Custody visits
Only a solicitor or trainee solicitor who has been instructed to do so may visit the client in custody.

GUIDANCE NOTE
This Statement restricts access to a person in custody in a Police Office, Prison and Cell Area.

There are occasions when a solicitor has taken instructions from the family or friend of an accused and has then visited a person in custody. It is the duty of every solicitor to check with the Police Station to ascertain if the person in custody has requested another solicitor or duty solicitor. If the person in custody has indeed requested the services of another solicitor or the duty solicitor, then the solicitor contacted by the family or friend may not visit the Police Station.

Moreover, instructions must come directly from the person detained and not by virtue of the Police arranging for a specific solicitor to be contacted who is unknown to and has not been requested by the accused.

6. Property to persons in custody
A business card and legal documents should be the only items given by a solicitor to a person in custody.

GUIDANCE NOTE
It has become apparent that certain solicitors have attended to the so called "needs" of their clients in custody by providing them with cigarettes, newspapers, meals and money. This Statement forbids any form of donation. In addition, this Statement shall include the giving to family or friends of the person in custody any items for onward transmission.

7. Mandates
All mandates requesting the transfer of papers and legal aid relating to a criminal matter shall be completed and executed by the assisted person in the form agreed by the Scottish Legal Aid Board and the Law Society of Scotland. The mandate should include the place and date of signing and a full explanation as to why the mandate has been issued.

GUIDANCE NOTE
The matter is governed by the Criminal Legal Aid (Scotland) Regulations 1987, paragraph 17(3), which states "where an assisted person desires that a solicitor, other than the solicitor presently nominated by him shall act for him, he shall apply to the Board for authority to nominate another specified solicitor to act for him and shall inform the Board of the reason for his application; and the Board, if it is satisfied that there is good reason for the application and, in the case of Legal Aid made available under Sections 24 or 25 of the Act that it is in the interests of justice or, as the case may be, is reasonable, for him to receive or continue to receive Criminal Legal Aid, may grant the application".

It seems clear from a plain construction of this Regulation that changes of agency where the client is legally aided in a criminal case can only take place if the Board gives the client authority to nominate another specified solicitor. Until the Board gives its authority the client cannot instruct another solicitor unless he wishes to do so without the benefit of legal aid, which fact should be notified to the Board.

Therefore the chronology of transfers of agency in criminal cases should be (1) the client approaches his proposed new solicitor to ascertain if he is willing to act; (2) client applies to Board for authority to transfer the agency; (3) Board grants authority; (4) client instructs new solicitor; (5) new solicitor serves mandate on previous solicitor.

The Board's authority to transfer must ante-date any mandate.

This Statement would solve many issues including inducements to transfer agency and "mandate wars". Adoption of this interpretation would of course meant that legally aided clients and fee paying clients will not be treated precisely equally. However, that objection has to be seen in the light of the need to comply with the Regulations which effectively impose a statutory suspensive condition on any mandate and the requirement that solicitors will require to inform a transferring client that instructions cannot be accepted until the Regulations are complied with.

8. Consultations with Clients at Liberty
A solicitor should not consult with a client, who is at liberty unless the consultation takes place in 1) the solicitor's office 2) a court or 3) a hospital; a solicitor may exceptionally attend the house of a client who is unable to attend the solicitor's office due to illness.

GUIDANCE NOTE
The solicitor should not visit a client within his home unless it is impossible for the client to attend the offices of the solicitor through ill health.

A solicitor leaves himself open to various allegations and indeed risks if he should attend at the home of a client. All solicitors should be aware that there is a risk. For example a solicitor could be within a house which contains drugs or stolen goods.

It will not always be possible to consult with an accused within a solicitor's own office. However, such consultations should take place within a similar office environment, such as the interview rooms within a Court building. However, it is accepted that there will be occasions when it is not possible or appropriate to interview a client within an office environment, for example when the client is in hospital. The onus is on a solicitor to justify an interview at any other place if called upon to do so. The geography and rural nature of Scotland will be taken into account.

9. Expenses
No payment in money or kind should be made to an accused person, a member of the accused person's family or potential witnesses.

GUIDANCE NOTE
It has suggested that solicitors have paid taxi fares, babysitting expenses and loss of earnings expenses to accused persons, their family and witnesses as an inducement for business.

These would seem sometimes to relate to the visit of these persons to a solicitor's office.

There is no rationale for making payment to any such persons. It is accepted that once a trial has ended, then only legitimate expenses may be paid to witnesses who were cited to appear at Court for the defence. A witness who is cited to give a precognition on oath is entitled to travelling and subsistence expenses.

It should be noted that for witnesses travelling far distances travel vouchers should be provided. Any payments made will require to be properly vouched.

10. Defence Witnesses
Only those witnesses relevant to a case should be cited to attend court.

GUIDANCE NOTE
Ideally, a witness should be interviewed before citation. A solicitor must take all reasonable steps to obtain directly from a witness the potential evidence in a case. It is accepted that this is not always possible and indeed a solicitor could leave himself open to criticism and complaint if he should not cite a witness when he has been specifically instructed to do so by an accused person. Nevertheless, a solicitor must at all times be in a position to justify the citation of all witnesses in a case.

In providing a citation, a solicitor should advise the witness of their right to claim legitimate expenses. These include travelling to and from Court. Neither witnesses nor indeed an accused person should be transported to Court by a solicitor.

In recent times it had been suggested that some persons with no involvement in a case have been cited to attend court only to provide these persons with expenses. Additionally, it has been asserted that parties have been brought to Court from custody, who have no relevance whatsoever to the case but who are cited simply to allow them to meet other prisoners at Court. Such actions cannot be tolerated.

A solicitor should keep a contemporaneous record of his actings and financial dealings in terms of this Code and provide this if so requested by the Law Society of Scotland.

Other Rules of Professional Conduct
A solicitor should at all times comply with good professional practice and the ethics of the solicitors' profession as set out in practice rules, other codes of conduct and textbooks on professional ethics.

GUIDANCE NOTE
The essence of professional ethics is such that it cannot be codified. Many texts provide guidance on the professional behaviour expected of solicitors. Solicitors have a duty to inform themselves of these texts and to approach their work in a manner consistent with the principles of good ethical practice. A solicitor acting outwith the terms of this Code may be called upon to justify his conduct.

11. Sensitive material and the client[1]
11.1 A solicitor should not show a client sensitive material related to his case at all, other than in circumstances where the solicitor is present and it is possible to exercise adequate supervision to prevent the client retaining possession of the material or making a copy of it.

11.2 A solicitor should not give a client for retention by him, even on a temporary basis, copies of witness precognitions; witness statements; productions or like documents relating to his case, unless there are exceptional circumstances justifying such a course in a particular case. If the solicitor believes that such exceptional circumstances exist he should, when giving the items to the client, explain that the items must be retained securely by the client; must be kept confidential; must not be shown to others, let alone released to others; must not be copied and must be returned to the solicitor by a fixed date, which must be as soon as possible having regard to the circumstances justifying giving the items to the client in the first place.

11.3 "Sensitive material" for the purposes of article 11.1 above includes:—
(a) a precognition or statement of a victim of a sexual offence;
(b) a photograph or pseudo photograph of any such victim or a deceased victim;
(c) a medical or other report or statement relating to the physical condition of any such victim or a deceased victim;
(d) any document, other than a document served on the client by the Crown or by a co-accused, containing the addresses or telephone numbers of witnesses or their relatives/friends or information from which their addresses and telephone numbers could be deduced.

GUIDANCE NOTE

From time to time the Society has been asked to give its views on the practice of giving to accused persons copies of the precognitions or statements of witnesses and of other documents associated with the accused's case.

In the vast majority of criminal cases the accused is in receipt of Legal Aid and it has been judicially declared that the accused has no proprietorial claim on the case papers. These belong to the solicitor. Where solicitors have sought to justify the practice of giving copies of precognitions and other documents to an accused, they have usually done so by seeking to rely on the duty which a solicitor has to communicate information to a client and thereafter to take instructions in respect of that information.

The view of the Society is that a solicitor should not give copies of precognitions/statements or documents to an accused, unless there are exceptional circumstances justifying a departure from this general practice. Exceptional circumstances might include a case of a particular length or complexity, necessitating giving the accused copies of documents to allow the formulation of a response. Even in this situation, the solicitor should only allow the client limited controlled access on the clear understanding that the client must keep the documents confidential and as to how long they may be kept.

In the view of the Society, under no circumstances should a client ever be given possession of sensitive documents such as precognitions and statements of victims in sexual cases, medical or post mortem reports, explicit photographs, or any documents which might disclose the private address or telephone numbers of witnesses.

There are unfortunate and worrying examples of problems which can arise if these guidelines are not observed: *e.g.* copies of witness statements could be circulated in the public domain, leading to witnesses being intimidated; the statements of victims of sexual crimes could be used as a form of pornography within prison; an extract from a firearms register complete with addresses and types of weapon has been circulated in a prison.

In addition, those solicitors who observe best practice find themselves coming under pressure from clients who indicate that instructions will be withdrawn if they are not provided with copy precognitions.

NOTE
[1] The Council has recently approved the following amendments to the Code of Conduct for Criminal Work. These amendments shall have effect from 1st April 1998.

12 Retention of Papers[1]

12.1 In murder cases and other cases involving life imprisonment, the papers should be retained indefinitely.

12.2 In other Solemn and in any Summary case, the papers should be retained for 3 years.
As a general rule, solicitors might regard it as good practice in every case to retain indefinitely a copy of the Complaint or Indictment and a copy of the Legal Aid Certificate.

GUIDANCE NOTE

Another issue associated with case papers is the question of the length of time such papers should be retained once a case has been concluded and how such papers should ultimately be destroyed if at all.

The options for retention are—
(1) indefinitely;
(2) destruction after a fixed period;
(3) destruction at the discretion of the solicitor; or

(4) a combination of the above, depending on the nature of the case and the likelihood or risk that reference to the original case papers will be necessary.

The Society is conscious of the consequences of recommending retention of too many papers for too long, having regard to the difficulties of office storage and the expense of "off-site" storage. On the other hand, certain types of cases involve offences of such gravity, complexity or high public profile, that the possibility of issues arising in future years is a real one. Other offences may have sentence implications in the short to mid-term: *e.g.* petitions for restoration of a driving licence after disqualification; reimposing the unexpired portion of a sentence after re-offending. Solemn cases might be expected to throw up more difficulties than Summary.

Destruction of Case Papers

Solicitors should note that when case papers are being destroyed it is vital that this is done in a comprehensive, secure and confidential way. If the solicitor does not destroy the papers personally, then they should be destroyed by a suitably qualified commercial firm.

NOTE
[1] The Council approved these amendments to the Code of Conduct for Criminal Work, with effect from 1st April 1998.

Practice Guidelines

Guidelines for the Recruitment of Staff to Undertake Investment Business

[November 1992]

In May 1990 the Securities and Investments Board (SIB) published consultation paper no. 40 on Training and Competence in the Financial Services Industry (The McDonald Report). Among the recommendations made by the SIB were several relating to the recruitment of individuals engaged in financial services work.

As required by the SIB the undernoted guidelines have been prepared by the Society's Investor Protection Committee and apply where solicitors' firms recruit staff to conduct or assist in conducting their investment business—staff for this purpose include those who are not solicitors.

The Guidelines which are to be complied with prior to conclusion of a contract of employment are:

(1) The firm requires to be authorised by the Law Society of Scotland to conduct investment business.

(2) The responsibility for compliance with the Society's Conduct of Investment Business Rules remains with the partners of the firm, who are also responsible for the supervision and discipline of their staff.

(3) The firm is expected to take up and be satisfied with personal and employment references of those members of staff recruited to work directly, or indirectly, in the firm's investment business area.

(4) If such staff have previously been employed by another authorised person, it is recommended that the firm check and be reasonably satisfied with the response from the relevant regulatory agency, such as the Financial Intermediaries, Managers and Brokers Regulatory Association (FIMBRA).

(5) The firm should ask the applicant whether he has a criminal record, excluding minor convictions such as road traffic offences. In the event of a criminal record being disclosed the Society should be consulted.

(6) The firm should seek to ensure that new staff are familiar and conversant with the Society's Conduct of Investment Business Rules and/or Accounts Rules as appropriate before they commence work in the firm's investment business area.

(7) It is recommended that the firm should keep a written record of compliance with the Guidelines.

Conflict of Interest in Commercial Security Transactions

[March 1994]

The Scottish banks have confirmed that they all now intend to introduce policies in the very near future whereby in commercial security transactions they will instruct separate solicitors to represent them. Their solicitors will, as has been the custom recover their fees and outlays from the borrower. It is the intention of the Scottish banks that they will use solicitors throughout Scotland and will not centralise their commercial security work. Furthermore the banks have indicated that they will expect those solicitors whom they instruct to charge reasonable fees.

[The President] understands that while this agreement has been reached with the Scottish banks, other banks operating in Scotland and members of the British Bankers Association will adopt similar policies.

Notwithstanding this general policy, the Scottish banks wish to reserve the right to instruct the borrower's solicitor to act for them, in what they described as *de minimis* cases. Each bank may adopt a different view on what constitutes a *de minimis* case, but the Council expects that the banks will act responsibly when deciding on their individual policies.

The Council believes it would be helpful if a definition is provided of a commercial security transaction. It is:

"A commercial security transaction relates to the secured lending to a customer of a bank or other lending institution where the purpose of the loan is clearly for the customer's business purposes."

However we must remind you, that should you receive instructions to act for a lender and a borrower in *any* type of transaction, but particularly a commercial security transaction you must exercise your judgment standing the provisions of the Solicitors (Scotland) Practice Rules 1986 (the Conflict of Interest Rules) as to whether you can properly act for both parties. It is appropriate that in exercising that judgment you take account of the circumstances which might arise. There follow certain examples which you may find helpful when you exercise your professional judgment. You should not forget, that should you decide to act for both lender and borrower (even in what purports to be a *de minimis* case) and ultimately a claim arises, you may have exposed yourself and your firm to the risk of bearing a double excess/deductible and the possibility of a loading on your master policy premium.

Finally, please do not hesitate to contact the Society if you feel you require further advice or guidance in this type of transaction.

Examples of conflicts of interest in commercial security transactions
The following illustrate some of the instances where lenders and borrowers have separate interests in commercial security transactions.

Disclosure of all relevant circumstances
1. Either:
   (*a*) the solicitor may know more of the borrower's position than has been communicated to the lender or *vice versa*; or
   (*b*) there may have been a reluctance by the borrower or lender fully to disclose their respective positions because of dual representation.
This clearly affects the extent to which impartial "best advice" can be given.

Ongoing negotiations
2. Negotiations between the borrower and lender may have only reached the "Outline Terms' stage—requiring further detailed consideration or negotiation of covenants/undertakings/events of default. In such negotiations the borrower and lender may have different negotiating strengths—and thus there may be competing pressures on the solicitor as to whose interests are to be promoted.

Defects in title
3. While a borrower may be prepared to "live with" a minor defect in title or some lack of planning or building consent the lender may take an entirely different stance.

Security by companies
4. Apart from the complexities and time restraints for registration of security, companies may well be subject to negative or restrictive covenants or powers affecting the security on which the borrower but not necessarily the lender, may be prepared to take a commercial view. This may merit separate consideration and advice.

Competing creditors ranking agreements
5. The circumstances as to the inter-relationship/enforcement of security between lenders may merit separate consideration and advice. Banks may not have "standard forms" of ranking agreements and this clearly may involve a solicitor in preparing a document and negotiating its terms on points which have a bearing on the borrower's position.

Security over commercial property
6. The permitted use, associated licences/quotas and specific standard conditions may merit separate consideration and advice as they may not be covered by pre-printed "standard" bank forms. Particular risks arise on the

transfer of a licence where the lender's interests will sometimes conflict with the borrower's commercial ambitions.

Leased property as security

7. The circumstances in which a lender requires protection in the event of irritancy may merit separate consideration and advice. Invariably the borrower is trying to strike the best deal while he is in occupancy while the lender needs protection in the event of the borrower's failure through insolvency or otherwise.

Enforcement of security

8. The solicitor acting for both borrower and lender may be placed in difficulty in the event of subsequent enforcement of a security. For whom does the solicitor act in such circumstances? Do both clients know and understand their respective positions?

Powerful clients

9. A major business client may bring subtle or even open pressures on a solicitor to follow a particular course or to turn a blind eye to a matter which could prejudice a lender's position, *e.g.* discrepancies between a valuation and purchase price.

All sums due: securities

10. Solicitors should be mindful to advise fully, joint obligants (husbands and wives) of the nature of an "all sums due" security. In particular it should be drawn to their attention that additional loans for example in respect of one obligant's business, may give rise to further secured borrowings without the other obligant requiring to sign the documentation.

Companies—*ultra vires*

11. Following changes to the *ultra vires* doctrine lenders may be able to rely on the provisions of what is now section 35 of the 1985 Companies Act.

If the solicitors involved act solely for the lender they would, as a generality, be entitled to rely on these same provisions if asked to do so by the instructing lender. On the other hand if the solicitors act also for the borrowing company it is quite clear that the solicitors would require to carry out a full examination of the company's memorandum and articles of association, since section 35 only provides protection for third parties—it does not for example excuse the directors from any liability arising from acting *ultra vires*. In such circumstances the solicitors, as agents for the lender, would become aware of any *ultra vires* aspect of the arrangements and the lender could be similarly tainted with this knowledge.

Guide to Professional Conduct and Ethics in Insolvency

[July 1995]

The Council has resolved that the Society of Practitioners of Insolvency Ethical Guidelines (the SPI Guidelines), shall, with effect from 1st September 1995, apply to all work carried out by an Insolvency Practitioner authorised by the Law Society of Scotland.

The SPI Guidelines are in addition to the obligations incumbent upon solicitors arising out of the Code of Conduct for Scottish solicitors and, in the event of any conflict between the two, the Law Society of Scotland Code of Conduct shall have precedence.

The SPI Guidelines may be varied from time to time and all variations must be observed by Insolvency Practitioners.

(In the event of any conflict between the SPI Guidelines and the Code of Conduct, the Insolvency Practitioner should consult the Law Society of Scotland).

GUIDE TO PROFESSIONAL ETHICS IN INSOLVENCY

Introductory note

1. [This paragraph refers to the revision of the Guide and its adoption by the Society of Practitioners of Insolvency with effect from 1st July 1993.]

2. The fundamental principles direct the attention of each member to the overriding importance in his or her professional life of integrity and objectivity. These elements are as important in the acceptance and conduct of insolvency work as in any other area of professional life. In certain insolvency roles the preservation of objectivity needs to be protected and demonstrated by the maintenance of a member's independence from influences which could affect his or her objectivity. Before a member accepts or carries out those roles, which are detailed in the guidance which follows, the member must not only be satisfied as to the actual objectivity which he can bring to his judgment and decisions but must also be mindful of how his or her acceptance and conduct will be perceived by others.

3. For the purposes of this Guide, "principal" means a sole practitioner, a partner in a firm or a director of a corporate practice.

OBTAINING INSOLVENCY WORK

4. The special nature of insolvency appointments makes the payment or offer of any commission for, or the furnishing of any valuable consideration towards, the introduction of insolvency appointments inappropriate.

5. The attention of members is also drawn to section 164 of the Insolvency Act 1986, which creates an offence punishable by a fine of offering to a member or creditor of a company any valuable consideration with a view to securing nomination as a liquidator, and to the Insolvency Rules 1986, which provide for remuneration to be disallowed to a liquidator (rule 4.150) or trustee (rule 6.148) whose appointment has been procured by improper solicitation.

Solicitation for proxies

6. In addition to any statutory consequences which it may incur, solicitation for insolvency work in any way amounting to that which a reasonable person would regard as harassment, renders a member liable to reference to the Investigation Committee.

PROFESSIONAL INDEPENDENCE AND THE ACCEPTANCE OF INSOLVENCY APPOINTMENTS

General

7. The following paragraphs refer to specific situations in which a member may not properly accept appointment. In situations other than those dealt with, a member should only accept office in any insolvency role sequential to one in which the member or his or her practice or a current employee of the practice has previously acted after giving careful consideration to the implications of acceptance in all the circumstances of the case and satisfying him- or herself that objectivity is unlikely to be compromised by a prospective conflict of interest or otherwise. If he or she remains in doubt as to his or her position, the member should seek advice from the Ethics Committee via the Secretariat.

8. The attention of members is drawn to the statutory disqualification on acting as an insolvency practitioner in section 390 of the Insolvency Act 1986.

Joint appointments

9. A member who is invited to accept an insolvency appointment jointly with another practitioner should be guided by similar principles to those set out in relation to sole appointments. Where a member is specifically precluded by the guidance which follows from accepting an insolvency appointment as an individual, a joint appointment will not render the appointment acceptable.

Appointment as supervisor of a company voluntary arrangement, administrator, administrative or other receiver

10. Where there has been a material professional relationship (as to which see paragraphs 13 to 16 (below)) with a company, no principal or employee of the practice should accept appointment as supervisor of a voluntary arrangement, administrator or administrative or other receiver in relation to that company. (See also paragraphs 17, 18, 30 and 31 (below).)

Appointment as supervisor of an individual voluntary arrangement, trustee in bankruptcy or trustee under a deed of arrangement

11. Where there has been a material professional relationship (as to which see paragraphs 13 to 16 (below)) with a client, no principal or employee of the practice should accept appointment as supervisor of a voluntary arrangement or as trustee in bankruptcy or as a trustee under a deed registered under the Deeds of Arrangement Act 1914 in relation to that client. (See also paragraphs 30 and 31 (below).)

Appointment as liquidator

12. Where there has been a material professional relationship (as to which see paragraphs 13 to 16 (below)) with a company, no principal or employee of the practice should accept appointment as liquidator of the company if the company is insolvent. Where the company is solvent, such appointment should not be accepted without careful consideration being given to all the implications of acceptance in the particular case and a member should satisfy him- or herself that the directors' declaration of solvency is likely to be substantiated by events. (See also paragraphs 30 and 31 (below).)

Material professional relationship

13. A material professional relationship with a client, such as is referred to in paragraphs 10, 11 and 12 (above) arises where a practice or, subject to the provisions of paragraphs 30 and 31 (below), a principal or employee of a practice is carrying out, or has during the previous three years carried out, material professional work for that client. Material professional work would include the following:

(i) where a practice or person has carried out, or has been appointed to carry out, audit work for a company or individual to which the appointment is being considered; or

(ii) where a practice or person has carried out one or more assignments, whether or a continuing nature or not, of such overall significance or in such circumstances that a member's objectivity in carrying out a subsequent insolvency appointment could be or could reasonably be seen to be prejudiced.

14. A material professional relationship with a company or individual (as referred to in paragraphs 10, 11 and 12 (above)) includes any material professional relationship with companies or entities controlled by that company or individual or under common control where the relationship is material in the context of the company or individual to whom appointment is being sought or considered. A material professional relationship could also arise where a practice or person has carried out professional work for any director or shadow director of a company of such a nature that a member's objectivity in carrying out a subsequent insolvency appointment in relation to that company could be or could reasonably be seen to be prejudiced.

15. In forming views as to whether a material professional relationship exists, members should have regard to existing or previous relationships with firms with which they are, or have been, associated which might affect or appear to affect their objectivity, including relationships whereby they or their firm are held out by name association or other public statements as being part of a national or international association.

16. A member should take reasonable steps prior to his or her acceptance of any insolvency appointment to ascertain whether any of the above work has been performed.

Appointment as investigating accountant at the instigation of a creditor
17. A material professional relationship would not normally arise where the relationship is one which springs from the appointment of the practice by, or at the instigation of, a creditor or other party having an actual or potential financial interest in a company or business to investigate, monitor or advise on its affairs, provided that:
  (*a*) there has not been a direct involvement by a principal or employee of the practice in the management of the company or business; and
  (*b*) the practice has its principal client relationship with the creditor or other party, rather than with the company or proprietor of the business, and the company or the proprietor of the business is aware of this.

18. If the circumstances of the initial appointment are such as to prevent the open discussion of the financial affairs of the company with the directors, an investigating member or other principal in the practice may be called upon to justify the propriety of their acceptance of the subsequent appointment.

Conversion of members' voluntary winding up into creditors' voluntary winding up
19. Where a member has accepted appointment as liquidator in a members' voluntary winding up and is obliged to summon a creditors' meeting under section 95 of the Insolvency Act 1986, because it appears that the company will be unable to pay its debts in full within the period stated in the directors' declaration of solvency, the member's continuance as liquidator will depend on whether he or she believes that the company will eventually be able to pay it debts in full or not.
  (*a*) If the company will not be able to pay its debts in full and the member has previously had a material professional relationship with the company such as is set out in paragraphs 13 to 16 (above), he or she should not accept nomination under the creditors' winding up.
  (*b*) If the company will not be able to pay its debts in full but the member has had no such material professional relationship, he or she may accept nomination by the creditors and continue as liquidator with the creditors' approval, subject to giving the careful consideration as to the implications, etc., referred to in paragraph 7 (above).
  (*c*) If the member believes that the company will eventually be able to pay its debts in full he or she may accept nomination by the creditors and continue as liquidator. However, if it should subsequently appear that this belief was mistaken the member must then offer his or her resignation and may not accept re-appointment if he or she has previously had a material professional relationship with the company.

Insolvent liquidation following appointment as administrative or other receiver

20. Where a principal or employee of a practice (subject to the provisions of paragraphs 30 and 31 (below)) is, or in the previous three years has been, administrative receiver of a company or a receiver, under the Law of Property Act 1925 or otherwise, of any of its assets, no principal or employee of the practice should accept appointment as liquidator of the company in an insolvent liquidation. This restriction does not apply where the previous appointment was made by the court. However, before a court-appointed receiver accepts subsequent appointment as liquidator, he or she should give careful consideration as to whether his or her objectivity could be open to question and, if so, the appointment should be refused.

Liquidation following appointment as supervisor of a voluntary arrangement or administrator

21. Where a member, or any principal or employee of his or her practice, has been supervisor of a voluntary arrangement or administrator of a company, the member may, if the considerations indicated in paragraph 7 (above) are satisfied, accept appointment as liquidator if so nominated by the creditors or appointed by the Secretary of State under section 137 of the Insolvency Act 1986.

22. However, where the relevant previous role is that of administrator, the member should not accept nomination or appointment as liquidator unless either:

    (*a*) the member has the support of a creditors' committee appointed under section 26 of the Insolvency Act 1986; or

    (*b*) he or she has the support of a meeting of creditors called either under the Act or informally, of which all known creditors have been given notice.

Bankruptcy following appointment as supervisor of individual voluntary arrangement

23. Where a member, or any principal or employee of his or her practice, has been supervisor of a voluntary arrangement in relation to a debtor, the member may, provided the considerations indicated in paragraph 7 (above) are satisfied, accept appointment as trustee in bankruptcy of that debtor provided that it is effected by a general meeting of the creditors under the provisions of section 292(1)(*a*) of the Insolvency Act 1986 or if the member has been appointed by the court under section 297(5) of the Act or by the Secretary of State under section 296 of the Act.

Administration following appointment as administrative receiver or LPA or other receiver

24. Where a principal or employee of a practice (subject to the provisions of paragraphs 30 and 31 (below)) is, or in the previous three years has been, an administrative receiver of a company or a receiver, under the Law of Property Act 1925 or otherwise, of any of its assets, no principal or employee of the practice should accept appointment as administrator of the company, unless the previous appointment was made by the court.

Supervision of a voluntary arrangement following appointment as administrative receiver

25. Where a principal or employee of a practice (subject to the provisions of paragraphs 30 and 31 (below)) is, or in the previous three years has been, an administrative receiver of a company, no principal or employee of the practice should accept appointment as supervisor of a voluntary arrangement in relation to that company.

Audit following appointment as supervisor of a voluntary arrangement, administrator or administrative or other receiver

26. Where a principal or employee of a practice (subject to the provisions of paragraphs 30 and 31 (below)) has acted as supervisor of a voluntary arrangement, administrator or administrative receiver of a company or receiver of any of its assets, no principal or employee of the practice should accept appointment as auditor of the company for any accounting period during which the supervisor, administrator or receiver acted.

Pension schemes of companies in liquidation, administration or receivership—appointment of "Independent Trustee"

27. A member should not appoint a principal or employee of his practice, or any close connection of any of the above or of himself, as "Independent Trustee" of the pension scheme of a company of which he is the liquidator, administrator or administrative or other receiver. A member should be aware of the threat to objectivity if he were to engage in regular or reciprocal arrangements in relation to such appointments with another practice or organisation.

Other potential conflicts of interest

(i) Group, associated and family-connected companies
28. Members should be particularly aware of the difficulties likely to arise from the existence of inter-company transactions or guarantees in group, associated or "family-connected" company situations. Acceptance of an insolvency appointment in relation to more than one company in the group or association may raise issues of conflict of interest. Nevertheless, it may be impracticable for a series of different insolvency practitioners to act. A member should not accept multiple appointments in such situations unless he or she is satisfied that he or she is able to take steps to minimise problems of conflict and that his or her overall integrity and objectivity are, and are seen to be, maintained.

(ii) Relationships between insolvent individuals and insolvent companies
29. A member who, or a principal or employee of whose practice, is acting as insolvency practitioner in relation to an individual may be asked to accept an insolvency appointment in relation to a company of which the debtor is a major shareholder or creditor or where the company is a creditor of the debtor. It is essential, if the member is to accept the new appointment, that he or she should be able to show that the steps indicated in paragraph 28 (above) have been taken. Similar considerations apply if it is the company appointment which precedes the individual appointment.

Transfer of principals and employees including practice merger
30. When two or more practices merge, principals and employees of the merged practice become subject to common ethical constraints in relation to accepting new insolvency appointments to clients of either of the former practices. However, existing appointments which are rendered in apparent breach of the guidance by such merger need not be determined automatically, provided that a considered review of the situation by the practice discloses no obvious and immediate conflict, such as a potential need to sue a new colleague.

31. Where a principal or an employee of a practice has, in any former practice, undertaken work upon the affairs of the company or debtor in a capacity which is incompatible with an insolvency assignment of his or her new practice, he or she should not personally work or be employed on that assignment, save in the case of an employee of such junior status that his or her duties in the former practice did not involve the exercise of any material professional judgement or discretion.

Personal relationships
32. The current legislation includes specific duties to report on the conduct of directors or shadow directors of an insolvent company. (See for

example the requirement under section 7(a) of the Company Directors Disqualification Act 1986 to report "unfit" conduct to the Secretary of State and sections 213 and 214 of the Insolvency Act 1986 on fraudulent trading and wrongful trading.) A member should have regard at all times to the spirit of the guidance on independence set out in paragraph 2 (above) and should not accept an insolvency appointment in relation to an individual or a company where any personal connection with the individual or with a director, former director or shadow director is such as to impair or reasonably appear to impair the member's objectivity. The attention of members is also drawn to the definitions relating to the persons "connected" with a company in sections 249 and 435 of the Insolvency Act 1986.

Relationship with a debenture holder

33. A member should, in general, decline to accept an insolvency appointment in relation to a company if he or she or a principal or employee of the practice has such a personal or close and distinct business connection with the debenture holder as might impair or appear to impair the member's objectivity. It is not considered likely that a "close and distinct business connection" would normally exist between an insolvency practitioner and, for example, a clearing bank or major financial institution. However, such a close and distinct business connection would exist where a member, or a principal or employee of the practice, holds an insolvency appointment in relation to such a bank or financial institution.

Purchase of the assets of an insolvent company or debtor

34. The Insolvency Rules 1986 contain prohibitions on members of a liquidation or creditors' committee acquiring any asset in the estate of an insolvent company or debtor (save with leave of the court or the committee). Save in circumstances which clearly do not impair his or her objectivity, a member appointed to any insolvency appointment in relation to a company or debtor should not him- or herself acquire directly or indirectly any of the assets of the company or debtor nor knowingly permit any principal or employee of his or her practice, or any close relative of the member or of a principal or employee, directly or indirectly to do so.

35. Where a contract is already in existence between the insolvent company or debtor and a principal or an employee of the member's practice, the member should seek guidance from the Ethics Committee via the Secretariat as to the propriety of accepting the appointment.

Guideline on Advertising Fees

[September 1995]

[This Guideline is printed at the end of the Solicitors (Scotland) (Advertising and Promotion) Practice Rules 1995, *supra*.]

[1] Law Society Guidance Notes on Exhibition of Title Deeds

In a conveyancing transaction, the seller/landlord's solicitor should, other than in exceptional circumstances, forward the title deeds for examination by the purchaser/tenant's solicitor at the latter's office.

If a title is likely to be in heavy demand, the seller/landlord's solicitor should make up sufficient sets of extracts and/or copies to ensure that the progress of transactions is not impeded by the unavailability of deeds. In such a case, it is acceptable to send copies of deeds, provided the originals or extracts are available for examination at the offices of the seller/landlord's solicitor if so desired.

Exceptional circumstances would include, for example, the situation where an extract did not contain the plan annexed to the original deed, which was in particularly heavy demand, or in fragile condition; or where the number of relevant deeds involved would render compliance with the guideline impracticable.

NOTES
[1] Reproduced with kind permission of the Law Society of Scotland, Conveyancing Committee. The Guidance note first appeared in J.L.S.S., vol. 41, No. 5, May 1996.

[1] Law Society's Guidance Notes to the Investment Business Rules and Regulations

NOTE
[1] Reproduced with the kind permission of the Law Society of Scotland.

CONTENTS

PART I

INTRODUCTION

PART II

INVESTMENT BUSINESS TRAINING

PART III

INVESTMENT BUSINESS COMPLIANCE CERTIFICATE RULES

PART IV

GENERAL OBLIGATIONS AND RECORD KEEPING REQUIREMENTS

PART V

INVESTMENT MANAGEMENT

Part VI

Trusts and Executries

Part VII

Part VIII

Safekeeping of Clients' Documents of Title—Custody

Part IX

Discipline

Part I

Introduction

A. *Regulatory Structure*

The financial services industry within the United Kingdom is governed by the Financial Services Act 1986 (FSA) which became fully operational in October 1988. The purpose of the Act is to regulate all investment advisers and to provide protection for investors. The Act distinguishes between two types of advisers:—

1. Independent Financial Advisers (IFAs)—provide independent advice and are not tied to any one financial services company.

2. Appointed representatives—can only act and provide advice on the products of the company they represent.

The overall regulator in the United Kingdom is the Securities and Investments Board (SIB). The SIB is ultimately responsible for the regulatory environment although it has currently delegated the day to day management of investment business to a number of other organisations which can be divided into two broad groups:—

1. Self-regulating organisations (SROs)—there are currently three SROs who are:—

(i) The Securities and Futures Authority (SFA)—regulates firms which deal in or advise on securities, futures and options;

(ii) Investment Management Regulatory Organisation (IMRO)—regulates firms whose main function is managing funds *i.e.* investment fund managers; and

(iii) Personal Investment Authority (PIA)—regulates life companies, unit trust companies and independent financial advisers.

2. Recognised Professional Bodies (RPBs)—there are currently nine RPBs who are responsible for regulating their own professional members who conduct investment business.

The Government has announced that it is its intention to establish a new regulatory authority (NewRO). NewRO will be a "Super SIB" as it will take over the responsibility of front line regulation from the SROs which will be abolished. NewRO will also take control of the supervision and surveillance division of the Bank of England and it will assume the regulatory functions of the Building Societies Commission, the Friendly Societies Commission, the Insurance Directorate of the Department of Trade & Industry and the Registry of Friendly Societies. At the time of going to press, the Government has not yet made a policy decision as to whether the RPBs are to be assumed into NewRO. It is anticipated the NewRO will be fully operational by the beginning of the year 2000.

B. *The Law Society of Scotland Regulatory Structure*
The Law Society of Scotland has been an RPB since 1988. The Society therefore authorises firms who wish to conduct investment business. There are currently 550 firms out of a total of 1,258 authorised by the Society to conduct investment business. The Society's detailed procedures on how firms must conduct investment business are contained in the following Rules:—
1. Solicitors (Scotland) Investment Business Training Regulations 1994—these came into force on 1 July 1994.
2. Solicitors (Scotland) (Conduct of Investment Business) Practice Rules 1997—these Rules come into force on 1st January 1998. These rules are known as the CBRs.
3. Solicitors (Scotland) Investment Business Compliance Certificate Rules 1997—these Rules come into force on 1st January 1998. These rules are known as the CCRs.

A firm which wishes to conduct investment business has to apply to the Society, who on receipt of this request will send the firm the appropriate application form. On approval of a firm's application to conduct investment business the Society will issue that firm with an Investment Business Certificate (IBC). This certificate must be displayed in the firm's offices.

A firm must pay an annual subscription to the Society in November each year in order to maintain its IBC. The fee for 1997/98 is £135 per authorised person.

C. *Types of Investments and Investment Business*
The definition of an investment is given in FSA Schedule I Part 1. Bank and building society deposits, most national savings products and term assurance policies (i.e. mortgage protection policies) are not investments for the purposes of the FSA. The FSA lists five different types of activity which constitute investment business and these are:—
1. Dealing in investments on behalf of others;
2. Arranging deals in investments;
3. Managing investments;
4. Advising on investments; and
5. Establishing or operating a collective investment scheme (*i.e.* unit trusts).

It is FSA Schedule II, Parts 2 and 3 which lists the activities which constitute investment business.

D. *Involvement of Solicitors in Investment Business*
The types of investment products solicitors will generally deal with are (a) shares; (b) Government Bonds (Gilts) and local authority loan stock; (c) life assurance policies; and (d) pension policies.

There are four levels of involvement which a firm may have in conducting investment business and these are:—

1. Execution only—this is where a firm effects a transaction for a client but the client does not rely on the firm to advise him on or to exercise any judgement on his behalf as to the merits or suitability for him of the transaction (*e.g.* the client comes in and give a clear instruction to the solicitor to buy 10,000 Marks & Spencer shares).

2. Taking instruction but giving no advice—here the client wishes to make an investment and the solicitor merely obtains the advice of a specialist financial adviser (*i.e.* a stockbroker) and then communicates the specialist's advice to the client but gives no comment on such advice. This activity does not fall within the definition of investment management.

3. Taking instruction but giving advice—here the client seeks the solicitor's views on what investments he should make. The solicitor again obtains advice from a specialist financial adviser, but this time the solicitor comments on the advice of the specialist.

4. Investment management—there are two types of investment management which a firm may enter into:—

(i) *Portfolio management*—this is where a firm has assumed responsibility for advising on or commenting upon the investments comprised in a client's portfolio.

(ii) *Discretionary portfolio management*—as in (a) above, but the firm has the authority to effect transactions for the client's portfolio at its own discretion without taking the advice of the client.

Most portfolios are made up of shares and/or gilts but it is possible for a portfolio to include unit trusts and life policies.

E. *Two Principles of Investment Business*
There are two basic principles which underline the conduct of all investment business and these are:—

1. Best advice (Rule 4.4)—To provide best advice a firm must know its clients and the market.

In order for a firm to know its client, a client fact sheet must be prepared for that client in advance of conducting investment business. A client fact sheet is not required where investment business is undertaken on an execution-only basis. The client must also be informed of the nature of the risks involved in any investment transaction. Furthermore, a firm must be able to demonstrate that it knows the market in relation to the investment products on which it provides advice.

The net result of this process of best advice—knowing the client and knowing the market—will be that a firm will be able to make a recommendation on a particular investment which is most suitable to a particular client in order to ensure that the client's particular investment objectives are met.

2. Best execution (Rule 4.5)—Once a firm "knows its clients" and "knows the market" and has therefore given best advice, the next step is to acquire or sell the product for the client in line with best execution. Best execution means that any transaction is effected/arranged with due timeliness and on terms that may reasonably be regarded at the best available at the time in the best interests of the client.

PART II

INVESTMENT BUSINESS TRAINING

A. *Introduction*
In 1994 the Society was required by the SIB to introduce a training regime for those individuals (both solicitors and non-solicitors) who conduct investment business within a firm. The requirements are incorporated in the Solicitors (Scotland) Investment Business Training Regulations 1994 which have been in operation since July 1994.
The two principal requirements under the Regulations are:—
1. Any individual who wishes to conduct investment business must be qualified by way of an examination or an exemption from the examination; and

2. Any individual conducting investment business must undertake a certain amount of continuing professional development in investment business per annum.

B. *Exemption from the Examination*

The Regulations contained transitional provisions under Regulation 7 that allowed a solicitor or a non-solicitor employee who had sufficient investment business experience to apply for an exemption from the examination. The exemption procedure was however a limited "window of opportunity" as the deadline for submission of an exemption application to the Society was 30th November 1994. Any individual who does not hold an exemption from the examination must pass the appropriate examination.

C. *Investment Business Examination*

The Society has recognised two examinations as investment business qualifications which are appropriate for those who wish to conduct investment business. These qualifications are:—

1. The Investment Advice Certificate of the Securities Institute—This is a three paper examination run by the Securities Institute. The first two papers are multiple choice while the third paper is a case study paper. All three papers must be passed for an individual to conduct investment business within a firm.

All details of the examination together with guidelines, application forms and study packs are available from the Securities Institute and not the Society. The Securities Institute address is:

> The Securities Institute,
> Centurion House,
> 24 Monument Street,
> London. EC3R 8AJ.
> Telephone: 0171 626 3191
> Fax: 0171 626 7432

This examination is suitable for those individuals who wish to specialise in stock exchange investments.

2. The Financial Planning Certificate of the Chartered Insurance Institute—This is also a three paper examination with the first two papers being multiple choice papers and the third being a case study paper. Again, all three papers have to be passed before an individual can conduct investment business within a firm. All details of this examination together with study packs are available from the Chartered Insurance Institute and not the Society. The Chartered Insurance Institute's address is:—

> The Chartered Insurance Institute,
> 31 Hillcrest Road,
> South Woodford,
> London. E18 2JP.
> Telephone: 0181 989 8464
> Fax: 0181 530 3052

D. *Qualifications Equivalent to the Society's Principal Two Examinations*

In addition to the above two examinations, the Society has recognised a range of other investment qualifications which are deemed equivalent to both the I.A.C. and the F.P.C. If a solicitor or non-solicitor holds one of the following qualifications they will not be required to sit and pass the I.A.C. or F.P.C.

To date the Society has recognised the following qualifications as equivalent to the I.A.C. and F.P.C.:—

1. The Securities Product Certificate of the Securities Institute.
2. The Securities Institute Diploma.
3. Membership of the Securities Institute.

4. The Investment Management Certificate of the Institute of Investment Management & Research.
5. The Associate Examination of the Institute of Investment Management & Research.
6. Membership of the Life Insurance Association.
7. The Advance Financial Planning Certificate.
8. Associateship of the Life Insurance Association.
9. Fellowship of the Life Insurance Association.
10. Associateship of the Institute of Financial Planning.
11. Fellowship of the Institute of Financial Planning.

If an individual holds another qualification outwith the above list that individual may apply to the Society's Council to have his investment business qualification recognised as being of a standard equivalent to one of the above examinations. Such an application must be made in terms of Regulation 6 of the Training Regulations.

E. *Continuing Professional Development*

The investment business C.P.D. requirements for all those solicitors and non-solicitor employees undertaking investment business came into force on 1st November 1995. The requirement is that all such individuals must undertake 5 hours of investment business C.P.D. per annum. The C.P.D. can either be in the form of private or group study and a record of compliance with the Training Regulations must be maintained.

For solicitors who are required by the general C.P.D. Regulations to undertake 20 hours of C.P.D. per annum, the 5 hours investment C.P.D. is part of and *not* in addition to this 20 hours. A solicitor can record his investment business C.P.D. on their general C.P.D. record card. A non-solicitor employee will have to make a separate record of his investment business C.P.D.

F. *Notification of Investment Business Qualification to the Society*

A firm, under Rule 9.5 of the 1997 C.B.R.s, must notify the Society of the following circumstances in relation to qualification under the Training Regulations.

1. A firm must notify the Society *in writing* of the identity of any individual within the firm who becomes qualified by passing the appropriate examination. This notification must be made within two months of such qualification.

Copies of the individual's pass certificates must be sent to the Society. In addition, where the individual who has become qualified is a non-solicitor, that individual's date of birth, National Insurance Number and date of commencement with the firm must also be provided to the Society.

2. Where a non-solicitor who did conduct investment business for a firm ceases to be an employee of that firm, the Society must be notified of such cessation within one month.

PART III

INVESTMENT BUSINESS COMPLIANCE CERTIFICATE RULES

A. *Introduction*

The Solicitors (Scotland) Investment Business Compliance Certificate Rules (CCRs) come into operation on 1st January 1998. From that date the Solicitors (Scotland) Compliance Certificate Rules 1994 are repealed and will no longer be in force.

B. *Self-Certification*

The principal change which is introduced by these new CCRs is the introduction of self-certification. What this means is that a firm can self-certify that it has complied with the Conduct of Investment Business Rules and it will no longer be necessary for a firm to employ an accountant to verify such compliance. A firm can, if it so wishes, employ an accountant to assist in the preparation of the Investment Business Compliance Certificate under the CCRs. Such assistance may involve the external accountant checking a firm's records to confirm the contents of the Compliance Certificate.

C. *Investment Business Compliance Certificate*

The Rules require a firm to submit to the Society the new style Investment Business Compliance Certificate which is reproduced in the Schedule to the CCRs. This certificate has to be produced for each six-month period of a firm's accounting year. This means that two such certificates have to be submitted to the Society. Furthermore, each certificate must be submitted to the Society within one month of the end of each six-month accounting period.

The certificate has to be signed by two partners of the firm, at least one of whom has passed, or is exempt from the investment business examination. Where the firm is a sole practitioner this signature requirement is reduced to one. **Where a firm has two or more places of business and where each maintains separate investment business records a separate Investment Business Compliance Certificate must be delivered in respect of each place of business.**

D. *Questions Within the Investment Business Compliance Certificate*

The new style Investment Business Compliance Certificate is a mixture of the old Management Letter and Compliance Certificate. It contains nine questions most of which have explanatory notes.

Question 1. Extent of investment business—A firm has to verify that its gross income did not derive wholly or mainly from investment business. Under the FSA, a firm can only derive up to 49% of its total income from investment business.

Under Question 1, the firm is asked to estimate the percentage of its total income arising from investment business. This percentage is calculated on the total fees rendered to the date of the certificate.

Question 2. Scope of investment business—This question lists 11 different categories of investment business and the firm has to identify which of the 11 categories it has conducted in the accounting period.

Question 3. Scope of securities, transactions and discretionary investment management—This question is made up of five constituent parts. Within part 3 the firm is asked to confirm that it has maintained the necessary transaction records in respect of purchases, sales and transfers in shares. The firm is then asked to confirm how many statements of terms of business/written contracts/client agreements were in force at the date of the Investment Business Compliance Certificate.

For those firms which conduct discretionary investment management there are three additional questions and these are:—

1. Identification of the number of discretionary managed portfolios in excess of £100,000 at the date of the Investment Business Compliance Certificate.
2. The number of individual share transactions in excess of £100,000 affected or arranged on a discretionary basis during the accounting period.
3. The total value of all the funds comprised in the discretionary portfolios at the date of the Investment Business Compliance Certificate.

Question 4. Life policies and unit trusts—In this question the firm must identify the number of life policies and transactions in unit trusts placed both directly or indirectly through another intermediary. The name of the life company or unit trust operator must be given together with the number of life policies and unit trust units placed with each body respectively.

Question 5. Individuals authorised to conduct investment business—The firm must identify all individuals both solicitor and non-solicitor who are authorised to conduct investment business within the accounting period. The firm must also state whether those individuals are authorised by way of an exemption from or a qualification in the appropriate examination. The firm must also identify whether the individuals have undertaken the appropriate amount of CPD.

Question 6. Investment business records—Under this question a firm must confirm that it has maintained all proper records under the CBRs.

Question 7. Assistance of an external accountant—The firm must confirm whether or not it has employed an external accountant to assist in the preparation of the Investment Business Compliance Certificate.

Question 8. Other matters which require to be reported—Such other matters include the receipt of an investment business complaint during the period.

Question 9. Compliance—Finally, a firm must confirm that it has complied with the FSA, the CBRs and the Training Regulations during the accounting period.

PART IV

GENERAL OBLIGATIONS AND RECORD KEEPING REQUIREMENTS

A. *Compliance Officer*
Every firm is required to appoint a Compliance Officer under Rule 4.1(2). The officer will either be a partner or sole practitioner. The Compliance Officer will be responsible for securing compliance with all the investment business rules and regulations. Firms are advised to appoint a Compliance Officer who either holds an exemption from or a qualification in the appropriate investment business examination.

B. *Disclosure of Certification*
Under Rule 3.8 a firm must state on all its stationery, terms of business and other publications relating to investment business the following (or words to the same effect):—
"Authorised by the Law Society of Scotland to Conduct Investment Business".

C. *Terms of Business*
Where a firm has assumed responsibility for portfolio management (non-discretionary portfolio management) a client must be provided with a statement of the terms of business under which its non-discretionary portfolio management will be undertaken. See Rule 4.6(1). The terms of business must comply with the relevant parts of Schedule 1(1).
Under Rule 4.6(2), where a firm undertakes discretionary portfolio management a client must be given a written contract which complies with Schedule 1(2).
A firm must retain copies of all terms of business provided and all written contracts entered into until the expiry of ten years from the time when the terms of business provided or written contracts cease to be effective.

D. *Client Fact Sheet*

This is a simple question and answer form which shows that a firm knows its client and has undertaken sufficient investigation into a client's financial affairs in order to make the appropriate investment recommendations. Individual client investment file must contain the original client fact sheet.

A number of situations can arise when a client fact sheet is being prepared:—

1. **Client refuses to provide details**—in this situation, the firm must obtain the client's signed acknowledgement of the fact he refuses to provide some/all information and a detailed note of this should be retained in the client's file. If, as a result of this the firm is not able to give best advice, the firm should decline to act for the client.

2. **Client gives the firm incorrect/misleading information (either innocently or on purpose)**—in these circumstances firm must make an accurate record of what information has been provided and that the firm throughout has acted in good faith.

3. **Client asks the firm to complete the client fact sheet**—in this situation the client must read over the fact sheet carefully and check all the details are correct before signing it.

E. *Commission Disclosure*

The disclosure of commission for sales of life policies and unit trusts is contained in Rule 4.10. Clients must be advised that commission will be received on the sale of life policies and unit trusts. The disclosure must be made in writing to the client and give the value of the commission in cash terms. This disclosure to the client must be made before the application or proposal form is signed by the client.

The only exception to the above disclosure is contained in Rule 4.10(2). This provides that where unit trusts are purchased by a firm acting as a discretionary investment manager or on an execution only basis, the amount of commission need only be disclosed as soon as practicable after the transaction is effected or arranged.

Nothing in the Rule 4.10 overrides the general law of agency and secret profit and the requirement that, unless the client agrees otherwise, the benefits of any commission received must be passed to the client either directly or indirectly by restricting the firm's fee for investment business by the amount of commission received (and the client notified accordingly) *or* returning it to the client or reinvesting that commission in the investment product of the client.

F. *Key Features Documents*

Rule 4.4(2) is concerned with the disclosure of product information for both life policies and unit trusts to clients. A firm must ensure that whenever it recommends a packaged product (life policy or unit trust) to a client, the client is provided with a written statement of the key features relating to the product, including the product's prospective surrender value. This key features statement will normally be provided by the product provider. These key features statements must be client specific, *i.e.* the statement must relate to a particular product for a named client. It is the responsibility of the firm to ensure that the client receives the key features statement.

Where a product provider does not produce a key features statement, a firm must produce the statement itself. Furthermore, where a firm does not obtain quotations for a product from a product provider or through another intermediary, a firm must produce from its own resources such quotations.

It is only where a firm buys a packaged product when it is acting as a discretionary investment manager or makes a purchase on an execution only basis that it is permissible for the key features statement to be despatched to the client as soon as practicable after the contract or change is made.

G. *Cancellation Rights*

A firm must ensure that included in any key features statement for any product is written notice of any cancellation rights attaching to the product. The cancellation rules on life policies which came into force on 1st January 1995 should be drawn to a client's attention and the main provisions of this cancellation regime are as follows:—

1. A client who enters into a life policy with a life company has the right to cancel the agreement if the prospective policy holder is habitually resident in the United Kingdom at the time when the relevant agreement was made.

2. The life company must send by post to the policy holder notice of his right to cancel and the notice must be sent within fourteen days from the making of the agreement.

3. Once the policy holder receives the notice he has fourteen days in which to decide whether to cancel it. If the policy holder decides to post the notice of cancellation to exercise that right, the decision is valid from the moment of posting.

4. Where the policy holder cancels, the agreement is rescinded and both parties give up what they have obtained and get back what they have paid ("back to square one").

H. *Reason Why Letter*

Rule 4.4(3) details the circumstances when a Reason Why letter should be given to a client. Whenever a firm recommends to a client to:—

1. take on a long term commitment; or
2. relinquish a long term commitment; or
3. transfer rights held under an occupational pension scheme into a personal pension; or
4. elect to make pension fund withdrawals from a personal pension fund, the firm must explain to the client in writing the reasons why the firm believes the commitment (or relinquishment) to be suitable. A copy of the "reason why" letter must be retained in the client file for a period of at least three years from the date on which the recommendation was given.

I. *General Record Keeping Requirements for all Transactions*

Rule 6.1 requires that a firm keep records of:—

1. All instructions received from clients to effect investment transactions and all decisions to effect transactions which are taken on behalf of clients;
2. All instructions given to other persons to effect investment transactions on behalf of clients; and
3. All investment transactions which have been effected on behalf of clients (which for a share transaction means keeping a copy of the relevant contract note).

A firm's record of compliance with the above general obligations must be kept for at least ten years.

J. *Record Keeping for Share Transactions*

In respect of the record keeping for share transactions a firm can either maintain individual file records for each client in relation to their share transactions or, alternatively, maintain a daily record book.

1. **Daily Record Book**—the daily record book is an "audit trail" of all share transactions carried out by the firm. The Compliance Officer should have overall responsibility for the daily record book.

The daily record book (which can of course be computerised) will contain entries for all mail relating to share transactions and thereafter records of telephone calls, meetings etc. The daily record book is vouched by letters, records of telephone calls, records of meetings, contract notes, share certificates etc.

Where a daily record book is maintained, this will also have to be backed up with a central record of all client transactions, which will entail a record card for each client showing the various share transactions carried out on their behalf.

2. **Individual Client Investment Files**—under this system each client is provided with their own investment file which will contain the vouchers for each transaction on a client by client basis. Such individual client files could be opened for each investment year.

Additionally, Rule 6.2 requires a firm to send a copy of the contract note to the client evidencing the purchase or sale of the shares. A copy of the contract note and the letter sending it out to the client should be kept on the client's file. It should be noted that in terms of Rule 3.3 the contract note should state that the transaction is to be effected on behalf of the client.

K. *Life Assurance and Unit Trust Record Keeping*

Under Rule 6.5 a firm must maintain a separate central record of the number of life policies and transactions in unit trusts placed directly or indirectly with each life office and/or unit trust company—postings to the central record should be done on a daily basis. The central record respect of each transaction will contain:—

1. the name and address of the client;
2. date policy/transaction effected;
3. the name of the life policy/unit trust operator; and
4. type of product/unit trust.

A typical entry in the central record book would be as follows:—

Client Details	Date policy arranged/ transaction effected	Life office/operator	Type of policy/ units
Mrs A. B. Smith (address)	1st December 1995	Scottish Widows	Low cost endowment
Mr C. D. Jones (address)	30th November 1997	Foreign & Colonial	Far Eastern Trusts 1,000 units

L. *Life Assurance—Typical Client File Paperwork*

The typical paperwork to back up a life policy will consist of:—

1. client fact sheet;
2. copies of the quotations obtained;
3. the quotations selected should be marked with the reasons for its selection;
4. copy of the reason why letter;
5. copy of the key features statement from the life company;
6. copy of the completed and dated proposal form;
7. copy of the covering letter sending the proposal form to the life company;
8. copy reply from the life company detailing cover arranged; and
9. appropriate record made in the Central Record.

M. *Unit Trusts—Typical Client File Paperwork*

The typical paperwork to back up a unit trust transaction will consist of:—

1. client fact sheet;
2. details of the information sources used to select a unit trust (*i.e.* Unit Trust rankings from Money Management);
3. copy recommendation on unit trust selected in the form of a reason why letter to the client;
4. confirmation that the unit trust company has provided the client with a Key Features document for that particular unit trust;
5. confirmation that client accepted the unit trust recommendation;

6. confirmation of firm placing the order with the unit trust company. The contract note will be issued by the unit trust company. Client submits cheque to firm to pay for the unit trust purchased;
7. record recording the effecting of the purchase of the required unit trusts for the client, recording in the Central Record when the transaction was effected, name and address of the client, names and type of units bought and from which company;
8. update client's Documents of Title List.

N. *Record of Investment Business Income*

A firm must maintain sufficient records to ensure that its investment income does not exceed 49% of its total income.

PART V

INVESTMENT MANAGEMENT

A. *Introduction*

There are two forms of investment management which firms are permitted to conduct under the Society's Rules and these are:—

1. **Discretionary portfolio management**—where a firm manages a portfolio of investments in the exercise of discretion; or

2. **Non-discretionary portfolio management**—where a firm has assumed responsibility for advising or commenting on the investments contained in a client's portfolio.

A firm which communicates stockbrokers' reports on a portfolio to its clients without commenting upon the investments comprised therein, is not a portfolio manager.

B. *Rules for Non-discretionary Portfolio Management*

Where a firm is acting as a non-discretionary portfolio manager, the firm must send to a client a statement of the terms of business which form the basis of the firm's actings. This terms of business statement can be in the form of a letter containing the relevant parts of Schedule 1(1). The letter needs only to be sent to the client who does not need to sign or return it.

Additionally, under Rule 6.6, where a firm is acting as a non-discretionary portfolio manager a client must be sent a report at least once a year stating the value of his portfolio at the beginning and the end of the period to which the report relates and the portfolio's composition at the end of the period.

C. *Rules for Discretionary Portfolio Management*

A firm which wishes to conduct discretionary portfolio management must obtain the specific prior approval of the Council of the Society. (Rule 11.1).

The Society in considering such discretionary portfolio management applications will consider both the competence of the firm in discretionary portfolio management and its operational procedures for conducting such investment management. The Society would expect such firms to have detailed internal controls, including procedures for checking titles to shareholdings each year. A separation of the investment management staff (*i.e.* those individuals who give investment advice) from the investment administration staff (*i.e.* those who actually place the orders and handle the cash administration) is expected.

A firm which wishes to conduct discretionary portfolio management will also require to be audited annually in respect of discretionary portfolio management operations at the firm's own expense by the Society's Inspecting Accountants. For the purposes of Rule 11.1, a firm is acting as a discretionary portfolio manager when it actively manages a client's portfolio without requiring the approval of the client for any investment decision. An essential feature of discretionary portfolio management is that investment decisions are generated internally by the firm's own investment staff.

A firm need only apply for permission to act as a discretionary portfolio manager where it is acting as such a manager to a significant extent. The Council of the Society will be the sole judge of what is meant by "significant extent". The guidelines which the Council currently uses in determining when a firm is acting as a discretionary portfolio manager to a significant extent are as follows:—

1. The firm manages on a discretionary basis one or more portfolios of a value in excess of £500,000;
2. Manages on a discretionary basis portfolios of a total value of £5m or more;
3. Arranges for the effecting of one or more transactions of a value of over £250,000 for any discretionary managed portfolio.

A firm which does undertake discretionary investment management for its clients must provide such clients with a written contract complying with Schedule 1(2) of the CBRs. These clients must sign and return the written contract to the firm. Furthermore, these clients must be sent a report at least once a year stating the value of their portfolio at the beginning and end of the period, to which the report relates, the composition of their portfolios and changes in composition between these dates.

PART VI

TRUSTS AND EXECUTRIES

A. *Introduction*
Where a firm is involved in non-discretionary or discretionary portfolio management involving trusts and executries, the following procedures apply:—
1. **Executries**—unless a transfer or sale of all of the holdings in an estate is intimated at the time of the initial interview, a client terms of business/ written contract should be concluded between the executors and the firm.

If the eventual beneficiaries of the investments are either clients of the firm (or indeed become clients of the firm) or are the executors of the estate a separate terms of business/written contract is required between the individual beneficiaries and the firm.

2. **Trusts**—in a trust a terms of business/written contract is required between all the trustees and the firm. If one trustee has been nominated to receive contract notes etc, this fact should be incorporated into the terms of business/written contract which must be signed by all trustees.

If the liferentrix or other trust beneficiary is a client of the firm, he may also require to conclude a terms of business/written contract with the firm, but this would be for a personal portfolio not the trust assets as the beneficiary has no right of investment over the liferented trust estate which would normally be invested to provide a balance between income and capital.

If any of the trustees are clients of the firm in their own right and wish the firm to deal in investments for them as individuals, they should conclude a separate terms of business/written contract with the firm.

3. **Power of Attorney**—the terms of business/written contract is concluded between the attorney and the firm even if the attorney is a partner in the firm.

4. **Curatory**—the terms of business/written contract is concluded between the curator and the firm even if the curator is a partner in the firm.

B. *Client Fact Sheet*
  1. **Executry**—not required as the Will speaks for itself.
  2. **Trusts**—not required as the Will or trust deed speaks for itself.
  3. **Power of Attorney**—required. The client fact sheet will be about the person who signed the power of attorney—not the attorney.
  4. **Curatory**—the client fact sheet is for the incapax—not the curator.

PART VII

PENSION BUSINESS—TRANSFER OR OPT-OUT FROM OCCUPATIONAL PENSION SCHEMES

A firm which wishes to give advice or make arrangements for clients in relation to transfers or opt-outs from occupational pension schemes must obtain the specific prior approval of the Society to give such advice or make such arrangements (Rule 3.2(2)(c)).

With regard to an opt-out from an occupational pension scheme it is SIB's opinion that:—

"An opt-out is presumed to be adverse to the interests of the individual investor concerned unless the contrary can affirmatively be shown."

It is the Society's opinion that an opt-out is never in the best interests of a client.

PART VIII

SAFEKEEPING OF CLIENTS' DOCUMENTS OF TITLE—CUSTODY

A. *Introduction*

A new Part 7 has been introduced to the CBRs which deals with the safekeeping of a client's documents of title. The Part 7 Rules are only applicable where a firm either itself or through a third party custodian both holds and administers a client's documents of title of investments. Administration means settling investment transactions, collecting and dealing with dividends, carrying out corporate actions such as proxy voting etc.

The mere safekeeping of documents of title of investments (*i.e.* where a firm holds share certificates in a safe but does not administer such shares) does not come within the scope of the Part 7 Rules.

Documents of title for the purposes of Part 7 means share certificates, statements relating to certificated or uncertificated securities (that is shares held under the CREST settlement system), life policies, statements relating to unit trusts and entitlement to other investments as defined in the FSA.

B. *Requirements for firms which both hold and administer investments*
Rule 7.2—Holding of Client Investments

The essential provisions of Rule 7.2 are:—

1. A firm must keep safe client documents of title of investments and ensure they are both readily accessible and separately identifiable from the firm's own investments.
2. A firm must not part with a client's documents of title unless it has the instructions of the client.
3. The client investments must either be registered in the client's own name or in the name of a nominee company approved by the client.
4. Where the firm itself is acting as the custodian of the client's investments, there must be a clear definition of the responsibilities of the firm in respect of those investments.
5. At least *once in each calendar year*, a firm must give to each client a statement of the investments held on the client' s behalf. This statement

must identify which of the investments (if any) have been lent or are held as collateral for loans and are therefore not free to be delivered to the client.

Rule 7.3—Client Documents of Title of Investment held by a Firm's Own Nominee Company

The basic requirements of Rule 7.3 are as follows:—

1. The firm's nominee company must only act on the instructions of the firm. Accordingly the firm must accept full responsibility to its clients for the actings of its nominee company.

2. A client must agree to the holding of his investments in a firm's nominee company.

3. Where a client has agreed that his investments can be held in the firm's nominee, the client's investments will be in the name of the nominee and if the firm has any of its own investments held in the nominee, these must be separately identifiable from the investments of clients.

4. Where a firm uses a pooled nominee (*i.e.* where a client's investments are not separately designated in individual accounts within the nominee) the firm must advise the client of its intention to pool and of the implications of pooling.

5. At least *once in each calendar year*, the client must be provided with a statement of the investments held on his behalf within the nominee company.

Any nominee company set up for investment business purposes after 1st January 1998 must be dedicated solely to the holding and to the activities related to the holding of documents of title of investments. Existing nominee companies which are often multi-purpose nominee companies, (*i.e.* the nominee is used not only for the registration of investments), can be maintained and continue to operate.

Rule 7.4—Use of a Third Party Custodian

The principal requirements of this Rule are that:—

1. Where a firm appoints a third party custodian to hold a client's investments, the services and duties to be rendered by the third party must be put in writing.

2. Where a firm appoints a third party custodian, the agreement between the firm and the firm's clients must state the respective responsibilities of the firm and of the third party custodian particularly with regard to any potential losses of a client's investments and the appointment of sub-custodians.

3. Furthermore, the agreement between the firm and any appointed third party custodian must provide written undertakings as to the latter's responsibility for meeting the general record keeping and reporting requirements under Rules 7.2, 7.3 and 7.7.

Rule 7.7—Record Keeping

The record keeping requirements under Rule 7.7 are as follows:—

1. For each client there should be a record of the documents of title kept for the client and the place where such documents are kept.

2. In addition, for each client the record should include a description of the investments to which the client's documents of title relate. (*i.e.* 10,000 Marks & Spencer ordinary shares of 28p).

3. The record must detail the movements of a client's documents of title into or out of the custody of the firm. If the documents of title have left the possession of the firm the identity of the person to whom possession has passed must be recorded.

It is essential that each client's record is adequately maintained to ensure that, at all times, it is possible to clearly identify each client's entitlement to investments. A firm is *not* expected to "back-track" and record the date on which client investments held before 1st January 1998 (the commencement date of the CBRs) came into the firm. What is expected is that client investments coming into the firm's possession after 1st January 1998 have such "possession dates" recorded.

Rule 7.8—Checking of Client Documents of Title

At least *once in each calendar year* where a firm acts as custodian it must check and reconcile each client's documents of title against a client's actual investment holdings. The firm is responsible for any shortfall between the record of the client's documents of title and the record of the client's actual investments.

Where a firm appoints a third party custodian it must ensure that the third party carries out such checking and makes good any shortfall.

PART IX

DISCIPLINE

A. *Introduction*

As the Society authorises firms to conduct investment business any breach of the Rules and Regulations will be the responsibility of the relevant partners in the firm against whom any disciplinary action will be taken. Rule 8.3 of the CBRs provides that any breach of the Rules may be treated as professional misconduct. Any breach of the Rules will be reported to the Society's Investment Compliance Committee. This Committee is independent of the Society's Council and has 33% lay representation. The Investment Compliance Committee considers both breaches of the Rules and complaints against firms which have been notified to the Society by either the Society's own Inspecting Accountants, a firm's accountants or members of the public.

B. *Complaints from the Public*

The various stages through which a complaint can proceed are as follows:—

1. A firm against whom a complaint is made must ensure that the complaint is investigated promptly and thoroughly and, where practicable this investigation should be carried out by a partner not concerned in the action or inaction complained of;

2. A firm must inform the complainer that it is open to him to report the matter to the Investment Compliance Committee;

3. The Investment Compliance Committee has a number of options available to it as to how it may dispose of a complaint:—

  (i) if the complaint is unfounded it will be dismissed with no further action;

  (ii) if the complaint is valid but does not amount to professional misconduct a letter may be sent to the solicitor responsible for the breach in question (or for the supervision of the member of staff concerned), deploring or regretting the conduct in question;

 (iii) if the complaint amounts to an inadequate professional service the Committee can:—

   (a) order the firm to reduce or waive its fee;

   (b) order the firm to correct the client's affairs at the firm's own expense; or

   (c) order the firm to take any other action which the Committee may specify.

  (iv) if a complaint does amount to professional misconduct, a solicitor may be reprimanded and a note of this will be made on the solicitor's record; or

  (v) the complaint may be referred to the Scottish Solicitors' Discipline Tribunal. If the Tribunal finds there has been professional misconduct it can fine the solicitor up to a maximum of £10,000; it can restrict or suspend the firm's Investment Business Certificate; it can order that the solicitor be suspended from practice or it can strike the solicitor off the Roll.

If a complainer is dissatisfied with the Investment Compliance Committee's disposal of a complaint he can refer the matter to the Scottish Legal Services Ombudsman who oversees all the Society's complaints handling.

C. *Other Disciplinary Powers*

In various circumstances the Society can suspend or withdraw a firm's Investment Business Certificate. Such circumstances are:—

1. Where a firm ceases to practice as solicitors or ceases to be managed and controlled by solicitors:

2. Where a firm ceases to comply with the Investment Business Training Regulations;

3. Where the firm is employing a non-solicitor employee (who is conducting investment business) who is not a fit and proper person or is not qualified to conduct such investment business;

4. Where the firm becomes insolvent;

5. Where the firm does not pay the fee for authorisation within thirty days of it being charged;

6. Where the firm does not deliver an Investment Business Compliance Certificate within one calendar month of the completion of the accounting period;

7. Where the Society's Council is satisfied that after a reasonable enquiry investors would not be adequately protected if the firm's Investment Business Certificate was not withdrawn/suspended; and

8. Where the firm's gross income is derived wholly or mainly from investment business.

A firm cannot conduct investment business while its Investment Business Certificate is suspended. To do so would amount to professional misconduct. Transacting such business in these circumstances may lead to a criminal prosecution under the FSA.

Law Society's Guidance Notes on Capital Adequacy

Introduction—Why issue guidance on this subject?
Following a period of consultation and discussion the Guarantee Fund Committee Working Party has recommended the production of Guidance Notes on the subject of Capital Adequacy in legal practices. The Guidance Notes are thought to be a valuable and confidential method of allowing solicitors to measure their own firm's financial standing. The problem of not having any standard to apply to the firm's balance sheet and profitability means that each firm is forced to make a personal decision about its level of reserves. This healthy independence has drawbacks in dealing with banks and other financial institutions because there are no opportunities for solicitors to make comparisons with other equivalent businesses.

The Law Society is increasingly aware of market pressures and tighter lending policies combining to give real problems to practices where these questions have never been faced before. The Guidance Notes are intended to help the independent firm to check on its financial health. Help and advice is also available if the standard is not being met by the practice. Telephone 0131 226 7411 and ask to speak for Leslie Cumming or one of his team on the subject of Capital Adequacy.

The Guidance Notes are intended to help solicitors to assess their financial position by fixing realistic values in areas where business optimism can traditionally over-rule prudence. It is also recognised that many solicitors have adopted conservative accounting policies in dealing with debtors and work in progress. If the test check produces a negative or poor Balance Sheet result because of these accounting policies *e.g.*, cash based accounts or nominal work in progress values, it is recommended that a realistic value be included in the adjusted figures in order to produce the most accurate result.

The trend of the business measured consistently and regularly can be a powerful management tool. In addition to testing earlier years accounts, the ratios can be done quarterly or half-yearly to measure the rate of improvement and decline. The more regularly this check is carried out the better judgment can be made on the state of the practice's financial health.

The Basic Standards
The standard measures are intended to look at balance sheet ratios and profitability. The results of the tests should be considered in three stages, action being taken or advice being sought depending on the results of your firm's own calculations.

1. *Is the practice solvent?*
If the method of calculating the value of your Balance Sheet as set out in Schedule I is applied to your firm's balance sheet, does the result show a negative value? If the answer is yes, get some advice on how to deal with the situation. The position is serious and must not be ignored.

2. *Are the capital reserves inadequate?*
The standard measures should be applied to the balance sheet figures. If the firm is solvent but the partner's capital does not achieve 20% of the value of total assets then the balance sheet needs some action to be taken in order to strengthen the position. Again, advice should be sought if the remedial action to be taken is not obvious.

3. *Profitability*
The net profit before tax should be at least 20% of income.
If equity partners charge salaries to the Profit and Loss account these should be added back to the profit.

If the results of the calculations do not achieve the 20% level on both balance sheet and profitability calculations the practice is considered to be in a marginal position. If this is the case, then action must be taken to improve the ratios without delay. Again, advice should be sought if the remedial action is not obvious.

The Benchmark Tests
The two key tests are defined as follows:—

(1) *Partnership Solvency Test/Capital Adequacy Test*

$$\frac{\text{Total partners capital reserves} \times 100}{\text{Total gross partnership assets}} = X\%$$

where X% is less than 0% the partnership is deemed to be insolvent and advice must be sought at once. Where X% is a positive figure, this measures the extent of capital cover in the practice. A target of over 20% is thought to be prudent.

(2) *Profitability of the practice*

$$\frac{\text{Total annual profits before tax} \times 100}{\text{Total annual income}} = Y\%$$

where Y% is targeted to be more than 20% of income.

The higher the assets and profitability ratio are, the stronger the firm's position is. Results in the 0%–20% range are a cause for concern and indicate a lack of financial stability. Well run partnerships may be targeting annual profit ratios in excess of 30%

Strong balance sheets will include a 50% partnership funding of working capital and at least a 30% stake in any properties owned by the partnership.

It will be helpful to check the equivalent figures in the previous 2 years in order to measure whether the position is stable, improving or declining. Any reduction in performance even in a strong set of accounts should be treated as an early warning.

Conclusion: If you are unable to meet the basic minimal standards as set out above you must take advice from another experienced solicitor, accountant or the Law Society. The smaller the ratios, the more urgent is the need for advice. Firms with losses or negative capital reserves must act at once.

Schedule II shows three examples where the original profit and partnership reserves range from adequate to strong. The tests show up inherent weaknesses in the figures. Complacency is dangerous in these circumstances.

SCHEDULE I

Benchmark Tests

Definitions and calculations to be used

Step 1. *Valuing assets*

—*Fixed assets*. Using written down values per your balance sheet is generally acceptable and will include properties, office equipment and cars.
—*goodwill*. This asset is ignored for the purposes of the test.
—*work-in-progress*. This must be prudently valued. Any estimate of work-in-progress must be capable of being confirmed by reference to time records or files and should not exceed 3 months average fee income (excluding any element of profit).

—*debtors*. The value must exclude any bad or doubtful debts. The total for this asset must be linked to the annual fee income. The test value should be the lesser of the actual total or 3 months fee income.

—*cash*. Actual value on deposits.

—*listed investments*. Cost or market value. If market value is the lesser figure this should be used.

The total assets value which has resulted from these calculations are used for the balance sheet ratio calculation.

Step 2. *Calculating liabilities*

This will include any bank overdrafts, loans or business mortgages or personal loans by third parties to the partnership or the sole practitioner in his business.

Also to be included are creditors of the business hire purchase liabilities on the firms assets and income tax and VAT liabilities on the profit and income figures included in the accounts.

Step 3. *Adjusted Balance sheet Partnership reserves*

The partnership capital reserves which form the balancing figure to the revised balance sheet calculations will reflect the balance sheet adjustments for the value of any assets which require to be written down or excluded as set out under Section 1 above. The gross balance sheet value of assets including current assets and the net partnership capital figures devised from the adjusted balance sheet are used in the calculation of the balance sheet ratios required under Test No. 1 and 2. The resulting figure is used for the balance sheet ratio calculation.

Step 4. *Calculating the ratio*

The revised capital reserves figures (Step 3) should be divided by the adjusted gross assets (Step 1) and expressed as a percentage.

Step 5. *Total income and net profit*

The figures for total income should be as per the annual accounts and may include fees, commissions, interest earned or other income generated by the practice.

The figure of annual profit after all overheads and operating charges including finance and depreciation charges but before tax and partners drawings is used for this calculation.

Step 6. *Profitability in the Practice*

The calculation of the annual figure of profitability as a percentage is done by using the values set out in Step 5.

SCHEDULE II

SAMPLE CALCULATIONS—EXAMPLE I

(a) Balance sheet adjustments

	Actual	*Test*
Goodwill	£100,000	£NIL
Property at valuation	120,000	120,000
Other fixed assets	60,000	60,000
	280,000	180,000
Current assets		
W.I.P.	140,000	61,000
Debtors	45,000	45,000
Clients account surplus (net)	1,000	1,000
	186,000	107,000
Total assets	£466,000	£287,000

Liabilities		*Actual*	*Test*
Trade creditors		£ 15,000	£ 15,000
Bank overdraft		50,000	50,000
Term loan		100,000	100,000
Total liabilities		165,000	165,000
Partner capital		301,000	122,000
		£466,000	£287,000

Comparative ratios
—capital/assets   65%   43%

(b) Profit and loss statement

	Actual	*Actual*
Income—fees		£280,000
—commissions		20,000
		300,000

Expenses		
Salaries	£160,000	
Office expenses	30,000	
Car expenses	15,000	
Professional fees	7,500	
Miscellaneous	12,000	
Interest	6,000	
Depreciation	15,000	245,500
Net profit before tax		£ 54,500
Profit ratio		18%

(c) Benchmark ratios

Balance sheet

$$\frac{\text{Capital} \times 100}{\text{Total Assets}} = X\%$$

$$\frac{£122,000 \times 100}{287,000} = 42.5\%$$

Profitability

$$\text{Net Profit} \times 100 = Y\%$$

$$\frac{£54,500 \times 100}{300,000} = 18.2\%$$

Note: The WIP figure is replaced by 3 months' costs as a reduced valuation. The strong balance sheet is being threatened by a weak profit position. If this three partner firm can't live on the profits a slow decline in the balance sheet position will result in a problem.

(c) Benchmark ratios

Balance sheet

$$\frac{24,000 \times 100}{149,000} = 16.1\%$$

Profitability

$$\frac{43,500 \times 100}{300,000} = 14.5\%$$

Release 46: 21 November 1997

Note: Balance Sheet. The strong position shown per the original Balance Sheet is undermined by the lack of property assets, the high goodwill and work in progress figures. Revalued WIP is included in the revised Balance Sheet at an actual valuation of files.

Note: Profit and Loss statement. Below average results. The problems have to be addressed before they get worse. Profits must be improved and the balance sheet strengthened. There is very little leeway.

SAMPLE CALCULATIONS—EXAMPLE II

(a) Balance sheet adjustmentrs

	Actual	*Test*
Goodwill	£100,000	£NIL
Fixed assets	60,000	60,000
	160,000	60,000
Current assets		
WIP	140,000	43,000
Debtors	45,000	45,000
Client account surplus (net)	1,000	1,000
	186,000	89,000
Total Assets	£346,000	£149,000
Liabilities		
Trade creditors	£ 25,000	£ 25,000
Bank overdraft	100,000	100,000
	125,000	125,000
Partners capital	221,000	24,000
	£346,000	£149,000
Comparative ratios		
—capital/assets	64%	16%

(b) Profit and loss statement

	Actual	*Actual*
Income—fees		£280,000
—commissions		20,000
		300,000
Salaries	£160,000	
Office expenses	42,000	
Car expenses	15,000	
Professional fees	7,500	
Miscellaneous	12,000	
Interest	5,000	
Depreciation	15,000	256,500
Net profit		£ 43,500
Profit ratio		14.5%

SAMPLE CALCULATIONS—EXAMPLE III

(a) Balance Sheet adjustments

	Actual	*Test*
Goodwill	£50,000	£NIL
Fixed assets	15,000	15,000
	65,000	15,000
Current assets		
WIP	25,000	13,000
Debtors	15,000	15,000
Client account surplus	1,000	1,000
	41,000	29,000
	£106,000	£44,000
Liabilities		
Trade creditors	10,000	10,000
Overdraft	35,000	35,000
	45,000	45,000
Partners capital	61,000	(1,000)
	£106,000	£44,000
Comparative ratios		
—capital assets	58%	Negative

Note: WIP is revised to actual values from the original estimate used. The reduction in asset value has produced a negative capital value—insolvency on this benchmark test.

(b) Profit and loss statement

Total Income	£85,000
Total expenses (not set out in detail)	65,000
Net profit	£20,000

(c) Benchmarks ratios

Balance sheet   **Insolvent**

Profitability $\dfrac{20,000 \times 100}{85,000} = 23.5\%$

The sole practitioner's profitability is acceptable but modest. Take advice on the apparent insolvency. How can the weak balance sheet be improved. Action to reduce borrowings and improve profit should be taken now.

Simple Guide to the Solicitors' (Scotland) Accounts Rules 1997
Solicitors' (Scotland) Accounts Certificate Rules 1997
Money Laundering Regulations 1993

THIS IS ISSUED AS A GUIDE AND IS NOT A SUBSTITUTE FOR THE RULES
AND REGULATIONS OF WHICH ALL SOLICITORS SHOULD HAVE A
THOROUGH KNOWLEDGE

Some Questions and Answers

1. *What is the main purpose of the Accounts Rules?*
To protect clients' money and to ensure that at all times Solicitors identify and record client funds so that they may be clearly identified from the Solicitor's own monies and to ensure that at all times Solicitors have enough money in their client bank accounts to meet the total amount that they are due to clients (irrespective of any money due to them by clients) both as a Solicitor and as a Trustee in the course of their practice.

2. *What is a Client Account?*   **(Rule 2(1))**
It is any account with a recognised Bank or Building Society in the name of the Solicitor but specifically identified in its title as being for clients or for a named client or trust etc. You can have as many client accounts as you need. The client account may also be a loan (but not a general deposit) to a Local Authority but in this case it must be in the name of the Solicitor for a specific client. In the case of a joint deposit this should be recorded in the books of the first named firm.

3. *Can the Client Account be with any Bank or Building Society?* **(Rule 2(1))**
No. It must be with an authorised institution within the meaning of the Banking Act 1987 or the Bank of England, National Savings Bank or the Post Office. It may also be an authorised Building Society under the Building Societies Act 1986. Any such institution must be able to operate within the bankers automated clearing system. Details of "recognised" institutions can be obtained from the Society or the Bank of England. If you deposit a client's money with an institution that does not come within the definition of a client account then you must have the client's written consent.

4. *Clients' Funds outwith the U.K.*   **(Rule 2(1))**
Client account funds may only be invested in accounts outwith the U.K. with the express consent of the clients and suitable risk warnings must be given to the clients in advance of any decision to place funds in accounts which are outwith the scope of the Accounts Rules.
Note that the Channel Islands and the Isle of Man are deemed to be *outwith* the U.K.

5. *What books must we keep and can they be electronic?*   **(Rule 12)**
You must keep a cash book and a ledger in which there must be an account for every client in respect of whom you have any financial intromissions. The Rules also require a separate record to be kept for inter-client transfers within the client ledgers. You must also keep a record of all other financial dealings of the Firm and all accounting information must be up to date. The narrative for the entries needs to be clear and each entry should be self explanatory. If the books are on a computer it must have software to allow the accounting information to be printed out on request. Alternatively, books can be handwritten. This must be in indelible ink and not in pencil.

6. We only do Legal Aid Work, do we need to keep Clients' Accounts?
(Rules 4 and 6)
It is common practice for cheques paid by The Scottish Legal Aid Board to be paid directly into the firm's bank account or another special bank account set up for this purpose. Many firms do not have a client bank account for this. However, it is important to note that when SLAB's cheque or telegraphic transfer is paid into the firm's bank account it is essential that you have already paid out the outlays due to third parties and these funds are simply reimbursements. If some, or all of the outlays have not been settled then that portion of SLAB's remittance in this respect is clients' funds and should be treated as such. Settlement of such outlays on the date of receipt is acceptable. If you are not able to do that then you must have a client bank account or you will be in breach of the Accounts Rules. Similarly contributions received from clients who are in receipt of Legal Aid or Legal Advice and Assistance *must* be treated as client funds until an account has been rendered in accordance with Rule 6(1)(d).

7. Should we have a surplus or float in our General Clients Bank Account?
(Rule 13)
Yes. Most firms do as a simple precaution to cover minor mistakes which may occur from time to time. The reconciliations have to be listed and the statements kept for at least three years.

8. Do we need a Compliance Partner?   **(Rules 16 and 18)**
Yes. You require a designated cashroom partner who is responsible for compliance with the Accounts Rules.
You also require a money laundering reporting officer to be appointed.

9. What do we do with money coming into the firm?   **(Rules 4(2) and 12)**
Immediately clients' money comes in to the office, ensure that appropriate entries are made in the Cash Book; **do it today and not tomorrow!** Clients' money must be lodged in a properly designated bank account—it must not go through the office Bank Account.

10. What do we do about money going out?
Firstly ensure that you have funds to make the payment, normally by cheque. If you do not have sufficient client funds from the client account then you must use the firm's funds to meet any shortfall. If clients' funds are in a Solicitors Special Deposit Account or similar they must be uplifted and paid into the Bank Account on which the cheque is to be written before you issue the cheque or make payment from that account.

11. Why must we record entries for funds not paid through the Client Bank Account?
(Rule 7)
The Rules now emphasise the need to record entries which are needed for completeness and to ensure that the client accounting records deal with the whole consideration involved in conveyancing transactions. If part of the price of a property is paid to the solicitor in the form of a cheque made out to a third party, the cheques should be recorded on the face of the ledger card as a contra entry.

12. How do we deal with bridging loans?   **(Rule 8)**
You must not enter into a bridging loan agreement on behalf of a client in circumstances which may impose on you personal liability for repayment in the event of default by the client. Bridging loans must always be in writing and you must give the lender full details of the client and what the arrangements are for repayment.

13. *Can we lend money to a client?*
   Yes, but you should consider whether a conflict of interest might arise.

14. *Can we borrow money from a client?* **(Rule 9)**
   No, unless the client has been independently advised about the loan or is in the business of lending money. (*N.B.* Personal and business loans are not covered by the Guarantee Fund.)

15. *Do we need to keep a list of Powers of Attorney?* **(Rule 11)**
   Yes, each year the designated cashroom partner must complete a list of active and dormant Powers of Attorney in the name of any Solicitor.

16. *What records do we have to keep to operate a Power of Attorney?*
   (Rules 11 and 12(2))
   A clear record of money paid in or out of the client's own bank account should be kept in a client ledger and cash book. Where you have exclusive control of the client's bank account then that bank balance should be treated as client funds which should be included in invested funds held for named clients.

17. *What do we have to do on a daily basis?* **(Rule 12)**
   For a manual system ensure that the cash book entries are also entered in the clients' or the firm's ledger. The cash book and the ledger should be summed up to date and regularly balanced. They should clearly identify monies which you hold in separate client accounts.
   A computer system will do this automatically provided you enter the information accurately and daily.

18. *What are other funds?* **(Rules 2(1), 12(1) and 14)**
   These are funds which you hold in individual accounts in the firm's name or in a Solicitor's name in Trust for a client. These include funds held under Powers of Attorney. Keep an extra column or section in your Cash Book or Day Book to record these. There must also be an additional column in the client's individual record headed "Other Funds" or you could have a separate ledger card dealing with investment funds only. You are required to keep this separate record and to reconcile (physically check the balances in the account against the records) at least four times a year (many firms do this monthly).

19. *What do we have to reconcile?* **(Rule 14)**
   You check that all interest earned on Building Society or SSD Accounts has been written up in the passbook or bank statements and that there is an equivalent entry on the face of the client records. You then prepare a list of investment funds and check this against the total of funds held in the Investment account for the various authorised bodies. Any differences between the figures must be identified and adjusted to the correct amount. You must also keep the reconciliation for at least three years.

20. *What do we have to do about interest on a Client Account?* **(Rule 15)**
   As a general rule when you have received money from a client you should put it into some form of interest bearing account for that client. This, however, depends upon the amount of money being lodged and/or the time it is likely to be held. You must always act fairly and reasonably. Smaller sums (under £500) which should be paid out within two months do not require to earn interest for the client. However, larger sums, even for short periods, do. Particular attention should be paid to executry funds. Make sure that they too earn interest for the client.
   You need not account to clients for interest earned on your general clients account(s), subject to the above rule.

RECENT SCHEMES introduced by banks or building societies offer differential rates for client funds. Arrangements to retain any element of the interest should be agreed with the client.

21. *What about the money laundering regulations?* **(Rule 16)**

(a) *To whom do they apply?*
Everybody.

(b) *To what do the provisions apply?*
To every one-off transaction which involves the payment by or to the client of an amount of ECU 15,000 (approximately £12,000) or more, and to any one-off transaction for a smaller amount which appears to be linked with others where the aggregate of the amounts involved is in excess of ECU 15,000.

> — to every case where the firm forms or resolves to form a business relationship for relevant financial business only,
>
> — if you suspect that your client is engaged in money laundering, or that a transaction is being carried out on behalf of someone else who is engaged in money laundering.
>
> "Relevant financial business", "business relationship" and "one-off transaction" are defined in the Regulations. The definitions are wide and any transaction which involves the handling of money of ECU 15,000 or more, is likely to be subject to the money laundering provisions.

(c) *What does this mean in practice?*
Some matters are **exempt**. Examples are:—
  • Existing clients do not require identification checks.
  • Instructions from other solicitors who confirm to you that they have complied (Reg. 10).
  • Cheques drawn on the client's own UK bank account (Reg. 8).
  • Criminal work, wills, licensing and gaming work, insurance claims, certain matrimonial matters etc.

(d) *Can you give us one or two practical examples?*
Matters which are unlikely to be exempt and therefore covered would be:—
  • House purchase (unless all funds from client's own UK bank account).
  • Investment of client's funds.
  • Receipt of funds for onward transmission to the client or a third party.

(e) *When did the Regulations come into effect?*
The Money Laundering Regulations 1993 (the "Regulations") came into force on 1st April 1994.

(f) *What are the Regulations supposed to do?*
Prevent the proceeds of unlawful activities being legitimised by being applied to carry out legitimate transactions.

(g) *What do we have to do under the Regulations?*
  1. Verify the identity of every person with whom you intend to form a business relationship, or carry out a one-off transaction;
  2. maintain record keeping procedures; and
  3. maintain internal reporting procedures.

(h) *What happens if we do not comply?*
Failure to comply with the Regulations constitutes a criminal offence, punishable by a fine and/or imprisonment for a term of up to two years.

(i) *What else do we have to do?*
Set up and maintain a procedure for establishing the identity of a client where required in terms of the rules and regulations (see (b) above).

(j) *Do we have to identify clients?*
Yes. If satisfactory evidence of the identity of new clients is not obtained then the business relationship or one-off transaction as the case may be shall not proceed any further.

(k) *How do we go about deciding if we need to comply and also in identifying new clients?*
Common sense.
However, if in doubt there is a style of Verification of Identity Flowchart annexed at Schedule 1 and an evidence of identity form at Schedule 2.

(l) *When is evidence of identity satisfactory?*
1. When it is reasonably capable of establishing that the client is the person he claims to be; and
2. When the person who obtains the evidence is satisfied, in accordance with the procedures maintained under the Regulations, that the evidence does establish that the client is the person he claims to be.
For **individual clients** it is suggested you obtain:—
- the true name and/or names used
- current permanent address, including postcode
- "wherever possible" the date and place of birth
- a document from a reputable source which has a photograph of the applicant *e.g.*, a current valid full passport or national identity card should be requested and the number recorded.

Other suggestions:—
- check the voters' roll
- make a credit reference agency search
- see an original recent electricity, gas, telephone, council tax bill or bank statement
- check a local telephone directory
- visit their home.

For **corporate clients**
No specific steps are needed if clients are:—
- a listed company or a subsidiary of a listed company
- a private company or partnership one or more of whose directors/partners are already known to the firm.

Steps are needed if clients are:—
- an unquoted company or a partnership and none of the directors/partners is already known, then the firm should verify the identity of one or more of the principal directors/partners and/or shareholders as applicable as if they were individual clients (see above).

It is suggested you also obtain copies of:—
- Certificate of Incorporation/ Certificate of Trade or equivalent and perhaps for Companies their latest report and accounts (audited where applicable).

(m) *What records do we have to keep and for how long?*
The evidence of identity you obtained needs to be kept for at least 5 years from completion of the relevant business or transaction concerned.

Release 46: 21 November 1997

(n) *Do we have to have a Money Laundering Reporting Officer?*
    Yes.

(o) *What do we have to tell him/her*
    Any information or other matter which comes to the attention of a person handling relevant financial business which in the opinion of the person handling that business gives rise to a knowledge or suspicion of money laundering.

(p) *What does the Money Laundering Reporting Officer have to do?*
    Consider all such reports and any other relevant information and decide if this gives rise to a knowledge or suspicion of money laundering. If so pass that information to NCIS.

(q) *How?*
    Use the style of form in Schedule 3
    In serious cases telephone or fax NCIS to get guidance on how to proceed with a suspicious transaction.

Telephone Number: 0171 238 8274
Fax Number: 0171 238 8286

(r) *What else should they do?*
    Keep a record of what they decide to do and why.

22. *Inter-Client Loans—Are they protected by the Guarantee Fund*
                                                          (Rule 6(1))
    Normally not. Make sure the lending client gives written consent to the loan and written confirmation that they understand that they will have no claim on the Guarantee Fund. Consider very carefully the question of conflict of interest in any such transaction.

23. *When can we take fees?*   **(Rule 6(1)(d))**
    After you have rendered a fee note and if you have funds in the client account. Do not draw fees when you do not have a balance to meet them as this is likely to result in a deficit in the client bank account and lead you to being in breach of the Rules. Take care to ensure that interim fees are fair and reasonable and reflect the work which has already been done.

24. *Do we have to balance the firm's books?*   **(Rule 12(4))**
    Yes. You must keep all your accounting records up to date at all times and balance your books monthly. That is all your books, your clients' account, your own funds and your assets and liabilities. The obligation is to have them balanced throughout the practice year and certify that this has been done by submitting an Accounts Certificate every six months. You must also properly maintain your own firm's records so the true financial position of the practice can be ascertained at all times. If in any doubt of this aspect of the Rules contact your own Accountant or the Accountants' Department of the Law Society (see below).

25. *What is an Accounts Certificate?*
    The annual Certificate produced by your Accountant under the Accountant's Certificate Rules had to be produced annually and within six months of the end of your year. **This requirement has been completely removed and replaced by a form of Accounts Certificate completed by two partners one of whom should be the designated cashroom partner (sole practitioners require only one partner). The forms of interim and final certificates are in the Schedule to the Certificate Rules.** You may retain the services of an accountant to check all or part of your records as frequently as you consider

to be needed. The Certificate is due to be completed every six months and sent to the Law Society within <u>one month</u>. The very tight time limit is a key part of the control over client accounts. **Do not leave it until the last minute!**

26. *What information is needed for the Certificate?*
   The Certificate should be prepared on the solicitors own letter headings and disclose the following details:—
   (a) The start and finish dates of the accounting periods.
   (b) The list of Powers of Attorney should be included. A separate list can be attached to the Certificate if the volume of Powers held is large.
   (c) Cashroom partners should be disclosed.
   On the reverse of the Certificate, information taken from the accounting records each quarter should be included as follows:—
   (a) Total sums due to clients in the general client accounts.
   (b) Total monies held in general client bank accounts.
   (c) Surplus or deficit which results.
   (d) Total sums due to named clients.
   (e) Total monies held for named clients.
   (f) The firm's financial position shown as a total. Monies held in the practice balance sheet for the firm should be shown in total. If the firm has term loans, practice loans, overdrafts or other borrowings shown in the balance sheet then these must be disclosed. Hire purchase liabilities which fund partnership assets are included but unexpired leases are not. Personal loans arranged outwith the firm are excluded.
   If an Accountant is instructed to help with the work of preparing the new Certificate, an explanation of the extent of help is needed. This is best done by attaching a copy of the Letter of Engagement as arranged between Accountant and Solicitor.

27. *Do the Rules and Regulations apply to Incorporated Practices?*
   Yes.
NOTE
   This brief guide has been prepared by the Guarantee Fund Committee who are Solicitors just like yourselves. None of us likes rules but they are there to help us all keep proper records, to protect clients' money, to reduce the risk to the Guarantee Fund and to keep the Guarantee Fund contributions to a minimum.
Please play your part
   If you are at any time in doubt about what you are doing, please do not hesitate to contact the Society's Chief Accountant, Leslie Cumming, or one of his staff at:

The Law Society of Scotland	Telephone: 0131 226 7411
The Law Society's Hall	Fax: 0131 225 2934
26 Drumsheugh Gardens	E-mail:
Edinburgh	Document Exchange DX ED 1
EH3 7Y	Edinburgh

who are always willing to help and advise.

SCHEDULE 1

VERIFICATION OF IDENTITY FLOWCHART

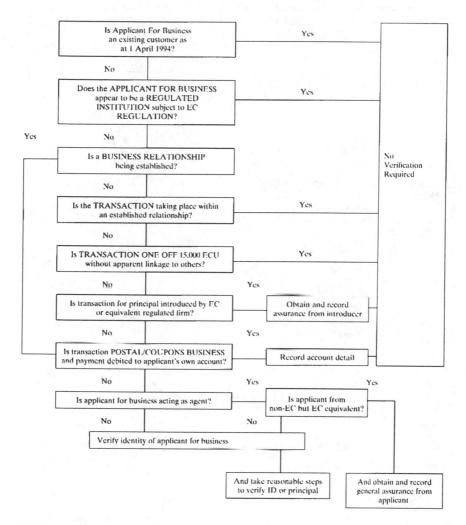

NOTE
If money laundering is known or suspected then a report must be made to NCIS and verification procedures undertaken if not already done so.

SCHEDULE 2

The Money Laundering Regulations 1993. Verification of client identity. Identity should be verified by obtaining **at least two of the following**, of which one should be from the list above the dotted line. Wherever possible, documents including a photograph of the holder should be obtained.

A. EVIDENCE OBTAINED TO VERIFY NAME AND ADDRESS

☐ Full National Passport   Ref No:_____
☐ Full National Driving Licence   Ref No:_____
☐ Pension Book   Ref No:_____
☐ Armed Forces ID Card   Ref No:_____
☐ Signed ID card of employer known to you   Employer Name & Address:_____

☐ Young persons NI card (under 18 only)   Ref No:_____
☐ Pensioner's travel pass   Ref No:_____
☐ Building Society passbook   Roll No:_____ BS:_____
☐ Copy Company Certificate of Incorporation   Incorporation No:_____

....

☐ Gas, electricity, telephone bill   Ref No:_____ Region:_____
☐ Mortgage statement   Ref No:_____ Lender:_____
☐ Council tax demand   Ref No:_____ Region:_____
☐ Bank/building society/credit card statement   Ref No:_____ Issuer:_____
☐ Young persons medical card (under 18 only)   Ref No:_____
☐ Home visit to applicant's address*
☐ Check of telephone directory*   (Copy entry required)
☐ Check of voters' roll*   (Copy entry required)

* Suitable for proof of address only

B. EVIDENCE NOT OBTAINED   Tick box as appropriate

Existing customer 1.4.94

Evidence provided previously on date_____

Other (please state reason)_____

I confirm that:
(a) I have seen the originals of the documents indicated above and have identified the above Customer(s), or
(b) In accordance with the Regulations, evidence is not required for the reasons stated.

Signed_____ **Date**_____

NOTES TO CHECKLIST:
   1. Where funds are coming other than from the client, the verification criteria will be relevant to the funds provider. For example, if a house is being bought in the name of X for £15,000 but the funds are paid by Y, then a verification form would need to be completed for Y if an individual or other appropriate check made with the issuer of the funds.
   2. A "business relationship" is defined as any arrangement between two or more persons designed to govern the dealings between those persons where the dealings are to be on a "frequent, habitual or regular" basis and where the monetary value is not known or capable of being known at outset.
   3. Under the regulations, if a transaction is considered to be a one-off transaction, the funds must be linked to any other transaction made by the same applicant/fund provider to assess whether the total funds over the last 3 months is in excess of £12,000.
   4. In terms of the regulations a calendar year means a period of twelve months beginning on 31st December.

SCHEDULE 3

O++N++   NCIS FINANCIAL DISCLOSURE

Please be careful to align typing on the same line as the plus sign coding

Test typing on this line ++   ++T++

___

Disclosure Type ++   ++1++Category++   ++2++

Name of Institution ++   ++3++

Your Reference No. ++   ++4++

Sort Code ++   ++5++

Town or Branch ++   ++6++

Surname ++   ++7++

Forename(s) ++   ++8++

Address ++

___

++9++ Do not type on this line

Postcode ++   ++A++ Date of Birth   ++B++

Other searchable Factors ++

___

++C++ Do not type on this line

Information ++

___

++D++ Do not type on this line.

Key:	Disclosure Type	DTOA 1986/CJScot/CJA 1988/POTA 1989
	Category	Type A for New or B for Update
	Surname	Surname of subject of disclosure or business name
	Date of Birth	Enter date as DD/MM/YY
	Other Searchable Factors	Identification Procedure, Associated Names, Tel Nos, Fax/Mobile Tel Nos, Passport No. Etc.
	Information	Details of Transactions arousing suspicion and other information considered to be relevant to disclosure *i.e.* Accounts details, Occupation/Employer. Continue on next page if necessary.

Release 46: 21 November 1997

Suggested List of Items that Should be Special Areas of Concern to Designated Cashroom Partners

Consider:—
1. The methods used to record incoming funds and make sure that all funds are lodged in the bank on the day of receipt.
2. Your arrangements to handle cash handed in by clients.
e.g. Do you have special arrangements to cope with larger cash sums brought to you by clients?
Do you see the detailed workings of the client account balances each month?

How much checking do you do each month on:—
  (a) List of client balances
  (b) Bank reconciliation working papers
  (c) Statements of surplus/deficit?
Do you have an automatic reporting and investigation procedure set up if your accounting system discloses a temporary shortage?
Can you confirm at least quarterly that all client funds including funds invested for named clients are properly accounted for? What checks are done to verify the position?
Are all large fees reviewed to confirm they are fully charged but not excessively or prematurely charged?
Do you have any controls over the level of interim fees being charged during an ongoing piece of business?

Guidance on Retention/Destruction of Files and Records

Specific obligations regarding the retention of financial records are noted in the Solicitors (Scotland) Accounts Rules. The client ledger records and day book records of journals must be retained for a period of ten years. The Law Society therefore recommended that any documents which may be required to be produced to vouch payments or receipts within the client ledger account should be retained for a period of ten years.
Client files which deal with conveyancing, executry or trust accounting matters would contain within the general correspondence files matters of importance which would require to be kept for the full ten year period. Bank statements, cashed cheques, VAT fee notes or any passbooks or print-outs which relate to funds invested or borrowed on behalf of clients would fall directly into this category.
Those solicitors who use a system of debit/credit posting slips to instruct the cashroom in their work should also ensure that these documents are retained safely for the ten year period. Previous advice from the Society had suggested that these posting slips might not require to be retained for the full ten year period. Police enquiries into matters of employee or solicitor fraud have now indicated that these documents are of vital significance to their enquiry since the handwriting will give significant evidence as regards the source of instructions in respect of any misleading or false entries. You may wish to take account of this advice.
The only financial records which are not covered by the ten year rule are the documents which comprise lists of client balances, bank reconciliation workings and statements of surplus/deficit prepared in respect of the monthly client ledger account reconciliation. These working papers are now required to be kept for a period of three years.

The Society is aware that a convention has grown up amongst solicitors who carry out a significant amount of Criminal Legal Aid whereby files which relate to completed cases are routinely destroyed twelve months after the matter has been concluded. The Society has no concerns regarding this procedure provided there are no client account funds involved in the transaction. In the event that the solicitor is dealing with client funds any relevant vouchers would require to be separated and stored for the full ten year period prior to the contents of the file being destroyed.

Generally if you are in doubt with regard to the destruction of specific client files or papers then every effort should be made to retain all documents for the minimum ten years.

Law Society Guidelines on Retention of Funds

The Professional Practice Department at the Society receives a substantial number of inquiries about solicitors' obligations in relation to funds retained at settlement of conveyancing transactions. Solicitors frequently find that they are unable to get instructions from clients who either decline to reply to letters or who have disappeared. Some general guidance may be of assistance in these situations.

Where a sum of money is to be retained at settlement of a conveyancing transaction, the conditions upon which it is retained should be set out in writing at settlement. The agreement should specify the time-limit for implementation. Matters should not be left to recollection of telephone conversations which may become vague with the passage of time.

If funds were retained pending fulfilment of certain conditions by the seller, they should be released when those conditions have been fulfilled in terms of the written agreement. The purchaser's solicitor does not need to seek instructions from his or her client at that stage.

Solicitors are entitled to rely upon agreements reached with other solicitors at settlement which set out conditions on which funds will be released. If the client instructs the solicitor not to release funds there could be a conflict of interest between solicitor and client requiring the solicitor to withdraw from acting.

It may be that the conditions for release of the funds have not been fulfilled by the seller. In these circumstances if the purchaser's solicitor produces vouching for the actual or estimated expenditure required to fulfil the conditions, the seller's agent does not require the seller's instructions to agree to the release of the funds as so vouched. Again solicitors are entitled to rely on the reciprocity of such agreements.

Law Society Guidelines on Faxed and E-Mail Documents

The Professional Practice Committee and the Council have looked again at a solicitor's duty in relation to a fax of a contractual document such as a Missive. The Committee re-affirmed its previously published view (Council Report—December 1991) that there is a duty on a solicitor to follow up a fax of a contractual document with the original as soon as possible. If the solicitor is instructed by the client not to send the hard copy that fact must be communicated to the other solicitor immediately and the solicitor must withdraw from acting if the client cannot be persuaded to withdraw such instructions. Furthermore, if a solicitor is not sure if a contractual document can be sent, a fax should not be sent of it. It has been held in the sheriff court that a bargain was concluded where the final Missive was communicated by fax.

Release 48: May 1998

The Committee also considered the question of E-Mails. They observed that normally an E-Mail is more akin to a phone call than to a fax and that solicitors should ensure they have an appropriate security level to deal with the question of confidentiality. If a solicitor is dealing by E-Mail with a matter and which instructions need to be recorded, written confirmation should be sent of the instructions received by E-Mail putting the onus on the client to correct the instruction if it has been wrongly noted. The E-Mail should be printed out and put on the file if it contains instructions.

E-Mails which carry attachments containing facsimile signatures should be treated as faxes.

Law Society Guidelines on Property Schedules and Mortgage Advice Service

The Professional Practice Committee has issued the following Guideline on Property Schedules and the promotion of a firm's Mortgage Advice Service:

Rule 5 of the Solicitors (Scotland) Practice Rules 1986—commonly known as the Conflict of Interest Rules—prohibits the same firm from acting for buyer and seller of heritable property "at any stage". The Professional Practice Committee have decided that giving advice about a mortgage or finance to a prospective purchaser of a property is acting at a stage. The firm selling the property can therefore only give such advice when the prospective purchaser is an established client or a client otherwise exempt from the general prohibition on acting for buyer and seller in the Rules.

The Committee has therefore decided that solicitors should take care about the wording of Property Particulars. If the firm's own Mortgage Advice Service is promoted to prospective purchasers in the Schedule, the Schedule must include a warning advising that the firm may not be able to act for the would be purchasers in giving mortgage advice or in any other matter connected with the purchase. Firms can offer to arrange for such prospective purchasers to see another solicitor thus keeping the business within the profession rather than going to external mortgage brokers or estate agents.

Law Society Guidelines for Compliance with Continuing Professional Development Regulations

The Regulations came into full effect on 1st November 1996. They apply to solicitors holding a Practising Certificate. The Guidelines will be reviewed periodically and may be amended in the light of experience.

Annual Requirement

Solicitors to whom the Regulations and Guidelines apply will require to undertake 20 hours Continuing Professional Development in each practice year. For solicitors practising in Scotland, England or Wales, a minimum of 15 hours will require to be in Group Study and up to five hours can be by Private Study, except for authors of published books or articles (see below). Solicitors practising outwith Scotland, England or Wales may comply with the Regulations by undertaking 20 hours Private Study.

Trainees

Trainee solicitors in their second year who have a restricted practising certificate are admitted solicitors and will require to undertake C.P.D. in accordance with these Guidelines.

Definition

In the Regulations Continuing Professional Development is defined as "relevant education and study by a solicitor to develop his or her professional knowledge, skills and abilities".
This means education and training in:
1. Specific legal areas and topics.
2. Management and organisation.
3. Communication and client care skills.
4. Other areas relevant to the solicitor's practice.
5. Any area designed to improve an individual's ability to operate properly and effectively as a solicitor.

Method

The Society wishes solicitors to have as much control and responsibility for their own development as possible. The parameters are therefore expressed in broad outline.

Private Study

Private Study means study undertaken by less than three persons together. No more than five hours private study per annum will count towards fulfilling the C.P.D. requirement.
Private study includes:
1. Distance learning by audio/visual/correspondence courses, television and radio courses, and computer-based learning.
2. The reading of relevant periodicals and books.
3. Writing relevant books or articles in periodicals or text books which are published (in which case the time occupied may be up to ten hours of the total C.P.D. requirement for the particular practice year).

Note: This list is not exhaustive but merely illustrative.

Group Study

Group study means study in a group of three or more people which lasts for a minimum of half an hour. For solicitors in Scotland, England or Wales, with the sole exception of authors of books or articles as stated above, it must occupy a minimum of 15 of the required hours per annum and must be in a form which can be verified.

Group study includes the following: discussion groups; tutorials; study meetings of special interest groups; workshops; seminars; or courses.

These may feature in house training or training by outsiders and may be run by firms; departments of organisations and/or firms; local faculties and societies; groups of firms; the Society's UPDATE Department; or other providers.

Group study may take place within or outwith Scotland and does not require to be in groups which only comprise solicitors. It does require to be relevant to the solicitor's practice.

The Law Society does not intend to award accreditation to any courses or course providers nor will it guide solicitors on what is relevant to them. Solicitors should exercise their own judgment on what training is relevant to their particular practice requirements. Such judgment will require to be exercised reasonably.

The preparation and delivery of training for others is a very effective means of learning. Solicitors involved as lecturers, tutors or leaders in any form of relevant group study may count preparation time up to a maximum of four hours towards the C.P.D. group study requirement, in addition to actual presentation time.

Some group study will involve workshops and role play. Courses requiring delegates' active participation in these ways are more effective than traditional lecture-based courses. Solicitors undertaking such participation may count an additional one-quarter of the actual time of the course towards their C.P.D. requirement.

Management and Professional Development Skills

A frequent cause of difficulty for solicitors arises out of lapses in management either of the office or the case and/or poor communication with clients, rather than simple ignorance of law or procedure. For this reason at least five hours of the total annual requirement (of which a minimum of three hours must be in group study) shall be spent on training in management (including self-management), organisation, client care and communication skills. These include Professional Ethics, Financial and Business Management, Budget Control, Computer Skills, Foreign Languages, Interview Techniques, Setting Priorities and Time Management. This list is only illustrative not exhaustive.

Double Training Relief

Solicitors who require to undertake compulsory training other than by reason of the Continuing Professional Development Regulations may count such training as part of the requirement for C.P.D. in that particular practice year. The following are some examples. They are not an exhaustive list:

Practice Management Course: Solicitors who require to attend a Practice Management Course by virtue of the Solicitors (Scotland) (Practice Management Courses) Practice Rules 1989.

Extended Rights of Audience: Solicitors who require to attend a Training Course in terms of the Solicitors (Scotland) (Admission with Extended Rights of Audience) Rules 1995.

England and Wales: Solicitors practising in England and Wales who require to undertake continuing training in that jurisdiction will not require to undertake further C.P.D. to comply with these Rules. Solicitors who do not require to undertake such continuing training shall undertake C.P.D. in accordance with the above requirements.

Solicitors Not Working Full Time Throughout The Year

Solicitors who do not work full time throughout the year will be exempt from the requirement to undertake 20 hours C.P.D. per annum as follows:
1. Solicitors, other than locums, working *150 hours or less* during the practice year—total exemption.
2. *Part-time* solicitors who work for more than 150 hours in the practice year will undertake one hour's C.P.D. per annum for every two hours per week worked with a minimum of ten hours C.P.D. per annum.
3. *Locums and Solicitors who only work part of the year* will undertake 1½ hours C.P.D. for every four weeks worked in aggregate with a minimum of ten hours C.P.D. per annum.
4. Solicitors who are *unemployed* for part of the year will undertake 1½ hours C.P.D. for every four weeks worked in aggregate.
5. Solicitors suffering *long-term* illness for ten weeks or more in respect of the same illness in any practice year may reduce their C.P.D. requirement in proportion to the number of weeks worked during the practice year rounded up to the nearest complete hour. To calculate the required number of hours divide the number of weeks worked by 2.6 and round up to the nearest whole number. (*e.g.* solicitors who work between 37 and 39 weeks in a practice year will require to undertake 15 hours C.P.D. in that year).

6. Solicitors taking *maternity leave* may reduce their C.P.D. requirement in proportion to the number of weeks worked in the practice year rounded up to the nearest complete hour in accordance with the formula in No. 5 hereof.
7. Solicitors who take *sabbatical* leave of six weeks or more in the practice year may reduce their C.P.D. requirement in proportion to the number of weeks worked in the practice year but with a minimum of ten hours C.P.D. per annum.
8. Solicitors *admitted during the practice year* (1st November to 31st October) will be exempt in the course of *that* practice year, but will require to undertake full C.P.D. in the following practice year.
9. Solicitors *retiring during the practice year and not renewing their practicing certificate* will be exempt in the course of that practice year.

Note: In all of the above the proportions of group study, management and professional development skills and private study will be reduced pro-rata.

Monitoring and Enforcement

Solicitors will be expected to complete the record card honestly and truthfully, and will be required to produce their record card at the end of the practice year.

The Society will study in detail a random sample of 5 per cent of returned record cards to check that the required hours of C.P.D. have been properly completed and will take steps to verify that the solicitors in the sample have undertaken the group study part of C.P.D. Group study may be verified by for example an Attendance Register.

If a solicitor has not complied with the requirement and is not entitled to exemption, further time will be given for compliance as a first sanction and independent evidence of group study will require to be produced to show that compliance has been achieved. Continued failure to comply may be referred to the Society's Complaints Department for consideration as professional misconduct. Records of compliance will be maintained by the Society.

[1] **Law Society Guidelines on Conflict of Interest**

NOTE
[1] As amended in May 1999.

Conflict of interest
It is a well established principle that solicitors should not act for clients where there is a conflict of interest between them. This was codified in the 1986 Practice Rules (*Parliament House Book*, Volume 3, Page F 328) in which Rule 3 states, "a solicitor shall not act for two or more parties whose interests conflict". That statement is entirely unqualified and is the guiding principle which governs the rest of those Practice Rules. Conflict of interest was amplified in the Code of Conduct published in October 1989 (and now printed as a Schedule to the Code of Conduct Rules (*Parliament House Book*, Volume 3, Page F 823). Article 3 of the Code of Conduct states, "Solicitors (including firms of solicitors) shall not act for two or more clients in matters where there is a conflict of interest between the clients or for any client where there is a conflict between the interests of the client and that of the solicitor or the solicitor's firm."

Neither the Rules nor the Code of Conduct contains a definition of conflict of interest. As somebody said it is hard to define but you know it when you see it. Unfortunately many solicitors only seem to see it long after it has appeared and when it is too late. There is a straightforward way of looking at this. If you would give different advice to different clients about the same matter there is a conflict of interest between them. It does not matter that the clients may be agreed about what they wish to do.

Conflict of interest is not a matter for the judgment of the client—it is a matter for the judgment of the solicitor. Only the solicitor has the breadth of experience, training and knowledge to fully advise a client where his interest lies. Jane Ryder in her book Professional Conduct for Scottish Solicitors states, "Where facts are disclosed to a solicitor on behalf of one client which may be prejudicial if disclosed to another client without the authority of the first, there is almost certainly a conflict of interest ... the critical test is whether the solicitor can adequately discharge all duties to his or her respective clients equally." (Pages 61 and 62).

The Discipline Tribunal expressed concern in their Annual Report for 1998 about continuing failure to recognise a conflict of interest and follow the Practice Rules.

Conflict of interest in court matters:

1. *Matrimonial*
It is trite to say that you should not sue your own client, but the question of conflict in court matters goes further than that. In matrimonial cases the same firm of solicitors should not act for both husband and wife in negotiating a separation agreement—or even in preparing a document that reflects the parties' own agreement. The parties have separate interests and the same firm should not act for both of them. If one of them refuses to get separate independent advice, they cannot be forced to do so but you should ensure that you only act for one.

You would be entitled to deal with the other as an unrepresented party—in which case you *must* (in terms of Rule 7 of the 1986 Rules) advise the unrepresented party in writing when sending a document for signature that such signature would have legal consequences and they should seek independent legal advice before signing. You should not spell out what the consequences might be as that would be giving advice. If the unrepresented party does not obtain separate advice and signs and returns the document to you, you would be entitled to treat it as delivered on behalf of your client and to deal with it accordingly. In 1998 the Discipline Tribunal found a solicitor guilty of professional misconduct for failing to comply with Rule 7 and said that whatever pressures might be put upon the solicitor ... "Where professional obligations arise it is not sufficient for a solicitor merely to follow the instructions of his client."

In many separations the matrimonial home will require to be sold. The Professional Practice Committee issued a Guideline about this in February 1994 and again in July 1998 (page F 977). Unless the parties have agreed in writing how the sale proceeds will be distributed (either as part of a wider agreement or as a separate stand alone agreement) neither of the solicitors' firms acting for the individuals should act in the sale. A separate firm should be instructed. This was emphasised in a recent reported case (*Dawson v. R. Gordon Marshall & Co.*, 1996 G.W.D. 1243 issue of 21st June) where Lord Osborne held that by not accounting to the husband for his share of the proceeds in accordance with the title, the solicitors had acted improperly. In that case the solicitors in fact had retained the balance of the proceeds and were in a position to implement the court's decree but they required to meet the expenses of a defended proof in the Court of Session.

If the parties *have* reached an agreement dealing with the free proceeds, and that means an agreement signed by the parties themselves, the solicitors acting for one of the spouses in the matrimonial affairs may act in the sale but must account to both parties in accordance with the signed agreement. They cannot accept unilateral instructions from one of them to alter that. That would be a conflict situation requiring them to immediately withdraw from acting. The mirror image is that if you are consulted by a married couple in connection with the sale of their property and at that time or subsequently you discover that they are separated you would be entitled to accept the instructions to act in the sale but you would require to advise each of them to seek separate independent advice in relation to their matrimonial position. Unless and until a written agreement dealing with the free proceeds is intimated to you, you would require to account to the spouses in accordance with the title.

2. Criminal matters—acting for co-accused
The Code of Conduct for Criminal Work states in Article 2, "A solicitor shall not accept instructions from more than one accused in the same matter." The Code was drawn up by the Criminal Law Committee who were of the view that there is always a potential for conflict between co-accused. For example if one pleads guilty he becomes a compellable witness against the other. Witnesses do not always come up to precognition. A solicitor who accepts instructions and subsequently has to abandon one of the clients is placed in a compromised position not only by virtue of having potentially breached the Conflict of Interest Rules but also by virtue of being likely to possess confidential information relating to the client for whom he has had to cease acting. The Rules of Conduct for Solicitor Advocates prohibit them from acting for more than one accused person "save in the most exceptional circumstances".

Conflict of interest in conveyancing
Conflict in conveyancing transactions is dealt with in Rules 5, 6, 7 and 8 of the 1986 Practice Rules. Rule 5 is without prejudice to the generality of Rule 3 (above) and states—reading short—that the same firm of solicitors shall not *at any stage* act for both seller and purchaser, landlord and tenant, or assignor and assignee in a lease of heritable property for value provided that, where no dispute arises *or might reasonably be expected to arise*, and the seller of residential property is not a builder or developer, the rule shall not apply in certain particular situations. It is worth bearing in mind that when something goes wrong and a complaint is made to the Society or a claim is made under the Master Policy, the circumstances will be looked at with the benefit of hindsight. With hindsight it is clear that the disputes that regularly arise in conveyancing transactions are all disputes which could reasonably have been foreseen such as difficulties with the title; unauthorised alterations; or problems with the purchaser's funding. If a dispute does arise in the middle of a transaction where the same firm are acting for both sides, the solicitors must take immediate steps to cease acting for at least one of the parties and advise them that they should consult an independent solicitor. It is almost always a mistake to attempt to resolve matters and solicitors are generally digging a deeper hole for themselves if they try and do so. It must always be remembered that the Rules are there not only for the protection of clients but also for the protection of solicitors.

The exceptions to the general prohibition are—again reading short—(a) associated companies or public bodies; (b) connected parties within the meaning of a now repealed section of the Income and Corporation Taxes Act (since replaced by Section 839 of the ICTA 1988); (c) parties related by blood, adoption or marriage; (d) established clients; and (e) where there is no other solicitor in the vicinity whom the client could reasonably be expected to consult.

Categories (a) and (b) of the exemptions do not cause any difficulties. Category (c)—parties related by blood etc—is not restricted to any particular degree of relationship but it is unwise to stray beyond the forbidden degrees of marriage.

The most commonly used exemption is the established client—category (d). An established client is defined as "a person for whom a solicitor or his firm has acted on at least one previous occasion". The Professional Practice Committee are of the view that this does not mean that the solicitor requires to have ceased acting in the previous matter—it can be a continuing matter. It must however be a matter in respect of which the solicitor has opened a file with something that the client could be charged for even if he has not in fact been charged for it or may never be charged for it.

Category (e)—no other solicitor in the vicinity—has been interpreted by the Committee as restricted to isolated rural and island communities. It is not applicable anywhere in central Scotland. The matter was raised in connection with a small Highland town which had one full time and one part time solicitor's practice. The Committee decided that this exemption was not available even in that situation, where the nearest other town with a firm of solicitors was nine miles away.

In every case where the solicitors are acting for both parties by virtue of categories (c), (d) or (e) the second part of Rule 5 requires that both parties be advised by the solicitor at the earliest practicable opportunity that the firm have been requested to act for them and that if a dispute arises they or one of them will require to consult an independent solicitor. This advice must be confirmed by the solicitor in writing "as soon as may be practicable thereafter". This does not mean when the offer has been submitted or is about to be submitted. It means when you are first instructed by the purchaser in respect of a property you are selling or in which you know you are to be instructed by the seller if the sale is being dealt with by an external estate agent.

These letters—known as Rule 5 (2) letters—are mandatory and even if you are entitled to act and there is no conflict of interest, failure to send out such a letter is a breach of the Rule. Although you may think that that will not matter if there is no actual difficulty, when the Society's accountants carry out a routine inspection of your firm they will ask for files where the firm has acted for both buyer and seller and report back to the Society where no Rule 5 (2) letters appear in the file. That may lead by itself to a complaint of professional misconduct. Indeed in its Annual Report for 1998 the Discipline Tribunal highlighted a case where they found a solicitor guilty of misconduct for not complying with this Rule. The Tribunal said "it does not mitigate the gravity of any breach that none of the clients involved had been prejudiced or were dissatisfied with the solicitor's conduct of the transaction".

"At any stage"

Rule 5 prohibits the same firm from acting "at any stage". This is interpreted strictly by the Professional Practice Committee. For example:

(1) acting as an estate agent only is acting at a stage for the seller even if all offers are to be submitted to a different firm of solicitors. You would not be entitled to act or give any advice to a prospective purchaser who does not fall within one of the exemptions.

(2) Giving advice about a mortgage or finance for a property is acting at a stage. Again you would only be able to give such advice to a prospective purchaser who is an established client or in respect of whom one of the other exemptions is available. This means you have to be careful about what you say in your property particulars if you are selling the property. The Committee published a Guideline (see page F 958) that if you market your mortgage advice service in your property particulars you must include a notice that you may not be able to act for the recipient. You would be entitled to say that you will arrange for the prospective client to see another solicitor—so that he stays within the Profession for such advice rather than going off to a mortgage broker.

Builders and Developers

Of course you cannot give any advice to a purchaser at all if you are acting for a seller who is a builder or developer. "Developer" has been considered by the Professional Practice Committee. Firstly, a Housing Association is a developer. Secondly, a person who is by trade a builder or developer selling in the course of his business houses or plots which are part of a larger development is clearly a developer but such a person selling a site or house as a single unit and not part of a larger development has also been treated by the Discipline Tribunal as a developer. For example a builder selling a house which has been bought as a trade-in would still be a builder for the purposes of Rule 5.

Thirdly, a person who is not by trade a builder or developer but is selling individual plots or houses which are part of a larger development has the temporary status of a developer (*e.g.* a farmer selling residential plots in a field).

However, a person who is not by trade a builder or developer but is selling a single plot or site is no longer regarded as a developer. A solicitor acting for such a seller who is consulted by the purchaser would be entitled to act for the purchaser if he falls within one of the exemptions to the rule. That is again always provided there is no actual conflict of interest between the parties and no dispute is reasonably likely to arise—which will remain a matter for the judgment of the solicitor. In such transactions there could well be conflicting interests *e.g.* rights of access; other servitudes; maintenance of private roadway; etc. The safest way to avoid such difficulties is to decline to accept instructions from both parties in the first place.

Conflict of interest in relation to loans

1. *General:*

Rule 5 also deals with acting for lender and borrower. In terms of Rule 5(1)(f) the terms of the loan must have been agreed between the parties before the solicitor has been instructed by the lender and the granting of the security is only to give effect to such agreement. You must always remember that the lender is also a client. The lender/borrower rule is still subject to the question of an actual conflict of interest or a dispute which may reasonably be likely to arise. Difficulties have arisen in a number of cases which have been reported—mainly in relation to commercial securities—but the lessons are also relevant to domestic security transactions. There are some extremely valuable articles by Professor Robert Rennie in the Journal of April 1994 (the lender's need to know); February 1995 (the expanding duty of care) and October 1995 (certificates of title). There was also a useful item in the caveat column in the Journal of February 1995 at Page 71.

2. *Commercial securities:*

In relation to commercial securities there was a Presidential circular in March 1994 advising that banks would normally instruct their own solicitors except in what they regarded as *de minimis* cases. The letter—which is printed in the *Parliament House Book*, Volume 3 at Page F 904—contained a number of examples where there is a greater scope for conflict of interest in commercial transactions. It is worth noting that about 25 per cent of all claims on the Master Policy arise out of defective security work.

As stated above if it goes wrong it will all be looked at with the benefit of hindsight. A breach of the conflict of interest rules will lead to a double deductible (excess) as well as a potential finding of professional misconduct. The current excess is £2,000 per partner up to a maximum of ten partners. Double that at £4,000 and the firm could be uninsured for £40,000 as well as having to face a loading of up to 250 per cent of the premium over a period of five years. Remember there are only about 1,200 firms of solicitors in

Scotland and there is therefore a very small insurance pool to fund the Master Policy. Because of the discount/loading position, unless you have a very substantial claim you will find that the policy is really an instalment payment plan.

3. *Home secured for business loan:*

Another area of difficulty in relation to loans is where the jointly owned home is to be put up as security for a business loan to only one of the owners. There is a clear conflict of interest between the owners and you should not act for both of them. Not only must you make it clear that you are not acting for the owner who is not getting the benefit of the loan—when sending the standard security for signature by that person you must accompany it with a letter in terms of Rule 7 of the 1986 Rules as stated earlier (see Matrimonial). In the case of *Smith v. Bank of Scotland* (1997 S.L.T. 1061) the House of Lords decided that the lender has a duty to advise such a joint owner to seek independent advice.

The matter was further considered by the English Courts in *Royal Bank of Scotland v. Etridge and Zwebner v. Mortgage Corporation Ltd* in relation to the duties owed to a spouse who is asked to put up her share of the matrimonial home as security. (See Article by Alistair Sim in Journal of March 1999 at Page 40: Reproduced at **F** 982 *infra*.)

4. *Council house purchase funded by relative:*

A further specific area in relation to loans to be wary of is the council house purchase by the elderly entitled tenant which is being funded by other members of the family. There are clearly different interests to be protected in these situations. The entitled tenant is entitled to the discount as a statutory right. He or she may also be entitled to security of tenure. The person putting up the money is entitled to have that investment protected or at least to get advice about that. Should this be by Standard Security? What about interest and terms of repayment? It is essential to recognise that these interests may not have been addressed by the parties themselves, and you need to make sure that these matters are fully understood by the parties and that there is no dispute between them about what is to happen before you can act. Although in these situations the clients will want it all done as cheaply as possible, that is their problem.

The golden rule in this as in all other professional practice matters is never to convert your client's problem into your own professional problem. If you are faced with a finding of professional misconduct and/or an expensive insurance claim, it could be the most costly fee you have ever earned.

5. *Your own security:*

Finally, in relation to loans—and not strictly speaking conflict of interest—the Society gets a considerable number of enquiries from solicitors about their own purchase and sale. The matter is governed by Rule 10 of the Accounts Rules. That Rule means that the firm cannot act for the lender in the creation, variation or discharge of a Standard Security where the borrower is a partner, the spouse of a partner, or a company or a partnership in which either of them have an interest. The definition of loan is wide enough to include a guarantee or a loan to children, parents or others. In relation to discharges there is an exception where the borrowers' obligations under the Standard Security have been fully implemented before a discharge is obtained from the lender. That means where the loan has been repaid in the natural course or out of funds not deriving from the sale of the property. Although the Council have power to waive this Rule where the borrower is a partnership (but not including a firm of solicitors) or a company—there is no power to waive the Rule where the borrower is a partner, the spouse of a partner or the firm itself.

[1] Law Society Guidelines on Confidentiality

NOTE
[1] As amended in May 1999.

Confidentiality

General

Confidentiality is frequently confused with conflict of interest but is in fact a separate and distinct question. There are no Practice Rules dealing with this but the position is set out in Article 4 of the Code of Conduct which states, "The observance of client confidentiality is a fundamental duty of solicitors. This duty applies not only to the solicitors but also to their partners and staff and the obligation is not terminated by the passage of time."

Confidentiality is a privilege which is exercisable by the client and which can therefore be waived by the client. It covers matters which are actually confidential and not in the public domain. For example, the contents of a document which has been registered in a public register can never be confidential, although the circumstances in which it was entered into, the advice given to the client and the instructions which were received from the client will be confidential so far as not set out in the document.

Specific situations:

1. *Party in dispute with former client:*

Where a solicitor's firm used to act for one party and is now instructed by another party with whom the original client is in dispute, if the original client has instructed a new solicitor there will be no breach of the Conflict of Interest Rules, but you may not be able to act for the new client. If you are in possession of confidential information about your original client which would be of benefit to the new one, you must make certain that this is not disclosed and not made use of. The best way to achieve this is to decline to act for the new client.

You should always remember the client's perception of the matter which will be different from your own. He may make a complaint to the Society anyway. While it will be a matter for your own judgment, you would not be criticised for declining to act. If the former client has not instructed a new solicitor, you should exercise even more caution before accepting new instructions as the original client may wish to instruct you in the matter anyway.

2. *Solicitor moving firm:*

A solicitor who had moved from one firm to another was the subject of a case in England which was reported in the Law Society Gazette in June 1995. He had been a partner in one of the foremost firms specialising in the field of intellectual property and a firm which at all times had acted for the plaintiff in a patent case. The solicitor was not in any way involved in those proceedings and was engaged on work for different clients. He left the firm to join a different firm who were acting for the defendant in the patent case.

The plaintiff sought an injunction to prevent the individual solicitor—but not his new firm—being involved in any part of the patent case on the grounds that he might be in possession of confidential information. The High Court in London did not grant the injunction and set out the test relating to solicitors who move firms. A solicitor will only be disqualified from acting in a contentious matter against his previous firm's clients if he or she has (or there is a real risk that he or she has) relevant confidential information; that is, information which was confidential at the time of communication and which remains both confidential and relevant. The onus of proof is on the solicitor. While the matter may not have been tested in the courts in Scotland the test set down in England is a valid one.

3. *Statement to the police:*

The Professional Practice Committee regularly receives calls from solicitors who have been asked to give a statement either to the police or to the solicitors acting for the former client's opponent. The authorities on confidentiality were reviewed in the reported case of *Micosta v. Shetland Islands Council*, 1983 S.L.T. 483 where Lord President Emslie giving the opinion of the court stated the general rule, "that communications passing between a party and his law agent are confidential". He then went on to say, "So far as we can discover from the authorities the only circumstances in which the general rule will be superseded are where fraud or some other illegal act is alleged against a party and where his law agent has been directly concerned in the carrying out of the very transaction which is the subject matter of enquiry." In the particular case the court refused a motion to open up a confidential envelope which had been recovered by specification in a civil action.

The principle was taken slightly further by Lord Macfadyen in the case of *Conoco v. The Commercial Law Practice* in 1996. In that case the Commercial Law Practice had been consulted by a client who had asked them to write to Conoco without mentioning his name but advising them that he was aware of circumstances in which they had made substantial overpayments on a contract which he would be willing to provide further information about in return for a proportion of what was recovered.

Instead of responding positively to this invitation, Conoco brought a Petition under the Administration of Justice Act to require the solicitors to disclose their clients' name and address which was granted. Lord Macfadyen stated, "The public policy consideration which underlies the fraud exception may be capable of extension to a situation in which a party and his solicitor, not themselves either guilty of fraud or involved in carrying out a fraudulent transaction, are involved in a transaction the purpose of which is to derive for the client benefit from his knowledge of a fraud committed by another party."

If you are asked to give a statement to the Police or the Procurator Fiscal the Professional Practice Committee view is that you should offer to be precognosced on oath before the sheriff. If you answer a question on the direction of the court you would not be subject to a complaint of breach of confidentiality, as the matter is fundamentally one of law not of practice. The High Court in 1999 refused a Bill of Suspension in the case of *Kelly and Sarwar* where the Solicitor appealed against a citation to give a precognition on oath.

You should not hand over your file or papers to the Police or the Fiscal unless they have obtained a warrant. You should pay close attention to what is called for in such a warrant and only deliver that. If you feel the material is confidential you should put it in a sealed envelope and mark it as such. If the authorities complain about the difficulty in obtaining a warrant, then *a fortiori* you should not hand over your papers voluntarily.

If you are cited to give evidence at a trial you must appear but again should follow the judge's directions. If you are required to answer a question you should do so. Whether the evidence is admissible is a matter for the courts to determine and might form grounds of appeal.

4. *Crime about to be committed:*

You may receive information from your client about a crime which he is threatening to commit. In those circumstances the client is *not* entitled to the privilege of confidentiality and you would be quite entitled and some would say obliged to draw the circumstances to the attention of the authorities. For example, if Thomas Hamilton—who had consulted a number of different solicitors about different matters—had advised any of them of his intentions at Dunblane primary school, those solicitors would have been duty bound to alert the authorities so as to prevent the tragic events from happening.

5. *Insolvent client:*

Finally, you may find yourself asked to produce information to a trustee in sequestration or a liquidator. If you acted for the bankrupt or the company which has gone into liquidation, the trustee or the liquidator steps into the client's shoes and is entitled to all the papers which you hold for the client— although in a sequestration only so far as relating to the bankrupt's financial affairs. You do not need to take your client's instructions on whether such information should be given.

You should however be careful to separate out papers in relation to individual directors or shareholders where you were acting for a company and only deliver those papers in relation to your acting for the company— unless of course the same person has been appointed trustee to the individual directors or shareholders.

Law Society Guidelines on Mandates in Executries

In 1986 the Council published a Guideline on a solicitor's duty to implement a mandate where the solicitor is one of the executors and also acting as agent in the executry. Two partners of a firm were executors along with the deceased's widow. The widow consulted other agents and a mandate from her was sent to the solicitor executor's firm. They declined to implement it which led to a finding of professional misconduct.

As part of their recent Review of Practice Guidelines the Committee considered this matter and re-affirmed the Council's view as follows:

1. Where there is a combination of solicitor and non-solicitor executors, a solicitor executor should not use his power as executor to secure the continuity of his acting as solicitor in the winding up of the estate. In such circumstances the solicitor may either cease acting or resign as executor.
2. If the solicitor ceases to act but remains as executor, he should bow to the wishes of the other executors on which firm should take over the administration of the estate. Failure to do so gives rise to a conflict between the interests of the executors and the interests of the solicitor's practice.
3. If the solicitor decides to resign, he should seek a discharge and obtemper any mandate if the remaining executors resolve that another firm should act.

Law Society Guidelines on Conflict of Interest and Ranking Agreements

The Professional Practice Committee have agreed that a Guideline should be published on conflict of interest in relation to a Ranking Agreement. The Committee are of the view that there is a conflict of interest between lenders in relation to a Ranking Agreement and that the same firm should not act for more than one lender even in *de minimis* cases.

Consideration should also be given to whether there is a conflict of interest between lender and borrower in relation to a Ranking Agreement. Whether there is will depend on the particular circumstances of each case.

Law Society Guidelines on Closing of Files

The matter of a solicitor's duty on closing a file was discussed in 1992 and a brief note on the subject appeared in the summer "Council Report" of that year. The Professional Practice Committee agreed:—

"That there is a professional duty upon a solicitor to advise a client in writing that the file will be closed in the absence of his instructions within a specific period of time."

This is clearly sound common sense in the situation where the solicitor is sitting waiting for further instructions. There must be some way of bringing the matter to a close so that the filing cabinet can be cleared of dormant files, accounts can be rendered either to the client or SLAB and both solicitor and client know the matter has come to an end. However there are cases such as old conveyancing transactions after the delivery of the Search and other cases where the matter is obviously concluded where the duty is not the same.

The matter has now been reviewed and the Committee have agreed that:

In cases where the matter in which the solicitor was instructed has not come to an obvious and natural conclusion there is a duty upon a solicitor to advise the client in writing that the file will be closed in the absence of his instructions within a specific period of time.

Law Society Guidelines on Terms of Business

As soon as instructions are received from a client or when tendering for business, a Solicitor should issue a terms of business letter of engagement. The content of the letter will vary depending on the status of the recipient and the type of work which may be undertaken. The letter should be clear and unambiguous using straightforward language thus ensuring that the recipient will be in no doubt as to the meaning of the content.

On all occasions, the following matters should be addressed in the letter of engagement:

1. The Source of authorisation of the Solicitor—Law Society of Scotland.
2. Method by which instructions should be given and received.
3. Authority of the client to instruct (*e.g.* who is the authorised person if the client is a company or a partnership; husband/wife or other multiple clients).
4. Supervision of client business. (*i.e.* name and status of person responsible for day-to-day conduct of matter and principal responsible for overall supervision if different).
5. Conflict of interest.
6. Requirement of confidentiality.
7. Procedures for resolving problems.

The following matters would normally be included in addition to those listed.

1. Holding client money.
2. Fee estimate (except in legal aid cases) to include VAT and prospective outlays.
3. Timing of payment of fees.
4. Outlays.
5. Timescale in general.

In addition, it is good practice for the following matters also to be included:

1. Indemnity/liability for loss.
2. Client's right to taxation.
3. Separate agent and client account in court matters (including legal aid).
4. Lien over titles and papers.
5. Level of service to be provided.

Clients who provide a regular flow of instruction of the same type of business and subject matter may not require a separate letter of engagement each time they instruct the Solicitor. In these cases, clients should receive a letter of engagement at least once a year and every time the terms of the letter of engagement are amended by the Solicitor.

Law Society Guidelines on Mandates

The Professional Practice Committee has recently reviewed the current guidance to the profession on the subjects of Mandates. This is contained in several sources and the purposes of this article is to update the guidance. The main guidance at the present time may be seen as being Scott Galt's article in the Journal in 1989 (see n. 1 at end) and an article on behalf of the Professional Practice Committee in 1995 (see n. 2 at end).

Times have changed since 1989. Clients now shop around more than they did and at times it may be difficult to draw lines between a response to advertising, competitive quoting and touting.

It remains the case, however that a Solicitor should not directly approach someone else's client (see n. 3 at end). We therefore have to look at both sides of the Mandate situation, the obtaining of a Mandate and the response to a Mandate.

Obtaining Mandates:

Since a Solicitor cannot approach another Solicitor's client other than as part of a general circulation, mail-shot or advert, the initial approach must come from the client. The exception to this, the situation of Partnerships breaking up, is considered below. There may be a variety of reasons why a client may wish to change Solicitors.

(a) **Client Moving:**

The simplest situation which will seldom cause any difficulties is the obvious one of the client moving from one part of the country to another and wanting to instruct a local Solicitor, *e.g.* in an ongoing matrimonial case.

(b) **Client Dissatisfied:**

The client may or may not be moving but wants a new Solicitor. This should be straightforward enough but points to note include:—
  (i) Ensuring that the instruction to the new Solicitor is from the **client** as opposed to a relative or friend who has suggested the change of Solicitor; and
  (ii) The client should be asked if the dissatisfaction should be communicated to the previous Solicitor and, if so, whether in general or detailed terms.

(c) **New Cases:**

For a variety of reasons, (moving, dissatisfaction, lower quote, personal connection or recommendation) a client may give instructions to a new Solicitor at the beginning of a new piece of business although that client was represented by a different Solicitor in previous matters. Most commonly this would be the situation where a property has been bought using one Solicitor and a few years later is to be sold through another who then has to obtain the titles. Obviously if the titles are with a Bank or Building Society the new Solicitor just requests them and gets on with it and no Mandate is needed. If the titles are with the previous Solicitor a Mandate will be required.

The situations outlined at (a), (b) and (c) above are relatively straightforward. For whatever reason the client has instructed a new Solicitor. Things
are much less straightforward, however, in the situation where the Solicitor's
Partnership is breaking up. There are two slightly different situations here.
One is the Partner leaving the continuing firm and the other is the firm itself
dissolving.

Partner Leaving:
The Partners of the firm involved should agree on the procedure to be
adopted in advising clients of the change in the firm. In some cases it may be
agreed amongst the partners that the departing Solicitor should carry on
with certain cases. In others it may be desired to leave it to their clients to
decide whether to stay or go with the departing Partner. It makes sense to
agree the approach in advance. An unseemly squabble may well alienate the
client from all of the Partners. The terms of a joint communication should be
agreed and sent to the client who should be invited to indicate a preference
to stay with the established firm or go with the departing Partner. In an age of
ever increasing competitiveness, however, it may be that the established firm
and the departing Partner wish to set out their respective stalls in their own
distinct ways. It is to be hoped that they can at least agree to send their letters
in the same envelope.
Particular difficulties arise where there is no co-operation between the
departing and remaining Partners. Some Solicitors take the view that all
clients are clients of the firm rather than individual Solicitors and maintain
that a departing Partner has no right to try to take clients away from the
continuing firm. If that were the case then the departing Partner would not
be allowed to seek Mandates from the clients. The Committee has
re-affirmed its view however that subject to what the Partners may
themselves have agreed a departing Partner is entitled to contact clients for
whom he or she has acted personally as the responsible Partner and invite
them to continue to be clients at the new firm.
The right to contact clients applies both while the departing Partner is still
a Partner of the firm whose clients are being contacted; and also for a
reasonable time after the Partner has left. What is a reasonable time will
depend on the circumstances but in a case in the early 1990's the Committee
decided that 3 months was still within a reasonable time.

Associates and Assistants Leaving:
All of the above applies only to Partners, (*i.e.* Partners in the previous
firm). Unless there is a specific agreement which allows it, a departing
Assistant/Associate is not entitled to contact clients of his or her employers
to seek Mandates with the sole exception of those who are Nominated
Solicitors on a Legal Aid Certificate. The Professional Practice Committee
accepts that an Assistant may very well attract business to a firm. However it
is the firm, and the Partners thereof, who have the authority to deal with the
clients. An Associate/Assistant does not act for the client. It is anticipated,
however, that where there is a significant element of *delectus personae* the
clients may wish to follow the Assistant elsewhere. The approach has to be
from the client however.

Nominated Solicitors:
In terms of the Legal Aid Act, legal aid is available through individual
Solicitors not firms. The Court of Session has held that "so long as a
nominated Solicitor remains in that position he is under a clear professional
duty to render all normal services provided by a Solicitor" (see n. 4 at end). It
follows that an employed Solicitor who is a nominated Solicitor is obliged to
advise the client of a move and if the client wishes, is entitled to continue as
nominated Solicitor.

Dissolution of Partnerships:

Occasionally a firm may be dissolved completely with various Partners going in various directions. If the firm ceases to exist then it can only be the personal relationship between an individual Solicitor and the client which is important. In most cases arrangements would be made for each Partner to take certain files etc. and the client would be advised of this and given an opportunity to instruct otherwise.

In the odd situation where there is no agreement between the Partners the proper course is for the client to be advised of the position, told the new business addresses of all the relevant Partners and asked to choose which, if any, to instruct to hold files etc. All of the Partners of the dissolving firm have a duty to ensure proper arrangements are made for the retention of all necessary files and documents.

Receiving Mandates:

The simple rule (except that there is no specific practice rule on the matter) is, and always has been, that when you receive a Mandate you must respond to it "timeously" either by sending the items requested to the new Solicitor or stating that you are exercising a lien pending settlement of fees and outlays. A delay in doing so will normally be misconduct. You cannot retain papers, even if you have a right of lien, if to do so would prejudice the client (*e.g.* in a continuing Court case or transaction) but you can deliver the papers reserving your right of lien and requesting the papers to be returned when the case is concluded. Prejudice is more than inconvenience and will depend on the particular circumstances of the matter.

Any Solicitor receiving a Mandate will usually want to know why. Sometimes the reason is obvious but various questions and problems can arise.

1. **Did the new Solicitor tout for the business?**—It is not for the established Solicitor to judge. You may suspect and if you have evidence you may report but you must, in any event, take the Mandate at face value and hand over the papers.

2. **There is an outstanding fee note.**—You can exercise your lien but you must still respond to the Mandate by writing to the new Solicitor immediately to say you are doing so.

3. **Work has been done for which a fee will be payable but no fee note has been sent out.**—One sometimes gets the response when sending a Mandate that the file has been sent to the Law Accountants and will be forwarded in due course once the fee has been advised and paid. Whether this is acceptable depends on the case in question. If a few weeks without the file will make no great difference then it may be acceptable for the established Solicitor to do this but if the new Solicitor needs the file quickly it is not. The file etc. can be delivered reserving the right of lien. A reasonable time to render an account is in order but it should not exceed four weeks unless the circumstances are truly exceptional. It may be that having extracted such information as required the new Solicitor does not need the actual file in which case it should be returned. This imposes a duty on the new Solicitor to say whether the file is needed urgently and to return the file for feeing as soon as reasonably practicable. If the new Solicitor gives an undertaking (not the clients undertaking) that the account will be paid out of the proceeds of the matter in hand, that should normally be accepted by the original Solicitor and the file and papers delivered.

4. To whom should a fee note be sent when a Mandate is received.—Views differ but the Professional Practice Committee decided in March 1997 that it is not a breach of Article 9 of the Code of Conduct for a Solicitor to send a fee direct to the former client. This followed the view that the debt was due by and would require to be enforced directly against the client. If a lien is being exercised the new Solicitor should be informed anyway. If a lien is not being exercised it might be wondered whether there is a duty on the established Solicitor to tell the new Solicitor that a fee note has been/is being sent. One doubts if it could be categorised as misconduct not to tell the new Solicitor this was being done but it might be seen as a matter of professional courtesy. It should be emphasised, however, that if anything at all is to be sent directly to a client who has instructed a new Solicitor then there should be nothing in that communication which invites the former client to resume the original connection. If fee notes can be sent direct to the client after a Mandate it seems to follow that reminders can also be sent direct but these should be just that, reminders and nothing more. Any invitation to discuss or the like would be a breach of Article 9 of the Code of Conduct and any such matters should be raised through the new Solicitor.

5. Can the established Solicitor ask why the Mandate has been sent?—Yes, but only after the mandate has been implemented. Implementation means delivery of the papers and not simply telling the new Solicitor that a lien is being exercised. The idea behind this is that no undue pressure should be brought to bear on the client and the danger of that happening clearly still exists while the established Solicitor still holds the papers.

6. To whom should the request for reasons be made?—In his article Scott Galt considered that a request for reasons for a Mandate should be addressed to the new Solicitor. The May 1995 Journal article states, however, that a Solicitor having implemented a Mandate "may write to the former client making a reasonable enquiry as to why the client has instructed a new Solicitor". The Solicitor can ask for information but must not in any way invite the former client to resume the original connection. Many Solicitors may disagree with the view that the Solicitor can write directly to the former client at all. On the other hand it may be one of the few ways in which touting might come to light. The current position is, therefore, that the established Solicitor can write directly to the client once the Mandate has been implemented but must be extremely careful in the wording of any such communication.

7. Criminal legal aid cases.—Specific rules apply and are set out at Article 7 of the Code of Conduct for criminal work. (See Schedule attached.)

8. Civil legal aid cases.—Again specific rules apply relating to SLAB's approval of the transfer of Legal Aid Certificates.

In both criminal and civil cases the guidance on request for reasons would apply. With regard to the payment of fees, it can be a source of great frustration in Advice and Assistance cases that SLAB will not consider an account until the whole matter is completed. The original Solicitor may have no way of knowing the matter has been completed unless this information is received from the new Solicitor and is therefore entitled to exercise a lien until a satisfactory undertaking from the original Solicitor is received. There is a clear duty on the new Solicitor to tell the original Solicitor when the account can be submitted or to pay the account out of the proceeds recovered or preserved.

9. Assistants leaving.—As noted above, the general rule here is that the client is a client the firm and not the individual and so the Assistant should not approach the client. A Mandate received in these circumstances however still has to be treated at face value and still has to be implemented, although the Solicitor's conduct could be brought to the attention of the Law Society.

10. Partial Mandated and General Mandates.—A difficulty which may occasionally arise is the situation where the client wants a particular firm to do a particular transaction without in any way intending to shift allegiance in general. Sometimes this has not been reflected in the Mandate which followed which might request "all title deeds and documents" leading to misunderstandings and quite possibly a falling out between Solicitors, none of which tends to impress the client very greatly. It is not uncommon these days for clients to use different Solicitors for different types of business or even for the same type and a new Solicitor should not simply assume that he or she is going to be acting for a new client in all matters. This difficulty could be addressed by producing a *pro forma* Mandate along the following lines:

I hereby authorise and instruct you to send:—
* *All title deeds and documents and files*
* *The title deeds of (specify property)*
* *The documents and papers relating to (specify matter concerned) held by you to (new Solicitors)*
* **Delete where applicable.**

NOTES
    [1] Journal February 1989 p. 54—Article by Scott Galt.
    [2] Journal May 1995 p. 207—Article—"The Departing Assistant and Mandates".
    [3] Code of Conduct—Rule 9. (Also Rule 5 of the Advertising and Promotion Practice Rules 1995)
    [4] *per* Lord Osborne in *McKinstry v. Law Society of Scotland*, 1995 S.L.T. 191.

SCHEDULE

MANDATES IN CRIMINAL WORK (ARTICLE 7 OF THE CODE OF CONDUCT FOR CRIMINAL WORK)

All Mandates requesting the transfer of papers and legal aid relating to a criminal matter shall be completed and executed by the assisted person in the form agreed by the Scottish Legal Aid Board and the Law Society of Scotland. The Mandate should include the place and date of signing and a full explanation as to why the Mandate has been issued.

Guidance Note

The matter is governed by the Criminal Legal Aid (Scotland) Regulations 1987, paragraph 17(3), which states "where an assisted person desires that a solicitor, other than the solicitor presently nominated by him shall act for him, he shall apply to the Board for authority to nominate another specified solicitor to act for him and shall inform the Board of the reason for his application; and the Board, if it is satisfied that there is good reason for the application and, in the case of Legal Aid made available under Sections 24 or 25 of the Act that it is in the interests of justice or, as the case may be, is reasonable, for him to receive or continue to receive Criminal Legal Aid, may grant the application".
    It seems clear from a plain construction of this Regulation that changes of agency where the client is legally aided in a criminal case can only take place if the Board gives the client authority to nominate another specified solicitor. Until the Board gives its authority the client cannot

instruct another solicitor unless he wishes to do so without the benefit of Legal Aid, which fact should be notified to the Board.

Therefore the chronology of transfers of agency in criminal cases should be (1) the client approaches his proposed new solicitor to ascertain if he is willing to act; (2) client applies to Board for authority to transfer the agency; (3) Board grants authority; (4) client instructs new solicitor; (5) new solicitor serves Mandate on previous solicitor.

The Board's authority to transfer must ante-date any Mandate.

This Statement would solve many issues including inducements to transfer agency and "Mandate wars". Adoption of this interpretation would of course mean that legally aided clients and fee paying clients will not be treated precisely equally. However, that objection has to be seen in the light of the need to comply with the Regulations which effectively impose a statutory suspensive condition on any Mandate and the requirement that solicitors will require to inform a transferring client that instructions cannot be accepted until the Regulations are complied with.

Form of Mandate approved by the Council

Dear Sir,
I write to inform you that the Scottish Legal Aid Board has transferred Legal Aid Certificate No.   from you to my new nominated solicitor who is   I authorise and instruct you to transfer to   all papers, documents and files which you hold on my behalf in relation to this matter.
Yours faithfully,

Law Society Guidelines on Avoidance of Delay in Concluding Missives

It is increasingly common for Missives to be in an unconcluded state until shortly before—or even at—the date of entry. While solicitors require to have regard to the interests of their clients and to take their clients' instructions, they must have regard to the principles of good professional conduct and may not accept an improper instruction. They should not knowingly mislead professional colleagues and must act with fellow solicitors in a spirit of trust and co-operation (Code of Conduct for Scottish Solicitors articles 2, 5(a) and 9).

In residential property transactions solicitors acting on behalf of both purchasers and sellers have a professional duty to conclude Missives without undue delay. Clients should be advised at the outset of this duty and of the consequences.

Where a solicitor for a purchaser is instructed to submit an offer but to delay concluding a bargain until some matter outwith the selling agent's control has been resolved—e.g. the purchaser's own house has not been sold; a survey or specialist's report is required; or funding arrangements are to be confirmed—these circumstances should be disclosed to the selling solicitor. If the purchaser instructs the solicitor not to disclose such matters to the selling solicitor, the purchaser's solicitor should withdraw from acting. To continue acting could amount to a breach of article 9 of the Code of Conduct by knowingly misleading a fellow solicitor. Where a purchaser instructs his solicitor to delay concluding a bargain without giving any reason the solicitor should similarly withdraw from acting.

Where a selling client instructs a solicitor to delay concluding a bargain having given an indication that an offer is to be accepted, the reason for that delay should be disclosed to the purchaser's solicitor. If the seller instructs the solicitor not to disclose the reason, or does not give a reason for such an instruction, the solicitor should also withdraw from acting.

If a solicitor—whether for seller or purchaser—withdraws from acting in terms of this Guideline, the confidentiality of the client should not be breached without the client's authority but when intimating withdrawal that should be done by stating that it is in terms of this Guideline.

Law Society Guidelines on Fixed Price Offers

The Professional Practice Committee published Guidelines on Closing Dates in 1991. At that time the Committee decided not to issue a Guideline in relation to fixed price offers, but after reviewing the matter in the light of more recent developments, they have now issued the following Guideline:

The use of fixed price offers should be considered carefully. Problems can arise when two or three prospective purchasers attempt to express interest simultaneously or when offers are submitted subject to conditions.

A sale advertised at a fixed price is an invitation to prospective purchasers to submit offers at that price. In the Committee's view it does not imply an undertaking on the part of the solicitor that the first such offer will be accepted.

If a solicitor is instructed to advertise a property at a fixed price, the Property Particulars should state if the date of entry is material and whether offers subject to survey, subject to finance being obtained, subject to the purchaser's own house being sold or subject to some other suspensive condition will be considered. Other matters material to the seller should also be clearly stated.

Law Society Guidelines on Powers of Attorney

[(July 1998)]

In 1995 the Society's Professional Practice Committee considered a complaint from a consultant psychiatrist that a solicitor, in setting up a Deed of Power of Attorney, did not satisfy himself that the grantor had the capacity to grant such a power. It was alleged that prepared paperwork was passed to the family, who obtained the signature from their elderly relative in hospital. There were no discussions with those in charge of her treatment. In this particular case the Mental Welfare Commission was satisfied after inquiry that the patient had not suffered and decided not to challenge the extant Power of Attorney.

The Professional Practice Committee reminds solicitors (a) that a solicitor must have instructions from his or her client (b) that the client is the granter of the Power of Attorney and (c) that solicitors are not the judges of mental capacity. That is for the medical profession from whom advice should be sought if there is any doubt as to a client's capacity.

Law Society's Guidelines on Acting for Separated Spouses

[(July 1998)]

Separation Agreement

Sale of jointly owned property

1. In 1994, the Committee published a Guideline in relation to the sale of the matrimonial home where the spouses are separated. That has now been reviewed in the light of experience. The Committee have re-affirmed the basic principle that unless the parties have agreed in writing—i.e. an agreement signed by the parties themselves—how the sale proceeds will be distributed, neither of the solicitors' firms acting for the individual spouses in their matrimonial affairs should act in the sale. A separate firm should be instructed. The agreement to be signed does not have to be a full separation agreement. It may be an agreement about the free proceeds alone.

2. The guidance applies where the property is in joint names. Where the property is in the name of only one entitled spouse, there is a clear conflict of

interest between the spouses and the same firm should not act for both of them. The firm acting for the entitled spouse may accept instructions in the sale of the property, but must not act for the non-entitled spouse.

3. Where a firm are acting in the sale of jointly owned property and in the course of the transaction it transpires that the spouses have separated or are about to separate, the firm can continue to act in the sale, but cannot act for either of them in relation to their matrimonial affairs. The clients must be referred to other agents for such advice. The firm acting in the sale should distribute the free proceeds in accordance with the title, or in accordance with the spouses subsequent written agreement. The firm cannot advise either of the spouses on such an agreement as there is a clear conflict of interest between them in relation to that.

4. The same firm of solicitors should not act for both spouses in relation to a separation agreement. Again there is a clear conflict of interest and even if the spouses have agreed on matters, a firm of solicitors should act for only one of them in preparing an actual agreement. If the other refuses to seek separate advice, the firm can deal with that spouse as an unrepresented party. In that case—whether or not the agreement deals with heritable property—the solicitor sending any document for signature by the unrepresented spouse must advise that spouse in writing that signature of the document will have legal consequences and he or she should seek independent legal advice before signing it.

5. Where solicitors are acting for one of two separated spouses and the jointly owned property is to be sold, unless the parties have signed an agreement dealing with the free proceeds of sale, the parties must be referred to a separate firm of solicitors to deal with the conveyancing. It would not be improper for the firm acting for one of the spouses to accept instructions to market the property, but unless there is a signed agreement by the time an offer is received, they should not act in the conveyancing.

6. If the parties have signed an agreement dealing with the free proceeds, the solicitors acting for one of the spouses may act in the sale but must account to the parties in accordance with the signed agreement. They cannot accept unilateral instructions from one of the parties to alter that. There is a clear conflict of interest between the parties in that event. Where solicitors are not acting for both parties in the sale, they are able to accept instructions from their own client to do diligence on the dependence of an action or in execution of an agreement.

Law Society Guidelines on Comments to the Media by Solicitors

[(September 1998)]

The media continue to show great interest in legal matters, particularly cases of a sensational nature. The media is increasingly seeking the views of solicitors involved in court proceedings and also those representing special interest groups or with recognised experience in a particular field. While it is quite proper for solicitors to assist the media in conveying accurate information to the public, there should be no infringement of solicitors' obligations to their clients, the courts, the profession or the administration of justice. The Professional Practice Committee have therefore approved the following Guideline:

(1) Solicitors presenting information to the media in relation to their clients' affairs are acting in a professional capacity. Solicitors should conduct themselves in their public appearances and public statements in the same manner as they would with their fellow practitioners and with the courts.

(2) Before making a public statement concerning a client's affairs, a solicitor must first have the client's authority to do so and must also be satisfied that any communication is in the client's best interests. Solicitors should nor permit their personal interests or those of other causes to conflict with their client's interests.

**Law Society Guidelines on Sending Document to Unrepresented Party
for Signature**

[(October 1998)]

In April 1998 the Committee published a Guideline on the question of
documents being signed by unrepresented parties. In response to views
expressed by the profession, the Committee have amended that Guideline
so that it now matches more exactly the wording of the Practice Rule. An
additional paragraph has been added at the end advising that notice may be
given in a separate letter or contained within the document to be signed. The
full text of the amended Guideline is as follows:

Rule 7 of the Solicitors (Scotland) Practice Rules 1986—the Conflict of
Interest Rules — requires a solicitor dealing with an unrepresented party in
a transaction involving heritable property to advise the unrepresented party
in writing when issuing any deed, missive or other document for signature
that signature will have legal consequences and the party should take
independent legal advice before signing it. There is no equivalent Rule for
other types of transaction.

The Professional Practice Committee have agreed that there is no
justification for distinguishing between transactions involving heritable
property and other types of transaction, and have decided that as a matter of
proper practice solicitors dealing with unrepresented parties in any kind of
transaction on behalf of a client should not issue any document for signature
by the unrepresented party without advising that party in writing that
signature may have legal consequences and to take independent legal advice
before signing it.

Such a notice may be in a separate letter or may be contained within the
document to be signed. It does not require to be acknowledged.

**Law Society Guidelines on Settlement Cheques Sent to be Held as
Undelivered**

[(October 1998)]

As part of their Review of Practice Guidelines, the Professional Practice
Committee have considered Guidelines which were issued in 1992 and 1994,
and have agreed that there should be no change to the most recent
Guideline, which was published in 1994. The Committee reaffirmed that
such matters should be agreed in advance if at all possible, and that it is
improper professional practice to impose unilaterally a condition that a
cheque in settlement of a transaction be held as undelivered pending
confirmation that the sender is in funds. The Committee accepted, however,
that while as a matter of law the seller's solicitor may be entitled to encash
the cheque and ignore the condition, such action would not be good
professional practice as it would destroy the professional trust between
agents. The text of the Guideline is as follows:

In the 1992 journal at page 323 a note was published after a purchaser's
agent, without prior agreement or discussion, sent the selling agent a cheque
for the purchase price "to be held as undelivered" until the purchaser's agent
telephoned to say it could be cashed. The chief accountant's advice as
contained in the note was that the selling agent should have ignored the
unilaterally imposed condition relating to delivery of the cheque and should
have cashed it.

Exception was taken to this view and the matter was extensively debated within the Society's Conveyancing Committee, the Professional Practice Committee and the Council. The considered view of the majority, approved by Council, contradicted important elements in the chief accountant's note.

It is not competent unilaterally to impose a condition, whether made verbally or in writing, in a contract such as for the sale of heritable property. In the absence of subsequent agreement, the missives prevail. It is professionally wrong for an agent to impose a unilateral condition, the first intimation of which to the other side is in a letter on the morning of settlement. Prior discussion and agreement is necessary. Professors Cusine and Rennie touch on this at para. 6.15 of their recent book, Missives, where they state: "It is not open to the purchasing solicitor, at the time of dispatch of the cheque, to require the cheque to be held as undelivered where the seller's obligations under the contract are unimplemented, unless of course that has been agreed with the seller's solicitor".

It is acknowledged that a practice that has developed of sending cheques to be held as undelivered with both sides being agreeable to this. This practice avoids alternative courses of action such as bridging or effecting settlement in person, all of which can be viewed as adding expense, though agents should be aware of the benefits of electronic transfer of funds. Assuming trust between practitioners, arrangements which rely on mutual acceptance of an undertaking nor to cash the cheque can be made. It is analogous to the customary sending of the settlement cheque to be held as undelivered pending dispatch of a duly executed disposition, etc.

It is also important to bear in mind that the question of conditional delivery of a cheque is dealt with in s.21 of the Bills of Exchange Act 1882.

The Society's view is that it was wrong and improper professional practice for the purchasing agent to impose the unilateral condition which he did. However, that did not entitle the selling agent to cash the cheque, given that it was sent subject to the words "to be held as undelivered". The Professional Practice Committee and the Council have confirmed that where money or deeds are sent to be held as undelivered pending purification of a condition, they should be so held if the condition is not purified. Settlement will not take place until they can be treated as delivered, with consequent penalty interest if provided in the missives. The matter is one of practice between agents rather than of law.

Law Society Revised Guidelines on Closing Dates and Notes of Interest

[Note important changes from previous Guidelines]

[(February 1999)]

Following publication of the revised Guideline on Closing Dates and Notes of Interest in the Journal of June 1998 (page 43) a number of representations were received from Members which have now been considered by the Professional Practice Committee. The Committee agreed to amend the Guidelines by removing the possible contradiction between paragraphs 1 and 2. The Committee adhered to the view that the closing date system has been successful and that a Practice Guideline remains appropriate. The Committee accepted that it is neither able to change the law nor to impose moral values on the public. The Committee also decided that a solicitor acting for a seller who accepts a note of interest from a prospective purchaser's solicitor has not given an implied undertaking that the prospective purchaser will be given an opportunity to offer. That part of the earlier Guideline has therefore been deleted.

The full text of the amended Guideline is as follows:

Closing Dates

Selling solicitor
1. There is no legal requirement on a selling solicitor to fix a Closing Date when more than one interest is noted. Selling solicitors are entitled to accept their client's instructions to accept an incoming offer without having a Closing Date and without giving other parties who may have noted an interest an opportunity to offer although every effort should be made to give them such an opportunity if at all possible. If, however, in acknowledging a Note of Interest the selling solicitor has given an undertaking to the prospective purchaser's solicitor that they will be given an opportunity to offer, the selling solicitor should withdraw from acting if the client insists on taking a different course of action.

2. Where possible when fixing a Closing Date, the client should be advised to make him/herself available to consider the offers received. If this is not possible (*e.g.* Executries, Trusts, Companies etc.) prospective offerers should be told this when being advised of the Closing Date.

3. In taking instructions from the selling client to fix a Closing Date, solicitors should advise the client that, although not bound to accept the highest—or indeed any—offer, if the client instructs the solicitor to enter negotiations with a view to concluding a bargain with a party who has submitted an offer at the Closing Date, the solicitor will not be able to accept any subsequent instructions to enter negotiations with or accept an offer from another party unless and until negotiations with the original offerer have fallen through. Unsuccessful offerers should, of course, be advised as soon as possible after the Closing Date of the situation.

4. In the event of the selling client subsequently attempting to instruct the solicitor to discontinue such negotiations in order solely to enter into negotiations with or accept an offer from another party the solicitor should decline to act further in the sale unless the client reconsiders and adheres to the original instructions.

5. Where, at a Closing Date, two or more offers are received in terms that are such that they cannot be distinguished by the selling client, the solicitor may revert to those offerers and give them equal opportunity to revise their offer.

6. These Guidelines apply equally to solicitors acting a estate agents as well a solicitors acting in the conveyancing. Different considerations may apply, however, to sales of commercial property and to sellers owing statutory fiduciary duties to others.

Solicitors acting for prospective purchasers
7. Where a prospective purchaser instructs the solicitor to submit an offer at a Closing Date, the solicitor should advise the client that if the offer is unsuccessful the solicitor will not be able to accept subsequent instructions to submit a revised offer or formal amendment unless expressly invited to do so by the seller's agent.

8. In the event of an unsuccessful prospective purchaser subsequently attempting to instruct the solicitor to submit a revised offer or formal amendment after a Closing Date has passed and without an express invitation by the seller's agent, the solicitor should decline to implement those instructions. The solicitor may accept instructions to intimate to seller's agent that in the event of negotiations with the successful party falling through, the prospective purchaser would be willing enter negotiations, but no indication of any increased bid should be given.

9. Solicitors acting for purchasers who have received a verbal or qualified acceptance—whether following a Closing Date or not—should advise

clients that although an initial acceptance may have been given by the seller, the contract will not be binding until Missives are concluded.

Notes of interest
Solicitors acting for prospective purchasers should advise their clients that noting an interest will not guarantee the clients an opportunity to offer, and if the clients are not in a position to put in an early offer they may not be allowed an opportunity to submit an offer at all.

Where a Closing Date has not been fixed the selling solicitors should advise their clients of any offers received—whether before or after negotiations with another prospective purchaser have commenced—and should intimate that the clients are entitled, but not obliged to accept the second offer notwithstanding that an acceptance may have been given to another prospective purchaser either verbally or in qualified form in writing. The seller's solicitor is entitled, but not obliged, to withdraw from acting if the seller wishes to withdraw from the acceptance of the earlier offer.

Law Society Guidelines on Duty to Lodge a Joint Minute and move for decree

The Professional Practice Committee has reaffirmed a Guideline originally published in December 1996. The Committee was asked for guidance about a divorce action where the wife defender had agreed terms with her husband in a Joint Minute which was signed by her solicitors. The action was allowed to proceed as undefended, but when the affidavits and Minute for Decree were lodged by the husband's solicitors, decree was not sought in terms of the Joint Minute, which had included a payment of periodical allowance.
The Committee agreed that a solicitor acting for a pursuer has a duty not only to lodge the Joint Minute, but also to seek decree in the terms of the Joint Minute. The solicitor for the defender is entitled to rely on that being done without requiring to check the Court Process.

Law Society Guidelines on Conflict of Interest between Borrower and Spouse

[(March 1999)]

ALISTAIR SIM considers the lessons that can be learned from two English cases involving issues of enforceability of securities

Claims regularly arise out of problems over enforceability of securities. Some of these problems arise out of alleged deficiencies in advice tendered to the parties or information reported to the lender. The duties of solicitors in relation to the latter have been the subject of a great deal of litigation in recent times. A certain amount of this litigation has gone on south of the border, however it has a potential impact here.
Two cases raise issues of interest and concern. The decisions in these cases do not necessarily represent the law in Scotland, but it is well worth considering the cases to establish whatever lessons can be learned.
The case of *Royal Bank of Scotland plc v. Etridge (No. 2), The Times*, August 17, 1998 (CA) involved spouses who were contesting proceedings for repossession of matrimonial homes on the basis that their signature of mortgages were procured by misrepresentation or undue influence on the part of the borrower.
How could solicitors be at risk in this situation? A lending institution will inevitably consider alternative remedies in the event of its inability to

enforce a security. If the security relates to matrimonial property and the difficulty in enforcing the security arises because the spouse alleges that the security was procured by misrepresentation or undue influence on the part of the borrower or lender, the lender may well consider possible remedies against the solicitor instructed to advise the spouse and procure the spouses signature.

Zwebner v. Mortgage Corporation Limited [1997] P.N.L.R. 504, Lloyd, J., Ch D involved a loan to be secured over a property belonging to the borrower and another party. The solicitor instructed to act for the lender issued a report on title in which there was an undertaking that all appropriate documents would be properly executed on completion. The solicitor sent the security deed to the borrower for execution by both the borrower and his co-proprietor. On the borrower's insolvency, the co-proprietor alleged that she was not bound by the security deed as her signature on the security deed had been forged. The lender was successful in recovering from the solicitor on the basis that, whether or not the solicitor had been at fault, the report on title amounted to a warranty that the security deed had been properly executed.

The terms of the judgment suggest that in England and Wales at least, the solicitor's duty of care to the lender may require the solicitor to be satisfied that the signatures of all signatories to a security deed are genuine.

It is beyond the scope of this note to consider the implications of these decisions in legalistic terms. While readers are encouraged to consider the full implications of the decisions the comments here are limited to managing risk.

The objective as always must be to do as much as reasonably practicable to minimise the risk of a problem arising at all. On this basis, should a problem still arise in spite of the precautions you have taken, you will be in a far stronger position to defend any claim.

The impact of the English cases may well be reflected in developments in the law here; in changes in the rules or practice regarding separate representation in security transactions and in changes in the terms of lenders' instructions. It is in the interests of practitioners to consider now what implications these developments and changes will have and to consider how the conduct of security work can be made as free of risk from the practitioner's point of view.

What does this mean in practice?
There are many issues that need to be considered routinely when instructions from a lender involve arranging signature of security deeds. A checklist which prompts you to consider relevant issues may be helpful. This might include the following points:
- Are you quite clear which party/parties is/are your client(s)? Lender, borrower, borrower's spouse? Are your instructions such that you could have a duty of care to more than one of these parties?
- Should you act for/advise more than one party?
- Is there an actual conflict of interest? If so, have you made it clear to the other parties that they should seek separate legal advice?
- Has the borrower's spouse been advised to take independent legal advice and, if so, has such advice been given?

If you are acting for the spouse
- Have you ensured that the spouse knows and understands who has instructed you and the basis on which advice has been given?
- Are you satisfied that the spouse was not subject to undue influence on the part of the borrower or the lender?

- Have you considered the implications of Rule 7 of the Conflict of Interest Rules (issuing deeds, etc., for signature by a party who has chosen not to instruct a solicitor)?
- Have you ascertained whether the spouse will receive direct financial benefit from the loan to which the security relates?
- Have you ascertained whether the spouse is involved in any way in the business to which the loan relates?
- Have you made other enquiries with a view to establishing whether the spouse might be advised not to sign the security deed? (Note: it may be only by examining the finances/accounts of the borrower's business that meaningful advice could be given in this regard)
- Has the spouse been advised of the implications of securing business borrowings over the matrimonial house/other matrimonial property?
- Has the spouse been advised that the security is an all sums security/a security for a fixed amount?
- Have you ensured that there are letters/attendance notes recording advice given?

When acting for the lender
- Have you considered whether it may be appropriate to qualify your report on title (to note, for instance, concerns in respect of potential conflict of interest)?
- If your instructions require you to warrant that the security deeds are properly executed, how have you satisfied yourself before reporting to the lender that the signatures are genuine? If you cannot warrant that signatures are genuine (*e.g.* by seeing the spouse sign and seeing evidence of identity), do not do so.

Remember, if a claim a rises and the cause of the claim is or is attributable to breach of the Conflict of Interest Practice Rules, the self-insured amount will be double the standard amount.

For guidance see comments at page F965 *supra* under "Home Secured for Business Loan".

The information in this note is (a) intended to provide guidance on matters of practical risk management and not on issues of law and (b) is necessarily of a generalised nature. It is not specific to any practice or to any individual and should not be relied on as stating the correct legal position.

Alistair Sim is *Associate Director of Marsh U.K. Ltd*

Law Society's Risk Management Flowchart and Procedures

(March 27, 1999)

Starting a Piece of Work

Common Failures	Good Service	How to Ensure Excellence	Model Procedures
Not finding out what the client wants us to do for him/her	**Ensure** that you always listen and ask questions when taking instructions	Use a questionnaire, checklist/aide-memoire	See examples in the Client Care Manual and Ensuring Excellence
Not telling the client what we will do— and not do	**Ensure** that the client knows what you will (not) do for him/her	Issue Letters of Engagement/Terms of Business	**Model** Procedure 1 See examples in the Client Care Manual and Ensuring Excellence

Common Failures	Good Service	How to Ensure Excellence	Model Procedures
Not telling the client the fee or basis of feeing and not being paid/complaint about fee	**Ensure** the client understands the basis of charges and why/how that may vary	**Explain** basis of fees in Letter of Engagement/Terms of Business	**Model** procedure 1 See examples in the Client Care Manual and Ensuring Excellence
Not avoiding conflicts of interest [complying with the Conflict of Interest Rules]	**Ensuring** that conflicts of interest are identified as soon as they arise and are avoided	**Establish** a file opening procedure. Maintain a full and accurate record on any database	**Model** procedure 2
Not complying with Money Laundering Regulations	**Ensure** consistent observance of the Regulations	**Establish** a set procedure and use standard forms/checklists	See procedures in Client Care Manual

Doing the Work

Common Failures	Good Service	How to Ensure Excellence	Model Procedures
Not communicating	**Ensure** that the client is kept informed at all times	**Establish** a policy regarding reporting	
Not recording a discussion	**Ensure** that proper notes are made of all conversations	**Use** a standard format of attendance note	
Not recording/acting on a time limit	**Ensure** that critical dates are verified at the outset and a system of reminders set up	**Use** a critical date diary	**Model** procedure 3
Not being able to locate a file/papers/titles/Wills etc.	**Ensure** that there are good safe procedures	**Establish** a formal office procedure	**Model** procedure 4
	Ensure that there is a system for tracking files, papers etc. outside the safe	**Use** a system of borrowing cards	**Model** procedure 5
Not following instructions	**Ensure** that proper notes are made of all conversations	**Use** a standard format of attendance note	
	Ensure that work is planned from the start and reviewed at intervals	**Use** a checklist/case plan	**See** sample case plans and commentary on planning of work in Client Care Manual
	Confirm oral instructions in writing immediately		

Common Failures	Good Service	How to Ensure Excellence	Model Procedures
Not doing the job properly	Ensure that an absent fee-earner's work is dealt with promptly	Establish a set procedure/ contingency plan	Model procedure 6
	Ensure that work is planned from the start and reviewed at intervals	Use a checklist/case plan	See sample case plans and commentary on planning of work in Client Care Manual
	Ensure that the styles and pro formas you/your colleagues use are up-to-date styles and pro formas	Monitor and review all styles and pro formas Create a record of all styles and pro formas	Model procedure 7
	Ensure that partners supervise incoming and outoing mail	Establish a formal office procedure and stick to it	Model procedure 8
	Ensure that good instructions are give to third parties	Follow proper procedures when engaging and instructing third parties	See commentary in Client Care Manual
Not avoiding unreasonable obligations	Ensure that partners supervise incoming and outgoing mail	Establish a formal office procedure and stick to it	Model procedure 8
	Ensure that only standard formats of undertaking are ever granted by the firm, ideally undertakings which will be treated as "classic"	Establish an approved office style and ensure that this is only deviated from with partner approval	Model procedure 9
Not reviewing work regularly	Ensure that files are reviewed regularly	Follow a standard format of audit checklist/audit record	Model procedure 10
Not recording securities/charges timeously	Ensure that work is planned from the start and reviewed at intervals	use a checklist/case plan	See sample case plans and commentary on planning of work in Client Care Manual
	Ensure that critical dates are verified at the outset and a system of reminders set up	Use a critical date diary	Model procedure 3
Not following accounts Rules and other Regulations	Ensure that work is planned from the start and reviewed at intervals	Use a checklist/case plan	See sample case plans and commentary on planning of work in Client Care Manual
	Ensure that files are reviewed regularly	Follow a standard format of audit checklist/audit record	Model procedure 10

Finishing a Piece of Work

Common Failures	Good Service	How to Ensure Excellence	Model Procedures
Not storing and recording papers	**Ensure** that there are procedures for concluding a piece of work and closing a file	**Establish** and follow a set office procedure	**Model** procedure 11
Not advising client of conclusion	**Ensure** that there are procedures for concluding a piece of work and closing a file	**Establish** and follow a set office procedure	**Model** procedure 11
	Ensure that an accounting is provided		
Not rendering fee	**Ensure** that there are procedures for concluding a piece of work and closing a file	**Establish** and follow a set office procedure	**Model** procedure 11
	Ensure that files are never closed unless fee rendered and client account balance is Nil	Use a simple checklist and auditing procedure to ensure files are not closed without account being clear	
Not closing the file	**Ensure** that files are never closed unless fee rendered and client account balance is Nil	Use a simple checklist and auditing procedure to ensure files are not closed without account being clear	**Model** procedure 11
Not dealing adequately with complaints	**Ensure** that complaints are handled in a consistent, prompt and clear manner	**Establish** and enforce a documented complaints procedure to be handled by a nominated Complaints Partner	See guidelines in Client Care Manual

RISK MANAGEMENT PROCEDURES

Model Procedures
1. Letters of Engagement/Terms of Business
2. File Opening
3. Critical Date Diaries
4. Safe Custody of Document Procedures
5. File Tracking
6. Fee Earner's Absence
7. Control of Styles/Pro Formas
8. Supervision of Incoming Mail
9. Undertakings
10. File Review
11. Concluding a Piece of Work & Closing a File

Model Procedure 1

Letters of Engagement/Terms of Business

Ensure that the client knows what you will (not) do for him/her.
Issue Letters of Engagement/Terms of Business

- Give the client the terms under which you work

- Advise a client when the terms of business change

- A Letter of Engagement allows a firm to tell a client what it will and will not do, what the cost will be and so on. It gives the terms of business. It may also deal with things which appear mundane but are actually important to the client, such as opening hours. The Letter of Engagement allows the firm to manage the expectations of a client as well as reduce risk of misunderstandings.

- A Letter of Engagement should therefore ALWAYS be issued to a new client.

- A Letter should IDEALLY be issued at the start of a new matter/transaction/case. For the work that has been done for the client before may be different, the fee structure not the same and so on.

- Where acting for a client with similar, multiple cases, *e.g.* debt collection, then issue a Letter of Engagement periodically. This might be once a year or when the fee structure changes.

- Refer to the Law Society's Guideline on Letters of Engagement (page F970, *supra*) when making up your style. The Society could provide suggested wording but there would never be agreement about exact wording, layout etc. Your version is best for you!

Model Procedure 2

File Opening

Ensure that conflicts of interest are identified as soon as they arise and are avoided.
Establish a file opening procedure.

- Establish that you can do the work

- Obtain basic information from client and record (see below).

- check that there is no conflict of interest with any other client. Consider what the client objective is and whether the process of attaining that objective could affect any other Firm client. Normally, when the conflict has arisen it is too late.

- Check that you or the firm are able to carry out the agreed action

- Verify client's identity for Money Laundering Purposes and to be sure as to whom you take instructions from

- Enter basic information on a database and allocate a client account/new matter number

- Issue a file bearing name, type of work, account number and name of fee earner (except where cash transactions only)

- Create a plan for the work

New Client Record

Full Name:	
Address incl Postcode:	

Phone Nos:	Home:		Work:	
Fax No:			E-Mail:	

Client Type:	Single/Joint/Married:
Fee Earner Name:	
Conflict of Interest Check carried out (Tick)	
Work can be done by me/us (Tick)	
Money Laundering form completed (Tick or N/A)	

Model Procedure 3

Critical Date Diaries

Ensure that critical dates are verified at the outset and a system of reminders set up.
Use a critical date diary.

- A Critical Date is a date on which or by which an action should be taken or specified so as to ensure that the client is not seriously prejudiced. This may be a date some days or week before the last date on which it is possible to take time-barred action.

- Examples are given in the appendix. These are not exclusive.

- Critical Date diaries may take several forms. Those described below are examples:—

- The simplest system is a desk diary kept by the fee-earner. This is easy to administer but can be lost and is not necessarily reviewed by another fee-earner. Therefore, it should be supplemented by another system.

- An enhancement of the individual diary system is one to be kept by department or firm. Each fee earner is responsible for entering their own critical dates in to it. One person is given the responsibility to monitor the diary and to remind the fee-earner of an action to be taken.

- A wall chart is also simple but has the advantage that other fee-earners can easily refer to it. Coded stickers enable different types of Critical Dates to be identified. Someone must be given the responsibility to monitor each day/week so as to remind a fee-earner that some action must be taken.

- A computerised system is within reach of any office having straightforward software. Many office systems have a diary. Each fee earner notifies a person of a Critical Date which that person enters on to the diary system. When the diary for that day is consulted in due course. The Critical Date appears and is notified to the fee earners. Some fee earners will wish to operate the system themselves but, in any event, anyone may consult the diary.

- It is good practice to have the fee earner confirm that a necessary action has been taken Failing that, a person must be responsible for reminding them. In the event of no response, someone else in the organisation should be told.

Appendix

LITIGATION
Personal Injury Triennia
Defamation Triennia
Quinquennia
Proofs/Jury Trials/Tribunals Hearings
Appeals
Debates/Procedure Roll Hearings
Criminal Pleading Diets
Criminal Trial
Criminal Appeals
Inhibitions
Industrial Tribunal Applications
Options Hearings
Procedural Hearings

COMMERCIAL
Notice to Quit—all types of Leases
Notices of Rent Reviews—all types of
    Leases
Registering changes at Companies House
Annual Returns and Accounts—Companies
Resiling Notices—Missives
Dates by which Disposition and/or Standard
    securities must be recorded in order to
    keep "live" the seller's and/or debtor's
    letter of obligation
Liquor Licensing Applications

AGRICULTURAL
Notice to Quit
Notices to Rent Reviews
Intimations of bequests of Tenancies
Applications to transfer agricultural quotas

PRIVATE CLIENT
Executries: Inheritance Tax Interest Charge
Executries: Deed of Variations and a
    Disclaimer of Legal Rights
Discretionary Trusts; charge to tax
Trusts: Vesting Dates

RESIDENTIAL PROPERTY
Closing dates for offers
Dates of entry

Model Procedure 4

Safe Custody of Document Procedures

Ensure that there are good safes procedures.
Establish a formal office procedure.

- Good practice dictates that there should be in place a simple and workable procedure for storing, locating and tracking Title Deeds, Wills, Securities and other documents held for client and Third Parties. The following is an example of a good-practice system.

- Safeguard all papers relevant to a matter

- The movement of Titles within and outwith the Office should be recorded on a database or register.

- All Title Deeds coming into the Office either from a Lender, client or Third Party (other than Titles received for examination in connection with a purchase transaction) should be recorded on this database/register.

- Titles should be stored within a "Title" envelope. The envelope should be marked on the outside with the identity of the client, the client file reference, and the address of the property.

- Each envelope should be allocated a number.

- Envelopes should be held in safe storage in numerical order.

- All movements in relation to Titles should be recorded on the database including lending of the Titles to Third Parties, delivery of the Titles to Lenders and other institutions, and delivery of the Titles to clients.

- The envelope retains its allocated number until Titles finally leaves the custody of the firm's offices.

- The number allocated is then freed for use in respect of other Titles.

- The data relating to the outgoing Titles is still however retained on the database/register.

- Date is recorded both in relation to identity of client and location of property.

- To prevent loss of data, a hard copy is printed on a regular basis. A disk back-up should be made regularly and stored in an appropriate safe or off-site.

Model Procedure 5

File Tracking

Ensure that there is a system for tracking files, papers etc. outside the safe.
Use a system of borrowing cards.

- Prevent loss of papers and files outside the safe

- Create a file for each matter and keep all papers with it or note in the file where they are

- Create a borrowing card (see sample below) and place one in each file as it is opened

- Whenever a files is taken by someone other than the fee earner or his/her secretary, the person so borrowing fill in the card and puts it where the file was

---

Style Borrowing Card

Clients Name:

A/C Number:

Case Title:

Fee Earner:

IF YOU REMOVE THIS FILE FROM THE CABINET AND YOU ARE NEITHER THE FEE EARNER NOR HIS/HER SECRETARY PLEASE COMPLETE BELOW

Name	Date Removed	Name	Date Removed

Model Procedure 6

Fee Earner's Absence

Ensure that an absent fee earner's work is dealt with promptly.
Establish a set procedure/contingency plan.

- It is important that progress is made on client's work despite the absence of the fee earner.

- A fee earner should, if possible, make a temporary or permanent arrangement for some other person(s) to look after his/her work or in the case of illness or holiday.

- Someone in the firm/department should always know what that arrangement is. In an emergency and failing allocation of responsibility, that person should do so.

- Arrangements should be made to divert phone calls.

- An absent partner's mail should be seen by another partner.

- The fee earner's mail should be checked by say 9.30 in the morning of absence by either another fee earner or preferably a partner.

- A fee-earner leaving the building temporarily should advise his/her Secretary and the receptionist. They should divert their phone to their secretary.

- A notice board in *e.g.* a secretary's room noting the whereabouts of fee earners/meetings is valuable.

- Advise the client that someone else is looking after his/her work.

- A basic checklist/case plan inside the front cover of the file to be filled in with the most up-to-date information could prove to be beneficial.

Model Procedure 7

Control of Styles/Pro Formas

Ensure that the styles and pro formas you/your colleagues use are up-to-date.
Monitor and review all styles and pro formas.
Create a record of all styles and pro formas.

- Introduce and enforce an office rule discouraging the use of styles and pro formas other than those which have been approved by [   ]

- Ensure that all styles and pro formas used throughout the firm are reviewed on a regular basis and whenever there is a change in law. Changes should be approved by a partner.

- To assist in the control and review of styles and pro formas, maintain a record of all styles and pro formas [for each area of work] **See sample below**

- Use the record of styles and pro formas to ensure that regular reviews of all styles and pro formas are carried out and logged

- On each style and each pro forma the author and the date of the latest review/update should be noted. These particulars should also be noted in the record of styles and pro formas

- Responsibility for maintaining the record of all styles and pro formas; checking that it is kept updated and ensuring that regular reviews of styles and pro formas are actually carried out should be allocated to a nominated fee earner

Record of Styles & Pro Formas

Style/ Pro Forma	Author/ Drafted	F/E resp. for review	Review Frequency	Review Date/ Review Done	Review Date/ Review Done	Review Date/ Review Done	Etc, Etc.
Offer to purchase (residential)	AJS 1/11/96	BKT	6 monthly	5/97 4/5/97 (BKT)	11/97 9/11/97 (BKT)	5/98 7/5/98 (BKT)	11/98
Lease—furnished residential	BKT 10/1/98	BKT	6 monthly	7/98 2/7/98 (BKT)	1/99	7/99	1/2000
Will (simple form)	CGD 9/2/97	CGD	Yearly	2/98 19/2/98 (CGD)	2/99	2/2000	2/2001
Power of Attorney	BKT 10/1/98	CGD	Yearly	1/99 17/1/98 (CGD)	1/2000	1/2001	2/2002
Etc Etc							

Model Procedure 8

Supervision of Incoming Mail

Ensure that partners supervise incoming and outgoing mail
Establish a formal office procedure and stick to it

- It is important that a partner sees all items of mail. They own the business and they take the risk.

- Mail should be opened in the presence of a partner (on a rota basis if more than one partner!)

- All mail should then go to the relevant partner (if there is more than one) before going to any other fee earner

- Any complaint should be immediately referred to the [Complaints Partner] and any letter indicating a claim to the [Senior Partner]

- If the partner cannot be identified from the letter/mail then the person dealing with it should refer to the firm's client listing. Any unidentified mail should be left in the mail area for identification.

Model Procedure 9

Undertakings

Ensure that only standard formats of undertaking are ever granted by the firm, ideally undertakings which will be treated as "classic"
Establish an approved office style and ensure that this is only deviated from with partner approval

The provisions of the Master Policy Certificate of Insurance relating to "classic" letters of obligation are as at March 1999 as follows:
- "Classic Letter of Obligation" shall mean an undertaking given by a solicitor in connection with the settlement of any transaction for the disposal for onerous consideration of any interest in property or the granting of security over any such property by a client of that solicitor in terms of which the solicitor personally undertakes any one or more of the following
  (i) to deliver a clear Search in the Property and Personal Registers or a Letter of Obligation in or substantially in the styles of Letter of Obligation set out in the Registration of Title Practice Book (HMSO Edinburgh) paragraphs G 2 20 to G 2 25 with reference to the later of (a) the date of settlement of the transaction or (b) where the disponee, feuar, tenant, assignee or lender as the case may be requires to complete title by recording in the Register of Sasines or registration in the Land Register the date of recording of that title or the Land or Charge Certificate (as the case may be) provided that in the case of (b) such undertaking is effective for no more than a reasonable period after settlement of the transaction (which in the case of an undertaking granted on or after 1st November 1994 shall be a period not exceeding fourteen days)
  (ii) to deliver a duly executed (and recorded if appropriate) discharge to be registered in the Land Register provided that the solicitor granting the undertaking has or will on settlement of the transaction to which it relates have control of sufficient funds to discharge in full the Obligations to which that security relates or
  (iii) to deliver a redemption receipt in respect of ground burdens in circumstances where the solicitor granting the undertaking is aware of the identity and whereabouts of the party entitled to the redemption monies and has available sufficient funds with which to redeem the ground burden in question

- The Self-Insured Amount shall not apply to any claim which arises (or to the extent that it arises) from having granted a Classic Letter of Obligation provided that
  (i) such claim is intimated to the practice after 31st October 1991 and
  (ii) in so far as the claim relates to an undertaking as described in (i) or (ii) above the practice provides evidence to the reasonable satisfaction of the Insurers that proper enquiry as to outstanding securities was made of the client and that immediately prior to settlement of the transaction to which the undertaking relates an up to date Search in the Computerised Presentment Book (after 6th April 1992 only) and an Interim Report on Search in the Property and Personal Registers or equivalent Form 10 11 12 or 13 Land Register Report (as the circumstances may require) was obtained which were clear except only as regards any security to which on or before settlement the provisions of (ii) above applied

- The foregoing shall not apply in the event that the solicitor granting a Classic Letter of Obligation
  (i) is aware of any outstanding security and
  (ii) has control of sufficient funds with which to discharge the obligations to which the security relates but fails to procure that a discharge of such security is recorded or registered as the case may be

Model Procedure 10

File Review

Ensure that files are reviewed regularly.
Follow a standard format of audit checks/audit record

- The purpose of the procedure is to set out the system for monitoring progress and quality of work by means of regular file reviews.

- Each fee earner must

  - Keep the file in order

  - Make sure that other relevant papers are kept together and are easily identifiable

  - Ensure that the file can be easily located (See Model Procedure 5)

  - Keep the checklist up-to-date

  - Complete a Critical Date Diary, where appropriate (see Model Procedure 3)

- Fee Earners are responsible for their own file reviews.

- At least once every three months, the fee earner will be issued with a list of current files for which he/she is responsible. The fee earner reviews all these files, marks the list to show the review has taken place and returns the list to [the Senior Partner]. Any action required should be carried out immediately.

- Each fee earner must review the files of another fee earner in order to ensure that work is being carried out properly. That should be done on a sampling basis and at least once every three months. The reviewer marks each file and makes a separate report to [the Senior Partner]

- The fee earner should review each file before closing it/completing the matter, Ideally, a partner should always see a file before it is closed.

Model Procedure 11

Concluding a Piece of Work & Closing a File

Ensure that there are procedures for concluding a piece of work and closing a file
Establish and follow a set office procedure

- Ensure that work has been completed properly, that the client knows the position and that the firm has received all moniés due to it.

- A firm should have a common method of closing and archiving files, dealing with cash balances etc.

- Fee earners should close files regularly so as to ensure that dead files are not littering up their room. They will be encouraged to do so if there is a secure system of storage and speedy means of retrieval of a file in storage.

- The fee earner must carry out a review:
  A checking that the work has been fully completed
  B ensuring that the clients' requirements have been met
  C making sure that the client has been advised of the outcome and any further action required
  D dealing properly with documents and other material
  E checking that the clients' details in the database are correct

- To close a file the fee earner shall first ensure:
  A that the work has been feed
  B that the cash balance is Nil
  C that the time record, if any, is Nil

- The fee earner then sends the file and any papers to storage, indicating how long they are to be kept

- The method of storage is one for the firm to determine. Usually, it will be on-site, in which case there must be:

  A a database or list of all files closed, with classification as to *e.g.* Name of Client; Client Account Number; Fee Earner; Date of Destruction

  B a secure method of storing the files

  C an efficient means of retrieving them

  D a borrowing index

- A good method of on-site storage is in boxes. These have a list of contents on the top. There should also be kept a separate, central list by box number and some other classification such as client or account number.

- At the end of each calendar year, the firm will list all files whose destruction date fell during that year. That list is reviewed and either a file destroyed or a new destruction date attached to it.

Law Society Secretariat

Douglas R. Mill, LL.B, B.A., M.B.A., (Direct Dial No. 0131 476 8146
(E-mail: drmillsec@msn.com) (The Secretary/Chief Executive)

Leslie H. Cumming, C.A., (0131 476 8141) (E-mail: lcumming@msn.com)
(Chief Accountant)

Miss Liz Campbell, B.A.(Hons), (0131 476 8145)
Deputy Director, Education & Training

Michael P. Clancy, LL.B, LL.B(Hons), LL.M, FRSA, (0131 476 8163)
(E-mail: lawscot1@nildram.co.uk)
Director, Parliamentary Liaison

Mrs Iona Cockburn, LL.B, (0131 476 8157) (E-mail: drmillsec@msn.com)
Personal Assistant to the Secretary and Conference Manager

David Cullen, B.Com(Hons), LL.B, AIIMR, (0131 476 8160) (E-mail:
update@nildram.co.uk)
Director, Education & Training

Mrs Lorna Davies, LL.B, Dip.L.P., (0131 476 8130) (E-mail:
update@nildram.co.uk)
Deputy Director, Education & Training

David Dickson, LB(Hons), (0131 476 8102)
Case Manager, Client Relations Office

Hannah Dolby, B.A.(Hons), (0131 476 8115) (E-mail: hdolby@aol.com)
Press & Public Relations Officer

Mrs Alison Gordon, LL.B, Dip.L.P., (0131 476 8183)
Case Manager, Client Relations Office

Duncan Hamilton (Maternity cover for Alison Gordon) (0131 476 8183)
Case Manager, Client Relations Office—from May to December

Mrs Morna Grandison (0131 476 8191)
Deputy Director, Interventions

Mrs Anne Keenan, LL.B(Hons), Dip.L.P., (0131 476 8188) (E-mail:
lawscot1@nildram.co.uk)
Deputy Director, Law Reform

Mrs Linsey J. Lewin, LL.B(Hons), Dip.L.P. (0131 476 8174) (E-mail:
linseylewin-lawscot@nildram.co.uk)
Deputy Director, Members' Services

Mrs Linda Lyall (0131 476 8140)
Deputy Director, Guarantee Fund

Mrs Jan McAlister (0131 476 8162)
Manager, Legal Education

Mary McGowan LL.B(Hons), Dip.L.P., (0131 476 8152)
Deputy Director, Client Relations Office

Peter McGrath, LL.B(Hons), Dip.L.P., (0131 476 8184) (E-mail: lawscot
1@nildram.co.uk)
Research Assistant

Miss Sarah Fleming, LL.B(Hons), Dip.L.P., (0131) 476 8153) (E-mail:
lawscot@nildram.co.uk)
Head of International Relations (from 1.10.99)

Miss Gillian Meighan, LL.B, Dip.L.P., Cert (Management) Open, (0131 476
8167) (E-mail: gmeighan@msn.com)
Head of Press & Public Relations Office

Mrs Olga Pasportnikov, LL.B, N.P., (0131 476 8116)
Case Manager, Client Relations Office

Bruce A. Ritchie, LL.B, (0131 476 8124) (E-mail:
linseylewin-lawscot@nildram.co.uk)
Director, Professional Practice

George C. Samson, (0131 476 8136) (E-mail: lawsoc2@nildram.co.uk)
Director, Administration

Miss Tricia Sim, M.A., (0131 476 8133) (E-mail: update@nildram.co.uk)
Manager, Update

Mrs Margot Walker, LL.B, (0131 476 8158)
Case Manager, Client Relations Office

Philip J. Yelland, LL.B, Dip.L.P., (0131 476 8131)
Director, Client Relations Office

OFFICE: 26 Drumsheugh Gardens, Edinburgh EH3 7YR. Tel. 0131 226
7411. Fax. 0131 225 2934. DX ED 1. E-mail: lawscot@lawscot.org.uk

Website: http://www.lawscot.org.uk

Brussels Office address—The Law Society of Scotland, 141/142 Avenue de
Tervuren, 1150 Brussels (DX 1065 BDE, Belgium) Tel. 00 322 743 8585. Fax
00 322 743 8586.

Index

Professional Practice—Where Can I Find It?

Index to practice rules, journal articles etc. on aspects of professional practice. Compiled by Bruce A. Ritchie, Deputy Secretary (Professional Practice), The Law Society of Scotland, who will be pleased to receive users' suggestions for further items for inclusion.

ABBREVIATIONS
Bus. L.B.: Greens Business Law Bulletin.
G.W.D.: Greens Weekly Digest.
Journal: Journal of the Law Society of Scotland.
P.H.B.: Parliament House Book.
Prop. L.B.: Greens Property Law Bulletin.
S.C.L.R.: Scottish Civil Law Reports.
S.L.T.: Scots Law Times.

Advertising
Solicitors (Scotland) (Advertising and Promotion) Practice Rules 1995 with Guideline on Advertising Fees. P.H.B., Vol. 3, page F 614.
Consumer Credit (Advertisements) Regulations 1989 (S.I. 1989, No. 1125).

Bankruptcy
Register of Undischarged Bankrupts—Journal October 1990.

Builder/Developer
1986 Practice Rules—Rule 5 (P.H.B. page F 329)
Article—Journal November 1994, page 423. (See also Guidelines on Conflict of Interest—P.H.B. Vol. III, page F 964).

Building Society Flotations/Mergers
Journal May 1997, page 206.

Books
1. *Professional Ethics and Practice for Scottish Solicitors* by Janice Webster (T. & T. Clark).
2. *Professional Conduct for Scottish Solicitors* by Jane Ryder (Butterworths).

Certificate of Title
—*See* Commercial Securities.

Closing a File
Journal April 1998, page 44

Closing date guidelines
P.H.B., page F 901. *See also* Journal February 1999, page 42.

Code of Conduct (See also Code for Criminal Work)
P.H.B., page F 823. Additions in Journal February 1999, page 43.

Code of Conduct for Criminal Work
P.H.B., page F 839. Additions in Journal February 1999, page 43.

Comments to the Media
Journal September 1998, page 8.

Release 52: May 1999

Commercial Security Transactions
Guidance Note—March 15, 1994 (P.H.B., page F 904).
Articles—Journal of April 1994 (Lenders' Need to Know); February 1995 (Expanding Duty of Care) and October 1995 (Certificate of Title).
President's letter of July 25, 1995—Copies available from Professional Practice Department.

Confidentiality
Code of Conduct, Paragraph 4 (P.H.B., page F 827).
Micosta v. Shetland Islands Council, 1983 S.L.T. 483.
Conoco v. Commercial Law Practice—Journal April 1996, page 132 also 1996 G.W.D. 12—731.
Guidance Notes—P.H.B., page F 966.

Conflict of Interest
Solicitors (Scotland) Practice Rules 1986 (P.H.B., page F 328/9).
Code of Conduct, para. 3 (P.H.B., page F 827).
Prop.L.B., December 1994, page 7.
Guidance Notes—P.H.B., page F 961.
Journal March 1999, page 40.

Conveyancing Committee Snippets
Journal May 1997, page 193.

Court Work—Duty to Lodge Joint Minute
Journal June 1998, page 43.

Criminal Work
See Code of Conduct for Criminal Work

Destruction of Files
Client Care Guidance Manual page 9.2.
See also Code of Conduct for Criminal Work (P.H.B., page F 844—Article 12).

Developers
Journal November 1994, page 423.

Discount Standard Securities—Discharges
Journal January 1987, page 4 and July 1998, page 8.

Employees' Names on Notepaper
Solicitors (Scotland) (Associates Consultants and Employees) Practice Rules 1996 (P.H.B., page F 635).

European Law—Where to find it
Journal April 1994, page 127.

Executries
Solicitor required to implement Mandate from co-executor—Journal July 1998, page 42.
Solicitor's duty to account to executors—not beneficiaries—*Loretto School v. McAndrew & Jenkins*, 1992 S.L.T. 615.

Faxed and E-Mailed Documents
Journal April 1998, page 44.

Fees—Liability for other Solicitors Fees
1. Solicitors (Scotland) Act 1980 S.30 (P.H.B., Vol. 3, page F 14).
2. Cross Border Code of Conduct Rules 1989 Rule 5.7 (P.H.B., Vol. 3, page F 461).

Fees—Duty to Agree to Taxation
Table of Fees, Chap. 2, Para. 2(b).
See also Written Fee Charging Agreements.

Fixed Price Offers
Journal June 1998, page 42.

Hived-off Financial Services Companies
Guidance Note—February 1994—Revoked with effect from April 1, 1999.

Incorporated Practices
Practice Rules (1987) (P.H.B., Vol. 3, page F 530).

Joint Minute
See Court Work

Legacies to Solicitors
Journal article—October 1989, page 389.
Drafting Wills in Scotland, Para. 6.150, page 347 *et seq.*
Webster on Professional Ethics at para. 2.11, page 20.

Lender—Duty to where also Acting for Borrower
See Commercial Securities. (The articles and cases are also applicable to domestic securities).

Letters of Obligation
Journal articles April 1973, page 121 (Professor Henry), May 1991, page 171, November 1993, page 431 (Professor Rennie).
Circular by The Secretary January 30, 1995 with style "Classic Letter of Obligation". (Copies available from Professional Practice Department).
For definition of Classic Letter of Obligation, see page F 993.

Living Will
Style available from Professional Practice Department.

Mandates
1. From client—Journal May 1998, page 46.
2. From banks, creditors etc.—Journal May 1993, page 185.

Media
See (Comments to the Media).

Missives—Avoidance of delay
Journal June 1998, page 42.

Money Laundering
Journal May 1998, page 40.

Mortgage Advice
See Property Schedules.

Multi Disciplinary Practices Prohibited
Solicitors (Scotland) (Multi Disciplinary Practices) Practice Rules 1991. P.H.B., page F 499.

Notary Public
Article—Journal February 1997, page 50.

Notes of Interest
See Closing Dates.

Ownership of Files
Article—"Mandates"—Journal May 1998, page 46.
Copies of Opinion of C.K. Davidson Q.C. in 1982 available from Professional Practice Department.

Powers of Attorney—Taking Instructions from Granter
Journal July 1998, page 43.

Release 52: May 1999

Precognitions in Criminal Cases not deliverable to Client
Code of Conduct for Criminal Work—Article 11 (P.H.B., Vol. III, page F 843).
Swift v. Bannigan, 1991 S.C.L.R. 604.

Precognoscing Untried Prisoners
Journal item—March 1993, page 115.

Property Schedules and Mortgage Advice
Journal April 1998, page 44.

Ranking Agreements—Conflict of Interest
Journal April 1998, page 44.

Redemption Statements
Guidelines issued by Council of Mortgage Lenders May 1994. (Copies available from Professional Practice Department).

Restriction on Practising as a Principal
Practice Rules, P.H. Book, page F 620.
Journal Item—June 1997, page 214.

Retentions
Journal July 1998, page 42.

Sale of Matrimonial Home where Spouses Separated
Guidance Note Journal July 1998, page 43.
Dawson v. R. Gordon Marshall & Co. G.W.D. 21/6/96 No. 1243.

Secured Loans to Solicitors—Prohibition on Acting for Lender
Rule 10 of Solicitors (Scotland) Accounts Rules 1997 (P.H.B., page F 639).
Journal August 1997, page 334.

Settlement Cheques Sent to be Held as Undelivered
Journal item—October 1998, page 47.
Prop.L.B.—August 1994, page 6.

Sharing Fees with Non Solicitors
Solicitors (Scotland) Practice Rules 1991 (P.H.B., page F 498).

Signature of Missives etc.
Journal article—February 1991, page 73—"Who signs for the firm?" (signature by assistant)
Journal item—April 1996, page 158 "Requirements of Writing (Scotland) Act 1995".

Signature of Documents by Unrepresented Party
Journal October 1998, page 47.

Small Claims—Extra Judicial Fees
Journal July 1989, page 271.

Speculative Actions
Solicitors (Scotland) Act 1980, Section 61A (P.H.B. page F 34.1).
Court of Session—Rule 42.17 (formerly Rule 350A). Blue Book, page F 68 or White Book Fees Supplement, page 51.
Sheriff Court—Act of Sederunt (Fees of Solicitors in Speculative Actions) 1992. (White Book Fees Supplement, page 66).
Article by Walter Semple—Journal February 1994, page 57.

Terms of Business Letters
Journal April 1998, page 44 and February 1999, page 43 re addition to Code of Conduct.
Better Client Care Guidance Manual, pages 1.3 and 25.1.

Title Deeds—Exhibiting to other Agents
Journal May 1996, page 195.